▲ 1: *Sketch of downtown Larkspur along the east side of Magnolia Avenue from Ward Street looking south, by artist Audrey Hulburd, 1980. The artist's sketches appeared on the front and back covers of the 1991 edition of* Larkspur Past & Present.

Larkspur
Past and Present

A History and Walking Guide

Larkspur Heritage Preservation Board

The Larkspur Heritage Preservation board gratefully acknowledges the financial support provided by the City of Larkspur and by the Larkspur Centennial Committee for this edition of *Larkspur Past and Present: A History and Walking Guide*.

LARKSPUR CITY COUNCIL, 2009:

Ronald M. Arlas, Mayor

Joan L. Lundstrom, Vice-Mayor

Larry Chu, Council Member

Kathy Hartzell, Council Member

Dan Hillmer, Council Member

Larkspur Past and Present: A History and Walking Guide

EDITOR: Helen Heitkamp

WRITERS: Helen Heitkamp, Richard Cunningham

DESIGN & GRAPHIC COORDINATION: Dena Van Derveer

CHIEF COPY EDITOR: Linda Chauncey

COPY EDITORS:
  Karen Deist
  Lelia Lanctot
  Rosine Reynolds
  Marilyn River
  Terry Ulin
  Dena Van Derveer
  Jack Wilson
  Sallyanne Wilson

RESEARCHERS & FACT CHECKERS:
  Nancy Curley
  Lelia Lanctot
  Mary Dale Scheller

PHOTO & BUSINESS COORDINATOR: Marilyn River

PHOTO PREPARATION: John Gillespie Jr.

COVER DESIGN & PRINTER SELECTION: Peter E. Martin

CARTOGRAPHY: Dennis Wuthrich, Farallon Geographics

PUBLISHER: Larkspur Heritage Preservation Board

PRINTER: McNaughton & Gunn

COVER PHOTO CREDITS:
  Front Cover: Gil Dubuc *(lower right)*;
    Jay Graham Photography *(upper right & lower left)*;
    William Costello Family *(upper left)*
  Inside Front Flap: Jack Wilson
  Inside Back Flap: John Gillespie Jr.
  Back Cover: Courtesy of Newall Snyder Collection

COPYRIGHT © 2010 Larkspur Heritage Preservation Board

ALL RIGHTS RESERVED. No part of this book may be reprinted or reproduced or utilized in any form or by any electronic, mechanical or other means, now known or herein after invented, including photocopying and recording, or in any information storage or retrieval system, without permission in writing from the publisher.

LEGAL DISCLAIMER. The Larkspur Heritage Preservation Board assumes no legal responsibility for the completeness or the accuracy of the contents of this publication nor any legal responsibility for appreciation or depreciation of the value of any premises listed or not listed herein by reason of their inclusion or an omission in this publication.

CATALOGING-IN-PUBLICATION DATA is on file with the Library of Congress

LIBRARY OF CONGRESS CATALOG NUMBER 2010937338

HARDCOVER EDITION ISBN 978-0-615-39511-1

SOFTCOVER EDITION ISBN 978-0-615-39512-8

Printed in the United States of America

DEDICATION

A toast to Larkspur on its 100th Birthday

This book is dedicated to Larkspur's Centennial Celebration.

Beginning with the March Centennial party, followed by the Fourth of July parade and the spectacular Rose Bowl dance under a full moon, the whole town celebrated its colorful past.

A hundred energetic citizens overcame generators that wouldn't power our sound system, runaway horses, 100-year-old vehicles sputtering to a halt, and two years of meetings to produce a year filled with festivities. Not only did the events celebrate what Larkspur is today, but also the contributions of citizens over the years who have preserved the small town's history despite threats of massive development, floods, slides, and fires.

The publication of *Larkspur Past and Present* is the culmination of the tributes that have been made during the year including the dedication of Centennial Park, the installation of a memorial plaque in front of City Hall, and sealing of a new time capsule.

The Centennial has been a tribute to the love of Larkspur by its citizens.

Kathy Hartzell, Member, Larkspur City Council
Centennial Committee Chair

▲ 2-5 (top): *Centennial Parade*; 6: *Kathy Hartzell, Centennial Chair*; 7-10 (bottom): *Centennial Celebrations, 2008.*

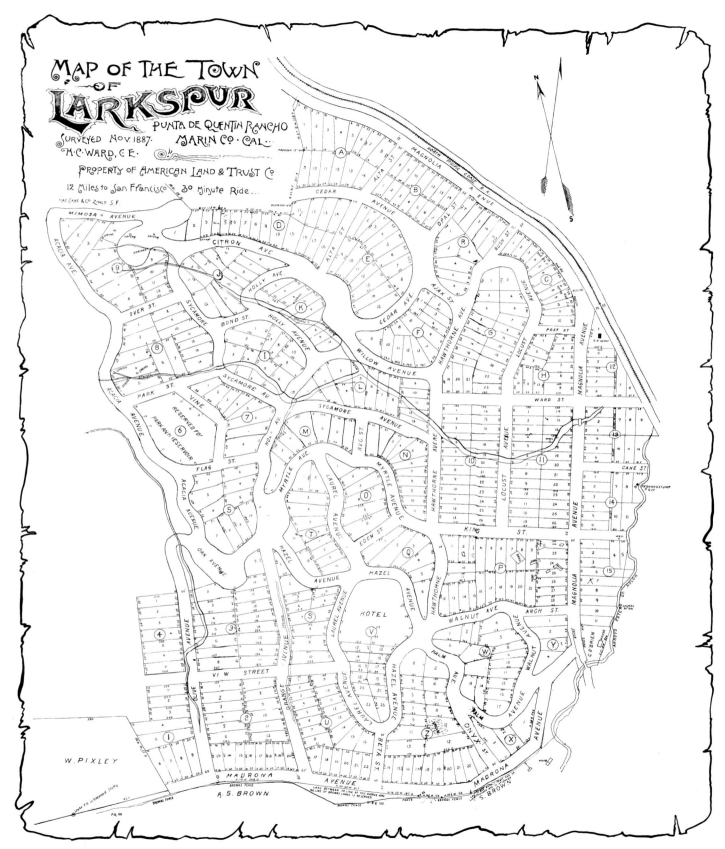

▲ 11: *This original 1887 Ward survey map created central Larkspur's street system and lot lines; many features beyond the downtown blocks were later changed or never developed.*

PREFACE

In these days of homogenized cities where diversity has all but disappeared, Larkspur has retained its variety of housing types, its old downtown, its redwood canyons, and its wooded hills. Although many of the structures are modest versions of architectural styles popular in the late 1800s and early 1900s, they are historic resources worthy of preservation as examples of the way people lived and worked in small communities at the turn of the last century.

With the high cost of housing in Larkspur the pressure for remodeling our older structures has increased. Modest summer cabins, bungalows, and 1940s tract houses are being expanded into large homes.

How do you differentiate between old things that matter and those that do not? How do you distinguish between resources that should be preserved as a link to the past and those that should be discarded to make room for the future? We hope this book will help you recognize buildings and resources that are truly connected to the people, the spirit, and the traditions of Larkspur; that exploring Larkspur's past will help you feel part of an ongoing fabric of family and community.

Since the older sections of Larkspur were developed in the days before automobiles, walking tours are a logical way to trace the town's history. They allow you to sample Larkspur's past and appreciate the community's historic value.

To make these walks both historically factual and fun, the functional history approach has been used – historic data is integrated with old timers' tales of prizefighters, bootleggers, and colorful early residents.

The search for a hometown can take a lifetime. Some lucky people have found one in Larkspur. Our mission is to introduce newcomers to Larkspur and reinforce longtime residents' love of their hometown.

This book updates the 1979 and 1991 editions of *Larkspur Past & Present* that were outgrowths of earlier walking tour brochures. The original edition and the revisions are the work of local volunteers.

▲ 12: *Created as a promotion for the city, this informal map of Larkspur featured local businesses and landmarks, 1953.*

INTRODUCTION

Larkspur's 2008 Centennial Year activities celebrated its official incorporation as a city in March of 1908. But Larkspur really began some sixty years earlier, when Gold Rush-era loggers started toppling thousand-year-old redwoods and sawing lumber on land previously visited only by the Coast Miwok Indians who hunted and fished along the salt marsh that extended as far as today's Magnolia Avenue and Doherty Drive.

It wasn't long before the big trees were gone and farmers and ranchers replaced the lumbermen, gradually giving way in their turn to hoteliers, saloonkeepers and merchants serving a growing community of summer visitors and weekend residents escaping San Francisco's fog. Larkspur became known as a playground for fun-seekers who picnicked in the cool canyon, swam and paddled in the creek, and enjoyed the libations poured by numerous drinking establishments.

Larkspur got its name and its first push toward development when mover-and-shaker Charles W. Wright, president of the American Land and Trust Company, bought the King dairy ranch in 1887. Wright auctioned off lots "large enough to pasture horses and raise chickens," according to sales brochures. Hoping to persuade the North Pacific Coast Railroad to locate a station in the town, Wright built five Victorian cottages and asked his wife Georgiana to suggest a name for the station. When the station was built in 1891 the railroad agreed to call it "Larkspur," after the flower which Mrs. Wright had seen growing on the hills. Later residents insisted she had mistaken lupine for larkspur -- but both wildflowers are native to our hills.

During the years leading up to its incorporation, Larkspur gradually built the trappings of a full-fledged city. The railroad linked the little town with the ferries that plied San Francisco Bay and attracted the first wave of commuters – later to become a flood with the construction of the Golden Gate Bridge. More and more cottages climbed the hills while hundreds of flat-bottomed houseboats anchored on the creek. Commercial buildings, many still standing, went up along Magnolia Avenue, the one-time county road that meandered from Sausalito to San Rafael. With a population approaching 600 – double that during the summer – Larkspur was ready to take its place as a full-fledged California city.

Only 12 miles from San Francisco and 30 miles from Oakland, Larkspur has been greatly affected by transportation improvements that helped make the city an increasingly popular bedroom community. In the period from 1960 to 1970 the population jumped from 5,700 to 10,487. Today, with a population of about 12,000, Larkspur is almost completely built out.

This book is intended to serve both as a history and as a walking tour guide to Larkspur's historic neighborhoods, a dual purpose made possible by the preservation of many homes and structures dating from the earliest days of settlement. The downtown in particular provides a capsule history of the town in just two-and-one-half blocks. It doesn't require much imagination to see Magnolia Avenue as the sea of mud it became in winter before it was paved in 1913 and to recognize many buildings as early centers of commerce.

The 1913 City Hall still anchors the downtown district, and dozens of well-kept buildings ranging from 70 to 110 years old contribute to its historic status. In fact, every Larkspur neighborhood retains important reminders of the city's history. In all, more than 75 residential properties that have contributed to Larkspur's essential character are recognized on the city's *Historic Resources Inventory*.

Change is history in the making. In 2010 development plans for the 16-acre Niven land on Doherty Drive are under city review. A new police headquarters is rising at Piper Park. A revamping of Larkspur Landing shopping center is pending. Despite changes every Larkspur neighborhood reveals traces of its history, just as each neighborhood has retained at least some of the small-town character that makes Larkspur special. Not every historic home has been researched, and many stories remain untold. We hope that this book will encourage residents and visitors to explore our town and discover for themselves the qualities that make living in Larkspur such a joy.

REFERENCE MAP of Larkspur's Neighborhoods

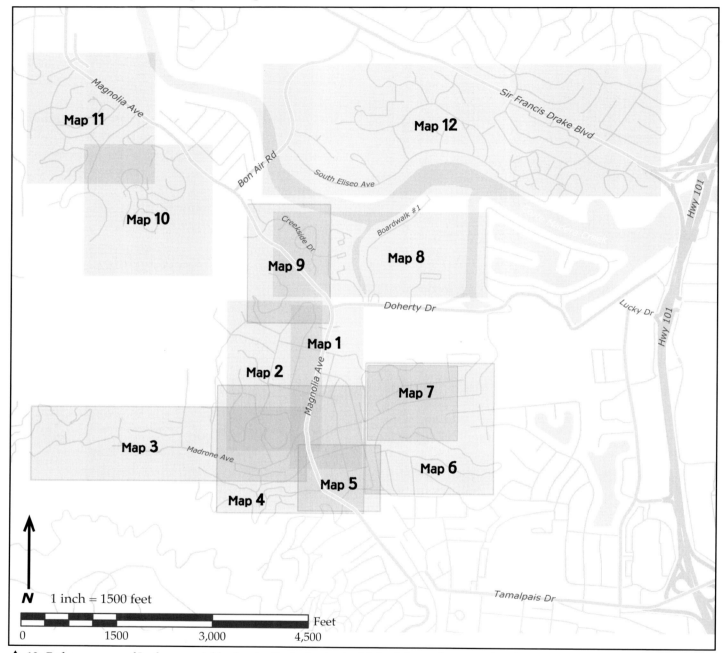

▲ 13: *Reference map of Larkspur neighborhoods. Each chapter in this book has at least one detailed companion map (see key) featuring general and specific points of interest highlighted in the text. All maps were created for this book by local resident Dennis Wuthrich.*

MAP KEY

1 Downtown *page xii*

2 Old Homes in Central Larkspur
   North Loop *page 58*
   South Loop *page 78*

3 Baltimore Canyon *page 96*

4 Baltimore Park *page 142*

5 South Magnolia *page 174*

6 Palm Hill *page 192*

7 Heather Gardens & Meadowood *page 204*

8 Piper Park, Boardwalk #1 & Creekside *page 218*

9 North Magnolia *page 238*

10 Hillview & King Mountain *page 254*

11 Murray Park *page 262*

12 Greenbrae & Bon Air *page 280*

13 San Quentin Peninsula *page 296*

CONTENTS

Dedication v
Map of the Town of Larkspur, 1887 vi
Preface vii
"Friendly Greetings" Map of Larkspur, 1953 viii
Introduction ix
Reference Map of Larkspur's Neighborhoods x

Chapter 1: DOWNTOWN 1
Chapter 2: OLD HOMES in Central Larkspur 59
Chapter 3: BALTIMORE CANYON 97
Chapter 4: BALTIMORE PARK 143
Chapter 5: SOUTH MAGNOLIA 175
Chapter 6: PALM HILL 193
Chapter 7: HEATHER GARDENS & MEADOWOOD 205
Chapter 8: PIPER PARK, BOARDWALK #1 & CREEKSIDE 219
Chapter 9: NORTH MAGNOLIA 239
Chapter 10: HILLVIEW & KING MOUNTAIN 255
Chapter 11: MURRAY PARK 263
Chapter 12: GREENBRAE & BON AIR 281
Chapter 13: SAN QUENTIN PENINSULA 297

Epilogue 345
Appendices
    Appendix A: Preserving Larkspur's Past 346
    Appendix B: Typical Homes of Larkspur 350
    Appendix C: Paper Streets, Stairs & Pathways 351
    Appendix D: Gustave Nagel - Larkspur's Architect 352
    Appendix E: Larkspur Woman's Improvement Club 354
    Appendix F: Timeline - Summary of Larkspur's History 355
    Appendix G: Credits 359
    Appendix H: Contributors 362
    Appendix I: Addresses & Places of Note 363

Index 367

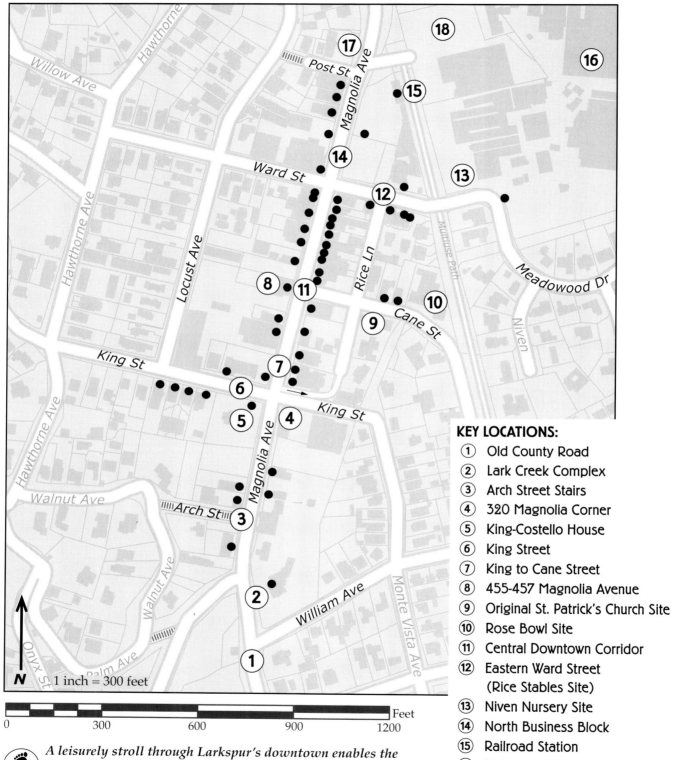

DOWNTOWN

Many of Larkspur's downtown buildings date to the 1890s, a period of rapid development that was undertaken by a handful of immigrant families. Those original buildings were erected within sight of the little railroad depot on the rural county road that became Magnolia Avenue.

• • • • • • • • • • • • •

Building lots had been created a few years earlier, in 1887, when the American Land and Trust Company optimistically laid out a town site. By the early 1900s our downtown encompassed two hotels, bakeries, a blacksmith, a cobbler, a large livery stable, meat and grocery stores, real estate offices, a bustling lumberyard, and at least three saloons. Small houses were set along the side streets, with grazing horses and cows nearby.

By the 1930s the several blocks between Post Street and Madrone Avenue had become a vibrant commercial and residential area, offering a full range of goods and services to the local community.

▲ 1.1: *A banner featuring Downtown's Blue Rock Hotel commemorated Larkspur's 2008 Centennial.*

▲ 1.2: *Larkspur's downtown on the morning of September 6, 1909, as citizens make ready for their first Booster Day celebration. Today's Blue Rock Hotel is visible at right center, facing Magnolia Avenue; all the buildings in center-left of the photograph still stand today.*

So it remained until the early 1960s when changed patterns of shopping and commuting spelled the end of small stores that supplied a walking population. The downtown businesses began a slow and difficult transformation to serving a population that arrived by automobile. Historic buildings that once housed butchers, plumbers, and hardware stores now offer distinctive clothing, catering services, and artisan pastries. Originally designed for very different purposes, those venerable structures have been subjected to physical demands that their builders never could have foreseen. The result was an ongoing tension between emerging retail trends and a desire to acknowledge the substantial history represented by our downtown buildings.

Remarkably, nearly all of Larkspur's early buildings continue to survive today, on streets that would be recognized immediately by one of our original citizens. The substantial historical integrity of the area was recognized officially in 1982, when Larkspur's Old Downtown was listed as a district in the National Register of Historic Places, and then protected by provisions of a special zoning ordinance enacted in 1987. More than twenty years later the city's 2008 Centennial celebrations showed the success of those efforts.

⊃ *This chapter describes the core of Larkspur's downtown, proceeding from south to north in accord with the street address numbers.*

① Old County Road

For more than a century the route now known as Magnolia Avenue was the only available north-south travel route between Sausalito and the mission in San Rafael. Used regularly during the Mexican period, it became a wagon and stagecoach route in the 1850s, and by the 1870s had become an official county road. Its route was dictated by topography – coming north from Corte Madera, it skirted around two deep ravines near Alexander Avenue and King Street, using a narrow point to cross the creek that drains Baltimore Canyon. To the north of today's downtown area, going toward Kentfield and "Ross's Landing," the road was forced to hug the foothills adjacent to the broad salt marshes of Corte Madera Creek.

The dirt road featured deep mud in the winter and choking dust in the summer. Pedestrians had to use boardwalks that were laid along its edge.

The central portion of Magnolia Avenue was paved in 1913, one of the first municipal paving projects in Marin County. In the 1920s, after much political maneuvering, Larkspur's central street was designated as a part of the state's original Redwood Highway. Larkspur officials balked when state engineers demanded the removal of three large redwood trees in order to widen the bridge over the Arroyo Holon, protesting that the trees were part of "the only redwood grove from Sausalito to the Humboldt County line." The trees were removed with great reluctance in late 1926; the concrete bridge was built, and remains there today.

▲ *1.3: This E.H. Mitchell postcard view, about 1912, looks north along the unpaved county road (now Magnolia Avenue) where it crossed the Arroyo Holon; the Arch Street stairs are visible beyond the wooden bridge. Note the utility poles and three-plank sidewalks.*

② Lark Creek Complex

The landmark building at **234 MAGNOLIA AVENUE**, now "The Tavern at Lark Creek," and known from 1972 to 2009 as "The Lark Creek Inn," dates to a far earlier time. Originally a part of the farm established by pioneer Patrick King in the 1860s, this land was sold by King to San Francisco schoolteacher Catherine O'Brien in 1881. Nine years later Catherine's sister Margaret purchased adjoining property to the north, thus creating an enlarged parcel that remained in family hands well into the 1920s. The early history of the two-story house itself is unclear; its construction is traditionally dated to about 1888, and it carries many of the Italianate features of homes of that period – a narrow and tall design with drop siding, projecting eaves supported by concave brackets and decorative blocks, pediments above the windows, and a small crest (probably originally made of iron, now wood) atop the roof. By 1910 owner Catherine O'Brien was living in the house, joined by her elderly widowed sisters, Ellen Crowley and Anna Murphy; it was Anna's large family that was remembered by neighbors. The Murphy family apparently included disabled children, and bars on some of the windows reinforced the community's

▲ 1.4: *The O'Brien-Murphy-Probert house in 1971, shortly before its transformation to The Lark Creek Inn. Note the absence of a dining room on the south (right) side.*

inclination to avoid contact with the family, considering them crazy. By 1930 only Anna's youngest son, Charles Murphy, remained in the house, finding work as a laborer at the nearby Schmitt chicken ranch.

The modern history of the house began in 1937 when it was purchased by England-born Hildred "Hil" Probert and his wife Mildred. The adjoining land to the north was purchased by Mildred's older siblings, Frances and Ethel Kelsey, who agreed to finance the construction of a gasoline service station, which was then leased to Hil Probert. By 1938 Probert's advertisements proudly offered Mobilgas products and personal service at his elaborate new station. The service station's stylish *porte cochère* survives today as the hair salon at 238 Magnolia; the service bays to either side became the small shops at 236 and 240 Magnolia.

PROBERT'S UNDER CONSTRUCTION

"Contractor A.C. Wheeler is rapidly pushing to completion the Hildred Probert salesroom and service buildings at the mouth of Larkspur Canyon. The buildings will be painted white with a light green trim to match the cement driveways and the floors of the salesrooms…. The new buildings match in color and design the service station and the Probert home … one of the oldest homes in the city."

— *Larkspur-Corte Madera News*, May 16, 1946

▲ 1.5: *Probert's under construction, 1946.*

At the close of World War II, Hil foresaw the postwar demand for new cars and became a dealer for newly available Kaiser-Frazer automobiles. The Proberts purchased the adjoining land held by the Kelseys, and Hil designed a new automobile showroom that eventually became the large building currently numbered as 242, 250, and 270 Magnolia. Because new lumber wasn't available immediately after the war, much of the showroom was built of recycled materials, with heavy timbers and skylights gleaned from the disused railroad ferry terminal in Sausalito.

Shortly after the showroom opened, Probert's complex was selected as the primary location for a new motion picture. Brian Donlevy, Ella Raines, and Charles Coburn starred in *Impact*, a film noir shot in Larkspur and San Francisco; both the service station and house were prominent features of the film. The script was expanded to include memorable footage of Larkspur's volunteer firemen, including slapstick scenes of a groom leaving his bride to answer a fire call. A short cameo even included Hil and Mildred Probert as customers at their own gas station. The film is treasured today for its colorful local scenes, many including Larkspur citizens as extras.

When Kaiser motorcars went out of production in the mid-1950s, Probert made another strategic shift, becoming the nation's first Toyota dealer. The new agency prominently featured a metal rack with a boxy Land Cruiser set at an improbable angle that promoted the car's hill-climbing ability. Alan Probert, Hil's grandson, recalled: "The highlight of my grandfather's pioneer Toyota dealership was a personal visit to his home and showroom from Mr. Toyoda, the president of the company. His visit was to thank him for his being the first dealer in the U.S. He presented my grandfather with two Seiko watches which I still possess."

Probert also became a serious collector; metal sheds behind the display room, where the parking lots are located today, held dozens of classic cars. During the war the same area had operated as a trailer park. Hil and Mildred were features of the community for three decades, raising their two children in the house at 234 Magnolia. Not long after Hil's death in 1968 the Toyota dealership closed, but Mildred stayed on in the house. Skip Sommer, a would-be restaurateur who was looking for a suitable site for a new Marin County enterprise, approached Mildred two years later. A deal was struck, with Sommer, Alan Ryan,

▲ 1.6: *The* Impact *film crew on location, about 1948, at Probert's gasoline station, with his Kaiser-Frazer showroom and service department on the left. The seated person at center probably is the female lead, Ella Raines, costumed in her service station coveralls.*

and other partners purchasing the house for use as a restaurant; when they learned Mildred owned many adjacent structures as well, they expanded their plan to include a mixture of shops that one of the partners described as "a miniature Ghirardelli Square." A local carpenter revamped the outbuildings, and a kitchen was tacked onto the rear of the house, which otherwise remained essentially unchanged except for the addition of a recycled wooden bar and relocation of the front door. A Lord & Burnham greenhouse was appended on the south side, to serve as a main dining room with views of the redwoods; it was enclosed with exterior siding and trim to match the house. The developers then coined the term "Lark Creek," a name never previously used to describe Larkspur's central waterway. Local shop operators, many of them amateurs, completed the eclectic mix, identified by the yellow paint scheme of the Lark Creek Shoppes complex.

After several years of operation the restaurant was turned over to others, and the real property to local realtor Sue Schaeffer. In 1989 chef Bradley Ogden and partner Michael Dellar assumed control of the restaurant, which eventually became the nationally renowned cornerstone of the Lark Creek Restaurant Group. Describing the old Inn as "prim and proper," the owners redesigned its menu and interior, reopening it in mid-2009 as The Tavern at Lark Creek.

San Rafael developer George Barnett built the four-unit apartment structure at **245 MAGNOLIA AVENUE** in 1961.

③ Arch Street Stairs

Larkspur's best-known stairs, used for training by generations of athletes and walkers, run for 139 steps between Magnolia and Walnut Avenues, but have always been designated as Arch Street *(see Appendix C)*. Although most streets were named for trees, the American Land and Trust Co. appears to have had a practice of using four-letter, non-tree names for any steep connecting routes that weren't likely to be used by vehicles. A few of those "paper streets" were outfitted with concrete stairways.

The contemporary office building at **265 MAGNOLIA AVENUE** was constructed in 2002 on what had been a gravel parking lot, used from the late 1930s through the 1960s as the site for some of Hil Probert's used car sales. The unsightly lot had been a downtown fixture for most of the

▲ 1.7: *This 1962 view shows City Hall through the trees at far left, with the Durston home at 282 Magnolia Avenue, the Lanouette house at 274 Magnolia, and Probert's used car lot and showroom.*

twentieth century, enclosed occasionally by a loosely draped steel chain; it was finally replaced by this handsome structure, designed and occupied by Pacific Design Group, Inc., an architectural firm. It was the first new commercial structure to be built in the downtown area in about 35 years.

Number **275 MAGNOLIA AVENUE**, a professional office building on lands originally a part of Patrick King's pear orchard, was built in 1967 for Peter J. Wikel, CPA, for use as his own office. The builders took special pains to preserve the valley oak on the front sideline, including a retaining wall built with the cooperation of the neighboring owner.

The small building facing Magnolia at **274 MAGNOLIA AVENUE**, now part of the Lark Creek complex, was for many years a private home. Built sometime before 1909, it was the main house for a group of seven tourist cabins grouped downhill to the rear of both 274 and 286; only one of those cabins remains today, the small structure near the creek numbered 276 Magnolia Avenue. For several decades the land was owned by Annie Lanouette and her husband Frank; after Annie's death in 1921, Frank stayed on in little 276, renting the 274 house to others. Frank Lanouette was part of a large family that figured importantly in early Larkspur history *(see page 39)*. In later years Ernest Probert and his wife Grace lived here while their son's adjacent Probert automobile showroom was constructed.

The small bungalow at **282-286 MAGNOLIA AVENUE**, used as a restaurant since the early

> **WHILE LARKSPUR SLEPT**
>
> "With a blast that aroused the populace, a huge revolving dryer in operation at the Golden Gate Cleaners in Larkspur exploded last Friday [at 7:40 a.m.], causing a loss estimated by insurance adjusters to be about $5,000. The tumbler was filled with a load of Army uniforms which were damaged and the dryer itself was rendered useless…. The Larkspur Fire Department arrived at once from across the street and quickly checked the flames."
>
> — *Larkspur-Corte Madera News*, June 27, 1946

▲ *1.8: The Golden Gate Cleaners at 320 Magnolia Avenue as it appeared in about 1955.*

▲ *1.9: Remodeled, the 320 building housed Katherine Eubanks' Florist, 1983.*

▲ *1.10: Java's outdoor dining tables in 1998. Cyclists and walkers made Java the place to be seen in Larkspur.*

1970s, was built about 1922 by George and Jean Durston. During construction of the bungalow, the Durstons lived across the street in their home at 9 Arch Street on the Arch Street stairs. Shortly after the construction of this five-room house they rented it to the Pacific Telephone and Telegraph Company, which occupied the building pending completion of a new brick office in the next block at 464 Magnolia. After George Durston's 1925 death, his widow Jean moved here with other family members. The building then passed through interim owners, eventually becoming part of the Lark Creek complex, and serving most recently as the Yankee Pier.

④ 320 Magnolia Avenue

The brick structure at **320 MAGNOLIA AVENUE** – one of several built downtown in the fall of 1925 by developer William F. Granger – was erected for L. V. Waymire and his wife Martha. They moved their Golden Gate Cleaners here from San Rafael, personally operating that business into the 1940s, then were succeeded by various operators for the next two decades.

The cleaning business was eventually replaced by Katherine Eubanks' florist shop, which moved to this location in 1960 from 479 Magnolia. The Eubanks family eliminated the industrial appearance of the structure, expanding the front door and windows. Their imaginatively designed window displays marked the unofficial southern end of the downtown retail area.

When Eubanks' Florist moved to a different downtown location in 1991, the 320 building was reconfigured for restaurant use and retrofitted for earthquake safety; thus transformed, it opened in 1992 as "Java," an innovative and hugely popular coffee house/restaurant. The outdoor tables at Java became a prime people-watching location that subsequently attracted the attention of other entrepreneurs. Adjoining structures, formerly operated as small shops, were then merged into the corner location, and in 2002 the enlarged site became a cutting-edge raw-food restaurant named "Roxanne's." Since 2004 the site has been chef Bruce Hill's Picco Restaurant, with an adjacent Pizzeria Picco at 316 Magnolia.

⑤ King-Costello House

Patrick King, born in Ireland in 1825, started farming here in 1866; his lands eventually became the basis for all of downtown Larkspur and the hills above it. His farmhouse, rebuilt as the gracious Queen Anne structure at **105 KING STREET**, has been a witness to most of Larkspur's recorded history.

Patrick and his wife Catherine had emigrated from Ireland's County Galway; Patrick then "engaged in the business of stock selling" with William Murray of Ross Landing. In 1866 King and Murray leased extensive acreage, including this site, from the Ross family, intending to farm it. In 1869 they purchased that land for $4,500, and two weeks later split their holdings, King taking the southern 701 acres, and Murray retaining the northern 533 acres. King's extensive farm thus encompassed most of the land from "the Baltimore Gulch" (today's Baltimore Canyon) northward nearly to modern-day Kentfield.

By the time of the July 1870 census Patrick and Catherine occupied their home on this gentle hillside, living here with a nine-year-old daughter and twin four-year-old boys, all born locally. Only seven weeks after that census Catherine died, leaving a dispirited Patrick to raise their family.

In 1873 King sold some land for the tracks of the new North Pacific Coast Railroad Company, and over the ensuing years sold other portions of his farm to various early families whose names still appear on our landscape. Patrick eventually remarried; in September of 1880 he and his new Irish wife Bridget sold all their remaining land to a San Francisco speculator, William F. Mau. Seven years later Mau and other investors formed the American Land and Trust Co., and formally began development of their subdivision, known as "the Town of Larkspur" in 1887. After that sale Patrick and Bridget retired to San Rafael; in their later years they each made a variety of gifts to Larkspur, including the lands for the original St. Patrick's Church structure on Cane Street. Patrick died in March of 1896, and Bridget followed in 1905. The street name "King" memorializes the important role of this pioneer family.

King's original farmhouse had been small and modest, located somewhat to the southwest of today's structure. In 1889 the house and its lands were sold to the extended Burtchaell family, who

▲ 1.12: *The James Costello family on the steps of "Woodstock," their country home at the corner of King Street and Magnolia Avenue. The portrait was probably made in 1898, shortly after their purchase, and shows James, wife Ellen, and daughter Eileen, with a domestic helper.*

apparently had been tenants on the farm after King's departure. The Burtchaell children became involved in a variety of commercial enterprises in Marin, including the Tamalpais Grocery Company on Magnolia Avenue. James T. Burtchaell contracted with Gustave Nagel in February of 1892 to build a new house closer to the street corner, while relocating and incorporating some portions of the original King home within that new structure. The current house thus dates to 1892, while its south-central bedroom wing dates to the late 1860s. Nagel's design used many aspects of the exuberant Queen Anne style, including a broad front porch with complex latticework, spandrels, beaded siding, steep and jerkinhead gables, fishscale shingles, and framed plaster friezes. The rock wall around the lot, made of local blue rock with sculpted grout, has pillars linked with stout iron chain.

About six years after the house was enlarged the Burtchaells sold the entire property to Ireland-born James and Ellen Costello of San Francisco, in March of 1898. The Costellos named their new summer home "Woodstock," using it only occasionally, except when forced to occupy it for an interval following damage to their San Francisco home caused by the 1906 earthquake.

▲ 1.11: *The original King farmhouse and outbuildings, viewed in this undated photo facing to the northeast across the county road with marshlands in the distance. The ravine opposite the house is now the dip in King Street as it approaches the creek, and cows graze where City Hall now stands.*

"James Costello and family took advantage of the good weather to motor over and spend Sunday at his comfortable home 'Woodstock.'"

—Marin County Tocsin, May 10, 1913

▲ *1.13: The 1948 rectory for St. Patrick's Church is an elaboration of the Spanish Colonial Revival style used in the adjacent church, 2009.*

▲ *1.14: The three Costello houses shortly after completion of the Mews project to the rear, 1997.*

▲ *1.15: The ancient barn behind 115 King Street, 2009. "It was nice of my grandfather to leave me a barn," said Jim Costello.*

▲ *1.16: The 1963 archdiocese house at 127 King Street, 2009.*

A prominent San Francisco businessman, James Costello owned and operated the O'Connor, Moffatt & Co. department store in San Francisco, but also made some investments in Larkspur. He and Ellen acquired the three adjoining lots on King Street in 1898, building handsome rental houses there about 1908. Costello also invested in the downtown Hotel Larkspur in 1901, owning it until 1910, when it was sold and reopened as the "Blue Rock Hotel." This house remained in the Costello family for decades, and finally saw permanent occupants in 1941 when newlyweds William Costello and his wife Barbara moved into the cold and drafty house. (Reportedly, they had been the first couple married in the new St. Patrick's Church across the street; construction had not yet been completed, so the wedding party entered through a side door!) Over the decades the family added central heating, a sunroom, sleeping porch, and bedroom at the rear. The concrete foundation of an old water tower remains in the rear yard, and next door, at the rear of 115 King Street, the early King barn continues to hold itself together precariously. In 2008 new owners began a thorough renovation of the landmark house, retaining most of the exterior portions of the structure in essentially unchanged condition.

⟴ *The downtown corridor includes several sites on the first western block of King Street. Turn west on King, then return.*

⑥ King Street

Designed by architect Arnold Constable, the rectory of St. Patrick's Church was constructed in 1948 at **114 KING STREET**. It replaced a small cottage previously on the site that was used as the rectory from 1922 until its demolition to make way for this structure. The elaborate architectural details were designed to complement the Spanish Colonial Revival style of the adjacent church, built in 1941. Minor modifications to the rear of the building in 1991 have left its elaborate front features intact.

The James Costello family, owners of the adjacent landmark house at 105 King Street, had three identical structures – **115, 117, AND 125 KING STREET** (sometimes called "The Three Sisters") – built as rental units in 1908. The neoclassic rowhouses were designed by Thomas J. Welsh, a prominent Bay Area architect and cousin of the Costellos. Each house is clad in brown shingles, with a hipped roof and covered front porch. The original double-hung windows have lattice panes above a single pane. Modifications to 125 King involved an additional dormer added in 1998.

The original builders were a bit too casual about lot boundaries, and in the 1980s a complex process of lot-line adjustments was used to alter the boundaries to satisfy legal requirements. Further changes came in 1997 when a proposal to demolish the houses was amended instead to allow the addition of three new units in a rear area previously used as a tennis court. The resulting planned unit development, called the "King Street Mews," created new houses numbered 119, 121, and 123. Those structures are accessed by a driveway between 117 and 125, replacing an earlier route that once led to a double garage behind the homes; new garages inserted under the 117 and 125 houses provided additional parking. Special conditions were imposed to preserve the Monterey cypress heritage trees at the rear of the lot. The result was an imaginative adaptation that preserved the appearance and utility of these handsome old homes.

For many years, descendants of the Costello family retained possession of the houses; James and Joanne Costello continue to reside in 115 King Street, which has an early barn from the Costello grounds located in its rear yard. That barn, of uncertain but ancient origin, has been strengthened from within to preserve its external appearance and remarkable roofline.

During the 1950s the families of St. Patrick's began preparations to establish a parish school. San Francisco architect Vincent Buckley prepared plans that included a school building at **120 KING STREET** and a new parish hall on Magnolia Avenue. Although the St. Patrick's School building was completed in April of 1961, it was unable to open immediately due to a shortage of teaching sisters. Eventually, the Dominican Sisters were hired to teach, and classes opened on September 3, 1963, with four grades.

Number **127 KING STREET** was the site of an early house, reportedly one of the five built about 1890 to induce the railroad to open a passenger station at Larkspur. It had been the home of Hugo and Sophie Stolzenberg from the 1920s until about 1940, after they retired from the butcher shop they had founded at 467 Magnolia Avenue. The current large stucco structure was built in 1964 as a convent to house Dominican Sisters who taught in the new St. Patrick's School. No longer used for that purpose, it remains the property of the Roman Catholic Archdiocese of San Francisco.

⊃ *Return on King Street to Magnolia, then turn left (north).*

⑦ King to Cane Street

On the evening of July 2, 1913, the members of Larkspur's Board of Trustees (forerunner of the City Council) recessed their regular meeting, marched two blocks south along Magnolia Avenue to **400 MAGNOLIA AVENUE**, and officially resumed their business here in "New Town Hall" for the first time. Two days later this structure was formally dedicated as part of the 1913 Independence Day ceremonies. It had taken only about ten months to purchase the land, prepare plans, and construct this building, now called City Hall.

From the time of the city's 1908 incorporation, the official meeting place for the Board of

TOWN HALL DEDICATION

The Marin Journal reported that school children marched and sang songs, and Reverend J.A. Gardiner made "a beautiful and eloquent invocation." Mayor M. T. Gardiner "gave quite a lengthy address," explaining that he "knew the people wished a fine building, and that it would be finished in a practical, artistic, and durable manner; that it would be built strong enough to last for an indefinite period." Finally, trustee Charles McLeran's son, John Ralph McLeran, "born three hours after his mother voted for the bonds which made [Town Hall] possible," was baptized on the spot, and one of his baby shoes was included within the cornerstone's time capsule.

▲ *1.17: Proud citizens of Larkspur gathered on Sunday, April 20, 1913, to celebrate the new Town Hall and lay its cornerstone.*

WEEKLY MOVIES AT CITY HALL

▲ 1.18: *Ad from the* Larkspur-Corte Madera News, *May 3, 1929*

Town Trustees had been Lynch's Hall, a large downtown building on Magnolia Avenue located several doors north of Ward Street. Within a few years the city leaders made plans for a permanent structure of their own; on August 12, 1912, Larkspur voters approved a bond measure providing $35,000 for street improvements and $10,000 for a new town hall. The street improvement funds were intended to provide grading and paving for all of Magnolia Avenue, and Madrone Avenue as far west as Jones Way. The *Marin County Tocsin*, praising the energetic Board of Trustees, noted that the "first paved streets in Marin County will be those built in Larkspur." In truth, much of that spirit of civic improvement had been impressed upon the Board by the recently established Larkspur Woman's Improvement Club, organized the preceding April; the women, having received the right to vote in 1911, were making their new political power felt in the community, and are generally credited with passage of the bond measure. Negotiations soon began for town hall locations, and by late December the Trustees had paid $2,750 for this site "above the main street and on the proposed State Highway overlooking the Town." Charles O. Clausen, a prolific young San Francisco architect, was selected to design the structure as the winner of a design competition entered by a dozen well-known architects. A construction bid was accepted in February of 1913, and the building was finished five months later. As completed, the entire structure, including its interior furnishings, cost $15,110.50.

The building was designed in the popular Mission Revival style, with a stucco exterior, a broad shaped parapet, wide arches on the entry porch, and prominent use of red tiles. An elaborate quatrefoil window is centered in the parapet, framed by tile-roofed twin towers that have projecting eaves supported by detailed bracing. Another tiled roof is cantilevered over the second floor balcony. One of the building's intended purposes was revealed when the trustees voted in May to "have it fitted with wiring for a moving picture machine." Indeed, the entire upper floor was intended for gatherings and theatrical events; early directories listed the "Town Hall Theatre," and many residents recalled movies, whist parties, minstrel shows, and themed dance nights held there, with the volunteer firemen sponsoring dances and vaudeville performances. It later became the Twin Cities Theatre, with motion pictures shown every Friday night. City offices occupied most of the lower floor, with the council meetings held in what is now the main room of the library. Large doors at the building's southeast corner admitted the firemen's wheeled apparatus to the rear of the building. Decades later those fire doors were replaced by a new exterior entrance for the library.

Larkspur's Centennial celebrations in 2008 recalled the city's formal incorporation on March 1, 1908. Five men constituted the original Board of Town Trustees: Frank Craig, a San Francisco coffee importer, was selected as the first chairman; he was joined by John T. Foley, a water company inspector, William J. Kennedy, a telephone company

▲ 1.19: *An arched door at the rear of Town Hall admitted the volunteers' fire equipment; the library took over that location in 1939. Note the original drinking fountain at the sidewalk that remains today, about 1914.*

auditor, Alfred E. Woods, a steamship company clerk, and Baron Wilhelm Von Meyerinck, a bank teller. Changing times (and state law) later transmuted the "town" to a "city," and the corporation's "Board of Trustees" to a "City Council."

City Hall has proven to be a remarkably good investment, serving the city's needs through nearly a century. A citizen's advisory committee in 2001 recommended that a seismic retrofit of the building be given a high priority, a project that is likely to occur sometime after completion of the new police station at Piper Park.

Libraries in the early 1900s were in a state of evolution; many were private, some were run for profit, and a few were experimenting with opening to the public free of charge. Belle C. Brown, a founder of the Larkspur Woman's Improvement Club, is generally credited with spearheading the effort to create a free library, and in 1913 that library was assigned space within the new Town Hall. The new library was managed as a volunteer institution, with donations and fundraising events used to provide funds to purchase books. In 1923 the library became a part of the young city's government structure.

Between 1932 and 1968 (with time out to serve as city clerk from 1956 to 1961), librarian Helen C. Wilson's name was synonymous with the library. She greatly enlarged its collection and services and created a reciprocal agreement with the countywide library system. With her strong personality and sense of humor, she put her personal stamp on the library in more ways than one. Joan Lundstrom, a long-serving member of the City Council and frequent mayor, remembers that Mrs. Wilson "had a big rubber stamp that she put on the inside cover page of books that said, 'Please wash your hands before using book.' Another said, '50 cent fine for turning down the corners of pages.'" Mrs. Wilson even was known to have levied fines on the nuns from St. Patrick's Church.

When the fire department moved to its new building at 420 Magnolia in 1939, the library was allowed to move into the vacated space. During the 1970s the library's board of trustees and Friends of the Larkspur Library began a campaign for improvement of the library's services and expansion of its facilities, and in 1983 those efforts were rewarded with dedication of a dramatically renovated space. Architect Sally Swanson & Associates provided for greatly expanded open stacks, with plush and welcoming furnishings for patrons. The library remains a vital focal point of the community, but a future move to larger space is considered inevitable, particularly as seismic renovation of City Hall becomes more pressing.

The landmark corner structure at **401 MAGNOLIA AVENUE** was built in 1941 as the second St. Patrick's Church in Larkspur. The original church had been built nearby at 505 Cane Street in 1899, but that wooden structure was later moved to the northeast corner of King Street and Locust Avenue.

By 1938 the original church structure had proven inadequate. The pastor, Father Crowley, consulted with San Francisco architect Henry A. Minton, who had been the architect for numerous churches and schools elsewhere in the San Francisco diocese.

▲ 1.20: *The 1941 Spanish Colonial Revival St. Patrick's Church, 2002.*

Minton designed this building using some of the same elements of Spanish Colonial Revival style, particularly the green-tiled tower, as he had employed earlier for the basilica of the Mission Dolores Church in San Francisco.

Ground for the new reinforced concrete church was broken on June 9, 1940, and the building was completed and dedicated on February 23, 1941. The nearby original wooden church building continued in use as the parish hall until 1961, when it was torn down to make way for a new St. Patrick's School.

The plans for the nearby St. Patrick's School included development of a recreation and meeting hall, called St. Patrick's Center, which was completed in December of 1960 at **409 MAGNOLIA AVENUE**.

· · · · ·

THE LARKSPUR FIRE DEPARTMENT

"The Larkspur Fire Department is one of the most unique ones in the United States. It costs the taxpayers of the town not a cent to maintain. The department owns the famous "Rose Bowl" where dances are held weekly during the summer months, and the dance place, one of the few out-door ones in the Bay region, takes in sufficient during season to pay all the expenses of the fire department. It is not thought that any other town in the United States of like, or larger size, can boast a self-supporting fire organization."

–*Larkspur-Corte Madera News*, January 13, 1939

▲ 1.21: *Shown here in 2009, Larkspur's firehouse remains essentially unchanged from its original 1939 appearance.*

Plans for a new firehouse, "as modern as the streamline train," were announced by Larkspur's volunteer firemen in February of 1938; as part of the deal, the City Council provided the site on a city-owned lot adjacent to City Hall. A new building would allow the fire department to vacate its former space in the rear of City Hall, making that space available for the city's library, at an expected alteration cost of about $2,000. Almost a year later this concrete firehouse at **420 MAGNOLIA AVENUE** was opened for public tours on Sunday, January 15, 1939, with Dolph Doherty, president of the volunteers, promising that there would be "no formal dedication ceremonies and no speechmaking." Designed by architect Samuel Heiman of Ross, it was built at a cost of about $25,000, paid entirely by the receipts from the Rose Bowl dances (*see page 19*). (The same Capt. Heiman later designed an Honor Roll erected outside City Hall in 1944 to commemorate those in the armed services.)

▲ 1.22: Larkspur's volunteer firemen pause for the camera while on parade in San Rafael in 1909. A century later the same banner is displayed in the Council Chambers in City Hall; Ally Podd was the banner bearer. Many of the founders of the later Larkspur Association of Volunteer Firemen appear here, as identified in 1955 by Dolph Doherty. Arranged behind the banner were Albert Volla, Albert C. LeCornec, Ernest Seadell, J. Frank Murphy (also the Town Marshall), Unidentified, George Belamy [Beleney?], Charlie Murphy, Leonard Young, Billy Taylor, John Frizzi, Prosper Zaro (in white chief's helmet) and Frank Ambrose. They will pull by hand their cherished chemical engine, with Leonard Young's six-year-old daughter Mildred riding atop the engine beneath the wreath.

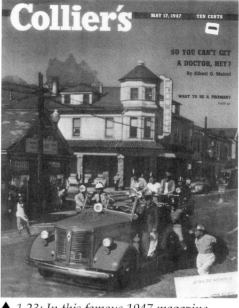

▲ 1.23: In this famous 1947 magazine cover, Larkspur volunteer firemen race to board their engine with the Blue Rock Hotel in the background. The staged photo features an engine driving on the wrong side of the street, and toward the firehouse in which it was stored.

Designed to be architecturally compatible with City Hall, the firehouse has a stucco exterior and red-tiled false roof. It originally contained an upstairs dormitory and showers for six men, a kitchen, a firefighters meeting room, and an apartment for use of the chief's family. Downstairs, two jail cells were provided (the better to contain inebriated Rose Bowl patrons) behind the engine bays. Those jail cells are long gone (although the window bars remain), and administrative offices have replaced the apartment, but much of the structure has retained its original features, updated as necessary with current information technology.

Formed in the early 1900s in response to well-publicized fires in San Rafael, San Francisco, and Sausalito, the Larkspur Volunteer Fire Department began with a bucket brigade and a hand-drawn hose cart. Shortly thereafter they acquired a new machine called a "chemical engine" that utilized tanks to produce carbon dioxide that propelled a stream of water.

For about a decade the volunteers operated as a loosely organized group with earnest, but changing, membership. Having finally attained permanent space within the new Town Hall, the group was formally incorporated in December of 1913 as the Larkspur Association of Volunteer Firemen (LAVF). The Association's first meeting was chaired by chief Prosper Zaro; after formal transfer of assets from the old to the new organization, new officers were elected. Randolph C. "Dolph" Doherty was elected chief, a position he would continue to hold for more than two decades. The founding directors were Doherty, John Frizzi, William Wegner, A. C. DeWitt, and J. F. Murphy. Members included Prosper Zaro, A. Volla, Arthur W. "Cap" Larsen, E. Seadell, John B. Colin, Albert C. Le Cornec, Leonard Young, and Henry Bain.

Without its volunteer fire department, Larkspur's history would probably not be very different than that of many small towns – but the firemen put Larkspur on the map. They operated the Rose Bowl dances, thus raising funds for a well-equipped department that made Larkspur famous.

A lead article in the May 17, 1947, *Collier's* magazine included a front cover photograph of volunteers rushing to board a moving fire engine, a scene repeated two years later in the 1949 film *Impact*. For many years an invitation to join the Association was highly prized, as the organization was considered the social and political arbiter of the city; waiting periods for new members often dragged on for years.

From 1913 until 1957 the LAVF operated as a private corporation, always solicitous of, but also distinct and independent from, the city's government. When the city assumed ownership of the fire department in 1957, the Association turned over equipment worth almost $500,000 to city control.

In their early years the volunteer firemen were called to duty by a bronze bell mounted in front of the original St. Patrick's Church on Cane Street. When the fire equipment was moved into City Hall in 1914, a powerful compressed air horn was installed in a 70-foot-tall tower at the rear of that building. The horn, called a "Gamewell Diaphone," remains operational (but unused) today. The Diaphone blew in coded patterns; Nancy Anthony, born in Larkspur and later the city clerk, remembered "You often waited apprehensively for the complete [horn] sequence to know just how close the fire was to your neighborhood." The same horn was blown daily at 8 a.m., noon, and 5 p.m. Audible over a seven-mile radius, the horn was universally used to order the affairs of life. "There's not a kid in the city," said former fire chief Bill Lellis, "who doesn't listen for that five o'clock whistle to know when to go home." The loud horn's daily blasts were finally discontinued as too noisy and no longer necessary; their disappearance closed another small town tradition.

The building at **426-428 MAGNOLIA AVENUE** is a concrete-block structure that was built in 1950 as a dental office, and has remained so to this day. It was built for (Mrs.) Ada Y. Ingalsbe, whose modest house survives far to the rear of this lot. Ada, who lived here from the 1920s until the mid-1950s, had been a dental nurse by profession, and apparently invested in a familiar concept; the first tenants of her new building previously had occupied dental offices in the professional space at 465 Magnolia. Before the office building was erected, Ada's house sat behind a white picket fence, hidden by dense masses of cedar that appear in many period photographs. The house's original 426 street address now refers to the dental offices, and Ada's house became 15 Rice Lane.

Ada's house and a nearby cottage, now numbered 13, 15, and 17 Rice Lane, were built sometime before 1909, apparently by Mary and George Madison of San Francisco; for a while their little complex of rental cottages was called "Madison Square." The

▲ 1.24: *Downtown Larkspur at 1 p.m. on June 7, 1954; the Little brothers' two stucco bungalows are on the left, with the Rose Bowl Chateau beyond. Larkspur Automotive is on the right. The banner above the street advertises the Rose Bowl dances.*

Madisons' two town lots now include the dental office structure, its adjacent parking lot, and the houses above.

Two similar stucco bungalows were built at 447 and **435 MAGNOLIA AVENUE** about 1924, in a period when the downtown retained a rich mixture of both residential and commercial structures. They were owned for many decades by David and Frank Little, who stored materials for their roofing business in the spacious rear yards behind both houses.

David C. Little, initially a shingler, expanded into a general roofing business with shingler Harry Booth about 1923; David soon acquired the entire operation, but kept the "Booth & Little" name thereafter. He was joined later by his brother Frank, and the Littles lived in these houses and operated their business here until 1970, when the house at 447 was razed (the site now provides parking for the restaurant at 455). Their business then moved to Redwood Highway, where it continues today as a family-run operation. David also served on the Larkspur City Council for 16 years, including three terms as mayor; he died in 1981 at age 93.

The remaining house, at 435 Magnolia, has retained much of its original exterior appearance, despite intervening commercial uses downstairs as a plumbing office, café, and in recent decades, a restaurant. The broad porch, with concrete floor and a stucco façade, is typical of California bungalows of the mid-1920s. Note that this structure has two entry doors on the porch; local dentist Dr. Thurlow C. Jaegeling rented this home for his family in the late 1930s, using the left door for his residence, and the

▲ 1.25: *The Alpine Garage, about 1928. The signs advertise both Erskine and (parent-company) Studebaker motorcars; Erskines were produced only between 1927 and 1930. Note the dense cedar trees on the adjacent Ingalsbe lot.*

▲ 1.26: *Reconstruction of the 444 Magnolia Avenue building in December of 1984. Only the ill-fated façade remained standing, and collapsed soon after.*

right door to enter his dental office. (Precisely the same pattern was used for the home the Jaegelings later built at 125 Magnolia Avenue.)

The house was purchased in the late 1980s by restaurateur Shih-Che Hsu, who phonetically named his operation "C.J. Chinese Cuisine." In 2007 the business changed hands and, now operated by former long-term employee David Sek and his wife Joanna, became "DJ Chinese Cuisine."

The Alpine Garage at **444 MAGNOLIA AVENUE** was erected on this corner in about 1925, and remained as an auto repair facility well into the 1980s. The original building had a single story with a distinctive stucco false front topped by red tile, done in a simple curved espadaña style, a simplified example of the Mission Revival style popular at that time.

By the early 1940s the business had become the Larkspur Garage, and later Larkspur Automotive Reconstruction. Four decades later, however, demand for office and retail space surpassed that for automotive services, and in 1984 the city approved reconstruction as a creative two-story office and commercial design that would have retained much of the structure's external historic character. Unfortunately, the signature façade collapsed during construction and is replaced today by a replica; historic preservation has numerous vexations.

⑧ 455-457 Magnolia Avenue

The second-story portion of **455 MAGNOLIA AVENUE** is the sole survivor of four identical residential structures built by Giacomo Costa about 1908. The distinctive shape of the roof has remained consistent since it was built; the building originally was only one story high, but later was elevated to provide commercial space on the ground floor. Remodeled numerous times, the lower portion is best remembered as the Rose Bowl Chateau, a popular cocktail lounge that was opened here about 1934, shortly after the repeal of

THE ROSE BOWL CHATEAU

"There was another bar on Magnolia, ... painted a calamine pink. It was named the Rose Bowl Chateau and we usually patronized it during the dance intermissions. Mixed drinks were twenty-five cents, a bottle of local beer fifteen. Nobody ever asked our age, and most of our crowd were four or five years under twenty-one, the drinking age minimum."

— Jerry Flam,
Good Life in Hard Times (1977)

▲ 1.27: *A rare snowfall, probably in 1913, decorated the luxurious garden of the Costa residence, next door to Stolzenberg's Meats.*

Prohibition, by locally-born Otto Guetter. The Rose Bowl Chateau was considered a vital hard-liquor adjunct to the soft drinks and beer available at the Saturday night Rose Bowl dances on nearby Cane Street. The Chateau was a small, stucco-covered structure, awkwardly jutting out to the lot line in front of (and under) the older wooden house.

The Rose Bowl Chateau managed to outlive its namesake; the Rose Bowl dance floor ceased operation in 1963, but the Chateau persevered until 1972. The space was then remodeled as Canzona's Restaurant, succeeded in turn in 1981 by Fabrizio Ristorante.

The older history of the site intertwines with most of this west side of the street. Giacomo Costa, born in Italy in 1852, immigrated to San Francisco and operated a boarding house there. He soon became a dealer in real estate, and with his wife Rosa, began investing in Larkspur properties. They acquired this lot in 1902 and built four residential structures arranged behind one another, after extending the lot's back line to better accommodate the buildings. A long driveway, located parallel to the structures, was named "Cane Court." Known as the Costa houses, the four buildings provided rental housing for Larkspur's downtown workers and residents until 1961, when three of them were removed for construction of the St. Patrick's schoolyard. The Costa family also acquired and developed most of the land in the center of this business block *(see page 32).*

Giacomo and Rosa's two sons were Roy and Enrico "Henry"; Roy worked in Larkspur for a while as an "automobile operator," and Henry served as a member, and president, of the Larkspur Board of Trustees from 1914 to 1918. It was Henry who proudly placed a business card for his San Francisco real estate and insurance business inside the 1913 City Hall cornerstone, and he reportedly co-owned the first automobile in Larkspur with Dolph Doherty; Henry would give other Town Trustees a ride when they did their Sunday inspection tours in 1914. The Costas' only daughter, Ida, married and remained in San Francisco. Giacomo and Rosa had their own home built here on the main street about 1900, between current addresses 457 and 465 Magnolia, where the thrift store's parking lot is now located.

Giacomo died in that house in 1921, remembered as a wealthy and prominent resident of Larkspur. Following Giacomo's death, his widow Rosa borrowed heavily against her many Larkspur properties; by 1928 those debts were foreclosed, and all her remaining Larkspur lands were sold at auction. Eventually the Costas' home was torn down, the lane was abandoned, and the resulting frontage was used to build the commercial structure at **457 MAGNOLIA AVENUE**.

Karl Schmalfeld first opened his Larkspur Cash Grocery across the street, in the little frame structure (452) that is now known as the "annex" to 450 Magnolia. In 1931 Karl was able to purchase this entire lot (today incorporating both 455 and 457), and by the mid-1930s he had moved his grocery operation to this new building. Like the building next door at 455, located on the same lot, this structure was squeezed in adjacent to the older Costa rental unit; that building's high roof remains visible to the southwest.

▲ 1.28: *Seen here about 1957, Kirby & Yates operated in the Karl's Grocery building as a package liquor store at 457 Magnolia Avenue from about 1952 to 1965, closing not long after the Rose Bowl dances were terminated. The space eventually became the St. Patrick's Thrift Shop. The adjacent Rose Bowl Chateau operated from 1934 to 1972.*

▲ 1.29: In this early view, probably photographed in 1900, the original St. Patrick's Church is at right center, facing northward toward the town. The house opposite the church became 502 Cane Street. Further north near Ward Street were (right to left) the livery stable, railroad buildings, and hotel, while Corte Madera Creek meanders across salt marshes in the distance.

A "cash grocery" was a phenomenon of the late 1920s and early 1930s, involving a shift from proprietor-service to self-service, with purchases no longer made on credit. Harry Richards, who grew up in the Larkspur-Corte Madera area in the 1920s, recalled the early days of small-town retailers who extended credit as a regular means of operation: "No cash changed hands. Everything was charged to a monthly account, which was paid in person at the end of each month. I tried to be along on settlement day, because there were gifts for small children." Karl's was one of several cash groceries in town, and by the time he moved his operation to this location, it probably was no longer necessary to use the "cash" term as part of the store's name. Instead, he simply used his own name – as everyone else did – to identify the new store.

Born in Germany, Karl had immigrated to the U.S. in 1912, moving to Larkspur in 1925. (His sister, Henrietta Vogt, lived with her husband at 488-490 Magnolia Avenue.) A sudden heart attack in 1951 ended both Karl's life and his grocery. The building soon was taken over by Frank G. Kirby and George Yates, operating it as Kirby & Yates Liquors until 1965. The notable checkerboard tile front of the liquor store reportedly was destroyed when a police car crashed into the building during a chase along Cane Street. After interim service as Cunningham Press, the building was acquired by the nearby St. Patrick's and since 1985 has operated as St. Patrick's Thrift Shop. The structure was then remodeled, a new brick façade applied, and the transom windows restored.

⊃ *The downtown corridor includes several sites on Cane Street, a one-block segment of the 1887 Larkspur subdivision that runs eastward from Magnolia Avenue.*

⑨ Original St. Patrick's Church Site

The gentle hillside overlooking the wooded creek bed and the town was the first site of St. Patrick's Church, located from 1899 until 1922 at **505 CANE STREET**.

In the 1890s Larkspur's Catholic vacationers and residents who wished to attend Mass had to travel to St. Raphael's Parish in San Rafael. James Costello (who was soon to purchase the King-Burtchaell house at 105 King Street) started a fund to create a church within Larkspur. Some Catholic families gave a series of "entertainments" to raise additional funds, and in 1896 a Mass was celebrated in the Larkspur School hall, using a piano for the altar.

Pioneer Patrick King, whose farm once included all of today's downtown *(see pages 6-7)*, had purchased back from the land developers the lots in this block. Shortly before his 1896 death, King transferred the lots to his wife Bridget, who later donated the land to the church in memory of Patrick's three children who had died in the late 1880s of tuberculosis.

Once the land had become available, Rev. Hugh Lagan, the priest at St. Raphael's Parish, undertook to provide a new structure on this site, to be

ST. PATRICK'S CHURCH

"A grand concert will be held in the school-house at Corte Madera on the evening of the 25th... The entertainment will be followed by an ice cream, coffee and cake luncheon and a dance.... The people of Larkspur and vicinity are raising a fund to build a Roman Catholic church. They already have about half the money required for this very deserving purpose. The admission to this social will be 50 cents. The proceeds of the evening will go to the church building fund."

— *The Sausalito News*, July 18, 1896

operated as a mission of San Rafael. Father Lagan hired Bryan Clinch, an architect who had designed many churches in the Bay Area, to design the new structure; it was constructed of redwood lumber, with the pews and altar railing recycled from the old St. Raphael's Church.

Father Lagan named the new church in honor of Patrick King. Prominent local residents Mary and Belle Brown, James Costello, and Ellen Callot Escalle donated stained glass windows. The new structure had neither a spire nor a bell tower; after Ellen's 1903 death, Jean Escalle had a separate bell tower built in front of the church and donated a bell in memory of his deceased wife. For the next two decades that bell also served as the town's alarm for its volunteer firemen; much later the Escalle bell was relocated to the present church tower at 401 Magnolia Avenue.

In 1915 St. Patrick's became a parish and acquired a full-time pastor, Father John G. Conlan, who promptly ordered the construction of a rectory on land behind the church. He contracted with Gustave Nagel in July of 1915 for $2,000 to construct the small shingled structure that survives today as 10 Rice Lane. That house has been expanded and remodeled repeatedly over the ensuing decades. However, by 1921 a new pastor decided that the original location was unsuitable for a parish church, probably because of physical limitations of the site itself, or due perhaps to the crowds and activity attendant the nearby Rose Bowl. In 1922 the church purchased larger space on King Street, and in March of that year the original church structure was removed from this site to the northeast corner of King Street and Locust Avenue, where it remained until it was demolished in 1961 to make way for the new buildings of St. Patrick's School.

The church later sold this site, and a two-story apartment structure was built here with a mixture of retail spaces. Although three of those retail spaces later were converted to residential apartments, the Larkspur Shoe Repair remained in the northwest corner location (505) until the mid-1980s.

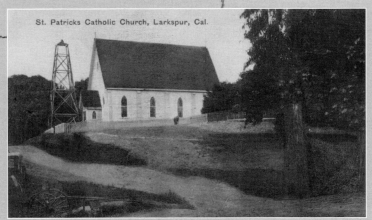

▲ 1.30: *A postcard view of St. Patrick's Catholic Church and bell tower, about 1905.*

"The new Catholic Church at Larkspur was dedicated last Sunday [July 9] the ceremony being performed by Archbishop Riordan. Mass was celebrated by the Rev. Father Hugh Lagan, assisted by Father Cleary, Father Mulligan, Father Lynch and Father Casey."

— *The Marin Journal*, July 13, 1899

▲ 1.31: *The homes at 508 and 502 Cane Street, dating to about 1909 and 1897, still retain much of their original street-front appearance in 2009.*

▲ 1.32: *The Cane Street entrance to the Rose Bowl, 1944. The dense redwood grove to the right remains unscathed, and many of the pipe handrails still exist on the concrete bridge over the creek. The two lanterns atop the entry posts are now in the custody of the fire department's history collection.*

The modest little shingled house has occupied its spot at **508 CANE STREET** since at least 1909. It was probably built for James J. Ryan of San Francisco, the owner during that period.

The two-story house located at **502 CANE STREET** probably was built about 1897 by John and Adelina Frizzi, both Swiss-Italian immigrants. (The similarly named August "Gus" and Julia Frizzi operated commercial enterprises at 499 and 501 Magnolia Avenue.) John had been a locksmith in San Francisco and then worked in Larkspur variously as a liquor dealer and day laborer. His primary community contribution was as a fireman; he was a founding director of the Volunteers, and a very active member of that group through the 1930s. John and Adelina sold this house in 1909, moving to 117 Locust Avenue. The house later was occupied by the extended Eatherton, Guetter, and Benz families from the mid-1920s until 1998. Throughout most of that period its exterior shape changed very little, easily recognizable from turn-of-the-century photographs. Operated as duplex residential units since the mid-1950s, the structure was revamped in 2003 with replaced exterior cladding and substantial changes to the north (rear) side.

⑩ Rose Bowl Site

Larkspur's legendary Rose Bowl – a spacious outdoor dance floor – was located at **476 CANE STREET** from about 1913 to 1963. The Rose Bowl Apartments, built in 1968 by Bette and Richard Peters, perpetuated the name, and managed to retain many of the bay, buckeye, and redwood trees that once enveloped the celebrated dance floor.

On December 4, 1963, the Volunteer Firemen announced with deep regret that they had decided to close the Rose Bowl permanently, after more than 54 successful years of operation. The name "Rose Bowl" reportedly derived from a rose-covered fence around the dance floor, and Cane Street itself, according to one theory, was named for wild rose bushes that grew there in the 1880s. The name came into use sometime in the late 1920s – before that it was simply the "outdoor dance pavilion" or the "open air platform."

As the Larkspur Volunteer Fire Department began to organize during the early 1900s, its members staged several impromptu dances to raise funds to purchase fire equipment. Perhaps the first formally advertised dance was held in September of 1909, as a featured part of the young town's Booster Day celebration. A temporary wooden dance floor was erected in the open area between the Hotel Larkspur (later known as the Blue Rock) and the train station, and in the shade of a large oak, surrounded by bunting, a small band (led by fire chief Prosper Zaro) provided music for dancers.

The success of additional dances prompted a search for a more permanent site, and by summer of 1913 a small "open air platform" had been built in "the Larkspur Grove" at this Cane Street site. The following August the Volunteers

THE ROSE BOWL

"Omnipresent firemen, nattily attired in spotless blue uniforms and dress white hats, keep a close watch on any overly-relaxed adult or on the high stepping teen-ager groups. Solicitous parents have no fear that their progeny will run into trouble at the Rose Bowl — its high standing record means too much to firemen."

— *Independent-Journal,*
May 2, 1952

contracted to buy that location for $1,475, and after making payments of $15 per month, received a deed in 1917.

The relationship between the young town and its firemen was unsettled. In December of 1913, at about the time the Larkspur Association of Volunteer Firemen became officially incorporated, the Town Trustees passed two ordinances; the first would have required regulation of all "open air entertainments and dances," and the second authorized the creation and organization of a volunteer fire department. Taken together the ordinances were seen as an attempt to close the dances and control the firefighters. Within two weeks citizens petitioned to vote on those ordinances, prompting a referendum election the following April that overturned both measures by two-to-one margins. At the same time four new Trustees were elected to the Board, ending abruptly any attempt to control the Volunteers' activities; within four days the Volunteers began preparations to enlarge their "open-air platform" for the coming dance season.

Over time the floor was increased in size, and included benches and seats along two sides, with the band platform, hat room, and

▲1.33: *Dancers paused on a Saturday evening in July of 1918; military uniforms on several men provide a sobering reminder that the final battles of World War I were raging then in Europe. Dolph Doherty, the chief (and later, president) of the Volunteers, stands at center in a dark suit, glancing toward the camera.*

▲ 1.34: *The origin of the Rose Bowl tradition is generally believed to have been Larkspur's Grand Celebration Booster Day held downtown on September 6, 1909. Onlookers and bunting ring the oak-shaded dance platform, and the firemen's chemical engine sits on prominent display in the foreground. The original train station provides shade at the rear.*

THE ROSE BOWL

"On clear, summery nights the crowd-pulling music can be heard as a nostalgic whisper as far as the lookout tower atop Mt. Tamalpais four miles away. The Rose Bowl, they say, is made for romance and memories."

— Undated news clip

refreshment bar backing onto the railroad tracks. Dancers learned to accept the shaking that occurred when the Interurban Service electric railroad cars came swooshing along. The exposed outdoor floor had to be replaced occasionally (using vertical-grain lumber from Dolph Doherty's Larkspur Lumber Company), and each spring the Volunteers had the floor sanded and "paraffined;" they applied "dance powder" weekly.

As word of the Saturday night dances spread, dancers arrived from all over the Bay Area on the two-lane roads, or on the ferries and train. The train crowds were sometimes rowdy, so the conductors and crew were deputized and given the authority to determine whether or not the crowds would be allowed to disembark for the dance. If they were too disorderly, they were returned to Sausalito to take the ferry back to San Francisco. "Larkspur was simply flooded with people on weekends," recalled Miriam Austin in a 1985 interview. "They came from all over the Bay Area. The town was just jumping Saturday nights. It was fun … out under the big redwood trees, the big dance floor and the good bands."

Dear Harry: Am having a swell time up here although it's a small hick town. Am going to the dance Sat. night, so won't be in for Sunday. Give my love to the family – will see you all next week. Love, Amanda

— From a 1932 postcard

Dancers foxtrotted, jitterbugged, and waltzed beneath strings of colored lights that were hung from the trees. The style and complexity of the music grew over time. On the opening night of the 1915 season, John F. Bena, an accordion player from San Francisco, brought an orchestra consisting of his accordion, a coronet, trombone, drums, and piano; that piano player was Henry Costa, who served then as a town trustee. Other bands were often little-known college groups, but by the late 1930s included well-known orchestras that played the Bay Area hotel circuit, such as Ernie Heckscher, Ray Hackett, Walter Krausgrill, Ray Tellier's San Francisco Orchestra, and the Del Courtney Band.

Arthur W. "Cap" Larsen, who was secretary of the Volunteers until 1947, served as master of ceremonies at the dances, announcing on-the-spot engagements, and perhaps the anniversaries of couples that had met at an earlier dance. Willie Frizzi *(see page 35)*, who was a one-man electrical company, designed an elaborate system of switches, dimmers, floodlights, and electrical displays. For a few years the dances featured the famous Rose Bowl "Firefall" at 11 o'clock; while the lights dimmed and the band drummer beat a long staccato roll, a blazing shower of white sparks cascaded from about 40 feet in the sky (while a fireman stood by with a hose, should one prove necessary).

In the earliest years no jail was available, so those dancers who were too drunk or disorderly to return to San Francisco were held overnight in a boxcar on a siding by the station. After the 1939 construction of the firehouse, its small jail was used for that purpose. Following the last dance, or perhaps the next morning, the sobered occupants would be loaded onto the train for return to San Francisco.

Many longtime Larkspur residents recall that local youngsters would scour the dance floor early on Sunday morning, searching for (and keeping) lost change near the refreshment stand, and then later, when adults arrived, helping in the official clean-up process, thereby earning a free pass to the movie at City Hall the following Friday night.

The Volunteers enjoyed financial success, and were generous in sharing the dance proceeds. On designated evenings the open air platform was made available to various worthy causes including the Larkspur Woman's Improvement Club, St. Patrick's Church, and the Corte Madera Fire Department.

Various theories have been offered to explain the demise of the Rose Bowl, including changes in the weather, high musicians' union wage scales, or the advent of television, but by 1963 the operating expenses far exceeded the income. Perhaps it is sufficient to note, as the *Independent Journal* described it, "a changing society lost interest in outdoor dancing on summer evenings." It's a pity.

On special occasions the Rose Bowl is lovingly recreated, most recently as a centerpiece of the city's 2008 Centennial. Tickets sold out within hours to 1,000 dancers who gathered on a clear summer evening on the historic grounds of Mary Tiscornia's Escalle winery. Outdoor lanterns were strung up, special bars were staffed, and an exact replica of the original moon lantern was commissioned and installed for the event. The bands played, and another generation discovered Rose Bowl romance and memories. There won't be another evening like it for a hundred years.

➲ *Cane Street now becomes Holcomb Avenue, discussed in the Baltimore Park chapter. Return to Magnolia Avenue.*

⑪ Central Downtown Corridor

Hungary-born Joseph A. Ambrosy operated, and probably built, a blacksmith shop on the corner of **450-452 MAGNOLIA AVENUE** at least as early as 1905. He and his Austrian wife Marie lived in the quarters above the shop. In later decades Joseph described himself as a veterinarian, a tendency suggested by several 1908 newspaper advertisements:

> "J.A. Ambrosy, General Blacksmith and Expert Horseshoer. Having served twelve years as blacksmith in the Army I am prepared to deal with the worst kind of corns on horses' feet and all kinds of impediments caused by unskillful shoeing. Carriage and Wagon Builder."

For several years Joseph was active in local affairs, but departed abruptly in 1910 to work as the blacksmith for a Siskiyou County lumber company, apparently never to return.

▲ *1.35: Metropolitan downtown Larkspur, about 1911. J. A. Ambrosy's blacksmith building is on the right (now 450 Magnolia Avenue), with Frank Murphy's Canyon Express Co. in an adjacent lean-to where the firemen's hose cart has been parked; note the large decorative cornices on the façade of the blacksmith building. Cane Street is simply a rough dirt area leading between the tree stumps. Stolzenberg's meat market and a candy shop are across the street.*

In the Ambrosys' absence, their shop was turned over to J. Frank Murphy and his wife, Catherine, who lived here for a few years with their teenage daughter Millicent. The Murphys seem to have made a mark in the community; Frank served several years as a town marshal, worked as a blacksmith, and operated the Canyon Express Company here in the period about 1911-1914.

Catherine Murphy was a formidable woman; Marjorie Woods recalled in a 1976 interview that Mrs. Murphy was "a huge woman who was very capable of going to the railroad to pick up large containers of butter and then delivering them to customers." She reportedly once marched to the Larkspur-Corte Madera School, upset that teacher Henry Hall had reprimanded her daughter, stood outside the picket fence, and swore loudly that she would wipe him up and down the street.

With the coming of automobiles, the role of the building began to shift from horses to cars. In 1919 the structure was purchased from the Ambrosys by Giuseppe "Joseph" Zampetti, another blacksmith, who lived here with his wife Josephine and son Gino. Zampetti earlier had converted the business into the Larkspur Garage, and in 1918 had received city permission to install an underground gasoline tank under the sidewalk. The Zampettis later divorced and sold their Larkspur Garage to William and Elizabeth O'Brien in 1923.

Through the mid-1920s the corner building was used for auto repair and storage; sometime earlier a small frame building had been added on the north side, and used as part of the auto storage enterprise. That adjacent structure (sometimes called the "annex") acquired its own address of 452/454 Magnolia, but always remained as a part of the same building lot. In addition to his garage business, William O'Brien operated a taxi company here, and in 1931 allowed his boarder, Karl Schmalfeld, to open the Larkspur Cash Grocery at this site, where it operated until Karl moved across the street to 457. After Karl's departure, the structure became a beauty and barbershop operated by Nardene and Jack DeLegons, then a 5 & 10 Cent store. In later years the annex housed small coffee shops (Faye's, Lucille's), and in the early 1960s was subsumed into the bar on the corner.

The corner building retains recognizable features of its original lines. The original v-channel siding was covered on the first floor by stucco in the mid-

▲ 1.36: At center, the Larkspur Hardware at 460 Magnolia Avenue, about 1960. Lucille's Coffee Shop is on the right at 452, and the unadorned brick structure to the left is 464 Magnolia Avenue.

1930s, to accommodate a new tavern, and keyhole windows were added in a vaguely Moderne style. The tall, Italianate false front once had large cornices with curved brackets; those design features remained in place until the mid-1950s, removed perhaps when the upper story was covered by protective asbestos shingles. A wide door on the south side, betrayed by lines in the concrete of the sidewalk and panels on the exterior, was not part of the original structure, but instead appears to date to the automobile uses of the 1920s.

Final transformation of the two buildings began in the mid-1930s, after the repeal of Prohibition, when the O'Briens leased the corner structure, first to Joe Jossa (Joe's), and then in 1938 to Robert and Olive Dooney, who promptly opened Bob's Tavern on the site. Bob's morphed into Jim's Tavern by 1954, and eventually became the Silver Peso in 1962. One version of the Silver Peso's creation myth invokes the Japanese invasion of the Philippines early in World War II. Retreating government forces supposedly dumped silver pesos into the Bay of Manila. After the war, divers returned to the area and recovered enough pesos to fund purchase of the bar. Or so the story goes. Another version holds that a bag of silver pesos was discovered under the floorboards during remodeling. Both stories improve with sufficient beer.

The Silver Peso has survived for nearly a half-century as a link to Larkspur's more flamboyant past, easily recalled when crowds spill into the street, or large Harley-Davidsons are parked at the curb.

Built in 1925 by owner-developer William F. Granger, the brick building at **460 MAGNOLIA AVENUE** was designed for its first tenant, Ralph L. Kokjer, who opened the Larkspur Hardware here.

▲ 1.37: *Firehouse construction volunteers, about 1908. From the left, Christian Muender, a railroad carpenter; the three Guetter boys, Max, Richard, and Otto; an unidentified man (perhaps Richard Guetter?); Detlef "Dick" Wessel; Frank Ambrose, a local house painter; Jim Bain, an early leader of the volunteers; Dolph Doherty, owner of the lumberyard and donor of the site and building materials; Jacob "Jack" Wessel, a building contractor; and Joe Ambrosy, the blacksmith at the adjacent shop. Onlookers at right are unidentified. Note the railcar in front of the shed, seen through the lumberyard's picket fence.*

◀ 1.38: *The completed firehouse, whitewashed and decorated for a Fourth of July, about 1909-1910. John Goeppert on left, Robert Murray, a local plumber, in bowler hat; Nell Doherty in center, accompanied by Carolyn Rice and Catherine Murphy; Clara Goeppert in foreground.*

▲ 1.39: *The western block of central Magnolia Avenue, looking north, about 1911. On the left, Stolzenberg's "meats, fruits and vegetables" store, a candy store, and Charles Hargens' Model Bakery. Note the high balcony and cornices on the bakery building.*

(Kokjer also served as census enumerator for the April 1930 federal census in Larkspur.) Ralph and Helen Kokjer ran their hardware store until the mid-1940s, raising three children in the residential quarters in the rear. The hardware store later passed through a succession of owners, finally closing in the early 1960s. In 1973 this space took on new life as Artist's Proof, a small bookstore whose owners, Maryjane Dunstan and Harriette Francis, supported numerous community activities. Eventually the building became an adjunct to Emporio Rulli.

On a larger scale, the 460 address marks the southern edge of what had been the extensive yard of the Larkspur Lumber Co. during the first three decades of the 1900s. The lumberyard occupied the whole of this block, except for the blacksmith's shop at 450 Magnolia. It was in this southwest corner of that yard that Dolph Doherty, the operator of the lumber company and chief of the volunteer firemen, donated space and materials for a small frame firehouse to contain the volunteers' hose cart and new chemical engine. This first firehouse was no longer needed after the fire equipment was transferred to City Hall in 1914. Although vacated by the firemen, the simple little structure continued in use as a part of the lumberyard until its demolition in 1924.

Hugo and Sophia Stolzenberg erected a retail meat and fruit store at **465-471 MAGNOLIA AVENUE** in 1907-1908, soon after they had purchased the two lots between Magnolia and Locust Avenues. A large barn that stood behind their shop still stands today, numbered as 469 Magnolia. Both Hugo and Sophia were German immigrants; Hugo was active in early civic affairs, agreeing to serve as a surety for the faithful performance of various elected officials during the town's early formation.

The barn at 469 served for hay storage and as a slaughterhouse. (The stream coming from Sycamore Avenue flows in a culvert beneath the barn, where a drain added waste material to the flow.) In intervening years the structure has had varied uses, including a self-service laundry, first opened in 1952 and still extant today. The old barn has been expanded and remodeled numerous times, although it still displays some of the original beveled drop siding on its east face, and the broad doorway to the laundry reveals the dimensions of an earlier barn door.

▲ 1.40: Bill Howard in 2008 at the history box he built to display the story of his building at 465-467 Magnolia.

Yet a third structure, present in the very early 1900s, was a small candy store, located immediately to the north of the meat shop. By the mid-1920s the candy store had disappeared, and was replaced much later by today's parking curb and plantings.

After Stolzenberg retired, his meat market was purchased by Andrew Gilardi in 1921. Hugo and Sophia then lived at 127 King Street until about 1940, and both died a few years later. The Gilardi family operated the Larkspur Meat Market here until the late 1940s, then used this address as Gilardi's Delicatessen and Catering, while moving their meat enterprise into Epidendio's market at 483 Magnolia Avenue. About 1957, the 467 address was transformed briefly into a television and appliance store, while Gilardi's catering operation moved to larger quarters at 489 Magnolia. This building then went through a series of uses, primarily as John Barry's and Bob Schoenhoff's insurance agencies, from the late 1960s to the mid-1990s.

In 1977 the old butcher shop and barn were connected by a covered walkway, landscaped parking, and a new building which became Donut Alley at 471 Magnolia Avenue, and used ever since as a popular doughnut bakery with office space above. Other small shops and services are tucked in nearby.

The upstairs portion of the meat market, numbered 465 Magnolia, originally was used as a residence for the Stolzenbergs, and then served for decades as doctors' offices. Its interior features befit a well-designed and comfortable home. In the late 1920s dentist (and later, City Council member) Dr. Thurlow C. Jaegeling practiced here, sharing surgical equipment with Dr. Louis L. Robinson; both were then followed by Dr. David Schmidt, a

▲ 1.41: At center, the elegant original Emporio Rulli building with white pediment at 464 Magnolia Avenue; the revamped 460 is at right, with 468 and 472 to the left, 2010.

DOWNTOWN, 1925

"The Larkspur business district is booming. With the new telephone building [464] and the dry goods store [468] and hardware store [460] buildings nearing completion and the side walls up for the drug store [472] ... it surely looks like business."

— *Marin and San Anselmo Herald*, September 18, 1925

▲ 1.42: 468 Magnolia Avenue, built as an identical twin of the structure at 460, as it appeared in 1960. It had been built and operated as the Larkspur Dry Goods until months before this photograph was taken, when it still retained its original appearance, including painted-over transom windows. The storefront has since been altered to provide outdoor café seating.

physician and psychiatrist (also a Council member), who had an office here until the early 1960s.

Former City Council member H. William "Bill" Howard acquired all the structures at 465 to 471 in 1996 and began a process of meticulous reconstruction and restoration. He had the brick facing removed from 467 Magnolia, which was then rebuilt to match early photographs. Asbestos shingles, probably applied in the 1950s and still seen on many of our downtown's similarly dated buildings, were removed, and the underlying original v-channel siding restored. Careful examination of the building's framing revealed numerous tobacco tins discarded by the carpenters, and a signed scrap of paper that recorded November 19, 1907, as the date of completion of the walls.

Owner-developer William F. Granger made a ten-year lease with the Pacific Telephone and Telegraph Company in July of 1925, promising to construct a "one story brick building" to the company's exacting specifications; **464 MAGNOLIA AVENUE** was finished and occupied by November of the same year. Special provisions for skylights assured ample light for the telephone operators inside. Although Granger built a group of four structures (460, 464, 468, 472) simultaneously, it was this building that received the greatest attention to detail and design, including the elegant recessed entry with a pediment over the doorway. A small alcove provided space for a coin-operated public telephone.

The telephone office (then called the "Pioneer Corte Madera Telephone Exchange") had a long history in Larkspur, operating from a sequence of locations in town as telephone service evolved and expanded. Eda Nagel recalled the Exchange's early location within the Tamalpais Grocery Co. at 489 Magnolia when she managed that store about 1910. The only way to know when a line became free was to listen in on the conversation; Eda knew who had gone into town that day, or where they were if not at home. Pacific Telephone eventually left this building when their services were consolidated in San Rafael.

In spring of 1973 the space was taken over by a pioneer of Larkspur's emerging restaurant renaissance; Michael Goldstein opened his 464 Magnolia restaurant here, operating until 1987, when the building was acquired by Gary and Jeannie Rulli for a wholesale pastry business named "Pasticceria Rulli." The following year they opened an elegant retail operation, Emporio Rulli, which since has incorporated adjacent buildings.

England-born Violet Henderson's Larkspur Dry Goods was the original tenant of **468 MAGNOLIA AVENUE**, one of several structures built by owner-developer William F. Granger in fall of 1925. Not only were the structures at 468 and 460 Magnolia built at the same time, they probably had

▲ 1.43: *The Larkspur Pharmacy, at 472 Magnolia, about 1948. Note the ceramic tile above the sidewalk and the transom windows beneath the folded awning. The brick facing and parapets are shown here in their original condition.*

▲ 1.44: *Commercial buildings evolve as fashions change; here, 472 Magnolia Avenue undergoes modernization in 1949. Workers complete installation of Ken Anderson's new storefront as passer-by Dolph Doherty watches their progress.*

essentially identical plans; notice particularly the shape of the rooflines.

Mrs. Henderson and her two teenaged sons lived in residential space in the rear of the store. In 1929 she married another downtown business proprietor, Robert C. Haake, who was the pharmacist next door at 472 Magnolia. Haake then joined his new family in the 468 space. After her husband's death in 1938 Violet Haake turned the store over to Mabel G. Stephens who operated it until the early 1950s. The dry goods store was followed by a series of insurance agencies and retail uses, and in the late 1990s the building became an addition to Emporio Rulli at 464 Magnolia; the front wall was opened to provide covered outdoor seating, and the interior rearranged and remodeled as a food service area. Negotiations with the city assured that the old storefront retained aspects of its historical integrity, a difficult accomplishment while the downtown evolves into the twenty-first century.

Built by developer William F. Granger in late 1925, the brick structure at **472 MAGNOLIA AVENUE** was originally occupied by the Larkspur Pharmacy, first operated by Robert C. Haake, who later married the proprietor of the adjacent dry goods store. Thirteen years later his widow Violet became the proprietor here after Robert's death, but she soon turned the pharmacy over to a succession of operators. In 1949 it was taken over by Kenneth R. Anderson, who added stucco facing over the brick, removed the transom windows, altered the parapets, installed a large glass display window, and relocated the door to the south end of the building's face. Ken Anderson, an active

THE LARKSPUR BAKERY

"Completely remodeled and re-decorated, the Larkspur Bakery has installed tables and will serve coffee and soft drinks with its bakery products. Christian Stoll, who took over the shop last August, has made great improvements, both in the bakery and store."

– *Larkspur-Corte Madera News*, April 30, 1937.

JUST WHAT WE NEEDED AND WE HAVE IT—

A MODEL BAKERY

WITH A GOOD REPUTATION

CHAS. HARGENS, Proprietor

Boost your bakery and you have him to STAY

▶ 1.45: *An advertisement for Charles Hargens' newly established Model Bakery from the 1910 Booster Day pamphlet. The ad encourages patronage to support a new enterprise.*

citizen and a conscientious local pharmacist, also was an accomplished photographer – several of our mid-century images are from his collection. Ken Anderson operated the town's central drugstore until 1978. In 1991 the building became the final location for another of Larkspur's iconic businesses, Katherine Eubanks' Florist, which operated here until 1994. Much later the structure became another portion of the Emporio Rulli.

Several buildings in the center of this block (**473-475-477-479 MAGNOLIA AVENUE**) share similar colors and a brick façade installed about 1961 that obscures their separate identity. Thus, the barbershop and hair studio, currently at 475 and 479, form a separate, freestanding building of uncertain history. That building was constructed sometime before June of 1909, but by spring of 1910 a large oven had been added at the rear of the building, and Charles Hargens opened his Model Bakery here.

Charles and Margaret Hargens, both German immigrants, had moved to Larkspur from Petaluma, where Charles had worked as a baker. Shortly before Charles arrived, another bakery had failed in town, and hope ran high that this new enterprise would succeed. Wilfred "Biff" Harris, a resident of the time, recalled that the Hargens' son John was nicknamed "Doughnuts." After school Biff and other Larkspur kids would accompany Doughnuts to his father's store where John would duck in, scoop up a handful of doughnuts, and give them to his friends.

In 1924 the Hargens turned over the bakery's operation to Oscar and Marie Schindler; Oscar, too, had been a baker in Petaluma. The Vienna-born Schindlers continued to live in Larkspur until their deaths in the late 1940s, but kept the bakery only until 1929. The business then went through a succession of changes and operators, ending with Christian Stoll in 1937.

In the early 1940s the bakery-café space became the Country Kitchen, operated by L. V. Waymire, who simultaneously was the proprietor of the Golden Gate Cleaners at 320 Magnolia Avenue. At about the same time part of the building was rented to a barber, William P. Sanderson; the barber's area was the southeast corner of the building (475), while the bakery occupied the north and west portions (479), a physical division that still pertains in the building today. Thus, a barbershop has occupied the corner space continuously since 1939; perhaps William was the source of the name Bill's Barber Shop. In 1950 the 479 space became the first location for Katherine Eubanks' new enterprise as a "floral decorator,"

▲ 1.46: *Looking north along the central block of Magnolia Avenue about 1936. The Larkspur Bakery at 479 Magnolia is on the left, Nardene DeLegons' Nardene Beauty Shop and Jack DeLegons' Sanitary Barber Shop at 454 on the right, adjacent to Ralph Kokjer's Larkspur Hardware.*

a trade she developed here until moving to 320 Magnolia in 1960. Since the mid-1970s several hair design studios have occupied the location.

The narrow **PASSAGE BETWEEN 472 AND 474 MAGNOLIA AVENUE** – only 59 inches wide – has seen an odd mix of uses over the years. In the late 1920s a gate there was labeled "Railway Express Agency." It later had an entrance faced with the same stonework as the adjoining structure at 474. For a short time in 1958 Woody Hilbert operated a stamp and butterfly collectors' shop here in a small structure squeezed under its own low roof. More recently the passage served as an entrance to a rear garden that was part of the Garden of Eatin' restaurant located in the building at 474 during the mid-1990s.

Unlike the west side of Magnolia Avenue, which began to develop with a variety of commercial uses in the late 1890s, the eastern portion of the street remained undeveloped until the very early 1900s. Held by a series of investors, eventually the land was sold in February of 1904 to Nicholas Yost, a Mill Valley lumber dealer. Yost leased the property in April of 1905 to a merchant named Morton, including "the large building consisting of two stories, used as a store and dwelling … and the fixtures and counter now being in said store." We thus know that the structure at **474-476-478 MAGNOLIA AVENUE** existed at least as early as spring of 1905. More intriguing is the unknown identity of its builder; an identical shingled structure stood on Throckmorton Avenue in Mill Valley in the early 1900s, suggesting the same plans were used for both.

At about the same time Earle Doherty, a friend of Yost's from Mill Valley, made arrangements to open his Doherty Lumber Company here, using this large building as its office. After establishing the lumberyard, Earle invited a young cousin, Dolph Doherty, and his new wife Nellie, to take over its management while Earle continued to run his other lumber business and investments in Mill Valley and Corte Madera (he and Yost later cofounded the Mill Valley Lumber Co., still active today). Dolph and Nellie arrived in Larkspur in January of 1906; they moved into the upper floor of this structure, where they lived until 1925. Their arrival marked a pivotal moment for the young town; Dolph soon was appointed to an open seat on the town's Board of Trustees, and served as one of our most energetic and influential citizens for the next five decades.

▲ *1.47: The office of the Larkspur Lumber Company (labeled a "sash and door" store on early maps,) and residence of Dolph and Nell Doherty, about 1910. Note the adjacent picket fence and stacks of lumber in the yard. Now remodeled as 474-476-478 Magnolia Avenue, the current building retains its twin doors.*

The Dohertys' re-named "Larkspur Lumber Company" thrived here for two decades; this block contained large storage sheds, a planing mill, a cement storage building, and stacks of lumber and pipe. The yard, faced by an unpainted picket fence, was supplied by a spur railroad track that ran parallel to today's Rice Lane, terminating near Cane Street. (A small segment of similar track was discovered

▲ *1.48: The Larkspur Lumber Company's yard in downtown Larkspur, as it appeared about 1909, well before Magnolia Avenue had been paved. The large water tower to the rear was part of the Rice Stable complex (see pages 38-39).*

beneath Magnolia Avenue during its reconstruction in 1991, and has been framed in City Hall.)

Judge Samuel Gardiner, born in Larkspur in 1902, remembered visiting the yard as a boy. "It was a very intriguing place … pulleys and motors and saws and everything you can think of operating. They were somewhat frightening, but very interesting. I liked to stand there and watch the operation. He got rough lumber and cut it and finished it and delivered it."

Nicholas Yost, then age 67, decided to sell the entire tract of land; the pending sale prompted the Dohertys to relocate their company across the railroad tracks, to an 11-acre site north of the railroad station (much later that area became the Larkspur Plaza shopping center). In May of 1925 a Corte Madera realtor and contractor named William F. Granger acquired this structure and set out to modernize it. He covered the shingled exterior with stucco, and added plate glass windows. The original doorframes and interior bead-board paneling have remained intact to the present. Within a few months Granger's new stores, at addresses 474 and 476, welcomed their first tenants. The first occupant of the remodeled 474 was a Swiss barber named Charles DeGeller, who remained in that location through the 1930s. Robert Mistron ran Bob's Fixit Shop there until the late 1950s. (Robert's son Warren later served for several decades as Larkspur's director of public works.)

"A new and up to date barber shop under the management of Mr. De Geller opened in one of the new stores on Saturday. Mr. de Geller comes highly recommended from San Francisco and will make a specialty of ladies' bobs."

– *Marin and San Anselmo Herald*, November 20, 1925

The 476 storefront became a tiny radio shop, and then in short order it served as a shoe repair shop, a lunchroom, and a cleaners. More recently the combined spaces became the Casa de Arte, and since 1999, Margaret Von Treskow's L'Ambiente gift store.

William F. Granger not only remodeled this building, he orchestrated the sale and development of the remainder of the block, thus becoming a one-man building boom. He created the new lots that became 472, 480-482, 484, and 488, making possible their sale to different individuals; he also personally purchased and developed the land that became the store sites at 460, 464, and 468 Magnolia. When he died four years later at age 54, the *Larkspur-Corte Madera News* reported: "He constructed a large number of store buildings in Larkspur, which added a great deal to the business district appearance of the town."

The little building at **480-482 MAGNOLIA AVENUE**, constructed sometime between 1900 and 1905, shares an uncertain history with its larger neighbor to its south. It may have been built by Wallace T. Morton, who operated the W. T. Morton Co. in this area in 1905, and seems to have been used briefly as a paint store in conjunction with the adjoining 474-476-478 building. For the next three decades, however, it served as a cobbler shop.

The primary occupants were Joseph P. and Rosa Steffe, two Italian immigrants who arrived sometime after 1910 to establish Joseph's cobbler shop in the retail portion at 482, and to raise their three California-born daughters in the living quarters above the store at 480. For part of that time the leased building was part of the large lumberyard parcel owned by Nicholas Yost; after Yost sold his interests to the corner bank, the Steffes purchased this site in 1925. The Steffes then expanded the structure and created a second upstairs window facing the street.

The interior of the shop still bears the early entry door, display windows, and small transom windows that appear in old photographs. The stucco façade is a later alteration to the older v-channel siding that remains on the exterior sidewalls, and along with the red roof tiles, suggests modest attempts at updating the structure.

▲ 1.49: *Joseph P. Steffe in his cobbler shop at 482 Magnolia Avenue, probably about 1918.*

▲ 1.50: *The rooflines shown here in 1955 reveal the three distinct buildings that comprise the current streetscape from 475 to 489 Magnolia. The bakery's building at left had a high false front with a large sloped cornice, supported by curved brackets. The middle structure was flat-roofed, with two bay windows. The third had a peaked roof, elaborate shingling, and a porch with turned railings that was inset between two bay windows. All were rebuilt after an upstairs fire on September 6, 1959.*

▲ 1.51: *Prosper Zaro, on the right, stands in his plumbing shop on July 5, 1909, accompanied by his helper, Walter Frizzi. The wall displays banners for the congressional campaign of William Kent, a Progressive Republican later famous as the creator of Muir Woods. This shop occupied the north space on the ground floor of 485 Magnolia Avenue.*

The building's best-known occupants were Donald and Beverley Agner, who operated the Agner Variety Store here from 1945 until 1956. They later combined their activity here with sales of outdoor products on the adjacent open lot to the north, then built and moved into a structure there (484 Magnolia) in 1956. After several other businesses operated here, the Agners sold this building to Marty Weissensee, the current proprietor of Country Gardens gift shop.

The historic "Rainbow Market" sign over the door of **483-485 MAGNOLIA AVENUE** links us to that market's heyday during the 1930s to 1960s, and hides the true nature of the structures beneath. The single entry door in fact serves two separate

POLES, PAVEMENT, TREES & STREETS

Decades of constant use took a toll on the downtown blocks, where street pavement and building exteriors suffered from lack of maintenance. In the 1970s the City Council and local merchants began a series of steps that allowed the inherent charm of the buildings to shine again. Worn wooden utility poles, laden with generations of bulky wiring, were removed from Magnolia Avenue in 1978, and the utilities placed underground. Street trees were introduced along the sidewalks to provide shade and create a softer ambience. Pedestrian-friendly dining was encouraged in 1993 when the City Council allowed outdoor seating at food service establishments. Magnolia Avenue itself, buried under multiple layers of patched pavement, was completely reengineered and rebuilt in 1991, culminating with a grand street party called to celebrate its completion; on September 28, Larkspur citizens danced the night away on new pavement at the Moonlight on Magnolia Blacktop Ball.

▲ 1.52: *In summer of 1978 unsightly utility poles were removed from Magnolia Avenue.*

buildings, now cosmetically joined as one. Both buildings initially contained small storefronts with dwelling spaces above.

These conjoined buildings have lost much of their original appearance; the current brick façade at street level and unornamented siding above make them appear to be a single structure. However, they were originally quite distinct, sandwiched between the bakery building to the south (475-477) and the bay-windowed structure to the north (489). A structural fire in 1959 gutted the upstairs apartments, ruining the upper façade of these structures, damaging as well the market space below and parts of the bakery building next door. The structures were then rebuilt with little regard to the original exterior design.

Various tenants occupied the retail space in the early years. In 1909 a clothes-cleaning establishment was at 483; the adjacent space at 485 was the shop of Prosper Zaro, a plumber and one-time chief of the volunteer firemen.

The early history of these buildings derives from the efforts of Giacomo and Rosa Costa, Italian immigrants who acquired this lot and its neighbor to the north directly from the town's subdividers in February of 1902. They also bought scattered parcels of nearby land at roughly the same time, thereby creating the large and irregularly shaped parking lot and access lanes at the rear of these structures. Giacomo probably had both of these buildings erected about 1904, and at least number 485, if not both structures, was called "The Costa Building."

The space took on its best-known significance when Pietro "Peter" Epidendio opened his fruit and vegetable shop here in the early 1920s. Peter and his wife Mary, both born in Italy, maintained an extensive vegetable farm near today's Niven Way, and opened the shop at 483 as a retail outlet for their produce. In 1923 the Epidendios purchased the 483 building from Rosa Costa, followed by the 485 building in 1925. In the early 1930s Peter retired to his farm, and the fruit and vegetable store was taken over by his son Ernest who expanded the store into both spaces, naming the enlarged operation the "Rainbow Market."

Ernie Epidendio, known to generations of Larkspur shoppers, continued to operate the Rainbow well into his eighties. Another fixture in the building was native son Charlie Young, a well-known butcher who operated the Larkspur Meat Co. (in partnership with Stephen Gilardi) at a meat counter in the market from 1955 to 1988; he taught many a housewife the difference between a tri-tip and a cross-rib roast. Like other small downtown groceries of the era, the Rainbow fell victim to competition by larger retail operations, finally closing in 1999; Ernie died a few months later, in January of 2000, at age 84. In recent years the space has been operated as Gallery Bergelli, featuring contemporary original paintings and sculptures.

The structure at **484 MAGNOLIA AVENUE**, substantially remodeled in 2007 by Dennis and Susan Gilardi, began life as a decidedly modest, single-story concrete-block building. It was built in 1956 by Donald and Beverley Agner, who operated the Agner Variety Store next door at 480, and then shifted their operation into this building. The remodeled structure was designed to be harmonious with the older structures nearby.

▲ 1.53: *Interior of the Rainbow Market on April 21, 1955. Will Penna took this photograph of his father, Guy, working at the Rainbow in a white apron.*

▲ 1.54: *The 1925 Vogt-Schmalfeld building at 488-490 Magnolia Avenue, as it appeared in 1960.*

▲ 1.55: The Tamalpais Grocery Company in April of 1906, with a line of earthquake refugees waiting for distribution of emergency supplies of bread and milk. The wagon contains 5-gallon milk cans to be poured into smaller containers. The doors and windows to the left identify a saloon, offering "billiards & pool;" Julia Frizzi's building at 499 Magnolia can be seen on the right.

▲ 1.56: The newly remodeled Larkspur Food Store in July of 1938. The staff included Charles Whiting, Charles Zuffinetti, Melvin Cevilli, "Babe" Cevilli, Amadio Tosi, Robert Tosi, "Mr. St. Johnson," and Jack Lynch.

Built in 1925 the stucco building located at **488-490 MAGNOLIA AVENUE** initially was intended to be a delicatessen operated by its brother-in-law owners, Engelbert Vogt and Karl Schmalfeld. The building instead saw a variety of uses over the years, as Engelbert and his wife Henrietta tried different enterprises, including a candy store. Karl Schmalfeld, the younger brother of Henrietta Vogt, worked elsewhere in town as a grocer, eventually opening Karl's Grocery at 457 Magnolia. In the late 1930s and early 1940s the Vogts operated the Old Heidelberg Inn here while living upstairs, and rented office space in the building to a succession of doctors. From the mid-1950s to the 1970s the front space was used as a Christian Science Reading Room, and since then has been used by several real estate offices.

For nearly a century **489 MAGNOLIA AVENUE** has been occupied continuously by food-service establishments. It has changed little from its original appearance; although the exterior was clad with asbestos shingles in the mid-twentieth century, obliterating some architectural ornaments, the building's essential features have remained intact. Several parts of the interior have never been altered. Two large upstairs residential units stretch the full depth of the building, each with a coal-burning fireplace. Many of the original upstairs features, such as five-panel doors and stamped hardware, remain in place.

This lot, like its neighbor to the south, was first acquired from the town's subdividers by Giacomo and Rosa Costa in 1902; the building was constructed for them soon after. By early 1905 the two street-level portions of the building were occupied by the Tamalpais Grocery Co. on the north, and a saloon on the south. The manager at the Tamalpais Grocery Co. was James Bain, a leader of the early volunteer firemen; the company's president was Egbert C. Burtchaell, a member of the prominent family then represented in the house at 105 King Street.

By 1909 both the saloon and Tamalpais Grocery Co. had been replaced by Buckley & Company, a grocery business that remained here through the mid-1920s, managed by John McNaboe. The Buckley & Company store later moved to the Lynch building (at 515 Magnolia), and its space was taken by Rufus H. Bonham's Twin Cities Grocery, to be followed in 1938 by the Larkspur Food Store.

The store was acquired in the early 1950s by Fred T. Schefer, who operated it as the Larkspur Food Center until about 1957, when Andrew Gilardi Jr. moved his catering operation into the building. Thus, during most of the 1930s to the late 1950s, Larkspur had two full-service food markets in adjoining locations; every resident could describe in detail their preferences for one store over another.

The Nicol family moved their Red Robin Catering Company from Kentfield into this location in 1965, purchasing the building from Stephen and Aletha Gilardi in 1971. The Nicols have carefully maintained their landmark downtown structure to the present.

▲ 1.57: *The Larkspur Branch of the Mercantile Trust Company of California, about 1925.* "This is without a doubt the most beautiful business building in Larkspur and it is held to be a credit to the town and to the Bank itself. The interior is finished in marble and in cream-colored wood-work. The exterior is of Spanish Brown stucco, roofed with red tile." – The Marin and San Anselmo Herald, *June 23, 1923.*

WHILE LARKSPUR SLEPT

A few minutes before 2 a.m. on May 14, 1974, a powerful bomb exploded in the crawl space beneath this building, breaking windows in surrounding structures and waking neighbors. A domestic terrorist group called the "New World Liberation Front" claimed credit for the blast, having similarly bombed other branches of Bay View Federal Savings and Loan, accusing that company of "not providing safe and adequate housing for the people." A parrot, on a perch in a plant store across the street, may have been the only witness, but wasn't talking. Police chief John M. Dineen said the blast caused about $25,000 damage to the bank building and nearby structures.

During the economic boom of the early 1920s this bank building at **494 MAGNOLIA AVENUE** signaled to the world that Larkspur finally had achieved economic consequence. The building opened to great fanfare on June 23, 1923, as the Larkspur Branch of the First Bank of San Anselmo. Within a year that bank was acquired by the much larger Mercantile Trust Company of California. Mercantile Trust began almost immediately to sell the bank's extensive Larkspur real estate, which included the entire lumberyard that previously occupied the majority of this block. The sales, arranged by local developer William F. Granger, were finalized on May 15, 1925, sparking the development of the block. The bank soon changed corporate hands once again; by 1927 it had become the American Trust Company, and continued under that name through the difficult economic times of the 1930s, but finally closed in March of 1938.

The Mediterranean Revival structure, with tile roof and arched windows, is richly ornamented with twisted columns, shields, and an encircling frieze with cherub faces and festoons. Dentils under the eaves transition to the stucco walls. A window and clock over the front door, both visible in the 1925 photograph, have been replaced by blank stucco.

Municipal economic pride returned to Larkspur with the reopening of the bank, now as a branch of the Bank of America, in the late 1940s. The bank's corporate logo, the ship U.S.S. Portsmouth under full sail, was applied to plaster medallions on the front of the building, but later removed when the Bank of America moved to a new structure at the corner of Magnolia and Bon Air Road. The altered medallions remain, still blank and a little the worse for wear. The building since has been occupied continuously by a succession of financial institutions, including Bay View Federal Savings and Loan, Atlantic Financial, and Bank of the West.

· · · · ·

The little structure at **499 MAGNOLIA AVENUE** was built about 1894, probably for Julia Frizzi, and may have been the first building in this block. Julia operated a bakery here, changing it over time to an ice cream parlor and candy store, and eventually to other retail uses. It has remained a recognizable part of our downtown ever since. Its plain false front and steep roof maintain their original lines; the original drop siding remains unchanged on the south wall, but the entire storefront has received numerous remakes, including the addition of stucco sometime in the 1940s.

The story behind this building began earlier. About 1880 two young teenage sisters named Julia and Elizabeth Guscetti, born near Nevada City, California, were sent to San Francisco to live with relatives. A decade later Julia met and married a Swiss-Italian locksmith named August Frizzi; her sister Elizabeth married Serafino Marilli, another Italian who worked in San Francisco as a waiter. These sisters would become leading citizens of Larkspur for nearly five decades.

▲ 1.58: *Julia Frizzi's bakery is in center of this picture, near the intersection of Ward Street and Magnolia Avenue, with the Frizzi home to the rear, about 1897. Note the Frizzi saloon has not yet been erected on the corner. Across Ward Street, the Hotel Larkspur is obscured by a tree, the Lynch building appears to the north, and the Brazil building is cut by the right margin of the photograph. The prominent hilltop house was the Beleney home at 234 Hawthorne Avenue. This photograph is credited to William Stringa, later a partner in the Blue Rock Hotel.*

Julia and Gus Frizzi bought a corner lot here in 1891, only three years after town lots became available. They acquired this structure while Gus continued his trade in San Francisco, and moved their family here in 1894. Their first home, built about the same time, was a small structure to the rear of their lot (now numbered 115 Ward Street); much later they built a larger home up the hillside at 30 Cedar Avenue. Several years after opening the bakery at 499, the Frizzis erected another building, now numbered 503, on the corner of their lot at Ward and Magnolia, where Gus opened a saloon about 1901.

For a short period about 1905 the Frizzis leased this bakery building to others – it was used variously as a barbershop or real estate office – but Julia later resumed management of the structure, operating it about 1910 as an ice cream parlor, but later moved that business into the adjacent 503 Magnolia.

▲ 1.59: *Julia Frizzi's Ice Cream and Candy Parlor, about 1910.*

By the late 1920s this building had become the Frizzi Electrical Works operated by Julia and Gus's son William (known to everyone as "Willie"). Willie Frizzi was born in Larkspur in 1896 and died here in 1988; he was a stalwart supporter of the volunteer firemen, one-time mayor of the city, and by all accounts, a character of the first order. Willie soon moved his electrical shop to the rear, accessed through the walkway (then labeled 499½), and rented this structure to a sequence of beauty shops beginning in the mid-1930s. From the late 1930s until 1955 this was the Larkspur Beauty Salon; it then became the Coral Beauty Salon, painted in a bright coral color that remains an indelible memory for residents of the period. After intervening uses, it has become a retail clothing store.

The tiny shop at **501 MAGNOLIA AVENUE**, operated in recent decades as a florist, is best understood in its original role as a path between the Frizzis' adjacent buildings, used first for access to the summer gardens and "Ladies Parlor" behind the Frizzi saloon.

▲ 1.60: *The Coral Beauty Salon, as it appeared in 1970. Under various names, a beauty salon occupied Julia Frizzi's 499 building from about 1938 until the mid-1970s.*

▲ 1.61: Gus Frizzi's saloon, or "exchange," about 1902. Note the broad wooden sidewalks and recently planted trees along Ward Street. The small girl is the Frizzis' daughter Helen (holding her father's hand), and the boy probably is their son Willie.

The gardens were partially covered by wooden latticework that supported honeysuckle and grapevines, and included a shuffleboard court that may have doubled as a bocce ball court. In later years the walk led to a shed that served as Willie Frizzi's electrical shop.

Built as a saloon for Julia Frizzi's husband Gus, probably in 1901, **503 MAGNOLIA AVENUE** was a focal point in Larkspur's bustling downtown. The building, almost dainty in detail, has retained its classic Greek Revival lines, including dentils and boxed eaves. The three-lap siding has faced the traffic on Ward Street for more than a century. Within ten years after its construction the original open porch and posts had been partially enclosed, first with a conventional wall across half the building, and later by a windowed storefront with a central doorway.

For several years Larkspur held a spot on the boxing circuit. Joe Walcott "The Barbados Demon," a highly versatile fighter who was Welterweight Champion several times in the early 1900s, briefly lived and trained at the Frizzi home, making runs on foot to Billy Shannon's saloon and training facility in San Rafael as a part of his fitness regimen. Considered "Larkspur's Own," Walcott was fondly recalled by the Frizzi family. "I remember Joe Walcott bouncing me on his knee," reminisced Willie Frizzi. "His arms hung down so long that his hands were at his knees." A punching bag hung under the porch of the family home.

Not long after Gus opened the saloon, Julia's sister Elizabeth and her husband, Serafino Marilli, moved to Larkspur from San Francisco. Serafino became a partner in Gus's saloon, but in 1905, as Gus's health failed, Serafino leased the operation from Gus, and took on a new partner, another Swiss-Italian named William Stringa. The enterprise thereafter became known as the "Marilli and Stringa" saloon. Months later, on April 18, 1906, Gus died at home, only minutes before that day's great earthquake. The new firm of Marilli and Stringa prospered, helped in part by the operation of a famous slot machine they installed in June of 1908.

The saloon continued to operate here until mid-1910, when Stringa and Marilli seized the

▲ 1.62: Porch of the Frizzi saloon, with Barbados-born boxer Joe Walcott sitting at left among other "sportsmen," about 1902.

Grossman and Lewis Matched.

"A red-hot boxing contest will be held at the San Rafael Athletic Club on the 9th of May. Rudolph Grossman and Henry Lewis yesterday signed articles and will do battle on that date.... Henry Lewis is in training with the famous Joe Walcott at Gus Frizzi's Larkspur resort."

– *Marin County Tocsin*, April 26, 1902

▲ 1.63: *Industrious citizens of Larkspur in front of Marilli and Stringa's saloon, about 1909.*

opportunity to buy the Hotel Larkspur across Ward Street. By late fall they had moved their business across the street, and reopened that building as the Blue Rock Hotel. Julia Frizzi, who continued to own both the 499 and 503 buildings, then moved her candy store into the site of the former saloon, reopening it as Frizzi's Sweet Shop. Julia's shop was the sole means of support for herself and her daughter Helen for many years. Julia Frizzi died at the age of 87 in 1954, having seen her little town grow from a single crossroad to a busy regional center. After the 1988 death of her son Willie, the Frizzi land and buildings finally were sold; they had been held in the same family for almost 98 years.

Variously, and under different proprietors, the corner building later became the Primrose Sweet Shop, the Thoroughbred Sweet Shop, and finally, Florence's Sweet Shop. It eventually morphed into a lunch fountain, newspaper, and tobacco shop, serving for most of that period as a Greyhound Bus stop as well. The 503 building finished the century as clothing and household furnishing stores, and is now Coquelicot.

⊃ *The downtown corridor includes several sites on the eastern portion of Ward Street.*

SIX HUNDRED DOLLARS STOLEN FROM A SAFE.

Larkspur Sleeps While Glass is Shattered And Dynamite Roars.

The safe in the saloon of Stringer & Morrilla at Larkspur was blown open some time Wednesday night or Thursday morning and some $600 were carried away by the thief or thieves.

The saloon is the one formerly conducted by the late Gus Frizzi and is in the center of town and across the street from the Larkspur hotel. The robbers effected an entrance by smashing in the front window. Once inside they attacked the nickel-in-slot machine with a pick ax and tore the back of the machine out. Only brass slugs rewarded this part of the work and the safe was the next victim. The knob was knocked off with a heavy sledge hammer and a hole was drilled through the lock. Nitroglycerine did the rest. There was over $600 in the safe. The thief left behind the hammer and the pick. Both were taken from the railroad. Suspicion in Larkspur is directed to several Italians who were formerly employed on the road. The town authorities believe that they can find the man.

– *Marin County Tocsin*, January 2, 1909

▲ 1.64: *Gus Frizzi's saloon later housed a candy store, a soda fountain, and in 1957 the Wagon Wheel restaurant (see above); more recently it has harbored a succession of retail stores.*

(12) Eastern Ward Street (Rice Stables Site)

A lime and cement storage building stood at **25 WARD STREET** in the early 1900s when this area was part of the Dohertys' lumberyard. In 1925 this corner lot behind the bank was carved out and sold to Robert Murray, a well-known local plumber who had a single-story store and apartment erected here a few months later. Much later the structure was used by his son Elmer as the site for Murray's Radio Shop. By the mid-1940s the building housed several small tradesmen's shops, including the Nichols Brothers Glass Works. Oakley Dexter took over the location about 1951, operating there for three decades as Dexter's Radio & Television; it was Dexter who added a stucco exterior and a second story in 1959. When the building was acquired by Zel Realty in 1983, window casings, a cornice, and other details were added to the façade to emulate the architectural style of the downtown. The second story is now used as small office spaces, while neighborhood restaurants have occupied the street level. Fernando Plazola's Ward Street Café has been here since 2005.

The Rice family's large livery stable once occupied this southeast corner of Ward Street and Rice Lane. Located at **11 WARD STREET** across from the railroad depot, the Rice Livery & Express Company provided essential delivery services for goods and passengers arriving by train. An adjacent house

▲ 1.65: *An advertisement for C. W. Rice's many services appeared in the first Booster Day pamphlet, 1909.*

at **7 WARD STREET** was the home of Charles and Carolyn Rice, and a larger house at **5 WARD STREET** may once have been the residence of Joseph B. and Julia Rice, Charles' parents. A fenced corral was located behind the barn, where residential parking garages stand today.

Patriarch Joseph B. Rice had a colorful personal history; shipwrecked on the Marin coast at age 27 in 1856, he swam ashore, established himself in San Rafael, and married there. He served as Marin's representative in the State Assembly in 1871-1872, was a city trustee in San Rafael from 1874 to 1882, and became a Marin deputy sheriff. As a businessman he owned a large brick-making enterprise and then a prosperous hay and grain business in downtown San Rafael (where Julia Street is named for his wife). He and Julia raised three children in San Rafael, but by 1882 the family had left San Rafael; Joseph suffered business reversals elsewhere, and sometime in 1892 Joseph, Julia, and their son Charlie settled in Larkspur. The Rices then acquired (but perhaps did not build), their splendid 45-foot-wide, 100-foot-long barn and stable. Joseph Rice's business success was sporadic; although his stable was advertised "to be sold at auction" in July of 1893, he instead retained it, and at Joseph's death in 1901, Charlie assumed full operation of the Rice Livery Stable.

The Rice stable provided a remarkable range of vital services to early Larkspur. A basic offering, of course, was rental of horses and vehicles (a livery service). As recalled by Judge Samuel Gardiner, "Travel by automobile was very rare until close to 1920 … My folks sometimes rented surreys-with-the-fringe-

WHAT'S THE ADDRESS?

Street address numbers were not adopted in Larkspur until 1926 and mandated in 1929. The City Council ruled that residential lots were to be numbered each 25 feet, but land in the business district would have numbers every 12½ feet. Throughout the city, numbers were to progress from east to west, and from south to north. However, no one seems to know why the "500" series of numbers on Magnolia Avenue began between the two Frizzi buildings, rather than at Ward Street. Inconsistent assignment of the numbers appears to have created substantial disarray in many older areas of the city; sequential numbers often are physically distant from each other, as widely evidenced in this downtown area.

▲ 1.66: *Charles and Carolyn Rices' shingled home at 7 Ward Street, 1904-1995. The livery stable had been to the right.*

▲ 1.67: *Charles W. Rice's Livery Stable on Ward Street, about 1904; his home is visible through the tree to the left.*

on-top to join with horseback riders for picnics to Muir Beach and elsewhere. These came only from Rice Livery Stable." Katherine Solomons Lilienthal remembered that her mother would ring Charlie Rice to tell him when her house guests were due to arrive, and he would have his surrey waiting at the train station to deliver them and their luggage to the family home on Walnut Avenue. On other occasions Rice would prepare a large wagon to take residents on a hayride to dances at San Quentin Village.

Rice also provided the muscle power for a growing town. As a drayman, he hauled pianos and heavy materials on his wagons. The early volunteer firemen depended on an available team of horses to draw their apparatus to a fire, using a team provided by either Charlie Rice or Frank Murphy. Rice usually received the city contract to sprinkle the dirt streets in order to reduce the summer's dust, and he regularly provided road-grading and dirt-hauling services.

Charles W. Rice personally built the house at 7 Ward Street, probably in 1904. He and his wife Carolyn lived there until his death in June of 1958, at age 91; she died in 1962, at age 85. According to his obituary, Charlie "could remember when Larkspur boasted only 12 houses. He recalled them well because he hauled their supplies from the railroad station." Carolyn Rice added her own rich story to Larkspur's history; born in San Francisco in 1876 as Carolyn "Carrie" Lanouette, she was the sister of Emilie Lanouette, who later married Gustave Nagel. After the catastrophe of the 1906 earthquake, Emilie and Gustave Nagel abandoned San Francisco, found shelter in the Rices' home, and remained in Larkspur thereafter. The Rices and Nagels were prominent citizens of early Larkspur – Charlie hauled the materials for our buildings, roads, and businesses, and Gustave built many of our notable structures. Charles and Carolyn had one child in 1899, a son named Joseph B. Rice, after his grandfather. That Joseph Rice became a wealthy San Rafael businessman and developer, who later built a showplace home at 130 Elm Avenue on Palm Hill.

As horses were replaced by gasoline engines, the livery stable was converted to automobile storage, and Charlie retired, with his last horse, in 1941. The barn gradually became dilapidated; at a local meeting, Charlie's son Joseph advocated demolition of the barn, calling it a "symbol of antiquation." The old barn was razed in early 1959 to make way for a proposed shopping center that never materialized. Some of its whitewashed lumber was recycled into the structure directly across the street, at 12 Ward Street.

In the late 1980s owner Richard Peters began the process of redeveloping the site; new residential condominiums were designed by architect Brock Wagstaff, and received final approval in 1993. Finally, in 1995 Charles and Carolyn's little house at 7 Ward, by then worn and neglected, was demolished, along with the nondescript house at 5 Ward, and the new Rice Stable Court houses were constructed on the site of the Rices' once-proud enterprise. A brass plaque memorializes the location.

This triangular area between **12 WARD STREET** and 500 Magnolia Avenue was once the southern end of Larkspur's railroad depot. During the 1920s nearby railroad buildings included a bunkhouse directly across the tracks and a freight building

▲ 1.68: *In the early 1900s this structure was home to a railroad foreman's family; it is now one of a cluster occupied since 1947 by the Twin Cities Post of the American Legion, 2010.*

closer to the passenger station. In 1947 the Northwestern Pacific Railroad Co. sold this site directly to the Twin Cities Post 313 of the American Legion. The core building in the complex is a steep-roofed structure at 500 Magnolia, once a house for the railroad's section foreman. Early drop siding, exposed on the back gable, is elsewhere covered with asbestos shingles. Shortly after the Legion took over the building, local carpenters Edward Kerbs and Alvin Ahlers attached a large meeting room on its north side. We know little about the third structure, a small residence at the rear (504 Magnolia), that seems to have been yet another depot outbuilding. At the rear parking area (12 Ward Street), the Legion now maintains their clubroom in a building that was first erected in the late 1950s by John Raggio to house an ambulance service; that structure incorporated barn wood recycled after the 1959 demolition of the Rice Livery Stable.

Although occasionally called "the station master's house," the main structure, built some time prior to 1909, was used primarily by Ireland-born Michael Cloney, the railroad section foreman, his wife Katherine, and their large family. (Rather than living on the depot grounds, the railroad's station agents usually lived in private housing elsewhere.) Originally oriented parallel to the tracks, the foreman's house later was rotated into alignment with Ward Street. After about two decades in this house the Cloneys moved in 1925 to a home built for them at 19 Monte Vista Avenue.

13 Niven Nursery Site

Ward Street originally terminated at the railroad tracks, which marked the eastern edge of the 1887 Larkspur subdivision. The street was later extended to provide access to the Niven nursery properties, approximately 17 acres of greenhouses and attendant structures. The nursery entrance became the driveway currently at **2 WARD STREET**, and the street was altered to connect to Meadowood Drive.

The family-operated nursery was founded by James and Ada Niven in 1921. James, a Scottish immigrant, was a professional gardener who selected this site after scouting Marin for a location with the most favorable climate. An avid baseball fan, he placed thermometers in trees whenever he traveled to ball fields, and discovered that Larkspur's baseball diamond provided the best combination of sunlight and consistent temperatures.

James initially was assisted by his two sons, Walter and George. Walter was killed in a boiler accident here in 1929, and George, who was also a roofing contractor, managed their wholesale florist enterprise, overseeing its expansion and growth until his death in 1962. George's son Jim then managed the business and was prominent in civic activities; he died in a fire engine accident while serving as a volunteer firefighter in 1978. Jim's daughter, Cyndi Niven, became the fourth generation to manage the nursery in 1982.

The Nivens' neatly maintained glass greenhouses eventually became a distinctive feature of central Larkspur. The earliest greenhouses occupied about five acres south of the Larkspur Lumber Co. (a site now occupied by today's supermarket in the Larkspur Plaza). The nursery area was later expanded eastward when tidal salt marshes that had surrounded the old Bickerstaff adobe and Azevedo house and barn were filled with earth scraped off those high spots; Doherty Drive now marks the northern edge of that enlarged site. At the peak of its operation in the early 1990s, the nursery occupied approximately 250,000 square feet of greenhouse space and employed about 25 people, producing roses and orchids for the wholesale market.

The nursery effectively ceased production in the late 1990s, thus prompting a complex planning process, known as the Central Larkspur Specific Plan (CLASP), to determine appropriate development of the site and adjacent downtown properties.

↩ *From this spot, walkers can proceed into the Meadowood neighborhood, or reverse along Ward Street to continue the downtown tour on Magnolia Avenue.*

▲ 1.69: *An early 1890s view of Larkspur's downtown hotel, with three ladies sitting on an upper veranda that encircles the entire building. The adjacent Lynch home is visible through the hotel's downstairs railings. Note that the dirt streets have not yet been raised to the level of the entry porch.*

⑭ Northern Business Block

For more than a century the Blue Rock Hotel structure at **505-507 MAGNOLIA AVENUE** has symbolized Larkspur to the outside world; it was designed for precisely that purpose.

In 1890, when only a few homes had been built in the area, the investors of the American Land and Trust Co. realized that their new "town" of Larkspur needed the recognition and prestige that a good hotel could provide. They decided to sponsor the construction of a hotel and to turn its operation over to private proprietors. Architect J. H. Littlefield of San Francisco designed this building, prominently located on the main county road. A builder named B. L. Wallace, also of San Francisco, began

HOTEL LARKSPUR

"Larkspurites are on [alert] as Hotel Larkspur nears the opening day. Carload after carload of beautiful furniture disappear[s] in its spacious halls, under the generalship of Mr. Hepburn, the genial proprietor. Each day sees the handsome house grow more charmingly beautiful."

— *The Sausalito News*, June 12, 1891

◀ 1.70: *Magnolia Avenue north of Ward Street, about 1895. The early hotel occupies the corner, and Merwin's General Merchandise building appears on the right. The small house between them was the home of Richard and Bessie Lynch. A white fence on the other side of the county road enclosed the grounds of the railroad depot. The vantage for this unusual view was the upper portion of the Rice livery stable on Ward Street. (The prominent hilltop house was the "Beleney Castle" at 234 Hawthorne Avenue.)*

construction in January of 1891, with a contract calling for completion in 88 working days at a cost of nearly $20,000.

The Hotel Larkspur was formally opened to the public on Saturday, June 13, 1891, and reportedly was booked for the season. Ten days earlier special guests had signed the first page of the hotel's register. Those guests were the friends and families of Hermann J. Sadler, then the president of the American Land and Trust Co., and the Company's secretary, William F. Mau, the same man who had purchased Patrick King's farm in 1880. Other guests included the two Badlam brothers from San Francisco, who had installed a 20,000 candlepower gas plant to provide illumination for the hotel and nearby street lamps; unfortunately, their Badlam Gas Machine proved unreliable, and was taken out a month later, to be replaced by "a fine machine ordered from the East."

Other businesses soon opened nearby. *The Sausalito News* of August 24, 1895 reported: "Larkspur has been embellished by the new and complete emporium of E. L. Merwin, who dispenses a fine grade of groceries and general merchandise. He is within easy reach of the R.R. station."

The unheated hotel operated only during summer months; its early years were marked by constant management turnover. In June of 1896 it was sold to

▲ 1.72: *The Hotel Larkspur, as it appeared in the period 1898-1909. Metal signs advertise the availability of a public telephone. The adjacent building on the right was Lynch's Hall, the social and commercial center of town.*

a Portuguese businessman named Ignacio Faustino Azevedo, who operated the building under the Anglicized name "Foster." By January of 1897 his Foster building housed both a grocery operated by J.S. Hopkins & Co., and the hotel, now conducted by storekeeper Edmund L. Merwin as the Hotel Merwin. Merwin soon departed, and in 1898 operation of the hotel was taken over by Harry Hopkins, who changed its name back to Hotel Larkspur. Meanwhile, Richard Lynch had erected his large hall and storefronts on the adjacent lots to the north.

The structure eventually was acquired in January of 1901 by James M. Costello *(see pages 7-8)*, who held the property for nearly ten years. Costello's ownership brought some stability to the hotel, and he turned its management over to a respected new proprietor, James McCormick. McCormick operated the Hotel Larkspur until 1910; he and his wife Mary Jane "Jennie" raised their four daughters nearby in a home at 577 Magnolia Avenue.

In April of 1910 William Stringa and Serafino Marilli, operators of the saloon across the street at 503 Magnolia Avenue, purchased the hotel and began plans to move their saloon into grand new quarters. They immediately hired Gustave Nagel to expand the structure and face its ground floor and pillars with locally quarried blue rock. The upper veranda was removed and rooms extended into its space, while the downstairs office was eliminated to allow expansion of the saloon and restaurant area. Stringa and Marilli's new hotel became Larkspur's most enduring landmark, as the delicate features of the Hotel Larkspur were replaced by the solid masonry of the Blue Rock Hotel.

▲ 1.71: *Proprietors Mary Jane and James McCormick at the entrance of the Hotel Larkspur, about 1905. The corner entry door behind the McCormicks led directly to the main office. In the background, a railroad car bears a load of cordwood.*

▲ 1.73: Gustave Nagel is shown at far right in summer of 1910, overseeing expansion of the hotel and installation of its blue-rock facing. Note the freshly quarried stone lying in the street to be hand-selected by masons.

▲ 1.74: A very early photograph of the new Blue Rock suggests this is one of the first business cards designed for its proud new owners.

William Stringa and Serafino Marilli were active on-site managers of their new Blue Rock Hotel, until Serafino suffered a paralytic stroke about 1919, whereupon his wife Elizabeth assumed his role. Elizabeth Marilli became a local legend; she was a tiny, dark-haired woman, respected for her business acumen, compassion, and strong convictions. "My grandmother became known as 'Ma Marilli'," Dorothy Barton wrote in 1991, "because she would stand for no nonsense and was deeply concerned about the welfare of the guests." The Marilli children, who washed dishes, waited on tables, and carried suitcases for guests, remembered a soda fountain made of two-tone marble where the dining room is today and a large attic where the hotel's employees lived. Elizabeth Marilli's daughter-in-law Helen (Mrs. Theodore) Marilli reported that Lee Dock Siu was the chef at the hotel for 19 years; "he could make the best Italian dishes," she added.

Elizabeth's husband Serafino died in October of 1930, and the Stringa-Marilli era of the Blue Rock finally ended eight years later when William Stringa and Elizabeth Marilli sold the hotel, with its entire contents, to Lloyd H. McLaughlin, a restaurateur from Crescent City. William Stringa, remembered as the "genial host" of the Blue Rock, died the following year, in April of 1939, at age 76, from injuries received in a severe automobile accident. Elizabeth Marilli died at age 90 in February of 1959, outliving her sister, Julia Frizzi, by nearly five years; those Guscetti girls were tough.

The Blue Rock then began its passage through a succession of owners and operators. After Lloyd McLaughlin suffered health setbacks, Ray Hobard

WHAT IS "BLUE ROCK?"

"Blue rock," or "bluestone," was widely used to build garden walls and chimneys in turn-of-the-century Larkspur. Once quarried informally at a number of locations in town, its formal name is graywacke, which is essentially dirty sandstone; when freshly broken, the rock appears dark gray – or even blue – in color, but it later weathers to light brown and gray. It can be seen at the large quarry pits behind San Quentin Prison and Larkspur Landing. The facing stone used for the Blue Rock Hotel reportedly came from the nearby Varsi Hill, which once rose at the site of today's Meadowood homes.

▲ 1.75: Co-proprietors William Stringa and Elizabeth Marilli operated the Blue Rock through its heyday period of the 1920s and 1930s. Here, William Stringa holds Dorothy Marilli, while her grandmother Elizabeth Marilli stands on the right, about 1916. The waiters and urchins around the main entrance are not identified.

Boggs acquired the building in 1942, adding the massive stone fireplace to the dining room. Construction of the fireplace was a community effort; patrons were encouraged to donate a stone to the enterprise. At least three stones bear etched names – one stone commemorates the November 11, 1939 birth of Linda Ann Lauterwasser, the infant daughter of city treasurer Russ Lauterwasser. Another recalls Hil Probert (see pages 3-4), and the third stone, marked "Ernie," reportedly referred to Ernie Epidendio, a well-known downtown butcher. Rumor has it that a gold coin was embedded in the mortar.

Major alterations to the hotel's appearance occurred in 1959, when contractor-owner Hugh C. Wood added a third story to the building and created the adjacent 12-unit Larkwood apartment complex facing Ward Street. Wood also created a parking lot on Magnolia Avenue, and completed the transition from transient hotel to apartments. When Nino Marchisiello took over the restaurant operation in 1984, he further remodeled the first-floor interior and added awnings to the building to accommodate outdoor dining.

The Blue Rock's current appearance is the result of a damaging fire that swept the top floor in July of 2002, made worse by the tiny rooms and narrow hallways that had been crammed into the third floor. Encouraged by the city, architect Thomas Bateman Hood designed a new pitched roof that evoked the hotel's appearance during the first half of the nineteenth century, complete with dormers. The corner tower was elevated slightly to retain its projection over the floor surrounding it, and the historic neon sign reinstalled. (The sign

▲ 1.77: *A crowd raises the flag in the new downtown park on May 1, 1908 as a May Day ceremony. Note in the background a road-sprinkling wagon parked on Ward Street, the extensive lumberyard, and the Rice Livery Stable with the adjacent home of Charles and Carolyn Rice.*

inexplicably proclaims the building an "inn," but it's been a "hotel" for most of its history.)

The restaurant space at 507, occupied since 1994 by renown chef Roland Passot's the Left Bank Brasserie, has continued the building's pivotal role in downtown Larkspur; William Stringa, the "genial host" of the Blue Rock, would feel comfortable there today.

The city parking lot at the northeast corner of Ward Street and Magnolia Avenue is a central location that was retained for many years by Larkspur's developers, the American Land and Trust Co. By 1908, however, residents were anxious to present a cultivated appearance to visitors arriving by train at the nearby station, and in spring of that year a deal was made to allow development of a public park on the corner. The Doherty Lumber Co. donated a flagpole, several women's groups paid for a flag, and a simple little park was developed. The *Marin County Tocsin*, with unfounded optimism, proclaimed that the new park would be "the largest and prettiest in the county." For many years distinctive tapered-top wooden fence posts enclosed the park.

In the era 1910-1925 the eastern edge of the park was bordered by a railroad spur line providing service to the downtown lumberyard. That spur track crossed Ward Street about 25 feet to the east of the bank building, and was removed when the lumberyard relocated in 1925.

▲ 1.76: *The Blue Rock Hotel in January of 1950. Its appearance had remained essentially unchanged over the last four decades. Note the fishscale shingles that remain on the tower.*

▲ 1.78: *Walter Frizzi, son of Julia and Gus, stands in the entry road (Branch Street) to the railroad station about 1910. The city park is behind him, trees line Ward Street alongside the Marilli and Stringa saloon, and the Hotel Larkspur and Lynch Hall face Magnolia Avenue.*

▲ 1.79: *The original Chevron station on Magnolia Avenue, adjacent to Mabelle and Archie Culpepper's real estate office, as it appeared in the late 1950s.*

▲ 1.80: *Cliff Archer and his son Doug at their modern station, about 1968. Doug later went on to a long and successful career with the Larkspur Fire Department, retiring as deputy chief in 2002. Doug continues as founder and curator of the fire department's history room.*

By the mid-1920s a modest Mission Revival-style stucco structure had been erected on a northern portion of this area, containing a real estate office, first occupied by Mary L. Courtright, then Mabel G. Stephens, followed later by the real estate, notary, and insurance offices of Corte Madera residents Mabelle and Archie Culpepper. For a few years part of that office space was allotted to a small Larkspur lending library, one of several for-profit libraries of the period. The Culpepper office building remained here into the late 1960s. In 1974 the City of Larkspur acquired several lots at this corner, and in 1975 opened the current parking lot for the benefit of downtown merchants.

A small gasoline service station appeared at **532 MAGNOLIA AVENUE** (now an empty lot) in the mid-1940s; operated for a while by Axel Jensen as a Chevron dealership, it was acquired by Clifford G. Archer in 1947. Cliff Archer soon had the structure moved a short distance from its original location (then labeled 522) to this site directly facing 543 Magnolia Avenue. Cliff operated his well-known station here until his retirement in 1972.

The original station was a small, flat-roofed, stucco building with two service bays, similar in appearance to the nearby stucco Culpepper realty office.

Demolition of that original station made possible the construction of a much larger structure in 1962, with four lanes for the pumps. That building served as a central element of the downtown from 1962 until 1988. Paul Penna, who grew up in Larkspur in the 1950s and 1960s, recalled that it seemed as though every teenage boy in town, at one time or another, found employment pumping gas at Cliff Archer's.

Under Jim Walker, the station survived until June of 1988; it was later demolished and the large raised parking area around it removed. The land since has remained undeveloped while various redevelopment proposals are considered under the Central Larkspur Specific Plan (CLASP) process.

The site that is now a paved parking lot at **515-529 MAGNOLIA AVENUE** was once occupied by one of Larkspur's most important structures, built by Richard Lynch. Ireland-born Lynch and his Scottish wife Bessie arrived in California with their three daughters about 1888, having lived previously in New Zealand. After the birth of a fourth daughter,

▲ 1.81: *Winter in early Larkspur, about 1897, with the railroad depot, Lynch's Hall, and Brazil building. Trees and the water tank obscure the hotel. The open space in the foreground later served as the community's baseball field, and decades later as a lumberyard. Note the northbound steam locomotive at the passenger station.*

LYNCH'S HALL

"The campers are having a fine time and a social hop was given in Lynch's Hall last Saturday night. Supper was served at midnight and all had a good time."

— *Marin County Tocsin*, July 16, 1898

they purchased two lots here in 1891, and built a home on their land at about the same time. Their house was set back from Magnolia and adjacent to the hotel building site. Richard was a carpenter-builder; it is quite likely he built several of the early structures in this area. By 1895 a small grocery and general merchandise store, operated by Edmund L. Merwin, had been erected on the northernmost of the Lynches' lots. Within a short time Lynch replaced that store with conjoined commercial structures that blocked off the front of his house and obliterated the site of the former store. For the next decade or so the two-part Lynch Hall was the largest, and probably most important, structure in town.

The Lynches' new structure instantly became the community's social center. It had four retail spaces on the ground floor, and a large room spanning the second floor that served as a general purpose meeting

◀ 1.82: *The Blue Rock Hotel and two-part Lynch building, about 1912. This view is taken from the railroad station, accessed by the dirt road in the foreground, with its wooden planked sidewalk. The spur track to the Larkspur Lumber Company crosses the road, and the fenced city park appears on the left. Magnolia Avenue was not yet paved, so a water wagon (seen parked at the Blue Rock) was used to sprinkle the dirt street. The shops shown here include a café, two real estate offices, and the Blake Brothers Grocery.*

hall and auditorium. In 1897 a meeting was held here to consider the formation of a volunteer fire department, and the room served as the site for at least one "grand ball."

The Hall later became the obvious choice for the new city's official meeting place; the Board of Trustees met here from 1908 to 1913, at a rent of $15 per month, before moving to the newly built Town Hall at 400 Magnolia Avenue.

Richard died in May of 1909; the *Marin County Tocsin* reported: "Richard Lynch, one of the first settlers to build a house in Larkspur, died at his home there last Wednesday. For years before the place was incorporated he was known everywhere as the 'mayor of Larkspur.' … His funeral was the largest ever held in Larkspur." His widow Bessie moved to San Francisco about 1915, where she died in 1941, at age 91. The Lynch building was eventually removed, its space finally becoming the parking lot adjacent to the Blue Rock Hotel.

In late 1891 Fritz Goerl, a prosperous Bavarian brewer in San Rafael, had a large commercial structure erected for him by Gustave Nagel at **531-533-537 MAGNOLIA AVENUE**. It was one of several investments that Fritz and his wife Josephine held across Marin County. Josie sold the property in 1908, not long after Fritz was killed in a runaway horse accident in San Rafael. The building has housed a variety of retail tenants throughout its long existence, with a residential unit (533) above, and another (now labeled 529) to the rear.

The building's distinctive false front hides a conventional ridged roof; note that the slight bulge above the decorative beams originally was clad in scalloped shingles; it is now covered by modern roofing material. That false front once had an additional, higher peak that disappeared in later decades. Some windows on the south face have been closed in, and a massive chimney removed.

Today's 531 Magnolia retail space, in the southern half of the structure, once operated as the Larkspur Drug Store; from about 1909 to 1911 its proprietress was a pioneering woman pharmacist named Evans Montgomery. For about two decades, from the late 1920s through the mid-1940s, it served as the headquarters and production facility for a family of local weekly newspapers. William G. Weaver owned, published, and printed the *Larkspur-Corte Madera News*, the *San Anselmo Herald*, and the *Fairfax Gazette* from the street-level floor of this building. The 531 space became the Lark Creamery from the late 1940s until 1954, followed by S & N Auto Parts in the early 1960s, and has seen a succession of small restaurants ever since, most recently as the Little Village Café, followed by today's Burritoville.

The space at 537 Magnolia Avenue was an early location for the real estate offices of Fred W. Ammann, then served through the 1940s as the production and printing shop for the adjacent newspapers, and since the mid-1960s has been occupied by a series of real estate offices. Niz Brown Realtors has been at this location since 1992.

The Goerl building, together with the adjacent building on the north, has anchored this northern block of Larkspur for more than a century. The southernmost structure is the older of the two; although the two buildings were erected separately, for many decades they have been held under the

▲ 1.83: The Goerl building on Magnolia Avenue, about 1913.

▲ 1.84: Commercial buildings in downtown Larkspur on September 6, 1909, looking south. An excited Booster Day parade crowd lines the street outside the (right to left) Brazil-Azevedo, Goerl, and Lynch buildings; the Hotel Larkspur is out of sight at the Ward Street intersection.

EVOLUTION OF A DOWNTOWN

After the American Land and Trust Co. subdivided the area and named it "Larkspur," lots throughout the newly created town were offered for sale. Most of them were offered for residential use, but the area that became today's downtown was treated differently. The company's officers hoped that prime locations along Magnolia Avenue would be used for commercial purposes; long before zoning or city planning existed, they simply wanted to create a viable economic structure.

Magnolia Avenue, with its long history as the primary land route between Sausalito and San Rafael, provided the basic corridor for economic activity. The original 1887 subdivision map recognized the location of the county road (Magnolia Avenue) near a "railroad depot" of the North Pacific Coast Railroad, thus designating the expected center of economic activity. That location prompted development of the hotel at the corner of Ward Street, to accommodate commercial and recreational visitors, and the nearby livery stable, to provide essential transportation. In short order, the Merwin, Lynch, Frizzi, Goerl, and Brazil buildings were located nearby; the pattern for downtown Larkspur thus was established well before 1900.

Many of the buyers who acquired land on Magnolia Avenue had clear commercial intentions; those early purchasers included the Lynches, Frizzis, Brazils, and Costas, who developed their lots for their own commercial enterprises. Other tracts were sold to speculators, such as Azevedo, Goerl, and Yost, who expected that commercial enterprises would be undertaken by leaseholders and future buyers. Some lots were retained by individual officers of the American Land and Trust Co. (or their family members), who sold their land years later as conditions became favorable. As a result, in much of the downtown area, the users and occupants of buildings were different than the formal owners of the land.

same ownership, maintained with similar external color and cladding. Except for the mid-century addition of asbestos shingles, the buildings have retained much of their original appearance, and provide a direct link to Larkspur's early commercial period.

Various landowners held the property at **539-545 MAGNOLIA AVENUE** until March of 1905, when it was acquired by Antonio "Antone" Brazil and Ignacio Azevedo, who each owned nearby downtown buildings. They probably had this structure erected in 1908. The distinctive three-part Italianate façade has a mansard cornice with supporting corbels, disguising a conventional ridged roof. That façade, and the arrangement of the upstairs windows, remains unchanged from the building's original appearance. A passage penetrates under the building's south edge, barely wide enough for modern vehicles. On a July morning in 1929 the elderly Mr. Azevedo fell to his death from the roof of this building, after attempting to repair a radio antenna and losing his balance.

The two retail spaces on the ground floor have long histories. The retail space at 539 Magnolia was a tailor's shop in the 1920s, and Larkspur's Taste Good Bakery in the late 1940s. The northern space, 545 Magnolia, was a drug store (The Larkspur Pharmacy) in the early 1920s, and by 1930 had become Frederick W. Ammann's notary and real estate office; he later became postmaster, and operated the U.S. Post Office here, where it remained until 1955. For the next three decades, the space was Fred and Edna Schefer's Larkspur Food Center, a small grocery store that stubbornly clung to life in a modern world until Fred's death in 1989. The old double doors now open to retail uses.

▲ *1.85: On the right, the Brazil-Azevedo building, 539 and 545 Magnolia Avenue, about 1916-1918.*

▲ 1.86: *The Lark in 1968, with the 1895 Brazil building visible to the right.*

In May of 1937 the Blumenfeld family, owners of numerous motion picture theaters in the Bay Area, announced plans to erect a new theater in Larkspur. It wasn't until June 21, 1940, however, that the new Lark Theater opened to rave reviews at **549 MAGNOLIA AVENUE**.

Plans for the structure had been prepared by William B. David, who designed 17 theaters in northern California, many of them for the Blumenfelds in Art Deco or Streamline Moderne styles. Two of David's other theater designs, the Park in Lafayette and the Noyo in Willits, appear to have been built with plans identical to the Lark's. (It may not be a coincidence that all three structures used four-letter names that fit neatly above the marquee.)

The Lark played on until 1999, when it finally went dark, a victim of the corporate consolidation and multiplex theaters of the period. Optimistic citizens began to discuss revival of one of the last small-town, single-screen theaters, and led by Bernice Baeza and Heidi Hillenbrand, they created a non-profit corporation and began the process of restoring the premises. The building's owners, real estate investors Terry Andrews and Michael Gottlieb, agreed to the restoration, and eventually to the purchase of the structure.

LARK THEATER OPENS IN 1940

"The new theater seats 400. It is of streamline design, the lobby wall covered with colorful tile, and the furniture made to order and elaborate. The interior of the house is modern, down to the last minute, and thermostatic heat keeps the theater at an even temperature in chilly weather, while the air conditioning system does the same for summer weather."

— *Larkspur-Corte Madera News,* June 21, 1940

"With crowds that jammed the new Lark Theater for a full evening, Larkspur's new playhouse made its bow last Friday night. Between the two shows Nate Blumenfeld welcomed those present in well-chosen words. Mayor Welter of Corte Madera and Councilman Lauterwasser, representing Larkspur, expressed the appreciation of the Twin Cities and pledged continued cooperation. A number of leading citizens of the two towns were introduced and took a bow, amid applause of the audience."

— *Larkspur-Corte Madera News,* June 28, 1940

▲ 1.87: *Painters apply final touches to the revived Lark, 2004.*

LARK THEATER REOPENS IN 2004

The Lark reopened on July 9, 2004, with a showing of *Impact*, the 1949 motion picture filmed in Larkspur. The restored Lark now serves as a community film center, presenting first- and second-run pictures, art film classics, independent films, and simulcasts of opera performances and major events. In August of 2007 a capital campaign enabled the corporation to acquire title to the building, and arrange long-term financing. An active membership program supplements ticket sale and concession revenues.

"Fund-raising efforts yielded $500,000 from community and corporate supporters, and renovation began with an outpouring of services from local professionals who offered their time pro bono or at reduced rates. Larkspur residents, from local architects and contractors to volunteers of all ages, pitched in to return the theater to its former grandeur. The theater's exterior was restored to its original Art Deco design with new neon lighting and a floor of refurbished terrazzo tiles... The auditorium's original decorative lights were hand-restored, and a mural was added to reflect the theater's vintage design motifs."
— *San Francisco Chronicle*, April 15, 2005

◀ 1.88: Larkspur's 1891 station, with a blurred southbound electric train just departing. The adjacent landscaped area has matured, suggesting a period about 1915. Train buffs will notice three rails to provide both narrow- and broad- gauge service, and a fourth for electric power.

⑮ Railroad Station Site

The narrow gauge North Pacific Coast Railroad, running then from Sausalito as far as Tomales, began regular service through this area in 1874. A simple freight depot was located on this site, adjacent to the county road. A decade later, when the American Land and Trust Co. laid out its "Town of Larkspur" in 1887, the developers determined to have regular passenger service made available as well, and received a promise from the railroad that passenger service would commence when five additional houses were built and inhabited. The developers fulfilled their part of the agreement with construction of small houses on Locust Avenue, King, and Ward Streets, and in July of 1891 a wooden North Pacific Coast station was completed at **552 MAGNOLIA AVENUE**. That building shared essentially the same design as others on the line, including the nearby Mill Valley (1889) station. It consisted of a passenger waiting room on the north end, a center office, and a small baggage room. A large windmill and water tank, necessary for steam-driven locomotives, were adjacent to the tracks.

The underfunded North Pacific Coast Railroad was reorganized in 1902 as the North Shore Railroad, and altered the system to broad gauge track and the addition of electric interurban trains. The electric commuter cars required installation of an electric third rail that received widespread attention. Judge Samuel Gardiner, raised in Larkspur in the early 1900s, remembered the dangerous third rail well, "because it was walked on by daredevils who jumped onto it with both feet at once and then left the rest of us open-mouthed with admiration." With the advent of electric trains in 1903, commuter service to San Francisco became much faster and more reliable. In 1926, 60 electric trains stopped in Larkspur daily, 30 each way. Some of them dropped off and picked up mail. Freight trains also used the track, the number depending on how much freight needed to be handled.

> ### THE NEW TRAIN STATION
>
> "Work of wrecking the old N.W.P. station at Larkspur began on Thursday morning of this week. The new station is ready for occupancy and is a decided credit to the town and railroad."
>
> — *Larkspur-Corte Madera News*, Friday, May 3, 1929

▲ 1.90: *In this undated photo, the open archway of Larkspur's main station opens to the tracks and warming room beyond. A parked baggage handcart contains a passenger's steamer trunk, and a lumberyard building shows at the rear.*

▲ 1.89: *Original ceramic heralds survive on the 1929 railroad station, 2010.*

In 1907 the company was reorganized yet again, to become the Northwestern Pacific Railroad, and remained so for the next several decades. By 1909 this site contained the passenger station, a small bunkhouse for rail workers, a handcar stand across the tracks, a freight building, and the section foreman's house *(see page 40)*.

Increased passenger traffic and political pressure to improve service prompted the Northwestern's decision in 1929 to install five stations along the Marin line, one of them built here to replace the old wooden structure.

Locals believed the replacement was due to a persistent campaign waged by Elizabeth Marilli, the stalwart co-owner of the Blue Rock Hotel. The new station building, still standing today, was typical of the Mission Revival style of architecture with a stucco exterior, red tile roof, and arched windows. It is one of the few remaining that has the original Northwestern Pacific ceramic heralds still mounted on the north and south exterior walls. A matching stucco warming room was also erected on the eastern side of the tracks to service northbound passengers. Both the station and warming room face broad concrete boarding platforms that constitute contributing resources to the Downtown Historic District.

After the Golden Gate Bridge opened in 1938, rail passenger service to San Francisco was doomed, and it ceased in February of 1941. Gradually, the old station fell into disrepair, with boards over its windows and weeds in the roadbed.

In 1991 the railroad station buildings were given a new lease on life with replacement tile roofs, structural repairs, and paint; since that time they have been occupied by a succession of small restaurants and offices.

▲ 1.91: *Weeds obscure the single remaining set of tracks, and boards cover the windows of Larkspur's station as seen here in the late 1940s. The steep embankment seen at the rear was lowered and landscaped in the early 1970s.*

LARKSPUR'S FIRST RESIDENTS

The broad salt marshes that once edged Corte Madera Creek near downtown Larkspur provided abundant foods for our original Native American inhabitants. The Coast Miwok people who lived in Marin and southern Sonoma County had both seasonal and permanent villages at places where fresh water and diverse food sources were available. A survey undertaken in 1908 recorded eight "shellmounds" – now known as middens – in the area stretching from today's Baltimore Park north to Murray Park. Those middens, comprised of charcoal and organic material such as shellfish, waterfowl, and fish refuse, marked sites that represented thousands of years of human activity. Two officially recorded sites were located in the immediate area of the old Bickerstaff knoll, and probably were part of a loose assemblage that stretched south through Meadowood to Chanticleer Avenue. That entire area provided sheltered weather and access to fresh water in the Arroyo Holon, the same elements that attracted Larkspur's settlers in the 1860s.

No aboveground evidence of the Miwoks' dwelling sites remains visible today, due to widespread agricultural and construction activity early in the nineteenth century; the Bickerstaff knoll itself was obliterated by land-leveling work for the Nivens' nursery greenhouses. Early residents in this area frequently found arrowheads, pestles, and similar artifacts, and occasional human skeletal materials were reported as well. Despite the urbanization in intervening years, artifacts and human remains are still scattered in small places that escaped earlier alteration of the soil. Thus, during the land-clearing phase of the Niven Nursery development, intensive archaeological monitoring activity will be a required part of the process. Those investigations will include monitors from the federally recognized Federated Indians of Graton Rancheria, who represent present-day descendants of the Coast Miwoks.

▲ *1.92: Looking eastward in early 1900s toward the Bickerstaff family's adobe ranch house, built in the early 1850s on a knoll above the salt marsh.*

⓰ Bickerstaff Ranch Site

Located far to the east of today's Lark Theater, and directly south of Hall Middle School, the Bickerstaff family's adobe house occupied a prominent knoll at the edge of the salt marsh. The odd old building was a county landmark for about 70 years.

Missouri-born Jonathan Bickerstaff and his Irish wife Ann Teresa arrived here in the early 1850s, perhaps following Ann's sister, Helen Brown, whose husband Richard Samuel Brown had established a house and farm at the mouth of Baltimore Canyon. These two pioneer families controlled all the lands to the east and south of what later became Patrick King's farm *(see pages 6-7)*. Indeed, the Bickerstaffs' prosperous dairy farm stretched south to the approximate location of today's Corte Madera Town Hall. By 1870 the Bickerstaff family consisted of Jonathan, his wife Ann, and four California-born children, ages seven to fourteen. Their farm included a barn and an extensive system of fences; the Arroyo Holon entered the marsh nearby, as did a smaller stream that flowed from today's Sycamore Avenue.

Tradition holds that the Bickerstaff house, built of sun-dried adobe bricks, had been constructed in 1852 – variously attributed to the labor of Indians or hired San Quentin prisoners. Documentary evidence instead suggests that the house was built sometime after 1855, as a single-story building. The second floor, and yellow fired-brick facing remembered by early residents, was added in later decades.

In the 1840s the same area had been used briefly as the site of a sawmill and barn operated by the U.S. government, processing redwood logs cut from the nearby canyons and then loaded onto boats at a landing where Boardwalk #1 is located today. A persistent tradition recounts that U.S. Army Captain John C.

▲ 1.93: In this 1890s view the Bickerstaff adobe appears behind the new railroad station and freight building. This photograph was probably taken from the veranda of the Hotel Larkspur.

Frémont chose the knoll as the site of an encampment during the hectic days following the 1846 Bear Flag Revolt in Sonoma. Frémont traveled from San Rafael to Sausalito on a raid during that period, and the nearby road was the only land route between those towns; this knoll would have provided a convenient and easily defensible location.

By the mid-1870s the Bickerstaffs had divorced, selling their property to land speculators Alexander Forbes and William Coleman. For several years their daughter Josephine remained on the ranch as a renter with her family. Ann Bickerstaff eventually moved to San Francisco, where she died in 1889, and Jonathan died in March of 1912, in a home he had acquired in Mill Valley.

After the Bickerstaffs' departure, the dairy land was transferred to Ignacio Azevedo, a Portuguese farmer and astute local businessman. He operated the Larkspur Dairy on the hillsides around today's Meadowood and Palm Hill; its buildings were located close to the original Bickerstaff knoll, and may have utilized the same barn. Ignacio, his wife Rosa, and their five children lived in a wooden house on the dairy farm for several decades in the early 1900s. Much later some of that land became the site of the farm operated by vegetable grower Pietro Epidendio, other portions were acquired by the Niven family's nursery and roofing business, and the northern tip became the site of the Larkspur Lumber Company.

The precise time and manner of the demise of the Bickerstaffs' adobe house and its oak-topped knoll is unclear; the house is absent from 1930s photographs, and the knoll had been flattened by the mid-1940s to create more space for the extensive greenhouses of the Nivens' nursery.

CENTRAL LARKSPUR SPECIFIC PLAN (CLASP)

A 22-acre area to the east of Magnolia Avenue, including the separately owned service station site, the railroad buildings, Larkspur Plaza, and the Niven nursery properties, has been involved in a complex planning process that began in 1997. Extensive public participation and comment during more than 40 workshops and meetings preceded formal hearings before the Planning Commission and City Council. Detailed Environmental Impact Reports were prepared to inform the deliberations, and another 15 hearings preceded the City Council's formal adoption of a Specific Plan for part of the area in September of 2006. The plans will guide the city's eventual zoning and other land use decisions for development of the area, which will have both commercial and mixed residential components. That process is ongoing as this book goes to press.

▲ *1.94: The ornate Brazil building established the northern end of Larkspur's commercial area, located adjacent to Post Street, about 1910. A heavy wagon, or perhaps a stagecoach, is traveling southbound in the distance, and two ladies in the center are standing on the eventual site of the Lark Theater. Against the stairs, a water trough for horses bears a sign for A. P. Hotaling's "Old Kirk" whiskey.*

AT THE BRAZIL BUILDING

"Saturday evening, the road from Larkspur station to M. Brazil's was illuminated by hundreds of Japanese lanterns. A surprise party was given to Senor Brazil by his numerous friends from the Azores. The old country dance, the 'Chamarita,' was rendered with all the grace and music of the old world."

— *The Marin Journal*, February 7, 1895

(17) Brazil Building Site

What is now an empty lot at **557 MAGNOLIA AVENUE** (the northern corner of Magnolia Avenue and Post Street) was the site of a vital component of Larkspur's early economic center, owned by Antone and Rose Brazil. Like many other early residents, Antone was a naturalized citizen, born in the Azores Islands. He purchased this site in October of 1894 and opened a small saloon.

Brazil's saloon apparently prospered, and in late 1895 he contracted with Gustave Nagel to dramatically expand his structure, building an elaborate two-story saloon and dwelling that opened in early 1896. That building had delicate spindle work above a 44-foot-wide porch, and second-story bay windows set behind a scroll saw railing. Ample glass windows opened to the saloon area.

In that early period a set of white wooden stairs mounted the steep bank from the train tracks to Magnolia Avenue in front of Brazil's building. Antone operated his saloon here into the early 1900s, and then moved to other endeavors, investing in the nearby building at 539-545 Magnolia. By 1905 the saloon had been taken over by Leonard Young, who with his wife Jessie eventually raised six children in the upstairs living quarters. (One of their sons, Charlie, went on to become a well-known butcher and operator of a meat counter in the market at 489 Magnolia Avenue.) Len Young's Larkspur Bar eventually morphed into a café, and continued to be operated by him into the mid-1920s. Len can be seen in old photographs standing in his doorway, watching games in the baseball field across the road. Len was an active citizen and a 1913 charter member of the volunteer firemen; he died in 1937.

What had been Len Young's café eventually became Marie Avedano's "Marie's Tavern" in the late 1930s, and during the late 1940s was operated as Leo and Ruth Martinez's "Leo's Restaurant and Cocktail Lounge." The structure was crudely modified in later years, becoming apartment units, and then burned in 1970 – twice in the same day.

The cause of the second fire was never confirmed, but always considered suspect by Larkspur's fire officials. The badly damaged building was razed soon after and has never been replaced.

(18) Lumberyard Site & Larkspur Plaza

When Dolph Doherty died in October of 1959, the Larkspur City Council promptly resolved to name "the new road to Hall School" after "a man who gave so much to the city." Doherty had been a central figure in Larkspur's community life, serving first as chief, and then for decades as president, of the Larkspur Association of Volunteer Firemen. Today's Larkspur Plaza shopping center, built in 1972 at **570-600 MAGNOLIA AVENUE**, is located on the site that had been Doherty's Larkspur Lumber Co. between 1925 and 1970.

The lumber company previously had occupied most of the downtown block between Cane and Ward Streets *(see pages 29-30)*. The Dohertys moved their operation to this 11-acre site, across the tracks from the rest of the downtown, in 1925. They purchased the site directly from the Coleman and Forbes families, who had acquired it in the mid-1870s as a portion of the pioneer Bickerstaff farm. Before the lumberyard moved here, the land

WHILE LARKSPUR SLEPT

"Two Larkspur residents dashed from a burning apartment house clad only in their pajamas last night as flames engulfed the building in the second of two fires yesterday. The two fires at the 75 year-old converted office building at 557 Magnolia Avenue caused damage estimated at $55,000 according to the Larkspur Fire Department. The first fire, its cause unknown, erupted at 2:49 p.m. ... At 11:57 p.m. the firemen were called to a second fire at the same address.... Approximately 40 men and five trucks from the Larkspur and Kentfield fire departments battled the flames for three hours."

– *Independent Journal*,
February 3, 1970

▲ *1.95: Randolph Doherty in his lumberyard office on the site of today's Larkspur Plaza, March 1959.*

▲ 1.96: *An undated early view of Larkspur's baseball field, looking north toward the oaks on what became the Doherty home site, with the salt marsh and Greenbrae hills beyond.*

▲ 1.97: *Larkspur's baseball field as it appeared in the early 1900s, looking southeast (where the batter has hit a single to left). Spectators are sitting on the knoll that later became the Doherty home site, with their backs toward the county road that became Magnolia Avenue. (The railroad tracks ran in a trench between that knoll and the roadway.) The Azevedo dairy barn and home are in the middle distance, with Varsi Hill (long since removed) in the center, and Palm Hill to the right. Today's Lucky Supermarket, at 570 Magnolia Avenue, is located near the ball field's second base.*

served informally as Larkspur's baseball field, hosting visiting teams from San Rafael or Sausalito.

The new lumberyard, numbered 554 Magnolia Avenue, was served by a short spur railroad track, which entered from the north and curved eastward. Lumber sheds were arranged in concentric curves to match the configuration of the railroad spur. The Niven family's greenhouses were immediately adjacent to the south. The entry road to the lumberyard sloped away from Magnolia Avenue on the route (then called "Marsh Road") that is still used today to approach the supermarket, although the revised grade requires that shoppers with low-slung cars have to use the roadway with caution lest they scrape their bumpers.

Moving the lumberyard from its downtown location gave the Dohertys the opportunity to build a new home for themselves. Dolph and Nell vacated the rented building at 474 Magnolia

THE DOHERTY HOME

"A building permit was granted Fire Chief R.C. Doherty for one of the handsomest homes in the county which he is about to construct on the knoll adjoining his lumber yard. Its outstanding location coupled with its wonderful architecture will make it one of the show places of Marin county."

— *The Marin and San Anselmo Herald*, October 16, 1925

1.98: *A steam shovel removes the upper portion of the knoll in preparation for construction of the Doherty home in 1925. A trench between the fences in the foreground allowed the train tracks to retain a level grade between the station and the salt marshes to the north. At the upper edge of the photo, an early model "parachute" street lamp overhangs Magnolia Avenue.*

and moved into their new home at 568 Magnolia Avenue in February of 1926.

Taken over by the federal government during World War II, the lumberyard served as a staging area for construction of the housing projects built for shipyard workers at Marin City. After the war the yard was returned to Doherty and his partner, Burt Wheeler, only after extended negotiations.

Nell Doherty sold her home in 1969; the lumber company closed in 1970, and preparations began for redevelopment of the site. Extensive earthmoving completely removed the Doherty home and knoll and broadened the intersection of Magnolia Avenue and Doherty Drive. The reconfigured site now contains a gasoline service station at 600 Magnolia Avenue and a small Doherty Park, dedicated in 1972. Nell lived on in Larkspur, overlooking the downtown from The Tamalpais, until her death at age 99 in 1984.

▲ 1.99: *The 1926 Doherty home sits alone on its knoll in right center, with San Quentin Peninsula in the distance. A curved driveway connected the home to Magnolia Avenue (out of view in the foreground). Glass greenhouses of the Niven Company are arrayed to the east beyond the house, with Doherty Drive at left of the image. This photograph was taken from the upper gardens at 599 Magnolia Avenue, 1964.*

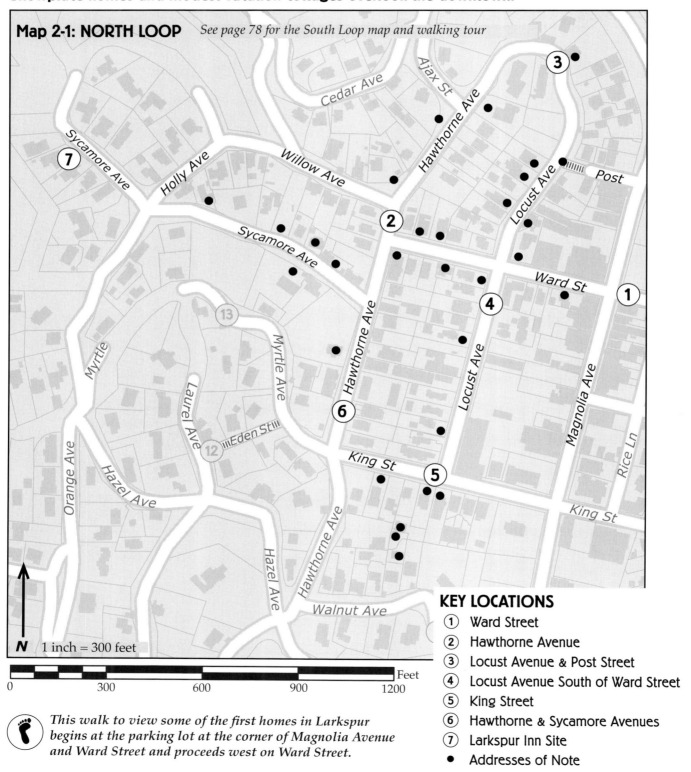

OLD HOMES IN CENTRAL LARKSPUR
Showplace homes and modest vacation cottages overlook the downtown.

Map 2-1: NORTH LOOP *See page 78 for the South Loop map and walking tour*

1 inch = 300 feet

KEY LOCATIONS
1. Ward Street
2. Hawthorne Avenue
3. Locust Avenue & Post Street
4. Locust Avenue South of Ward Street
5. King Street
6. Hawthorne & Sycamore Avenues
7. Larkspur Inn Site
• Addresses of Note

This walk to view some of the first homes in Larkspur begins at the parking lot at the corner of Magnolia Avenue and Ward Street and proceeds west on Ward Street.

OLD HOMES IN CENTRAL LARKSPUR

Only 1,800 people lived in Larkspur in 1907 when Maybelle Schneider moved into her home at 101 Locust Avenue, according to a 1975 interview. Homes at that time sold for as much as $4,000.

• • • • • • • • • • • • •

NORTH LOOP

After the redwoods were clear-cut in Larkspur in the 1850s to 1860s, the hills west of Magnolia Avenue were almost treeless. By the early 1900s some native oaks, madrones, and redwoods had begun to fill in the open spaces, but the vistas from the hills stretched east to San Quentin and the bay, and west to the slopes of Mt. Tamalpais. Local drayage man Charles Rice grazed his horses on the bare slope below Locust Avenue. Trees were prized. In 1911 citizens required a permit to cut any tree.

The bare slopes not only allowed vistas, they caught the eye of early real estate entrepreneurs. Thorpe Wright, C. W. Wright's son, stated that his father paid $21,000 to $22,000 for all the land shown on the 1887 Ward Survey Map for the American Land and Trust Company *(see page vi)*. The purchase included the land west of Magnolia Avenue between Madrone Avenue and the Escalle vineyard. Lots that were

> *"Larkspur was really country when we came here in the 1900s."*
> — Maybelle Schneider

▲ 2.1: *View looking across downtown and up Ward Street (center) to homes on Locust and Hawthorne Avenues, Big and Little King Mountains, and Mt. Tamalpais; illustration dated between 1896 and 1901.*

▲ 2.2: *View over ballpark (where Larkspur Plaza is today) to the Brazil Building, Beleney house on the hill, Big and Little King Mountains, and Mt. Tamalpais, about 1913 to 1914.*

"large enough to pasture horses and raise chickens were laid out at prices ranging from $200 to $500," according to sales brochures.

A young Irish engineer named Michael M. O'Shaughnessy who was "as green as grass" professionally, according to Thorpe Wright's mother, installed the sewer system in town – his first big job. He later went on to have a large firm and business in San Francisco, and engineered San Francisco's Hetch Hetchy water system.

Large ads ran in the San Francisco newspapers promoting the auction of properties. Since the North Pacific Coast Railroad did not have a stop in town, special excursion trains were arranged to bring people to see the properties. A platform was built so people could detrain. The first parcel was sold to Ann Dolliver at the entrance to Baltimore Canyon *(see page 106)*.

In 1890 C. W. Wright discovered that the railroad would build a passenger station if five more homes were built in town. Four of these five homes are included on this walk. The fifth house has been torn down.

After the five Victorian houses were built, the station was constructed in 1891. The name "Larkspur" was given by the railroad company that selected it over the name "Graystone" after the town's blue-gray rock. Many residents believe it might have been named "Lupine" had Wright's wife, Georgiana,

▲ 2.3: *The North Shore Railroad Station with the Brazil building behind it, early 1900s.*

▲ 2.4: *Some of the earliest homes were built on and above Magnolia Avenue, north of the center of town, 1895. Note Corte Madera Creek in the foreground.*

correctly identified the flowers growing on the hillsides. However, both wildflowers can be found here.

From 1890 to 1910 Larkspur was a bustling, robust resort center that catered to summer vacationers, and attracted fun-loving people from all over the bay area.

Maybelle Schneider, who attended the Rose Bowl dances where her husband was a traffic officer, recalled, "It was so crowded on weekends that you could walk faster than you could drive along the highway [Magnolia Avenue]. You could get a drink at the Blue Rock and get back in your car before the traffic had moved."

In the early 1890s and 1900s impressive turreted Victorian homes were built on the low ridges surrounding downtown. Closer to downtown more modest Victorian-style farmhouses and bungalows were built. A tour of the old homes of central Larkspur includes both. Today some are famous for their architectural flourishes, some for the prominent people who lived in them, and some for the activities that took place in them.

① Ward Street

Ward Street was the major road access from the station to the new hillside homes. Named for H. C. Ward, Wright's surveyor, the street is one of the few not named for trees in the original Wright tract. The three houses at 115, 117, and 119 reflect three generations of a notable local family, and three successive styles of modest residential architecture from the 1890s to the 1940s.

The wooden Greek Revival-style house at **115 WARD STREET** is the oldest of the three. It is located behind the early structure at 499 Magnolia Avenue, and was built around 1894 by Gus Frizzi, who

JAG TOWN

"When I was a young girl living in Mill Valley, I was not allowed to come to Larkspur. It was called 'Jag Town' in those days, and it was very rough on weekends with all the drinking places."

— Leslie Ezekiel

▲ 2.5: 115 Ward Street before remodel, 1988.

LARKSPUR RECOLLECTS

"In those days [early 1900s], people called Larkspur 'Hungry Hollow.' One reason was the big barbecue. They would build a fire in the well up beyond the house, and get it going good and hot. Then, they would take a bull's head, wrap it in burlap, soak it well with the hose, and lower it into the well onto the coals. The good smells would drive people crazy."

— Willie Frizzi

▲ 2.6: 115 Ward Street after a snowstorm. Note the elm and cypress trees on the street, 1913.

came from Switzerland to Larkspur in the late 1800s. The house has a gable roof, grooved shiplap exterior, and main entry from a second story porch. Originally there was a barn with a water tower and windmill behind the house.

In its heyday the house was the center of a wide variety of festive and often raucous activities. A beer garden with lath and netting was located between the house and the saloon on the corner of Magnolia Avenue. In the 1890s prizefighters, such as Jim Corbett, a relative of the DeWitts who lived at 134 Ward Street, and welterweight Joe Walcott, trained in the basement of the house.

Later, the large basement in the house contained ham radio equipment used by Theodore Marilli and Willie Frizzi in the "spark gap days" from 1910 to 1915. During this time they were credited with saving a boat sinking off Point Reyes when they relayed its SOS to the Coast Guard. According to Serafino Marilli's wife Elizabeth, in the early 1900s blackbirds used to nest in the elm and cypress trees that lined the street and would attack people as they walked by.

A number of prominent people lived at 115 Ward Street through the years, including Charlie Rice and Serafino Marilli, owner of the Hotel Larkspur, when he first came to town. Although Willie Frizzi was born here on November 8, 1897, he lived most of his adult life in a house formerly located at 30 Cedar Avenue, where he grew grapes, strawberries, and rhubarb in his garden, and raised pigeons. He took pride in his electrical skills, and invented an electric flycatcher that he used around his home. As an electrician and early member of the Larkspur Volunteer Fire Department, Willie wired the town's first box pull-type fire alarm on Magnolia Avenue. He literally lit up the Rose Bowl, creating an elaborate system of switches, dimmers, floodlights, and stage lighting that gave the dances their pizzazz. Along with Cap Larsen, he masterminded the "Firefall" display of white sparks that fell 40 feet as part of the finale at the dances.

In his later years Willie was a familiar figure at the Magnolia Avenue and Ward Street bus stop, where he loved to chat with commuters waiting for the early morning bus. Before he died in April of 1988, he boasted that he was the oldest native-born Larkspurian.

The house at 115 Ward Street was sensitively reconstructed after a partial fire in the late 1970s. From 1989 to 1990 the house and the three other buildings in the Frizzi parcel (503 and 499 Magnolia Avenue, and the old bocce ball shed located behind today's 501 Magnolia but formerly numbered as 499½) underwent major structural remodeling to bring them up to code. Multipane windows replaced the mix of windows that dated from different periods. New front steps were added to match those in old photographs.

Historical architect Dan Peterson reported, "The scale and basic design of the building has been maintained. The building is representative of the unpretentious, small houses that dotted the landscape in the 1900s."

Originally the Julia and Gus Frizzi property extended from Magnolia to Locust Avenue, encompassing what are now numbers 115, 117, and 119 Ward Street as well as 499 and 503 Magnolia Avenue. In the early 1920s Frizzi's oldest son Walter inherited the two vacant lots behind number 115 and built a stucco California bungalow with bracketed roof gables and long overhanging eaves at number 119 in 1925. Longtime Larkspur City Council member and mayor Walter Frizzi planted a lawn and vegetable garden between his home and the family home. In 1941 he built the hipped and gable roof house with horizontal detailed siding on the site at 117 for his daughter, Betty Frizzi Krause. Walter Frizzi lived at 119 Ward Street until he died in 1970.

The five houses built by Wright beginning in 1890 in order for the town to qualify for a railroad station comprised a subdivision ahead of its time. Each was identical in architectural detailing and floor plan. The home at **122 WARD STREET** is still in prime condition. When the original owners, the Cazateaus, who had a laundry business in San Rafael, sold the house in the 1900s, the new owners hung a sign with the name "The Wigwam" on

WILLIE FRIZZI

"Willie was always a character, even as a kid. One time the priest told him he should go to church, and he replied that where he lived was close enough to heaven already."

— Alice Ambrose Krogman

▲ 2.7: *A farewell party at the Blue Rock Hotel on September 19, 1917 honored some of Larkspur's finest before they left for Camp Davis to fight in World War I: Serafino Marilli in background, leaning on railing, William Stringa, in car with dog. The other men are identified as Horace Poley, Mert Bain, Walter Frizzi, Wyndham Barnes, Charles Dodge, and Tony Rose.*

▲ 2.8: 122 Ward Street, 2003.

the front porch. According to Willie Frizzi, the sign indicated possible hanky-panky.

In 1939 the house's past reputation was cleansed when Larkspur's former police chief, Howard Clark, became its owner. At that time the interior was museum-quality with the original gaslight fixtures, a typical Victorian parlor and sitting room with metal embossed paneling below the plate rail, and ten-foot-high ceilings. The old iron fence can still be seen beneath the shrubbery in front of the house. A two-story addition was made at the rear and respects the integrity of the front elevation of the house.

Many of the early homes have been given a new life without losing their small-town scale. The 1900s California Craftsman-style bungalow at **133 WARD STREET** succumbed to the enemies of old houses – dry rot, termites, and the lack of a foundation. The house had to be jacked up, the joists and walls redone, and a new lower floor tucked under it in the 1980s. Period windows were installed and the period design replicated.

Although originally built in 1907, the home at **134 WARD STREET** has been extensively remodeled. Its claim to fame is that Ken Kesey, author of *One Flew Over The Cuckoo's Nest*, rented the house in the 1960s and lived there with his Merry Pranksters. The two 1920s hipped-roof cottages at 135 and 141 Ward Street, built in the 1920s for speculation, are typical of the many small homes that were built throughout Larkspur during that period.

One unique feature of Larkspur architecture is the mix of details from all periods in individual homes that often makes them difficult to date. Since Larkspur had its own lumberyard, early

▲ 2.9: *View to downtown with 141 and 143 Ward Street in the foreground, date unknown.*

builders could copy elements from San Francisco homes. Commented architect and former Larkspur Design Review Board member, David Jones, "Their simplistic and modest approach of mixing architectural details is their strength compared to today's mass-produced, consumer-oriented housing market."

The hipped-roof house at **136 WARD STREET** is an example of a mix of styles that includes Queen Anne, Colonial Revival, and classical features. The exterior has shiplap siding on the upper floor, broad-faced clapboard with splayed channel joints on the lower floor, and a heavy pediment and projecting eaves over the bay. The Palladian windows have a clear lower section with ten-pane ribbon windows in the upper section.

Contractor Joseph Jossa built the hipped-roof house at **143 WARD STREET** in 1908. This is an example of the contractor using the above-mentioned styles as well as Willis Polk-like features in the house. Key features are the heavy pediment projection over the front door, the window projections, the molded cornice at the eaves, and the narrow-faced, shiplap siding. The Jossas later lived in the Beleney house at 234 Hawthorne Avenue.

At one time John McNaboe, who managed Buckley & Company on Magnolia Avenue, owned the house. Another prominent local who lived at 143 Ward Street in the 1920s and 1930s was "Cannonball," the railroad station agent. "We called him 'Old Sourpuss'," said Bill Weaver Jr., son of the local newspaper owner. "He didn't like children and all the kids had to take the train to Tamalpais High School every day. On the day we had to buy our commute books, it was wild."

Former Larkspur City Council member and mayor William Howard, who owned 143 Ward Street, lived there from 1996 to 1998, and then sold it to his daughter, called it a "shotgun cottage" since you could open the front door and shoot a shotgun through to the back door without hitting anything. The side section with a shed roof facing Hawthorne Avenue is an addition.

⊃ *Turn north on Hawthorne Avenue, then follow Locust Avenue south to King Street.*

② Hawthorne Avenue

During the early 1900s **201 HAWTHORNE AVENUE** was a popular boardinghouse called the "Larkspur Villa Hotel" with country-inn type rooms, wide verandas, and a lovely front garden. The cross-gable country Victorian, with the shingle detailing in the gables and hipped-roof tower, was spruced up in the 1980s, including enclosing the verandas. According to Harold Kelly, Almon Wheeler, father of Burt Wheeler who ran the Larkspur Lumber Company in its later years, lived here before moving to Palm Hill.

Some of the houses that appear in early photographs, such as 207 Hawthorne Avenue, have since been torn down. Others still remain, but have lost their individuality. The home at 220 Hawthorne

LARKSPUR ARCHITECTURE

"The people building in Larkspur were more sophisticated than in more rural areas and were aware of more architectural details. Each home has something very personal and individualistic … A very casual, personal touch was like a trademark left behind."

— David Jones, architect

▲ *2.10: Larkspur Villa Hotel, 201 Hawthorne Avenue, early 1900s.*

▲ 2.11: *The Daveler house at 219 Hawthorne Avenue, 2001.*

Avenue, for example, no longer has its original octagonal shape.

A house highly visible in early 1890 photographs of Larkspur is **219 HAWTHORNE AVENUE**, at the corner of Hawthorne Avenue and Ajax Street, which boasts Swiss farmhouse chalet elements, as well as classical and colonial influences. Although not as impressive as its neighbor across the street, the house, with its hipped-gable roof and front and rear shed dormers with windows and eyebrow sash windows punched below the roofline, is typical of the homes of the period. The exterior has a mix of broad-faced horizontal clapboard and shingles under the gable ends. The front porch with a spindle railing wraps around the side of the house.

The first owner was Wyndham Barnes. His son Ed later built a house at the corner of Alexander and Pepper Avenues. Lesly Daveler, a former planning commissioner and mayor of Larkspur, and his wife Sarah bought the house in 1947. After Daveler's death in 1993 Sarah lived in the house until her death in 2007.

The most prominent home today, as well as in all the early photographs, is **234 HAWTHORNE AVENUE**, a Victorian lady with a checkered past. In 1897, when the five-bedroom, four-bath house was built, its tall towers and turrets stood out on the treeless hill dubbed "Knob Hill" by locals at the time. The residence of architect B. Allen Brown was described in the January 1897 *Sausalito News* as "a study in architecture and a very comfortable and substantial home." A caretaker's house and/or stable were on the adjacent lot to the north.

In 1899 when Brown couldn't pay for the house, C. W. Wright took possession and sold it to George Beleney who had asparagus farms in the Sacramento Valley. The Beleneys used it as a summer residence. In addition to tall turrets, it boasted an elaborate aviary and a huge fish tank. Locals nicknamed it "The Castle." George Beleney, as described by Mrs. T. Marilli was "a very proud, well-dressed man" who had a son, George, and two daughters, Blanche and Marie.

The Jossas owned the house in the 1920s and furnished it lavishly. According to Alice Ambrose

▲ 2.12: *An early view from the top of Laurel Avenue looking towards the top of Hawthorne Avenue. Hipped-roof house (219 Hawthorne Avenue), towers (234 Hawthorne Avenue), and Larkspur Villa Hotel (201 Hawthorne Avenue), lower left, early 1900s.*

▲ 2.13: *The towers are gone now, but one turret remained on the 1897 house at 234 Hawthorne Avenue in this 1956 photograph.*

Krogman, the house was rumored to be a place where women in trouble could go for illegal surgery. The yard had a big iron fence around it with a gate that was kept locked. During Prohibition a distillery on the property reportedly supplied Larkspur with most of its liquor.

Mrs. Jossa died poor in a convalescent hospital. The towers and several turrets on the house burned in a suspicious fire in 1933 after the Jossas moved out. In 1938 Dr. D. G. Schmidt, a local psychiatrist at San Quentin prison, purchased the house, and it was later bought by Mrs. Slocum in 1945, who converted it to an 18-room convalescent home in the 1950s.

William Slocum purchased the home from his mother in 1960 and restored many of its Victorian details. During the 1960s and 1970s a commune known as "One World Family of the Messiah's World Crusade" lived in the house, followed by the Ali Akbar School of Music. One World Family opened The Mustard Seed restaurant in Mill Valley, the first natural food restaurant in Marin. In the 1990s Heritage Board member Kathleen Kearley-Green and her husband Robert bought the home and did major maintenance work on it under a Mills Act Contract, as well as adding space at the rear, without jeopardizing its historic integrity. They later moved to 21 Hawthorne Avenue.

A lot-line adjustment in 1994 created a building site for the new home that was built at 250 Hawthorne Avenue. The contemporary house has its own version of a clock tower and was built by prominent Larkspurians Dennis and Susan Gilardi.

③ Locust Avenue & Post Street

The homes along the downhill and uphill sides of Locust Avenue are more modest than their hilltop relatives and are difficult to see from the street as they were built before roads existed. They were accessed via steps from Magnolia Avenue. Most of them, such as **148 LOCUST AVENUE**, the Elie Berthinier house, were built in the early 1900s. An early contractor named Liebert built and lived in the house that had an enclosed porch, a standard feature in homes of this period. Since the homes were primarily for summer use, the porch was used to sleep extra guests and dubbed a "sleeping porch." A remodel in the 1980s added a gabled dormer and changed the street-side façade of the house.

The Berthiniers built a large barbecue area and horseshoe pitching courts adjacent to the house; the upper court for the men, the lower for the ladies. Mr. Berthinier built what he called "The Burma Road" halfway down the slope, a wide trail that wound around the hill to Opal Street where his grandson lived. The path was designed so his grandson could visit without walking on the streets.

The rear of the shingled house visible just south of the Berthinier house and down the slope is 146 Locust Avenue *(see page 243)*. Music, film, and theater critic Stephanie von Buchau lived in this house, halfway between Locust and Magnolia Avenues, until she died in December of 2006.

Early planning in Larkspur consisted of grids laid over hill and dale with little concern for steep slopes, gullies, or access roads. The surveying and platting of the city done by H. C. Ward in 1887 looked very tidy on paper and, since most people walked to their homes, these issues did not present any problems until roads were built. The plotted streets that are inaccessible to cars are called "paper streets" *(see Appendix C)*. One of these is **POST STREET**, just northwest of the Lark Theater. It is still marked as a street on county maps, but it is really just a long flight of steps connecting Magnolia and Locust Avenues, emerging between 114-116 Locust and the garage adjacent to 128 Locust. Before cars and paved streets homeowners accessed their hillside homes by steps and paths. Homes built on this slope are still accessed by this pathway. In 2008 the Post Street stairs were recognized as a valuable pedestrian connection and received a Federal grant of $186,875 for repairs as part of a drive to encourage people to drive less and walk more.

The house at **127 LOCUST AVENUE** was built in 1906 by Mr. Honisberg whose son Billy was a cartoonist. The house had only three rooms with nine-foot ceilings, oak floors, and wainscoting in the living room. Floor joists were 16- x 16-ft beams. The fireplace was made from the Larkspur quarry's blue rock. Cabinets were made of tongue and groove redwood. Originally the house had a veranda around it, which has been partially enclosed.

At a later date Julian Wild, who owned racehorses at Golden Gate Fields, bought the house. He did the concrete work in the back of the house that extends to the adjacent homes. Wild bought the Frizzi sweet shop at the corner of Magnolia Avenue and Ward Street in 1933 and added a drinking fountain in front. Confusion still exists concerning a lot at 7 King Street, across from City Hall, that he is said to have either donated to the city (for a public swimming pool) or to the telephone company

Many early homes were built in a rustic fashion. H. C. Ward's house at 125 Locust Avenue was originally built on tree stumps with no foundation. Ward surveyed the town for Wright after Wright bought the King Ranch. The house has been remodeled and owned by winemaker, musician, and violin/bass maker Pierre Josephs for years.

The Theodore Marilli house at **113 LOCUST AVENUE** originally had three bedrooms but was remodeled to accommodate his wife Nellie and their five children. Theodore was the son of Serafino and Elizabeth Marilli, who came to Larkspur in the 1890s and owned the Hotel Larkspur (later the Blue Rock Hotel) from 1910 to 1938. The Marilli children were drafted by their grandmother Elizabeth into the hotel service to wash dishes and do odd jobs such as making sandwiches on the nights of Rose Bowl dances.

From the street, only the back of **108 LOCUST AVENUE** is visible. This was the home of William Stringa, who arrived in this country in 1883, went to Sonoma and then to San Francisco where he was in the umbrella business. He came to Larkspur in 1890 and later went into partnership with the Marillis. Together they owned and operated the Blue Rock Hotel after it was remodeled in 1910.

④ Locust Avenue South of Ward Street

The house at **51 LOCUST AVENUE** is one of the five houses built in the early 1890s to help the town qualify for a railroad station. It retains the distinctive shingled gable common to the five Wright homes. Although the front porch has been enclosed and the front stone pillars removed, no other changes have been made to the exterior.

Originally owned by a family named Cazneaux, the house was later owned by John Foley, one of the first Larkspur Trustees for whom a street is named in the Canyon, and then by the Gaffney family. From 1952 until the 1980s, Leslie Ezekiel lived in the house. Miss Ezekiel, a teacher for 35 years at the Larkspur-Corte Madera School, reported in a 1975 interview that her first salary was $135 a month "and they still owe me for the first month." Her first class was the "greatest" because it included former Corte Madera

▲ 2.14: *The value of the Post Street stairs as a pedestrian connection was recognized by a Federal grant to repair them, 2008.*

▲ 2.15: *The modest 1890s Victorian home at 51 Locust Avenue has had its porch enclosed but still retains its small scale and major features, 2001.*

▲ 2.16: Two of the homes on Locust Avenue beyond the vegetable garden buildings in the foreground are 37 Locust at the far left and 51 Locust at the top right. They are two of the five houses built by C. W. Wright in order for Larkspur to qualify for a railroad station, early 1900s.

MISS EZEKIEL REFLECTS

"Larkspur's grown, it's changed. Some of the changes are not for the best, but there are improvements. At least we've got paved streets!"

— Leslie Ezekiel, schoolteacher and resident of 51 Locust Avenue

police chief Frank Nelson, Dick Seaton who lived at 258 Madrone Avenue, and Biff Harris, who lived at 627 Magnolia Avenue.

Due to multifamily zoning, the section of Locust Avenue between Ward and King Streets is a mixture of single-family homes, apartments, and condos. This zoning allowed even one of the houses that had been built to qualify for the railroad station, the Country Victorian with a cross-gable roof and decorative trim at **37 LOCUST AVENUE**, to be squeezed by new construction. Although the house has been preserved, a new garage overwhelms its street view. In the 1900s the house belonged to Al Newman, a song and dance man dubbed "Happy Al," who worked professionally in San Francisco.

Another one of the Country Victorians built in 1890 to qualify for a railroad station is at **11 LOCUST AVENUE**. The best preserved of the original five, it is identical to the homes at 37 and 51 Locust Avenue and 122 Ward Street, with a cross-gable roof and decorative trim. In the early 1900s Frank Ambrose, who was town constable, tax collector, and fire chief, rented the house from Mrs. Flemming. Of his various jobs, his daughter Alice Ambrose Krogman commented, "In those days everything was thrown in together." Constable Ambrose used to patrol the canyon with his Airedale. "That dog went everywhere with him," said Mrs. Krogman.

Frank Ambrose came from an old Italian family that had immigrated to San Francisco long before the quake, and lived on Greenwich Street. After the fire in 1906 the family stayed first in tents at the Presidio, and then "we were all put on a boat like cattle and brought here," said Mrs. Krogman. There were five Ambrose children: Alice, William, Kathleen, Nita, and Rowena. When they settled in Larkspur, Frank Ambrose and other early settlers formed

▲ 2.17: The remaining stone pillars on the Ward Street side of 51 Locust Avenue are composed of local jasper, serpentine, and basalt, 2008.

the Larkspur Volunteer Fire Department that began with one piece of equipment and no firehouse.

The house has a large kitchen "where we ate," said Mrs. Krogman. "There was a painted tin dado and in the bathroom, a tub with feet."

⊃ *Turn west on King Street.*

BUILDING LARKSPUR THE WRIGHT WAY: Five houses that brought a railroad station

- **122 WARD STREET**
- **51 LOCUST AVENUE**
- **37 LOCUST AVENUE**
- **11 LOCUST AVENUE**
- **127 KING STREET:** A convent for the teaching nuns of St. Patrick's School replaced the fifth original house at 127 King Street. No longer a convent, the property is owned by the Roman Catholic Archdiocese of San Francisco.

▲ 2.18: *37 Locust Avenue before remodel and garage addition, 2003.*

▲ 2.19: *11 Locust is the only one of the original five C.W. Wright houses that retains its original form, 2003.*

⑤ King Street

The California Craftsman-style bungalow at **131 KING STREET** was built in the 1920s with an expansive, shallow roof gable that is echoed in a gable over the screened front porch. Typical of the bungalow style, the rafters are exposed, and roof beams with carved ends project through the gables. The triple windows are six panes over one. The exterior is narrow, horizontal shiplap siding. The interior includes an eight-sided dining room with built-in cabinets. In the 1930s a bedroom and half bath were added at the back of the house.

The homes at **133, 135A,** and **135B KING STREET** were built on a pathway that used to connect King Street and Walnut Avenue.

The second house from the corner of Hawthorne Avenue and King Street is **143 KING STREET**. It was built by Charles McLeran's father in 1906 after "we got burned out in the city," said Charlie, whose father was a teacher at Lick-Wilmerding School in San Francisco. Before the quake the family had spent summers in Larkspur. They lived in the house for several years and then bought a house at 114 King Street that stood where the parish rectory now is located. When they sold that house to the archdiocese, they moved back to 143 King Street and lived there until Charlie built a house on Palm Hill in 1936.

⊃ *Turn north on Hawthorne to Sycamore, then west on Sycamore to its end.*

▲ 2.20: *Many old homes in town, such as 145 King Street, seen here in 2001, were built in the early 1900s but are not on Larkspur's Historic Resources Inventory.*

▲ 2.21: *View from Walnut Avenue to the rears of (center left to right) 135, 133, and 131 King Street. The Costello house, water tower and barn are in the right foreground, 1908.*

⑥ Hawthorne & Sycamore Avenues

Built prior to 1890, the house at **121 HAWTHORNE AVENUE** has 12-foot ceilings. The dining and living rooms have oak floors and redwood paneling. In the living room there is a dado with diagonal paneling above it. At one time a porch extended around the front of the house. The house is now completely obscured from the street by trees, but the house is still visible from City Hall and other downtown locations.

According to Alice Ambrose Krogman and Charlie McLeran, the Vesarias lived in the house in the 1920s. Ernest W. Hewston wrote, between 1895 and 1897, about "Graybeard Vesaria whose daughters, Lillian and Larkspur, were the town's belles." Another newspaper report on January 30, 1897 referred to Louis Vesaria, who was a school trustee, and mentioned his house on the hill. The house was later owned by a banker who reportedly hanged himself between the living and dining rooms when beset by financial reverses. Since 1941 the house has been owned by the Gmahling family: first Carl and Blanche, who raised their family there, then George and Georgene, who were active in the Redwoods Presbyterian Church, and now their son, Gary.

At the turn of the last century there was a two-story, shingled building at the edge of a creek that ran down from Sycamore Avenue where 132 and 134 Hawthorne Avenue are located today. A Chinese laundry operated in the building. According to Alice Ambrose Krogman, the family wore their hair in queues, and the children of the area liked to watch them work and listen to them chat in their native tongue. Glenn Courtright reported they had two wagons and toured the area up to Kentfield to pick up and deliver laundry. The family lived on the second floor of the building until it burned.

Behind the laundry to the south was the Dell'Era dairy. Louis Dell'Era came to this country in 1906 and was caretaker and gardener for early residents. From 1919 to 1925 he was caretaker of the Bon Air Hotel, the present site of Marin General Hospital, and lived next door.

▲ 2.22: *121 Hawthorne Avenue, 1975.*

▲ 2.23: *The remodeled house at 12 Sycamore Avenue was designed with elements that relate to the older homes of the neighborhood, 2008.*

12 SYCAMORE AVENUE

"I set the two-story addition below the existing house with a modern interpretation of old-style elements. The cupola tower which contains the stairs to the various levels is a transitional element between the old house and the new addition."

— Dan Peterson, architectural historian

The walk up Sycamore Avenue is a journey into the past and the present. Old homes mingle with new ones. The home at **12 SYCAMORE AVENUE**, with an addition and remodel designed by historical architect Dan Peterson, has a hipped-roof cupola tower and gable and hipped roofs, and shows how the new can echo the old and fit into an established neighborhood.

About 1890 to 1891 local architect Gustave Nagel built **15 SYCAMORE AVENUE** as a summerhouse for the Henry Thorntons who lived there year-round in the early 1900s. Dorothy Thornton was a good friend of the McCormicks, managers of the Hotel Larkspur. Henry Thornton was the president of Baker-Hamilton, a hardware and farm machinery catalog firm in San Francisco.

Michael O'Rourke, whose parents owned the house from 1947 to 1987, was the owner in 2008. The senior O'Rourkes remodeled the house in 1964, at which time the redwood paneling was removed from all the rooms in the house except the dining room, the ceilings were lowered, and a bedroom added at the west side. The house has an octagonal-shaped living room. A Canary Island date palm in the front yard probably was planted when the house was built. Michael and his wife Kathleen have restored the house by opening up the ceilings, re-installing the original front door, and replicating its window. A bedroom gable was added on the east end of the house, but the two original gables at either end still exist. When they converted the attic to livable space, they did so without changing the exterior, retaining the tower and porch.

Over the years Michael talked to Thorpe Wright about buying Avon Street, west of the house. He reported that when Thorpe's father was subdividing Larkspur, Thorpe's mother asked that 64 rights-of-way, or paper streets, be preserved as open space, but revert to the Wrights' ownership in the future. When Thorpe Wright died, he left everything to his

▲ 2.24: *A new gable bedroom on the east end is the only addition to 15 Sycamore Avenue. Although the attic was converted to livable space, the 1890s tower, porch, and original two gables at either end of the house remain, 2008.*

▲ 2.25: *An unused military barrack supplied the lumber to build 16 Sycamore Avenue in 1948.*

caregiver. After negotiations, a lot line adjustment was made and the land was split between the Michael O'Rourke and John Lippitt at 26 Sycamore Avenue who posted his parcel as "Mt. Lippitt."

A unique feature along Sycamore Avenue is the mingling of the early summer cabins with the newcomers on the street. Some of the old-timers look unchanged, like the home at 18 Sycamore. Others, such as **16 SYCAMORE AVENUE**, have retained their basic bones. Built in 1948 by Carl and Sylvia Thoelecke of Green Gorilla fame (*see page 261*), the house had a unique construction history. Since building materials were in short supply in the post-war era, the couple bought one of the unused barracks from a military camp in Marysville and had it shipped to Larkspur for a total cost of $995. Unfortunately their 43-foot-wide house was too wide for the lot, so they set it on an angle and got the city's blessing. The Thoeleckes lived in the house until 1961.

Another owner was Dr. Elmo Shropshire, veterinarian and singer-songwriter and banjo player who gained fame for his hit Christmas song, "Grandma Got Run Over by a Reindeer." In 2008 he wrote and produced "The Larkspur Song" with Rita Abrams for the city's Centennial.

The home at 16 Sycamore Avenue has been given a modest facelift, with new shingles replacing the old asbestos ones, and a gable porch built over the front door.

The unique character of the hipped-roof California Craftsman-style bungalow that nestles between the redwoods at **22 SYCAMORE AVENUE** has been enhanced to highlight its Maybeckian tradition. The house retains its board-and-batten siding with the handmade wooden brackets at the base, the broad-faced horizontal shiplap siding at the foundation level, and the window design where lattice balances the triple panes. Darwin Reinhold, a song-and-dance man who earned fame in California's Gold Rush country, owned the house in the 1920s. The creek behind his house carried runoff from the hills. A Golden Gate Bridge float designed by Reinhold for the Fourth of July Parade, fourteen years before the actual bridge was built, gained him big newspaper coverage.

The 1890s modest, hipped-roof summer cottage with horizontal shiplap siding at **40 SYCAMORE AVENUE** and its neighbors, are a contrast to the new, large Craftsman-style home between them. The Canary Island date palm in the front yard was a favorite of this period. The home is one of the few houses of this style that has not been remodeled.

⑦ Larkspur Inn Site

The site of the Larkspur Inn encompassed the south side of Sycamore Avenue from **117 SYCAMORE AVENUE** to its end. In 1891 Charles W. Wright built the 80-room hotel complete with bowling green, croquet courts, riding paths, and bathhouses on Corte Madera Creek. The contract required completion within 88 days and the cost was $20,000. The four-story hotel had drawing rooms, bars, and dining rooms on the first floor. The second and third floors had 40 guest rooms each, and the fourth floor had 20 rooms for the employees. Furnishings came from W. & J. Sloane in San Francisco.

▲ *2.26: 22 Sycamore Avenue still retains its interesting lattice detailing, 2008.*

▲ *2.27: 40 Sycamore Avenue retains its original modest design, 2008.*

▲ 2.28: *The Larkspur Inn's letterhead shows its commanding location above the city, 1896.*

THE LARKSPUR INN

"The average in winter was about 50 guests, mostly from the East, attracted by the climate, and brought to the hostelry by a hotel bus drawn by four horses."

— Thorpe Wright, 1927

A 400-foot-long, two-story veranda wrapped around nearly the entire building. A round, five-story tower was located at one end of the building that had a four-story, cross-gable center and a square, five-story tower at the other end. Dormers were located at the towers and central roof section. The carriage entrance was on the first floor with two flights of stairs leading to the central main entrance on the second floor.

The hotel burned down on September 6, 1894. According to Thorpe Wright, his father did not rebuild "because it did not pay even though it was always full." He added, "it had been the idea of my father's partner, Mr. Sadler, to build it because he wanted a nice place to go on weekends." Instead Wright built a three-story, six-bedroom home called "Elfwood" on the hotel site covering a 75- x 100-ft area. The three-story house, with a cross-gable roof with pediments and a hexagonal tower, had a wide veranda across the front facing the view. B. Allen Brown, who also designed the Beleney house at 234 Hawthorne Avenue, was the architect. Around the house were gardens enclosed by a fence and a huge locked gate.

In 1975 Thorpe Wright traced his family's history back to Toronto where his father, who was born about 1852, lived until he ran away at age 10. After working on some of the farms in his home area and discovering that it was very difficult to farm on the rocky land, he took off for Alaska during its second gold rush. Even though he filed a mining claim, he disliked the cold so much that he retreated south, first to Seattle and then to Tacoma via an Indian canoe, the only mode of transportation he could find.

Wright bought some property in Tacoma, much to the amusement of his friends who felt it was a foolish investment. He started a general store that did very well, but after his brother's death he picked up stakes again and ground-leased his property. He had the last laugh when he sold the Tacoma property for $75,000, a fancy sum in the early 1900s.

His wanderings landed him in San Francisco, and he became associated with Mau, Sadler & Company, a wholesale grocery

▲2.29: *Larkspur Inn, early 1890s.*

firm. Again, land investment came into the picture when one of the company's accounts in Fresno paid its bill in lots instead of cash. The lots sold for a handsome sum. When William Mau purchased the Pacific Iron and Nail Company, he made Wright a part owner with a monthly salary of $500, very good money in those days. That, plus the profitable sales of land and other sources of income, allowed Wright to make his land investment in Larkspur.

The American Land and Trust Co. was formed by Mau, Sadler & Company and C. W. Wright in order to develop the lands of the King Ranch. However, Wright did not always agree with all the business decisions made by Messrs. Mau and Sadler, so they made a property agreement whereby Mau and Sadler took all of the Sunset District properties that the company held in San Francisco, and Wright took the King Ranch. In 1913 the company name was changed to Anglo-American Land Company, dropping the word "Trust," when a new state law made it illegal for a trust company to hold land in this manner.

C. W. Wright's wife, Georgiana Adamson Wright, was born in 1862. She lived in London and first came to the United States with her mother, stopping in New York, and then sailing on to Panama, crossing the Isthmus, and finally arriving in San Francisco. Since she was sailing on a Confederate ship and San Francisco sided with the north during the Civil War, they had to enter the San Francisco port without any lights. Although she went back to England, she returned to the United States when she was older. This time she crossed the country by train. Union soldiers guarded each train car carefully because Geronimo was on the warpath.

Thorpe Wright did not indicate in the 1975 interview how his parents met or when they were married, but he was born in the family home in 1898. He had a sister Elvira who, along with Georgiana Wright's parents, the Adamsons, and Mrs. Adamson's sister, Margaret Elvira Adamson, lived with the family.

Thorpe remembered that when he lived in Larkspur as a child, it was "country." His family had seven dogs, an orchard, a bowling

▲ 2.31: C. W. Wright, 1886.

LARKSPUR REMEMBERS MR. C. W. WRIGHT

"Mr. Wright was a "man who only talked to you on occasion."

— Glenn Courtright

"Mr. Wright always carried his papers in a straw basket."

— Helen Wilson

"Mr. Wright was short with a white moustache."

— Katherine Solomons Lilienthal

▲ 2.30: C. W. Wright's house "Elfwood" replaced the Larkspur Inn in the mid-to-late 1890s, but was equally as imposing and visible on the hillside.

alley, and a croquet court left over from the inn. They rented a bathhouse on the creek below Bon Air bridge, and had a stable operated by Mr. Hill. According to historian Helen Wilson, Elvira rode her horse sidesaddle with her riding habit flowing almost to the ground. Thorpe recalled that there were other youngsters in the neighborhood to play with, if he cared to. Once he and a neighbor girl rode their donkeys together. He did not go to public or private schools but received private instruction at home. He reported that his grandmother, Mrs. Adamson, was his teacher and was very good at arithmetic. Later he and his sister studied art at the old Hopkin's Art Institute that became the San Francisco Art Institute. He gave up art lessons at age 16 when he joined his father in business.

The Wrights were well-to-do, had servants, and held piano concerts and dances in the large entry hall of the home. The family seemed aloof to local residents. Mrs. Wright wore her hair in a bobbed style. She was considered very proper and cultured by contemporaries, and is reported to have once remarked, "What care I for the peasants of Larkspur?"

Judge Samuel Gardiner remembered seeing Thorpe Wright walking around town with a parakeet on his shoulder. "I can't say that I remember him dressed very well. The outstanding thing was his red hair, and his exclusiveness," he said. An interesting image of Wright family life can be derived from the remembrances of a number of longtime Larkspurians. Mrs. Wright served prospective property-buyers tea with cucumber sandwiches in her home. Harold Kelly, whose family started the Hibernia Bank in San Francisco, qualified as a guest and was invited to tea, but according to him, he was never asked back because he asked for a second piece of cake.

Marjorie Woods, who lived at the top of Walnut Avenue, recalled in a 1979 interview that when she was younger she was escorted to Thorpe's attic playroom that was well stocked with toys. In particular she remembered a wonderful butcher shop filled with all the equipment such a shop would have, plus carved figurines. She and Thorpe were served tea by a servant in a very proper fashion. Local old-timers remember a mean old rooster, the Wright family pet, who performed the role of watchdog for the house.

"When the Wright mansion went up in smoke and flames [in 1929] it took hours to extinguish," said Alice de Veuve Cagwin Heron whose family lived at 223 Magnolia Avenue. A tremendous amount of papers and magazines that were stored in one of the rooms smoldered for hours. After the fire the family moved to their San Francisco residence. For years they had reversed the common trend and maintained a weekend house in the city and permanent residence in the country.

Mrs. Wright's sister, Margaret Adamson, preferred to remain "in the country" so she lived in an adjacent barn with an abundance of pet cats until her death in the 1950s. Helen Wilson reported that she was "a pathetic sight, dirty, poor, and never had enough food. The grocery man would let her pick through the produce that was going bad and take what she wanted." Mrs. Wilson never could understand why Thorpe and Elvira didn't take better care of her, and provide for her.

C. W. Wright died in 1929. His son Thorpe, who lived in San Francisco, always caught neighbors' eyes when he drove up the street in his vintage Pierce Arrow car to visit his property. He reported that his father considered his Larkspur investment very profitable. Up until the 1906 earthquake the interest alone on the installment sales paid for carrying the Larkspur property. The Depression changed that. The county taxes became so high the family considered it unwise to continue to pay taxes on the unsold property. In 1932 they sold out to Adolph Tiscornia.

Longtime resident at 26 Sycamore Avenue John Lippitt remembers Thorpe Wright in his Salvation Army-style outfits in the 1970s and 1980s, driving down Sycamore Avenue in the vintage Pierce Arrow his father bought for him in 1915: "The upholstery was flapping out the window, and the car was a fugitive from the wrecking yard." He added that the one time he saw Thorpe in a suit and tie, he didn't recognize him. Wright died in 1987.

In 1957 the area near the end of Sycamore Avenue was bulldozed by Trevor Jones, who lived at 101 Sycamore Avenue. Homes were then built there. In the process of demolition at 117 Sycamore Avenue, the old, arched, brick wine cellar of the Wright house was uncovered. Unfortunately, the cellar was not stable enough to be preserved.

Many of the turreted estates with wide verandas visible on the hills above Larkspur in early 1900s photographs are gone, sometimes replaced by modern versions of mega-mansions. Harold Kelly lived in a house at 49 Holly Avenue built by Wright in the 1890s. "If my mother hadn't gone to San Francisco for my birth, I would be the oldest native son in Larkspur," he remarked. They shared a barn behind the house with his mother's sister who lived at 55 Holly Avenue. According to Mr. Kelly, after a family fight Harold's mother told him to go out and cut the barn in half. "And I did just that," he said. After the roof and top floor burned off of 55 Holly Avenue in 1939, it lost much of its original character, and local children called it "the haunted house."

Rentals were a booming business in Larkspur during the early 1900s. Many families moved into small back cottages during the summer in order to rent out their main homes. The larger homes rented for $150 for two months. Across the street from 55 Holly Avenue the Wessels at one time had several cabins they rented out for $25 a month.

Water supply was an issue in the early development days. When C.W. Wright originally had the town surveyed, he had a water dowser locate the springs to be included on the 1887 map *(see page vi)*. A water tank can be seen in old photographs above Wright's Larkspur Inn at the end of Sycamore Avenue.

According to Thorpe Wright, a water tunnel was drilled to supply the water for the hotel. He recalled that it was necessary to conserve water in the summer months, but no one ever ran out of water.

Other wells were located to catch the runoff from the hills. Thorpe also pinpointed a well at the corner of Alta and Cedar Streets that, although never used, had to be cleaned out occasionally. Another spring-fed pond located at the corner of Sycamore Avenue and Bond Street was dammed up near Holly Avenue when it was built. The pond was deep enough "to put a cat in a sack in it," according to Harold Kelly. The Larkspur Water Company had a reservoir at the top of the hill near Sycamore, Orange, and Myrtle Avenues to which they pumped up water from Arroyo Holon.

"Local fishermen paid kids to fish the carp out of Corte Madera Creek because they fed on the striped bass. The kids would collect their money and then throw the carp into the pond up here," reported Harold Kelly.

The story goes that there was a goldmine on the saddle of Little King Mountain above Sycamore Avenue. According to Thorpe Wright, the mine was

▲ 2.32: *C.W. Wright's "Elfwood" in the late 1890s, center back. Below and to the right, 49 and 55 Holly Avenue have been torn down and replaced by new homes.*

financed, run, and operated by a ferryboat captain who dug an open shaft about 60 feet deep. The ore mined there was assayed at about $2 a ton, so it didn't pay. Subsequently, rain washed away and filled in the shaft, but the timbers and opening of the mine were still visible in 2008 according to Jim Hogg.

James Sterling Rhodes, a Texan, had a string of horses that he pastured at the upper end of Willow Avenue, a wide-open area back then. Bill Weaver Jr. remembers when he and George Heierle would go up there and offer to do any kind of work just to ride the horses, even clean out the stable. Their favorite ride to the top of Mt. Tamalpais took all day.

Public access to the lower slopes of Little King Mountain is available at the end of Sycamore, above Holly, Citron, and Cedar Avenues.

⊃ *At this point walkers can return to the city parking lot via Holly, Willow and Hawthorne Avenues and Ward Street.*

• • • • • • • • • • • • •

OLD HOMES IN CENTRAL LARKSPUR: SOUTH LOOP

Begin this double-loop walk at the Arch Street stairs located across from 250 Magnolia Avenue.

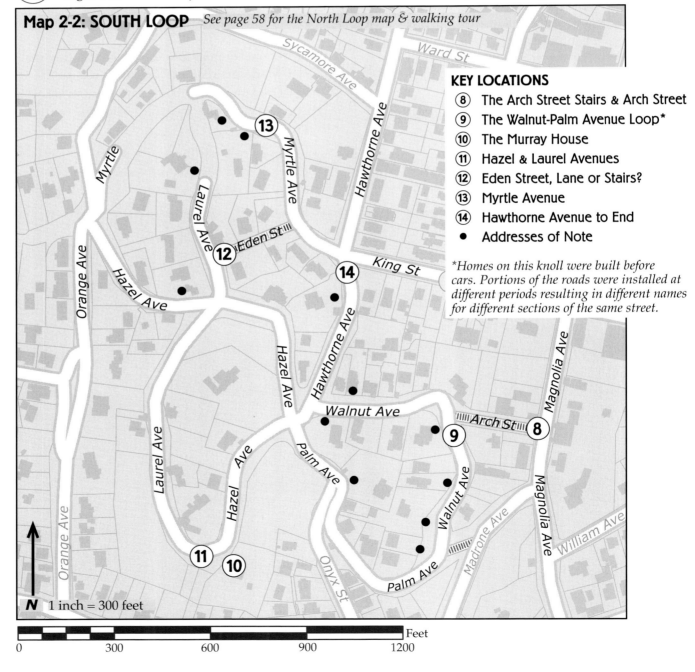

Map 2-2: SOUTH LOOP *See page 58 for the North Loop map & walking tour*

KEY LOCATIONS
- ⑧ The Arch Street Stairs & Arch Street
- ⑨ The Walnut-Palm Avenue Loop*
- ⑩ The Murray House
- ⑪ Hazel & Laurel Avenues
- ⑫ Eden Street, Lane or Stairs?
- ⑬ Myrtle Avenue
- ⑭ Hawthorne Avenue to End
- • Addresses of Note

*Homes on this knoll were built before cars. Portions of the roads were installed at different periods resulting in different names for different sections of the same street.

1 inch = 300 feet

SOUTH LOOP

As a boy during the early 1900s, Judge Samuel Gardiner hand-delivered milk to families on the hill above the downtown and Baltimore Canyon. Steps and paths up the hills, boardwalk sidewalks, and dirt roads were how early Larkspur settlers got from downtown to their hillside homes. Paths stretched up to Walnut, Hazel, and Laurel Avenues from Madrone Avenue, Magnolia Avenue, Ward Street, and King Street.

⑧ The Arch Street Stairs & Arch Street

The paths received official recognition as streets in 1887 when H.C. Ward included them on his survey map for the American Land and Trust Co. Over the years some have become overgrown, some reverted to the original owners, some were sold, and a few lucky ones became known as streets, such as **ARCH STREET**.

C. W. Wright donated the lot at **9 ARCH STREET** to the Larkspur Presbyterians for a church that was built in 1904. The pulpit was made from part of a huge redwood tree stump cut in 1849. Dr. James S. MacDonald preached in Corte Madera in the morning and in Larkspur in the afternoon. Thorpe Wright recalled that Dr. MacDonald's brash young successor once called on his mother. During the visit the man remarked that he was replacing the Reverend because MacDonald was too old and that

▲ 2.34: *Many of central Larkspur's old homes were built with architectural details such as the interior gables at 95 Laurel Avenue, which were filled with curved shingle surfaces, multipane windows, gable inserts and brackets with eyes, 2008.*

▲ 2.33: *View from Palm Hill, across Baltimore Park towards Big King and Little King Mountains. At center, large houses from left to right: Mahoney, Basebe, Wright; far center right: Beleney, about 1910.*

▲ 2.35: Arch Street stairs, 1999.

THE STAIRS

"Access by commuters and others was primarily straight up the hill by footpath from the junction of Madrone and Magnolia Avenues ... When these were slippery from rain, a boardwalk near the Arch Street church site was used."

— Judge Samuel Gardiner

the church needed a younger man. Responded Mrs. Wright, "When do you get too old to get into heaven?"

In 1912 the church building was sold due to low attendance and was rented for a time as a church assembly hall. George Durston bought the building in 1921 and remodeled it into five rooms with two attic bedrooms. "The belfry was screened in and my sister and I slept in the sleeping porch that was created," recalled his granddaughter, June C. MacCourt, who lived at 9 Arch Street from 1921 to 1928 with her parents and from 1933 to 1934 with her husband. In 1933 a kitchen was added at the rear and the attic was expanded to include one large and two small bedrooms and a gable dormer window. A new, brick-faced fireplace with an inset iron plaque made by Hugh McPhee, Durston's brother-in-law, was also added.

June MacCourt had fond memories of the Arch Street stairs. She recalled that the entire expanse on either side of the stairs was a sunny slope covered with dry grass. In the summertime she and her sister would coast down the hill on garbage can lids.

High school gym classes use the stairs as an outdoor StairMaster™. The stairs are the favorite run of "The Man in the Crooked Hat" octogenarian Zvi Danenberg who claims, "A run up and down the 139 Arch Street stairs takes me 20 minutes to do 1,000 steps." In 2009 he recorded his millionth step on the stairs.

Originally, thanks to the treeless slope, the 9 Arch Street house enjoyed a view to San Quentin. After 1934 when the Bonhams, who owned a downtown grocery store, rented the house from Mrs. Durston, they installed a large fishpond, complete with goldfish, below the front porch.

Guy and Cecilia Penna's family moved into the house in 1941 and enjoyed the property to the fullest. Their children, Rosemary, Will, and Paul roamed the streets and hills of Larkspur with their cameras recording the town from the 1940s through the 1960s.

"The 9 Arch Street yard wasn't just one yard," commented Paul Penna. "It was like many yards joined together. There was a formal entry garden, a tropical area around the fishpond, a desert area in the cactus garden, a blossom-filled cut flower garden, a patio and arbor, two separate vegetable gardens, a fruit orchard, and a vineyard."

The goldfish pond was demolished in 1955 and replaced by a smaller pond that retained the original waterfall, according to Paul.

Paul Penna created a tiny village in the yard with miniature plants, a miniature town with street signs for the garden paths, and water faucets painted like fire hydrants.

Will Penna recalled mushroom-foraging hikes up the canyon to gather porcinis that his mother would cook with oil and garlic and serve over pasta.

In the course of doing yard work, treasures from the past were unearthed, such as an Indian grinding bowl that was turned into a birdbath, and obsidian spearheads that Rosemary still owns. A later owner found a small glass communion cup when the porch was replaced. Although the bones of the original church are still part of 9 Arch Street, its pious look is now secular. The orchard continues to flourish on the slope between the house and Walnut Avenue.

The early plot maps that laid out the lots on steep slopes came back to haunt the city when two parcels on the north side of the stairs, and one on the south side at the base of the stairs, were faced with development proposals. Due to the tight constraints on the south-side parcel with its buckeye tree, the city purchased the lot in 1983 for possible future parking. The north-side parcel fronting on Magnolia Avenue was developed with office space. After a marathon series of hearings, a minimal square footage house was approved in 2004 for the land-locked upper lot 8 Arch Street. Although the two upper homes on the stairs have Arch Street addresses, their parking and mailboxes are on Walnut Avenue.

⟳ *From the top of the stairway walk clockwise to view Walnut and Palm Avenue homes.*

⑨ The Walnut-Palm Avenue Loop

The first people to build on the hills in the early 1900s were San Franciscans looking for a summer retreat from the fog. At that time, most of Larkspur's permanent population was made up of modest families of Irish or Italian descent who were primarily Catholic. They looked askance at the more sophisticated and wealthy summer visitors. Among some locals this loop was known as "Jew Hill," or shortened to "The Hill," along with a series of other names. In 1913 Gustave Nagel's daughter Eda ran for Rose Bowl queen as a "Hill" girl according to an interview with her in 1975.

Commented former schoolteacher Leslie Ezekiel, "The summer people stayed aloof as a rule. In the 1920s Larkspur was a hot bed of gossip, a regular Peyton Place."

Lillian Murray Dodge, in a March 4, 1975 interview mentioned that the Hazel-Laurel loop was dubbed "Snob Hill," because her mother would not let the children play with "just anyone."

As the Arch Street stairs, and others throughout Larkspur, were once the major access to houses on the hill, early homes were oriented towards them.

▲ *2.36: Presbyterian Church located on Arch Street, about 1915.*

▲ *2.37: 9 Arch Street when purchased by George Durston who turned it into a home, 1921.*

▲ *2.38: 9 Arch Street when the Penna family lived there, 1973.*

▲ 2.39: A black cast iron fireplace plaque depicting a man playing a dulcimer with his family had been painted bronze but was still at 9 Arch Street when the house was sold by Craig Scherfenberg and Paula Paskov in 2005.

AT 9 ARCH STREET

"One of my fondest memories was listening to the bands that played every Saturday night in the summer at the Rose Bowl. It was wonderful being serenaded to sleep by Ernie Hecksher and Del Courtney."

— Rosemary Penna

Although not visible from the street, the steps and front door of **33 WALNUT AVENUE** are on an axis with the Arch Street Stairs. The Henry and Delores Craner family, who built their first home at 55 Walnut Avenue, built this house after 1906, but didn't move in until 1912. Originally there was a driveway that encircled the house, and shingled arches supported the porch.

In the 1950s the interior of the house was remodeled into one big room downstairs. Family members occupied the two-story, ivy-covered, shingled house until it was sold in 1971. Since 1972 artist-sculptor Marcia Dalva and her husband, film editor-director Robert Dalva, have lived there.

The early twentieth-century homes on the hill could almost be called an informal development inspired by Lucius Solomons who built the first house on the east side at **7 WALNUT AVENUE** in 1902. Solomons, a San Francisco attorney, and his family, had spent a summer in a boardinghouse in Baltimore Canyon and had fallen in love with the area. The Solomons bought a lot on the east side of the hill from C. W. Wright for $800 and had a summerhouse built in the summer of 1902. It took six weeks and cost $1,200. Solomons decided to buy the lots on either side of his new home, paying $900 for one and $1,000 for the other, and they invited their San Francisco friends to build on adjacent lots. His family spent summers at their Larkspur home, and because Larkspur schools had only a six-week summer vacation, the children attended Larkspur-Corte Madera School until September when they returned to San Francisco. Lucius Solomons adopted Larkspur not just by raving about it and inspiring his friends to move there, but by helping with its incorporation in 1908.

The Solomons house was a typical summerhouse with a large porch, two bedrooms, a kitchen, an attic room, and a bathroom. A wooden platform was built for a tent where the children slept down the hill from the house. The house remained in family ownership until 1962.

▲ 2.40: Although an upper floor was added to 7 Walnut Avenue, the lower floors retained their early 1900s character, 1998.

HICK TOWN LARKSPUR

Mrs. Lilienthal's mother, Helen Frank Solomons, referred to Larkspur as a "Tinkle Town" because it was a little bit of a "hick town."

▲ 2.41: *Marian and Katherine Solomons in front of 7 Walnut Avenue with vegetable man Gow's wagon, 1910.*

Mrs. Katherine Solomons Lilienthal, daughter of Lucius Solomons, recalled that the family was at its Larkspur home during spring vacation in 1906. She was sleeping on the living room sofa when she was awakened by a swaying motion. She thought this was not too unusual as there were often tremendous windstorms. Her mother told her it was an earthquake and went up the undulating attic stairs to fetch Katherine's two-year-old sister. Neighbors convened and, as dawn approached, they watched the glow of the fire from the city. It was then that they realized the extent of the earthquake damage. The Solomons rented a boat to go to the city and returned with Katherine's cousins. The family remained in their Larkspur home until December when they were able to move back into their city home.

Homes on nearby lots, such as the A. E. Woods house at **19 WALNUT AVENUE** built in 1907 by a Midwestern carpenter, were built with redwood from the Larkspur Lumber Company. The house was constructed on a lot purchased from C. W. Wright at a cost of $300 to $400. "The way the note was written, the actual cost was close to $2,000," recalled Miss Marjorie Woods.

A. E. Woods assumed many civic responsibilities. He was one of the original five trustees for the newly incorporated City of Larkspur in 1908 and was elected president of the Board of Trustees in 1910. In 1913 he became city clerk, a position he held for five years.

From their hilltop home reached by climbing 67 stairs, the Woods enjoyed a breathtaking view of the bay and surrounding hills. The home remained in the family until 1971. It has had several subsequent owners and has since been remodeled.

Prior to the 1906 earthquake, San Francisco attorney Otto Wise and his wife built **3 WALNUT AVENUE**. It was, at that time, the only two-story house on the hill. Wise later gave it to the "Emmanuel Sisterhood," a San Francisco girls club. The home was partially destroyed by a fire that claimed one life in 1969 and was rebuilt by contractor Al Lamperti of San

A SUMMER DAY IN LARKSPUR

"My friends and I would take the path down Hawthorne Avenue over to Hill's boathouse. We would swim for the day and go home for dinner. Then we would go to the Rose Bowl Dance, which was great fun. If we were still feeling like it, we would go down to the Escalle Inn for a drink and sandwiches. … One of the popular drinks at Escalle was a 'Queen Charlotte,' made of raspberry soda."

— Katherine Solomons Lilienthal

▲ 2.42: *The path between Walnut and Madrone Avenues was marked as a street on the 1887 survey map (see page vi), 2008.*

GHOST AT 30 PALM AVENUE?

Maria O'Rourke claims that the ghost of Rabbi Voorsanger lived in a glass box made from one of the windows of San Francisco's Temple Emanu-El. The box was stored in the attic at 30 Palm Avenue for years until the attic was rebuilt.

Rafael. Hillside homes in this area were built by friends back then, so they had backyard gates opening into each other's yards. The gates still exist.

Jack and Sallyanne Wilson have owned the home since 1970. Sallyanne served on the Larkspur Parks and Recreation Commission, the Marin County Planning Commission, and the Larkspur Heritage Preservation Board.

Amy Wilson Maroney, who grew up at 3 Walnut Avenue, recalled, "We would play for hours in the 'Dark Park' (Dolliver Park) and run up the hill to our house when we heard the dinner bell."

The confusing progression from Walnut Avenue to Palm Avenue is a mystery that can be solved by checking Ward's 1887 survey map. It shows a street extending up from Madrone to Walnut and Palm Avenues. Since the survey map did not take into consideration the topography, such streets are called "paper streets" because they only exist on paper. At the junction on the map, the street to the east was marked Walnut, the one to the west was Palm.

Although changes have taken place in the homes at 2 and 12 Palm Avenue they retain tidbits of history. Two Palm, an early summer home built by Andrew Armer, was remodeled in the 1980s. Only its wide porch that wraps around two sides remains. Twelve Palm was one of four homes in the area belonging to the Solomons and was the summer residence of Katherine Lilienthal.

The large house at **30 PALM AVENUE** was built in 1908 by Henry Kahn, a San Francisco optician. It sits on a knoll that has a panoramic view of San Francisco Bay and Mt. Tamalpais. Originally built as a summerhouse, the Prairie-style house, with a cross-gable roof, had first and second floor porches on the south, west, and

▲ 2.43: *The large house in the center is 30 Palm Avenue, built in 1908 before Onyx Street was paved. Palm Avenue is the road across the middle, with the rear of 55 Walnut Avenue at the far left and 24 Palm Avenue at the far right. At center left are 23 and 19 Walnut Avenue. Date of photograph estimated to be between 1908 and 1913.*

north sides to capitalize on the views and provide sleeping areas for guests adjacent to almost every room.

The Kahns, their daughter Florence, and son-in-law Leon M. Voorsanger, lived in the house during the summers. They also shared a San Francisco home. Leon Voorsanger's father was Rabbi Jacob W. Voorsanger, who was the second rabbi of the Temple Emanu-El in San Francisco. The house is believed to have been designed by famous San Francisco architect Willis Polk, who had worked with Voorsanger on the Restoration of San Francisco Committee following the 1906 earthquake. However, another rumor circulated that it was architect Julia Morgan who designed the house.

The Kahns' house was situated directly behind the Solomons house at 7 Walnut Avenue, a fact that caused some hard feelings at the time. In 1913 when the Solomons family returned from a trip abroad, they were aghast to discover this huge, two-story structure, so out of scale with the summer bungalows in the area, and so close to their backyard. Apparently the Kahns had wanted to site their home to get the best bay and mountain views.

Leon and Florence Voorsanger raised their son Jacob "Jack" at 30 Palm Avenue, and their son Eric Voorsanger lived nearby in Baltimore Canyon until he died in 2009. After the Voorsangers sold 30 Palm Avenue in 1944, the house changed hands a number of times. In the 1960s, 19 people who needed to "crash" lived there simultaneously. They created temporary living quarters for themselves on the main floor and sleeping cubicles in the attic. If houses could talk, 30 Palm Avenue would be happy to have its current occupants, Maria and Terrence J. O'Rourke, represent its history since 1982. Maria, who was active on Larkspur Citizens' Advisory and Open Space committees, and Terrence, who was raised at 15 Sycamore Avenue, have meticulously preserved 30 Palm's story and integrity.

According to a 1996 report by architectural historian Geraldine Peterson and historical architect Dan Peterson, "The original image of the house has only been changed by closing in the porches." Although trees now block the southern views, the ones to the east from the second floor and to the west are still available.

▲ 2.44: *One of the first homes on the hill above downtown was 55 Walnut Avenue, built by Henry Craner. Although an addition was made at the rear, the house still retained its historic status, 1985.*

⊃ *At the junction of Palm, Walnut, Onyx, Hawthorne (unsigned), and Hazel Avenues, make a quick right turn from Palm onto Walnut to view two homes.*

The arrival of cars threw the hillside homeowners into a tizzy. Because streets were created after homes were built, there was limited flexibility in their configuration and size. Many could only be designed as one-way streets. The creation of the loop road of Palm and Walnut Avenues was a source of controversy for years. Residents futilely resisted the city's efforts to construct a road.

When Walnut Avenue was installed, Mrs. Katherine Solomons Lilienthal, whose family lived at 7 Walnut Avenue, recalled that property owners of the period were incensed that the city charged them for construction of a road they didn't want.

The first home on the Walnut/Palm hill was **55 WALNUT AVENUE**. Built from 1895 to 1896 by Henry Craner and Delores Carillo Jackson Craner, the Italianate-style house was designed by architect B. Allen Brown, who had designed other early Larkspur homes. The house is distinctive for its tall, narrow windows, the dormer on the rectilinear shingled hipped roof, the front porch with gable, and the paneled door design. Henry Craner, who had emigrated from Germany about 1866 at the age of 13, was an architect and designed the other homes they built at 33 and 39 Walnut Avenue.

Mrs. Craner was an aunt of the actor Leo Carillo. She had inherited a great deal of money and land from her Spanish relatives, who had a land grant for much of the Los Angeles area. In fact, "they owned

7th and Spring Streets in Los Angeles," according to Otha Craner, her daughter-in-law. Mrs. Craner recalled that Leo Carillo, the actor famous for his role as "Pancho," the sidekick to the Cisco Kid in the early 1950s TV series of the same name, always visited Granny (Delores Craner) when he was in San Francisco appearing in the theater. "One particular visit was typical of his antics," said Otha Craner. "He brought all the ladies appearing with him in his show to 'Granny's' for lunch, and regaled them all!" Granny Craner was a lively, witty woman who told stories of the Indians coming over the hills to attack her family's ranch in the Los Angeles area when she was just a girl. She had four children – Andrew, Ruth, and Carlotta Jackson from her first marriage, and Gerald H. Craner from her second.

The Craners lived at 55 Walnut Avenue until 1912, when they sold it to the Kellys, relatives of the family that founded the Hibernia Bank in San Francisco. The Craners didn't stray far from the hill and moved to 33 Walnut Avenue. Anne Kelly was listed as the owner in 1928 in the Marin County assessment book. In the 1960s Mr. and Mrs. Victor Bergeron of Trader Vic's restaurant fame lived in the house and did minor remodeling at the rear. In November of 2005 the Bergeron family sold the home to John and Carol Knorpp, who did major preservation work, such as stabilizing the brick foundation, replacing an addition at the rear, and modifying roof dormers to create livable attic space in 2008. The work meets the standards for historic preservation set by the U.S. Secretary of the Interior and therefore does not jeopardize the home's historic status.

In the 1920s Larkspur was a small town, and owners and renters jumped around from house to house. At one time Police Chief W. V. Nicholson lived at the hipped-roof home with a central dormer and a view that overlooks downtown at **60 WALNUT AVENUE**, across from 55 Walnut. In 1934 Biff Harris, whose family owned the home at 627 Magnolia Avenue, rented the house from Nicholson. In the typical informal style of rentals of the period, Harris made a deal to get a three year lease and ten months of free rent, and then $25 per month after that in exchange for installing the plumbing and electricity. "At the time, the house had burlap on the walls with battens over it and just one light bulb dangling on a cord in the center of each room," reported Harris. Another longtime resident of the house was San Francisco fireman William Smith and his wife, Mildred, who lived there for 50 years. Since 1974 the house has been occupied by Richard and Debbie Lundberg; Debbie has been active in the community, serving for several years on the Larkspur Library Board.

⤷ *To continue the tour, retrace your steps to the intersection and head south on Hazel Avenue.*

⑩ The Murray House

In 1900 Robert Murray, a son of William and Maria Murray who owned much of North Larkspur,

AT 60 WALNUT AVENUE

▲ *2.45: 60 Walnut Avenue still looks over downtown Larkspur, 2008.*

"[Nicholson was] the typical cop of those days. He expected kickbacks and shook down some Larkspurians, particularly during Prohibition. Nicholson always would appear when I was sheetrocking or working on the house. He would stop by and I would have to give him a drink."

— Biff Harris

▲ 2.46: *The steep-gabled house at 10 Hazel Avenue has a floor plan similar to a shotgun cottage, 2001.*

▲ 2.47: *The paneling in the rooms of 10 Hazel Avenue combines vertical and diagonal redwood strips for support, 2008.*

moved his family to this site and began to build the two-story Greek Revival-style house at **10 HAZEL AVENUE**. Their daughter, Lillian Murray Dodge, recalled that the family lived on the property in tents while the house was being built. They moved in before it was finished, "but we didn't mind." The Murrays had two Jersey cows, chickens, and many other animals. Katherine Lilienthal remembered getting her family's milk from the Murrays.

The house followed a popular architectural design of the period called "shotgun cottages." Designed with balloon framing, the cottages were relatively simple and quick to construct and had steep gabled roofs and stud walls that ran from sill to eave line. The design could almost be called an early green building as light is fed down from the roof skylight through a center light well in the attic, and heat flows from the basement through an open grate to the upper hall.

The exterior of the house has a balcony on the second-floor gable return. The railings on the balcony and porch are simple vertical elements. There is grooved shiplap siding on the first floor, and shingle siding on the second with moldings around the windows, doors, and building edges. The house also has an interesting ceramic flue on the chimney.

The property is covered with low walls composed of a variety of rocks, some brought from the quarry in Baltimore Canyon. A particularly interesting feature is a low-arched recess similar to Mexican shrines. Later owners of the home have discovered ponds and extensive plumbing on the property. Murray, a plumbing contractor for many of San Francisco's big hotels, had his shop at 521 Magnolia Avenue.

When the house was vacant in the mid-1960s, Robert L. Hamann, the owner of the Hamann Pet Shop on Cane Street who lived across the street at 7 Hazel, kept birds there. Different varieties of birds flew loose in each room, and the house was a "real mess." According to neighbors it was dubbed "The Birdhouse." Reports also circulated about both transients and deer wandering through the house.

When the Ceniceros purchased the house in 1966, they cleaned up both the interior and the exterior. On the outside they restored the Mexican grotto and the elaborate stone-paved path system. Inside they stripped off the wallpaper and the burlap-covered walls and exposed the redwood paneling, which runs horizontally in the central hall. There is a mixture of vertical paneling on one or two walls, and the paneling runs diagonally on the other walls of the rooms to provide lateral structural support.

Since the homes on the two loops in this area were some of the earliest ones built, paths between streets were plotted on early maps for walkers. Like the Arch Street stairs, Beta Street *(see Appendix C)* was originally plotted to connect up from Madrone to Hazel at the hairpin turn but was never developed.

⑪ Hazel & Laurel Avenues

A confusing road name switch, similar to the junction of Walnut and Palm Avenues, occurs after the sharp turn at 10 Hazel. The Hazel section of the road extended to 10 Hazel before the Laurel section was built. When the road was connected from Laurel to Hazel, it was given the name Laurel up to the hairpin turn.

A house called "Hilltop" at 34 Laurel Avenue was built by two bachelors of German ancestry in about 1910 and has not been researched.

The downhill, wooded section where Laurel begins – just beyond 10 Hazel – was originally part of the many small lots on the hill that Adolph Tiscornia had purchased from early developer C. W. Wright in the 1920s and 1930s. Canyon resident James Holmes reports that in the 1950s and 1960s, his father Jack unsuccessfully tried to buy the land above his home at 124 Madrone Avenue from Tiscornia. Years after Tiscornia's death in 1967, a subdivision map of the Orange/Tiscornia Lands was approved in 1984 dedicating an open space easement on the southwest 1.4-acre parcel at 45 Laurel, and placing a deed restriction on the property. The little-over-an-acre (49,546 square foot) open space parcel abuts the rear of homes from 112 to 124 Madrone Avenue and from 10 to 24 Orange Avenue leaving only an 11,726-square-foot parcel buildable on the steep 41% slope. The awkward panhandle-shaped lot between 10 Hazel Avenue and 47 Laurel Avenue was eventually sold, but construction is only allowed on the 100- x 100-ft panhandle section. The bulk of the lot is dedicated open space.

Farther along on Laurel, before 47 Laurel Avenue, View Street, another street marked on early maps, was abandoned after a lawsuit in the 1990s and sold to the adjacent owner.

To add to the street confusion in the area, Hazel and Laurel Avenues crisscross at the junction where they meet between the two loops. In hillside neighborhoods the level junction areas were popular recreation spots. In the 1920s colored lights were strung around the flat open space where Hazel and Laurel met to create an informal neighborhood dance pavilion between the four corners.

The top of this hill, surrounded by Hazel and Laurel Avenues, was marked on the early Ward 1887 survey map as the site of C.W. Wright's hotel. Eucalyptus trees were planted on the slope as wind protection for the future hotel. However, Wright opted for a more protected location on Sycamore Avenue for his hotel (see page 73-74). After a long series of hearings in 1982, the hotel site on the top of the hill was developed with just one home, and the density was reduced for the rest of the land. Due to the heavy tree cover on the hilltop, a large house was approved for the site but was exposed in the very prominent location when the eucalyptus trees were cut down.

The Hazel and Laurel neighborhood boasts some of the most substantial homes built in Larkspur prior to the twentieth century. While three of them – the Basebe house at 95 Laurel Avenue, the Von Meyerinck house at 33 Myrtle Avenue, and the Lucchetti house at 29 Myrtle Avenue – retain some of their original character, the one at **74 HAZEL AVENUE** is a sad example of the consequences of "modernization." The proud, classic revival-style house of Judge William Mahoney succumbed to 1930s-style changes.

Completed in 1884, the house had a bad start when a suit was brought against the original contractor, and Larkspur architect and builder Gustave Nagel was called in to complete the work. The house originally had a Victorian-style second floor porch

▲ 2.48: *74 Hazel Avenue, built in 1884, was the home of Judge William Mahoney.*

▲ 2.49: *The extent of remodeling at 74 Hazel Avenue can be seen in this 1975 photograph.*

JUDGE MAHONEY OF 74 HAZEL AVENUE

Old-timers recall that Judge Mahoney was a big man who wore a high silk hat, carried a gold-headed cane, and wore gloves, striped pants, and a frock coat as he waited for the train to go to San Francisco.

▲ 2.50: 74 Hazel Avenue, the Judge Mahoney house, at left; 95 Laurel Avenue, the Basebe house, at right, about 1890.

that wrapped around the front and side. At some point the original porch railings and column brackets were replaced by removing the railings and Greek Revival-style columns. In keeping with the classic revival-style of the period, the house had a truncated hipped roof, centered front door, and horizontal wood siding. When finally completed, Judge Mahoney buried a time capsule of mementos under a post.

Sometimes family histories are as fascinating as the history of the houses. Thorpe Wright recalled that Judge Mahoney was a difficult man for many people to like and that he was at odds with many of the townspeople. Alice Ambrose Krogman commented, "The kids thought of Judge Mahoney as mean because he chased them for going after the cherries in the trees that rimmed his property ... But if we didn't get them, the birds would have."

"Mr. Mahoney was known as a curbstone lawyer [because he didn't have an office]," said Wright. "He was a notary public and somewhat of an opportunist, business-wise." However, when a fire ravaged the house, in the days before the volunteer departments, all the townspeople came to extinguish it. Thorpe Wright reported that there might have been a little residual spite. A mattress was gently carried downstairs but a brand new treadle sewing machine was thrown out the window, smashing it to bits.

Mrs. Mahoney was something of a mystic. She and the Judge had three children – Ella, Jane, and Willard. She took the children to live in San Francisco after she and the judge divorced. Daughter Ella dabbled in art and then turned to the stage, first working as a chorus girl and then becoming Lillian Russell's understudy. Russell's opera company performed in 1892 at the Baldwin Theatre in San Francisco. Old newspaper clippings describe Ella Mahoney's many stage roles, including one as Lillian Russell in a playlet called "A Chorus Girl's Chagrin." Seemingly adept at stirring up publicity, Ella once accused an employer of failing to pay her $80. That incident resulted in a front-page story in the *San Francisco Chronicle*. Ella married twice and had one son, Gurney Robinson. Her brother Willard died at age 20, and it is thought that his ashes are buried beneath one of the trees in the yard.

Judge Mahoney died in August of 1933 following an incident demonstrating the chivalry of the era. He was riding back to Larkspur on the train and shared a compartment with a woman and a man. The window was open and the woman asked that it be closed since she was cold. The judge closed it but the other man re-opened it, saying he was too hot. The judge reminded him the lady wanted it closed, and with that a fistfight began. Judge Mahoney knocked out his opponent. The judge went home and died that night. He was 84 years old.

Upon his death the state took the old house for taxes in the mid-1930s, but Ella managed to buy it back and then sold the home to Alfred and Borghild

THE BASEBE MANSION

"G.A. Nagel has just completed Prof. Basebe's handsome mansion. It is a unique piece of architecture of the early English style, planned by the owner. Such a home only a true artist can build."

— *The Sausalito News*, May 8, 1891

▲ 2.51: *95 Laurel Avenue, the Basebe house, built in 1891.*

Finnila in 1936. Alfred Finnila, a civil engineer who worked on the Golden Gate Bridge and had a construction supply company, operated a miniature golf course across the street from 74 Hazel Avenue in the 1930s. The Finnilas extensively remodeled and modernized the house in the 1930s and covered the exterior with stucco, completely smothering its original character. Ella Mahoney remodeled the old barn and lived there until her death in 1968.

⟳ *Continue on Laurel Avenue, the street between 74 and 70 Hazel Avenue, until reaching the end.*

In 1888 Rosa Basebe purchased the whole hilltop surrounding **95 LAUREL AVENUE**. She purchased land from the American Land and Trust Company on the same day as Ann Dolliver *(see page 106)*. When her English husband, Charles Edward Basebe, designed their home, "Staplehurst," he drew true-to-size plans for it. Constructed by Larkspur builder Gustave Nagel, the completion date of the house was 1891.

The three-story, approximately 5,500-square-foot house was not built as a summerhouse, as were many of the early homes, but rather as a stately mansion with a full basement and attic, but no kitchen. The story goes that the Basebes sent a servant out nightly to the Hotel Larkspur, the site of today's Left Bank restaurant, to bring dinner home. Originally each room had a fireplace, but only four are now in working order. A kitchen and bathrooms were added in 1932.

The house is redwood throughout, built with lumber that came from Mill Valley's old mill.

▲ 2.52: *Locals used to call 95 Laurel Avenue, "The Big White House," 1955. The house is now yellow.*

▲ 2.53: *Flower and sunburst motifs were used to give houses a happy look, 2008.*

▲ 2.54: In this photo from 2008, the light-colored house (top) at 95 Laurel Avenue and the shingled, gabled house at 29 Myrtle Avenue are still prominent on the hillside above downtown, and 121 Hawthorne Avenue is visible at the lower right.

COLONEL BASEBE

"Col. Charles Edward Basebe, the Larkspur masher who has been so successful in achieving the infamy for himself, was sentenced to 60 days imprisonment and to pay a fine of $100... We trust it may prove sufficient to deter such human vermin from annoying decent, self respecting women in the future. There are an abundance of females who like to be mashed and the practice should be reserved for their exclusive benefit."

— *Marin County Tocsin*, 1893

Moldings around the ceilings are hand-designed plaster. Bryce and Ida Florence, the home's second owners, dismantled the original cupola because it leaked and the cost to repair it was prohibitive. According to one old-time sailor, the cupola, which always had a light in it, served as a landmark for navigators on the bay since it was visible from San Quentin Point.

The stained glass and ribbon windows are the originals. In 1959, when the third owner purchased the house, the property was self-contained, with chicken coops, many fruit trees, and vegetable gardens. Owners since the 1960s, such as Shirley Jones, and David and Donna Manahan, have appreciated its historic character and have taken steps to restore and upgrade the house. It has six working fireplaces and still retains a painting of a stormy coastal scene made by Basebe.

The original Victorian details that the house boasted have been enhanced. Victorians are thought of as prudish, but architectural historians report they secretly expressed their sexuality with anatomical architectural features such as button details for navels and brackets with eyes. The insides of gables were faced with a different texture than the house siding, such as shingles, to contrast with horizontal siding. The use of flower and sunburst motifs was done to give houses a happy look.

The bearded Colonel Basebe was a man of many talents – architect, engineer, artist, and author. He is thought to have built a railroad and steam engine in England. One of his published books was a novel, *The Remarkable Fledger*. An ex-army man, he stood very erect and used a walking stick as he took his daily walks to the post office.

Basebe was what was called a "remittance man," an exile living on money sent from home. His rakish lifestyle followed when he and his mistress (later his wife) left England, crossed the Atlantic, and arrived in Larkspur where they made their home. One old-timer recalled that he had a very nice wife whom he divorced. Following the divorce he hired a housekeeper who may have inherited his estate when he died in 1927. Another story is that his family disowned him.

➲ *Retrace your steps and take the concrete steps downhill on your left. At the base of the steps, turn left from Eden Lane onto Myrtle and walk up the hill to view the next stop from the driveway.*

⑫ Eden Street, Lane, or Stairs?

Officially named "Eden Street" on the 1887 subdivision map, this "street" has been signed as "Eden Lane" and serves as a stairway between Laurel and Myrtle Avenues *(see Appendix C)*.

▲ 2.55: *Eden Street, a paper street, provides a short cut from Laurel Avenue to Myrtle Avenue. Originally, the steps went through plum and apple orchards.*

"A side trip to Eden Street and a quick look at 95 Laurel Avenue was a regular feature of the walks my brother and I used to take around Larkspur."

— Paul Penna, who grew up at 9 Arch Street

▲ 2.56: *The gables of the 1903 house at 29 Myrtle Avenue are integrated with the side façades to provide attic rooms, 2008.*

⑬ Myrtle Avenue

Although the horizontal siding of the gabled house at **29 MYRTLE AVENUE** was covered over with shingles in the 1950s or 1960s, its distinctive profile competes with the big yellow house above it at 95 Laurel. When built in 1903 as a summerhouse, probably by San Francisco dentist Alfred F. Lucchetti, a hipped-roof porch wrapped around the north, east, and south sides of the house. The front door at the center of the second floor porch overlooked the downtown and opened into the open living room and dining room. A unique design feature is the gables on four sides of the hipped roof that are integrated into the sidewalls so that three attic rooms and the stair access are accommodated. The interior has four-inch vertical redwood paneling in the old sections of the house. The original brick fireplace is in the living room, although its brick chimney has been reinforced with an interior metal sleeve.

The Lucchettis summered in the house with their son Francis and daughter Alice. At some time prior to 1960 the east and south sections of the porch were removed so that the back door has become the front door, and a two-story addition was constructed on the east side of the house.

A court battle after the death of the parents divided the estate. Francis was awarded the upper parcel, with the house, and Alice inherited the lower portion. When Jean and Wally Colthurst bought the house from Francis in 1961, they restored the redwood paneling and house details but were required by their mortgage lender to replace the old wooden casement windows with aluminum ones.

According to neighbor Brenda McKowen, in the 1960s the house was known as an "Addams family"-type house. Today the house is not visible from the street.

European royalty arrived in Larkspur in 1904 when the Baron and Baroness Wilhelm Von Meyerinck built the impressive house at **33 MYRTLE AVENUE**.

The two-story shingled house entrance was off Myrtle and had a grape arbor entrance.

The diminutive Baroness was born Anna Hoffmeister in Dusseldorf, Germany in 1864, the daughter of a physician. An unconventional woman with a mind of her own, she objected strongly to a marriage arranged by her parents when she was about 18 years old. Selling her own jewelry, she booked passage to New York City. Her enormous musical talent and headstrong manner made her family think she was capable of "doing anything she set her mind to," according to one family member. In New York City she sang in concerts and was a teacher. In 1890 she married the Baron. Shortly after the birth of their only son, Herbert, in 1893, they came to San Francisco.

The Baroness maintained a music studio in San Francisco for many years. Equipped with a stage, her studio was the scene of a constant array of recitals, plays, and musicals. She played a number of instruments and was described as "always teaching and holding classes." Children throughout the area took piano lessons from her. Judge Samuel Gardiner recalled, "Madame Von Meyerinck, as she was generally known, was a motherly person."

The Von Meyerinck home in Larkspur was designed to accommodate the Baroness's musical talents, and the original music room on the lower floor held her two concert grand pianos, along with other instruments, and marble busts of great composers made by her brother Heinz, who served as court sculptor to the Kaiser in Germany.

In the back garden there was a little summerhouse containing a "shower" that consisted of a can of cold water the Baroness could tip over herself each day after her swim in the slough, a routine she followed in summer and winter. That, and her unsweetened juice made from berries she gathered in the surrounding hills, constituted her health routine.

Following their move to Larkspur, Baron Von Meyerinck took an active interest in the community. He was elected to the Board of Town Trustees, was the leader of the "wet" faction prior to Prohibition, and was collector for the municipal water system. He committed suicide on July 16, 1909, when he was falsely accused of juggling bank books. Later evidence indicated that his accounts were straight and that he had not been guilty of any wrongdoing in the bank's affairs.

Following his death, the Baroness continued to make Larkspur her home base, leaving it occasionally to pursue her musical interests. "Laddy" or "Sonny," as she called her son Herbert, was placed in the Hitchcock Military Academy (later called the San Rafael Military Academy) when she had the urge to travel. She toured in Alaska, China, and Russia. While in Russia she served in the Russian Court as piano teacher to Nicholas and Alexandra's children. She brought home a variety of jewelry that had been

▲ 2.57: *The entrance of the 1904 house built by Baron Von Meyerinck at 33 Myrtle Avenue was relocated from the south side to the north side so its two towers are now at the rear, 2008.*

BATHTUB FOR THE BARONESS?

Rumor had it that the Von Meyerinck home had the first bathtub in Marin County. The tub had to be hoisted into the house through the upstairs bathroom window. It sat in the middle of that room, a round cupola, as it was too large to put anywhere else.

▲ 2.58: *The round tower at 33 Myrtle Avenue may have housed the first bathtub in Marin.*

THE BARONESS

"She was very proud of being the Baroness Von Meyerinck and was always called the Baroness until her dying day. Even though she became disoriented at the last, she never let even the nurses in the hospital forget that she was the Baroness. All of her cards were printed that way, and her household belongings were monogrammed with a "V" set into an "M" and marked with the family crest containing a seven-pointed crown."

— A family member

presented to her by the Czar. One piece that contained around 50 stones was divided by the family and reset into individual pieces.

As Laddy grew up, he organized an orchestra that played for years in San Francisco at the St. Francis, Clift, and Palace Hotels. His orchestra had two musicians who later formed bands of their own – Phil Harris and Muzzy Marcellino. An account of Larkspur's third Booster Day in 1913 told of the parade with "Laddy Von Meyerinck, and others of the band, setting the tune."

During World War I, he decided it was to his advantage to change his name from Von Meyerinck to Meyerinck. His mother never forgave him.

Almost forty years after the Baron's death, the Baroness fell in her home and broke her hip. She was found when her family came to take her to the Blue Rock Hotel for the traditional Christmas Eve dinner she always held there. She died at St. Mary's Hospital on July 4, 1950. Her short obituary concluding with, "She taught music for years in San Francisco and had taught at Tamalpais High School and in Larkspur. She was a native of Germany. She first lived in Larkspur in 1906 [sic]." The writer obviously failed to capture the flavor of this woman who was so far ahead of her time.

After the Baroness died, her daughter-in-law, finally having a chance to react to her strong-willed "Mother Von," took the marble statues and busts into the backyard and destroyed them with a hammer, burying the fragments in the garden. Only pictures of Heinz's sculptures and one urn that survived are still with the family. Grandson "Bink" Meyerinck recalled Lee, the oriental houseboy, spending an entire day polishing the urn. Lee lived in the basement where the kitchen was located, and where the family said the stairs descended almost into the sink.

Llewellyn Dudley Crandall, known as "Lew," was Larkspur's postmaster from 1955 to 1968. He purchased the house and lived there in the late 1940s through the 1960s. He also operated a part-time weaving business, called "Lorellyn Weavers," from the house, which was noted on a 1953 sketch map. The name Lorellyn was a combination of his first wife Lora's name and his.

According to his stepson, Kevin West, Lew made looms that he sold nationally, and he had taught weaving at some point in his past. Joan C. Crandall, Lew's second wife and Kevin's mother, said Lew first became interested in weaving when he worked in the occupational development department of a federal prison. She had little to do with the looms except making string heddles. West reported that the weaving studio was in the corner tower with the hexagon bay windows in what had probably been the Baroness's former music studio, as it was large enough for two grand pianos and was accessed by a separate door below. The looms were constructed in the adjacent summerhouse.

⟲ *Proceed south on Myrtle Avenue to Hawthorne Avenue. At the corner look up the southwest hill to observe the last house on this tour.*

⑭ Hawthorne Avenue to End

In early 1900s pictures **21 HAWTHORNE AVENUE** was prominent on the hill when looking south down Hawthorne Avenue toward the Walnut and Laurel hills. Because the front door, main living areas, and porch were on the second floor, the driveway access was from Hazel Avenue. The brown-shingled house, built in 1907, is a mixture of 1890 features and early Craftsman details, architecturally bridging the two periods. On the south side, the hipped roof is punctuated by a bay-style dormer with small, multipane windows. Originally two sleeping porches wrapped around the south and east sides.

Although the original open verandas on the east and south sides have been enclosed, most likely around 1934, other original features remain, such as the multipane windows on the west side of the main porch, the tongue-and-groove redwood ceiling, and porch supports on the main floor. At some point two decks were added on the southern face of the house, accessed from the enclosed porches. A 2001 attic remodel added three gabled dormers and raised the existing bay-style dormer by a few feet to create two bedrooms.

The main floor double-hung windows with their simple molded trim and multipane upper sashes are original to the house. The main living areas have changed very little and retain the original redwood wainscoting, the clinker brick fireplace with wide arched niche above it, the walnut and mahogany flooring, and the built-in redwood lead glass cabinets in the living room.

From 1909 to 1947, the house was owned by Arthur W. "Cap" Larsen, who was described in a 1947 *Collier's* article as "a little pink-cheeked cherub of 74." As secretary of the Larkspur Association of Volunteer Firemen, he was a driving force behind the Rose Bowl dances, where he acted as master of ceremonies. Larsen dreamed up a wide variety of promotional stunts to publicize the dances. The most famous was a stunt that never came off – the promise of a girl who would jump from the top of a redwood tree into a fire net.

Larsen was involved in the big water scandal that erupted in 1910 and 1911. According to Judge Samuel Gardiner, Cap Larsen was prosecuted for "grand larceny" when it was discovered that the pipe system belonging to the Larkspur Water Company was filled with water siphoned off from

▲ *2.59: The 1907 Prairie-Craftsman house at 21 Hawthorne Avenue has overlooked downtown Larkspur for a hundred years, 1999.*

MYSTERY AT 21 HAWTHORNE AVENUE

Was the tiny closet room adjacent to the front porch, accessed by a trap door, and tucked into a false stucco chimney a hide-away for bootleg booze during Prohibition?

the Marin Water and Power Company and then sold back to Larkspur residents. Biff Harris who used to live at 627 Magnolia Avenue claimed that his father Joseph was the only reason that Cap Larsen didn't go to San Quentin. In a 1975 interview he recalled that one night, around the time of the scandal, his father and Cap Larsen met at Len Young's saloon, had a few drinks, and his father hauled Cap outside and knocked him cold.

Larkspur Heritage Preservation Board member Kathleen Kearley-Green and her husband Robert purchased the home in 1999 from prior owners Greg and June Hubit. A story reported by the Hubits was that Jerry Garcia lived in the house at one time during the 1960s or 1970s prior to their purchase in the 1970s.

Although this house has been upgraded and modified over the years, its historic integrity is intact. The Greens completed an upgrade of the foundation, seismic retrofit, and restoration of many of the house features before selling the house in 2010.

Commented Kearley-Green, "We had always wanted a brown shingle-style house and felt the house has been an important hillside structure in early Larkspur and should be brought back to that dignity."

BALTIMORE CANYON - An ancient canyon shelters giant trees and eclectic homes.

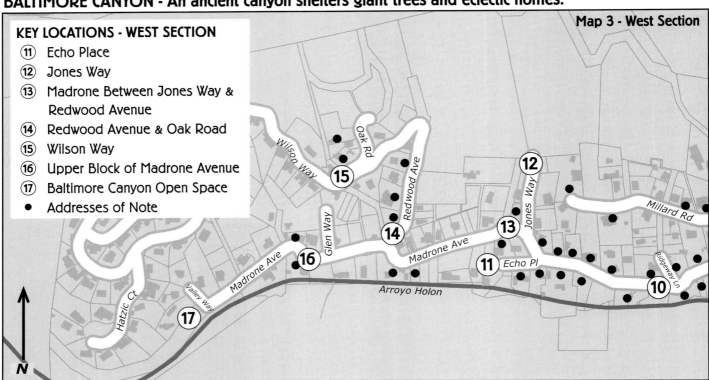

Map 3 - West Section

KEY LOCATIONS - WEST SECTION
- ⑪ Echo Place
- ⑫ Jones Way
- ⑬ Madrone Between Jones Way & Redwood Avenue
- ⑭ Redwood Avenue & Oak Road
- ⑮ Wilson Way
- ⑯ Upper Block of Madrone Avenue
- ⑰ Baltimore Canyon Open Space
- • Addresses of Note

 Beginning at the mouth of "The Canyon," walkers may experience babbling Arroyo Holon, cool shade, and the towering redwoods that lured visitors to early Larkspur and enticed them to build cabins and year-round homes. Bring a picnic to enjoy at Dawn Falls after viewing the houses hidden among the trees and hills above.

REMEMBERING BALTIMORE CANYON

"This is glorious weather for campers, and they are quite numerous just at this season.... The redwood canyon in back of Larkspur, one of the most inviting spots in the county, is quite crowded, and the healthy and jolly inhabitants as they ramble through the brush or lie lazily in the shade are enough to make a pale-faced city worker envious."

— *The Marin Journal*, July 5, 1894

▲ 3.1: *The original copy of this May, 1898 photograph contains a detailed list of the names of the merry visitors enjoying a "picnic in Redwood Canyon."*

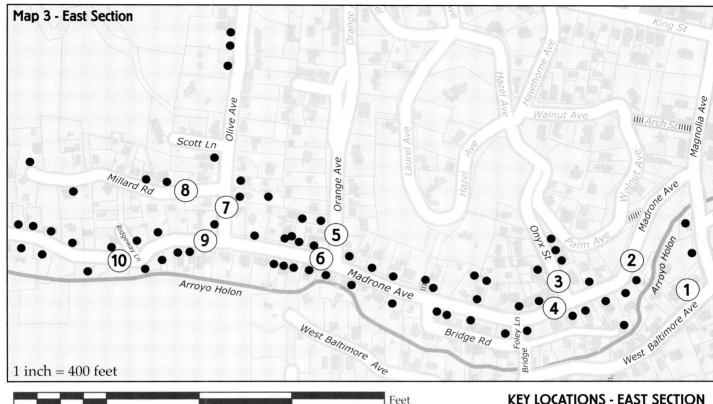

KEY LOCATIONS - EAST SECTION
1. Sawmill Site
2. First Block of Madrone Avenue
3. Onyx Street
4. Madrone Between Onyx Street & Orange Avenue
5. Orange Avenue
6. Madrone Between Orange & Olive Avenues
7. Olive Avenue
8. Millard Road
9. 200 Block of Madrone Avenue
10. Ridgeway Lane & the Glen Addition
• Addresses of Note

BALTIMORE CANYON

Larkspur's modern history began in this cool and verdant canyon that penetrates two miles into the lower slopes of Mt. Tamalpais. It was first described merely as the streambed of the Arroyo Holon, the creek used to mark the northern boundary of a Mexican land grant created in 1834. Giant redwoods lined the creek and marched up the hillsides, mingling with oaks, madrones, laurels, and California buckeyes.

• • • • • • • • • • • •

The name changed dramatically in 1849, when entrepreneurs from Baltimore, Maryland started a thriving sawmill operation at the canyon's mouth. The area became known as "Baltimore Gulch," and within a decade most of the majestic redwood trees had been removed. After the departure of the sawmill, only a few small farms and residences lingered in the gulch, which gradually came to be called a "canyon" as that Spanish word was adapted into American English in the 1870s.

The creation of "The Town of Larkspur" subdivision in 1887 introduced an alternate name. The area occasionally was called "Larkspur Canyon" to describe its location, or "Redwood Canyon" to describe its unique collection of second-growth redwoods, among the most accessible to pleasure seekers from San Francisco. Later residents, unaware of its history, sometimes have called it "Madrone Canyon," adapting the name of its predominant street.

Through the 1920s, published hiking maps labeled the central Baltimore Canyon area as "camp grounds." Summer camping involved either temporary tents or longer-term established campsites. An established camp, sometimes rented from landowners, usually included a tent platform, which was a rough wooden frame with plank flooring, occasionally including hip-high walls. Contoured canvas could be stretched over the frame. More than a few of those walled tent platforms were later converted into rustic houses.

"In 1923 the canyon was filled with tent houses. In the winter, people took down their tents, put all their furniture in the middle of the tent platform, and covered it. There was seldom a light in the canyon beyond Olive Avenue from Labor Day until Memorial Day."

— Helen Wilson, a long-term Canyon resident who moved to Larkspur in 1922

Although a few individuals had constructed homes on small land holdings, the sudden availability of formally-subdivided lots spurred a building boom that began in earnest during the early 1890s. Those first houses were nearly always summer retreats, built by fog-weary San Franciscans along the lower stretches of "Madrona" Avenue. Many of those early houses remain today, some as large homes built by the more well-to-do, and a greater number that began as very modest shacks, cabins, or cottages that were owned by, or rented to, ordinary tradespeople and their families.

During summer's heat the sheltered Canyon maintains a mild climate, so the informal vacation structures required only minimal protection from the elements. Most houses were single-wall construction – a basic framework covered with one layer of planks or shingles. Many houses had both entry porches for visiting and sleeping porches to accommodate simple beds and cots. The footpaths and roads, like those of downtown, were bare dirt, with winter's rivulets and mud making the routes impassable.

"Very few families lived all year 'round in the Canyon; it was too damp under the redwoods in the rain."

— Eleanor Rideout Fuller, recalling her summertime visits to the Canyon during the early 1900s

Two events, about thirty years apart, forced irrevocable changes. The first was San Francisco's great earthquake and fire of 1906. Many families who had lost their homes in San Francisco fled to the safety of Larkspur, taking up residence at campsites or vacation cottages owned by family or friends. Rudimentary structures had to be expanded and upgraded for permanent occupancy, and boardwalks added to the dirt streets. What had been a collection of informal and part-time structures evolved into a community that now included many permanent homes. The second change was caused by World War II and the need to provide housing for employees at the Marinship shipyard in Sausalito. The summer rentals became year-round homes, as it was considered one's patriotic duty to release an unused vacation house to the new wartime market.

The large number of modest structures rented during the war remained on the market during later decades, giving the Canyon a diverse and somewhat disorganized appearance. In the late 1960s and early 1970s, flower children, hippies, and "alternative lifestyle" folk were attracted by the Canyon's low rents and rustic housing, or merely by its woodlands. Outdoor campsites with poor sanitation and uncontained fires posed a threat to safety, and the raucous, drug-tainted lifestyle of the newcomers perplexed the longer-term residents, while raising the hackles of the recently arrived suburbanites.

As property values began to skyrocket in the 1980s, the Canyon's laid-back character was threatened not by hippies, but by yuppies. Older homes, often structurally substandard, were subjected to extensive remodeling, or simply torn down and replaced with far larger houses that catered to the greater Bay Area's housing market; little attention was given to the peculiar charm of the Canyon's historic styles. Larkspur's Floor Area Ratio ordinance now addresses the bulk and scale of a home in relation to its site and neighborhood, aiming to reconcile the old and the new. Similarly, a Heritage Tree ordinance seeks to protect the redwoods and other established trees that give the Canyon much of its unique atmosphere.

⊃ *The materials below set out a walking route from the landmark oak tree on West Baltimore Avenue, then around Dolliver Park, and up Madrone Avenue.*

① Sawmill Site

Here on the flat lands near the creek and adjacent the landmark oak, the Baltimore and Frederick Mining and Trading Company established one of California's earliest commercial sawmills in November of 1849.

Logs were hauled out of the Canyon by teams of yoked oxen and sawn in the mill; the milled lumber was then carried in wagons to the estuary leading to Corte Madera Creek (near the current location of Larkspur Plaza Drive), and from there it was shipped to a thriving market in San Francisco.

The mill's frame was constructed of massive hand-hewn redwood beams. It was described in Marin County Assessor's records of 1854 as a "steam mill with fifteen upright saws." By that time a small lumber camp had grown around the sawmill, including a blacksmith shop and several "dwelling houses" for the workers, who would have included loggers, bullwhackers, sawyers, and teamsters. The Company also may have briefly operated a trading post. Among the nearby buildings, recorded in May of 1852, was

REMEMBERING BALTIMORE CANYON

"In 1849 the tide water flooded all land up to Ross Landing and sloughs were very deep... When we arrived at Larkspur, there was no one to meet us. The country was a wilderness ... After the new mill was installed, we erected our dwellings and proceeded to get out the lumber. I can picture the majestic redwoods that covered the flat where Larkspur stands today. Some of the trees were eight feet in diameter and lifted their immense bulk 300 feet upwards."

— Daniel Taylor, last survivor of the Baltimore Company, quoted in the *San Rafael Independent* of December 8, 1914

▲3.2: *There are no known photographs of the sawmill or logging activity in Baltimore Canyon, but this early photo depicts a similar operation in a Northern California forest. A twelve-ox team is dragging a long line of cut redwoods along a "corduroy" road built of logs set horizontally into the ground. One man holds a grease bucket to grease the logs, thereby reducing friction.*

THE BALTIMORE COMPANY'S SAWMILL

As soon as news of the California gold discovery reached the eastern United States, various "companies" of ambitious men organized to seize new economic opportunities. In January of 1849 a group of thirty Maryland adventurers organized "The Baltimore and Frederick Mining and Trading Company." Each member subscribed $1,000 for the purchase of supplies and a variety of equipment, which included the complete workings of a steam-powered sawmill.

They shipped their bulky equipment aboard the ship *Andalusia* on April 18, bound for San Francisco around South America's Cape Horn. The members of the company personally took the supposedly quicker route across Panama; they left Baltimore on April 24 aboard the schooner *Creole*, heading to the sleepy little town of Chagres on the northern coast of the Isthmus of Panama. From there, they traveled up the Chagres River on boats, transferred to mules for a trip over the mountains, and then waited for weeks on the beach at Panama City, hoping to catch a ship bound north to California.

In mid-June they boarded the English brig *Corbiere* for a twelve-week voyage north on the Pacific, finally arriving at San Francisco on September 10, 1849. Less than two weeks later their equipment arrived on the *Andalusia*, and members of the company began searching for an appropriate site in the lumber country. In early November the group sailed up Corte Madera creek to a landing site near today's Bon Air Bridge. They hauled their equipment south to the mouth of a large wooded canyon where they erected buildings and assembled their sawmill. Decades later some of their buildings still stood on the land bounded by today's Baltimore, Madrone, and Magnolia Avenues.

Although the Baltimore Company disbanded after a few months, the mill continued in operation. In August of 1850 it was acquired for almost $16,000 by Benjamin Buckelew, a visionary San Francisco businessman with grand plans for new enterprises in Marin. In 1852 Buckelew sold the mill and timber-cutting rights for $18,000 to George H. Ensign, a lumber dealer in San Francisco. At about the same time, Richard Samuel Brown served as an engineer for the mill and, with his wife Helen, later laid claim to about 200 acres of land in the immediate area, building a succession of homes near today's lower Madrone Avenue.

In later years Buckelew regained title to the mill, then disassembled and moved it to Point San Quentin. Cut logs thereafter were floated to the beaches at San Quentin, processed at the sawmill, and the lumber shipped out from the deep-water wharf on the point. Eventually the old mill building became a social center for San Quentin Village; it was converted into the Red Mill Inn, and finished life as an Italian restaurant that burned to the ground in November of 1929.

▲ 3.3: Young John Beech sits in a wagon in the middle of unpaved West Baltimore Avenue in a family photograph taken about 1918. The heritage oak in the background is silhouetted against Palm Hill to the east.

one of California's earliest bowling alleys, a "Ten Pin Alley" that was "situated near Corte Madera Steam Saw Mill."

By the early 1860s, most of the Canyon had been clear-cut, and the area given over to small farms. Although the redwood trees were gone, their vestiges remained. Judge Samuel Gardiner, who was raised at the mouth of the Canyon in the early 1900s, commented: "One thing that is not appreciated today is the character of the redwood growth that existed here. There were thousands of redwood stumps ranging from 5 to 15 feet in diameter at the point of cutting, thousands of them." Many of those stumps re-sprouted, producing the large second-growth trees on today's Canyon floor.

Several of the Maryland men also remained, and became leading citizens of Marin County. A. Jerome Barney launched publication of the *Marin Journal* (forerunner of today's *Independent Journal*), Val Doub served as Marin's sheriff for three terms, David Clingan also served as sheriff, as well as in the state assembly, John Davis was county auditor and treasurer, Henry Baechtel served as a Marin County supervisor, and Daniel Taylor was county clerk. The last survivor of the company, Taylor died in San Rafael in 1916, where a small street was named after him. The

Company's name was later attached to the Canyon, the Baltimore Park subdivisions, and the avenues.

Larkspur's best-known landmark tree is the ancient valley oak, *Quercus lobata*, located mid-street fronting **205 WEST BALTIMORE AVENUE**. Valley oaks are the largest oaks in North America, prized for their massive trunks and broad arching branches. Professional arborists determined that this tree started growing about 1750, when this land was an unsettled frontier of New Spain. A now-missing plaque proclaimed that General Mariano Vallejo, eventually the Comandante-General of the Republic of Mexico's Alta California, once had camped beneath the tree. More than a half century later Larkspur's Board of Trustees ordered the construction of a protective concrete curb around "the historic oak tree" in 1918.

↪ *Walkers should exit West Baltimore Avenue and proceed north on Magnolia Avenue (toward downtown), then turn into the Canyon at Madrone Avenue.*

Both the Gardiner home at **215 MAGNOLIA AVENUE** and the de Veuve Cottage at **223 MAGNOLIA AVENUE** stand on land that was originally owned by R.S. Brown and his wife, Helen. The Rev. James Allen Gardiner, a Presbyterian minister, and Henry de Veuve, a San Francisco insurance man, purchased the property from the Browns' daughters Mary and Belle in April of 1896. The two families had camped together and bought the property in a single transaction, Henry purchasing the narrow parcel by the creek for $75. *(See pages 186-189 for details about these two homes and the families who built and lived in them.)*

Remnants of the great redwood forest logged by the Baltimore Company line the streambed that formed the northern boundary of the large rancho – including all of today's Mill Valley and Corte Madera – that was granted to John Reed in 1834. The rancho grant designated this streambed in Spanish as Arroyo Holon; an "arroyo" is simply a "stream," and "Holon" apparently was a proper name, probably Coast Miwok in origin, and might have referred to a Native American village area a few blocks to the east. The Arroyo Holon was later designated as the southern boundary of Samuel Cooper's 1840 Rancho Punta de Quentin. The name continues to appear today on city and county maps as the creek's official name, although it is more commonly called Larkspur Creek. The creek forms high on the eastern side of Mt. Tamalpais, cascades over Dawn Falls, and flows for nearly two miles next to Madrone Avenue, then parallel to Monte Vista Avenue, and finally past Meadowood to drain into the navigable Corte Madera Creek near Piper Park.

The Arroyo Holon is a seasonal creek, usually flowing by November or December, and drying completely by July. Although customarily placid, on occasion it turns into a turbulent, churning torrent. A 1925 storm saw floodwaters flow over the bridge at Magnolia Avenue. In January of 1982, when more than eight inches of rain fell in a 24-hour period following a week of rain, landslides cascaded down the Canyon hillsides and fallen trees dammed the creek. Once again the creek's waters covered the concrete bridge at Magnolia Avenue, flowed through the adjacent park, and swamped the smaller bridges upstream at Bridge Road and downstream at King Street.

▲ *3.4 & 3.5: The Arroyo Holon is quite capable of overflowing the bridge at Magnolia Avenue; these photographs show the floods of February, 1925 (looking north) and January, 1982 (looking south).*

↪ *The route turns left, westward, from Magnolia along Madrone Avenue.*

② First Block of Madrone Avenue

Shown on early maps as "Madrona" Avenue, the name of this street quickly changed to Madrone to match the popular spelling of that native tree. Dolliver Park straddles both sides of Madrone Avenue at its intersection with Magnolia Avenue. The portion north of Madrone Avenue was the gift of Ellen Dolliver Jewell to the City of Larkspur in 1922. Ellen was the oldest daughter of Ann and Thomas Dolliver, whose family had acquired a large tract from the American Land and Trust Company in April of 1888 *(see page 106)*. Ellen's deed restrictions specified that "no building be erected … that the redwoods be preserved and that the grounds be used for recreational purposes of the people of Larkspur." Three decades later the land south of Madrone Avenue was deeded to the city by Mr. and Mrs. C. S. Burtchaell in 1956, and named in memory of his grandmother, Ann C. Dolliver. Generations of children have dubbed this "Shady Park" or "Dark Park" because its wide creek bed and large bay laurel trees provide an ideal retreat on a hot summer day.

Drivers entering the Canyon for the first time must learn to avoid the redwood trees growing in the roadbed. When Madrone Avenue was paved in 1913, about forty redwood trees were enclosed by the pavement in the block between Magnolia Avenue and Onyx Street. Although concrete and asphalt are hardly their preferred growth medium, the trees persist, often to the dismay of impatient motorists who are forced to pull aside and allow others to pass through the narrow confines. Over the last century the trees and automobiles seem to have struck an uneasy truce regarding their respective claims to the road, but it wasn't always so.

Larkspur-born Bob Collin recalled that in the early 1930s a group of "self-appointed traffic safety experts" began to lobby for the trees' removal. He clearly remembered a meeting held by the indomitable Belle Brown, Bob's grandmother Marie C. Fleming, Angie Nicholson (the police chief's wife), and other stalwarts of the Larkspur Women's Improvement Club. Belle proclaimed that they would do "whatever is necessary" to prevent

▲ *3.6: The 41 Madrone Avenue summer home of Julius and Pauline Jaegeling, as it appeared about 1913.*

removal of the trees, a declaration that apparently ended the matter.

For many years the neighborhood's attitude toward the trees was reflected by a sign stating "CAUTION TREE CROSSING" that was tacked onto one of the redwoods at the entrance to the Canyon. However, in July of 1961, 39 signatures were presented on a petition to the City Council requesting the removal of fifteen redwoods, allegedly a hazard to motorists. At the Council's next meeting a standing-room-only crowd of Canyon residents appeared, all in favor of "letting these beautiful trees stand." The Council agreed, and the trees have remained ever since.

Just west of the park is the Jaegeling home at **41 MADRONE AVENUE**, a two-story summer home built by Dr. Julius P. Jaegeling, a San Francisco dentist, and his wife Pauline "Lena" about 1908. The land had been acquired by the Jaegelings from Mary and Belle Brown in 1908, and might have been used previously by the Browns as the site of their stable. (An ancient barn once stood on the adjacent lot at 39 Madrone, until it was removed in 1929. A notch in the concrete curb on Madrone reveals the barn's location.) In 1911 the Jaegelings acquired an adjoining lot that faces West Baltimore Avenue to the south, thus creating a single yard that spanned the Arroyo Holon.

The shingled house has double-hung windows with nine-pane windows in the upper sash. A picture of this house was featured in the 1913 Larkspur Booster Day pamphlet. The Jaegelings made various additions over the years, including a kitchen at the rear that was flooded by the creek on several occasions. Pauline Jaegeling died in 1946, and Julius in 1952. Dr. Jaegeling's second wife and widow, Emma Rose, sold the house in 1954 to former city councilman Robert Lee and his popular wife Bette,

▲ 3.7: *The Arroyo Holon provided entertainment for ducks and a pony in the Jaegelings' back yard, about 1912.*

who lived there until the mid 1980s. In 1960, a two-story wing was added to the original house, with a living room downstairs and a bedroom and bathroom upstairs. More extensive renovations and additions followed in recent decades, including a large garage erected in the front yard in 1995. The oldest of the Jaegelings' three sons, Thurlow, also became a dentist and prominent citizen of Larkspur, with a home at 125 Magnolia Avenue.

The landmark house at **47 MADRONE AVENUE**, known as "The Redwoods," is probably the oldest in the Canyon. Built in the early 1880s, it was the final family home of R.S. and Helen Brown, Baltimore Canyon's first permanent settlers. The Brown family occupied a central position in Larkspur and Marin history.

The lands surrounding the Browns' homesite stretched from Magnolia Avenue nearly up to Bridge Road, and once encompassed at least five buildings, a water tower, and several entry lanes; some of their structures apparently dated back to the 1850s operation of the nearby Baltimore sawmill. The

▲ 3.8: *The house at 47 Madrone Avenue, historically known as "The Redwoods," was home to the Brown family from the 1880s until 1925. It is probably the oldest house in the Canyon, 2008.*

THE PIONEER BROWN FAMILY

Richard Samuel Brown and his wife Helen "Ellen" owned (or at least claimed) most of the land south of Arroyo Holon. The Browns arrived in Larkspur in the early 1850s, when Samuel started work as an engineer for the Baltimore Company's sawmill. Samuel was English, born near Liverpool in 1815; his wife was born Helen Murphy in Athlone Parish, in Ireland's County Roscommon, about 1827. Although Samuel and Helen arrived in Marin separately, Helen probably came here with her younger sister, Ann Murphy, who married Jonathan Bickerstaff, and raised a family in the large adobe house that overlooked the salt marshes near today's downtown Larkspur. Mrs. Winifred Tierney, who with her husband had settled a large tract of land around today's old town Corte Madera, was a third Murphy sister. Samuel and Helen died at home two days apart, in January of 1892.

The Browns had four children: Alice, William, Mary, and Isabella. Only Mary (born circa 1859) and "Belle" (born circa 1863) survived to adulthood; Mary was quiet and reserved, but the industrious Belle played a major role in Larkspur's history. Mary died in 1926, after an arduous automobile trip with her sister, and Belle followed in 1940, eulogized as "Larkspur's most beloved pioneer resident, admired and respected throughout the entire county." Belle had started her career as an elementary teacher, served as Larkspur's city clerk from 1918 to 1928, and then served until the time of her death as city treasurer. She was a founder and mainstay of the Larkspur Woman's Improvement Club, and a founder and first president of the Marin County Historical Society.

After completing his work at the sawmill, Samuel turned to farming; he owned a 40-acre tract that included much of today's Meadowood area, as well as 160 acres of Baltimore Canyon and the flat lands of today's Baltimore Park. Samuel and his two brothers-in-law, Jonathan Bickerstaff and M. Tierney, also tried prospecting; they made a variety of mining claims in the local hills in the 1850s–1860s, but nothing came of them.

The Brown family eventually built and occupied a succession of homes, most of them located near the Sausalito-San Rafael county road that later became Magnolia Avenue. Beset by land title problems, in August of 1880 the Browns purchased 4½ acres to the north of Arroyo Holon from Patrick King, thus acquiring indisputable ownership of their permanent homesite. Mary and Belle managed to retain that land, and later speculated by buying and selling additional tracts throughout the area. For many years, they rented some of their several buildings to summer visitors and took in full-time boarders.

▲ 3.9: *Canyon matriarch Belle C. Brown, shown in an undated photograph.*

adjacent houses currently at 53 and 55 Madrone once were part of the immediate compound, and in later years were used by the Browns as summer rentals. A line of tall poplar trees, prominent in turn-of-the-century photographs, marked the southern edge of the Browns' lands. Prone to rot, fallen branches, and invasive roots, most of those trees have been removed, but a few remnants persist along the creek bed near West Baltimore Avenue.

The Browns' graceful old two-story house at 47 Madrone has retained much of its early appearance, with relatively few alterations. The drop siding used on the original portion was extended to each of the several additions to the kitchen wing on the west end. According to Aida Burke, who was a close friend of Belle Brown and whose father once had rented a room in the Brown home, the home's first kitchen was constructed on the large stump of a redwood tree. A cross-gabled roof with shed dormer drops down to incorporate the front porch. Many of the double-hung windows still contain old glass. At some time, perhaps in the 1950s, the porch was altered to include flagstone paving and a hooded brick façade on the foundation, which occurs also on the related structure at 55 Madrone.

▲ 3.10: *This north-facing photograph, taken sometime between 1901 and 1906, shows a broad meadow between today's Piedmont Road and West Baltimore Avenue. The visiting military unit, with round Sibley tents and field guns, has not been identified. All of the houses shown here still exist; on the left margin the Dolliver-Shula house on Onyx Street is visible through the trees, and at the top of the photo the Craner house sits on a knoll at 55 Walnut Avenue. The Brown house is at the center, with its prominent windmill and water tower. Nearby, a tiny portion of the Dolliver roof protrudes through the trees. Tall poplar trees wend along the creek bed, and the landmark oak tree stands barren of leaves at right. Beyond the oak, the Gardiner house is surrounded by a white wooden fence.*

A tall water tank tower and windmill served the several buildings that were part of the Brown compound. That tower was located to the southwest of this building, close to the small house that is now 53 Madrone. Another dwelling was located due south of the main house, approximately where a swimming pool is located today. That house had the benefit of a 5-foot easement over a footpath that connected to West Baltimore Avenue.

"The Redwoods, the residence of the Misses Brown, at the entrance to the canyon of the Arroyo Holon, is a remarkably picturesque place. The rustic idea is carried throughout in walks, bridges, etc."
— *The Sausalito News*, Jan. 30, 1897

After the deaths of their parents in 1892, sisters Mary and Belle Brown continued to live here in The Redwoods, although they reportedly would move to one of the smaller buildings near the creek when an opportunity arose to rent out the larger house. In 1925 the sisters sold the family home to Dr. Lester and Emma Newman for $5,750, then moved into their adjacent house at 55 Madrone. After his wife's death, Dr. Newman reluctantly sold the house in 1948, and it passed in 1965 to the present owners, Barbara and Norman Beal, making the Beals the longest-term residents of the house.

Despite its address, the home at **53 MADRONE AVENUE** no longer has a Madrone entrance but instead faces the unnamed private alley that branches from Bridge Road. The address reveals that this house once was another part of the Brown family compound. Originally served by an entry lane, the house had an access path that led from Madrone adjacent to the house at 55; it now can be reached only by the alley at the rear.

From 1947 until 1991 this was the home of Harry and Margaret Richards, who had been childhood friends in Corte Madera. Harry, who trained as an engineer, did extensive remodeling and expansion of the house during the late 1940s and early 1950s, often working late into the night. He recalls that the house had a very simple redwood 4 x 4 frame, with single walls of 1 x 12 redwood planks and battens. He gradually added modern plumbing, concrete foundations, and additional rooms. After the Richards family acquired the home, new fences on the adjacent lots prevented direct access to Madrone

▲ 3.11: 53 Madrone Avenue, the home of Harry and Margaret Richards, whose two sons are shown here in the early 1950s after the Richards completed their remodeling. The house originally may have been an adjunct to the nearby sawmill. It has since been expanded to cover the lawn shown here.

▲ 3.12: The home at 55 Madrone Avenue originally was part of the Brown family compound, and from 1925 until 1940 the residence of the Brown sisters, 2008.

Avenue, and Margaret had to walk to civilization by using the alley to Foley Lane, and then along Madrone towards town.

The shingled home at **55 MADRONE AVENUE**, built well before 1908, was a part of the larger Brown family compound, as indicated by the land's irregular eastern boundary that snakes between large redwood trees and the other Brown houses at 47 and 53 Madrone. The house originally had redwood siding and a cross-gabled roof. It was remodeled substantially in 2001, keeping only some of the original lines.

The original role this house served in the Brown family is unclear, but Mary and Belle Brown moved here in 1925 after they sold the family home at 47 Madrone. The sisters often would hold an open house at their home on Sunday evenings when they served biscuits, jelly, and tea. They traveled to Europe and Asia in 1915, a rare adventure for single ladies of that time. After Belle's death in 1940, the house passed to Robert and Geraldine Bowen, who lived here for another two decades.

The house at **59 MADRONE AVENUE** was probably built about 1931, on land that had long been a part of the Brown family compound. The long and narrow shape of the lot reflects its earlier use as an entrance drive that led from Madrone Avenue to the rear of numbers 47 and 55 Madrone, and provided access to the smaller house at 53 Madrone.

The home of Ann and Thomas Dolliver at **58 MADRONE AVENUE**, built in 1888, is listed in the National Register of Historic Places, as well as being a city and state landmark. This California Stick, Eastlake-style, home still has essentially the same footprint and appearance as when it was first constructed. The three-story house has a high gabled roof and a wide, double veranda with a hipped roof supported by 6 x 6 posts which are aligned through both stories. A dining room on the uphill side was added between 1910 and 1920, as was a bath that was tucked under the upper veranda space at the opposite end of the house.

The lower portion of the house is covered with redwood beveled-drop siding, while 2 x 6 redwood vertical trim caps the corners. The front gable has been shingled with a staggered, square butt pattern, while the small shed-roof addition on the east is covered with fishscale shingles. The peak and tips of the eaves are trimmed with bull's-eyes and decorative wood strips.

The house is typical of the simpler, utilitarian type of structures that were built as summer homes by upper-middle class San Franciscans in the late nineteenth century. The house appears to have been Ann's enterprise entirely; on April 2, 1888, she bought the first lots sold in Larkspur by the American Land and Trust Co., acquiring the entire block on the north side of Madrone Avenue to the east of Onyx Street. This house purportedly was the first one built in Larkspur by designer/builder Gustave Nagel.

Thomas Richardson Dolliver was a shoemaker, living in Lowell, Massachusetts, with his English-born wife Ann and their three children, when he decided to join the California Gold Rush. He walked from St. Louis cross-country in four months, apparently did some mining in the Sierra, and was joined by his family in San Francisco sometime before 1860. By 1875 Thomas was the proprietor of a new firm, Dolliver & Brother, with his younger brother Samuel R. Dolliver, and joined by his daughter Sarah's husband, Albert R. Church. The firm became a major importer and supplier of shoe manufacturing materials, surviving into the 1930s. The Dollivers, now prosperous, were able to maintain a large permanent home at 2201 Fillmore Street in San Francisco. Their youngest daughter, Clara, married Samuel W. Burtchaell in 1891, thus joining a prominent Marin County family that owned several grocery stores in San Rafael, Larkspur, and Mill Valley, as well as the notable home at 105 King Street. In later years, members

▲ 3.13: *The Dolliver house at 58 Madrone Avenue in about 1889, looking east. Ann Dolliver and her daughter Ellen are sitting on the upper veranda, daughter Clara Dolliver Burtchaell is on the steps, son Sewall Dolliver is standing on bank, and young Bert Church (Ann's grandson) is sitting mid-bank. The picket fence was still under construction. In modern times the house must be viewed from the south (the side to the right in the photograph).*

▲ 3.14: *The 1888 Dolliver house as it appears in 2010, seen on its south face.*

▲ *3.15: The circa-1903 Blair house at 63 Madrone Avenue has been meticulously maintained to retain its original street appearance, 2008.*

▲ *3.16: The small cottage at 69 Madrone Avenue dates to the early 1900s and shares architectural features with its neighbor at 63 Madrone Avenue, 2008.*

of the family bought additional lands nearby, as described in the Onyx Street materials below.

The one-and-one-half-story house at **63 MADRONE AVENUE**, known as "Blair" house, was probably built about 1903 and has been maintained in excellent condition by Roger and Rebecca Archey, the current owners. It was yet another part of the extensive Brown holdings, although it was not sold as a separate lot until 1921 when it was purchased by Louis and Helen Blair, who apparently had been tenants there for many years previously. The house probably had been built much earlier for Belle Brown's use as a rental property, perhaps at the same time as the very-similar adjacent house at 69 Madrone.

The house has a front gable decorated with fishscale and diamond shingles, a boxed cornice, and an unusual curved projection above the double windows, edged with sawtooth-notched shingles. The windows have delicate diamond-shaped muntins on the top sash. The current owners made additions at the rear in July of 1975, but with great attention to detail and minimum impact to the front of the house; they extended the central ridge line further south about 15 feet, changing the kitchen layout. The garage, located on the back alley, was demolished and rebuilt in 1991.

Louis Blair had a sign painting business in San Rafael, and his billboards appeared at many places in the county. His wife Helen was the sister of Rena Hanna, who owned several houses further up Madrone Avenue. The Blairs, married in Ross in 1913, raised their three children in the house; Helen died in 1940, but Louis remained in the house until shortly before its sale to the Archeys in 1972. Louis died in Corte Madera in 1975, at age 91. A copper plaque with the Blair name still remains on the front porch of one of the best-preserved houses in the Canyon.

The adjacent home at **69 MADRONE AVENUE** originally had a T-shaped floor plan and a porch that wrapped around three sides of the house; much of that porch space has long since been enclosed. The interior consisted of a long living room in front and three little rooms in the rear; additional rooms were added on the second level. The front gable, with fishscale and diamond shingles and curved projection above the double windows, precisely mirrors the similar details of the adjoining home at 63 Madrone Avenue. The same builder may have erected both houses.

This lot originally was another part of the larger Brown family holdings, and was first created on May 7, 1901, in a deed from the Brown sisters to Mary Amelia Martin of San Francisco. In 1923 Miss Martin sold the house and land to Emily Shine, who with her husband Jeremiah, lived in the home until about 1949. Jerry Shine was a blacksmith, first for the water company (where he also worked as a caretaker at Phoenix Lake), and later for PG & E; Emily was for many years the cook at the Larkspur-Corte Madera School's cafeteria. Emily's sister, Marie C. Fleming, lived further up the Canyon at 20 Olive. The Shines' daughter, Mabel Pimm, was a well-known local telephone operator who lived here with her parents during the 1920s.

⊃ *A short detour from Madrone Avenue proceeds uphill on Onyx Street, then returns.*

▲ 3.17: *An undated photograph of the Dollivers engaged in summertime croquet in a sun-dappled portion of The Grove.*

▲ 3.18: *Three homes on Onyx Street share similar histories and 1920s-period features, 2010.*

③ Onyx Street

The entire eastern side of Onyx Street was part of the original Dolliver parcel, acquired in 1888. The Dollivers' son-in-law, Albert Church, purchased four lots across the street that formed the western corner of Madrone and Onyx in October of 1888. Nine months later, in July of 1889, the Dollivers' son Sewall purchased the adjoining land on the upper west side of Onyx. Most of the Onyx area thus became an extension of the Dolliver family's summer retreat, and was known as "The Grove." The extended Dolliver family used the area for summer recreation.

The energetic Gustave Nagel purportedly built the three houses at **12/14, 16,** and **22 ONYX STREET** in the early 1920s. They share obvious elements of design and materials, and apparently all stemmed from a single speculative development project. All three houses had open porches, like the one remaining at 22 (drainage scuppers from the earlier porches remain visible on numbers 16 and 12). They also share identical three-lap siding on the upper stories, v-channel siding on the lower portions, and rectangular design details on the concrete foundations.

The Dollivers' daughter Ellen had succeeded her parents in management of the family properties, and late in life married a San Rafael man named William H. Jewell. Although William Jewell reportedly had a role in developing these homes, he died in 1920, too early to have had much impact. When Ellen died in 1924, her brother Sewall Dolliver took over as administrator of her estate; he formally subdivided the lots and sold the houses. The deeds for the houses range from 1924 to 1927, although all three homes appeared on an insurance adjustor's map of August 1924, and may have been built even earlier.

The tiny private road called Onyx Court, which leaves Onyx Street and curves up the hill to the west, provides access to a variety of homes that were squeezed into the original lot arrangement by re-subdivider Charles C. "Charlie" Dodge in 1912. Dodge halved two large lots facing Onyx, then split off the rear of each of them, creating eight lots in all; three of those were given new frontage on Onyx Court, becoming numbers 23, 25, and 27. In 1913, Dodge further split a group of lots that faced Madrone, creating nine lots in the process. The new road thus provided rear vehicular access to numbers 88, 94, and 96A, 96B, and 96C Madrone (more recently, a driveway uphill to 10 Hazel has been added). Dodge's two subdivisions provide woeful examples of poor lot design, applied with little regard to concerns of traffic or provision of utilities and services.

The Dollivers' son Sewall purchased a pair of adjoining lots on Onyx Street in July of 1889. Those lots, both facing Onyx, were unusually large, designed to accommodate an established grove of large redwood trees that precluded building on much of the land. It was Sewall who commissioned the construction of the elaborate landmark house at **17 ONYX STREET**, probably in 1893. However, Sewall married in 1894 and held his land only until March of 1895, when he sold the house and the lots to Anton ("Tony") Shula and his wife Alice; the area thereafter became known as "Shula's Grove." A series of additions were made to the 17 Onyx house over the years, including the shed-roofed addition on the north side and the two-story column on

▲ 3.19: *Sewall Dolliver built the house at 17 Onyx Street about 1893; from 1895 until about 1912 it was owned and occupied by the Anton Shula family, 2010.*

the south side. The current owners have made extensive modifications.

The houses at 21 and 29 Onyx Street occupy the remainder of the Sewall Dolliver's original large lots. A long-gone house at 19 Onyx is now evidenced only by a drive cut in the curb in front of the 1973 house at 21 Onyx. The 29 Onyx house, which may date as early as 1910, is remembered by neighbors as having been a tiny shack with its porch encircling a huge tree; that house was completely rebuilt in 2006.

Anton Shula operated a successful cigar and tobacco store at 100 Market Street in San Francisco in the 1890s and early 1900s; he would have been about age 35 when he purchased this handsome house and its grove. A few years later, in July of 1899, Shula added to his holdings by purchasing the land fronting Madrone Avenue from the Dollivers' daughter Sarah J. Church (by then a young widow). The Shulas thus held the entire lower portion of west-side Onyx Street and the adjoining lots on Madrone Avenue. Some of their extensive land may have been used as tent platform sites for summer campers. The Shulas remained here for another decade, but divorced and left the area about 1912, sometime after the death of their son. Anton then returned to San Francisco, where he remarried.

The homes at **1, 11,** and **15 ONYX STREET** are on the site of Shula's Bowling Alley. A detailed map of 1909 shows the bowling alley here, with an adjacent building labeled "billiards and soft drinks." Both buildings were managed by Anton Shula, who reported his occupation on the 1910 Census as "owner, bowling alley." The building was used extensively for dancing as well as bowling; the Dollivers' daughter, Clare Burtchaell, recalled (apparently with good cause) that the flimsy wooden building was "a great noisemaker." In later years it became something of a community center; on Friday, August 2, 1907, it was the site of "the mass meeting for the purpose of discussing the proposition of incorporating our town," and it was used for organizational meetings of the Larkspur Woman's Improvement Club in 1911.

The bowling alley was merely a part of the town's summer atmosphere. As early Canyon resident Helen Wilson said in 1975, "From the beginning Larkspur was a sporting town. People came here to enjoy themselves and the out-of-doors. There were the bowling alley at the corner of Madrone and Onyx ... dog races up Madrone as far as Jones Way, and the camp sites in the canyon."

THE BOWLING ALLEY

"The Sausalito bowling team spent Sunday afternoon at Shula's bowling alley."

– *The Marin County Tocsin,*
Feb. 20, 1909

▲ 3.20: *Anton Shula's bowling alley at the northwest corner of Madrone Avenue and Onyx Street, as it appeared sometime before the 1913 paving of Madrone Avenue.*

When was the bowling alley built? Although some neighbors assumed that Anton Shula had erected it, the simple style of the structure suggests it must have had a much earlier origin. Could it have been the pioneer "ten pin alley" described as "near the steam sawmill" in an 1852 deed? Whatever its origin, the building disappeared about 1913, when Charles C. Dodge acquired the land from the Shulas and re-subdivided the four lots facing Madrone into nine smaller lots.

After the bowling alley was razed, local builder William F. Wegner built the houses at 1, 11, and 15 Onyx Street in the early 1920s. Each has been substantially revised, with 11 being essentially rebuilt, but with period-appropriate design. Local tradition holds that a large set of windows on the west side of the house at 1 Onyx were recycled from one of Larkspur's early post offices on Magnolia.

⊃ *Return to Madrone Avenue. The sidewalk on Madrone Avenue's north side rises steeply away from the street, and is best walked separately; the southern sidewalk remains flat. Houses are discussed below in the order they actually occur while moving west, as the street address sequence is often inconsistent.*

④ Madrone Between Onyx Street & Orange Avenue

The houses at 68, 74, 82, and 84 Madrone Avenue were all parts of Charles Dodge's 1913 re-subdivision; their lots vary in size and shape. The distinctive hipped-roof house with two prominent hipped dormers, at **68 MADRONE AVENUE**, is located on the four lots originally acquired by Albert and Sarah Church in 1888. Sarah was one of the Dolliver daughters, and it is likely that Sarah and her husband Albert built this house in the early 1890s. Sarah, however, was suddenly widowed and sold the land to Anton and Alice Shula in 1899; Charles Dodge later acquired it in 1913. Dodge re-subdivided the land and allowed his new daughter-in-law, Mrs. Courtland Dodge, to live in this house as a bride before she moved to a new home nearby at 82 Madrone Avenue.

A large pair of double-hung windows faces Madrone Avenue, capped with an elaborate cornice. Broad front steps originally descended the Onyx Street side of the house, facing the bowling alley; the entry stairs now lead to Madrone, passing through

▲ *3.21: The circa-1890 home at 68 Madrone Avenue, probably built by Sarah and Albert Church. It has retained many aspects of its original street-side appearance, 2008.*

a flush-grouted blue rock retaining wall. The garage beneath the house was added in the 1950s. The building received substantial upgrading in 2008, when the original exterior porch was partially enclosed on the northeast side, and many interior changes occurred.

Although built in 1922 for Courtland and Lillian Murray Dodge, the two-story shingled bungalow at **82 MADRONE AVENUE** (on the hillside walkway) has retained little of its original appearance. Renovations in the 1990s removed an entrance gable from the east side, creating a new entry at the southwest corner. Courtland Dodge worked as a superintendent at a sugar refinery. His wife, Lillian Murray Dodge, was the granddaughter of William and Maria Murray, who once owned the entire northern section of today's Larkspur. Lillian's childhood home was located further uphill at 10 Hazel Avenue. After Lillian and Courtland divorced, she worked in real estate and lived in the house until the late 1970s when she could no longer climb the stairs. She died in 1984 at age 90.

The small stucco bungalow at **83 MADRONE AVENUE** dates to 1924, when Charles and Minnie Coburn became its first owners. The northeast corner of this lot (at the fencepost by the sidewalk) marks the precise point where the boundary line of Rancho Punta de Quentin first meets Madrone Avenue. To the north of that boundary were the lands developed by the American Land and Trust Co. (including much of the Canyon and downtown portions of Larkspur). To the south of the line was land derived from John Reed's Rancho Corte Madera Del Presidio, and eventually developed by representatives of the Coleman and Forbes estates.

▲ 3.22: *A 1924 stucco bungalow at 83 Madrone Avenue marks the edge of the Baltimore Park subdivision, 2008.*

This was Lot Number 10 of the ninety lots that had been laid out as Baltimore Park Subdivision Two. The modest houses from here to 109 Madrone were all part of that subdivision. *(See pages 143-146 and 165 for the full story of the subdivision.)*

This small structure is an excellent example of the modest bungalows of the mid 1920s, with a living area of only 978 square feet. Although earlier bungalows were usually shingled, stucco became popular as a practical and stylish exterior for houses built after the mid-1920s, as prominently displayed a few blocks away on Monte Vista Avenue. Two small windows flank the brick chimney, another signature design of the period. The board-and-batten extension at the rear of the house was originally an open porch, but was later altered to become a bedroom. An unusual garage at the rear conforms to the odd angles of the lot; it is one of the few structures remaining in Larkspur that has concrete channels to guide an automobile's tires through the doors.

The Coburns' daughter, Pearl Leftwich, succeeded them as owners, and in 1953 sold the house to Frieda Kates. The present owner is Frieda's daughter, Amelia De Mello, and her husband Albert.

For three decades the modest little house at **87 MADRONE AVENUE** was the home of Charles and Balbina Brady; they acquired it in 1953, while Charles operated the Larkspur Cabinet Shop downtown in the old freight depot. Mrs. Brady continued to live here until her death in 1984. Prior to the Bradys, Bierfeldt A. Fedde, a German-born secretary of a building and loan association in San Francisco, had owned the home and the adjacent lots to the west since the 1930s. The house is covered in simple v-channel siding and has a minimum of

FOLEY LANE

Little Foley Lane — a street only 82 feet long — was an afterthought. When Baltimore Park Subdivision Two was created in 1913, Bridge Road was the only connection between Baltimore and "Madrona" Avenues, meandering along parallel to both Madrone Avenue and the creek bed for more than 400 feet. Finally, at the City's request in 1922, the subdividers agreed to deed a 20-foot-wide portion of their Lot 10 to the city as a new street, and what remained of Lot 10 later became the site for the small house at 83 Madrone. The curbs were changed, and the "extension" was paved to a width of 14 feet, in November of 1922, at a cost of $365. Once complete, the City Council designated the new road as "Foley Lane, in memory of ... John T. Foley, who as a member of the first Board of Trustees of the Town of Larkspur and Trustee almost uninterruptedly till his death, worked untiringly for the best interests of Larkspur." Foley had died in August of 1920; read more about him on page 135.

Foley Lane connects to Bridge road; the several small houses located there were all developed as part of the Baltimore Park Subdivision Two. Although some of those structures date as early as 1911, most were built in the mid-1920s and early 1930s.

▲ 3.23: *Best-known as the Brady home, the little summer cottage at 87 Madrone Avenue probably was built in the early 1920s, 2008.*

BRIDGE ROAD

The intersection of Madrone Avenue with Bridge Road marks an early entrance to the Canyon. The road is named for the bridge that crosses the Arroyo Holon (Larkspur Creek) several hundred yards down-Canyon, described in greater detail in the Baltimore Park chapter. That bridge connected to an older route that joined Magnolia Avenue as early as the 1870s. Much of the land in this area served as campgrounds before its general development in the 1920s.

BETA STREET

One of Larkspur's many paper streets is represented at **110 MADRONE AVENUE** by a broad concrete stairway that rises twenty feet from the roadway to the nearby sidewalk. Beta Street is shown on the original 1887 subdivision map as continuing from Madrone Avenue further up the hillside, connecting to the loop formed by Laurel and Hazel Avenues, but only this concrete portion was built. Here, as elsewhere in town, a four-letter street name (not the name of a tree), apparently was used for those routes that connect major loop roads, and often were designed for foot, rather than vehicular, traffic. (*See Appendix C.*)

ornamentation; it thus appears to have been used for most of its years as a simple summer retreat. Two tall Norway spruce trees in this yard date from the early days of the house.

A small building on the rear of the lot, at **16 BRIDGE ROAD**, reportedly was a former tent platform that had been converted into a tiny house by Charles Brady. For many years this remnant of the Canyon's camping days served as an authentic reminder of another way of life; however, it was smashed nearly to oblivion by a collapsed bay laurel tree, and has since been substantially rebuilt – it even has a concrete foundation.

▲ *3.24: This house, seen in 2008 high above the street at 88 Madrone Avenue, probably was built about 1905.*

Back on the hillside walkway, the steep-roof house at **88 MADRONE AVENUE**, high above the street and barely visible, retains its original narrow three-lap siding. The front porch facing Madrone Avenue has four square posts, with two windows above it in the front gable. Four rooms and most of the downstairs were added in the 1920s. The house is now linked with an adjoining landlocked parcel and receives its primary access from Onyx Court.

Katherine Martin, the wife of Larkspur real estate agent William Martin, originally purchased this lot and the adjoining one at 94 Madrone in May of 1899. This modest structure may have been built about 1905. From the 1920s to the early 1970s this was the home of the Charles and Grace Schneider family. Mr. Schneider, a switch tower operator for the NWP railroad, was a tall and gaunt man who ran for the city council several times.

The two-and-one-half-story house at **94 MADRONE AVENUE** probably dates to 1899 and has retained many of its internal features. Elaborate plastered ceilings and ornate baseboards occur throughout the house, and the main fireplace has delicate beveled bricks with turned wooden uprights, finished in a dark varnish. The double-hung windows on the second floor are symmetrically placed above the front entry door below. As with its neighbors, vehicle access is available from Onyx Court at the rear.

Katherine Martin purchased this lot in 1899; it probably was the Martins who built the house, as the Census of 1900 recorded them as living in this immediate area with two nieces and a sister-in-law. However, by October of 1904 Katherine had remarried and conveyed the house to Larkspur's Frank Craig. In the early 1970s the home's architectural character was further altered when shingles were applied over the original siding.

The large parcel on the hillside walkway comprising **96A, 96B, AND 96C MADRONE AVENUE** originally was Lots 15-17 of the American Trust Co.'s Larkspur subdivision. Three houses are located here, all with vehicular access made possible by Onyx Court, a small private lane on the hillside to the rear. The older shingle-covered unit 96A, adjacent to the Madrone Avenue sidewalk, has multipane windows of a former sleeping porch facing the street. The other two structures are located higher on the hill to take advantage of views of Mt. Tamalpais, and may be reached by ascending a winding hillside stairway, or by descending from Onyx Court.

The 96B house has three-lap siding and flat casings, but its age is difficult to determine; 96C is a small and shingled structure reportedly built about 1935. All of the houses have operated as rental properties for many years, including a stint for one of the structures as a hippie commune in the 1960s.

The modest hipped-roof house at **105 MADRONE AVENUE** was built about 1918, probably for Edward and Mary Henderson, who lived there through the mid-1950s. Little changed in the front, it

▲ 3.26: 105 Madrone Avenue, one of the several Baltimore Park Subdivision homes that was built in the period 1915-1925 on Madrone Avenue, 2008.

has extensive additions at the rear, and was covered decades ago with asbestos shingles.

The western-most of the several Baltimore Park homes on Madrone Avenue is **109 MADRONE AVENUE**. The land was purchased originally in 1924 by Bridget and Patrick Kilcoyne, both immigrants from Ireland, who built this house the same year. The structure originally was covered in horizontal three-lap siding, and had an open porch on the northeast corner. The Kilcoynes had raised three daughters in San Francisco, where Patrick worked as a stevedore, then moved to Larkspur as their permanent home. Not long after Patrick's death in 1943, the house was acquired by Martin and Ellen Rosell, who remodeled it in 1953 to essentially its present appearance, installing the vertical board-and-batten exterior and enclosing the porch.

The house at **118 MADRONE AVENUE**, probably built in the early 1900s, has a porch on two sides

▲ 3.25: The house at 96B Madrone Avenue, set high on the hill adjacent to Onyx Court, 2008.

▲ 3.27: Major Martin Rosell in the front yard of his home at 109 Madrone Avenue in about 1946. Fresh sidewalk cement encloses a redwood tree still there today.

▲ 3.28: *The blue rock retaining wall below 118 and 124 Madrone Avenue, one of several masonry relicts of old Larkspur, 2009.*

▲ 3.29: *The Sheehan family's tidy little summer cottage at 123 Madrone Avenue probably dates to about 1917, 2009.*

and an unusual dormer in the gable peak that was added in the 1970s. Originally there were iron gates in the stone pillars leading up to the house. This lot was first sold to Grace and Franklin Heydenfeldt in February of 1900, and the house was occupied by them the same year. Franklin was an accountant; he and Grace raised four daughters here for about a decade. The Heydenfeldts had purchased other lots nearby in the same year.

William Deane was an Irish immigrant who worked as a land appraiser for a railroad, and dabbled in speculative land development. By January of 1920 he, with his wife Anna and their five children, had acquired this home and remained through the 1930s. In a 1974 interview, their son William Deane said that his family had added the large three-story tower on the front, as well as a kitchen and sun porch in the rear. In recent decades owners named Dean are unrelated to the earlier Deane family.

The Deanes' holdings eventually included several nearby houses. About 1915 they built the adjacent house at 124 Madrone Avenue, probably building the long stone retaining wall in front of both 118 Madrone and the yard at 124 Madrone at about the same time. The wall, made of local blue rock, has the same distinctive sculptured grouting (a "grapevine" pattern) as was used on much of the blue rock masonry of the period; that wall is listed as an element of Larkspur's *Historic Resources Inventory*.

The James W. Sheehan family owned the little cottage overlooking the creek at **123 MADRONE AVENUE** in the 1920s, using it as a summer retreat, and eventually passing it to daughter Maude M. Vizzard in 1949. Shortly after that, Maude (by now a widow) and her nearly grown children became year-round residents. When Maude died in 1967, the cottage passed through an intermediate owner, and to its current owner in 1974.

This is one of the least-altered classic Canyon summer cottages, probably built in 1917. Relatively small, at about 1330 square feet, it has benefited from the transformation of outdoor porches into enclosed space on the east and south sides. It has simple three-lap siding, a cross-gable roof, double-hung windows, and casings characteristic of modest structures of the period. The inviting front porch is set behind a low wall. More than twenty large redwoods are scattered across the grounds.

The hillside home at **124 MADRONE AVENUE** occupies two lots; the yard comprising the eastern part was deeded to Grace Heydenfeldt in 1901, and a 1905 deed for the main lot went to Sarah Foley, who served for a time as the Larkspur postmistress. Both lots were later acquired by William Deane (118 Madrone), who built this house about 1915 as a speculative venture. A hand-dug and brick-lined well, with metal water tower, is located at the rear of the yard, and served both 118 and 124. The shingled, hipped-roof house with overhanging gabled dormer was then rented out for a number of years. Its original front porch is now glassed in; a garage once occupied the ground floor.

Extending along one side of the house was a long living room paneled up to a plate rail with redwood, and a clinker brick fireplace at the rear. When water was piped in, the kitchen became a bathroom, and a large paneled kitchen was added at the back of the house. The lattice on the front of the house was salvaged from the demolished R.C. Doherty home on Magnolia Avenue in 1970.

According to neighbors, this was the home of one of the many local bootleggers during the 1920s; his still was located in a room behind the downstairs garage and had a separate entrance. The current small garage with three-lap siding was added later. Frances and Jack Holmes bought the house in 1950 and put up a traditional Canyon sign dubbing it "Holmestead." The house has remained in their family.

The house at **130 MADRONE AVENUE** has an obscure but colorful (and tragic) history. The 1900 Census shows Lizzie Marriott living in this immediate area with her husband, Andrew, and five children. We know little about them, but one story had it that Mr. Marriott, a day laborer, forgot to duck his head on exiting a stable, and died of a broken neck. His widow Elizabeth purchased this lot in January of 1906, and remained here at least through 1910. Neighbors say a man who wanted to duplicate his home in the Marina District of San Francisco remodeled the house in the 1940s with a Spanish-style stucco front. Unfortunately he spent only one night in the home after it was completed and died of a heart attack a day later.

In the late 1930s Vernon Thompson and his wife Ruth acquired the lot at 134 Madrone Avenue, reportedly moving a cottage to the rear of this site from West Baltimore Avenue. In later years they added the front portion of the house and developed a showplace garden and barbecue pit. The current owners added the gambrel-roofed garage facing Orange Avenue in the late 1980s, replacing the Thompsons' barbecue pit.

The streamside house at **143 MADRONE AVENUE** is squeezed onto a tiny parcel that was the result of confused land boundaries of the 1880s, altered further by later adjustments. It most probably was built about 1905 or 1906, using three-lap siding, a boxed cornice, and fishscale and diamond shingles on the street-side gable (features very similar to the homes at 63 and 69 Madrone Avenue, built in the same period). Known once as the "Honeymoon Cottage," the little structure has survived far longer than whatever marriage that name once celebrated.

This small house, with a living area of only 876 square feet, originally had four equal-sized rooms, and no bath. Like many older homes in the Canyon, external pipes reveal that indoor plumbing was added to the house long after its construction. The eastern veranda was added at a later date, and a portion of the south veranda was enclosed to make a bedroom, possibly when the bath was added at the southwest corner of the house.

The early history of the house revolves around Dr. George Cornet and his wife Fanny, both Russian immigrants who lived in San Francisco and acquired a deed for this site in 1909. George was a podiatrist who later traveled extensively to Siberia as the representative of a San Francisco machinery maker. He and Fanny were married about 1903, and might be the source of the "honeymoon" nomenclature. After intervening owners, the house was purchased in 1951 by Elizabeth and Patrick Glynn, and occupied until April of 2000 by their elderly daughter, Mrs. Alice Campe, who was fondly

▲ 3.30: *George and Fanny Cornet's "Honeymoon Cottage," built about 1905 at 143 Madrone Avenue, 2008.*

▲ 3.31: *The Rentschler home at the wide-open corner of Madrone and Orange Avenues (136 Madrone Avenue), as depicted in the 1909 Booster Day pamphlet. In later years the roadbed of Madrone Avenue was altered to a lower grade.*

remembered by neighbors. A new owner in 2007 began the necessary process of structural upgrades.

Located essentially in the bed of the creek, the lot at **147 MADRONE AVENUE** was first acquired in January of 1912 by Rena B. Hanna, her sister Helen, and their elderly uncle. The lot's unusual shape, with only 12 feet of frontage on Madrone, dictated that a narrow path lead from the street down and across the creek to the house. Shortly after their purchase, Helen married Louis Blair, and raised a family nearby at 63 Madrone. Rena, a tall, gaunt woman with henna-colored hair, had wanted to build a house directly on the street between 151 and 143 Madrone Avenue, but the city would not allow it. Instead she built this house sometime before 1930 with foot access via a bridge. In 1955, she built a large addition to the original bungalow.

The Brown sisters sold the land at **151 MADRONE AVENUE** in April of 1908 to George Hogan, who probably built the house and then sold it to the Hannah sisters, Rena and Helen, who acquired it in 1910 (and who later acquired the neighboring lot at 147 Madrone). Originally a small, brown-shingle bungalow, this home once had a square-pillared veranda across the front. After holding the lot for 35 years, Rena slightly revised the lot boundaries and sold the property to George and Gertrude Kelley in 1946. From that time until 1973, this was the site of the "Kelley Piano Studio," with a baby grand piano that nearly filled the small living room. Gertrude Kelley, known as "Betty," taught piano here to support herself and her husband George. Betty is fondly remembered as a vivacious and humorous woman, with bright-red dyed hair, much younger than her husband. She died in 1973, and the house then passed through a succession of owners and renovations.

Local tradition had it that George Kelley was retired from an earlier life in which he supposedly operated an infamous nightclub and dancehall known as "Spider Kelly's" in the heart of San Francisco's bawdy Barbary Coast. Under those theories, Betty was supposedly a piano player at the bar. Unfortunately, the documentary evidence lends little support to that colorful story.

⟶ *Walkers may proceed along Madrone Avenue, or turn up Orange Avenue to view several homes in the first block, and then return to Madrone.*

⑤ Orange Avenue

Several of the homes on lower Orange Avenue date to the early 1900s, but multiple ownerships and confused address numbers obscure their histories. In 1903 and 1904 Jacob and Dora Sellmer bought several lots in this area, and in December of 1905, William C. and Eva M. Rentschler purchased the corner lot. For many years their house at **136 MADRONE AVENUE** was known as the "Sunshine Villa" and bore its pink shingles cheerfully.

The various Sellmer and Rentschler lots originally faced Madrone, but were reoriented to face Orange Avenue. The lots' reorientation allowed an additional building site to be created facing Orange, now occupied by the two houses at 9 and 11 Orange.

▲ 3.32: *A current view of the former "Sunshine Villa" at 136 Madrone Avenue, 2010.*

Christian and Emily Schroeder, the parents of librarian Helen Wilson, bought the compound from the Rentschlers, and discontinued the rentals as family members moved into the cottages. The Schroeders sold number 136 in the late 1930s to Howard and Elizabeth Bray. To create a rental unit, the Brays imported a chicken coop to the rear of one of the small cottages here, where it was dubbed the "Chicken Coop House;" it remains there today, minus the fowls. Delightful, sparkling Elizabeth Bray, who was chosen Larkspur Senior Citizen of the Year in 1974 and served on the Larkspur Library Board for eight years, lived in the house until 1987. A variety of additions and changes have been made to the buildings in recent years.

The houses at **9** and **11 ORANGE AVENUE** share a driveway and an uncertain history, closely linked to the adjacent houses on the south. The rear house, number 11, is a modest guest house with a board and batten exterior hidden under asbestos shingles. A central hipped roof is supplemented by a shed roof addition covering a living room and carport. The simple but sturdy construction of that house suggests an early 1920s vacation or rental cottage. The shingled main house at number 9 is a much older structure, probably built during the very early 1900s, with interior walls of knotty pine paneling downstairs and beadboard or board and batten elsewhere. Both houses were owned from the mid-1940s until 2008 by members of the Belcher family, who in turn had purchased from the Brays, the owners of the adjacent complex at 136 Madrone.

↪ *Return down Orange Avenue to proceed further westward (up-Canyon) along Madrone Avenue.*

▲ 3.34: *Number 9 Orange Avenue, shown here in 2008, dates to the early 1900s.*

⑥ Madrone Between Orange & Olive Avenues

Orange Avenue's intersection with Madrone Avenue marks the lower edge of the Laurel Dell Tract, a small subdivision of nineteen lots created in the spring of 1907. Although the Brown family had once claimed 160 acres of the Canyon, and this small tract was within the early "Brown's Fence," it later became a part of the American Land and Trust Co. properties; sisters Belle C. and Mary A. Brown purchased the land only a year before they began its development. They probably chose the name Laurel Dell to evoke the aromatic bay laurel trees that dotted the sunny floor of the Canyon at the turn of the century. The new subdivision included all the lots along the south side of Madrone Avenue, from addresses 147 to 221, and stretched roughly from the intersection of Orange up to Ridgeway Lane. The south edge of all of the lots abuts the boundary line of the original Rancho Punta de

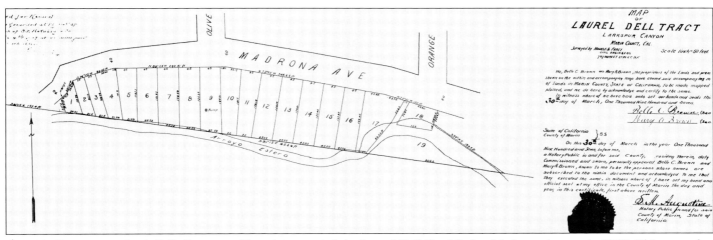

▲ 3.33: *Canyon matriarch Belle Brown and her sister created the Laurel Dell Tract facing Madrone Avenue in 1907. This map of the lots was filed in the Marin County Recorders Office, depicting each lot and the alignment of the "Arroyo Estero de Holon."*

▲ 3.35: Built in 1932, this Castilian-style stucco cottage is at 157 Madrone Avenue, 2008.

Quentin. Most of the lots were rather narrow, and today retain the 45-foot width first established in the original plat map.

1907 promised to be a good year for subdividing land in Marin; the 1906 earthquake and fire in San Francisco had created strong demand for lots in Larkspur, and local landowners were quick to oblige. The new Laurel Dell Tract was surveyed and platted by Nourse & Farey, civil engineers in San Francisco, with each of the lots facing Madrone Avenue. Belle Brown was widely respected for her shrewd dealings in real estate, and the Laurel Dell lots indeed proved popular, with most of the sales completed by 1912. Perhaps as many as six of the lots went to a single purchaser, Frank Craig, a town trustee who speculated in real estate.

The land at **157 MADRONE AVENUE**, one of the Laurel Dell lots, first sold in 1912 but was not built on until about 1932, by B. Karl and Jeanne Wolfe, as a retirement cottage. The Wolfes designed their tile-roofed home to resemble colorful Castilian cottages the couple had seen in Spain. Substantial rear additions, designed to match the Spanish flavor of the original, were made by the current owners in 1996.

The small board and batten home at **163 MADRONE AVENUE** was one of the first of the Laurel Dell Tract homes to be built. The lot was sold in 1910 to Grace M. Anderson of San Francisco. Grace was only 22 years old when she bought the house, working as a "municipal stenographer" in San Francisco. As with several other purchasers of lots from the Brown sisters, Grace was a single working woman; her father, Cornelius, was a carpenter, and may have built the house at about the same time.

The Tudor-styled home at **167 MADRONE AVENUE**, located on the original Lot 15 of the Laurel Dell Tract that first sold to Mrs. Annie Price of Larkspur in 1909. Annie and her husband George lived elsewhere on Madrone at the time of the sale; this house, however, was probably not built until about 1932. The home has a circle of unusually large redwoods in its rear yard. The basement was filled by mud and debris during the 1982 flood, when mud surged down Madrone Avenue and broke through a back window of the basement in its inexorable return to the creek bed.

Matching stone stairs lead to the three homes at **146, 148,** and **150 MADRONE AVENUE**, suggesting contemporaneous development of all three houses around 1910. The lot at 146 was foreshortened; it was first deeded to Jacob and Dora Sellmer in 1903, who later used its rear portion as part of the lot they created at 9 Orange. The house at 150 has drop siding typical of many houses at the turn of the century; its lot also has been truncated, with the rear portion cut off to create the smaller house at 148, which has a long "rat tail" strip to provide the stairway access to Madrone Avenue. Ruth Belcher, who lived for many years at the adjacent 9 Orange, believed that 148 had once been a carriage house for Frank Craig's nearby home at 160 Madrone.

The diminutive board and batten cottage at **171 MADRONE AVENUE** dates to about 1928. Frank Craig had acquired six lots here in the Brown sisters' Laurel Dell Tract, and then rearranged the lines to create fewer, but larger, parcels. This small lot, with a front footage of only 35 feet, was the remnant of that process.

Frank Craig, later the chairman of the town's first Board of Trustees, built the house at **160 MADRONE AVENUE** about 1903. It was located on a group of four lots that he acquired incrementally between 1902 and 1906. He named his new home "The Catalpas," after the sweet-flowered trees he planted along Olive Avenue; six of those trees remain today. He married about 1908; he and his wife Hattie raised their two sons, Beverly and Lansing, in this home, continuing to live here until the early 1940s.

The two-story house now has a front porch the width of the house, decorative shingles high in the gable, and coved drop siding on the walls below. The gable window has a mix of rectangular and arched panes. A tall structure at the rear of the lot, originally a water-tank tower, was remodeled into office space. Portions of the house were rebuilt in the early 1970s, and substantial interior remodeling in 1996 added side dormers but retained the upper parts of the original façade. The original brick foundation, replaced with modern concrete, was recycled into an outdoor brick patio, and the original brick-lined well was restored for garden irrigation. New homes were created from The Catalpas' grounds at 154 Madrone in 1974, and at 2 Olive in 1990.

Craig's career as a town trustee was rocky, at best. Newspapers and minutes of the Larkspur Board of Trustees (forerunner of today's City Council), told of a wild and stormy session of the trustees on February 25, 1909. Frank Craig was voted out of the presidency of the Board by the other trustees, but refused to relinquish his role. The newly appointed president, William J. Kennedy, attempted to proceed but the meeting first came to a standstill and then "went on with both Craig and Kennedy addressing the board in such loud tones that neither side could be heard." When Town Marshall Murphy was instructed to put Craig out of the hall, "[Marin County] Deputy sheriff George Ortman and Special Officer James Buckley stood up and stopped the riot that was sure to have started, as each side had their friends at their backs." The minutes laconically concluded that "Not much was accomplished at the meeting and an adjournment was taken until March third, when trouble is expected to break out again."

Days later Craig filed suit against Murphy on a number of charges, including failure "to bestir himself to save the town from the ravages of starving bovines and wandering dogs." At trial, the judge asked why the issue of the proper manner of removal of the mayor "was not taken to court and settled, instead of having riotous meetings of the board." For a time, two rival Boards – one composed of two members, one of three – attempted to meet simultaneously, each with its own clerk. Events bumped along until early April, when Craig and Kennedy both formally resigned, and the Board thereupon elected Kennedy as mayor. Somehow, our little city had survived.

In his later years Craig had done little to soften his reputation; some neighborhood children feared "Old Man Craig," who was usually dressed in an old felt hat and Big Ben suspender overalls, but others found him to be kind and understanding. Aida Burke said that many people remembered Frank as a cantankerous old man "who seemed to be against everything, although he had a lovely home, charming wife, and enjoyed caring for a very beautiful garden."

During the psychedelic 1960s, neighbors recalled, long-haired residents of the Canyon would tie small bags purportedly

TALL TREES IN THE CANYON

The Baltimore Canyon contains three types of exceptionally tall trees, all native to California. The giant sequoia (*Sequoiadendron giganteum*) growing at 1 Olive Avenue could be expected to reach a potential mature height of about 300 feet in another thousand years or so. Although tall, it nevertheless will never attain the height of the nearby coast redwoods, whose largest specimens exceed 360 feet, and are generally considered the world's tallest species. The third native (and second tallest plant in the world) is the coastal Douglas fir (*Pseudotsuga menziesii*), which occurs naturally in several areas of Marin. The prominent Douglas fir that grows near 2 Echo Place might attain a mature height of 200 to 250 feet.

▲ 3.36: *Tall conifer trees provide evening silhouettes in the Canyon, timeless.*

filled with "tea" onto the branches of a tree that overhung the sidewalk in front of 160 Madrone. In the evening other people would come and pick up the bags. Warren Mistron, then Larkspur's director of public works, directed his crew (dubbed "Mistron's Marauders" by the locals) to impede the traffic by lopping off the branches.

⊃ *Walkers may turn onto Olive Avenue, with side trips on Millard Road and Scott Lane, or continue westward along Madrone Avenue.*

⑦ Olive Avenue

Olive Avenue is the final and western-most of the streets called for by the original 1886 plat of Larkspur. Although designed to connect to the rest of the street system on the north, those links were never realized, and the pavement now dead-ends against a steep slope. Two side streets, Millard Road and Scott Lane, were later added on the west side to provide access to nearby lands. The houses in this neighborhood represent a number of styles and periods; a few houses date to the late 1890s, others to the 1920s, and the remainder to the 1950s.

The large contemporary home at **1 OLIVE AVENUE** also bears a 202 Madrone Avenue address and occupies a large portion of two original lots. An original house on this site dated to the late 1890s or early 1900s, when it was the summer residence for the family of Cornelius and Delia Kelly. California-born Cornelius Kelly was a San Francisco police officer, married to Irish-born Delia; their permanent residence was in San Francisco, where they lived with their eight children. The northern portion of those lots, originally facing Madrone, was later split off to create the adjacent lot at 9 Olive Avenue.

For many years, Thomas J. Acheson tended a spectacular garden here. One of the remarkable features of the house at 1 Olive is the splendid giant sequoia tree adjacent to the front gate. That tree was probably planted as a specimen in the late 1890s, and is likely to be the largest of its type in the Canyon (if not in Larkspur). Giant sequoias occur naturally only in the southern Sierra Nevada, where they grow shorter and more stoutly than the coast redwoods.

▲ *3.37: The showplace home at 24 Millard Road was built by contractor-owner Frank Knittle in 1907, 2008.*

⑧ Millard Road

Millard Road intersects the west side of Olive Avenue, providing access to a variety of homes arrayed across the upper slopes of the Canyon. A short but steep stroll here reveals unusual views and some interesting history.

In the late 1890s Frank B. Millard and his wife Martha learned of a knoll in the upper reaches of the Pixley lands that provided a sweeping view of Mt. Tamalpais and the Baltimore Canyon. They purchased about an acre of that land from the Pixley family in May of 1897. Over the next two years they acquired additional lands and rights-of-way from both the Pixleys and American Land and Trust Co., thus creating what would become "Millard Road." That road later became the template for the 1906 Pixley subdivision of the surrounding land. In addition to the Millards' own house at number 45 Millard Road, the other older houses that remain on the road date roughly between 1907 and 1923.

Cyrill and Marie Skala, who both had been born in the mid-1880s in portions of the Czech Republic (or as they were called then, Moravia and Bohemia), acquired the land at **20 MILLARD ROAD** in the early 1920s. Cyrill was the proprietor of his own barbershop in San Francisco; over a period of several years he pieced this parcel together from various neighboring lands, and then built this house around 1923. The basic placement of the house is unchanged, except for an easterly extension added in the mid-1970s. The original exterior entrance has been replaced by interior stairs, but the v-channel siding and outer appearance remain generally true to the original. This sunny home has had only three owners since it was built; the current owners discovered in a closet a large panoramic photograph of early twentieth-century Prague, which they remounted in tribute to the Skalas.

The nicely maintained home at **24 MILLARD ROAD** was built in 1907 by Frank and Marie Knittle, who continued to live here until the early 1940s. The site combines Lots 19 and 20 of the Pixley subdivision, and is set above a concrete retaining wall similar to others on Onyx Street and adjacent to City Hall. The house is covered in three-lap siding, and displays excellent examples of fishscale and diamond shingle patterns on the front gable with decorative brackets under the eaves, all popular elements of the period. Twin garages, added in 2001 to replace a burned original, were designed by architect Brock Wagstaff, as were internal second floor alterations not visible from the street.

A long concrete stairway leads to several landlocked homes high on the hill behind number 44, and constitutes the original "Path No. 1" as drawn on the early Glen Addition tract map of 1896. The lots there were created by the Pixley subdivision of 1906 and never had vehicular access. Consider a time in which residents thought nothing of climbing steep slopes by foot, perhaps having walked previously from the downtown railroad station. The small house at 44 Millard Road occupies two of the original Pixley Tract lots, and was built about 1913. Its exterior entrance has been enclosed, and the deck added in recent years.

The original Millard residence overlooks the Canyon at **45 MILLARD ROAD**. Frank Bailey Millard and his wife Martha "Mattie" built this house between mid-1897 and the end of 1898. Their residency marked a brief but brilliant period in the history of the Canyon.

F. B. Millard, born in Wisconsin in 1859, was a pivotal member of San Francisco's literary world during its "Golden Age." He began newspaper life as a typesetter, but quickly advanced as an investigative reporter for the *Chronicle*. By 1893 he was city editor for the *Morning Call*, and later was hired personally by William Randolph Hearst to become the Sunday Editor of Hearst's *San Francisco Examiner*. In those capacities he published early works of Jack London, Frank Norris, and Joaquin Miller, and knew personally many writers and poets of the period, including Upton Sinclair and Ambrose Bierce. A week after Edwin Markham had been a guest at this house in January of 1899, Millard first published Markham's "The Man With the Hoe," a phenomenally successful poem.

Most of Millard's own novels, short stories, poems, and other works were published under his middle name,

▲ *3.38: Noted journalist and author Frank Bailey Millard, whose 1898 house stimulated creation of Millard Road. This portrait was made in 1924.*

ILLUSTRIOUS VISITORS IN THE CANYON

Millard's daughter Gladys Dwiggins recalled famed naturalist John Muir's first visit to the family home in Larkspur: "We lived in a house on a hillside surrounded by woods. There was a good view of Mt. Tamalpais. It was a Mecca for all the poets and writers who used to come to visit us when I was small. One day in April, father showed up with Mr. Muir, and he immediately went out on our veranda to view the sea of mountain lilac. He said it was the most beautiful display of mountain lilac in California and for the next several years he would show up each April to visit us." She also remembered Jack London's visits: "When London visited our house my mother was always worrying that he would burn the house down with his smoking in bed." London is said to have read from his manuscripts while standing in front of the fireplace.

Bailey. In 1905 Hearst convinced Bailey to take the position of editor of Cosmopolitan magazine in New York, and by mid-year the family had left Larkspur permanently. He worked for several other magazines and newspapers while continuing to publish books of his own. Eventually, Bailey and Mattie moved to the Los Angeles area, where she died in 1922, and he wrote his largest work, *History of the San Francisco Bay Region*, in 1924. At the time of his death in 1941, Bailey was a columnist for the *Los Angeles Times*.

Although most San Franciscans used their houses in the Canyon as summer residences, by 1900 Bailey, Mattie, and their two children were living here year-round. The Millards retained ownership of this house until July of 1905, selling it then to Frank Murphy, a San Francisco attorney, and his wife Nonie. Over the next few years the Millards sold the remainder of the land in the area, incidentally creating the downhill lots at 246 and 250 Madrone.

Later occupants of the house realized that it had been built for entertainment. Sandi Gariffo, who lived in the house in the mid-1970s, reported "the large 35 by 25 foot living room with its recessed redwood paneling is more like a San Francisco house than a summer house." When the Gariffos bought the house, they thought something was strange about the front bathroom; they later discovered that it had been built in what had been a redwood-paneled entry hall. "There was a huge front door that led to the bathroom," she said. The hipped-roof house originally was designed to face Madrone Avenue far below; it was the Gariffos who created a main entrance and entry hall on the Millard Road side of the house, adding a series of turned columns and brick work along the driveway.

A house set high above the end of the road at **56 MILLARD ROAD** was owned and occupied for a short while by Garnet Holme, famous in Marin as one of the founders of the Mountain Play on Mt. Tamalpais, and its director for many years. Appropriately, he chose a homesite that features an unobstructed view of the mountain. Holme was widely known as a playwright and producer of outdoor pageants, and directed the Ramona pageant in Hemet, the Serra pageant in Carmel, and similar productions in Yosemite and Yellowstone National Parks. In 1924 he was named Pageant Master of the National Park Service.

▲ 3.39: *The hipped-roof cottage at 16 Olive Avenue, built in the early 1900s, was part of a group owned by the extended Hiniker family, 2008.*

▲ 3.40: *Marie (Hiniker) Fleming's home at 20 Olive Avenue, where she lived with her married daughter's family, the Collinses, 2008.*

▲ 3.41: *George and Julia Craig's rural home at 25 Olive Avenue was built in the mid-1890s, 2008.*

Marion Hayes Cain, for eight years the President of the Mountain Play Association and a personal friend of Holme, recalled the circumstances of his tragic death in February of 1929 at age 56. "He had a cottage in Larkspur on the lower slopes of the mountain. … The slopes of his little house were rather steep and in leading guests from his home down to the lower road he slipped and he grabbed for a little tree for support and it wouldn't hold his weight and he fell down a rather steep bluff and had a concussion and so he died in the Ross Hospital."

A large contemporary home now occupies the site of the little early 1900s cottage that Holme occupied. He had lived there only a year and a half.

◗ *Return from Millard Road to Olive Avenue.*

The homes at **16, 18,** and **20 OLIVE AVENUE** originated with George and Marie Hiniker, who began raising their family here in the late 1890s. George, a blacksmith in Marin, also owned land and cattle in Modesto. In 1905 he was killed at age 43 in a horse accident while driving cattle in Tuolumne Meadows, leaving 30-year-old Marie to raise their four children. A few months after his death, she completed the purchase of their home on Lot 5 (address 20) of the original Larkspur subdivision, adding the adjoining Lot 6 (address 16 and 18) in 1910, and proceeded to rent houses to sustain her family. George's father, brothers, and sister lived in town as well, and may have shared the several houses here.

The 16-18 addresses contain three small shingled houses: a hipped-roof structure at street side, a modest cottage in the middle, and a one-and-one-half-story house on the rise at the rear of the lot. All appear to be of similar vintage, dating to the turn of the last century. The larger hipped-roof house at number 20 served as the traditional family home; it has a box cornice and unpainted shingles, and once had an exterior stairway on the north side. An additional structure (20½) is located to its rear. The single garage now at number 16 once served the houses collectively.

Marie remarried in 1912 to John R. Fleming (her deceased husband's best man), but divorced him not long after, nevertheless remaining "Mrs. Fleming" until her death at age 80 in 1955. Marie and George's youngest child, Marie Arnita, married Ernest Collin, and together they joined Marie's household in the 1920s, living at 20 Olive until the mid-1940s. Marie Fleming was a resourceful and gracious woman, for many years a strong supporter of the Larkspur Women's Improvement Club, and active in other civic activities. Her younger sister, Emily Shine, raised a family at 69 Madrone.

The shingled house at **25 OLIVE AVENUE,** known as Julia Craig's home, was probably built around 1896 by George and Julia Craig. The house has retained much of its original appearance on the south and east sides, although expanded and remodeled by several successive owners. For many years the land was joined with the larger parcel behind it (now at 10 Scott Lane), as well as with the adjacent large lots to the south and the narrower area to the north from which Scott Lane was created *(see below)*. The house thus once commanded much of the east side of Olive Avenue. Old stonework in the hillside behind the house enclosed a natural cleft in the bedrock that formed a "cooling cave" for the storage of foodstuffs.

Julia's husband, George P. Craig, was the older brother of Frank P. Craig, later the owner of The Catalpas at 160 Madrone. Julia's mother, Mina, joined her in this house with her second husband, James Norton, a carpenter. After both George and James had died, Julia and Mina sold their lands in the area, and moved to Stockton about 1916.

Further uphill three distinctive homes at **53, 55,** and **57 OLIVE AVENUE,** known as the Harry Allen houses, or "Brantwood," were developed by Harris S. "Harry" Allen and his wife Alice, aided

SCOTT LANE

Donald E. and Ida Scott developed the short private road called Scott Lane in the early 1950s. They lived in several houses in this area during the mid-1940s, finally purchasing the home at 25 Olive Avenue. With a partner, Scott acquired the two large lots adjoining his to the north, combined them with his land behind 25 Olive, and then designed new lots to face the lane he created. The several houses on Scott Lane were built between 1953 and 1958. The Scott family left the neighborhood soon after these houses were completed.

by various family members, over a period of almost fifty years. Now owned individually, the houses evolved during the first half of the twentieth century as the summer home of a colorful, close-knit, and adventurous family.

The Allens lived full-time in San Francisco with their daughter Barbara and son Lewis, where Harry was the owner of the prosperous Allen's Press Clipping Bureau. Their granddaughter, Frances A. G. Davis, recalled that although "they were middle class people who led a very conventional life," they also managed to travel "far and wide." They went to Europe a number of times, and for one of their anniversaries spent almost a year going around the world; "China and Japan were of great interest." The eclectic materials incorporated in the house and garden at number 55 reflect their extensive travels and interests.

▲ 3.42: *The 1928 Brantwood "gardener's house" at 53 Olive Avenue, as it appeared with its original roof in 1954.*

"Mr. and Mrs. Harry Allen and son Lewis returned Sunday from a trip to Europe. The Allens came over Tuesday to spend a few weeks at their summer home on Olive Avenue, where they own several acres. Mr. Allen built the famous Alpine Dam trail starting from his home which is used by the Sierra Club. The Allens report a very interesting trip through Italy, Switzerland, England, and spent time motoring through the country."

– *Larkspur-Corte Madera News*, August 23, 1929

The site of **53 OLIVE AVENUE**, acquired by the Allens in 1907, originally was used for a barn and stable, and the house was not constructed until 1928, designed to face the nearby main house and share its architectural detailing. The lower floor served as a garage (thus sometimes called "the carriage house"), while the second floor was designed as a "very pleasant" home for the live-in gardener. The original roof of this house consisted of fire-resistant terra cotta tiles. Allen had a clear vision for the roof designs originally used throughout the estate: "The most striking feature [of Chinese architecture] is the curving roof, upturned at mitered corners, and with its splendid sweeps unbroken . . . ." This house has large, multipane, arched windows that open onto a second-floor deck. Scrolled iron brackets were added under the deck to mimic those of the gatehouse at number 55. When the entire estate was sold in the early 1950s, this structure was converted into a separate two-story house.

Harry first learned of this area in July of 1897, from "a mutual friend, Ben Lathrop, [who] wished to dispose of a bungalow with a fine spring and half an acre of hill at the base of Tamalpais. The following Sunday … I sought it out, and it was mine within the week." That initial purchase consisted of the two lots on which **55 OLIVE AVENUE** is located. Three years later, in March of 1900, Harry married Alice in this yard.

Harry was an accomplished Sierra hiker and a life-long walker. In 1893 he had traveled though England with his brother Lewis, and hiked into the Lake District to visit the artist and critic John Ruskin; Ruskin's estate was named "Brantwood," a name Allen later adopted for his Larkspur property. He eventually developed an extensive network of hiking trails that began in the garden of this house and led over Little King Mountain to Phoenix, Lagunitas, and Alpine lakes. On occasion, a lost hiker would descend the trails, only to be bewildered by a sudden entry into an exotic garden. Much of that route is now on private land or overgrown, but parts survive as the Harry Allen Trail near Phoenix Lake and a portion of the King Mountain Loop Trail. Granddaughter Frances recalled, "We children often had to go out with our granddad and great uncles to clear the trails on the hill behind the house." The yard and trails fascinated the neighborhood children. Gary Scott, who grew up at nearby 25 Olive in the 1950s, recalled the yard as "a magical place where we sailed imaginary Chinese junks and played pirate."

▲ 3.43: *Brantwood's 1929 "gatehouse" at 55 Olive Avenue, 2008.*

The trails led to "a safe, unspoiled, kid's paradise; we could run forever. It was wonderful."

The elaborate estate evolved over a long period; for much of that time, the original rustic bungalow built by Ben Lathrop in the late 1890s was the only structure on the number 55 site, and the adjacent house (now number 57) served as a residence for the extended family and guests. In 1929 Allen demolished the Lathrop bungalow, and designed and began building a two-story main house, capped by a turret bedroom. That house, like the garden, evolved over a period of several years, with Allen "using materials from the old house and from everywhere else." As he recalled in a 1930 letter: "The beams in the living room, stenciled by Alice and our friends, were made from the old gym of the San Anselmo orphanage, made available when Robert Dollar made them a gift of a new gym of brick. The large iron brackets at the entrance gate were from the old Mill Valley railroad station terminus. The tile roof was made in Richmond. The … tile throughout are the souvenirs of travels around the world."

The house features two gates; a small "moon gate," forming a circular entrance to the upper yard and house, and the double-decked "gatehouse" (now sometimes called the "teahouse") that opens to the garden. "The gate house front is made of green tile from China," Allen wrote. "Inside are tile from Italy and Mexico, a 'petite fontaine' from North Africa and the floor tile is [from a batch] made to restore Mission Dolores in the original way of 1776." Neighborhood tradition held that some parts of that gatehouse (built in 1929) had been recycled from the Chinese Pavilion at the Panama-Pacific Exposition of 1915 in San Francisco, but Allen's extensive writings never mentioned that detail, and diligent research by the current owners has failed to establish such a link; perhaps Allen merely adapted some aspect of the Pavilion's design. The timeworn original columns of the gatehouse had to be replaced with concrete replicas by the current owners. Allen himself planted "the little sprig that is now the *Sequoia sempervirens* by the moon gate," but ironically the roots of that tree, grown much larger, now threaten the very structure for which it was intended to be "the sentinel to guard the moon gate from all evil."

The Allens undertook a major remodeling of the main house in 1947, interrupted by Harry's death in July of that year. Only a month later, an accidental fire destroyed much of the interior, as well as the entire second floor and turret bedroom. Fortunately, Harry's tiled roof had contained the fire, preventing its spread to the surrounding area. The family then rebuilt the house, but at a reduced scale and with a conventional roof.

The extended Allen family sold the entire estate in 1953; Alice died elsewhere in 1958. The main house then passed through several owners, valiant attempts at repair, and a long period of neglect and misuse. When acquired by the current owners, this once-splendid structure was again in serious disrepair, occupied by a dissolute group of rock musicians.

Long-term rescue of the house began in February of 1987, when Stevie and Tom Serleth optimistically purchased a fascinating but badly dilapidated house, moving in with two small children a few months later. They have zealously guarded the home's history, and lovingly invested more than two decades in reconstruction of the house and restoration of its garden.

Long considered a part of Brantwood, the **57 OLIVE AVENUE** site was acquired in 1907 by Alice Allen's parents, Frank and Cara Mayhew, with whom the Allens had lived in the early years of their marriage. The house, called "Madrona Lodge," was built the next year and used by various members of the family for the next few decades; for much of the time it served generally as a summer guesthouse. In 1946, this house acquired its first full-time residents when the Allens' daughter, Barbara Gaskin, moved to Brantwood with her husband William and their children during the post-war years. Barbara's unexpected death in 1951 triggered the later sale of the entire estate in 1953.

The guesthouse was later altered to reflect many of the details used elsewhere in Brantwood. As with all the houses here, it has gone through additional changes in succeeding years.

⟳ *Walkers should reverse direction on Olive Avenue, return to Madrone Avenue, and continue up-Canyon.*

⑨ 200 Block of Madrone Avenue

Another of the original Laurel Dell Tract houses, the two-story shingled house at **205 MADRONE AVENUE** is hidden behind a dense family of six large redwoods that guard its front yard. The house has tall dormers and an unusually elaborate columned entry porch. It was nearly identical to another house that formerly occupied the adjoining lot to the east. Although its history is vague, it probably was built in the period 1910-1915. The lot itself is foreshortened; a separate parcel and house exist at the rear, connected to the street by a "rat tail" strip containing a driveway. That house, at 203 Madrone, was rebuilt after a 1986 fire only after substantial controversy.

The tiny yellow gem of a cottage at **207 MADRONE AVENUE** probably was built soon after sale of the land in 1907. As with many of the Laurel Dell lots, its front width measures only 45 feet; the house itself measures only slightly more than 900 square feet. The original purchaser, Charles Stanley, was a

▲ *3.44: The little cottage at 207 Madrone Avenue exemplifies the simple demands of early 1900s Canyon summer structures, 1990.*

▲ *3.45: Emma Pixley's gracious home at 222 Madrone Avenue, built about 1898, as it appeared in 2010.*

house carpenter who might have built the structure, but otherwise seems to have had little connection to the area. The cottage has painted shingles and a hipped roof, with a porch that wraps around the north and west sides. As with other simple homes of the era, the centered front door enters directly into the living room. It has undergone moderate internal modifications.

Original structures in the Canyon are subject to many risks, not the least of which is fire. An early home on the large lot at 208 Madrone was destroyed in a fatal fire early in 1973, and the current owners, Larry and Annie Aull, designed and built a replacement home there a year later. The site had been derived in 1903 from the extensive lands earlier held by the Millard family.

The landmark Pixley home at **222 MADRONE AVENUE** stands on land originally sold to William C. Pixley by Patrick King in September of 1880. King's ranch, which once covered most of today's Larkspur, had already been split into a number of smaller holdings when King agreed to sell this 4.68-acre parcel. The new Pixley land, which extended from 222 Madrone up to number 250, thus became an early "island" around which the American Land and Trust Co. developed the remainder of the Canyon in the late 1890s.

William Pixley was a brother of Frank Pixley, a celebrated editor and publisher in San Francisco who also owned the Van Reynegom "Owlswood" estate in southern Larkspur. William was age 57 when he purchased this land, but was described as "an old man" when he died here a year later in a spectacular brush fire that escaped his control and burned thousands of acres. The land remained in the Pixley family, and in 1898 the present structure was built for Emma Catharine O'Reilly Pixley, William's widow. Family descendants recall that lumber to build this and another house (perhaps the Zaro structure?) came from Duncans Mills on the Russian River, and cost about $500.

The house has a centered gable with the main eaves extending across its base. Fishscale and sawtooth shingles cover the gable's face, where a hood with brackets protects double-hung, nine-pane windows. The house is encased by coved drop siding, with flat casing around the windows. A porch extends across the front of the house with trellises at either end covered by original wisteria. A tall, rustic chimney on the rear of the house was built of locally quarried blue rock.

Emma Catharine was an artist who painted scenes of Baltimore Canyon on a four-panel door that still remains in the house. It's likely that her artist's sense of natural light led her to site the house at the rear of her land, where sunlight was unobstructed by the ridge to the south. As a devout Episcopalian, she invited founding members of Corte Madera's Holy Innocents Episcopal Church to hold some of their early meetings in her front yard. She later gave the church the two lots where that church stands today. *(See page 190-191 for more Pixley history.)*

By 1900 the house was occupied by Clare E. Pixley and her son Henry. Henry and his father (also named Henry) both were active speculators and developers of nearly lands. They purchased additional property, and in 1906 the family sub-divided their holdings into 36 lots encompassing both sides of Millard Road and Ridgeway Lane, thus creating the "Pixley Tract." Most of the homes currently on those two roads date to the period of the Pixley Tract development.

English-born Henry Lister, a prominent San Francisco attorney, and his wife Lydia, a playwright, purchased this house in 1908. According to Ernie Zaro, who grew up next door, there were two signs on the gate, the first saying "Henry B. Lister, Attorney at Law" and underneath it, "Elfdale." During the 1950s the "Elfdale" sign hung on a maple tree in the front yard. Ernie recalled that the Listers used this as a summer home and frequently entertained show business people. He particularly

▲ 3.46: *Annie Baker's "summer shack" at 217 Madrone Avenue has survived into modern times with minimal alterations, 1990.*

remembered Mrs. Lister's pump organ as it accompanied opera singers who were easily heard from outside the house. The Listers retained the house until the late 1950s.

Except for minor modification, the exterior of the house is unchanged. The original small carriage house is now a street-side garage, still bearing a pulley that hangs at the east end of the building, ready to admit hay into the attic. An antique carriage remained inside this structure until the early 1970s.

The lot at **217 MADRONE AVENUE** was first sold to Annie and Joseph Baker of San Francisco in February of 1910; the tiny cottage they built here has remained little affected by the passage of the ensuing century. It boasts perhaps the smallest front-footage of any house in the Canyon, measuring only 25 feet across. The house's age was poignantly revealed during kitchen remodeling, when a World War I "Doughboy" poster was found on the backside of plywood paneling. James Holmes, a life-long Larkspur resident and local history buff, has owned the house since 1984. The house is frequently described, without intended derision, as a summer shack.

Five months after acquiring number 217, Annie Baker purchased the adjoining lot at 215 Madrone. Joseph Baker, according to a directory of that time, was first a salesman and then switched to engineering after going back to school. As his means improved, the family built a larger home here and retained the 217 structure as a guest cottage. The Baker family continued to own those two parcels

FIRES IN THE CANYON

William Pixley's "Blackberry fire" was one of many to have swept the lower edges of Mt. Tamalpais, but it was probably the worst. Contemporary newspapers reported the tragedy in some detail. It started on Wednesday, September 14, 1881, while Pixley was attempting to clear his land. "Finding the underbrush very thick and troublesome to clear with the axe, he determined to burn it." Aided by a neighbor, Thomas Collins, Pixley set fire to a thick stand of blackberry bushes and poison oak, but the fire quickly spread into a laurel bush, "which crackled and blazed up very fiercely, as laurel always does in a fire, while its leaves shriveled and were floated off by the wind in large cinders." As he lost control of the fire, Pixley's wife Emma called to him; he started toward her, but was never again seen alive. Pixley's own small house was burned, but his wife managed to escape. The fire quickly spread down the Canyon, toward Patrick King's farm *(see pages 6-7)*: "King's place was swept of every blade and even to the clapboards of his barn. The barn, which was full of hay, was saved only by the greatest exertions, and its escape bordered on the miraculous. The dwelling of Mr. King also had a narrow escape from the flames." Other pioneer homes in the area barely avoided destruction.

In the afternoon of the 14th, residents of San Francisco were troubled by the unusual appearance of the sky. The *Daily Alta California* reported that "Crowds filled the streets, and expressions of wonder and even apprehension could be heard on every side." The *Morning Call* described the scene in detail: "The northern and western sky was gradually relinquishing its usual gold-tinted blue to a ghastly yellow tint that reflected its light over the entire city. Slowly the entire heavens, north and west of the city, assumed a strange color. When ... cinders and ashes began to fall in showers on the street, some as large as dollar pieces, a genuine fright took possession of those who had watched the phenomenon thus far." Ashes and cinders also were reported falling in Alameda.

As the winds shifted, the flames moved onto the upper slopes of Mt. Tamalpais, then worked along the ridges to spread into the Blithedale Canyon in Mill Valley and portions of the Tiburon peninsula, threatening parts of Sausalito. The burned area eventually was estimated to be twelve miles long from north to south, and seven miles wide.

William Pixley's burnt body was found the day after the fire started, fallen on a cow path where he had been using a shovel to fight the flames. Everywhere the fire was considered beyond human control. "No effort is being made to extinguish the fire; none can be made with any show of success." Gangs of men managed to beat back the flames at individual houses. The fire continued to burn until at least September 20, when it finally was turned back on itself by shifting winds. Photographs taken in Baltimore Canyon at the turn of the century show barren spars remaining from "the fire," and traces of that blaze remain evident even today on older redwood trees and stumps in the Canyon, which show thick patches of charred heartwood and bark. The hills above Larkspur's downtown had been scoured as well, and appear remarkably barren in photographs taken in the 1890s.

Over the years various smaller fires swept parts of the Canyon, often sparked by the wood-fired locomotives on the railroad; the *San Francisco Chronicle* of September 24, 1889 described a fire that started near the Corte Madera depot, then "soon spread and reached into heavy timber in the mountains where it raged fiercely." Weeks later, the October 3, 1889 *Marin Journal* reported that a series of fires once again threatened the area, and R.S. Brown and his family *(see page 103)* "only saved their home by hard work extending through several sieges by day and night."

Pixley's 1881 fire was sometimes confused with a fierce blaze in July of 1913 that started high on Mt. Tam and threatened both Larkspur and Mill Valley; Larkspur officials feared their town was in "imminent danger of complete destruction." Army units from the Presidio in San Francisco joined the fighting efforts, and their officers ordered the evacuation of Baltimore Canyon; only an upper portion of the Canyon actually burned, in a fire that lasted about five days. Mayor Gardiner later published a letter of appreciation "to all our friends who stood shoulder to shoulder with us in our hour of need and rendered such valued service for the protection of our valley."

The most damaging blaze was the 1929 fire in Mill Valley. On July 2nd and 3rd about a thousand acres burned in Cascade Canyon, destroying 117 homes. Crews from Larkspur helped to fight that blaze, which spurred renewed interest and concern for acquiring adequate equipment for Larkspur's volunteer fire department.

▲ 3.47: *Prosper Zaro, with his assistant Walter Frizzi seated on the wagon, posed in front of Zaro's home at 228 Madrone Avenue about 1913.*

until 1951 when the properties were sold separately. The house at 215 Madrone burned in the mid 1970s, and was replaced in 1977 by contractor-owner Ken Solvenson with a large contemporary home. That house was designed in a not-particularly-successful attempt to accommodate the many redwood trees on the site.

The original eclectic design of the cottage at **221 MADRONE AVENUE** was celebrated by a prominent name sign that declared it "The Shambles." Adelaide Bartlett began building this summer cottage by herself about 1910, after acquiring both Lot 1 (the house site) in 1908, and Lot 2 (the yard) in 1912 as part of the Brown sisters' Laurel Dell Tract. Adelaide was only 26 when she acquired the land; she worked full-time in San Francisco as a deputy county assessor, maintaining living quarters there with a sister during the workweek, and spending weekends in the Canyon. Documents show she traveled widely, including trips to London and Hawaii in the 1920s. She retired to The Shambles on a more nearly full-time basis in the late 1920s, and died here in 1934.

The cottage originally had siding of vertical board and battens, but was converted to shingles in the mid-1970s. One of its distinctive original features is an inglenook fireplace with benches alongside. The name sign reportedly was removed at the urging of an overly-cautious real estate agent who failed to appreciate the Canyon's colorful history.

In June of 2010 a fierce blaze destroyed one of the Canyon's best-known landmarks. An old shingled house that stood at **228 MADRONE AVENUE** was occupied about 1910 by Prosper Zaro and his new wife Hilma shortly after they vacated rented quarters downtown. Their small house (about 1,100 square feet) shared a yard with some of the largest redwoods in the Canyon, and remained in continuous family ownership for a century. This lot, purchased by the Zaros in May 1910 from Emma Catharine Pixley, occupies a prime level location adjacent to the Pixley home at 222 Madrone, and the structure itself might have had some earlier connection with that compound. The dangerous blaze that consumed the dilapidated structure was quickly contained by Larkspur's firefighters, but radiant heat severely damaged nearby giant redwoods.

Prosper Zaro was born in San Francisco in 1880 and raised in Sausalito, where his Austrian father, Ernest, was a fisherman. Hilma was a recent immigrant from Sweden; they married in 1908 and established

AVENUE OF THE GIANTS.

The tall coast redwood trees (*Sequoia sempervirens*) in the 200 block of Madrone Avenue are the largest in the Canyon, and for several good reasons. Rainfall on the lee side of Mt. Tamalpais often exceeds 50 inches per year, and the narrow Canyon maintains a relatively cool temperature year-round; both factors make the Baltimore Canyon very conducive to redwood growth.

Although logged extensively in the 1850s, these redwoods lost only their tall trunks; the vigorous root systems remained. When cut, the trees respond aggressively by sending out numerous small, rapidly growing sprouts from the base of the stump. Within only two or three years, a single stump will be surrounded by a dense thicket of green foliage that begins to compete for sunlight with nearby plants. Eventually a circle of young redwood trees will surround the decapitated parent, forming a family group (sometimes called a "fairy circle") of strong trees, each one a genetic clone of the parent. Nurtured by an already-established root system, the new trunks can quickly grow to as much as 50 to 70 feet in height in only a few decades.

Redwoods generally grow to their largest potential when located on flat alluvial valley bottoms with deep soil. In this part of the Canyon, the nearby Arroyo Holon maintains a high water table under the Canyon's flat floor. The redwoods spread their root systems into a large, interlocking, flat mass that can draw easily from the high water table. The impressive trunks in this portion of the Canyon are among the largest second-growth trees in Marin County.

No one alive today knows how large these trees may have been when they were first cut in the 1850s. Several eyewitness accounts mention trunks 8 feet or more in diameter, and a stump once located near Dolliver Park was reliably described as 23 feet in diameter.

themselves in Larkspur, where Prosper became a central feature of the community. His business card, found in City Hall's 1913 time capsule, proudly proclaimed that he had plumbed that entire building and noted that he was then Chief of the Larkspur Volunteer Fire Department. During the World War I years, Prosper worked as a pipe fitter at the Navy Yard in Mare Island. Oakley Dexter recalled that Zaro spoke in a highly erudite, eloquent fashion – more like a professor than a plumber.

Ernest L. ("Ernie") Zaro, Prosper and Hilma's only son, recalled that the old shed with v-channel siding near the intersection of Madrone Avenue and Ridgeway Lane, across from the family home, may be the structure that once housed a horse-drawn hose cart used to pump water from the creek in case of a fire in the Canyon. Prosper, along with "Dolph" Doherty and F. Sherman, was in charge of tending this fire wagon. When the wagon needed repairs, the group started what may have been the precursor of the Rose Bowl dances. Since all three men played musical instruments – Prosper was the drummer – they decided to put together an impromptu band to raise funds. "So they built a little wood platform in the redwood grove over across the way," recounted Ernie. "They charged a nickel, maybe it was a dime, and people came to the dance. That was the beginning of what later became the Rose Bowl." Ernie delivered groceries "all around town" as a youth using a Model T Ford, served in the Navy in World War II, and died in Marin in August of 2003 at age 88.

⑩ Ridgeway Lane & the Glen Addition

Walter K. Cazneaux and his wife Jean lived at **234 MADRONE AVENUE** from the early 1930s until about 1950. Walter's parents (Walter C. and Kathryn) had raised him in their nearby home at 17 Ridgeway Lane, where they lived from about 1927 until about 1942. The current owner remodeled the 234 house with great care in 1977, and further expanded the yard by acquisition of adjacent lots.

In 1957, a tramway was proposed to take passengers to the top of Mt. Tamalpais from Baltimore Canyon. A bridge was to be built across the creek adjacent the small house at 233 Madrone Avenue, which probably dates to about 1906. The developer claimed the tramway "would bring a great deal of new,

▲ 3.48: *The 1896 Glen Addition extended subdivided lots into the sunnier upper reaches of the Canyon; today's Echo Place occupies the curve in Madrone Avenue shown in this 1909 scene. Power poles in the roadway were not considered an impediment to travel.*

needed prestige to the city." The bridge would allow tram visitors to drive to parking areas scattered along the route, then board an elephant train and be driven to the tram station. A 6-minute tram trip would carry riders to a terminal and restaurant at the top of the mountain. To accomplish all that, an expert had recommended enlarging Madrone Avenue to two 12-foot driving lanes with an 8-foot parking lane, which would have required removing dozens of redwood trees from the roadbed. Citizens organized the Baltimore Park and Madrone Canyon Property Owners Association and successfully defeated the tramway proposal before both the City Council and the water district directors. The current lot is something of a remnant, being neither part of the Laurel Dell Tract to the east, nor the major Glen Addition lots to the west. The creek cuts perilously close to the rear edge of the house, which has undergone a variety of drastic changes.

A flood control dam located across the creek from 239 Madrone Avenue is a reminder of the disastrous 1982 flood, when the side canyon to the south of this house gave way under relentless rains. A debris flow of rocks, mud, and mature redwood trees surged down the channel, creating an immense pile of material that blocked the Arroyo Holon. That debris pile in turn exacerbated the flooding problems downstream. The Marin County Open Space District cleared the debris and during the following summer constructed an earthen dam designed to prevent any repetition of that event. The dam is accessible from the service road that runs along the south edge of the creek. The current house at 239 Madrone was built in 1974.

The large "Ridgewood" sign at the entrance to **250 MADRONE AVENUE** is one of the last house name signs remaining in the Canyon. Street address numbers were not used here until the late 1920s, and visitors found a house simply by looking for its name. As with the arks on the salt marsh, the names were

RIDGEWAY LANE

Ridgeway Lane is a narrow strip of pavement that somehow manages to provide access to about ten different lots; it was officially created as Path No. 3 on Pixley's 1906 subdivision map. In another of the mapmaker's physically impossible paper feats, the path/lane was supposed to connect to Millard Road, the narrow street high on the hill to the rear. Paths No. 1 and No. 2 were drawn yet higher on the hill above Millard Road. All three "paths" can be traced to even earlier notations on the 1896 Glen Addition plat, suggesting that they once operated as true footpaths in an era before vehicular traffic.

▲ 3.49: *This Ridgewood sign at 250 Madrone Avenue is one of the last survivors of the house identification signs that were used in the Canyon before address numbers were assigned, 2009.*

sometimes chosen because they were descriptive, but more often because they were whimsical or poetic. House address numbers were previously unnecessary, as mail was picked up at boxes in the downtown post office.

The land at 250 marks the western corner of what had begun as the Pixley Tract, and was later sold to the Millards, whose large home is still visible high to the rear. The Millards created this lot in 1906, shortly after they left the Canyon permanently, selling it to John and Elsie Doose of San Francisco, who apparently built a house here soon thereafter. Owner-contractor Steve Jones renovated and rebuilt the 250 home in the early 1970s, and later revisions have expanded it far beyond its modest origin.

* * * * *

Ten years after the American Land and Trust Co. first subdivided the downtown and lower Canyon portions of Larkspur, the company finally put its remaining lands on the market. The 1896 Glen Addition was just that – an "addition" to the already-subdivided area of the town, but massive in scale. It encompassed the entire upper reaches of the Canyon, stretching from Olive Avenue to the far western edge of the current city boundary.

Unlike the orderly lots of downtown Larkspur, most of the Glen Addition consisted of very large and irregularly-shaped parcels, arrayed across steep hills and narrow canyons. The company made little attempt to design individual building lots in that area, relying instead on purchasers to create smaller lot configurations according to their own desires and circumstances. Over the following decades, various speculative buyers created and sold new lots derived from the original parcels. The result was a confused array of housing sites, often with unrealistic access routes and too-steep topography. Several of the improbably designated streets and roads never came into existence, and three others (Jones Way, Glen Way, and Valley Way) were nothing more than short, steep watercourses that created flood problems for decades to come. The main access road – Madrone Avenue – stayed close to the creek, requiring that access to the upper reaches of the Canyon instead be provided by the confusing sequence of Redwood Avenue, as extended to Oak Road, and much later, to Wilson Way and the Madrone Highlands.

There was no monumental entry to the Glen Addition; the edge of the tract is unmarked, and along Madrone Avenue, began simply with the houses at 259 and 260 Madrone Avenue. A few doors further west, near the intersections of today's Echo Place and Jones Way, a barbed wire fence was once strung across the road, "to keep the cattle in and the people out," according to Edward Scherman, whose parents built one of the first homes on Oak Road. Opening of the Glen Addition thus necessitated what became known as "the Madrone extension;" the road builders decided that Madrone Avenue would hug the hillside, rather than continue along the creek bed. That "extension" was, of course, merely a dirt route. Writing in 1978 about her childhood in the early 1900s, Eleanor Rideout recalled, "We used to walk up a dirt road when the Foleys lived in the Canyon – finally a board walk about 4 planks wide was installed; it was quite an event."

Progress lagged; although the Glen Addition survey work was completed in 1896, the plat maps weren't officially recorded until 1899. Only a single sale occurred in the first year thereafter, and by the end of 1906, scarcely fourteen sales had been completed. The one exception to the Glen Addition's amorphous design was its "Block 1," a group of 22 rectangular lots between the creek bed and the newly extended Madrone Avenue. Those lots were among the first to be sold, and became the sites of several of the Canyon's notable homes. The first of those lots became 259 Madrone.

The large Schwarz-Seaton house at **259 MADRONE AVENUE** occupies Lot 1 of the Glen Addition's

▲ *3.50: The Schwarz-Seaton home at 259 Madrone Avenue, built around 1901, as it appeared in 1989.*

streamside Block 1. The entire parcel, which originally included the sites of the smaller houses to the west at numbers 263 and 265, was first purchased by Christine and Henry Schwarz of San Francisco early in 1901; the main house was probably built about that same time. After being widowed, Christine left San Francisco in the mid-1920s and moved into the little house at 265, allowing her daughter Ruth (and Ruth's new husband, Frank Seaton) to take over the large family home at 259. Ruth and Frank (who was a sales executive for the Foremost Dairy) lived at 259 the remainder of their long lives.

The house has beveled siding, a combination of four- and six-pane double-hung windows, and shaped rafter tips. As with other old homes, exterior pipes reveal that indoor plumbing was added long after the house was built. One door leads directly to Madrone Avenue (and the adjacent houses at 263-265); a larger door opens to a porch facing the garden. The large yard to the east (not a part of the original Lot 1, but acquired later) was maintained by Frank as a showplace garden, complete with a life-sized deer statute on the lawn that made passing motorists do a double take. Ruth Seaton died in 1963, and, when Frank followed in 1974, the current residents acquired the house.

Originally used as a part of the Schwarz-Seaton properties, the land at **263** and **265 MADRONE AVENUE** was first acquired in 1901, with streamside portions added later. Christine Schwarz's small house at 265, adjacent to Madrone Avenue, consists of an original eastern portion covered in beveled siding like the larger home at 259, with a western addition that used coved drop siding. Number 263 at the rear also used beveled material. Both modest structures reflect the unpretentious and simple construction typical of early Canyon summerhouses.

The two houses at **260** and **264 MADRONE AVENUE** occupy a lot first purchased in 1901 by Martha Millard, apparently as an adjunct to the Millard lands on the hill above. Number 260 was built in the mid-1950s, but some parts of number 264 apparently date to about 1907; an unfinished building on that site – probably number 264 – was expanded by local builder Gustave Nagel in 1918. The structure since has undergone numerous changes.

▲ *3.51 In this early 1900s photo Archie, Althea, and Donald MacKillop are gathered on the family lot at 271 Madrone Avenue, with an unidentified visitor behind them. Note the traditional Canyon tent platform in the rear.*

Beginning in the 1880s, San Franciscans Angus and Emily MacKillop and their family pitched summer tents on the two Glen Addition lots at **271 MADRONE AVENUE**, eventually purchasing the land in 1901. Scottish-born Angus, and his Swedish wife Emily, had six children and a number of close relatives. Eventually they erected a summer shack atop a tent platform; when the time came to build a permanent house, Angus moved the shack to the rear of the yard, where it was used to store tents and to house summer visitors. Nearly a century later, it remains today as guest quarters. In the course of re-landscaping the backyard, the current owners discovered that the ground was crisscrossed with various pipes that once led to the campers' tent sites and shower locations. The spacious yard, which incorporates a third parcel south of the Rancho boundary line and spanning the creek, contains several of the Canyon's larger redwoods.

Angus and Emily's oldest son, Angus W. MacKillop (Jr.), and his wife Althea, owned a hardware store in San Francisco; they became full-time residents here about 1931, retiring in 1942. It was they who undertook the building (or perhaps, the expansion) of the main house during the early 1930s, using unemployed friends (and perhaps persons who owed money to the hardware store) to work on the house, with the result that many things are out of kilter. The fireplace already had been built when Althea decided that she needed a bigger living room, so the end wall was pulled out and the room extended, leaving the fireplace off-center on the wall.

Althea and Angus Jr. died in 1960 and 1961; shortly thereafter their daughters rented the main house to an informal group that included musician Jerry Garcia, later the famed leader of the Grateful Dead. That arrangement ended when the renters nearly burned the house down. When Gerrit and Sandy Blauvelt purchased the house from intermediate owners in 1974, some rooms still had rainbows painted on the walls, and the floors had burn marks from untended clothes irons. Over the next three decades the Blauvelts carefully renovated both The Mackillop-Blauvelt house and grounds, protecting and enhancing one of the Canyon's landmark homes. Sandy Blauvelt has been a mainstay member of Larkspur's Parks and Recreation Commission since the 1980s.

Alex MacKillop, the youngest son of Angus and Emily, raised his own family in a house he and his wife Aimee built further up the Canyon, at 377 Madrone, where they lived from the 1930s to mid-1940s.

Henry O. Pixley originally acquired the lot at **268** and **272 MADRONE AVENUE** in May of 1904. The house at 268 may have been built about 1905; number 272 bore the name "El Cabana" for many years; its construction probably dates to about 1912.

ROCK AND ROLL IN THE CANYON

During the late 1960s and early 1970s, many of the Canyon's "counterculture" folk were also emerging as noted rock and roll musicians. Perhaps the best known were some of the Grateful Dead members who lived with Jerry Garcia in the large home they rented at 271 Madrone. Close by, across the creek at 380 West Baltimore, Janis Joplin purchased a 1965 house, living there until her death in 1970. Singer and actor Huey Lewis lived at 17 Ridgeway, working as a partner in a yogurt-distributing business, until major recording contracts funded his move elsewhere.

▲ *3.52: The circa 1905 Levis home at 1 Echo Place, as it appeared in June of 1978.*

⑪ Echo Place

Echo Place is a relatively recent addition to the Canyon; the little cul-de-sac wasn't created until 1972, and its contemporary-styled homes all were built in the mid-1970s. However, this area originally comprised five lots of the Glen Addition's Block 1, and two of the houses here date to that earliest period of life in the Canyon. The name itself is a gentle echo of the past; Isabella and Carl Holm acquired two lots here in 1900 and 1907, built a house, and operated a small summer resort. The name of their home was "Echo."

At one time seven to ten cottages, houses, and "sheds" clustered here, most of them located with little regard for the niceties of lot lines. A small seasonal stream flowed across the grounds, emitting from Jones Way and crossing the line of Madrone Avenue to join the Arroyo Holon. Because the redwoods had been logged years earlier, and the undergrowth burned by the fire of 1881, this area at the turn of the century was a meadow of small plants, bay laurel trees, and fruiting huckleberry bushes. It must have been a delightful location to while away warm summer days – maybe it even had an echo.

In later years the buildings had been used as substandard rentals, and during the 1960s hippie era they served as another of the commune complexes.

▲ 3.53: *Vernon Dale, the circa 1908 Canyon home of John and Eleanor Foley at 4 Echo Place, as it appeared in 1978; it was replaced with a new structure in 1994.*

The lots were purchased as a block by developer James Stice in 1971. In short order he razed many of the rustic structures, installed the present road and modern utilities, and built the surrounding houses at numbers 2, 5, 6, and 7 Echo Place.

A massive Douglas fir stands at the northwest corner of Madrone and Echo Place, perhaps the largest still remaining in the Canyon.

Alice and Thomas Levis first bought the lot at **1 ECHO PLACE** in September of 1905. Thomas was an Irish-born night watchman in San Francisco who later became a clerk for one of the street railways there. Because the Levises retained a city residence, this house appears to have been built and used as a summer retreat by people of modest means. Alice and Thomas retained the house until her death in the 1930s. The house has always faced Madrone Avenue, and before its inclusion in the Echo Place subdivision, once had its own house name, "The Maples," and a mailing address of 275 Madrone. The lot, like all the others in this area, once ended at the southern boundary line of the Rancho Punta de Quentin, but later was extended further south to the creek bed.

The house has a steep roof, drop bevel-channel siding, and flat window casings. Some alterations have occurred over the years, primarily involving the addition of a kitchen and bathroom to the rear of the home. The freestanding garage and loft was constructed in 1987 by the current owners, Peter Martin and Marianne Rafter, who took pains to assure its design would compliment the original house. Marianne serves as a member of Larkspur's Library Board, and Peter oversaw aspects of the design and production of this book.

The original "Echo" building at **3 ECHO PLACE** was once the home of Isabella and Carl Holm. It was Isabella, Carl's second wife and widow, a Scottish immigrant, who operated her summer resort here on Lots 5 and 6 for more than three decades. When she died in 1938 at age 88, Isabella made an earnest request to be buried in Larkspur, but there were (and are) no cemeteries in the city. After her cremation, her ashes were "brought back to Marin county;" perhaps a trace of Isabella still remains in Echo Place. The house was substantially renovated in 2006-2007, but retains some of its original exterior appearance.

The lot at **4 ECHO PLACE** was first sold to Eleanor Foley in 1907. The formal entrance to the lot was on Madrone Avenue, at the top of the steep curve, but pedestrians pragmatically went through the neighbors' lands below, where Echo Place eventually was created. Decades later the shingled house remained as one of the three original structures that had survived the re-subdivision of 1972. However,

▲ 3.54: *John Foley, Chairman of the Larkspur Town Trustees, as depicted in the Booster Day pamphlet of 1909.*

when the current owners undertook much-needed renovations, the task proved impossible, and in 1994 a completely new house was constructed on the site.

Eleanor's husband, John T. Foley Jr. was a highly regarded member of Larkspur's early Board of Trustees, serving from 1908 until early 1920, when illness forced him to resign. He served several terms as mayor, and was both a visionary and stabilizing presence in the city's early growth. John's parents, Irish-born John Foley Sr. and wife Fanny, had retired from San Francisco, and lived with John's sister, Sarah Foley, who owned a house at 51 Locust. Sarah was also important to our young city, serving as Larkspur's postmistress for about a decade before her death in 1915. John Jr. and Eleanor had come to Larkspur around 1905, first living downtown, adjacent to his parents and sister, but later built their home on this lot, and lived here as year-round residents. They named their new Canyon home "Vernon Dale."

The Foleys were joined every summer by Eleanor's young niece, Eleanor Rideout, who came from San Francisco. She remembered that her aunt "was one of the instigators of the early Booster Days and the Outdoor Dance Hall. She had me sitting on a float in one of the parades." She also recalled that the Presbyterian Church on Arch Street *(see pages 79-81)*, "was encouraged by Mrs. Foley Jr. In fact, the family dog attended church there with them." As a visitor in the Canyon, the niece had gathered "many a bunch of fern and huckleberry for camp decorations, and also many a bucket of huckleberries for pies." Eleanor and John Foley may have joined the Holms in operating summer rentals here, as several structures once stood on the southern portion of their lot, adjacent the houses managed by Isabella Holm. After John's death in August of 1920, Eleanor moved to Alameda, eventually selling the land to her neighbor Mrs. Holm at 3 Echo Place.

⑫ Jones Way

The tiny road named Jones Way was the first side street at the eastern edge of the Glen Addition, surveyed in 1896 by a civil engineer named Dunzy A. Jones, about whom little is known. Just as Ward Street in downtown Larkspur perpetuated the name of that area's surveyor, Mr. Jones was probably the inspiration of the name for "Jones Way." Surviving documents reveal that Jones was paid for his survey work in 1896 by scrip issued by C. W. Wright, President of the American Land and Trust Co., payable for $150 worth of real estate. In December of 1898, Jones cashed out that note by assigning it to F. B. Millard, who presumably used it in purchasing some of his lands on Millard Road.

Ironically, Jones' namesake street included a dangerous flaw; it was placed in the center of a storm channel that exploded in a spectacularly destructive mudslide in January of 1982. One home was totally destroyed, another badly damaged. Lynn Bellati, who lived at **300 MADRONE AVENUE** at the time of the storm, barely escaped with her life. "I heard what I thought was a huge bolt of lightning and thunder," she recalled. "I turned around and there was a wall of water coming down the street. What I had heard was . . . trees cracking and the [adjacent house] breaking up and the sound of the water coming down. It looked like everything was coming down the street – trees, rocks, mud." The effects of the Jones Way debris flow were felt far downstream on Madrone Avenue; rocks, mud and water coursed down the street, blocking gutters, filling low garages, and flooding the intersections. Many homes and yards were damaged. The widespread destruction, however, brought out equally broad community assistance. As Lynn continued, "The next day was one of the saddest and one of the wonderful days of my life. When I got here in the morning my husband was here ... and 50 or more people from all over as well as neighbors who pitched in to help us." The Bellatis proceeded to restore the house at 300 Madrone Avenue with only minor changes and retained its original character.

⑬ Madrone Between Jones Way & Redwood Avenue

Beyond Jones Way, the houses on the creek side occupy portions of the Glen Addition's Block 1; the hillside houses derive from larger tracts that were subdivided piecemeal. Most of the houses in this block have completely replaced their predecessors.

Two contemporary homes built in 1981 are located on a steep and controversial concrete driveway between 300 and 302 Madrone Avenue, high above little Jones Way. The drive occupies a route once designated as Nightingale Road. Below Madrone Avenue, steep drives descend to contemporary homes at numbers 323, 325, and 327, which replaced much smaller original structures located near the creek.

Like many San Franciscans, William Roy McMillan and his family camped on land overlooking the creek. In 1929 they built a little cottage at **337 MADRONE AVENUE**, identified for decades by its signboard as "Forget-Me-Not," named for the flowers on its hillside. It later became the home of William's daughter Marion and her husband Joseph Balestreri, the secretary for a plumbers' union in San Francisco. That cottage, subsequently used as rental quarters, has drop siding, no eaves, and four matching windows of six panes over one. Years later, the Balestreris purchased the adjoining house at **339 MADRONE AVENUE**. That large brown shingle house had been built about 1904 as a summer residence, and owned since about 1908-1910 by San Franciscans Francis and Anita O'Brien, in conjunction with Adolph Lien, Anita's brother. Anita, the family's last survivor, died here in 1967.

⊃ *Traffic splits at the intersection of Madrone Avenue and Redwood Avenue. Explorers on foot may continue on the relatively level final section of Madrone Avenue,*

▲ *3.56: Built about 1912, the shingled duplex at 33 Redwood Avenue still reflects its early design, 2006.*

▲ *3.55: The little house at 1 Redwood Avenue was probably built about 1913 on one of the lots created by speculator Morrison F. Pixley, 2006.*

or climb the ever-steeper Redwood Avenue as it rises to connect to the Madrone Woodlands on the hillside above.

(14) Redwood Avenue & Oak Road

Redwood Avenue began as a side street, but became a thoroughfare. When originally created by the 1896 Glen Addition subdivision, Redwood Avenue rose from Madrone Avenue and terminated near the top of a small canyon. Morrison F. Pixley, a Corte Madera real estate agent and active land speculator (who was also a son of Emma Catherine Pixley; *see pages 126-127*), bought most of the land in this area in 1906-1908, then re-subdivided and promoted it through the 1920s. He created an additional roadway, Oak Road, designed to climb steeply westward from Redwood Avenue and zigzag much further up the hillside through his lands. Although Pixley's Oak Road appeared on maps for the ensuing century, it was little developed, finally becoming important in the early 1960s when its link to Wilson Way provided a route into the populous Madrone Woodlands.

The few older houses directly on Redwood Avenue were developed about 1912-1915, and were used primarily as summer retreats; most of the area was given over to informal camping. One of the first houses was probably the little shingled, hipped-roof house at **1 REDWOOD AVENUE**, most likely constructed around 1913. For most of its 90-plus years the structure served as a duplex for short-term and seasonal renters. It has since reverted to a single owner-occupant.

Next door, the Gallatin family owned the handsome home at **11 REDWOOD AVENUE** for more than four decades. California-born Willis E. Gallatin was a captain in San Francisco's fire department; he and his wife Sarah acquired this house in 1913, and vacationed here in the 1920s with their family of eight children. By 1930 they lived here as full-time residents, with the family retaining the land until the late 1950s. The painted-shingle house has a flared skirt and shingled columns on its wide porch. The current owners made substantial modifications to the house in 1998, including significant alterations to the front porch area and external changes at the rear. The street-side garage, unlike the main house, is clad in coved drop siding.

Two other buildings reflect the early 1900s development of the area; 27 Redwood Avenue, reportedly built in 1908, has been updated repeatedly, while shingled **33 REDWOOD AVENUE** has retained some of its 1912 features, including centered gable dormers on the east and west faces and beveled brackets under the eaves.

As the road climbs further, two houses on the south side span the odd transition from Redwood Avenue to Oak Road to Wilson Way; 17 Oak Road is a 1915 structure far below the roadbed, while the adjacent small house at 33 Wilson Way is dated to 1940, and occupies a sunny prominence that was once – quite literally – the end of the road.

For more than ninety years the steep portion of Oak Road above Wilson Way was a partially paved track that served only a few permanent homes. Work began in 2008 to rebuild that roadway to modern standards, thereby making four reconfigured building lots available for new development. All of those lots have views west to Mt. Tamalpais and east to the Bay and Mt. Diablo.

One of the first structures here was located at 33 Oak Road, a tiny and dilapidated 1907 house, demolished in 2008 to accommodate the revamped road. For decades this had been the location of Larkspur's last chicken farm, operated by Eddie Scherman on land acquired by his parents in the 1930s. Eddie was fondly remembered as a walking encyclopedia of early Canyon history, a self-proclaimed "poultry man" who for years sold and delivered eggs throughout town. After his 1996 death at age 96, his buildings became uninhabitable. Another early home, at **45 OAK ROAD**, built around 1916, still clings to a knoll that enjoys a fabulous view. The house at **20 OAK ROAD** is a 1984 replacement of an earlier structure. Old directories mention several other addresses of long-gone structures in the lower Oak Road area.

(15) Wilson Way

In 1923 Helen and Edwin Wilson acquired a large tract of land that faced Madrone Avenue, stretching from Glen Way nearly to Valley Way. Their small house, located high on the hillside, was accessible from Madrone Avenue only by climbing a grueling set of 194 wooden stairs called

MADRONE WOODLANDS

Wilson Way continues westward as the central street of the Madrone Woodlands subdivision, with short side streets named Polhemus Way and Hatzic Court, both named after the investment groups that subdivided the area in 1961. Nearly all the homes in this area were built in the early 1960s and 1970s, but only after extensive grading and roadway construction had rendered the steep terrain accessible. The subdivision is bounded on the west by Larkspur's city boundary.

▲ 3.57: *A pencil portrait of Helen Wilson, Canyon resident and city librarian.*

"Bovin Way," once located between 422 and 434 Madrone. Those stairs were soon destroyed in a flood and mudslide, so in 1927 the Wilsons hired a tractor to create a new entrance road; the new route branched off from Oak Road and contoured westward along the hillside for almost a quarter mile to their house. Their house, located at number 125 Wilson Way, is now substantially modified and surrounded by the contemporary homes of the Madrone Woodlands subdivision.

The Wilsons' large tract first had been purchased in 1910-1911 by a group of San Francisco postal workers, who reportedly wanted to move to Larkspur "to get away from earthquakes." In a 1975 interview, Helen reported that the postal workers had the land surveyed, but failed to realize that their lots were too small to accommodate houses on such steep terrain. The scheme failed, and eventually the Wilsons acquired the former lots as a single tract.

By 1939 Helen Wilson was divorced, now the single parent of a young daughter. Juliet Kraegerhill, who rented a room from Mrs. Wilson then, recalled: "It was the house at the end of the road. It was so black; there were no streetlights. Mrs. Wilson had to maintain the road, and if she didn't she wouldn't have a road. She had to worry about cleaning the culverts. One bad winter the road washed out and you had to park the car blocks away and walk in. The water would be so heavy over the road that it was very dangerous. You could be wiped away, and no one would know." The advent of the Madrone Woodlands development in the early 1960s brought the opportunity to reshape, grade, and pave Mrs. Wilson's driveway, which became today's Wilson Way.

A spunky former schoolteacher, Montana-born Helen Wilson became a vital part of Larkspur. She served as secretary of the first planning commission, and for five years as city clerk, but her major love and devotion was to the library. Helen was Larkspur's librarian for 36 years, from 1932 to 1968. When remodeled in 1984 the city's library was dedicated to her; she died at her home a few months later, having lived a remarkably full and active life for 98 years.

⤴ *Return to the intersection of Madrone Avenue and Redwood Avenue; then turn west, going up-Canyon.*

▲ 3.58: *Built about 1905, the home at 370 Madrone Avenue overlooks Glen Way and the creek below, 2006.*

⑯ Upper Block of Madrone Avenue

Many of the large lots overlooking Arroyo Holon (Larkspur Creek) originated as parts of the Glen Addition, but most of the original structures have since been completely replaced. A group of contemporary homes all dated to 1979 at numbers 351, 355, and 359 Madrone occupy reconfigured portions of the original Block 1 lots. The original house at 359 Madrone, named "Kokosing," was used as a weekend camp by the Girl Scouts from 1939 to 1947. Similarly a large home now at 387 Madrone, built in 1996, replaced a much earlier structure on a streamside lot filled with large redwoods.

A surviving house above the intersection at **370 MADRONE AVENUE** probably dates to 1905. Reportedly built over time by John and Mary Wilson's family, it was used as a summer residence, and later occupied by their adult children into the mid-1980s. Portions of the exterior remain unchanged, but alterations have been made as recently as 2010. The house has three-lap or "teardrop" siding and overhanging eaves, with many original double-hung windows that have six panes on the upper sash. A modern carport encroaches into the original Glen Way dimensions.

Another of the improbable "ways" created by the Glen Addition mapping, Glen Way is a small stump of a road that provides access to only two contemporary homes. The stone steps that approach the front door of the home at number 9 Glen Way are set against a rock face that was one of many minor blue rock quarries during the early 1900s.

LARKSPUR WATER COMPANY DAM

About 350 yards to the west of the trailhead, the Dawn Falls trail overlooks the remains of a thick stone dam across the streambed, now breached at its center, allowing water to flow over the aged stonework. The dam consists of locally quarried blue rock and rubble, loosely mortared together, and measures almost twenty feet high. Rusted water pipes lodged in the streambed serve as reminders of the residential water system that the reservoir once supplied. Behind the dam, silt and gravel have filled the once-deep reservoir; the resulting gravelly meadow now approximates the configuration of the original impoundment.

The dam apparently was built by C. W. Wright's American Land and Trust Co. as part of its promotional activity for lot sales in the downtown area. The resulting Larkspur Water Co. operated a water system here for about a decade in the late 1890s and early 1900s. Although the 1896 survey that created the Glen Addition shows the dam and reservoir as an existing feature, we have no clear record of its date of construction. The dam's spectacular destruction, however, occurred by dynamite on the evening of Monday, May 24, 1926.

▲ 3.59: *Waters of the Arroyo Holon now flow over and through the old stone dam, 2010.*

> "The body of Christ[ian] Muender, 64, a building contractor of Larkspur, was found Monday evening in an abandoned reservoir in Larkspur canyon, where he apparently had committed suicide by drowning ... Witnesses, who had seen Muender making his way toward the reservoir, led the Sheriff's office and Larkspur officers to believe that his body might be somewhere in those waters. Preparations were made to dynamite the structure, known as Wright's dam. Shortly before the fuse was lighted, the body came to the surface. The dam was blown up anyway, as it was claimed to be a breeding place for mosquitos."
>
> — *The Marin Journal*, May 27, 1926.

The western-most surviving house of those in the streamside Glen Addition occupies a prime sunny site below the road that was first acquired in 1905, with the house purportedly dating to about 1918. Harry and Dot Mortimer of San Francisco probably built **377 MADRONE AVENUE**; Dot later sold the land, house, and furnishings to Alex and Aimee MacKillop in 1922. The MacKillops were permanent residents, with Alex working as a local carpenter; he was a brother to Angus MacKillop at 271 Madrone. Although the house has been updated several times, much of its northern and western exterior reflects the original configuration, including a large beam and pulley high on the northern gable.

Several homes above Madrone Avenue between Glen and Valley Ways, dating to the 1920s and 1940s, have been significantly remodeled. In their midst, between 422 and 434, is a steep and brush-covered patch that once contained a stairway named "Bovin Way," long since abandoned. It was part of an unsuccessful attempt to colonize the hillside, and led to the home of Helen Wilson, 194 steps above.

The final Glen Addition street, tiny Valley Way now serves merely as a drainage way and access drive for the late-1940s home at number 436. The contemporary homes to the west were developed as a part of the Madrone Woodlands subdivision higher on the hillside; although their address numbers (135, 139, 141) are labeled Valley Way, they actually derive from Wilson Way on the hill above. Madrone Avenue itself was optimistically proposed to continue up the hill from the Valley Way intersection, but that roadbed was never constructed. This intersection now marks the beginning of an undeveloped street, Water Way, whose route forms the initial trailhead for access to the open space lands beyond.

⑰ Baltimore Canyon Open Space

The upper Canyon's long history includes its use as a reservoir in the early 1900s and as illegal campsites during the turbulent 1960s. It has since settled into respectability as a portion of the Marin County Open Space system, thus continuing a century-long tradition of hiking in its cool depths.

The junction of Valley Way and Madrone Avenue forms a major signed trailhead to the vast open space preserves to the west. A narrow and rough footpath leads into the Canyon; for about 70 yards it follows the planned route of Water Way, a never-developed road (now badly eroded) that would have led directly to the dam and reservoir further upstream. The path instead drops downhill, crosses a timber bridge, and joins the main Dawn Falls trail that penetrates about one mile further up the Canyon to its namesake waterfall.

Rusted steel posts, the remnants of a chain link fence across the trail, mark what had been the eastern boundary of land owned for about three decades by Adolph Tiscornia, who also owned much of the King Mountain area and the Escalle estate in north Larkspur. That fence, which also roughly marks the Larkspur city boundary, was erected in 1971 to ward off hikers and illegal campers, but instead sparked a contentious process to acquire legitimate public access to an area that had been used for recreational

BLUE ROCK QUARRIES.

The large rocks used to construct the dam apparently were quarried from the hillside immediately to the north, an area now covered by soil and debris. Old maps show that site and another, much smaller, quarry located another 390 yards upstream. That last quarry remains readily visible from the Dawn Falls trail, which climbs abruptly over the quarry's debris pile shortly before arriving at the intersection of the Dawn Falls trail with the Ladybug Trail and bridge. The Ladybug Trail climbs steeply to join the King Mountain Loop Trail that wends around the summit of King Mountain, named for Larkspur's pioneer landowner.

hiking since the 1880s. An ambitious campaign to raise funds for the so-called Northridge lands narrowly missed voter approval in 1975, but created momentum that resulted in a negotiated purchase of 357 acres by the Open Space District a year later, jointly funded by the cities of Mill Valley and Larkspur and private donations including a generous gift by Larkspur citizen Clara-Belle Hamilton. Subsequent purchases created an unbroken span of open space preserves that includes Blithedale Summit, Baltimore Canyon, and King Mountain. The entire area is now managed by the Marin County Open Space District, which publishes hiking maps and information regarding the area's wildlife. ✦

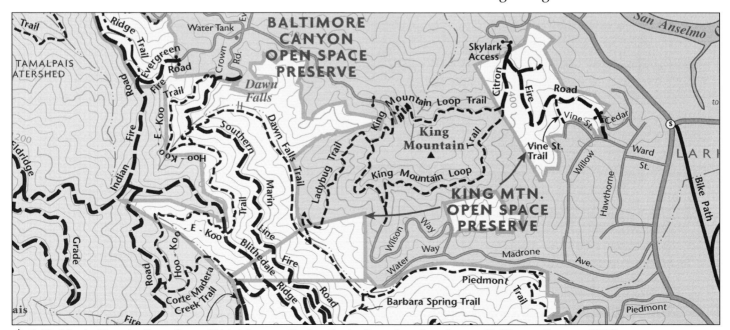

▲ 3.60: Marin County Open Space District maps display the trails and routes of upper Baltimore Canyon, 2010.

BALTIMORE PARK
Early twentieth-century homes exhibit a variety of architectural styles.

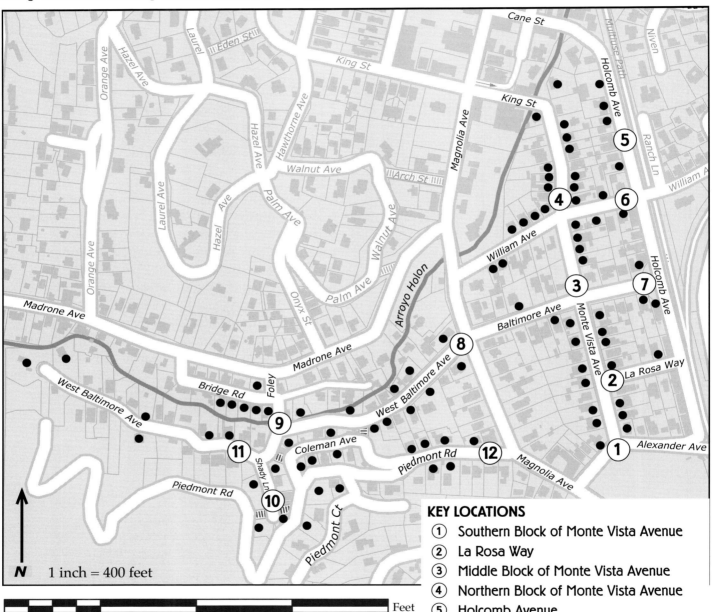

KEY LOCATIONS
1. Southern Block of Monte Vista Avenue
2. La Rosa Way
3. Middle Block of Monte Vista Avenue
4. Northern Block of Monte Vista Avenue
5. Holcomb Avenue
6. William Avenue
7. Baltimore Avenue
8. West Baltimore Avenue
9. Bridge Road Crosses Arroyo Holon
10. Shady Lane
11. Western Block of Baltimore Avenue
12. Piedmont Road
• Addresses of Note

This easy, mostly level walk begins at the intersection of Monte Vista and Alexander Avenues, and explores the variety of home styles east of Magnolia Avenue before wending up Baltimore Canyon on the south side of Arroyo Holon. Street parking is available on wide Monte Vista Avenue, and there is bus service along Magnolia Avenue.

BALTIMORE PARK

Most of south-central Larkspur was laid out by two "Baltimore Park" subdivisions in the early 1900s. The original 1907 subdivision included land generally to the east of Magnolia Avenue; the 1913 Baltimore Park Subdivision Two encompassed the Canyon floor between Madrone, Baltimore, and Piedmont Avenues. Together, those tracts created more than 200 lots.

• • • • • • • • • • • • •

This area has a very different history than the nearby downtown. R.S. Brown, who had worked at the early Baltimore sawmill in the 1850s, settled and farmed about 200 acres of Canyon lands that included most of this area *(see page 103)*. Jonathan Bickerstaff, Brown's brother-in-law, operated a dairy farm during the same period, adjacent to the salt marshes and including all of today's Palm Hill. Their holdings became embroiled in long-running legal proceedings brought by the heirs of John Reed, who claimed the same land as a rightful part of the Rancho Corte de Madera del Presidio. That litigation was finally resolved in favor of Reed's numerous heirs in 1885.

Before the law suits were concluded, sophisticated land speculators had negotiated an arrangement with the Reed heirs to settle the title disputes.

◄ 4.1: *This idealistic early illustration of south Larkspur includes the original 1895 Larkspur-Corte Madera School building at far left, with a steam-driven railroad train in the foreground. Two fences enclose the county road (now Magnolia Avenue) across the middle of the scene. The road that became Baltimore Avenue passes adjacent to the isolated oak tree in the center before entering Baltimore Canyon. The single house on the right likely is the home of R.S. and Helen Brown, now at 47 Madrone Avenue.*

Those investors were Alexander Forbes and William T. Coleman. Alexander Forbes was a wealthy Scottish shipping broker who had invested heavily in Marin real estate – extensive tracts in San Rafael still bear his name. William Tell Coleman, famous as a leader of San Francisco's Committee of Vigilance in the 1850s and later a successful merchant in New York, returned to California in the early 1870s to develop other areas of San Rafael. The two men's similar activities in Larkspur are less well known, but no less important. In a complex series of transactions during 1871 and 1872, Forbes and Coleman variously paid $9,000 to pioneer settlers R.S. and Helen Brown for about 218 acres of land, and $19,000 to Jonathan and Anna Bickerstaff (and another family member) for about 475 acres. The area they acquired constitutes much of modern day Larkspur and Corte Madera, and was known thereafter as the "Forbes-Coleman Tract." The two men's estates held and leased those lands for the next thirty years, finally settling on subdivision plans during the early 1900s.

Before the land was subdivided it remained available for casual use by others. Neighbors grazed cows there, and campers used it during summer. One resident recalled: "[People] came, year after year, to the camping grounds in what is now known as Baltimore Park. The land was owned by the William T. Coleman Estate, and a Mr. Rose was in charge and rented the space where tents were put up among the trees and poison oak shrubbery. In June and July, an area of perhaps 5 or 6 acres of the valley became a colony under canvas, and a most agreeable and peaceful settlement it was."

The Forbes and Coleman families had a nice sense of history; they recognized the memory of the 1849 Baltimore and Frederick Mining and Trading Company's sawmill that lingered in the name Baltimore Canyon, and adopted that label both for their subdivisions and the central street that linked them. Today's Holcomb Avenue was originally named "Maryland" Avenue, to commemorate the origin of the early loggers. Both Alexander Avenue and William Avenue were named to honor patriarchs (Alexander) Forbes and (William) Coleman, and tiny La Rosa Way, between Monte Vista and Holcomb, may have honored an obscure Mexican-Californian active in the early statehood period.

▲ 4.2: *The Marin County Recorder's official 1907 map for Baltimore Park Subdivision One. The newly renamed "North Shore Electric Suburban Railway" bound the area on the east. The Magnolia Avenue name (bestowed earlier by the 1887 subdivision of "the Town of Larkspur") has been extended to this southern portion of the former county road. Uniform-sized lots averaged 7,500 square feet, except in Block G to the north, where smaller lots measured about 4,800 square feet.*

The formal creation of Baltimore Park in 1907 introduced a whole new marketing outlet for land in Larkspur. Development of the original town remained under the control of the American Land and Trust

BALTIMORE PARK — YOUR OPPORTUNITY

"The property in and around Baltimore Canyon was jointly acquired some thirty years ago by two very shrewd and far-seeing capitalists, Mr. William T. Coleman and Mr. Alexander Forbes. These old pioneers of Marin had the pick of the choicest lands, and they readily saw that Baltimore Park afforded a really ideal site for country homes amid exquisite settings. During their lifetime they could not be induced to part with this gem, and it is only lately that their estates have concluded to offer the property in subdivisions. It is your opportunity. Come tomorrow and see Baltimore Park. You don't have to buy. Come and pick poppies or ferns. It will be a trip worth while."

— Advertisement by William L. Courtright, *The San Francisco Examiner*, April 9, 1911, p. 50

▲ 4.3: This 1911 full-page advertisement from the San Francisco Examiner assured potential buyers that "desirable people will be given the most reasonable terms. Undesirable people won't be given any terms. They are not wanted."

Company (later called the Anglo-American Land Company), with its primary sales office on Market Street in San Francisco. The Forbes and Coleman families instead created their own marketing arm, using an experienced local representative, William L. Courtright, who maintained a sales office near Baltimore Park Station and built his own showplace home nearby at 3 Elm Avenue. A third subdivision of the Forbes and Coleman lands, labeled Palm Hill, was launched in 1913.

The two Baltimore Park subdivisions developed different characteristics over time. Subdivision One had homes built primarily in the 1920s, usually as more substantial, permanent, homes for families adopting a new suburban lifestyle on large

MONTE VISTA AVENUE

Wide Monte Vista Avenue was clearly intended to be a main thoroughfare of Baltimore Park (and was designed to route its sewage pipes toward Corte Madera Creek). It runs from Alexander Avenue on the south to King Street on the north.

▲ 4.4: *Charles and Ida White built their "Whiteacres Cottage" at 9 Monte Vista Avenue about 1908, moving here from San Francisco with their three children that same year. This period photo, taken about 1911, may include their son Raymond peering through the window.*

sunny lots. Baltimore Park Two, with uneven boundaries and many small lots tucked into the Canyon, developed primarily as seasonal vacation cottages. By the end of World War II, housing shortages had filled the structures in both areas with full-time residents.

Early publicity stressed the attractive scenery of the area and genteel lifestyle of the residents, a feature supposedly assured by use of "covenants, conditions, and restrictions" that were just coming into practice in subdivision law.

Plans for Baltimore Park One (then also called the Brown Tract) were first prepared in 1897 by San Rafael surveyor George M. Dodge, but a slightly amended formal version wasn't officially recorded until 1907. Sales began then in earnest, with about 16 lots sold and built on within the first two years. Most of those original houses remain today; the majority of them are visible on Magnolia Avenue, and the others are primarily on Monte Vista Avenue.

⤷ *The following text describes Monte Vista Avenue, La Rosa Way, and Holcomb Avenue proceeding from south to north.*

① Southern Block of Monte Vista Avenue

Early photographs of the area show that the first homes to be developed here stood isolated in wide grassy spaces, while hay was farmed nearby on Palm Hill. The early homes at 8, 9, and 23 Monte Vista Avenue were all built with wooden exteriors. Certainly the most elaborate was the home of Charles and Ida White, at **9 MONTE VISTA AVENUE**, celebrated as "Whiteacres Cottage."

White was the assistant cashier for the Aetna Insurance Company in San Francisco, a position that apparently allowed him to invest substantial funds in his new home, built in 1908. He also served as Larkspur's town treasurer from 1908 until 1924. The house has elements of an eastern shingle cottage, and was maintained in excellent condition by Paul and Christine Elmquist who owned it from the mid-1980s until 2010; it still boasts original light fixtures, windows, interior paneling, and an elaborate clinker brick fireplace. A redwood grove in the rear of the yard once sheltered an active spring, used by early residents of the neighborhood for drinking and laundry purposes.

Across the street **8 MONTE VISTA AVENUE** was the home of the Robert J. and Lillian Finigan family, who lived here through the mid-1940s. The house's age is deceptive; although it is built of old-style beveled-channel drop siding, neighbors and family members believe that the lumber was recycled from a horse barn at the nearby Pixley family's Owl's Wood estate. Robert personally built the house, finishing it in 1920.

Probably the first home built on this block was **23 MONTE VISTA AVENUE**, built for Rose Pignaz, an Irish widow with three children, and owned by her daughter Ann for several decades thereafter. The house apparently was built in the very early 1900s. It has an eclectic mixture of elements befitting its transitional period; the three-lap siding was used on many turn-of-the-century

▲ 4.5: *The Finigan home at 8 Monte Vista Avenue, as it appeared in 1990.*

▲ 4.6: *In 1908 Rose Pignaz acquired the deed to this home at 23 Monte Vista Avenue, although construction likely had occurred several years earlier. Note the enclosed porch in this 2008 view.*

▲ 4.7: *The wooden home at 31 Monte Vista Avenue, seen here in 1990 before later renovations and landscaping.*

▲ 4.8: *The 1924 Tosney-Heierle home at 20 Monte Vista Avenue, as it appeared in 2009.*

▲ 4.9: *A nice example of a stucco California Bungalow of the mid-1920s remains at 28 Monte Vista Avenue, 2010.*

homes, and the porch (since partially enclosed) has classic columns resting on a low wall. The unusual front door has a single pane of beveled glass in a trapezoidal inset. A tiny gable vent with a decorative railing completes the picture.

A fourth wooden house, also of three-lap siding but attributed to about 1925, is at **31 MONTE VISTA AVENUE**.

The next generation of homes on Monte Vista Avenue was built using stucco, designed either in the California Bungalow or Mediterranean styles that were popular from about 1910 until the late 1930s. The modest homes at 20 and 28 Monte Vista, each having about 1600 square feet of living area, exemplify the understated California Bungalow style. Both have low-pitched roofs, modified bay windows, semi-enclosed front porches, and multipane windows. (A third small stucco house at 26 Monte Vista, erected about 1923, was completely redesigned by architect Brock Wagstaff in 2002; it originally was nearly identical to a house that remains at 219 Monte Vista.) **20 MONTE VISTA AVENUE** was built in 1925 by the widowed James Tosney, who moved in here with his mother Annie, his sister Mary, and his nine-year-old daughter, Mildred. Mildred later married George Heierle; the Heierles have lived in this house since 1947, perhaps establishing a Larkspur record for Mildred for longevity in a single home. George, like his Swiss father Otto before him, worked his entire career at the Niven Nursery. The house has a spacious corner porch overlooking the intersection; it has had relatively few changes made during its long existence here. **28 MONTE VISTA AVENUE** was built in 1924 for Frank P. Resek, a credit manager, and his wife Esther, who lived here through the mid-1940s. This house has a small detached garage, and retains most of its original features, including beveled brackets under the eaves.

▲ 4.10: *The home built in 1928 by John and Margaret Schafer at 5 Monte Vista Avenue, as it appeared in 1990.*

▲ 4.11: *The 1926 Mediterranean home at 2 Monte Vista Avenue, 1990.*

▲ 4.12: *The Mediterranean-style stucco at 12 Alexander Avenue, as it appeared in 2004.*

A stucco home of an entirely different style was erected at **5 MONTE VISTA AVENUE** about 1928 for John H. Schafer and his wife, Margaret. Schafer, who was an auditor at Crocker First National Bank in San Francisco, used a vaguely Tudor Revival style with decorative half-timbering for this well-kept home. Its exterior shows little evidence of alteration.

• • • • •

Mediterranean-style homes with red tile roofs are located at 2, 14, 19, and 32 Monte Vista Avenue, and on the corner at 12 Alexander Avenue. The houses at **2 and 14 MONTE VISTA AVENUE** were both built between 1924 and 1926 by local contractor William F. Granger. Number 2, built in 1926 for Harry and Emelie Boeddiker, retains much of its original size and features, while the nearby number 14 has undergone extensive remodeling at the rear.

The elaborate corner home at **12 ALEXANDER AVENUE** has original lantern fixtures at the entrance, with ornamental wrought iron railings, triple-arched windows on the recessed porch, and an arched front door with strap hinges. Built about 1925 for Albert and Minnie McGill, it has tall arched windows at the living room facing Monte Vista Avenue. A mature deodar cedar in the front lawn matches the house across the street, reflecting a popular tree style used in many yards of that period.

A variation on the Mediterranean (or Spanish Colonial Revival) designs appears at **19 MONTE VISTA AVENUE**. This unusual house was built in 1926 for the Michael and Katherine Cloney family, who then occupied it with seven of their eleven children; members of the family remained here until the mid-1970s. Twisted columns support the red tile roof over the recessed center porch, and urn designs on the parapet echo the baroque style of the sculpted frame around the porch.

The Cloney family had substantial roots in Larkspur, as Michael had been the Northwestern Pacific Railroad's section foreman for many years. The Cloneys also owned an adjacent house at 15 Monte Vista, which was razed and replaced with a much larger structure in 2006. That process of demolition and replacement has produced several controversial results on this street. Another house erected in the mid-1920s was replaced at 25 Monte Vista in 2001. Both new houses used Craftsman-style design elements, but their relatively large

▲ 4.13: *Elaborate twisted columns and a central arcade distinguish the Cloneys' 1926 home at 19 Monte Vista Avenue, 2010.*

TWISTED COLUMNS: Churrigueresque

Several Baltimore Park and Palm Hill homes bear elements of an architectural style that uses elaborate sculptural details, labeled Churrigueresque. A simplified version of the style, also known as Spanish Baroque, was revived by the Mediterranean style of early twentieth century California, particularly in San Diego, where it had been used in the Panama-California Exposition of 1915. It generally uses twisted columns or window frames, cupolas, and similar details.

The most exuberant local example is the home at 19 Monte Vista; similar features are visible on the stairway and living room windows of the home at 203 West Baltimore Avenue. A few features appear as well at 12 Alexander Avenue, 144 Magnolia Avenue, and 36 Acacia Avenue.

size and full utilization of yard space generated some neighborhood concern. A yet-larger house built in 2004 at 225 Monte Vista (also replacing a 1920s home) further altered the texture of this modest neighborhood.

The third of the Mediterranean-style stucco and red tile houses is the largest, at **32 MONTE VISTA AVENUE**, built about 1931 for Dr. Louis L. Robinson, who earlier had a surgery practice and residence at 465 Magnolia Avenue. He operated a medical practice in the downstairs portion of this house for several years. From the mid-1960s to 1980s, it was the residence of Larkspur city manager Harlan Barry and his wife Laurie. In 2004 Wagstaff Linsteadt Architects oversaw a new garage and significant expansion of the house.

The elegant wide-dormered stucco bungalow at **40 MONTE VISTA AVENUE** was featured prominently in early real estate advertisements. It probably was built about 1920 by Arthur D. Collman, a German immigrant who built houses in Larkspur during the early 1920s. It has an unusual covered porch with terrazzo pavement, an arbor supported by classic columns, and an oversized entry door. The broad roof has projecting eaves with brackets and exposed beams.

In 1925 Collman sold number 40 to Charles S. Gruver and his wife Mary, who lived here with their extended family. Although Charles described himself as "retired," neighborhood tradition has it that he used a large upstairs closet to stockpile bootlegged liquor. Those suspicions seemed confirmed in late 1929 when Charles was indicted by a grand jury for "conspiracy to violate the prohibition law." Months earlier his adult son Martin had been arrested by federal officers who raided a thriving liquor still on a Marin ranch. The Gruver family moved out soon after, and the house was repossessed and sold in 1933 to Robert Salkeld, a NWPRR employee, and his wife Lallage, who raised their family here. The home's best-remembered owners were Wilson and Harriett Weckel, who lived here for 45 years until 1999. It was probably due to "Bill" Weckel's prowess as a gardener that the yard boasts two fine examples of once-rare deciduous dawn redwood trees near the garage, and another specimen, a giant sequoia, adjacent to Baltimore Avenue.

▲ 4.14: *The graceful stucco home at 40 Monte Vista Avenue dates to about 1920; a recent gate and plantings now screen this 2004 view.*

2. La Rosa Way

The north side of La Rosa developed earlier than the south side, where homes were built in the late 1940s. The graceful home at **8 LA ROSA WAY** was probably built in 1927 for Edwin and Frances Ossman and their two daughters; Edwin was a postal clerk, and remained here into the late 1950s. The house is sheathed in three-lap siding, and has a wide, gracious, covered porch supported by tapered pillars resting on a half wall. The double-hung windows have delicate mullions dividing the upper sashes; v-channel siding surrounds the foundation. A 1924 home at the adjacent number 10 was razed in 2009, and replaced.

The house at 7 La Rosa was erected about 1947; the nearby structure at 21 La Rosa was built in 1947 for Ernie Epidendio, who operated the downtown Rainbow Market.

▲ 4.16: *The broad porch of the 1927 home at 8 La Rosa Way has distinctive and gracious design details, as seen here about 1990.*

3. Middle Block of Monte Vista Avenue

The western side of the block between Baltimore and William Avenues is shadowed by one of Larkspur's storied groves of second-growth redwood trees, now shared cautiously by several structures that face both Baltimore and William Avenues. For many decades the undeveloped land was known as the "Soroptimist's Grove," as it was owned by that group of professional women. A former owner had imposed a restrictive covenant requiring that a portion of the land "remain in its present natural state." Unfortunately, the land was poorly managed, and during the 1960s was occupied by hippie groups that created substantial disturbances. Neighborhood complaints and dissatisfied heirs of the grantor combined to force the sale of the land to a San Rafael builder, Paul Potts, who built four structures there in 1974. An easement applies to the rear of three of the lots to protect the trees, with questionable efficacy.

Two small houses, mirror images of one another, share a driveway at **112** and **116 MONTE VISTA AVENUE**. Both houses were built in 1941, probably by Frank B. Knittle, a local contractor who lived with his wife Marie in number 112 for several decades, after leaving an earlier home on Millard Road.

These houses, like others nearby on Baltimore and William Avenues, rest atop a low knoll; that knoll reportedly was scraped off in the early 1900s for use as road fill material nearby, and particularly to make way for Monte Vista Avenue itself. Numerous area residents have reported finding arrowheads and

▲ 4.15: *Standing on Palm Hill in about 1922, these men are looking at 23 Monte Vista (between their elbows), 40 Monte Vista (long roof), 107 Baltimore (two-story home with oak tree behind), and 19 Baltimore (at right margin of photo). Chances are good one of these men is William L. Courtright, the real estate agent for the Baltimore Park and Palm Hill subdivisions.*

▲ 4.17: *A 2009 view of 112 Monte Vista Avenue, built in 1941; a mirror-image house is located next door at 116 Monte Vista.*

other artifacts of Native American occupation in this area, and remnants of midden material currently remain in some yards.

The nearby railroad tracks were operated after 1902 as the North Shore Railroad, running electric interurban trains that required a signal and switching tower near the Baltimore Park station. That signal tower (Tower No. 3) was operated 24 hours a day; one of the operators was Harry G. Sayer, who lived in the tidy Colonial home at **118 MONTE VISTA AVENUE**. Harry and his wife Bertha had this house built about 1921, shortly after their marriage, living here into the early 1950s. The house has tapered porch columns and three narrow dormers, with clapboard siding. Windows facing the porch have delicate small panes on the upper sash. Note the concrete wheel guides built into the driveway, one of the few remaining

LARKSPUR MIDDENS

Archaeologists define a "midden" as a refuse heap representing decades, usually centuries, of repeated human settlement in an area. The Bay Area is ringed with "shell mounds" that contain shells, bones of marine animals, other organic material, and discarded utilitarian artifacts. Several middens were officially recorded in this immediate area by archaeological surveys in the early 1900s. Three of those sites are close to the salt marshes that once existed along the eastern end of William Avenue.

▲ 4.18: *Harry and Bertha Sayer's 1921 home at 118 Monte Vista Avenue, as it appeared in 2010.*

▲ 4.19: *The Baltimore Park signal tower, about 1940. Several operators lived nearby.*

▲ 4.20: A 1925 stucco home at 202 Monte Vista Avenue on the northeast corner of William Avenue, 2006.

▲ 4.21: 208 Monte Vista Avenue, built about 1926, is an excellent example of a well-designed California Bungalow; 2006.

▲ 4.22: The shingled home at 210 Monte Vista Avenue is another of builder William F. Granger's numerous Baltimore Park structures. Landscaping has matured since this 1990 view was taken.

examples of that early solution to the demands of steering an automobile up a narrow driveway. Additions at the rear have not affected the front elevation of the home.

④ Northern Block of Monte Vista Avenue

This block contains the oldest houses in the area, some on unusually large parcels, as well as a collection of homes built in the late 1920s by two local contractors. Unlike the grasslands to the south, this area has always been notable for its redwood groves.

Three small houses, all built in 1925-1926, appear at **202, 208,** and **210 MONTE VISTA AVENUE.** The stucco-clad corner house, number 202, typifies the Mediterranean style, using a partial red tile roof and enclosed porch. Tradition has it that Corte Madera contractor William F. Granger, who erected many of downtown Larkspur's buildings in the same period, built this house for his niece Bessie and her husband, Andrew C. Huntemann, who remained here into the 1950s. A rear addition has not changed the well-kept front appearance.

The neighboring number **208 MONTE VISTA AVENUE** was first occupied by William and Fagan Osborn, who each worked at the downtown telephone office at 464 Magnolia Avenue, where she was the chief operator. Their small stucco bungalow has low-pitched rooflines and a dramatic arched living room window that matches the arched porch entrance. A small detached garage at the rear of the lot typifies mid-1920s design, before accommodation for automobiles had come to dominate residential architecture. This structure most likely was built by William F. Wegner, a local contractor who built many houses on this block.

The shingled bungalow at **210 MONTE VISTA AVENUE** was also built by contractor William F. Granger in 1925, and originally occupied by the Frank Cunane family. Its tidy shingled exterior has kept its original shape. The current owner has meticulously remodeled the entire house to appropriate period style; several magazines have featured aspects of its interior.

In mid-block, the two houses at 218 (1947) and 227 (1951) were built in the late-1940s style; the nearby number 236 dates to 1961. Tiny **226 MONTE VISTA AVENUE**, a hipped-roof house with three-lap

▲ 4.23: *The tiny home at 226 Monte Vista Avenue probably was built about 1910 for Anna Schmitt and her husband Charles, a San Francisco plumber, 2009.*

▲ 4.24: *The Hurst and Durston families camping in the redwoods in 1898. Sisters Mary Hurst (at center) and Jean Durston (at right) were Scottish immigrants; the Durstons later moved to Larkspur in the early 1920s. Fred Hurst, who perhaps made the photograph, does not appear in this picture.*

siding, dates to about 1910; it was occupied by Anna M. Schmitt from the early 1920s until the late 1930s. Exposed exterior plumbing attests to an occupancy that predated modern conveniences.

The houses at **230, 232,** and **234 MONTE VISTA AVENUE** have interlocking histories. In the early 1900s the Frederick and Mary Hurst family of San Francisco had a summer camp in this area, to which they escaped after the 1906 earthquake.

The Hursts purchased the double lots at **232-234 MONTE VISTA AVENUE** in 1909, and at about the same time built the shingled house now hidden within the redwood grove and numbered 234. Fred eventually took on a range of official roles in Larkspur; he served as town marshal from 1917 to 1923, working periodically as recorder, tax collector, and street superintendent as well.

After her husband's 1923 death, the widow Mary Hurst vacated her home at 234 and moved into tiny number 232 next door (reportedly once a chicken house), where she lived for another decade while she rented out the large family home. The Hursts' son Eugene purchased additional land in the area in 1913, including the adjoining lot at **230 MONTE VISTA AVENUE**.

According to oral tradition, Eugene Hurst's father Fred built the house at 230 about 1915 using leftover materials from his work as a housing contractor in San Francisco. That house was sold in 1927 to the Chester and Catherine Lucas family, who remained there into the early 1950s. In 1998-1999 the number 230 house underwent an extensive remodeling designed by architect Brock Wagstaff.

▲ 4.25: *The Hursts' home at 234 Monte Vista Avenue as it appeared in 1990, prior to addition of a second story and other modifications.*

▲ 4.26: *The remodeled Hurst-built house at 230 Monte Vista Avenue, as it appeared in 2006.*

▲ 4.27: *203 Monte Vista Avenue, built about 1928, is probably another Wegner-built home, 2009.*

▲ 4.28: *William and Elizabeth Wegner in their yard at 219 Monte Vista Avenue on the occasion of their 50th wedding anniversary in 1959. Note Wegner's trademark slat vents at the gable.*

▲ 4.29: *The 1922 home at 219 Monte Vista Avenue, occupied by contractor William F. Wegner and his wife Elizabeth. The house was carefully refurbished in 2009, preserving its best period features, 2009.*

The west side of Monte Vista Avenue has irregular lots whose sizes vary widely; the lots were not created by the subdivision process that produced the rest of the neighborhood, but instead by the development activities of local contractor William F. Wegner and his wife Elizabeth. The corner house at **203 MONTE VISTA AVENUE** was built about 1928 for Thornton and Lillian Boggs, who remained there until the late 1940s. The bungalow at 205 Monte Vista was built about 1925 for Ruth and Arthur Monaghan; it was remodeled in 2005.

The small homes at **211, 215,** and **219 MONTE VISTA AVENUE**, all built by Wegner in the mid-1920s, have unusual shared driveways leading to a complex of attached garages spanning the rear yards. All the houses are stucco; while number 211 is Mediterranean, the next two are traditional California bungalows. After building these houses, Wegner apparently rented them until permanent buyers came forward.

Number 219 was occupied at various times by the Wegners themselves. The odd shape of this particular lot allowed preservation of a grove of large redwoods at the rear, adjacent the creek. "Bill" Wegner was an early and active member of the volunteer firemen, and responsible for most of the design and maintenance of the Rose Bowl's dance floor; in later years he served as Larkspur's building inspector. In 1928 Wegner also built and occupied an adjacent showcase home at 225 Monte Vista Avenue, which was razed in 2004 and replaced by a much larger structure.

The northernmost house on the west side, the steep-roofed little cottage at **237 MONTE VISTA AVENUE**, has a clapboard exterior, a tapered brick chimney with decorative tiles, an arch top planked door, and other elements of the Storybook style popular in that period. It was built about 1933 for Joseph Ebert, a tile contractor, his wife Olivia and their young son Robert; for most of the 1940s and 1950s it was the home of Samuel and Katie Parsons.

Several large parcels complete this northern block of Monte Vista Avenue. The house at 236 Monte Vista occupies a double lot; it was built in 1961 on lands first acquired in 1907. The early structure at **250 MONTE VISTA AVENUE**, probably built in 1909, was the home of Charles and Annie Holcomb. The original Holcomb house was a one-story, two-room house; it was later rotated to its current south-facing position, and enlarged with a second story and dormer, a living room, dining room, and kitchen. The Holcombs' six-lot parcel once extended east to what was then Maryland Avenue.

Baltimore Park 155

▲ 4.30: *211 Monte Vista Avenue, built in classic stucco by William F. Wegner in 1926, as it appeared in 2009. The arched porch and red tile parapet were notable features of the period.*

▲ 4.31: *The 1926 home at 215 Monte Vista Avenue as it appeared about 2006 before landscaping had matured.*

▲ 4.33: *Charles and Annie Holcomb's original house at 250 Monte Vista Avenue, seen about 1910 with Annie's sister, Hattie Pfluger, on the porch.*

Charles was an assistant city engineer for San Francisco but worked in Larkspur as well, surveying for the early paving of some of Larkspur's streets in 1913-1914. When King Street was extended eastward from Magnolia to Monte Vista, he paid personally for the necessary retaining wall. After Charles's death in 1923, Annie successfully requested the City Council to rename Maryland Avenue in honor of her husband's contributions to the city. Annie remained in the 250 home until her death in 1947 at age 71, and daughter Jennie (Mrs. David Scott) lived in the home until her death in 1993.

⑤ Holcomb Avenue

Lots on the southern end of Holcomb Avenue face the railroad bed, and contain a variety of small structures, many of them duplex units built in the 1940s and subjected to

▲ 4.32: *The Storybook-style entry of the 1933 cottage at 237 Monte Vista Avenue, 2009.*

▲ 4.34: *The Holcomb family home at 250 Monte Vista Avenue as it appeared in 1990.*

▲ 4.35: *In the early 1900s this house at 409 Holcomb Avenue occupied a much larger corner location abutting William Avenue, 2006.*

▲ 4.36: *About 1925 Harry Booth shingled the little house at 431 Holcomb Avenue, 2010.*

various alterations ever since. The older structures occur north of William Avenue. One of them has a sketchy history; **409 HOLCOMB AVENUE**, a tall brown shingle structure with hipped roof, dates to the early 1900s; its double lots were first sold in 1907 to a W. H. Gossip, and once included the entire corner now occupied by this building and the newer house (1974) at number 8 William Avenue. A driveway easement allows access to William Avenue from the old structure at the rear. Four small homes, all in general post-war style and dating to the late 1940s and early 1950s, appear at numbers 415, 419, 421, and 427.

A small home at **431 HOLCOMB AVENUE** was built about 1925 by Harry Booth, a shingler who for a short time was a partner in the "Booth and Little" roofing company downtown. As befitted his trade, he used a staggered-shingle style that requires labor-intensive precision. Much of the front exterior of this little home has been retained, reflecting many influences of the California bungalow style.

Nearby, the large two-story house on a double lot at **437 HOLCOMB AVENUE** dates to about 1910 or earlier, when it was owned by Margaret Horstmann, who in 1907 had also acquired the land to the west (now numbered 236 Monte Vista). Her son, Albert McGill, later owned many parcels in the area; McGill sold this house in 1924 to Mary and Charles Young, who lived there until about 1936, followed by the Spain family until 1970. The 437 house has a cross gabled roof with box cornices

▲ 4.37: *Looking northwest after the snowfall of January 9, 1913, with Charles Holcomb and his daughter Jennie standing near the Hurst home at 234 Monte Vista Avenue (at left), and the Horstmann house at 437 Holcomb Avenue (right).*

▲ 4.38: *A 2009 view of the early Horstmann house at 437 Holcomb Avenue.*

on the north, east, and south sides, with original large double-hung windows. A long wing of the home that stretched toward the west remains essentially unchanged today, with windows added to a once-open porch. The original exterior of the house has been enveloped by aluminum siding.

Most of the properties at this north end of Holcomb Avenue were once portions of larger tracts of land that carried through to Monte Vista Avenue on the west. The Holcomb family lands included the three lots now numbered **441 HOLCOMB AVENUE**. The large home here is an extensive 1990s remodel of an earlier home built in the 1920s.

The northern end of Holcomb Avenue merges into Cane Street; the formal transition between the two streets occurs at the creek bed of the Arroyo Holon, which also marks the northern boundary of Subdivision Two. The northernmost house had been a small frame dwelling near the creek at 461 Holcomb, owned by Minnie C. Learn from sometime before the 1920s until the mid-1960s. The lot to the east of her home once served as automobile parking for the Rose Bowl dance pavilion across the street. After the Bowl closed, George Brockman of Mill Valley removed her house and developed the entire site in 1969 as the El Guaycura studio apartments, but not without repeated hearings and negotiations to preserve the many redwood trees on the site. *The Rose Bowl's extensive history is presented in the Downtown chapter on pages 19-22.*

⑥ William Avenue

The short portion of William Avenue between Holcomb and Magnolia was an essential part of the 1907 Baltimore Park Subdivision One. As originally laid out, William Avenue stopped at the railroad tracks; the address numbers thus began at Holcomb, running west toward Magnolia Avenue. Years later, when William Avenue was extended across the tracks, the pattern had to be reversed and additional address numbers in those new blocks grew larger moving eastward. It may be confusing, but that's just how it is. *The portions of William Avenue east of Holcomb are described in the Heather Gardens & Meadowood chapter.*

The first house to be built on William Avenue was constructed about 1907 for John and Adele Norris; they sold it in January of 1908 to Teresa and Charles Martin of San Francisco. For the next 16 years, the solitary two-story house at **12 WILLIAM AVENUE** was known as "the Martin house," and appears in many photographs of the period. In 1910 Mrs. Martin bought two adjoining lots that were later subdivided to form present-day 202, 208, and 210 Monte Vista.

The Martins continued a permanent residence in San Francisco while they owned this house, and in 1924, after her husband's death, Teresa sold the house to William and Elizabeth Graham. William, a patternmaker for the railroad, sold the home in 1943 to Vernon M. Brown, remembered as the pastor at nearby Redwoods Presbyterian Church, who held it through the mid-1950s. The external form of the house is readily recognizable from early photographs, but the ensuing century of wear has not been kind to the structure. It is still shingle covered, with large centered dormers with three double-hung windows on both the north and south sides. What had been a covered entrance on the southwest corner has now been filled in with a door and an eclectic mix of recycled windows.

Other houses on the block represent a variety of styles; the unpretentious stucco home at **7 WILLIAM AVENUE** was an early wartime home, built in 1942. It had a mate next door at 11 William, but that structure was razed and replaced by a much larger house in 2005. Those houses were built slightly later than the two matching houses at **15 WILLIAM AVENUE** and **122 MONTE VISTA AVENUE**, both constructed in Colonial style on a shared lot in 1937.

The 100 block of William Avenue contains a collection of cottages, generally dating from the 1920s and early 1930s. Mary Bradbury owned the

▶ 4.39: *A postcard view of the Martin house on unpaved William Avenue, about 1910. Magnolia Avenue is hidden beyond the trees, and the main railroad route toward Larkspur station strikes off to the right. The eventual site of the Baltimore Park station is just out of this view to the left. Tracks of the newly opened Detour rail line show in the immediate foreground, heading around Palm Hill toward San Rafael.*

entire northwestern part of this block in the early 1900s, and it is quite probable that the small cottage at **106 WILLIAM AVENUE** was her home, built perhaps as early as 1913. Its appearance has changed over the years; sleeping porches were glassed-in, and more bedrooms and a carport were added in 1977. Irene Tomasi acquired that cottage in 1925, and at the same time, Irene's sister, Jennie Gilardi, purchased the adjacent lot at 110 William. Jennie and her husband Andrew built their stucco cottage in 1926, and thereby established an important Larkspur dynasty whose family members continue today as active contributors to the community. Andrew established the downtown meat market at 467 Magnolia Avenue, and later a catering service at 489 Magnolia Avenue.

The 1926 Gilardi house at **110 WILLIAM AVENUE** has a stucco exterior and low-pitched roof, with an unusual south-facing expanse of windows; it retains much of its original appearance. In 1926 the Gilardis also purchased a large wooded area to the north (now 120 William), which was used for decades for entertaining; with other trees on their adjacent lots, the area became known as the "Gilardi Grove." Damage to some of those trees caused extensive controversy in the neighborhood in 2005.

Next door, the handsome Colonial Revival (or Cape Cod Cottage)-style house at **116 WILLIAM AVENUE** was completed in August of 1923 for the family of Margaret G. and Charles R. Lemme. Margaret acquired the lot in February of 1923 and recorded completion of the house only five months

▲ 4.40: *The 1926 Gilardi house at 110 William Avenue bears many of the signature features used by builder William F. Wegner. Note the bevel-tipped brackets, slatted gable vent, and hooded chimney, 2009.*

▲ 4.41: *The 1923 home at 116 William Avenue was completed by the Lemme family in 1923, and remains in exceptional condition, 2006.*

4.42: A view north in newly created Baltimore Park, looking toward downtown Larkspur, about 1909. The new rail line toward San Rafael and Greenbrae branches to the right around Palm Hill. Notice the Martin house (12 William Avenue) in the open grass fields to the left. The vantage point for this photograph would have been the tall switch tower whose foundation is still visible near the rail bed opposite 121 Holcomb Avenue.

later. That fast construction time, combined with the oral tradition of later owners, indicates the house was built from a manufactured kit available through mail order catalogs that were popular in the period. The solidly built three-bedroom house remains in pristine condition, with no apparent exterior alterations.

Charles Lemme worked as superintendent of a San Rafael Studebaker agency's repair shop, and his son Rudolph became a salesman for a spark plug firm; later occupants often found discarded spark plugs in the garden. The house was acquired by the Stewart family in the early 1960s, and remains in that family today.

On the south side of William Avenue, the shingled number 111 is a 2003 reconstruction designed by Wagstaff Linsteadt Architects of a 1920s house. The adjoining 115 was built in 1928, but has been significantly modified. The next structure, at **121 WILLIAM AVENUE**, has been attributed to 1931. Its narrow three-lap siding exterior appears little altered, except that a large picture window has replaced smaller double-hung windows. This house had a cameo role in the 1949 film, *Impact*, featuring a bathrobe-clad volunteer fireman dashing from its door. Finally, tiny **123 WILLIAM AVENUE** was built about 1908 as an adjunct to the splendid Seegelken home at 214 Magnolia Avenue. The one bedroom and one bath cottage has the three-lap siding typical of that period, and simple flat window casings; there is an extension at the rear.

Two streets, Baltimore Avenue and Piedmont Road, provide the primary east-west travel on the western side of Magnolia Avenue. Both streets are discussed below, following the address numbers in a westward direction.

⑦ Baltimore Avenue

Anchored by the railroad station on the east, Baltimore Avenue pointed westward toward the Canyon of the same name, following a route pioneered by 1850s lumbermen and later used by quarry wagons in the 1870s.

The 5-acre site of the Baltimore Park Station at the intersection of Holcomb and Baltimore Avenues was purchased by the City of Larkspur in 1997, spurred by local residents' fund-raising efforts as the "Railroad Open Space Association." The site includes the final location of the passenger station and the massive power station near William Avenue.

The tracks of the Northwestern Pacific Railroad had been altered in 1908-1909 to provide a new route, named "the Detour Line" or "Cutoff," that allowed northbound trains to branch off directly toward San Rafael, rather than continue on the main line toward the Russian River area.

The new junction provided a natural transfer point for passengers, and the site was soon adapted as a passenger stop. An early accommodation for Baltimore Park passengers was a tiny wooden shelter located on the west side of the tracks, directly in the alignment of the new Baltimore Avenue. One

▲ 4.43: *Young Jennie Holcomb standing in the famous snowfall of January 9, 1913. The wheel marks on Maryland (now Holcomb) Avenue lead south toward the original Baltimore Park wooden passenger shed, with the switch tower visible beyond. Above her head looms the wooden Larkspur-Corte Madera School. To the right are the homes at 9 and 23 Monte Vista Avenue.*

account described that shelter as nothing more than "a tiny abandoned real estate shack." In December of 1913 the railroad built "shed stations" at both Baltimore Park and Escalle, further north on the tracks. The passenger shelters were vital to the promotional efforts to sell lots in Baltimore Park, which repeatedly stressed the convenience of a rapid 45-minute rail commute to San Francisco.

Both the Baltimore Park and Escalle stations later were replaced by handsome wooden structures with three broad arched bays enclosing multipane windows, surrounded by carefully tended landscaping. A commemorative stone and brass plaque today marks the main station site. About 1928 a matching structure was erected nearby, adjacent to the southbound tracks; the concrete foundation of that shelter remains visible today opposite the Calvary Baptist Church.

As part of their promotional activity, the subdividers planted the first two blocks of Baltimore Avenue with Mexican fan palms. Complaints soon followed from the Larkspur Woman's Improvement Club that the trees were "inappropriate," but a member of the city council personally interviewed residents and determined that local opinion favored the trees. They since have grown to near-maximum height and age; twenty of those trees still stand in the median, with three more near the curb that curves in front of the Calvary Baptist Church; others once stood near the opposite curb.

Only the site of the station remains today, but broad concrete waiting platforms exist on both sides of the trackways, revealing the dimensions of the wide double-track system.

George Niven, then a roofing contractor in Larkspur and a son of the founder of the Larkspur Nursery near downtown, purchased several lots at the southwest corner of Baltimore Avenue. He and his wife Inez finished their home at **5 BALTIMORE AVENUE** in September of 1927. The house combines

▲ 4.44: *The Baltimore Park station as it appeared in 1926. This important commuter's stop provided quick and efficient transportation to San Francisco or to Tamalpais High School in Mill Valley. It was also the preferred stop for Saturday night dancers attending the nearby Rose Bowl on Cane Street.*

HOMES ON BALTIMORE AVENUE

Baltimore Avenue, like its larger neighborhood, was a solidly middle-class collection of homes. Although successful professionals owned some of the houses, the majority of the residents were clerks and tradespeople, many working for the NWP railroad. Most of the houses on the first two blocks were erected during the 1920s. Further up the Canyon, in Subdivision Two, many vacation homes were built as early as 1912.

elements of French Revival and Tudor styles, with an exterior of painted shingles and a steeply pitched roof; their original roof consisted of "transite" shingles that provided an elegant slate appearance, appropriate to its owner's trade.

Elaborate multipane French doors set off the northeast corner of the house, with decorative wrought-iron balconies. An arched entry door is set into the porch, under a curved roof that continues from the second story. Inez designed and maintained an elaborate garden in the rear of the home. The Nivens occupied a central role in Larkspur's economic development, with George managing the family nursery for several decades.

Before the Nivens' house was completed, in 1927 George sold the corner lot to Burt Wheeler, the young manager of the Larkspur Lumber Company. Burt had his Mediterranean-style stucco home at **1 BALTIMORE AVENUE** built that same year, probably by a construction team working for his father, Almon Wheeler, a housing contractor who lived nearby at 18 Acacia Avenue. The covered porch had arched openings, with plaster garlands around oval shields on the parapet walls. Later additions carried those same design features to a rear second story.

The Calvary Baptist Church at **2 BALTIMORE AVENUE** was built about 1946 under Pastor Harold Hettema, with most of its members drawn from military families at Hamilton Air Force Base. The church's original building was the curved-front portion that follows the curb line; in 1958 a two-story addition with classrooms and fellowship hall was erected on the west side. The two prominent corner lots earlier had been acquired by Belle Brown in 1926, intended for a women's club structure, but that plan never came to fruition.

▲ 4.45: *George and Inez Niven's 1927 home at 5 Baltimore Avenue, as seen in 2000.*

▲ 4.46: *The 1927 Wheeler home at 1 Baltimore Avenue, as it appeared in 2000.*

▲ 4.47: *The original structure of the Calvary Baptist Church, at 2 Baltimore Avenue as it appeared in 1957.*

▲ *4.48: The mid-1930s Mediterranean-style home at 101 Baltimore Avenue, 2009.*

▲ *4.49: The 1920 Todsen home at 107 Baltimore Avenue, as it appeared in 2004 before modifications that extended the rear portions of the home.*

Numerous bungalows line the street; those nearby at 9 and 19 Baltimore Avenue, both built about 1921, had low-pitched roofs, with stucco and clapboard exteriors; both have been remodeled and expanded significantly. The small duplex across the street at 10/12 Baltimore was erected a few years later. The two houses at 16 and 26 Baltimore were built much later, in 1948 and 1941.

Another excellent example of a Mediterranean-style stucco home, this time with a complete red tile roof, occupies the corner of Baltimore and Monte Vista at **101 BALTIMORE AVENUE**. Built about 1934, apparently for Edmond and Louise Stengel, it has a flared chimney, arched front door and windows, and an unusual seven-sided entry room that faces Monte Vista.

One of the oldest houses on the street was built about 1920, probably by and for Theodore Todsen, a German-born carpenter who built several houses in Larkspur and Corte Madera. **107 BALTIMORE AVENUE** appears in period photographs as a nicely-proportioned, two-story Craftsman-style home, with a low-pitched roof over the large porch and living room, a matching rear entrance, and an upper bedroom floor at cross angles to the main area. Married late in life, Todsen appears to have designed and executed a showplace home for his bride.

Most of the initial features of the 107 house remain today, except that shingles were later applied over the original horizontal siding. The living and dining rooms have box-beamed ceilings and elaborate built-in cabinetry, accented by a stained glass window and doors. Todsen and his wife Marie lived here into the early 1950s, followed by Dale and Glenn Danley for the next 53 years. New owners Eliza and Michael Koeppel extended the rear of the house in 2005, aided by architect Brock Wagstaff and contractor Alan Buschert, maintaining the original façade and scrupulously matching its design features.

The roadbed of Baltimore Avenue has a deceptively level appearance; a substantial swale underlies the street, revealed currently by the low yards in 110, 118, and 120 Baltimore. Early photos show a dip in the grasslands that had to be filled by hundreds of carts of soil, moved by horse-drawn grading equipment. The homes at 111, 115, and 121 Baltimore sit atop the filled lands, and natural drainage and the sanitary sewer both follow that swale through underground easements in the yards. Numbers 111 and 115 date to 1951-1952, while number 121 was built in 1939 and incidentally was the residence of Ellis Brooks, a prominent San Francisco Chevrolet dealer and pioneer television pitchman, from about 1947 to 1952.

The grande dame of Baltimore Avenue is the elegant stucco home at **118 BALTIMORE AVENUE**, arranged in a planned garden on double lots. Built about 1926 by contractor Arthur D. Collman, who lived then at 40 Monte Vista, it was designed for Henry C. and Eva Meyer, who moved from Sausalito but lived here for only a short time. The well-to-do Mrs. Meyer kept her extensive collection of fur coats in the cedar-lined closets. In 1928 they sold the house to William D. and Edna Black; William was an accountant with Price, Waterhouse & Co. in San Francisco, and was able

▲ 4.50: *Virginia Slivka lived for five decades in the elegant 1926 home at 118 Baltimore Avenue, 2010.*

▲ 4.51: *Churrigueresque details of the 1934 Papajohn house at 203 West Baltimore Avenue, as seen in 2010.*

to afford a house valued at $15,000 in 1930, by far the most expensive in the neighborhood. Mrs. Black organized Red Cross relief workshops in the basement rooms during World War II; she sold her home in 1947, several years after William's death. The house next was acquired by Virginia and Joseph Slivka in 1951, who raised six children in the home; Joseph died in 1993, and Virginia, who had been raised in Corte Madera and worked as a nurse, remained here until 2007, praised by neighbors as a charming member of the community.

The house has scrolled eaves and unusual detailing around its covered doorway; the door is solid mahogany with glass insets, set above a terrazzo stoop. The living room's 18-foot ceilings set off three arched windows and an interior fireplace with fleur-de-lis designs, suggesting elements of a French Revival style for the home.

⑧ West Baltimore Avenue

Baltimore Avenue links Subdivisions One and Two; the western portion of the street, across Magnolia Avenue, was re-named West Baltimore Avenue in 1925. Two Mediterranean stucco homes occupy the corners; **203 WEST BALTIMORE AVENUE** was built about 1934 in the baroque Churrigueresque style, probably for Christ and Marie Papajohn, who lived here through the 1940s. Note especially the twisted porch supports, arched windows, and elaborate frames around windows that face Magnolia Avenue. A large deodar cedar occupies the front yard, as with several other houses of the period. The widowed Marie had the small house at 205 West Baltimore built about 1942, and later moved into it herself. On the opposite corner, **204 WEST BALTIMORE AVENUE**, a relatively unadorned Mediterranean stucco with a full red tile roof, was built about 1936 for Charles and Helen Neils, who lived here through the 1950s. It has been expanded and remodeled, but remains a good example of its type.

This part of the street has deep historical roots; the area surrounding the Landmark Oak Tree in the street near 205 West Baltimore was the location of a large steam sawmill erected in 1849 by the Baltimore and Frederick Mining and Trading Company. Drawn here by the redwood forests, the loggers lent their company's name to the Canyon and eventually to today's street and subdivision. *See pages 99-100 of the Baltimore Canyon chapter for more information about this spot.*

George and Laura Eckert moved to Larkspur about 1906, and in 1914 purchased four large lots now numbered as **215 WEST BALTIMORE AVENUE** that extended through to Piedmont Road, promptly building a showplace home there in 1915. They raised three children in the house, remaining into the 1950s. The flat-roofed home typified the horizontal Prairie style popularized by Frank Lloyd Wright, and may have been based on one of his designs in Illinois. A large sleeping porch occupied the southern side of the second floor. The front yard was arranged with two specimen redwood trees, one each of the native giant sequoia and coast redwood; the broad lawn was set behind a concrete retaining wall. The house was sold in the mid-1950s to Larkspur City Council member Daniel Allen and his wife Madeleine, a well-connected pair who entertained widely. The Allens in turn sold to Tom and Joan Day in 1970, who soon undertook an extensive remodel of the exterior, rebuilding the porch and removing the original stucco (by then damaged with dry rot) and replacing it with shingles. Joan Day was a master gardener, remembered by neighbor Dee Fratus as "a Martha Stewart before there was a Martha Stewart," and a tireless contributor to the Heritage Committee's initial research. After the Days' departure in 1999, the house was extensively remodeled and the yard completely rebuilt. A few years later the original concrete retaining wall was replaced by stonework, and a small garage was added on the west side.

The Eckerts had developed more than their own land; they also acquired the streamside lot across the street at **222 WEST BALTIMORE AVENUE**, building a shingled cottage there in 1924. Initially used as a rental, it later was sold to John and Opal Sharp, who owned the house until 1990. They gradually expanded the house, replacing a sleeping porch with a living room over the garage and extending the west wall.

Probably the first house on this block was named "Baltimore Lodge," at **223 WEST BALTIMORE AVENUE**. The shingled structure was built about 1907 by Ruth and John Birlem. John worked in various capacities for the railroad, and either he,

▲ 4.52: The "Baltimore Lodge" at 223 West Baltimore Avenue, as it appeared in 1910. The porch has since been enclosed, and the dormer removed. The original sign remains above the inner door.

▲ 4.53: The tiny Craftsman bungalow at 232 West Baltimore retained its original appearance in this 2009 view.

or a brother named Fred, was the captain of one of the railroad's ferryboats. They yielded the house in 1922 to John and Cora Jones, who remained there into the mid-1950s. The house has retained its basic external shape, although a small dormer facing the street has been removed. The original sign proclaiming the house's name is still mounted on the wall over the front door, since enclosed. The word "Lodge" seems to have spawned a number of misperceptions about the history of the structure; there is no evidence of its use as anything other than a conventional private residence.

The Craftsman (or Arts and Crafts) bungalow style typically included exterior shingles, exposed rafter tips, and a conscious simplicity of ornamentation; the little house at **232 WEST BALTIMORE AVENUE** is a nearly untouched early representative of that design. Note especially the double-exposure line on the shingles, and the cross-gabled dormer that suggests a second floor, but merely opens to attic space. Projecting beveled beams support the eaves, and original double-hung windows, with six panes in the upper sashes, remain throughout. A covered front porch invites leisurely conversation with passers-by. The house was built about 1912, on a small lot set hard against the Arroyo Holon to its rear; in fact, a stone monument survey point ("P.Q. 99") marking the boundary lines of the Mexican ranchos is buried in its backyard. It seems to have been used as a rental in the early years, and at 753 square feet, its two bedrooms provide only limited space. The tiny detached garage has two narrow concrete tire strips rather than a conventional driveway. Since the 1940s the home was occupied by Jack and Virginia

Curran, and later by Virginia and her second husband, George Ankers. A collection of rocks in the yard was gathered by Virginia on vacations through the west. George was born in Mill Valley, and lived in this area all his life; he was the last proprietor of the downtown Larkspur Hardware at 460 Magnolia Avenue.

Next door, two houses at 234 and 236 West Baltimore date to the early 1920s, and were substantially remodeled and expanded in the 1990s.

As Baltimore Avenue begins to dip toward the streambed it narrows dramatically, encountering redwood trees that constrict the road further. Crossing the boundary into Subdivision Two, streets that averaged 70 feet in width are now reduced to less than 30 feet, and remain so throughout the rest of the subdivision.

The large house at **233 WEST BALTIMORE AVENUE** was built about 1908 for Thomas and

▲ 4.55: *The Millars' Sequoia Lodge at 233 West Baltimore as it appeared in 1967, shortly before a substantial remodel.*

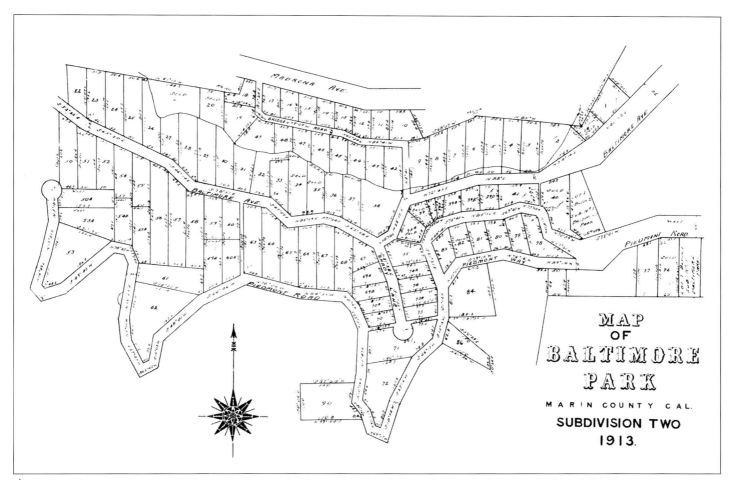

▲ 4.54: *Surveyor George M. Dodge's 1913 Map of Baltimore Park Subdivision Two, as formally filed with the Marin County Recorder on June 2, 1913. Narrow Baltimore Avenue runs across the center from right to left, with portions of Piedmont Road forming the lower edge of the map; the Arroyo Holon creek appears simply as a wavy line between Baltimore Avenue and Bridge Road. This map created about 90 distinct lots in the Baltimore Canyon area.*

Edith Millar, who named it "Sequoia Lodge." Thomas was a romantic figure; born in Scotland, he served as a U.S. Army captain in the Philippines. He operated a local insurance agency, and held office as a town trustee until 1914, but by the early 1920s Tom and Edith had left the area, divorced. The house soon was owned by John and Mary Perks, who occupied it for the following 30 years.

The spacious backyard contains a natural amphitheater, used for W.P.A. concerts by out-of-work musicians during the Depression. George and Fran Kohler substantially expanded the house in 1967; a massive blue rock fireplace and chimney remain from the original house. In 1926 John Perks altered his lot lines to reshape the adjacent small lot that is now **229 WEST BALTIMORE AVENUE**, and had contractor William F. Granger build a small California bungalow there for use of the Perks' son, Reginald. That house later was owned by music teacher Marjorie Whittlesy for about five decades, then significantly expanded in the early 2000s. The original porch and front eaves are unchanged.

Before automobiles dominated daily travel the subdividers designed walking routes for pedestrians. The long concrete stairway between house numbers 233 and 247, leading to Coleman Avenue, was named "Stradway Lane" by the city in 1915. Although the name persists on official maps, a street sign that once marked the stairs is long gone. A similar stairway is located between address numbers 265 and 273, and two more lead away from nearby Shady Lane; these four are the only public stairways in Subdivision Two.

The shingled two-story McKenna home overlooking the stream at **249 WEST BALTIMORE AVENUE** was built for Joseph and Margaret McKenna about 1912. Margaret had been born into a pioneer family; she was the youngest child of Winifred Tierney, who once owned more than 175 acres that were absorbed into the Forbes-Coleman holdings. As such, Margaret was a cousin to both the Brown and Bickerstaff families. Active in local affairs, Margaret died here in 1944, one of the last direct links to Larkspur's earliest period. The house is set to the rear of the lot, with several of its original features intact, including a clinker brick chimney and exposed beams under the eaves. The adjoining duplex structure at 253 West Baltimore has been on that site since at least 1924; it too has shingles above and clapboard siding below.

In the days before address numbers came into use a sign proclaimed the name of the house at **250 WEST BALTIMORE AVENUE** as "Twelve Trees." Those (redwood) trees remain, but the 1920s house essentially has been replaced by extensive remodeling done between 2003 and 2004. Nearby houses to the west were not developed until the 1940s, perhaps reflecting the flood threat caused by the meandering course of the creek. The creek eventually was forced away from the house sites, and into a channel against the road's bulkhead. An old wooden bulkhead had been a constant source of concern to neighbors until it was replaced by the current concrete structure about 1927.

Because of the creek, the north side houses here gain vehicle access from a small private alley that branches eastward from Bridge Road.

▲ 4.56: *Wooden bulkheads protected the narrow roadbed from the waters of Arroyo Holon in the early 1900s. This is the approximate site of 249 West Baltimore Avenue.*

Marin County's reputation took a decided turn for the worse in 1978 when NBC newsman Edwin Newman appeared in a televised special report that pictured Marin's residents as a collection of uniquely pampered, hedonistic, and rather foolish people. The program – featuring hot tubs, head shops, pop psychology, and massages using peacock feathers – was amusing to some and offensive to many. Newspaper editorials bemoaned the slight, and outraged Marin County Supervisors complained that the county's reputation had been badly and inaccurately slandered. The program included a brief interview with the owner of the 1963 house at **264 WEST BALTIMORE AVENUE**, a woman who described her desires as "Everything – I want everything, nothing less." That comment inspired the program's title: "I want it all now." Although the hot tub jokes lingered for years, the house acquired new owners in the late 1980s.

⊃ *Bridge road intersects West Baltimore Avenue here, and strikes westward up the Canyon toward Madrone Avenue.*

⑨ Bridge Road Crosses Arroyo Holon

Some form of bridge has been at this location since the 1890s or even earlier. Crossing the concrete bridge, the original route named Bridge Road turns left up the Canyon; tiny Foley Lane, only 20 feet wide, wasn't connected to Madrone Avenue until 1922. A private alley turns eastward, providing vehicle access to several houses whose formal addresses are West Baltimore Avenue or Madrone Avenue.

The houses on the north side of Bridge Road face Madrone Avenue, dating variously to the early 1920s or later. The desirable south-side lots overlooked the creek, on pleasant sunny sites that usually accommodated vacation houses. Two homes there, at numbers 25 and 27, date to the first decade of development in Subdivision Two. Number **25 BRIDGE ROAD** is a two-story shingle house, with hipped roof, two-window dormer, and

▲ 4.57: *The Rustic Bridge, freshly constructed of redwood logs in this undated postcard, was used to promote Baltimore Park Subdivision Two. It replaced a yet earlier structure; the current concrete bridge was built about 1927.*

exposed rafter tips, dating to about 1915. A covered porch shelters the entry, and numerous original double-hung windows contain six panes in the upper sashes. **27 BRIDGE ROAD**, a small, single-story home with a hipped roof, probably dates to 1911, when Gustave Nagel, one of Larkspur's active builders of the period, received a permit to build a house here. The adjoining home at 35 Bridge Road, built about 1924, was substantially altered in later decades, and number 39 wasn't built until about 1950.

Three of the houses share similar histories; the homes at **1, 15,** and **19 BRIDGE ROAD**, dating to the 1920s and 1930s, were built by Herman S. Meinberger, a San Francisco contractor who also used number 19 as his family's vacation home. Number 19, built in 1925, was expanded in the 1990s to a second story and additional rooms, but retains an elaborate original clinker-brick fireplace. Across the street,

▲ 4.58: *The Rustic Bridge about 1913. Real estate agent William L. Courtright's name appears on a banner displayed on the rear of a horse-drawn carriage used to take prospective buyers on tour.*

▲ 4.59: The hipped-roof portion of the small house at 27 Bridge Road probably was built in 1911 by Gustave Nagel, 2009.

▲ 4.60: Built in 1908, the Escobosa-Thomas house at 263 West Baltimore Avenue is seen here in 2009.

tiny number **16 BRIDGE ROAD** is reputed to have begun life as an early 1900s tent platform, gradually altered to permanent housing; unfortunately, it had to be completely rebuilt after being smashed by a giant bay laurel that collapsed in a 1990s storm. It was one of the last remnants of the widespread camping that filled the Canyon at the turn of the last century.

↩ *Return to West Baltimore Avenue*

Set among redwoods on the hillside overlooking the bridge, the house at **263 WEST BALTIMORE AVENUE** was built about 1908 for Ignacio and Marguerite Escobosa. Large outdoor porches (since enclosed) were built to obtain fresh air for her fragile health. The house is best known as the residence of Major Julius Thomas and his wife, Violet, from 1937 until their son Jim sold it in about 2005. A substantial remodel then by contractor Steve Crutchfield retained much of the home's exterior appearance and interior charm. The neighboring house at 265 West Baltimore, dating approximately to 1912, apparently was used as a summer house well into the 1930s.

273 WEST BALTIMORE AVENUE, at the base of Shady Lane, may be one of the oldest structures in the Canyon. It predates the 1913 subdivision, and the owner who substantially rebuilt the house in the early 1970s discovered it had been built upon a giant redwood stump as its sole foundation. It was occupied from the 1920s into the 1960s by the widowed Annie Landreville. The front portion of the house retains its original footprint.

⑩ Shady Lane

Aptly named Shady Lane is a short cul-de-sac whose address numbers start at the top; steep topography prevents a connection to Piedmont Road, which curves above it. The street harbors only six houses; numbers 2 and 10 were constructed in 1918 and 1926, and both have been rebuilt to varied degrees, while number 8 is a 1959 addition to the street. Set under tall trees adjacent to one of the stairways, **3 SHADY LANE** is attributed to about 1920. Across the way, **4 SHADY LANE** was built for Douglas and Virginia Duncan in 1948 as a rustic home; Virginia remained here until 2003. It has a split shake and brick exterior, and a little streambed that (usually) contains the seasonal runoff down the side canyon.

Tall **11 SHADY LANE** dates to the early 1900s, with a large exposed sleeping porch on the upper story, drop siding on its lower exterior, and a shingled exterior covering the original upper floor. John and Laura Ross lived here for three decades starting in the late 1920s.

↩ *Return to West Baltimore Avenue and head west (up-Canyon).*

SHADY LANE STAIRS

Tiny Shady Lane has two sets of concrete stairs rising to nearby Piedmont Road; a gentle path and stairs to the east, and extremely steep stairs to the west.

Baltimore Park 169

▲ 4.61: *The tall 1920s home at 3 Shady Lane coexists with redwood trees on a steep slope, 2010.*

▲ 4.62: *The Duncans occupied their 1948 home at 4 Shady Lane for more than five decades, 2009.*

▲ 4.63: *The Wilfert house at 330 West Baltimore Avenue, built about 1908, as it appeared in 2009. It has changed very little from its original appearance.*

⑪ Western Block of West Baltimore Avenue

The handsome two-story shingle at **320 WEST BALTIMORE AVENUE** probably was built about 1918; it has the projecting eaves of the brown shingle or Craftsman style, a wide dormer protruding through the low-pitched roof, and projecting window boxes on the sides that merit their own roofs. Next door is one of the Canyon's iconic houses, the Wilfert house at **330 WEST BALTIMORE AVENUE**. This level and sunny double lot was the first sale made in the new Subdivision Two, to Christopf and Emma Wilfert of San Francisco in 1908. They built this house as a vacation residence about 1908-1910. Like many early Canyon houses, it once had fruit trees in the yard before second-growth redwood trees reclaimed the sunlight. The house has the three-lap siding and flat window casings widely used around the turn of the last century. New York born Christopf Wilfert owned a successful meat company in San Francisco, and retained this house until 1922, when he sold it to Joseph Carew, a San Francisco dentist, and his wife Mary; the Carew family held the home into the early 1940s.

The steeply-sloped south side of West Baltimore initially did not encourage construction; all the houses from number 301 to 321 were constructed (with considerable excavation) between 1961 and 1967. Number 325 was built in 1927, and extensively remodeled since then. It has a conjoined redwood tree in the front yard that boasts one of the largest girths in the Canyon. The next house, **339 WEST BALTIMORE AVENUE**, occupies large grounds spanning the base of a side canyon. This small house was built about 1920, and expanded modestly over the years; its yard includes many significant redwoods.

During the 1870s and 1890s, a large rock quarry was sporadically operated in the upper reaches of this canyon, linked to a smaller quarry above Shady Lane. Both quarries were near the eventual route of Piedmont Road. The rock material was graywacke, the same "blue rock" that has been quarried at several locations around the Larkspur area. Called "Quarry Ravine," the land was first leased by landowner William T. Coleman and Richard S. Brown (his tenant, and former owner of the area) in 1877; the lease included the right to develop a wagon road leading to "the County Road and Rail Road," as well as to a potential "embarcadero" on the salt marsh channels. Documents from the 1890s mentioned cabins, horse stables, loading chutes, and rock crushers located here at the mouth of the ravine, and specifically described a roadway that apparently became the forerunner of West Baltimore Avenue. A broad exposed rock face and berm of spoil material high on the hillside marks the location of what must have been one of the largest quarries in the area.

Across the street, **346 WEST BALTIMORE AVENUE** was built in 1918 by Walter C. Thierbach as a vacation home for himself and his wife Georgia. Walter, a civil engineer in San Francisco, built the house himself during the summer months in the Craftsman style, with a false dormer and exposed rafters. He used 36-inch-long redwood barn shingles for both the roof and the exterior walls. A front porch supported by tapered posts was partially enclosed in the 1940s, and several additions were made at the rear of the house over later decades; the front and side exteriors remain unchanged. The home has been occupied since 1973 by former Larkspur City Council member Richard Cunningham and his wife Susan. The Cunninghams have introduced hundreds of residents to Larkspur's history with their walking tours of downtown and Baltimore Canyon. Thierbach also built the adjoining home at number 342; it was occupied from the early 1930s to 1967 by Trille M. Grube.

The western edge of Subdivision Two is marked by the cul-de-sac end of the street, where two

▲ 4.64: *The Thierbachs' 1918 vacation house at 346 West Baltimore Avenue, seen in 2010.*

▲ 4.65: *The classic shingle hipped-roof house at 374 West Baltimore Avenue, shown here in 1968, was probably built as a vacation home about 1908.*

lots occupy a flat bluff high above the stream; **374 WEST BALTIMORE AVENUE** was built here about 1908, with a hipped roof, exposed rafter tips, and a single attic dormer on a shingled exterior. As with some other early Canyon homes, the yard's massive redwoods shelter several old fruit trees. A former detached garage was converted to an artist's studio in the 1970s, and later became a second dwelling unit.

The last house on the street, set adjacent to a redwood grove above the stream, represents relatively recent history; built in 1965, **380 WEST BALTIMORE AVENUE** was for a few years the home of legendary rock songwriter and singer Janis Joplin. She is remembered as a polite neighbor and convivial feature at local taverns, whose house seemed always inundated by hangers-on, particularly when she was on tour. Neighbors recall large troops of motorcyclists rumbling along the narrow street to visit the house. After her 1970 death in Los Angeles, the house was acquired by Sue and Jack Lessin, who raised their large family here, remaining until 2008. The home's unique location at a previously-popular trailhead was then recognized by a successful campaign to purchase a slice of the land for access to the adjoining Marin County Open Space District lands. The house was rebuilt substantially in 2009, but retains its striking clerestory windows and high-ceilinged living room.

⑫ Piedmont Road

Piedmont Road begins at Magnolia Avenue and continues westward into Subdivision Two; it was not paved until the late 1920s. As with nearby West Baltimore Avenue, Piedmont shrinks suddenly in width as it crosses the boundary between Subdivisions One and Two and enters hilly terrain. At a fork, the lower (northern) loop becomes one-way Coleman Avenue, while Piedmont itself continues along the upper (southern) loop.

Beginning at Magnolia Avenue, the first four houses on the south side of the street are of varied ages and styles; all have been significantly altered over the years. The oldest house had been number 3, but it was completely rebuilt in 2008, retaining only a few stylistic features of the original early 1920s structure; numbers 7 and 15 both date to the late 1940s. Number 11, built about 1934, has minimal Mediterranean features, with much of the details lost to revisions, including a large rear addition. This house incidentally was a childhood home of Gavin Newsom, elected San Francisco's mayor in 2004 and 2008.

The small shingled cottage at **10 PIEDMONT ROAD** was built about 1926 by William F. Wegner, a local contractor active in the Monte Vista neighborhood. Its exterior remains essentially original, with only minor modifications to the arbored entryway. A wide expanse of multipane casement windows contributes to its country cottage style. The adjoining home at **18 PIEDMONT ROAD** was built in 1950 by Dan and Madeline Allen, intended as a guest house for their adjacent showplace home at 215 West Baltimore Avenue. Avid square dancers, the Allens built this structure with special bracing under its 24- x 40-ft living room and equipped it with a speaker system so Mr. Allen could call the dance instructions. Much later this house was split away from its parent parcel, with a majority of its land being retained as the large garden remaining behind 215 West Baltimore. It was substantially remodeled in 2008.

A small hipped-roof house at **24 PIEDMONT ROAD** probably was built sometime before 1924, and for many years was used in conjunction with the house to its north. It gained independent status in 1948, and its front exterior has changed little since then. Next door, the shingled Cape Cod-style house

▲ 4.66: *Number 10 Piedmont Road is little changed from its original 1926 appearance as seen in 2010.*

▲ 4.67: *The small hipped-roof home at 24 Piedmont Road originally was a part of the larger parcel to the north, facing West Baltimore, 2010.*

▲ 4.68: *Seen here in 2010, 30 Piedmont Road is one of many Kott houses built in Marin in the mid-1950s.*

at **30 PIEDMONT ROAD** was built in 1953, after the division of a single large lot that stretches north to Baltimore Avenue. It was one of the almost 250 distinctive cottages built across Marin during the 1950s by a colorful Mill Valley contractor named Gerald C. Kott. His builder's brochure stressed "choices, originality, tailoring [of] finances and the quality of custom homes for a modest, affordable investment." Sue Lessin, the current owner, says Kott's "everyman" homes have a continued appeal to aficionados in Marin.

The large house set back grandly on its lawn at **25 PIEDMONT ROAD** was built about 1913 by Jacob and Rebecca Wolf, who used it as a summer residence until 1918. By 1923 the house had passed through two other owners when Julia Luce of New York acquired it. This was a retirement home for Julia and her husband, Edgar Luce, who had been treasurer of a newspaper bureau in New York. After his death in 1941 Julia stayed on into the early 1950s. For many years the house remained essentially unchanged, until substantial revisions were made by new owners Nancy and Kirk Mulligan in 2002. The entry door was moved from the upper story at the rear to a new roofed entry at the front, flanked by paired stairs, in 2005. The little detached garage close to the street has beveled knee braces under broad eaves, suggesting that it dates to the early 1900s.

In 1923 the Luces also purchased the adjoining lot at **27 PIEDMONT ROAD** for use as part of their garden; the house now at that address was erected in 1959 and occupied for much of the time since by Chuck Kroeger and his late wife Mary Lou, who had been a stalwart contributor to early Heritage Committee activities. Their daughter, Sarah Garcia, has continued family tradition as one of the curators of the city's historic photographs.

As Piedmont forms a loop with Coleman Avenue, all the houses carry Piedmont addresses except one, at 5 Coleman, built in 1959. The house at number 50 Piedmont dates to 1933. The nearby home at **52 PIEDMONT ROAD** dates to 1918 but had a lower floor added under it in the 1970s, and further revisions since then. Number 58 was erected in 1998, replacing a much earlier home that burned. The house at **62 PIEDMONT ROAD** dates to 1910 and has an important literary history. Shortly after World War II – from about 1948 to 1952 – author Leon Uris lived here with his wife Betty. Leon, working as a circulation manager for a San Francisco newspaper, wrote his immensely successful first novel *Battle Cry* in an upper bedroom, writing late at night while his wife worked as a night nurse. Since then the house has been substantially rebuilt.

Two older houses sit above the roadbed, on a warm hillside with a view across the Baltimore Canyon. Shingled **57 PIEDMONT ROAD**, adjacent to Piedmont Court, has been updated frequently but still bears a few trademark features of its estimated construction date of 1917, including beveled braces under the eaves. This house initially was owned by a San Francisco hatter, Fred Bates, and his wife Martha. The adjacent **65 PIEDMONT ROAD**, overlooking "Ammann's corner," dates to 1925; it has exposed rafter tips and extensive casement windows, in a yard dominated by several mature Douglas fir trees. For many years this was the residence of George and Emma Boyd; George served as Larkspur's town treasurer in the 1920s.

The most authentic of the homes on the loop is the low-slung, shingled **66 PIEDMONT ROAD**, for decades the home of Frederick and Bertha Ammann

▲ *4.69: The 1913 Wolf-Luce house at 25 Piedmont Avenue as it appeared 2009.*

▲ 4.70: *The remodeled 1917 Bates house at 57 Piedmont Road, 2010.*

and their son Arthur. Frederick maintained his own hat store in San Francisco, was a member of Larkspur's Board of Trustees in the 1920s, and eventually operated a succession of real estate and notary offices downtown on Magnolia Avenue. This was the family's vacation home until they moved here full time in the early 1920s. By the late 1940s, after Fred's death, Arthur remained in the house, and Bertha moved to a smaller home at 19 Baltimore Avenue. A broad porch that wrapped around the southwest corner was enclosed by new owners in 1973, but much of the house has remained in its original configuration.

The hairpin turn in the road here was dubbed "Ammann's corner," and the story has it that the clockwise direction of the narrow one-way road was determined by a fire engine's inability to negotiate up the tight corner.

Once at the intersection of Coleman Avenue, Piedmont Road continues left (south) up the side canyon to two additional houses; the home at **81 PIEDMONT ROAD**, probably built in the early 1900s, and much further along, 260 Piedmont, located on an unpaved portion of the road high above Baltimore Avenue. Dated to 1923, this remote house has a sparse record of occupation, but was substantially remodeled and enlarged in 2007.

This portion of Piedmont Road has never been developed, and now forms one boundary of the Marin County Open Space District's vast holdings to the south and west. The land in this immediate area was acquired in 1988 as part of an open space purchase campaign. This portion of about 14.8 steep acres was known as the "Lauterwasser parcel," a tract that had been owned by Larkspur resident Russ W. Lauterwasser, a former Larkspur city treasurer and grading contractor. The larger area is now called the Blithedale Summit Open Space Preserve, contiguous to portions of the 196-acre Baltimore Canyon Preserve.

A walk beyond the 260 house leads past Quarry Ravine *(see 339 West Baltimore on page 169-170)* and eventually to one of the Marin County Open Space District's Baltimore Canyon trailheads at the end of the dirt track. Early promotional materials for Baltimore Park suggested that Piedmont Road would one day be extended to Mill Valley, but the technical and financial obstacles involved obviously ended that dream.

▲ 4.71: *Frederick Ammann, a San Francisco hatter, acquired the house named "Old Glory" at 66 Piedmont Road about 1906; this photograph may date to 1910. Notice the uniformed housemaid at the right margin. The fence was built in the Rustic style popular at the time.*

▲ 4.72: *81 Piedmont Road, another early vacation home with an enclosed sleeping porch, 2009.*

SOUTH MAGNOLIA
Larkspur's southern entrance includes its namesake school and period homes.

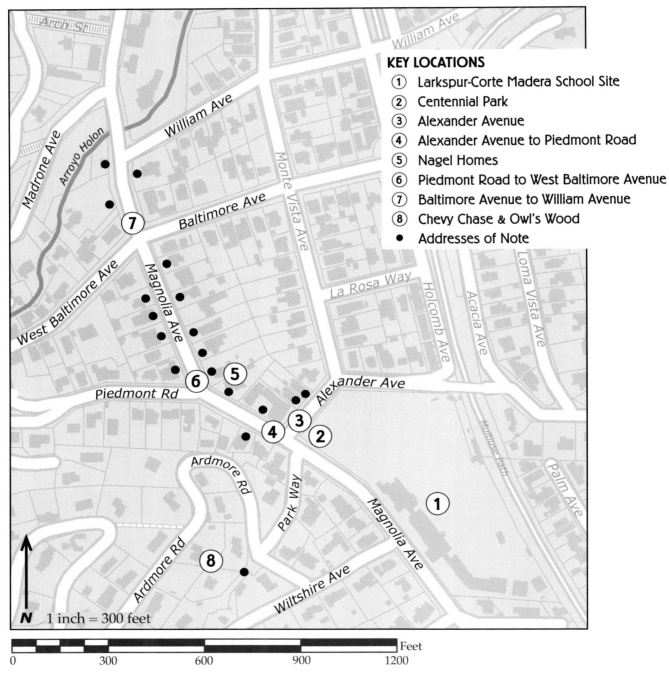

KEY LOCATIONS
1. Larkspur-Corte Madera School Site
2. Centennial Park
3. Alexander Avenue
4. Alexander Avenue to Piedmont Road
5. Nagel Homes
6. Piedmont Road to West Baltimore Avenue
7. Baltimore Avenue to William Avenue
8. Chevy Chase & Owl's Wood
- Addresses of Note

1 inch = 300 feet

 Park on Alexander Avenue and begin the tour at the school grounds on Magnolia Avenue. Walk down the east side of Magnolia Avenue to view homes on both sides of the street. Highlights of this tour include homes of some of Larkspur's most prominent early citizens and houses designed and built by Gustave Nagel.

SOUTH MAGNOLIA

The southern approach into Larkspur encapsulates the essence of a small town neighborhood and sets the stage for the entrance to the downtown. Following along what used to be known as the county road in the early part of the last century, Magnolia Avenue passes the old Larkspur-Corte Madera School (LCM) site, the Redwoods Presbyterian Church, a number of early 1900s homes, and enters the downtown area through an archway of tall redwoods.

• • • • • • • • • • • • •

Originally two Mexican land grants – the Rancho Corte Madera del Presidio in 1834 in the south, and the Rancho Punta de Quentin in 1840 in the north – had divided today's Larkspur acreage at Arroyo Holon (Larkspur Creek.) The earliest development took place in the northern section of town that was part of the Rancho Punta de

SOUTH MAGNOLIA HOMES

"When the houses in the south section of Magnolia Avenue are put together as a group, they give a sense of community even though, individually, they are not landmark quality."

— Dan Peterson, architectural historian

▲ 5.1: *Magnolia Avenue before paving in 1913. The house on the left is 143 Magnolia Avenue. At the center is the Gardiner house at 215 Magnolia Avenue.*

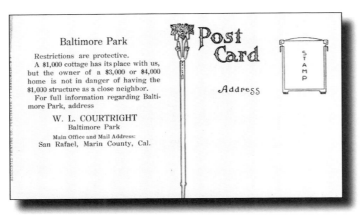

▲ 5.2: *An early 1900 advertisement for 130 Magnolia Avenue.*

Quentin. When Larkspur was incorporated in 1908, some of the lands south of Madrone Avenue that had been part of Rancho Corte Madera del Presidio were included.

The south Magnolia Avenue homes were planned to establish an upscale character for the future town. An early 1900 sales advertisement for the $3,000 and $4,000 homes by W. L. Courtright boasted of the exclusiveness of the future homes.

While the early homes with their wraparound front porches supported by columns, hipped roofs, and dormers don't rate high on the historical pecking order, they are a reminder of the town's history.

① Larkspur-Corte Madera School Site

In the 1860s the original school for the thirty Larkspur and Corte Madera students was located in a one-room structure at 214 Willow Avenue in Corte Madera that was later converted to a private home. In 1894 Agnes (Mrs. Alexander) Forbes and the Frank Morrison Pixleys donated the present site at **20 MAGNOLIA AVENUE** where a wooden-framed Larkspur-Corte Madera School was built in the late 1890s by Gustave Nagel at a cost of $5,000. The donation deed had the proviso that it should only be used for a school or it would revert to the original owners or their heirs. The school was located close to the redwood grove where the parking lot is now located. The two-story wood frame building, with a dormer and cupola, had a picket fence with a turnstile at the entrance and boasted four classrooms.

In 1916, when the school was deemed too small, a two-story stucco addition was built in front of the original frame building close to the redwood grove. A playground was installed within the grove with swings suspended from wooden uprights.

The similarity of the architecture to Larkspur's City Hall suggests that it may have been designed by San Francisco architect C. O. Clausen. Like the city hall, it was a Mission Revival-style building with two tile-roofed towers. The left tower held the library, storage

SCHOOL PRANKS

Nighttime raiders were known to physically change the school name from Corte Madera School to Larkspur School or vice versa.

One Halloween, according to Biff Harris, the entire side steps of the school were pulled away. Another year a garbage can was placed on top of the flagpole. Judge Samuel Gardiner recalled a time when pranksters took either a horse or a donkey up the stairs to the belfry tower at the school.

▲ 5.3: *Larkspur-Corte Madera School, about 1910.*

▲ 5.4: *Larkspur-Corte Madera School with Mission Revival-style addition, 1920s.*

▲ 5.5: *Larkspur-Corte Madera School with southern addition, early 1930s.*

room, and washroom; the right held the principal's office and another washroom.

Early school trustees were W. H. Eastman, James Broad, and Henry de Veuve. There were four classrooms downstairs and two upstairs with the center part of the second floor devoted to a high-ceiling auditorium and a basketball court. The stage was located behind the arched front windows *(see Fig 5.4)*. A wooden fire escape hung from the back of the building.

During these early years a great rivalry existed between the twin cities resulting in the school having various names – Larkspur School, Corte Madera School, Corte Madera Grammar School, and Larkspur-Corte Madera School. According to former LCM principal and Larkspur School District superintendent Gilbert Slusher, "the various names appeared to coincide with the town that had the majority on the Board of Education."

Prior to the 1920s the school year was split since the schools worked around agricultural seasons. Hence students did not attend continuously for a nine-month period. "It was not uncommon to find kids 15, 16, and even 17 years old still going to elementary schools because parents pulled kids out of school to work on crops," commented Slusher in 1989.

An addition in 1921 included kindergarten, first, and second grade classrooms as well as a cafeteria, and was located just south of the two-story main building. The addition was separated from the main building by a courtyard where the flag salute was held every morning. The original wooden building was torn down in 1929. In 1939 a building south of the current main entrance was added and the old stucco building was torn down. Lillian Murray Dodge recalled in a 1975 interview that the building was declared "too dangerous to withstand an earthquake, but they had a terrible time tearing it down."

The post-World War II baby boom made the existing structure inadequate, and in 1949 the final addition at the south end of the building was built. The kindergarten class that year had 107 students.

Two names are always mentioned when talking about the early days of the school – Henry Clay Hall and (Miss) Leslie Ezekiel. The two combined the rare qualities in a teacher that inspired respect and awe as well as admiration and warmth. "Pops" Hall, as he was fondly remembered, was both the principal and a teacher at the school until his retirement in 1929. Although a strict disciplinarian, he had a soft touch and made a point of making a personal, warm comment to students as he presented each of them with their diploma at graduation time.

"I shall often recall you as a gentle boy… yet you always held your own position with vigor and activity."

— Excerpt from a 1918 personal note from "Pops" Hall to Wilford "Biff" Harris with his diploma

---

Alice Ambrose Krogman, daughter of an early town constable, recalled that the influenza epidemic of 1918 to 1920 took a heavy toll. Larkspur passed an ordinance requiring people to wear masks when they went outside. At this time school principal Hall visited students at home to help them with their lessons.

Alice's sister, Rowena Ambrose Winkler, remembered that when they cut down the eucalyptus trees to build the new school in 1921, Pops Hall tricked the boys by hiding something in the dirt and sending them out to find it. "They ran all over and tramped down the field," she said.

Leslie Ezekiel, who spent most of her years as a fifth-grade teacher, fondly recalled the World War II years when she taught thirty or more boys to knit lap robes for military hospitals. The boys forgot their rowdiness and showed unusual patience. Some even knitted while on traffic patrol.

During the 1940s and 1950s the school building deteriorated. In 1960 a bond was passed to clean up its sorry state and add extra classrooms to accommodate the influx of students. Gil Slusher, who grew up in Heather Gardens, earned plaudits for his graceful handling of students, parents, and classroom logistics. During his regime, parent involvement mushroomed, spearheaded by Barbara Slusher, Ruth Anne "Queenie" Young, Fran Holmes, and Nancy Curley, who set up and ran the PTA that masterminded hot dog days, the Halloween carnival, and fund-raising events.

The strong nostalgia that many people in Larkspur and Corte Madera felt for old LCM made its closing in 1979 a wrenching experience. Despite strong protests, the economic reality of the declining student population and increased operating costs required the closure. Since the original deed required that the property be used for educational purposes, the school district has leased the property only for those purposes. The grounds have continued to be open to the public.

② Centennial Park

A stone-studded fountain, an artifact from the past, still stands near the redwood grove. Built by Corte Madera stonemasons of Italian descent between 1910 and 1915, the fountain was dedicated to Henry C. Hall and originally bore a plaque commemorating those who died in World War I. Although no longer working, the fountain had a special feature that catered to four-legged friends – a low opening where dogs could quench their thirst.

The original dirt tennis courts were located at the corner of Magnolia and Alexander Avenues. This was also the location of early maypole celebrations. Volleyball courts were installed in their place and new tennis courts were constructed next to them in the 1920s. During their prime in the 1930s and 1940s the tennis courts were lighted for nighttime use with a coin-operated system similar to a parking meter according to local historian James Holmes, whose mother Fran played on the courts. A raised center umpire's seat was set between the courts.

In 1991 Magnolia Avenue Park, a neighborhood picnic area, replaced the volleyball courts. In 2008 the park was renamed "Centennial Park" and the corner was given a grassy picnic area and new landscaping. The invasive Monterey pines were removed and the tennis courts received a new reconstructed surface.

"Larkspur-Corte Madera School was the center of the world on every other Sunday when baseball games were held there," recalled Judge Gardiner. "I was forbidden to go because it was Sunday and my father was a minister, but I sneaked out to them once in a while and got hell for it."

▲ 5.6: *Principal Henry C. Hall with students from the class of 1925.*

▲ 5.7: *Centennial Park at the corner of Magnolia and Alexander Avenues was dedicated on April 4, 2009.*

Early students recall playing on swings hung from the remaining eucalyptus tree and many remember it as a favorite shady lunch spot. The original playing field was north of the redwood grove and was moved east of the school after the original structures were torn down. The area, now called "Joe Wagner Field" in honor of a beloved elderly crossing guard who shepherded students across Magnolia in the 1950s and 1960s, was used by the eighth grade until it was transformed into the baseball diamond with bleachers and a concession stand in 1959.

The big surge of new, young families in the 1990s created a demand for a T-ball field. In 1995 the Twin Cities Little League created the Susan Johann Gilardi Field just east of the tennis courts. The funding was the result of Dennis Gilardi racking his brain for a birthday gift for his wife Susan. He decided that diamonds are a girl's best friend, but instead of the 4-carat type he invested in the Little League baseball diamond.

May Day was a major celebration in all of the Marin schools from about 1910 to the 1930s. The festivities featured dances, maypole winding by six boys and six girls in countywide contests, and a May queen with court and parade. The celebrations ended in 1947 when the U.S.S.R. adopted the day for their political celebration. A special maypole winding was done in 2008 in honor of Larkspur's centennial celebration.

At today's Marin Primary & Middle School (MPMS) children's voices echo in the halls of the single-story buildings. Little feet clamber over the base of the giant eucalyptus tree at the edge of the eight-acre site that has six buildings, including a library, art and music studios, a science lab, and a media center as well as outdoor sports fields. In 2008 a new fenced entrance with an intercom and keypad was added at the southern gate of the school complex. Marin Primary began as a pre-school, moved to 20 Magnolia Avenue in 1980, and has been expanded over the years. In 2009 enrollment was 325 students from pre-school through eighth grade.

The view across the street from the school has changed since the 1930s. In 1923, after a request for a tearoom and club by Abe Ruef, the area was

MAY DAY REMEMBERED

"The boys were not too happy to be included in the maypole winding… When Principal Neil Cummins* pointed to you and said, 'You, you, and you,' you volunteered. When he said, 'Put on a dress,' you put on a dress."

— Charlie Young

*Neil Cummins was teaching principal at LCM from 1924 to 1938 when he became superintendent. He retired as superintendent in June of 1956.

▲ 5.8: *Dancing around the maypole at LCM School, 1920s. Note the Alexander Avenue Bridge at center right, and the heritage eucalyptus behind the school, left.*

▲ 5.9: *Marie Arnita Hiniker, age 7, was Princess of the 1911 Booster Day Parade and valedictorian of the Class of 1919 at LCM.*

rezoned as a business district. Bob Collin, who attended LCM in the 1930s, recalled fondly that the cold drinks, sandwiches, and snow cones sold at Carl Wolfe's gas station across the street from the schoolyard were vastly preferred to the school cafeteria food produced by his aunt, Mabel Shine.

③ Alexander Avenue

In 1925 Gustave Nagel built the classic bungalows at **8** and **10 ALEXANDER AVENUE** for Helen Bain, an unmarried San Francisco schoolteacher who was the sister of his son-in-law Merton Bain. Family records indicate that the shiplap-sided homes, with their squatty front-porch posts and double-gable roofs, were built for $2,500 each. At the time they were built, the backyards joined with the Nagel home at 126 Magnolia Avenue and with 116 Magnolia, creating a compound that is still inhabited by family members. In 2009, 8 Alexander Avenue was in pristine condition with no changes. The porch on number 10 has been replaced with different columns and railings.

Several members of the large Bain family had substantial links to Larkspur. Helen's younger brother James had moved to Larkspur from San Rafael about 1903, working as manager of the Tamalpais Grocery Co. at 489 Magnolia Avenue. James was an early proponent and organizer of a volunteer fire company for Larkspur, and agreed to serve as its chief during that early period. When Larkspur incorporated in 1908, he became our first town clerk. The Tamalpais Grocery was succeeded by Buckley & Co. Grocers shortly thereafter, prompting Bain to leave his city position in order to devote himself to the grocery. He moved from Larkspur about 1910 to settle in San Francisco with his bride. On his departure, he was presented with a gold badge by the grateful city; that badge was returned to the city by his proud descendants in 2008. Two other Bain brothers, Henry and Merton, followed similar career paths; both worked with Buckley & Co., and Henry was a founding member in 1913 of the Larkspur Association of Volunteer Firemen. Merton, the youngest of the group, married Delma Nagel and operated local branches of the grocery; he too was a volunteer firefighter, serving for decades as treasurer of the Association.

▲ 5.10: *The Redwoods Presbyterian Church, shown here as it appeared in 2008, found its final home in 1951 at the corner of Magnolia and Alexander Avenues.*

④ Alexander Avenue to Piedmont Road

In the summer of 1896, 36 Larkspur and Corte Madera residents gathered at the Larkspur-Corte Madera School with two seminary students to form today's Redwoods Presbyterian Church at **110 MAGNOLIA AVENUE**. In the church's early years it played musical chairs between Corte Madera and Larkspur. The first services were held at the Larkspur Inn at the end of Sycamore until the hotel burned down in 1894. The services were then held at LCM School until 1902 when they moved south to a new steep-gabled church built at 271 Corte Madera Avenue on land donated by William Pixley. They remained at the Corte Madera location until 1938 when the 50-member congregation decided to build a church in Larkspur on land donated by C. W. Wright at Arch Street. The building was later converted to a home and is still standing.

"Churches formed the main centers of social and civic activity from 1896 to 1919."

— Judge Samuel Gardiner in a 1983 letter

The Magnolia and Alexander Avenue location was acquired as two parcels in 1917 and 1922. "The lot on which the Redwoods church was built was acquired by my family and others," said Judge Gardiner. "Some time before 1914 my father, a retired minister, and my brother Paul and I went up and leveled areas where the church sits now that were part of the redwood grove. We built tables and benches and it was used for an outdoor church and picnic area for many, many years before the church was built."

Judge Gardiner recounted, "... My father preached in the church irregularly and preached elsewhere in the county until the mid-twenties. Adda Estella Gardiner [his mother] was one of the organizers and a president of the Thimble Club, a club that centered on that church. ... My family was most active in the Sunday school where my brothers and I were superintendents, and in Christian Endeavor, Easter, and Christmas activities. Many of these groups held their functions in our home."

The Thimble Club, organized in 1907 by a group of churchwomen, was a social and service club that contributed funds to the church by having needlework bazaars, food sales, and luncheons. The group first met at the Corte Madera church location but felt the hard, straight-backed church chairs were not conducive to socializing.

In 1930 they moved to a new clubhouse that was erected on the church property on Magnolia Avenue. It was named Eastman Hall after charter church member Mary Eastman. In 1937 the church assumed responsibility for the building that had also been used for Sunday school, worship services, and community uses. In 1950 the church was re-incorporated as the Redwoods Presbyterian Church, and in 1951 a new building adjacent to Eastman Hall was erected. To make way for the present church sanctuary, Eastman Hall was moved first to the adjacent lot on Magnolia and then, in 1959, to the southeast corner of Holcomb and William Avenues where it was later razed by the fire department for safety reasons.

With the arrival of the boomer generation both the city and church population swelled. A new connecting wing with a deck and patio was built in 1965. The early work of the Thimble Club was carried on by The Sewing Group, and community services broadened to a national and international level.

"The challenge the Redwoods Presbyterian Church faces in 2008 is the competition with weekend activities, especially sports," commented the Reverend Lynn Penny, interim pastor.

* * * * *

Some older homes that were, as of 2010, smothered in greenery such as **93 MAGNOLIA AVENUE,** keep their architectural treasure out of sight. Hidden behind the trees and shrubs is Frank DePue's rustic hipped-roof bungalow built in 1913 by San Quentin convicts. The house has narrow wood siding and porches on two sides. According to Judge Gardiner, from 1906 to 1920 Frank DePue was well respected as the owner of bloodhounds that were used to track escaped prisoners from San Quentin and local jails. The dogs were ideal for tracking since, at that time, escapes were made on foot.

DePue, who headed up the State Bureau of Identification when it was at San Quentin Prison, was also an early user of fingerprints, although they were not well accepted as evidence at that time. In April of 1912 the City of Larkspur evidently thought enough of his talents to hire him "to investigate the mutilation of the clerk's books which had certain accounts torn out relative to the Marshall's account and licenses."

THE REDWOODS CHURCH

"The simplicity of the A-frame Redwoods Presbyterian Church design was intended to reflect the church's local environment. The vertical timbers at the end of the sanctuary... evoke the soaring trunks of the redwood trees. The green carpet reflects the mossy floor of a redwood forest."

— James Holmes, parishioner

▲ 5.11: *Stones collected by parishioners were fashioned into a large mosaic plaque, designed by Larkspur artist Irene Clark, which hangs in the church sanctuary, 2008.*

The fireplace in the house is low-grade white quartz with gold banding (now painted over) that came from the Empire Mine in Grass Valley. Arthur Giddings, an avid railroad electrician and later a guard at San Quentin State Prison, lived in the house for many years and made no structural changes to it. Giddings and his wife Gladys died in 1982 and 1983 respectively. In 2008 the occupant of the house was Gloria Wood, the Giddings' daughter, a talented singer who used the home as her voice studio.

⑤ Nagel Homes

Some early homes by Larkspur's master builder and designer Gustave Nagel are between the school and church and the downtown area. The Queen Anne cottage at **116 MAGNOLIA AVENUE** was built in 1925 for his daughter Delma. She married Larkspur grocer Merton Bain who died in 1981. Their daughter Dorothy and her husband, Thomas McCarthy, still live there. In a simplified manner the house repeats many of the traditional Gustave Nagel features that he incorporated in his home next door at 126 Magnolia Avenue.

The exterior has the same painted redwood dropped siding as the home at 126 Magnolia Avenue. Although the shallow, gabled roof over the body of the house and the separate roof over the veranda differ from the roof configuration of its neighbor, they have trim and extended cut-out end details and extended stepped rafters on both the main gable and the lower veranda gable. The column bases and the interior of the veranda are paneled with dropped siding. The beveled glass in the front door is rectangular-shaped. The double-hung front windows are dressed up with a pair of small, rectangular windows on the top and sides.

The interior of the house has a soft-toned brick fireplace flanked with cabinets that have leaded glass doors. Similar leaded-glass cabinets frame a window seat in the dining room. Although a rear addition has been made, it is not visible from the street and the house is in pristine condition with no other material or structural changes.

Gustave Nagel completed **126 MAGNOLIA AVENUE** for himself and his wife Emilie in 1907. Nagel, whose building career spanned a number of architectural periods, was a facile designer who latched onto whatever was the current trend. With

▲ 5.12: At one point during his career, Gustave Nagel opened the Oyster Depot in San Francisco, 1901. When it burned down in the 1906 earthquake and fire he returned to building homes in Larkspur.

▲ 5.13: A 1990 photo of 126 Magnolia Avenue, the home Gustave Nagel built for himself in 1907. It remains unchanged in 2010.

a lumberyard and mill in town, he could craft details from all periods and incorporate them in his designs. Many of Larkspur's landmarks are to his credit, from the King house (105 King Street) in 1892 and the Basebe house (95 Laurel Avenue) in the 1890s, to the remodel of the Blue Rock Hotel in 1910 and the modest homes for family members at 116 Magnolia Avenue, and 8 and 10 Alexander Avenue that are still inhabited by Nagel and Bain relatives.

Nagel originally built a cabin for himself near where 55 Walnut Avenue is today, but moved back to San Francisco when the cabin burned to the ground in the 1890s. After the earthquake, he returned to Marin and lived in a small rear cabin while he built his home on Magnolia Avenue. During this period the Nagels purchased their food and milk from Owl's Wood, according to Gustave's daughter Eda Nagel. She and her brother-in-law, Merton Bain, operated the McNaboe Company grocery stores in Larkspur and Corte Madera from the early 1920s until around 1956.

The Queen Anne cottage design of the Nagel house is a showcase for borrowed details of the Victorian and Edwardian periods done in a simple fashion. The 2- x 3-in railings of the porch with an

▲ 5.14: *Gustave Nagel decorated his home with a mixture of architectural details from different periods, 2010.*

CHARACTERISTICS OF NAGEL HOMES

The interiors and exteriors of the other Nagel-designed family homes have similarities. Most have stone or brick fireplaces, leaded or beveled glass in built-in bookcases, buffets, and dark stained wood paneling in the dining and living rooms. Some even have secret 6- x 8-ft rooms that were used for stashing contraband during Prohibition. Plumbing pipes are on the exterior of the houses. According to Nagel's relatives he used lots of nails in building his houses.

▲ 5.15: *Eda Nagel, shown in a 1970s photo, was an avid crocheter, and kept her 126 Magnolia Avenue home in vintage condition with original furnishings.*

open work created by middle half rails are mounted on tapered columns. The pattern is repeated in the bargeboard and dentils in the soffit. A front door with oval-glass insert is off-centered at the north end of the porch. (The glass window in the front door of 116 Magnolia is rectangular.)

Instead of shingles in the gable, the dropped siding is repeated. The framing of the center of the three gable windows arches over the center one. The roof has a gable dormer on the east side and a hipped-roof extension over the porch. The bricks of the front garden wall were salvaged from the 1906 San Francisco earthquake and fire. A chain is looped like a jump rope above the wall. In a Larkspur tradition, the gate pillars are topped with local stones, and the lacy iron gate between them has ornamental scrollwork.

The southwest side of the house has a cut corner with a simple version of a cornice with cutouts and a pendant. The chimney that pierces the end gable combines a base of Larkspur traditional blue rock with an upper section of salvaged San Francisco bricks. A unique touch is a mini cupola complete with a finial at its top. The interior of the gable pediment is paneled with dropped siding and the hipped-roof extension is trimmed with dentils at the junction of the soffit and the frieze.

"When we had a snowstorm one year, Nagel took the wheels off his horse and buggy and put runners on it and went touring down through town," recalled Judge Gardiner. Nagel's dog "Happy" tagged along with him on jobs and is visible in pictures of the remodel of the Blue Rock Hotel.

Eda Nagel, who ran for Booster Day Queen in 1913 and was an avid crocheter in her later years, lived in the house until she died in July of 1984 at age 96. All of her father's original furnishings were kept in place while she lived in the house. Now 116 and 126 Magnolia Avenue are owned by Gustave's granddaughter Dorothy Bain McCarthy and her husband, Thomas McCarthy *(see Appendix D)*.

▲ 5.16: *The famous magnolia tree at 125 Magnolia Avenue, 2008.*

▲ 5.17: *130 Magnolia Avenue, home of William J. Kennedy, an early Larkspur trustee, 1910.*

⑥ Piedmont Road to West Baltimore Avenue

The *Magnolia soulangiana* at **125 MAGNOLIA AVENUE** was planted in 1941 on this corner and was the inspiration of Bay Area landscape architect Gordon Courtright. Courtright had been hired by dentist Dr. Thurlow Jaegeling and his wife Margaret to design the yard in exchange for a set of dentures for Courtright's mother, Mary Courtright, who had been Larkspur's postmistress and city clerk. However, the magnolia was not part of the original landscaping plan and, much to Dr. Jaegeling's dismay, an additional $7.50 was added to the bill. Since the tree was already planted, it stayed. Commented daughter Joy Jaegeling Best, "Courtright assured the doctor that over time he would see the value of his investment."

Twenty years later Dr. Jaegeling confided to Courtright when he was sitting in the dentist's chair that he was very proud of the tree. The tree's fame and landmark status has spread far and wide so that even a postcard addressed to "The owner of the magnolia tree on Sir Francis Drake Boulevard" was delivered to Jaegeling.

Some people guessed that it must have had several trunks to account for its unusually large size. However Joy affirmed, "it is truly just one tree.... When the tree was young, the lowest branches must have rooted."

In the springtime owners have traditionally lighted the tree to display its full glory of lush bloom at night. The tree was in full bloom when the city celebrated its centennial on March 1, 2008.

Porches were a universal and distinctive feature of late nineteenth- and twentieth-century homes. Walking down Magnolia, the majority of the homes originally had porches that were used as cool summer spots, similar to today's patios, and were designed in a variety of sizes, shapes, and placements. One, such as **130 MAGNOLIA AVENUE** constructed around 1907 for William J. Kennedy, an early town trustee, has porches that wrap around two sides of the house. The porches are tucked under an extension of the main hipped roof supported by columns and enclosed with shingled railings. Over the years an addition enclosed the east porch, and the front porch has been enclosed with multipane windows. An extensive remodel in 2008 maintained the original footprint and character of the house.

Another house, **134 MAGNOLIA AVENUE** built in 1925 by Gustave Nagel, has a porch with a separate, shallow gable roof, and extended eaves and shiplap siding that repeat the shallow gable main roof. The typical Nagel roof details of the extended eaves and window treatment similar to 116 Magnolia are

▲ 5.18: *134 Magnolia Avenue, built in 1925, shows Gustave Nagel's favorite architectural details in this photo taken in 2000.*

repeated on the house. This is another example of the post-war trend to enclose porches to expand interior space.

Although the shingled, hipped-roof house at **141 MAGNOLIA AVENUE**, with two front hipped-roof bays and center gable dormer, was built in 1910 by George and Lucinda Bannan, it looks like a forerunner of the Prairie-style architecture of the 1920s. The hipped-roof porch on the north side of the house has been enclosed, and the original multipane windows have been replaced.

Of all the porches along this section of Magnolia, the one at **143 MAGNOLIA AVENUE** takes first prize. The house was originally built in 1909 for James B. and Bertha M. Donnolly. Mrs. Donnolly had been ordered by her doctor to move to Marin County. Weather permitting, she was advised to sleep outdoors, hence the spacious porch. A 70-foot, L-shaped porch with circular columns extends across the front and along the north side of the house under a separate roof. The house has a wooden, hipped roof incorporating such Colonial Revival-style features as dentil trim and a frieze band. A hipped-roof dormer with two four-pane windows and a wide overhang is centered over the main roof. Two stately Canary Island palms with distinctively marked trunks stand in the front yard. This species was a favorite landscaping choice in the 1920s.

The Kelly family began their thirty-year occupancy of the house in 1944. During their ownership the back carriage house received a foundation and concrete floor. Raymond and Hazel Guaraglia bought the house in 1974 and extensively restored their home to maintain its original appearance.

A sample history of Larkspur architecture is visible at the north end of the street with homes from the 1800s, early 1900s, and 1920s to 1950s side by side. When nearby Baltimore Park was being developed in the 1920s and 1930s a popular home design was the Mediterranean-style bungalow with a tile roof, stucco exterior, recessed metal-framed windows, and arched doorway and windows.

The home at **144 MAGNOLIA AVENUE** captures the prime details of the Spanish-Eclectic style that borrows elements from the history of Spanish architecture such as the cross-gable tiled roofs, detailed, arched focal windows, arched front doors topped with shallow arched pediments, and display

▲ 5.19: *141 Magnolia Avenue, about 1910.*

▲ 5.20: *The wrap-around porch at 143 Magnolia Avenue is supported by classical columns with a dentil trim and frieze band. A personal touch is an old telephone call box, 2008.*

▲ 5.21: *The Reverend James Gardiner and children playing in the snow in front of 143 Magnolia Avenue, 1913.*

niches. Built in 1926 by Gertrude Guetter and her sister, daughters of local baker Richard Guetter, the house retains it historic charm.

The steep-gable, stucco house with multipane windows at **145 MAGNOLIA AVENUE**, built around 1923, was originally a smaller pier-and-post structure. Diagonal exterior boards indicate that the walls were raised in one piece to install a foundation when a second story was added in the 1980s. The pottery shards imbedded in the concrete driveway may be related to the ceramic pot on top of one of the entrance pillars.

In the 1970s Royal and Berta Radke lived in the house. During World War II Royal was a Navy quartermaster whose quick action helped save 800 of his fellow crewmen on the USS *Astoria* (CA-34) during the 1942 Battle of Guadalcanal.

The Spanish design influence of adjacent Baltimore Park homes is visible at **150 MAGNOLIA AVENUE**, built in 1932 by Russell W. and Grace K. Lauterwasser. He served as both city council member and city treasurer simultaneously in the early 1940s. They owned

▲ 5.23: *Magnolia Avenue was macadamized in 1913, a first in Marin County. The house at 214 Magnolia is visible at center right.*

additional property on the northern slope of Baltimore Canyon and off Piedmont Court that was eventually acquired as part of the Marin County Open Space District's lands *(see page 173)*. Over the years gossip circulated that Lauterwasser and Adolph Tiscornia, who advised the city on legal matters at the time, collected acreage from leads about depression properties that were coming up for sale.

Spanish Revival-style homes are also represented at 201 and 204 West Baltimore Avenue in the Baltimore Park chapter. A 1950s house style is added to the period mix at 148 Magnolia Avenue.

⑦ Baltimore Avenue to William Avenue

Judging from many early twentieth century accounts by people who eventually built homes in Larkspur, the corner of Magnolia and William Avenues was a popular spot to pitch a tent while exploring the area to purchase a lot. It evolved from a tent site to a home site in 1908 when Henry and Anna Seegelken built the Queen Anne cottage at **214 MAGNOLIA AVENUE** with a shallow gable roof over the body of the house and a separate roof over the entrance. An interesting board-and-batten Tudor-like motif on the interior of the gable remains although it has been painted. A narrow, rectangular leaded window under the gable peak has been replaced with a pair of four-pane casement windows.

⮑ *Cross Magnolia Avenue at the William Avenue crosswalk.*

Early maps label this creek Arroyo Holon. "Arroyo" is Spanish for creek or brook and "Holon" is apparently a proper name. It is identified on contemporary maps as Larkspur Creek. Formed by natural springs and run-off from Mt. Tamalpais, the creek waters cascade over Dawn Falls, flow past the Tavern at Lark Creek, parallel Monte Vista Avenue to Cane Street, and then pass through the Niven property to drain into Corte Madera Creek.

▲ 5.22: *Residents liked to add personal touches to their homes such as the ceramic pot on top of the post at 145 Magnolia Avenue, 2008.*

▲ 5.24: *The Henry and Anna Seegelken home at 214 Magnolia Avenue has an interesting combination of Victorian and Tudor features (batten framing within the gables), 2008.*

Helen Wilson called the hipped-roof cottage at **223 MAGNOLIA AVENUE** "Red Riding Hood's grandmother's house." The Henry de Veuve house, built in 1895, was also called the "Hansel and Gretel cottage" because of its quaint character with leaded windows and shed dormer. The asymmetrical, hipped roof extends down over the front porch entrance and rear porch.

The Henry de Veuve family started camping in Marin in the late 1890s, according to a 1976 letter from Alice de Veuve Cagwin Heron, whose family had ties with other early Larkspur families. Her grandparents had camped across the street on what is now William Avenue. Her father, who built the house with Mr. Cooley, had camped on the Gardiner property, living in a tent and boarding at the Gardiners until he purchased the land at the corner by the creek for $75.

▲ 5.25: *The de Veuve house at 223 Magnolia Avenue with de Veuve children Arthur, Alice, and Henry, 1904.*

Alice's letter shows a graphic picture of life in the late 1890s and early 1900s. "Water was scarce and had to be pumped. On cold mornings, it was necessary to prime [the water pump] with hot water and warm up the works – very exasperating if one was in a hurry. ... The three-seater [outhouse], called a 'Chic Sale,' which came in varied sizes, was universal until running water was piped in. ... Coal oil lamps and candles were our only means of lighting. ... Cooking was done on old wood and coal stoves, as was most of the heating. ... Our laundry was taken care of by the Chinese laundrymen who also supplied much of our fresh food. One would come with a pole across his back with a basket suspended at either end. These contained fresh produce from the San Francisco markets. On special occasions we would be supplied with lichee nuts and coconut of a special kind." According to Katherine Solomons Lilienthal, who grew up on Walnut Avenue, the vegetable man was named "Gow" and came from Sausalito with his horse and wagon.

Henry de Veuve was in the insurance business. His brother Gardner was the first principal of LCM in the 1890s.

· · · · ·

The Reverend James Allen Gardiner purchased land in 1896 from Belle and Mary Brown and began building his home at **215 MAGNOLIA AVENUE** in 1898, completing it in 1901. Gardiner, who was born in Ohio in 1842, had degrees from Wooster College, and had taught in Ohio where he met 18-year-old Adda Estella Holtz (b. 1861) who was also a teacher. After they were married on June 30, 1879, they moved to Idaho and then to Portland, Oregon where Gardiner became assistant superintendent of schools. When he abandoned teaching in the 1890s to enter the Presbyterian ministry, the family moved first to San Pablo and then to Larkspur in 1896 after spending several summer vacations camping in Baltimore Canyon. Adda Gardiner was one of the organizers and a president of the Thimble Club. She was also an organizer of the Larkspur Woman's Improvement Club in 1910. The Gardiners celebrated their 50th anniversary with a large dinner in 1929 when the reverend was 87 years old. He died on July 8, 1940. Adda died at age 87 in 1948.

The house, designed and built by Reverend Gardiner with the help of his older children, has a unique star-shaped roof design. The framing was mounted

HOUSE MYSTERY AT 215 MAGNOLIA AVENUE

The 4- x 1- x 1-ft secret compartment. Was it for jewelry or booze?

▲ 5.26: *Treasures unearthed in the Gardiner garden: A compass with the date June 30, 1892 engraved on the back, square head nails, a bottle, and the biggest find, a pistol, 2008.*

▲ 5.27: *The 1900-era well is visible through a glass trap door in the pantry of 215 Magnolia Avenue, 2008.*

▲ 5.28: *The Gardiner house at 215 Magnolia Avenue, about 1911.*

on a circular foundation that Judge Gardiner saw as a child during excavations for the furnace. The foundation was composed of ten 1 x 6 and 1 x 8 redwood boards that were soaked in water until they were pliable and then laminated together to make the circular base. The unusual star-shaped structure evolved, Sam Gardiner surmised, because his father was building it as a permanent residence and was trying to compete with the Mahoney, Basebe, and Beleney homes already built. Until 1912 the house had no central heating or running water.

The family had a barn behind the house and an outhouse about 75 feet from the back door. Judge Gardiner recounted, "The old home was warmed entirely by fireplaces and the kitchen stove with wood that my brother Ed hauled by horse across the fields. He would hook onto a fallen tree and tow it down. It was my chore to cut it up. If I didn't cut the wood up, I was cold at night."

The family grew all of its own vegetables and fruit, kept chickens, and maintained several cows whose milk was stored in a cooler room on the north side of the house that is now a laundry room.

A brick-lined, circular well that is now visible through a glass trap door below the pantry floor was under the original kitchen and supplied the house with water. A second well about 9 feet across and about 25 feet deep was located in the lower corner of the property near the creek and supplemented the water supply. The well water was drafted into service during the 1975-1976 drought.

Judge Gardiner recalled in a 1983 interview that he, his brother, and his father built a pump house near the well and installed an electric motor to water their extensive garden, running it "all day long, every day, all summer." When they dug the well, they shoveled through 6 to 8 feet of redwood sawdust and chips and bark from the old Baltimore milling operation. Since Reverend Gardiner preached intermittently in the

▲ 5.29: *Although a new railing has replaced the original, the curved walls, distinctive hipped roofs and gables, and double front doors still exist at 215 Magnolia Avenue, 2008.*

Redwoods Presbyterian Church and around the county until the mid-1920s, the house was designed with two front doors, one for family use and one for persons visiting the Reverend professionally.

"My father was 60 years old when I was born," reported Judge Gardiner, who was delivered on the living room floor. "I was the eighth child in the family composed of seven boys and one girl. The older children were born in the 1880s and 1890s and then my brother Paul in 1900 and myself in 1902." With his teaching background, the Reverend Gardiner opted to tutor Samuel and his brother Paul in the Larkspur home. His father stressed history, mathematics, and Latin so when Samuel attended Tamalpais High School as a junior in 1917, he recalled, "I had had much more mathematics than they teach at high school so I helped teach the course at Tamalpais."

"The primary reason (for home schooling) was a feeling on my father's part that if we went to public school we'd get mixed up with girls and learn all about sex."

— Judge Gardiner, who was home schooled

During the 1906 earthquake, reported Judge Gardiner, "There was a single big shake and quite a lot of tremors, small tremors, afterwards. After the quake my brothers who commuted by electric trains to San Francisco invited a number of their friends over to our home as an escape. People continued to commute to San Francisco, but there was a lot of fire and smoke." Although the family worried about their two chimneys, they suffered no damage.

The life of Judge Samuel Gardiner spanned a major portion of Larkspur history. He played an important role in city and county affairs as Larkspur city attorney from 1933 to 1964 and as a Marin Superior Court judge from 1971 to 1973. Salty and well read, he once commented that he'd outlived all his friends; nevertheless, 160 other friends managed to show up for his 100th birthday party. Samuel Whittier Gardiner died in September of 2003, only a few weeks before his 101st birthday.

Two of Judge Gardiner's brothers played a role in Larkspur history. Edgar Gardiner photographed Magnolia Avenue before it was paved. His photos not only show the early condition of the county road with its boardwalk sidewalks, but also record the early-1900s homes.

Robert M. Gardiner, Samuel's oldest brother, and his wife Grace built a home at 12 Loma Vista Avenue in 1910. During his term on the Larkspur City Council, he introduced numerous ordinances in 1911, set up the offices of city engineer and city attorney, and served as mayor. His son, Robert S. Gardiner, and his wife Lemoine moved into 215 Magnolia in 1948 and raised their family there until 1977. Thus the Gardiner home remained in family control for nearly eight decades.

Over the years owners have left their mark on the property. The two cedars at the entrance were seedlings brought back from the Sierra by the Gardiners. The Hills family painted the "Hills Estate" on the chimney. Other changes were not as harmless. In 1977 the house suffered a number of unfortunate alterations to its historic features.

The current owners, Ellen and David Turner, have restored the house over the past 13 years to its former stately position. They have capitalized on the house and its setting by staging festive events, from a Fourth of July campsite with tents and sleeping bags for a crowd of friends to carrot hunts for children at Easter.

"There's a joyful spirit to the house design because it doesn't follow convention. I like the curved shape of the walls because the only reason to do that is for the pure pleasure of doing it," commented owner and graphic artist David Turner.

▲ 5.30: *The original 9 Ardmore Road, called "Owl's Wood," looking west from the site of LCM School, about 1887.*

▲ 5.31: *Orchard at 9 Ardmore Road, Owl's Wood, about 1920.*

▲ 5.32: *One of the cottages at Owl's Wood, about 1919.*

▲ 5.33: *Shown in this 2008 photo, 9 Ardmore Road is the last survivor of the homes that were part of Owl's Wood. It was formerly 7 Ardmore Road. The numbers changed when there was development on the street.*

⤴ *Walk back along the west side of Magnolia Avenue to Ardmore Road for an optional side trip to Chevy Chase.*

⑧ Chevy Chase & Owl's Wood

Although the major development of the Chevy Chase area took place in the 1920s, the land had been occupied by squatters in the earlier days of the Mexican land grants. Sea Captain John Van Reynegom had arrived in the area aboard his schooner, the *Linda*, in 1848. When his crew deserted for the gold fields, he settled on these lands, planted a vineyard and orchard, and developed his own cattle brand.

At this time many squatters settled in this section between Larkspur and Corte Madera because the original Mexican land grant boundaries were not precise. The original grant gave prominent Marin pioneer John Reed one league of land not to extend farther than Arroyo Holon, which then was owned by the San Francisco Mission. However, when the land was surveyed, it was discovered that one league came only to the top of Alto Hill. Reed was satisfied with that amount, and anything beyond was declared public land.

Under the Homestead Act, Van Reynegom was able to file a claim to his 160 acres in 1860 and 1862. Reed's heirs were later persuaded to claim payment from the squatters, and in 1885, after losing the court case, Van Reynegom's son-in-law, Frank M. Pixley, received a quitclaim to the land for $2,000 in gold. A few months later Pixley deeded the land to his wife Amelia to ensure the deed was recorded. He then purchased additional acreage so that his total lands were 191 acres extending from the Corte Madera train station to the top of Christmas tree hill, north to the Chevy Chase area and across Magnolia Avenue to the far side of the railroad tracks, thus including the site of Larkspur-Corte Madera School.

• • • • •

In the 1880s Owl's Wood, a cluster of homes at the cul-de-sac where only **9 ARDMORE ROAD** still remains, was the country estate of the Pixleys. Frank Pixley had ridden to California on a mule with a wagon train when he was 24 years old. He married Amelia Van Reynegom in 1853. He prospected for gold on the north fork of the Yuba River for a year before setting up a law practice in San Francisco. In 1877 he founded, owned, and edited the *San Francisco Argonaut*, a weekly newspaper that boasted among its contributors Gertrude Atherton, Mark Twain, and Ambrose Bierce. Pixley was also prominent on the state level. During vigilante days, Pixley was the San

▲ 5.34: *Until it was torn down and replaced by a new home, the simple Owl's Wood cottage at 5 Ardmore Road kept its original exterior features and was used as a piano studio with adjunct laundry, 1970s.*

Francisco city attorney; in 1859 he served in the state assembly, and by 1862 he was state attorney general.

In its heyday Owl's Wood had apple and apricot orchards, vineyards, and gardens surrounding the broad-porched Victorian farmhouse. Occupied by Frank and his brother William, the estate had a comfortable farm cottage, a spacious barn and corrals, a modern coach house, a dairy house, and enclosures for cows, pigs, chickens, and other farm animals. An 85,000-gallon stone reservoir and many springs supplied water to the estate.

Before his death in 1891, Frank Pixley had unsuccessfully tried to sell the lands and estate for $75,000. When Amelia Van Reynegom Pixley died, she left Owl's Wood to her adopted children, Farrington and Vera Pixley, who made the place a working ranch until Farrington died from tuberculosis, leaving Vera as the sole heir.

Corte Madera police chief Frank Nelson, who was also tax collector, fire chief, building inspector, and court clerk in the 1940s, was born in the farmhands' house at Owl's Wood in 1910. His father ran the dairy there and delivered milk to customers in Larkspur and Corte Madera.

When Vera Pixley sold the property to Abe Ruef and his partner in 1921, she retained the section immediately west of Park Way at Ardmore Road. The property included the honeymoon cottage that was the first house built (now 9 Ardmore Road), the stables, and a small house at 5 Ardmore, now replaced, that was part laundry room and part music studio for her granddaughter.

The barn and stables were both converted into a private home by the Sonnenbergs when they purchased the property in 1935. In a 1974 interview Dorothea Sonnenberg ironically recalled that she had been friends with the Pixleys' granddaughter and had once visited Owl's Wood for lunch, but had been bitten so badly by mosquitoes that she swore she would never live there.

Ruef, who had a checkered career ranging from political boss behind San Francisco mayor Eugene Schmitz's administration to serving time in San Quentin from 1911 to 1915, originally intended to turn the large Victorian Pixley house that once stood on Wiltshire Avenue into a nightclub. He removed the interior partitions of the house, built roads, surveyed lots, and gave the area the name Chevy Chase. He defaulted on the mortgage payments as well as his taxes and gave up the property before he could proceed with his plans. He died, bankrupt, in 1926.

Thomas Minto bought the property for back taxes in 1937 and, latching onto Ruef's name for the area, Chevy Chase, sold lots and put in a miniature golf course at 55 Magnolia Avenue.

All that remains of the original Owl's Wood is 9 Ardmore Road. After various lot splits, the other buildings were torn down and replaced with new homes. ✦

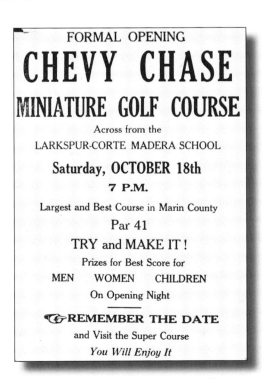

▲ 5.35: *Newspaper ad for the miniature golf course, 1937.*

PALM HILL
Palm Hill's limited roads lead to protected neighborhoods and paths.

▲ 6.1: Palm Hill, looking south from the Heather Gardens area, 1910. The cut made on the hillside for the railroad cutoff parallels today's William Avenue.

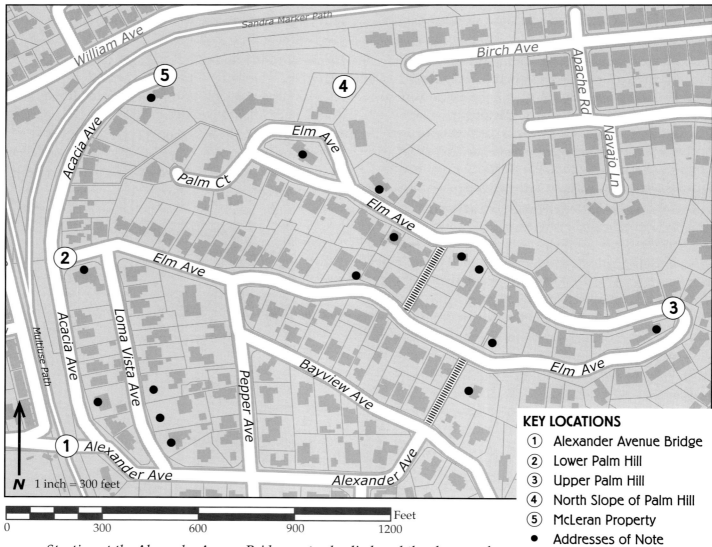

KEY LOCATIONS
1. Alexander Avenue Bridge
2. Lower Palm Hill
3. Upper Palm Hill
4. North Slope of Palm Hill
5. McLeran Property
• Addresses of Note

Starting at the Alexander Avenue Bridge, a steady climb and the absence of sidewalks present challenges, but explorers are rewarded with seeing a variety of home styles and tantalizing views through the trees growing on this once-bare hill.

PALM HILL

Palm Hill is bounded by the Northwestern Pacific Railroad right-of-way and Holcomb Avenue on the west, the NWPRR and William Avenue on the north, and the Corte Madera town limits on the south and east.

• • • • • • • • • • • •

Over the years, Palm Hill's topography has changed. In the early 1900s the northwest slope of the hill was a grassy knoll, except for a lone valley oak. Town blacksmith and liveryman Charlie Rice grew and harvested hay crops there for his livery of stable horses. From 1910 to 1913 the tall, thin Mexican fan palms of Baltimore Avenue marched across the railroad tracks and up the lower part of the hill, christening it Palm Hill. In the 1930s and 1940s elm trees were added to the upper part of Elm Avenue, pepper trees to Pepper Avenue, and acacia trees to Acacia Avenue. Dutch elm disease in the 1980s eliminated the canopy of elm trees that arched over Elm Avenue. In 2010 the hill was densely populated by a mixture of both trees and homes.

IN THE 1960s

"My sister Thorley and I ran loose in the neighborhood, but we knew that we had to go home when we heard the five o'clock City Hall horn blow."

— Susan Turner, who grew up at 60 Elm Avenue

▲ 6.2: *View of Palm Hill from Baltimore Park with station in the foreground, 1940.*

1) Alexander Avenue Bridge

The Palm Hill development was undertaken in 1913 by the Coleman and Forbes estates, developers of the Baltimore Park subdivision. William Courtright was again their agent. When it was opened for development, a wooden bridge spanned the railroad tracks to connect to the area.

Recalled Judge Samuel Gardiner, "I used to stand on that old wooden bridge when a steam engine went below and, with its protection, I was able to defy the power below. Other kids found this to be fun but horses did not."

The development ran into problems, and work was not started until January of 1920. Gossips at the time talked of kited checks. Others said the lots priced at $1,000–$2,000 were too high to sell. After these financial problems, William Courtright disappeared. To support the family, his wife Mary became postmistress and held that position from 1917 to 1928, when she became city clerk.

The Coleman and Forbes estates were further strapped when the old wooden bridge over the railroad tracks was declared in need of repairs in 1922. An assessment district was proposed despite the railroad engineers' insistence that the "structural portions of the bridge were in good condition." Robert Gardiner rallied his neighbors on Palm Hill to get cost estimates for a new Alexander Avenue bridge. City Trustee minutes regarding the bridge report that discussions dragged on with the city pressing to build a new one, and the Coleman and Forbes estates wanting to repair the old one with the railroad and themselves as principals. The new concrete reinforced bridge was designed by Larkspur city engineer John C. Oglesby, and was to be funded by an assessment district. Despite protests, the Larkspur Board of Trustees decided that the cost of the proposed road improvements, including the bridge, should be assessed to the property owners of Palm Hill. First authorized in August of 1925, the arched concrete bridge over the railroad tracks was not completed until 1927.

Listed in the National Register of Historic Places in 1983, the 163½-foot-long and 29-foot-wide bridge has two lanes within the 20⅓-foot-wide roadway. The reinforced concrete structure, with concrete arches that support the deck by means of suspended pillars and transverse floor beams, was a unique construction for its period. Only five similar bridges are known to exist in California. The name of the bridge was changed to the Charles Holcomb Bridge in 1991 in honor of the San Francisco assistant engineer who surveyed Larkspur's street alignment in 1913, but it is still referred to as the "Alexander Avenue Bridge."

The controversial tradition of the bridge has continued. In 1997 seismic stabilization of the bridge was proposed and an environmental study was made. After many meetings and studies, plans were approved. State funding was available, but work was not started by the deadline. By 2010 the project appeared to be on track for seismic work that would retain the historic character of the bridge.

BRIDGE ADVENTURES

ON TOP: Walking the top of the bridge has been a rite of passage for Larkspur children. Older boys have been known to practice rappelling off the center span.

BENEATH: "Frog epidemics" erupted in the standing water by the railroad tracks under the Alexander Avenue Bridge after a rainy winter, according to sisters Susan Turner and Thorley Murray, who grew up at 60 Elm Avenue in the 1950s.

▲ 6.3: *The arched roadway of the Charles Holcomb Bridge, commonly known as the Alexander Avenue Bridge, frames a view of Mt. Tamalpais, 2010.*

▲ 6.4: *Left to right: Homes at 20 and 12 Loma Vista Avenue, 18 Acacia Avenue in the foreground, upper Palm Hill in the background, 1920s.*

② Lower Palm Hill

Until the wooden bridge over the railroad tracks was built, lack of roads to Palm Hill was one of the stumbling blocks to its development. Lower Palm Hill developed first. An early access point, according to Judge Samuel Gardiner, was an extension of William Avenue near the Electric Booster Station that crossed a large slough west of the station. When Samuel's brother built the first house on lower Palm Hill in 1910, his father and brother cut logs, laid them down, and made a log road access.

Robert M. Gardiner, the oldest son of Reverend James Allen Gardiner, built the house with the center gable at **12 LOMA VISTA AVENUE.** The low, bungalow-style house was a gift from his wife Grace's father, George Seaton, a contractor in San Francisco. Their son, Robert S. Gardiner, was born in 1911 and reared there. After a move to San Francisco, he returned to Larkspur and lived at 215 Magnolia Avenue until his death.

Robert S. Gardiner recalled in a 1974 interview that the family planted the two redwoods and blue spruce in the front near the old entrance, and that there was a garage where the present driveway is located. The house was built with a balloon frame with each stud going from the floor to the attic. Originally, the attic may have been unfinished since he remembered laying flooring to prevent someone from dropping through the ceiling to the rooms below. His father's original workshop still stands at the rear of the house.

The house was extensively remodeled in the 1950s. The interiors were opened up, the stone pillars were eliminated, and the front porch was replaced with a deck. The front door was replaced with sliding glass doors and large windows, closing off the two windows on the south wall. A fireplace was added as was a new entrance at the rear of the house. The three dining room windows at the rear are the only remaining originals.

Another early Palm Hill home is the Courtright house, a California Craftsman-style bungalow at **3 ELM AVENUE** across from the Baltimore Park railroad station *(see pages 159-160)*. It was built in 1912 by William Courtright, a real estate agent for the Coleman-Forbes interests. The house has a cobblestone foundation composed of some of the 32 wagon loads of stones that had been used in the railroad bed when the spur was laid in 1908. Mary L. Courtright was reported to have tossed the stones over the railroad fence. The Courtrights had local Italian stonemasons lay the cobblestones and, according to her son, Glenn Courtright, one day when union masons showed up to claim the job, his mother ran them off with a shotgun.

Another of Mary's five children, horticulturist Gordon Courtright, planted the famous magnolia tree at 125 Magnolia Avenue in exchange for dental work from Dr. Thurlow Jaegeling. A magnolia tree in the Courtright yard was planted at the same time but has never achieved the same size or fame.

▲ *6.5: The Courtright house at 3 Elm Avenue, 1978.*

▲ *6.6: The Courtright house in 2007.*

Although a second story was added to the house in 1984, the addition was located to the rear of the building and could not be seen from the street. Inside the house are unique features, such as built-in cabinets in the dining and living rooms, Douglas fir flooring, a front door with beveled-glass panels, interior doors with transoms, and the most unusual element, rear windows that drop into wall cavities.

• • • • •

The early homes were built at the base of Palm Hill on Acacia and Loma Vista Avenues on a low ridge below the top of the hill. In 1914 Almon Wheeler, who was a 6-foot 3-inch-tall contractor, built the bungalow-style home at **18 ACACIA AVENUE**. Wheeler, who had been a teacher in Burlington, Vermont until he became deaf, had come to California in 1907. In 1922 he built the new dance floor for the Rose Bowl when it was moved to Cane Street. For years he was the Larkspur building inspector. His son, Burt C. Wheeler, a longtime employee of the Larkspur Lumber Company, became part owner with Dolph Doherty and eventually sole owner of the company.

A bay window and an addition at the rear have enlarged the house but have not jeopardized its historic front view from Acacia Avenue.

Many of the Acacia Avenue backyards extend to Loma Vista Avenue, where some of their garages are located, often creating parking challenges for both streets.

The Loma Vista homes that were built on a knoll above the street in the 1920s had views that stretched in all directions. The cross-gable frame house at **20 LOMA VISTA AVENUE**, built in 1925 by Bertha Smith and her physician husband, has a two-story section with a sleeping porch, and a one-story section with shiplap siding. Brackets support the multipane bay windows in the living room and bedroom. A small porch with modest capitals on the pillars frames the front door. Earthquake worries influenced the design of the house, which was bolted to the foundation and built with large, closely-set studs.

Emagene and Roger Boero bought the house in 1967. According to their escrow papers, Loma Vista Avenue was at one time called Palm Avenue, a continuation of the street by that name in Corte Madera. In 1970 they received a letter addressed to "Occupant" from Bertha Smith, who was at that time 86 years old and lived in Stockton. The letter said the house was designed by Mr. Sheldon and, "I bought the lot that extended front and back to a driveway up the hill. We had lots of tile in the house, linoleum, hardwood floors, two baths and a shower downstairs.... The kitchen was wired for electricity."

One of Bertha Smith's favorite features in the house was the mirror above the fireplace that allowed her

▲ *6.7: 18 Acacia Avenue, 2007.*

to see from the kitchen to the living room, so she could check if the children were practicing the piano.

Over the years, the Boeros have had visits from Jeanne Smith Daugherty, one of the Smith daughters, who liked to visit "her house." "Growing up in the house," she reported, "my sisters and I slept on the second-story sleeping porch which was open air, and had canvas rolled on dowels where the windows are today." When it rained, they would roll down the canvas. Dr. Smith was very concerned about tuberculosis, and felt the fresh air of the open porch was a preventative to the illness. If one of the girls was ill, she was moved into the middle bedroom that had an oil heater.

When the prices of Palm Hill lots were lowered in the 1920s because of the developers' financial problems, new homes sprouted along Acacia, Loma Vista, and Elm Avenues. These homes replicated the Spanish, Mission, and Craftsman bungalow styles and give the hill its distinctive character.

Home building entered a quiet phase on the hill until the late 1930s and 1940s when the World War II building boom triggered the development of infill homes on choice vacant lots on both upper and lower Elm. In 1937 the impressive Spanish-style house at **8 LOMA VISTA AVENUE** (on the corner of Alexander Avenue) was constructed for $15,000 – a hefty price in those days. The house was one of five residences designed by a Mr. Winner who specialized in commercial buildings and designed several Bank of America facilities. The house steps up the slope in a series of modules combining flat and tile roofs, cantilever timber and stucco balconies, tile chimney caps and metal casement windows. Decorative tile and stucco eyebrows extend over the lower floor roofs.

▲ 6.8: *8 Loma Vista Avenue, 2007.*

TYPICAL PALM HILL HOMES

▲ 6.9: *114 Acacia Avenue, 2007.*

▲ 6.10: *20 Elm Avenue, 2007.*

▲ 6.11: *56 Elm Avenue, 2007.*

▲ 6.12: *Sketch of 130 Elm Avenue.*

The original owner, Mrs. Waterbury, lived in the house until she was 93 years old. Then her daughter Ada and Ada's husband, Lewis Foster, owned and lived in the home until it was sold in 1961.

Many of the lots were long and narrow, and extended between lower and upper Elm. The early homes were alternately sited at the front and rear of the properties, providing maximum privacy. Early sewer lines were laid directly down the hill from upper to lower Elm, which caused future problems when the lots were split.

Early residents report that when they purchased home sites, they were allowed to choose their own street address numbers. Curiously, there are no 200 numbers.

The Spanish-style home at **70 ELM AVENUE** was built in 1929, after the price of lots was lowered. Rumor has it that the strongly textured, stucco, cross-gable house, with a combination of flat and shed roofs, was a model home at the time the upper hill was developed. Other exterior details include S-shaped Spanish roof tiles, flat roofs with parapets, tile vents and metal multipane casement windows of rectangular glass. The living room has a vaulted ceiling, a fieldstone-framed fireplace with a niche above, and a large focal window that originally framed a view to Mt. Tamalpais. Other details include arched doorways, a foldout, drop-down phone center in the hall, a built-in dining room china cabinet, crown moldings in the kitchen, and coved ceilings in the bedroom and hallways.

Ted and Helen Heitkamp purchased the house in 1960. Helen helped organize the 1970s Town Meetings, has served on the Planning Commission, and, in 2010 serves on the Heritage Preservation Board. Although an open front porch was added when the old stairs rotted, the bulk and mass have not changed.

With the development of microwaves, big screen TVs, washers and dryers, and other twentieth-century equipment, the modest 1,200-square-foot early homes faced the need to be remodeled. Much to the chagrin of neighbors, adding a second story often required an almost complete teardown to the foundation to support the second story.

▲ 6.13: 70 Elm Avenue, 2007.

One of the most dramatic teardowns was at **106 ELM AVENUE**. Around 1939 the U.S. government located a radio station there staffed by an F.B.I. agent named Frank Kellogg who set up a signal to catch illegal ham operators in the area. He would pick up the signals and then go out in his car with a tracking device to confiscate the radios. The station operated through World War II, when it was converted to a home. In 2001 it was purchased, torn down, and replaced with a large, contemporary, Mediterranean-style home.

On the southwest side of Palm Hill, the McWatters property, owned by artist and painter Lottie McWatters, was a large lot where she and her husband built **109 ELM AVENUE** in the 1940s. Over the years the lot, which extended between Elm Avenue and Bayview, was subdivided into three additional lots, and homes were built at 111 Elm and 60 and 64 Bayview Avenues.

Another home on a choice lot was built at 121 Elm Avenue in the late 1940s for John and Amy Keller. In 1968 Jean and Paul Knudsen purchased it and reveled in "the views of Mt. Tam, San Francisco, the East Bay, and sunsets and full moons." In the 1960s families would spread out blankets and sleeping bags on the slope adjacent to 121 Elm to watch Fourth of July rockets and fountain bursts being fired from the park below. According to Thorley Murray a favorite summertime activity for hill children was sliding down its grassy slope in cardboard boxes.

③ Upper Palm Hill

The 1940s introduced a change on Palm Hill from the Spanish bungalow style to simplified wood-clad homes with low-pitched roofs. One of Larkspur's earliest examples of California ranch-style architecture was built at the crest, above the hairpin curve, at **130 ELM AVENUE** in 1940 by Joseph B. Rice, son of Charlie Rice, who owned the livery stable on Rice Lane *(see pages 38-40)*. In 1974 Charles and Nancy Curley purchased the house and lived there until 2003, with their two sons, Kent and Craig. "When we first moved from the dark canyon to Palm Hill, I had to wear sunglasses every day for a month inside the house," commented Nancy.

Both Nancy and Chuck were stellar players in city activities and rode in the Fourth of July parade as Citizens of the Year in 1983. Their property was the site of many hill and city gatherings. Chuck served on the Planning Commission from 1966 to 1975, and served on the City Council from 1975 to 1983, including several terms as mayor, as well as numerous county boards and Larkspur's 2050 Committee. Nancy was a founding force behind Larkspur's Heritage Preservation Board, overseeing the writing of the early heritage ordinances and the production of editions of Larkspur histories while juggling terms as a PTA president.

· · · · ·

The combination of the assessment district for the concrete bridge, internal financial problems, and the Depression of 1929 were major blows to the development of Palm Hill. When the Coleman and Forbes estates defaulted on their bond payments in the early 1930s, the city seized the property. The Depression had stalled the real estate market so few lots sold, even at the bargain price of two hundred and fifty dollars. Charles McLeran, who had grown up at 143 King Street, bought 11 acres along the southwest ridge, and on the lower north side of the hill. In 1936, at age 25, he designed and built the house at **385 ELM AVENUE**, which was one of the first on the ridge top of the hill. "It was more or less a copy of a house I had seen in the Loire Valley," he commented in a 1979 interview. "We took the outlines of the house, kept the exterior the same, and redid the interior."

The interior has a high central area with a balcony. The steep gable roof has tile shingles, and the exterior is covered with durable asbestos. "I had originally planned to have a driveway go around the house," said Charlie,

PAPER STREETS ON PALM HILL

A network of what are called "paper streets" traversed the slopes of Palm Hill, providing shortcuts between the upper streets and the lower ones. Some were legal easements with steps, others paths and trails that "hill" children used to go to school, and adults to the train station and commute buses.

One that is still actively used connects lower and upper Elm Avenue (begins between 80 and 88 Elm and ends just north of 385 Elm). Another, between 101 and 109 Elm, which is lined by a row of large Monterey pines, connects to Bayview Avenue opposite the Alexander Avenue junction, and is used by children going to Neil Cummins School. County maps show it as "Short Path."

Sadly, more recent homeowners discourage their children from using the trails, and SUVs zip up and down the hill. Gone are the adventures that paper streets provided for previous hill children, as well as the more practical shorter routes to schools, and emergency exits during a fire or other natural occurrences.

For more information, see Appendix C.

▲ *6.14: Stairs from Lower Elm to Upper Elm, 2010.*

BUILDING ON PALM HILL AT 375 ELM AVENUE

▲ 6.15: 375 Elm Avenue (center). The small house at right was a monitoring station used by the government during World War II, 1939.

"Next door, at 385 Elm, the McLerans were constructing a home, and I remember their contractor asking, 'Why on earth would you want to buy a lot and build a house on this god-forsaken, windy hill?'"

— Gertrude Gadow

"but I was unable to buy the other lot, so the best view of the house is from the back." He, his wife, and their family lived in the house until 1961 when they moved to Kentfield.

Charlie and his brothers, Ralph and Robert, were active for years in the Larkspur Association of Volunteer Firemen. In 1945 Charlie started the McLeran Roofing Company, located in back of the Larkspur Lumber Co. (current site of Larkspur Plaza). The firm moved to Murray Park in 1946 and by the late 1980s it was located in San Rafael, where the business remains in the family.

Charlie's son, Brian McLeran, currently lives at 385 Elm Avenue. In 2006 and 2007, major updating was done, including an upgrade of the existing swimming pool and preservation of the house's historic character.

The house at **395 ELM AVENUE,** another early home on the Palm Hill ridge line, was owned by Theophile "Pop" Gorreaux, who moved in on Labor Day of 1936. He took advantage of the existing double lot and planted an orchard that extended down to the lower section of Elm Avenue. An avid gardener, he enjoyed grafting different varieties of fruit onto the same tree, and tended the park in front of the railroad station for years. He is said to have helped plot the street-to-street sewer layout on Palm Hill. The house has been remodeled and additions made.

The pressure for housing in the 1940s triggered some major changes on Palm Hill. Max and Gertrude Gadow bought their lot at **375 ELM AVENUE** in July of 1936, on their first wedding anniversary. The Gadows moved into their new home in February of 1939, and by 1991 they had been residents for 52 years. The house is currently owned by their sons, Roger and Bob. Their lot (that connects upper and lower Elm) and the lots at 57 and 85 Elm (that connect Elm and Bayview), are still through lots.

Another home on upper Elm at **410 ELM AVENUE** was built between 1936 and 1940 by Charlie McLeran for his wife's sister, Rose Stone, who was married to the German Count Cornelius Boecop. During the 1960s it was the home of Helen Gallentier who was known around the hill for

▲6.16: 385 (center) and 410 Elm Avenue (left) looking east from 455 Elm Avenue, 1947.

rescuing homeless cats and dogs. Monte Deignan, a Larkspur Planning Commissioner, and Mary Denton live there and have done an extensive remodel and addition.

Laverne (or "Suzy," as she is known on the hill) and Neil Ball bought the choice empty lot at the peak of Palm Hill at **455 ELM AVENUE** in the 1940s. Their lot was on an unpaved section of the road with no sewer and no trees, except for a single valley oak tree that still graces the entrance to their driveway on the north side of the property. Its shape appears to be the same as the one visible in old photographs of the bare hill. Construction began in 1946. Like other residents on the hill, Neil Ball commuted to his job at an insurance company in San Francisco by catching the Greyhound bus at the corner of Magnolia and Alexander Avenues.

While many of the early homes on the north side of the hill depended on septic tanks due to a lack of city sewer connections, some owners were able to connect to sewer lines via easements. For instance, the Balls secured a permit to place their sewer line under the street and down a five-foot easement on the then-empty lot at 419 Elm. The line extended around 74 feet, joining the line owned by Otto Heierle, who had developed the property on the south side of Elm. The line served two houses at the time and connected to the city sewer system at Elm and Loma Vista Avenues. Heierle, who was manager of the Niven Nursey at that time, reportedly owned the end of Palm Hill and Palm Court.

From the 1940s through the 1960s the original development lots with the stucco, Mission-style bungalows were split, creating substandard lots by today's standards. The result was that the new wood-sided homes were built bumper-to-bumper with

▲ 6.18: Oaks near 455 Elm Avenue.

TREES ON PALM HILL

"I remember building a fort and skywalk with boards that stretched between the branches of the oaks opposite my house [455 Elm Avenue] over to the grove of eucalyptus trees.

— Greg Ball

▲ 6.17: Laverne Ball's house under construction at 455 Elm Avenue in 1947.

▲ 6.19: The namesake elms on Palm Hill were removed in 1985 because of Dutch Elm disease.

the older ones. Views were often blocked. The original sewer lines created problems since, like the Balls' easement, some were located under the new homes or ran through their side yards. In addition the newer homes blocked foot traffic along old, unofficial easements between the upper and lower sections of the hill, such as the link between Palm Court and Acacia Avenue.

Sewer connections and geography caused another problem, called the "County Island," that was faced by infill homes on Palm Hill. The five homes built between 109 and 345 Elm Avenue, at the eastern hairpin curve point, were just outside the Larkspur city limits. The county, Corte Madera, and Larkspur all had an interest in this piece of land, according to Laverne Ball. "Some had their front yard in Larkspur and their back yard in Corte Madera," she reported. When confusion arose in 1959 over which department should respond to a fire at 129 Elm, a movement was begun to clear up the boundary question in order to have uniform public services for future hill homes.

The annexation was tricky since the sewers were not connected into Larkspur but went downhill and would require a tax assessment to connect them to Larkspur's system. Lengthy negotiations between city representatives dragged on but were finally concluded, and the annexation went ahead. In 2007 all houses were connected to the sewer line except 430 Elm Avenue.

④ North Slope of Palm Hill

For years, before the Elm Crest subdivision was approved in 1999, the wooded north side of Palm Hill was home to generations of black-tailed deer that raised their fawns there and made forays into

▲ 6.20: *The bulldozed slope and slide repair on the north side of Palm Hill, 2001.*

▲ 6.21: Collier's *magazine featured Larkspur with a photo of three of the four McLeran boys working on the roof of 200 Acacia Avenue, 1947.*

the rosebushes and other attractive garden plants that weren't fenced off. In the 1960s its dense vegetation was an ideal location for future engineers and builders to construct tree houses and create a rustic outdoor playground for the twenty or more children growing up on the hill at that time. Some still keep in touch and reconnect at the annual Fourth of July parade.

According to Greg and Ross Heitkamp, who grew up at 70 Elm Avenue, a heavy 2½-inch knotted rope hung from a big oak's branch on the back side of the hill. The branch extended over a steep slope. Five or six of the hill kids would clamber onto the rope and swing out over the steep slope below. Getting off was a challenge requiring extra swings to get back over the upper slope, or dropping off and suffering bruises.

Another time, shovels, pick axes, and clippers disappeared from various parents' workshops. The hill gang cut the Scotch broom and cleared an early mountain bike trail from Elm down to William, including a big jump.

This north slope site of fun and games has been replaced by the two homes of Upper Elm Crest. Because of the steep slopes and potential for landslides in the area, the original proposal for four homes was halved, creating over-sized lots. In 2002 large, contemporary, shingled homes were built at 420 and 440 Elm Avenue by Weiss & Company. To control the size of the homes, there were deed restriction caps of 3,200 square feet.

⑤ McLeran Property

Although Palm Hill is not large, the spectacular views it offers of Northridge, San Francisco Bay, Mt. Tamalpais, and Ross Valley have helped home prices soar from their original modest prices to a million dollars or more. The potential for teardowns of modest homes, often on substandard and steep lots, has sent the asking prices sky high. The one-story Spanish-style house of Ruth McLeran, Charlie McLaren's sister, at **200 ACACIA AVENUE** was sold for over two million dollars in 2007. Local builder James Giacomazzi constructed the original house. The four McLeran brothers, Charlie, Ralph, Hugh, and Robert, worked on the house and were pictured tiling the roof in a *Collier's* magazine article dated May 17, 1947.

· · · · ·

Now Palm Hill is a mixture of architectural styles that reflect the history of the hill. A number of the original Mission-style stucco homes remain, as well as some homes built in the 1920s and 1930s. When substandard lots did not allow enlargement above grade, basements were excavated, thereby more than doubling the square footages on the small lots. On the plus side, the street views of some of these homes have retained their original character. On larger lots, sizeable Mediterranean- and Craftsman-style homes have sprouted up.

Instead of rolling their sleeping bags out in tree houses, the current generation lays them out on trampolines. Even the local deer have gotten hemmed in by development, although they still make their daily treks around the hill to munch on *agapanthus*, dropped plums, and loquats, as well as any roses foolish enough not to be fenced. The milkman no longer delivers, jokingly asking kids what flavor they want, and then giving them ice. Local gossip is no longer picked up over the party line services by an operator.

In the 1960s, everyone knew everyone on the hill. Young people walked down the paper streets in groups to the three schools at the foot of the hill. Young people met and knew the hill elders. Commented Ross Heitkamp, "I had a paper route, so I knew everyone and they knew me."

Now, the way the neighborhood communicates has changed. Laverne Ball, Monte Deignan, and Mary Denton host neighborhood picnics. Catherine Way has organized an Emergency Preparedness List of residents, but interaction between the generations is limited. Parents drive their children to school. Gardeners tend the yards, so there are fewer opportunities for casual street conversations. ✦

▲ 6.22: *Neighbors Jim Hardsaw and Sara Laurens, right, greet 90-year-old Laverne Ball, left, who opened her yard for the annual Palm Hill picnic in 2010.*

▲ 6.23: *Palm Hill activist Catherine Way chats with longtime Hill resident Jean Knudsen at the yearly picnic hosted by Monte Deignan and Laverne Ball at 455 Elm Avenue, 2008.*

HEATHER GARDENS & MEADOWOOD
Wartime housing and a commuter railroad yielded to contemporary homes.

▲ 7.1: *A historic view from Palm Hill to what is now called Heather Gardens, with Varsi Hill at far right, from Palm Hill, about 1912-1915.*

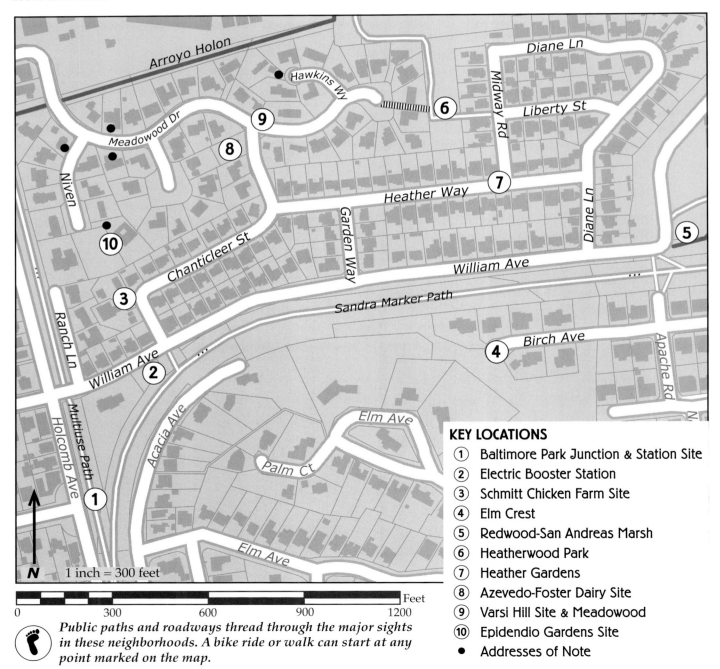

KEY LOCATIONS
1. Baltimore Park Junction & Station Site
2. Electric Booster Station
3. Schmitt Chicken Farm Site
4. Elm Crest
5. Redwood-San Andreas Marsh
6. Heatherwood Park
7. Heather Gardens
8. Azevedo-Foster Dairy Site
9. Varsi Hill Site & Meadowood
10. Epidendio Gardens Site
• Addresses of Note

Public paths and roadways thread through the major sights in these neighborhoods. A bike ride or walk can start at any point marked on the map.

HEATHER GARDENS & MEADOWOOD

A whole new window of opportunity opened up for Larkspur when the North Pacific Coast Railroad tracks were laid through the town in 1874. At first, narrow gauge steam trains hauled freight through town. After passenger service began in 1875, new neighborhoods, hotels, and resorts were built around the stations.

• • • • • • • • • • • • •

The original North Pacific Coast Railroad was reorganized as the North Shore Railroad in July of 1902, with the innovative concept of using hydroelectric power to propel electric commuter cars. The new railroad installed an electrified "third rail" to provide power, and simultaneously added another running rail to accommodate the wider standard gauge electric cars. The result was a four-rail trackway that carried both narrow and standard gauge cars. "They were the first in the U.S. to use alternating current [for their block signal system] and were the envy of many railroad systems," commented railroad buff Art Giddings. Railroad devotee Wilson Weckel explained further, "The AC was used to create the block signals that controlled the operation of the trains. The DC current powered the trains using a third rail."

In 1907 the railroad underwent another reorganization, emerging as the Northwestern Pacific Railroad (NWP). That company provided both freight and commuter services to Marin's residents for more than three decades. According to Giddings, riding the trains was "a civilized and efficient way" to get around Marin and to San Francisco. "The trains … made it possible for countless commuters to reach their destinations in less time and in a relaxed frame of mind," he said. Giddings, a former electrician-lineman with the Northwestern Pacific Railroad in Tiburon, died in 1982.

Daredevils jumped onto the third rail with both feet at once to impress their friends.

— Judge Samuel Gardiner in a 1983 letter

▲ 7.2: *Baltimore Park junction looking north at the foot of Palm Hill along the railroad tracks into Larkspur, with the station at center and "The Cutoff" at right, about 1927.*

▲ 7.3: *Eighty years later the tracks are gone, replaced by pathways used by pedestrians and bicyclists, 2007.*

REMEMBERING THE TRAINS

"In winter storms when tracks flooded, the train caused sparks to fly like crazy along the route."

— June Tanner, Corte Madera

▲ 7.5: Baltimore Park junction with tower. Baltimore Park on left, Palm Hill on right, 1939.

① Baltimore Park Junction & Station Site

Before 1909, passengers from Larkspur had to travel to San Anselmo and then via the Miracle Mile tracks to reach San Rafael. After its 1907 corporate reorganization, the revamped NWP shortened the commute by installing a cutoff track, descriptively called "The Cutoff," from east of Baltimore Park, parallel to today's William Avenue. At a new junction named "Detour" (located bayside of today's Industrial Way), this cutoff joined an existing track that went directly to San Rafael through the NWP's Tunnel #3 near the Green Brae Station, close to today's Marin Airporter parking lot. In 2010 the tunnel, now called the "Cal Park Hill Tunnel," was due to open for bicyclists and pedestrians, with public transit to be added later.

Once the cutoff was completed, the NWP built Larkspur's second stop – the Baltimore Park junction station – which triggered the development of the surrounding neighborhoods.

"The trains were so efficient," recalled Judge Gardiner. "It was a 15-minute train ride from here to Sausalito and then half-an-hour across on the boat to San Francisco. In 1917, when I went to Tamalpais Union High School, the whole school population traveled by the electric trains. I went from Baltimore [Park] Station to Almonte and transferred to the Mill Valley train. I spent my time on the train reading."

Others did not use their time so wisely. Recalled Bob Collin, who rode the trains in the late 1930s and early 1940s, "We traveled to school on an electric train called 'The Special' which had a boys' car and a girls' car and three mixed cars. The boys' car was not unlike a locker room on wheels. The guys would horse around, talk bad, and generally go out of control. … When the train went into the Chapman Tunnel someone would flip off the light switch and the air would be filled with flying bananas, oranges, apples, and assorted foodstuff. … Many a little 13- or 14-year-

▲ 7.4: In 1921, 77 trains a day left Sausalito to travel four different routes in Marin. A round-trip commute ticket book for a month from Larkspur to San Francisco was $5.95.

▲ 7.6: Baltimore Park Station and Alexander Avenue Bridge, about 1942.

A PATH FROM YESTERYEAR

Today, school children, joggers, bikers, dog walkers, baby strollers and the Larkspur Walkers make heavy use of the old railroad bed that connects with Corte Madera and downtown paths.

old freshman … was separated from his trousers and propelled into the girls' car and the door held shut. … The girls, of course, loved it."

Passenger rail service was discontinued in 1941, freight in 1967, and the tracks removed in 1977. The 1990 Larkspur General Plan designated the railroad right-of-way for open space and bike path use, but it was not a simple goal to achieve. The six acres of land within the triangle bordered by Holcomb and William Avenues and Diane Lane caught the attention of developers, while Larkspur citizens envisioned open space and bike and pedestrian paths.

In 1988 a Railroad Open Space Association (ROSA) spearheaded by Tina McArthur, James Holmes, Douglas and Carol Kerr, and Carol Schrumpf raised $12,000. The funds, combined with the city's ISTEA federal grant and state funds, purchased the five acres in 1998 for $397,000. Because the land had been subdivided, a one-acre building site had to be allowed. A stone and plaque on the rock at the Holcomb Avenue entrance to the station honors the efforts of ROSA.

Today, school children, joggers, bikers, dog walkers, parents with baby strollers, and the Larkspur Walkers make heavy use of the old railroad bed that connects with Corte Madera and downtown paths.

The concrete slab and slot for the electrical third rail, the station platform and steps, and the blue rock pillars are the only reminders of the trains that hissed to a stop at the Baltimore Park Station until 1967. The original modest 1910 wooden passenger structure constructed by the NWP was replaced with a handsome, open-sided shelter surrounded by gardens when Southern Pacific acquired the railroad in 1929.

This new station was centered on Baltimore Avenue to the west and the stone steps and pillars led to Elm Avenue and Palm Hill to the east. No train tickets were sold at the station. Since most roads in town were unpaved, boxes were provided at the station for passengers to leave their dusty or muddy footwear and change into a good pair of shoes for the trip to San Francisco.

② Electric Booster Station

When the 1909 cutoff was built, a large switching tower was located between the station and the Alexander Avenue Bridge. Judge Gardiner reported, "switching was done by hand to put the trains

▲ 7.7: In 1998 ROSA's involvement with the purchase of five acres was honored with a plaque alongside the bike and pedestrian path at Holcomb and Baltimore Avenues, 2007.

▲ 7.8: Mission Revival-style electric booster station, built in 1929 to supply additional current for the increase in train traffic, 1930.

on the right tracks. Switch handles were set in a row in the floor and stretched about eight feet. Each handle was about five feet long and these moved the switches through long bars without any electrical connections."

When the line was upgraded in 1929, more power was needed for the increased number of trains running through the county. To supply the additional current, the NWP constructed a Mission Revival-style electric booster station designed and built by Arend Louis "Buzz" Horstmeyer.

The two-story substation, located on the Sandra Marker Path across from the intersection of William Avenue and Chanticleer Street, has 10-inch-thick walls reinforced with pilasters, concrete-framed roof panels, and a thick floor slab. The fully automated plant, containing a synchronous motor generator and automatic control equipment built and installed by General Electric, supplied power to meet commuter rush-hour demands when as many as 60 trains rattled along the tracks daily.

Although the building was totally utilitarian, it boasted distinctive features such as shaped parapets, small cornices, blind-arched windows, and even its name inscribed in concrete, giving it strong architectural character. Large, handsome doors secured the building. After a similar one in Sausalito was torn down, this became the only substation still standing in Marin.

Over the years several offers have been made by private individuals to remodel the building into a home or other uses, but the City of Larkspur has retained ownership for the preservation of city files in its vault-like space.

A small adjacent parcel, approximately one-tenth of an acre, that was previously owned and used by PG&E as a parking lot for workers at the substation, was privately purchased by the Baltimore Park Associates and later sold to the city so it could be part of the open space bike path plan.

The purchase of this parcel foreclosed access from William Avenue to the property to the east and south of the railroad right-of-way. Earlier plans had proposed a youth and public recreation center and a low-income housing development for the elderly. The Elm Crest neighborhood was approved on this property in 1999.

After construction of the railroad station, the Coleman and Forbes estates sold most of the land east of the railroad tracks to three families: Frank and Caroline Schmitt in October of 1919, Pietro Epidendio in November of 1919, and Joseph and Elsie Varsi in 1930.

▲ 7.9: Schmitt chicken farm between Ranch Lane and Chanticleer Street, 1920s.

ELM CREST —

"When people ask me what part of Larkspur I live in, I tell them the Corte Madera part."

— Molly Wuthrich

▲ 7.10: *The Elm Crest development includes these homes at 200 and 202 Birch Avenue, as well as the home on the hill above at 420 Elm Avenue, 2007.*

③ Schmitt Chicken Farm Site

German immigrants Frank and Caroline Schmitt built the chicken farm with a 340-foot-long chicken house at **5** and **9 CHANTICLEER STREET** on land that stretched approximately from the railroad tracks on the south to the end of today's Ranch Lane. Now Chanticleer Street bisects most of what had been the chicken farm. Some suggest that Schmitt named his farm "Chanticleer" in honor of Chaucer's vain but clever rooster in *The Canterbury Tales*.

The family delivered their eggs regularly to customers in Corte Madera and Larkspur from their poultry coops, visible in early Larkspur photos. Although the coops have been demolished, the low, one-story Schmitt residence at 9 Chanticleer Street, with its porch on two sides, still stands just west of 11 Chanticleer Street. It retains some of its original character and is listed on the Larkspur *Historic Resources Inventory*.

Although William Avenue paralleled the railroad and was recommended as a possible major access road from downtown Larkspur to Highway 101 in 1965, citizens did not support the idea and it was never implemented.

④ Elm Crest

In the late 1990s, fifteen homes were proposed for the Elm Crest development on the 8.2 acres of land owned by the McLeran family north of Elm, west of Lakeside and Birch. Because of the steep slopes prone to slide problems, only eight lots were approved – two on the upper and six on the lower lands on Palm Hill.

This final approval of eight homes in 1999 marked the end of several years of contention between Larkspur and Corte Madera. A major controversy had centered on their size and on the access to the homes. The requirement to maintain the railroad open space right-of-way solely for the public dictated that, although the lower homes were in Larkspur, they had to be accessed via Birch Avenue in Corte Madera.

Two homes were located on Elm Avenue at the top of Palm Hill where slide repair and drainage improvements were required. The six homes constructed on Birch became a Larkspur "island" with their only access from Corte Madera. The homes on the cul-de-sac formed a friendly neighborhood where kids, rabbits, dogs, bikes, and basketballs shared the space, although delivery, emergency, and repair people had problems locating residents.

⑤ Redwood-San Andreas Marsh

Man has dramatically changed the geography between the railroad spur and what is now Doherty Drive and Redwood High School. A series of knolls projected into the old salt marsh: one at the corner of Doherty Drive and Magnolia Avenue, the Bickerstaff knoll south of today's Hall School, a large peak and ridge – Varsi Hill – that extended south between today's Meadowood and Heather Gardens, a small and large knoll at the site of today's Redwood High School, and one known as "Richardson Island" between today's Lucky Drive and Wornum Drive.

The high school knoll was bulldozed, and additional fill was taken from Varsi Hill. The 1950s block-design

▲ *7.11: View north from 455 Elm Avenue. Heather Gardens is at the lower left foreground. In the middle ground is the high school knoll at center left and the Richardson Island knoll at far right, 1947.*

school by Grommè, Mulvin & Priestley of San Rafael was opened in 1958. Built of reinforced concrete for $12 per-square-foot, it was one of the lowest cost high schools built at that time. Originally designed for 1,200 students, it was envisioned to serve 3,000 students when fully developed. In 2009, 1,441 students attended the school.

When the Community Fields were installed in 1987, bike path and marsh restoration projects were completed between the fields and the railroad right-of-way.

At the bend of William and Diane, the 15-acre Redwood-San Andreas Marsh between the former railroad tracks and the high school playing fields is the last survivor of the large marsh that had extended to the bay. According to Barbara Salzman, president of the Marin Audubon Society, a grant from the California Coastal Conservancy allowed creation of a remnant of the former marsh on the Tamalpais District lands. The marsh functions as a floodwater basin as well as a wildlife habitat.

▲ *7.12: Heather Gardens nestles between Palm Hill and the Redwood High School track and football field where a knoll used to be (shown above in Fig. 7.11, middle left). Greenbrae Marina, Corte Madera Creek, and the Greenbrae hills lie beyond, 2007.*

▲ 7.13: *The High Canal Bridge, shown here in 2009, was built in 2001 at the site of the old trestle (Fig. 7.14).*

"The funds enabled Marin Audubon to install a new tide gate and culvert to avoid flooding of adjacent properties," reported Salzman. "Channels within the marsh were excavated to improve circulation and habitat for fish, migratory shorebirds, and waterfowl."

When the railroad cutoff was built in 1909, a major portion of the north side of Palm Hill was chopped off leaving a 50-foot cliff on that side of the hill. Though now covered with growth, the dent in the hill is visible. Longtime residents guess that the fill was probably used to raise the level of the marsh where Madera Gardens was built.

▲ 7.14: *The wooden railroad trestle that was located west of today's Tamal Vista Boulevard and paralleled William Avenue, 1956.*

▲ 7.15: *The 15-acre Redwood-San Andreas Marsh has been preserved as a floodwater basin and wildlife habitat, 1958.*

⑥ Heatherwood Park

A block north of the Sandra Marker Path, Heather Way follows the westerly route of the old dirt road that had curved around Varsi Hill. The hill, which can be seen in old photos, poked up in the middle of the lands bounded by Midway Avenue on the east, Chanticleer Street on the west and Heather Way on the south.

In 1955 and 1956 a huge portion of the top and eastern end of Varsi Hill was removed to provide fill around the Redwood High School site. A hint of the hill's original shape is still visible today behind the homes on the north side of Heather Way, and on the steep north-facing slope beneath Hawkins Way. The slice off the hill is most dramatic at Heatherwood Park.

In the 1950s a small, unnamed park was created for Heather Gardens families at the eastern base of Varsi Hill with an entrance between 15 and 19 Midway Avenue, which was named after the World War II naval battle. The Rotary Club sold the land to the city for $1 and the Larkspur Lions Club purchased the play equipment. "I remember going with my Dad on Lions Club work parties to clear the weeds in the park," recalled Doug Archer.

▲ 7.16: *Looking north across Heatherwood Park, 2007. The west side of the park shows the cut that was made in Varsi Hill in the 1950s to provide fill for Redwood High School.*

By the late 1960s the park had become overgrown and the play equipment had been moved to Dolliver Park. When Meadowood was being developed beginning in 1976 and 1977, there was a scare that the park land was going to be sold to a developer for $1 to build apartments. In response to the threat, Meadowood and Heather Gardens residents rehabilitated the small park with new amenities, and it was re-christened "Heatherwood Park." The city obtained HUD funding to build a stairway to integrate the neighborhoods. According to Phil Terry, the HUD funds were justified because at that time, "almost everyone was retired and on a fixed income." Today Heatherwood Park remains a popular place for neighbors to meet.

HEATHER GARDENS —

"Heather Gardens was the outcrop of the war effort. People began coming in. This was a summer town and all the summer cottages were rented out and there was just no other place for people to live. So ... they started building Heather Gardens.

— former police chief Howard Clark in a 1985 interview

▲ 7.17: *Diane Newberry on her tricycle on Heather Way at Midway Avenue in Heather Gardens, 1943.*

⑦ Heather Gardens

The Varsi family, owners of a San Francisco florist company, held most of the land that abutted the Schmitt and Epidendio lands on the west and included a vast area extending to salt marshes on the north and east. The Varsis planted thousands of heather bushes on the hillside.

In 1941 Joseph and Elsie's son and daughter-in-law, Russell and Beatrice, developed the Heather Gardens homes to reduce the pressure for wartime housing and used the name of the hillside plant for their subdivision. Small lots averaging a little over 4,000 square feet were first laid out around Garden Way, Heather Way, and Diane Lane. The last four houses on Diane (74 to 88) were built in the 1950s

▲ 7.18: *45 Chanticleer Avenue, former home of Faye and Willie Wilson in Heather Gardens, 2007.*

▲ 7.19: *Old and new sit side by side in Heather Gardens, 2009.*

on larger lots and with a different design. Diane Lane was allegedly named for the Varsis' infant daughter who later became a Hollywood actress nominated for a 1957 "Best Supporting Actress" Academy Award for her role as Allison MacKenzie in "Peyton Place."

In 1942 additional lots were staked out along Chanticleer Street following the historic property line between the Schmitt and Epidendio farms. An ancient boundary oak still straddles the property line behind 45 Chanticleer Street. As late as 2007, this modest home retained much of its original cottage charm and was formerly known for its owners' collection of bird feeders and gnomes. Juncos, towhees, and sparrows still visit daily.

While Heather Gardens provided housing for Sausalito's Marinship wartime workers, locals were not thrilled with the five-room (two bedroom/one bath) homes with small covered porches. "Everyone was amazed at the houses sitting so close together because before that no one built next to his neighbor," recalled former police chief Howard Clark in a 1985 interview.

Because of the low water table a few feet below the ground surface, the section at the junction of Midway Avenue and Diane Lane flooded during the storms of 1952, 1978, and 1982, from the combination of high tides and very intense rainfall. The original pump at the corner was replaced with an automatic one with a backup generator and has coped with the situation as long as the drains don't become clogged. One family at 85 Diane Lane raised their home three feet after it flooded several feet above the floor level in 1978.

The water percolates under Doherty Drive and across Redwood High School's football field from Corte Madera Creek so much that even a levee at Doherty Drive does not hold back the tide.

Over the years, second stories, garage conversions, and additions have enlarged the 1940s houses. These homes, which originally sold for $3,000 to $4,000, were selling for about $300,000 in the 1990s. By 2007, the addition of second stories and more square footage skyrocketed prices to over a million dollars. In 2009 the majority of the original homes have been remodeled or replaced.

▲ 7.20: *Heather Gardens, 1996. The streets are still pedestrian friendly as demonstrated by longtime Councilman Dan Hillmer and an unidentified skater.*

FOSTER'S CHICKENS

"The Fosters used to keep the chickens in the front room of the house. They just closed it off and lived in the rest of the house."

— William Costello

VARSI HILL

"Where Meadowood is today there used to be a hill with a house on top of it. We used to think it was haunted because the fellow who lived there did magic."

— Nancy Anthony, former city clerk

Costs as well as the demographics have changed this working class neighborhood to a mostly professional one. Families are now struggling with the limitations of expansion on the small lots and the need to update the 1940s floor plans designed before microwaves, large TV screens, and computers.

Even with high prices, Heather Gardens still offers an opportunity for young families to get started judging by the number of baby strollers in the area. The streets are still closed off for neighborhood block parties and a big annual New Year's party.

Despite problems, residents of Heather Gardens bask in the warm friendly climate of the neighborhood. "The weather is fantastic," enthused neighborhood activist and Library Board member Phil Terry. "We have a bit of a micro climate and a very friendly neighborhood. It's flat and people are out walking all the time."

⑧ Azevedo-Foster Dairy Site

The Azevedo-Foster Dairy was located in the general area of Meadowood. Around 1892 Ignacio Azevedo settled in Larkspur with his wife Rosa and raised a family of five children, several of whom remained in the area most of their lives. Like many of the dairy operators in the Bay Area, the Azevedos had emigrated from the Azores Islands of Portugal.

Their dairy, sometimes called "Larkspur Dairy," was rented from the Coleman and Forbes estates on land that later became the Schmitt, Epidendio, and Varsi properties. After Ignacio's retirement around 1915, Enos Foster and his wife, also named Rosa, who similarly had five children, continued operating the dairy. Rosa did fine needlepoint work according to Alice Krogman. Foster may have been Ignacio's younger brother, who used "Foster" as a variation of the family name, "Faustino." According to Krogman, Foster died from a fall when he climbed on a roof to repair it.

▲ *7.21: Heather Gardens, right foreground, and Varsi Hill, right, viewed from 455 Elm Avenue in 1947.*

"We used to get chickens from the Fosters," remarked William Costello in a 1974 interview. He added, "Milk was loaded into big containers and Rosa would drive around town and people would come out with pots and pans and she would pour off milk for them."

Willie Frizzi made the daily milk deliveries at one time, and poured the milk into pans left on doorsteps by homeowners. "By the time people got up, the cream had settled to the top," commented Harold Kelly.

In the 1920s during Prohibition when the property was vacant, entrepreneurs installed a still that produced beer and brandy until government agents raided the site and blew up the still, according to Otto Heierle. "It caused a lot of commotion and excitement in the town," he said.

⑨ Varsi Hill Site & Meadowood

The modern Meadowood neighborhood, laid out between 1965 and 1972, included most of the old Epidendio farm and much of the former Varsi Hill. The remaining top portion of Varsi Hill was further excavated in the early 1970s to create Hawkins Way and the eastern end of Meadowood Drive.

"The hill was solid rock," recounted Bill Epidendio. "They had to dynamite to lower it and cut through for Meadowood Drive." An approximately two-acre parcel, with the redwood grove that had been adjacent to the farm, still remained in Niven family ownership in 2009.

Archeological sites have been recorded on the pasturelands at the western base of Varsi Hill between today's Meadowood homes and the end of the old creek inlet near today's Lucky supermarket. A 1995 Holman & Associates archeological review cited the existence of a Miwok settlement in the area prior to the 1776 arrival of Spanish settlers.

RECOLLECTIONS

"Varsi Hill, which was covered with eucalyptus trees and flammable brush, had a history of fires during the summer months. Juveniles used the hill as a play area, constructing tree houses and forts in the bushes. The Larkspur Fire Department nicknamed it "Five Dollar Hill" because the volunteers received five dollars every time they responded to fires on the hill."

— Doug Archer, longtime fireman

▲ 7.22: *The former Varsi Hill is topped with homes today. The house at the left is one of the original Meadowood homes, 2007.*

▲ 7.23: *Bill Epidendio, one of Ernie Epidendio's three sons, holds the sign that hung on a eucalyptus tree at the end of what is now Ranch Lane. The letters were cut from cardboard and nailed on, 2007.*

"My grandfather filled a coffee can with obsidian arrowheads, and found mortars and pestles and other tools and bones when they plowed the land."

— Bill Epidendio

The Epidendio structures were torn down for the new development. During the Meadowood subdivision's two-year construction, temporary access was granted from Holcomb Avenue, where Ranch Lane is today. According to Mr. and Mrs. J. R. Foster, that access was actually a portion of their backyard that they allowed by a "gentleman's agreement."

When the Holcomb access was closed, a petition signed by 139 Heather Gardens residents protested and demanded a second access because of the increased traffic. A dual access requirement for Meadowood filled many hours at 1969 City Council meetings. Former mayor Neil R. Brixon asserted that Meadowood was to have two entrances, one from Chanticleer Street and another from Ward Street. In October of 1969 the Larkspur City Council voted to abandon the Holcomb Avenue extension and provide a Ward Street connection.

A joint venture between the city and the subdivision developer required a bridge over Arroyo Holon (Larkspur Creek) resulting in splitting off two lots west of the new roadway that were left in Niven ownership. Homes were built there in the 1990s.

The requirement explains the awkward jog between Meadowood Drive, the eastern section of Ward Street, and the bridge. When the connection to Ward Street was made, a public easement was created along the edge of Arroyo Holon.

Meadowood homes were originally typical 1960s style with natural wood exteriors. Although the original deeds required that the homes have no exterior colored paint except for colorful doors, no clotheslines, and no TV antennae, other changes have taken place. In 2009 the Meadowood homes at **11 HAWKINS WAY**, **10** and **15 MEADOWOOD DRIVE**, and **3 NIVEN WAY** still retained the character of their original design. Homes that originally sold for $30,000 to $60,000 are now on the market for almost $2 million.

⑩ Epidendio Gardens Site

The original access to Epidendio Gardens was from William Avenue just east of Holcomb Avenue on a dirt road parallel to the railroad tracks behind the Azevedo-Foster Dairy. The entrance was there because it was one of the few places where the tracks could be crossed. Pietro's grandson Bill has the wooden "Epidendio Road" sign that marked the entrance, now named Ranch Lane.

Pietro "Peter" Epidendio, who immigrated from Buto, Italy, arrived in San Francisco just hours before the 1906 earthquake. After working on a produce ranch in Colma, he moved to Larkspur in 1915 and did gardening work for real estate agent William L. Courtright. He lived in a farmhouse on the property leasing it from 1915 to 1919 when he purchased 40 acres of the rich, fertile soil from the Coleman and Forbes estates.

Historian Dr. Leo Stanley reported in a 1971 Marin Historical Society publication, "The upland behind and east of the old (Azevedo-Foster) barn was a rich rancheria and the site of a large shell mound. The lowlands had received silt annually washed from Madrone Canyon by Larkspur Creek. It was open land of extraordinary fertility with a magnificent grove of redwoods." The Epidendio farmhouse and the adjacent four family homes and barn were east of the redwood grove at the end, where **24 NIVEN WAY** is today. Bocci ball was the sport of the ranch and homemade wine the refreshment. Salami and peppery ham, the specialties of the house, were served with Mary Epidendio's home-baked round bread. A stucco outhouse was located in the redwood grove.

The 1971 Stanley article reported that the land was dry farmed with crops dependent on the weather. The gardens were particularly colorful since gladioli were interspersed with vegetables, and fields of heather stretched to the east. Horses and cows were pastured on the land. Pietro's vegetables were in demand. In addition to selling at the San Francisco produce market, he sold to the people of Larkspur as well as to a wide area stretching from Tiburon to Stinson Beach. When business grew, he opened a fruit and vegetable shop at 483 Magnolia Avenue in the early 1920s and another in Corte Madera.

Pietro Epidendio died in 1952 when he drowned in a large well adjacent to Arroyo Holon. When Pietro was first reported missing, local authorities speculated that he might have impetuously accompanied some friends on an airplane trip to Italy. A week later the family became concerned when they noticed a water pump had been turned on for several days and insisted the well be examined. His body was finally discovered after a third search of the 20-foot-wide well, a loose safety rope attached to his waist. Bill Epidendio was eight years old at the time of his grandfather's death. Records at this time show that Pietro had an interest in the Blue Rock Hotel.

In 1954 Pietro's wife Mary sold the Meadowood section of the gardens to Jim Niven who, with his wife Lorraine, moved into the old Epidendio farmhouse. In order to maximize the usable land for the nursery, as well as prevent the yearly flooding, the shallow winding Arroyo Holon was straightened and relocated along the base of the old Varsi Hill by Jim Niven.

Pietro's son Ernest was born at the ranch. He went to Larkspur-Corte Madera School and Tamalpais High School, and then worked at Rainbow Market, the market he took over from his father and later expanded. Ernie continued to operate the Rainbow Market until he retired in 1984. Ernie didn't stay retired for long and lived above Rainbow Market since he liked to be "near the action." He was a familiar face on Larkspur streets and later at his job at Woodlands Market in Kentfield. In his off hours he was an avid baseball fan and frequently drove to visit his sister, Alice Becker, in Santa Rosa and his brothers in San Rafael and Corte Madera between feeding the birds above Rainbow Market.

Ernie died at age 84 on January 28, 2000. "My Dad didn't talk much about the past," recalled Bill Epidendio. "He worked in the store 54 years from 1930 to 1984 and once commented, 'It's neat to find the thing you love to do.'"

Bill's brother Richard, who owns Rich Readimix Concrete and bought his own home on Sycamore Avenue, has fond memories of growing up in Larkspur. "Growing up in Larkspur was truly special," he commented. "I'm glad that my own son is having the opportunity to grow up in Larkspur. There's nowhere else better to grow up."

▲ 7.24: A photo of Ernie Epidendio, taken by his grandson Anthony, shows his love of feeding birds, and was displayed at his memorial service in 2000.

▲ 7.25: Big and small feet as well as bicycles follow today's Sandra Marker Path where trains once clattered down the rails. Mt. Tamalpais still guards the Larkspur valley below, 2007.

PIPER PARK, BOARDWALK #1 & CREEKSIDE
Historic floating arks, now ashore, have been joined by homes and a park.

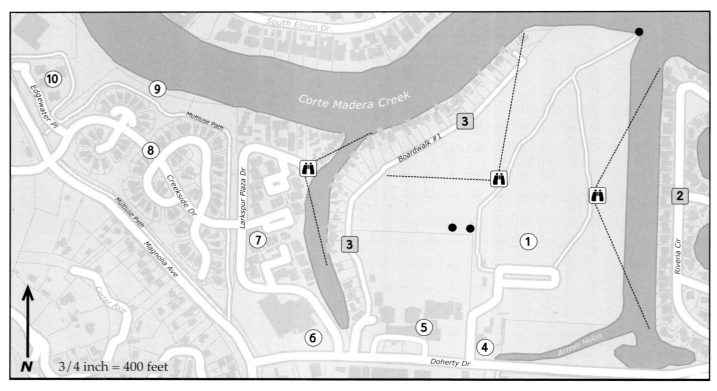

 This level tour is appropriate for walkers and bicyclists. Circumnavigate Piper Park clockwise, then continue along streets and creekside paths westward towards Bon Air Road. Key locations ② and ③ should not be visited directly – they are best seen from the viewpoints indicated by the binoculars.

KEY LOCATIONS
- Viewpoints
- ① Piper Park
- ② Larkspur (Greenbrae) Marina
- ③ Boardwalk #1
- ④ Police Station
- ⑤ Hall Middle School (Henry C. Hall School)
- ⑥ Mt. Tam Racquet Club
- ⑦ Larkspur Plaza
- ⑧ Creekside
- ⑨ Marsh
- ⑩ Edgewater
- • Locations of Interest within Piper Park

PIPER PARK, BOARDWALK #1 & CREEKSIDE

Larkspur's topography has changed dramatically since a large Miwok rancheria was located at the edge of the marsh. Meandering streams and creeks fed by water from the surrounding hills crisscrossed the marsh on their way to Corte Madera Creek creating a delta. Early settlers built their homes on the hills. When the demand for more homes grew, the hills were topped, the marsh was filled and the streams were re-channeled or buried to create buildable land.

• • • • • • • • • • • • • •

In 1855 Ross Landing on Corte Madera Creek was an active shipping point, according to a February 9, 1915 article in *The San Rafael Independent*. Captain Charles Mastron had the lease for the San Quentin terminus and erected the first wharf at San Quentin and one at Ross Landing. Originally his steamer *Contra Costa* plied between Ross Landing, Petaluma, San Quentin, and San Francisco. Later, Captain Mastron's old steamer *Tamalpais* made the trip each way from San Francisco in four hours and charged $2. Captain Paul Treanton operated a Marin schooner business in the 1850s

> ### ABOUT CORTE MADERA CREEK
> "[In 1855] the channel was deep, and the steamer landed at the point where the county road to Kentfield Station encounters the old bridge. Ross Landing was a busy point with as many as forty scows in the creek at one time and about 106 oxen and mule teams unloading hides, tallow, cord wood, rough lumber, tan bark and swine and cattle."
>
> — *The San Rafael Independent*, Feb. 9, 1915

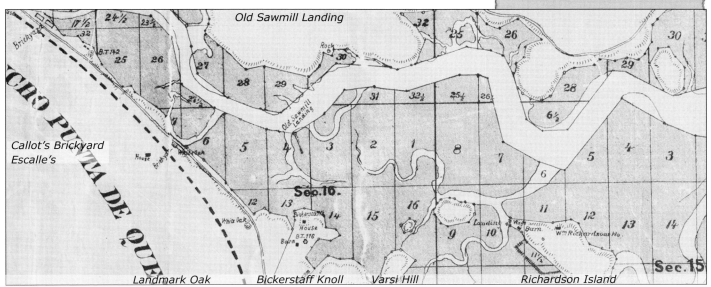

▲ 8.1: On this 1871 map, sections 3, 2, and 1 mark the general area where Piper Park is today. The knolls at sections 9 and 16 were bulldozed down to create the Redwood High School site. The land south of 11, 12, and 13 was known as Richardson Island.

MARSH FILL FROM MANY SOURCES

▲ 8.2: *The unsupervised discarding of household appliances and car parts created a problem of differential settlement when Piper Park was created.*

"*People brought old tree stumps, anything they wanted to get rid of and left it on the site.*"

— Bob Smith, former city councilman

transporting brick from the Callot brickyard (later Escalle winery) to San Francisco.

The cutting of lumber and firewood from the hills during the 1850s and 1860s not only shifted Larkspur's industry from lumbering to ranching, it also exposed the bare hills to erosion. The winter rains washed down the soil and filled the creek with silt so that a flood plain was formed with barely a trickle of water flowing through.

Periodic dredging was required to keep the channel open. In 1919 early Larkspur resident Belle Brown reported, "A plan for dredging Larkspur Creek [today's Corte Madera Creek] so that freight may be brought from San Francisco by boat has been under consideration." She told of thrice weekly trips of the *Ida* up the creek from San Francisco. The *Ida* discharged freight at the wharf near where Boardwalk #1 now is located. A long bridge led to the wharf in Larkspur. Until 1939, when the final dredging was done, the creek was considered navigable up to the old Ross Landing.

As the population increased in the Ross Valley, more and more homes were built in the flood plains making flooding from winter storms a

▲ 8.3: *Overall view from King Mountain showing salt marshes and the Redwood High School site (knoll at center). An uncontrolled dump existed on the Piper Park site in 1956, just to the left of the greenhouses.*

▲ 8.4: *When high tides and heavy winter storms combined, the marshes flooded, 1956.*

▲ 8.5: Kite view of Piper Park area, looking west, 2008. Beyond the parking lot and ball field in the foreground are (left to right): Hall Middle School, Hall ball field, community garden and dog park, restored marsh and the beginning of Boardwalk #1.

major threat. In the 1950s and early 1960s water skiers were pictured on the College of Marin football field. Hillview and Heather Gardens subdivisions suffered water damage. In 1965 and 1966 the U.S. Army Corps of Engineers moved in dredgers to create a deeper channel and realign the creek course for better flushing of storm runoff waters. Today, the police station, Piper Park, Hall Middle School, Larkspur Marina, Larkspur Isle, Creekside, and the Redwood High School playing fields are all built on the dredging spoils from the creek.

On the plus side, new buildable sites were created. On the minus side, the sites often require pile foundations and may be subject to settlement, seismic problems, flooding, and rising water tables. In the storms of 1952, 1982, and 1998 many of the old streams reasserted themselves and flooded their new neighbors. Only the Boardwalk #1 arks outfoxed nature by having a community designed for its marsh location.

Portions of the marsh were filled with everything from car parts to tree stumps, creating a modern-day midden that was first located on the Henry C. Hall School site and then moved east.

The combination of the dredged creek fill and the unsupervised dumping of old household castoffs made the site not only structurally difficult, but also created differential settlement problems. The tennis courts were consequently designed with a nontraditional slope that local players called "a home court advantage." Out-of-town opponents still complain about the sloping courts.

① **Piper Park**

In 1969 the city considered the idea of a yacht harbor but instead drew up plans for a park on the site. In 1971 Piper Park, named for Ron Piper, the city manager at the time, was established on 22 acres of the marsh and dump site, extending from Doherty Drive to Corte Madera Creek.

The marsh was not forgotten in the process of creating park facilities. A 14-acre marsh preservation area surrounds the active section of Piper Park and is home to nesting mallards who waddle up to the children's playground for handouts, and great blue herons who swoop over the tennis courts to feed at low tide. Unfortunately the Canada geese that came for the winter decided to stay, much to the distress of outfielders in the ballpark.

The park is home to a variety of activities for the entire community. With the increase of young families in Larkspur, the playing fields have been expanded and are used heavily on weekends. Activities at the park include: baseball, softball, Little League, soccer, cricket, golf, kite flying, volleyball, horseshoes, flying radio-controlled airplanes, fishing from the pier, picnicking, BBQ, birthday parties, and summer movie-viewing.

The Larkspur Walkers, a social walking group, meet regularly at Piper Park to explore Larkspur neighborhoods or take field trips within the county or San Francisco. Organized by Nancy Spivey in 1987, the group has grown from four people to over a hundred members.

▲ 8.6: The Larkspur Walkers begin a walk from Piper Park, 2010.

▲ 8.7: Piper Park is a place for wildlife and people.

▲ 8.8: Piper, a Maltese poodle named for the park, enjoys a romp in the fenced dog park, 2010.

▲ 8.9: Longtime Parks and Recreation commissioner Sandy Blauvelt (left) and former Parks and Recreation director Nancy Spivey (right) spearheaded the creation of the Community Garden in 1982, shown here in 2007.

In 1982 the **COMMUNITY GARDEN** was created with 42 12- x 17-ft plots on land that had been used by Public Works to dump dirt, sand, and woodchips. The garden, originally funded by the Marin Community Foundation, the Marin County Board of Supervisors, and the Larkspur City Council, has been expanded twice for a total of 74 plots in 2010. In 2007 a scarecrow welcomed visitors inside the gate. An orchard with 24 fruit trees, a compost pile, and a tool shed are at the north end. No spraying is allowed. Most people plant a combination of vegetables and flowers. Tomatoes are the most popular vegetable grown.

According to former Parks and Recreation director Nancy Spivey, "The thought behind the community garden was that gardening is a form of recreation. Families living in Madrone Canyon without much sunlight and nearby apartment dwellers need a plot of land for flowers and vegetables." She proved right. The garden has been a popular addition to Piper Park from the start.

The one-third acre **CANINE COMMONS** was dedicated on May 6, 1990. The dog park faced threats of a possible corporation yard relocation, but wagging tails and happy barks prevailed, and it was enlarged to a half-acre and reopened in 2006. Dog owners enjoy views of Boardwalk #1, Mt. Tamalpais, and the marsh while their furry friends frolic.

THE PIER at the north end of the park, donated by the Headlands Foundation in 2001, is not heavily used because of the hauling distance from the parking lot. Walkers, however, have a good view of Bon Air Hill and the buildings along South Eliseo Drive.

▲ 8.10: *The wailing sounds of bagpipers float across the park during practices, 2008.*

▲ 8.11: *Piper Park tennis courts, 2003.*

▲ 8.12: *Aerial view of diking and filling of Greenbrae Marina, 1955. The marsh area at center is the site of the future Piper Park. The Heather Gardens subdivision is at the lower left.*

▲ 8.13: *Greenbrae Marina, now known as "Larkspur Marina," 1975. The northeastern edge of the Piper Park marsh is in the foreground.*

② Larkspur (Greenbrae) Marina

This marina can be seen across the inlet from the east side of Piper Park. From 1964 to 1965, when the creek was dredged by the U.S. Army Corps of Engineers, the marsh was filled to create the lagoon development. Many of the original homes were designed with unpainted shingle and redwood exteriors popular during the late 1960s and early 1970s and sold for an average of $34,500. Today some are on the market for over a million dollars.

Although the marina's filled land had the usual problems of settlement, flooding, and potential seismic issues, developers faced an added physical limitation of what could be built on the lots. Property lines extended to the middle of the lagoons, and the underwater land limited the buildable portion of the lots, resulting in a denser look than the average subdivision. The trade-off was the benefit of views of the lagoon, creek waters, Mt. Tamalpais, Greenbrae, and Northridge.

The name "Greenbrae Marina" became controversial in 2007 when a change to the name "Larkspur Marina" was proposed. Although the sign at the entrance was changed to Larkspur Marina, a formal name change has not been approved in 2010.

⤴ *The best place to view Boardwalk #1 is from Piper Park just north of the dog park or from the end of Larkspur Plaza Drive. The water views of many of the arks retain the typical historic ark character. In many cases the original architectural designs of the façades on the boardwalk side have dramatically changed.*

③ Boardwalk #1

In the 1880s the floodplains along the creek and around San Francisco Bay became an ideal spot for the unique development of houseboating. The flat-bottomed boats, like the hay scows of the period, were raked at the bow and stern and could be anchored on the water, on the mud flats, or even on dry land.

With their flexibility, the boats had a great appeal for summer vacationers and squatters because of the freedom from taxes and sewer hookups. Judge Samuel Gardiner commented, "The ark community near Escalle was a separate world and seemed to want nothing to do with the rest of the town for the probable reason that they feared control and taxes. Most arks had no vehicular access and were reached by plank walks running from Bon Air Road or across the salt marsh from Magnolia Avenue. Those who lived in the arks paid personal property taxes rather than real property taxes to the city. There was a serious sanitary problem until sewer connections were compelled in the 1940s and 1950s."

In their heyday, there were around 400 arks in Marin's ark communities according to houseboater and noted cartoonist Phil Frank. "Each was built

▲ 8.14: *Arks at Boardwalk #1 and #2 along Corte Madera Creek. In the middle distance, Escalle winery nestles in the lower flanks of Little King Mountain, early 1900s.*

with a distinctive style and with craftsmanship that enabled many to survive the ravages of time and weather for nearly 100 years."

The arks were popular vacation homes from 1906 through the 1920s, enjoyed by many, including the socially elite of San Francisco. Arkite Jim Nevil, whose parents owned *Ark Eerie* on Boardwalk #2 in 1918, remembers Martin The Clam Digger who dug clams every day, packed them in 5-gallon cartons and sent them on the evening train to the Palace Hotel in San Francisco. The clams, he reported, were "as big as the palm of my hand." This was before the sewage polluted the creek in the 1920s.

Boating traffic was ended when the runoff from the clear-cut hills filled the creek with mud and silt. About that time the ark communities of Boardwalks #2, #3, and #4 moved onto the mud flats at high tide. The arks of Boardwalks #2 and #3 were at the edge of the creek opposite Escalle winery. Boardwalk #4 was just north of Bon Air Bridge. Access to all the

▲ 8.15: *Arks along the south section of Boardwalk #1, viewed from near the dog park in Piper Park. Mt. Tamalpais on the far left, Big King*

communities was via boardwalks from Magnolia Avenue across the marsh, but they were linked to each other by plank walkways that crisscrossed the marsh.

The living areas of the early arks were mounted on boat hulls and had an efficient use of space similar to a ship's cabin. Skylights, windows that slid into the walls, decks that encircled the house, and arched roofs were common features. Although the arched roofs are considered a key architectural feature of ark homes, longtime resident Herb Launer of the *Pacific Striped Bass Club* (Ark #9) explained, "It's just the fact that the roof is a gentle arc to keep the water off. … It hasn't anything to do with 'two animals' and all that."

In the 1870s a wagon road ran along the edge of the slough to the head of the inlet. Dolph Doherty told longtime Boardwalk resident, John Lynch, that wagons went down along the road to Old Sawmill Landing, which was located at the site of the *Mud Lark* (Ark #16). The Board of Tidelands Commissioner's map of 1871 also indicates that location for the landing. In this early period, the slough ended where Ark #5 of Boardwalk #1 is today. The boardwalk began opposite the end of what is now the parking lot.

The homes were viewed more seriously after the San Francisco earthquake. Phil Frank quoted a 1906 article by Blanche Parkington in *The Pacific Monthly*: "The country home of the sea lover is this year his only home. … To this place of refuge, where, before, their lightest

▲ 8.16: *Corte Madera Creek Ark Colony, looking east from Little King Mountain, 1910. Hill's boathouse is the long building in the left foreground. Old Sawmill Landing would have been at the creek bend on the far right.*

▲ 8.17: *An aerial view of arks along Corte Madera Creek taken about 1937, looking south. Boardwalk #4 was north of the rickety Bon Air Bridge at lower right. Boardwalk #3 was just south of the bridge on the west side of the creek, and Boardwalk #2 was at center left, also on the west side of the creek.*

(cont.) and Little King Mountains on the left, and The Tamalpais retirement community on the far right provide reference points, 2009.

CORTE MADERA "LAKE"

In the early 1900s a channel was dredged in a loop and back to the creek (in the general area of today's Hall Middle School) with the idea of creating a Venice-type development. "The creek was a regular lake in the area from Bon Air Bridge to Larkspur Plaza," recounted Mrs. Randolph Doherty.

▲ 8.20: *Boardwalk #1 (foreground) and flood control spoils (center), 1965.*

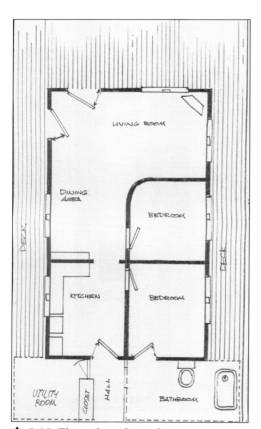

▲ 8.18: *Floor plan of an ark.*

moments were spent, came hundreds in their direst need, flying before earthquake and fire they came, naught left of their wealth but these little places of pleasure, now their only home." When the cost of upkeep of the aging boats became prohibitive, many were beached or perched on pilings above the bay and converted to summer cottages or year-round homes.

The forty arks of Boardwalk #2 were located between today's Larkspur Isle north to the Tiscornia (Escalle) property. Twelve arks in this area were leased from the state in 1963; a few others were privately owned. All the arks of Boardwalk #3 between Escalle and the Bon Air Bridge were leased from the state. Boardwalk #4, with 20 to 27 homes, was located just north of the Bon Air Bridge. All the arks of Boardwalks #2, #3, and #4 were removed as part of a flood control project in 1965 and 1966, except for the one that was privately owned.

In a foreshadowing of future protests, Boardwalk #2 Arkite Phyllis Lahargoue chained herself to a bulldozer in a vain attempt to prevent the destruction of the arks in 1968. Her son, Bill Ford, was the author of *The Woggle Bug,* a story of growing up on an ark at Boardwalk #2.

* * * * *

Boardwalk #1 is the last survivor of the four houseboat colonies along the west banks of Corte Madera Creek. A questionable opportunity for residents to acquire ownership of their marsh lots in 1939 may have spared Boardwalk #1 from demolition in 1965. Only

▲ 8.19: *Central section of Boardwalk #1 as viewed from the western marsh near the grass playing fields in Piper Park, 2009.*

Piper Park, Boardwalk #1 & Creekside   227

▲ 8.21: Boardwalk #4, 1966.

the highlands above the salt marshes and tidelands were part of Punta de Quentin. For years, summer squatters anchored their arks along sections of the creek. Various owners claimed the marshes. On a deed dated December 24, 1938, Hugh B. Porter and Frances L. Porter were granted title to 1,500 acres of creek frontage on the west side of the creek for the bargain price of about $225,000. The original subdivision is noted as "not recorded" on the current Assessor's parcel maps. The lots were based on a survey made by city engineer John Oglesby in which a 25-foot ark had a 35-foot lot and in some cases overran the line into the creek. In later years problems with lot lines developed.

At a special meeting of the Arkites Association of Boardwalk #1 on April 2, 1939, the minutes indicated that "a Mr. Leitch appeared stating he was representing Mr. Porter whom he claimed was the owner of the land on which all or a majority of the arks were located. He stated that Mr. Porter wished to dispose of sites in accordance with the maps he displayed, at a price of $10 per foot frontage on Corte Madera and Doherty Creeks." The sale of the lots to the Arkites spared the residents from State condemnation because the residents had purchased their land and homes in 1939. Only seven houses at the far end of today's Piper Park marsh preserve were removed by the flood control project.

"Hugh Porter did claim the whole area," reported Judge Samuel Gardiner in a 1983 letter. He "made some deals which may or may not have been appropriate. The city fathers and most of the upland community looked down on the Arkites as just leeches who wanted police service but gave little, and who would not clean up the disposition of garbage and sewage." In 1947 Porter's interests were sold to James Wilson of Ross.

Records of the Arkites Association, the group of homeowners who maintain Boardwalk #1, go back to about 1922, but there is pictorial evidence that the arks occupied the area long before that. According to Mrs. Theodore Marilli, the arks on the creek were called "Arksville" in 1918 and had their own mayor, George Franzen.

The boardwalk has an unusual lifestyle where people are willing to wheel in their groceries and haul out their garbage in makeshift carts. Helen Wilson remembered that even by 1923, when she came to Larkspur, the arks area was popular for swimming and boating. "It was really a vacation area," she said. "Only a few stayed most of the year because most of the arks were not geared for year-round living. People came on the weekends for boating and to get drunk."

▲ 8.23: Destruction of Boardwalk #4, 1968.

▲ 8.22: Kite-view of arks along the eastern section of Boardwalk #1, 2008.

EBB AND FLOW OF POPULATION OF BOARDWALK #1

❖ In 1963 there were 28 dwellings and 10 vacant lots.

❖ In 1979 there were 35 residences.

❖ In 1991 there were 38 lots total, 2 vacant.

❖ In 2007 there were 36 homes and 60 people living on Boardwalk #1.

Prohibition played a big part in the popularity of the ark communities. Stills cropped up in the marsh and bootleggers set up shop in the arks because of their inaccessibility. Jim Nevil, who spent summers on Boardwalk #1, remembers that at night, during Prohibition, if a stranger approached along the boardwalk, especially if he had a hat on, everyone "threw their booze overboard." Apparently the hat, a fedora, tagged the person as a government agent. The next day Jim and his young friends would dive for the bottles, getting five cents for each one retrieved.

"When people had too many at a party, they were just loaded into wheelbarrows and wheeled home."

— Willis Carroll LeVan, better known as "Bill," who lived on the Boardwalk from age 7 until he died

---

A distillery on the marsh caught fire during Prohibition, according to former teacher Leslie Ezekiel. "It was a huge fire."

Other fun seekers visited *The Buffalo*, later called *Cosy*, an ark at the end of the Boardwalk that was removed by the Flood Control District in 1966. Reputed to have been a house of prostitution in the Delta area before it was moved here, its interior was divided into tiny cubicles which perhaps lent credence to the story.

Over the years, arks from other waterfront communities have found a refuge at Boardwalk #1. *The Argonaut*, originally part of the Belvedere ark community, had been moved to Antioch where it was purchased by ark buff Phil Frank and his wife, Susan. They brought it to lot #7 at Boardwalk #1 in 1979. To get the 24- x 44-ft ark onto the lot, it was pulled up inclined beams, using blocks and tackles, at an equinox high tide. The Franks lovingly restored the ark to its original 1886 to 1890 period of construction. The ark is constructed of 1- x 4-inch tongue-and-groove fir and redwood, and has a walkway completely encircling it. Unfortunately remodeling and an addition have drastically altered the restoration. Only the view from across the slough allows a glimpse of the arched roof of the original ark.

Herb Launer's ark the *Pacific Striped Bass Club* (**ARK #9**) also traveled around the bay before finding a home at Boardwalk #1. It was anchored at Corinthian Island in Belvedere from 1911 until 1954, then on dry land at Blackie's Pasture in Tiburon. From there it traveled across the bay to Point Richmond. In 1979 Launer latched onto the ark for the bargain price of a dollar and moved it to a vacant lot at #9. He added with a chuckle, "The following fall I got a triple set of paperwork from the state asking for the sales tax on the purchase. I sent them a check for seven cents and they actually cashed it. I've kept the paperwork." To get the ark onto lot #9, Launer laid down a pressure treated wood foundation and a ramp greased with Crisco® oil. At a high tide, he used a tow truck with a cable and winch to haul it onto the foundation. The *Pacific Striped Bass Club* is one of the few arks whose original barge is visible underneath it.

▲ 8.24: The Buffalo *and* Cosy *signs salvaged by John Lynch, 1977.*

▲ 8.25: Pacific Striped Bass Club *(Ark #9), 1990.*

In the 1950s Boardwalk #1 began approximately where Larkspur Plaza now meets Doherty Drive. Before Doherty Drive was built, vehicle access was via a road through the Larkspur Lumber Company, located where the Larkspur Plaza grocery store is today. In 2007 the Central Larkspur Area Plan (CLASP) proposed connecting Boardwalk #1 access to Larkspur Plaza Drive.

Over the years the Arkites have been actively battling for their community. Hassles over the repair of the actual boardwalk have been a constant issue. The leaky water line, as well as the potential cutting off of access from Doherty Drive, fill pages in the Arkites' book of minutes. The group suffered with a city dump on its doorstep.

In a 1942 letter to the County Assessor, Caroline Burk gave a graphic picture of the problems of creek-side living when she explained why Boardwalk #1 should have a lower assessment than had been proposed: "Some arks are in bad shape, leaking and off the level. Many have only single boardwalks. None of them have the foundations that land houses have. The wear and tear of the elements down here is unusually severe necessitating much repair work. The boardwalk is sometimes flooded so that winter residence is not always feasible. There is no access road and the art of walking has to be cultivated, as well as skill in hauling provisions in little wagons along the narrow walk. The walking distance is, in some cases, half a mile at least. There is no gas for cooking and heating. Most of the arks are used for weekend or summer residences."

Today, since many of the boardwalk-facing sides of the arks have been remodeled, their creek sides present their most historic view. The view at the end of Larkspur Plaza Drive looks across to the *Green Gate* (Ark #13), a hipped-roof farmhouse that was towed here from Petaluma. The approximately 720-square-foot ark, surrounded by a porch, was left on the boat hull on which it was originally towed until after the 1950s when a foundation was built.

A porch wraps around the beveled clapboard building with French doors on the west side and a single door framed by high windows on the east side. Slats have been added to the original 2- x 4-in railing. The interior has beams defining the angles of the ceiling, wainscoting, and

ARK NAMES ON BOARDWALK #1

Most of the arks have retained their original colorful names.

Ark #6 - *Green Pasture*

Ark #7 - *The Argonaut*

Ark #8* - *Star*

Ark #9* - *Pacific Striped Bass Club*

Ark #13 - *Green Gate*

Ark #15* - *Redwing*

Ark #16 - *Mud Lark*

Ark #17 - *Anchor*

Ark #18 - *Dolphin*

Ark #20 - *Ramona, Catalina*

Ark #21 - *Sleepy Lagoon*

Ark #22* - *Standard*

Ark #23 - *Glocca Morra*

Ark #24 - *Regal*

Ark #26* - *Sea Gull*

Ark #28* - *The Mooring*

Ark #32* - *Sea Lark*

Ark #35 - *Sunny Skies*

*Listed on Larkspur's *Historic Resources Inventory.*

▲ 8.26: *Great egret drawn by Brian Collett while visiting his sister Joan Brown at Ark #6 in 2007.*

BIRDS IN THE MARSH

In 1965, the Audubon Society survey indicated the following species of birds in the marsh:

- Brewer's blackbird
- Coot
- Great blue heron
- Great egret
- Greater yellowlegs
- Killdeer
- Kingfisher
- Mallard duck
- Red-winged blackbird
- Snowy egret
- Song sparrow
- Swallow
- Western meadowlark
- Western sandpiper
- Willet
- Several kinds of rails

▲ 8.27: *Green Gate (Ark #13) from the end of Larkspur Plaza Drive, 2007.*

paneling. There is a kitchen and a bath at one end, a living room through the center by the French doors, and two bedrooms at the creek end. The nine-pane windows contain old rolled glass. On the boardwalk side, a storage building appears to have been part of the original building, and has the same beveled siding.

According to architectural historian, Dan Peterson, "this hipped-roof bungalow, surrounded by a veranda, is unique in that it is representative of the earliest bungalows in California that were built in the southern part of the state. It shows a relationship back to the theory of the form coming from the South Seas."

From the end of Larkspur Plaza Drive, two arks to the north, the *Redwing* **(ARK #15)** has retained its ark roof and basic ark shape, with horizontal clapboard siding. The middle section of the building is the approximately 12- x 20-ft original ark, with a door at each end. A remodel included removing non-original composition siding, raising the elevation for flood protection, and installing new windows that reflect the design of the originals. Some of the traditional arched-roof arks can be spotted to the south, such as *The Argonaut* (Ark #7), the *Star* (Ark #8), the *Pacific Striped Bass Club* (Ark #9), and the *Redwing* (Ark #15).

Seven homes at Boardwalk #1 are included on Larkspur's *Historic Resources Inventory*: the *Star* **(ARK #8)**, the *Pacific Striped Bass Club* **(ARK #9)**, the *Redwing* **(ARK #15)**, the *Standard* **(ARK #22)**, the *Sea Gull* **(ARK #26)**, *The Mooring* **(ARK #28)**, and the *Sea Lark* **(ARK #32)**.

Longtime resident, Tom Wertz, commented in a 1998 memo, "On the boardwalk it is tough to mind your own business. Thirty-six families share a common water meter, gas line, driveway, parking lot, garbage dumpsters, and a rickety wooden walkway. A quick ten-minute trip out the boardwalk often becomes a twenty-minute meeting."

None of the homes along Boardwalk #1 are floating anymore, and most of the original arks have been greatly modified over the years. New infill structures have post-and-pier foundations.

"As overall property values have risen, homes on Boardwalk #1, once seen as relative bargains, have gone up as well," commented Arkite and Planning Commissioner Chris McCluney. Not just costs have changed but also the demographics, according to longtime resident, Kay Washburn. "In 2007 there was only one family and four old-timers. Most of the people are 60 and older, retirees and professionals, but there are still a few artists and a few characters who add spice to the area."

Improvements have taken place due to the changes in demographics. Maintenance is now complete for the above-ground gas, water, and sewer lines that were replaced in 1998. The widening of the boardwalk from 4 to 6 feet is an ongoing project. Another important safety addition is the installation of a subsurface community fire protection line and hydrant so fire fighters don't have to carry a hose down the boardwalk. Delivery people still have a long hike to #35.

According to Chris McCluney of #25, "The biggest upgrade in the last 10 years was raising the parking lot 2½ feet and paving it in 2005. Up till then, we had to keep an eye on the tides and keep our cars out when it got to a 6.8 tide. "

The Arkites Association worked actively for the preservation of the adjacent marsh, and in 1965 persuaded the city council to declare it a bird sanctuary instead of allowing additional fill to be placed there. The somewhat uncommon brackish water in this area attracts some special birds.

Former longtime ark resident and activist, George D. Washburn of *The Mooring* (Ark #28), said in a 1963 report on the area, "Corte Madera Creek is on one of the main flyways of migrating waterfowl, and during the migrating seasons is frequented by mallards, canvasbacks, teal, and other species of ducks. There is a small resident population of semi-wild mallards, pekins, and mud hens. This is probably one of the few localities in the center of a city where egrets may be observed feeding in their native haunts." Early Arkites minutes also indicated a weekly fee of $1 to residents for feeding baby ducks.

Kay Washburn, also of #28, fondly remembers rescuing ducklings and raising them in a sheltered area near her ark to protect them from the large water rats. She would release them when they were teenagers.

ARKS WITH TRADITIONAL ARCHED ROOFS

▲ 8.28: *The* Star *(Ark #8), 2007*.

▲ 8.29: *The* Redwing *(Ark #15), 2007*.

▲ 8.30: The Argonaut *(Ark #7) seen from Larkspur Plaza Drive, 2007*.

▲ 8.31: *Sunny Skies (Ark #35), owned by the Thierbach family, 1900s.*

A recent invasion of spartina grass was hand removed and hauled out by a local crew. Other local invaders, Canada geese, visit the marsh but seem to prefer the grass at Piper Park. Several clapper rails have returned to the area although some Arkites are not happy about their "god-awful squawk."

Under threat of Bay Conservation and Development Commission controls, and to preserve its unique scale and setting, a Larkspur Tidelands Ordinance was passed in 1975. The special Larkspur zoning ordinance was tailored specifically for the boardwalk community and its unique problems. Standards were set for setbacks, height of structures, foundations, and other controls to maintain the scale and character of the area.

Although changes have taken place on Boardwalk #1, Dan Peterson feels the unique character of the strip of homes along the boardwalk deserves preservation, and recommends it as a historic district. Besides the arks listed on the Larkspur's *Historic Resources Inventory*, several have historic story value if not architectural value. According to John Lynch of Ark #5, the *Sleepy Lagoon* (Ark #21) was occupied by Howard Gilbert, a concert singer at one time. Legend has it that the *Regal* (Ark #24) was the hideaway for the controversial lobbyist Artie Samish when the state legislature was trying to subpoena him to testify about influence peddling.

The *Glocca Morra* (Ark #23) was formerly located on the Schultz property in the area of the creekside edge of Niven Park in Drake's Landing. When Neils Schultz bought the Green Brae lands from the Roman Catholic Archdiocese of San Francisco in 1946, Andrew Jorgensen floated this ark and the *Sleepy Lagoon* over to this location. Although not a true ark, the *Regal* (Ark #24), is an ark reincarnated. The 1936 Arkites minutes reported they had acquired an old ark, *Rockaway*, on this site. Sea Captain John Mattson of the *Standard* (Ark #22), "agreed to tear it down, clear the ground, and receive in payment thereof all the wreckage." Mattson constructed the *Regal* with the timbers from the old ark, perhaps one of Larkspur's first "green" buildings.

Willis Carroll LeVan recalled the story about "Whiskey Bill" who was sent to fix a leak on the *Rockaway* before it was torn down. At that time there were two trap doors at each end of the boat. One went into the bilge and a second, center one that opened to the creek. Whiskey Bill bailed for hours until someone finally asked him if he was trying to bail out the creek since he was taking water out of the center trap door.

Over the years new homes have filled in the vacant lots along the boardwalk. Many, such as the *Sunny Skies* (Ark #35), have had their exteriors completely remodeled. Other new ones, such as #0, #1, and #2, all designed by architect John O'Brien, echo the design spirit of arks. Even with changes and additions, the intimate character of this unique area has persisted over the years. "Larkspur Boardwalk #1 is a wonderful, hidden gem with its homes on tidal water, the beautiful view of Mt. Tam, the numerous shorebirds, and the pastoral setting, but right in town," summed up Chris McCluney. "We continue to enjoy somewhat of a bohemian sense out here. The boardwalk almost enforces a sense of serenity because the walk out to the homes allows ample time to wind down from a commute."

▲ 8.32: *The first three homes at the beginning of Boardwalk #1, including Ark #2 pictured here, were designed with ark character by architect John O'Brien, 2007.*

④ Police Station

When the old junkyard on the land where Piper Park now stands was filled to capacity, the first new tenant on the south side of the property was the city's corporation yard. After Piper Park was established in 1971, the police station became the next tenant.

The 1972 requirements for a police station were a far cry from when Howard Clark started the job as chief of Larkspur's one-man police force in 1941 in a cramped office in City Hall. His main responsibilities were acting as dogcatcher and settling Rose Bowl Dance fights. "It was fist-to-fist combat," he recounted. "I got knocked down many times." In those days drunks were stashed in a boxcar and then put on the last train to Sausalito, or held overnight in a small room behind the fire station. Clark was officially named chief in 1948.

By 1971 Chief Clark headed a force of 15 officers, yet he occasionally retained some small town fun. According to Public Works superintendent Joe Monestier, Chief Clark delighted in sneaking up behind workers when they were painting the white lines on the street and blasted his siren to make them and the line jump.

By 1972 Larkspur police got a new $60,000 home in the City corporation yard at the entrance to Piper Park. The Schultz Foundation contributed $35,000 towards the new building. Dubbed a "relocatable/temporary" building, it replaced what critics called the 586-square-foot "broom closet"-sized quarters at City Hall. Designed to house 13 police officers and 5 office personnel, the "temporary" 3,000-square-foot building lasted 37 years.

Phil Green became chief in 1978 and was involved in the consolidation of the Larkspur and Corte Madera police forces in 1980. According to Dan Hilmer in a July, 2008 article in the *Marin Independent Journal*,

▲ *8.34: Twin Cities Police Station at the entrance to Piper Park, 2007.*

the joint Twin Cities Police Authority is unique in California – the only shared police department in the state. "It was a big challenge to meld the two philosophies," Chief Green commented in a 1985 Larkspur Heritage Preservation interview. "Larkspur had a by-the-book type of enforcement and Corte Madera had a laid back, pro-active enforcement approach." Salaries, benefits, work schedules, and the officer mix had to be worked out, but the consolidation has continued to work successfully.

At that time Chief Green commented that different areas in Larkspur and Corte Madera had different problems. "East of 101 has car thefts, burglaries, robberies and traffic; the west side of 101 has a general law enforcement approach. The second area of concern is traffic," he added.

In 2007 traffic-related issues, complaints, and enforcement were still the #1 priority, according to then-captain Todd Cusimano, who became chief in 2010. Law enforcement operations have changed drastically over the past 30 years. "We have computers in cars and communicate with one another by radio from as far away as 50 miles," added Chief Cusimano.

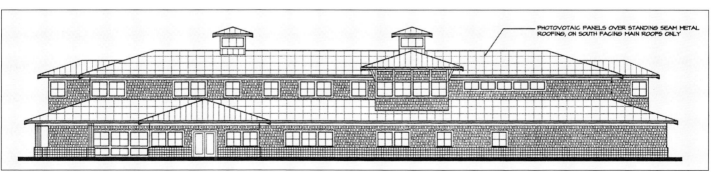

▲ *8.33: Proposed new police station, 2008.*

POLICE FACTS*

❖ Juvenile crimes are mostly committed by community residents

❖ Serious crimes and identity thefts are committed by persons outside Larkspur/Corte Madera jurisdiction.

❖ Major increase in identity theft and fraud-related crimes in the past 15 years due to the use of computers and the Internet.

* as of 2007

▲ 8.35: *2010 was the end of an era for both longtime chief Phil Green and the 37-year-old "temporary" modular police station.*

A $20 million ballot measure to finance a new police station passed in 2008. Construction of the two-story "green" building in the same location at the entrance of the park was begun in 2010, and will accommodate a larger staff and new, up-to-date equipment.

⑤ Hall Middle School (Henry C. Hall School)

After World War II, Larkspur saw a surge in housing and new residents. When the baby-boom children reached school age, new schools were needed to accommodate them. Henry C. Hall School opened in 1959 with kindergarten through sixth grade classes.

David "Doc" Little, who served on the city council for various terms from the 1920s until World War II, commented, "I was on the council when we bought the area where the Redwood and Hall Schools are now. We paid $25 an acre for the land back then, and the people damned near kicked us off the council for spending that kind of money."

"The only available site in Larkspur, unless the district became involved in lengthy condemnation litigation, was the Larkspur city dump," explained former superintendent of the Larkspur School District Gil Slusher. "This property was purchased from the city, and the debris from the dump was removed and replaced with granular fill on which the Hall School was constructed. The adjacent swampland was filled with dirt which was transported all the way from Fairfax by truck." Doherty Drive was connected to Lucky Drive when Henry C. Hall School was built in 1959. The school was named after the principal (and artist) who had worked at Larkspur-Corte Madera School for 20 years from 1906 to 1926.

Over the years the school has evolved from a K-8 school, when the boomers were moving through, to a middle school. When district enrollment declined and San Clemente School in Corte Madera was closed in 1982, Hall was reorganized as a middle school for the sixth, seventh, and eighth grade students in the district. As of that year the students in the lower grades attended Neil Cummins Elementary School in Corte Madera. In the fall of 2006 a fifth grade was added to Hall's sixth-to-eighth grades, and an approximately 10,000-square-foot building was constructed to accommodate the additional students.

▲ 8.36: *Henry C. Hall School, 1973.*

▲ 8.37: *Hall Middle School, 2007.*

▲ 8.38: *Value World under construction at the corner of Magnolia Avenue and Doherty Drive, about 1966.*

▲ 8.39: *The Disco store at the corner of Magnolia Avenue and Doherty Drive, 1972.*

⑥ Mt. Tam Racquet Club

Mt. Tam Racquet Club is an example of an adaptive reuse of a 1965-1966 building originally built for discounter Value World. Its bright red fascia emphasized its height and a stone façade made it totally out of character with Larkspur's old downtown. The original proposal, which was approved in 1966 after only five hours of discussion, was based on the revenue that would be produced for Larkspur which, at the time, was casting a jealous eye at the new Corte Madera centers. In 1974 the large building that had since changed hands to Disco, a "big-box" store, was transformed into the Mt. Tam Racquet Club. The stone façade was spray-painted and a new arched façade of vertical siding was added. Today, tennis balls instead of packing crates lob into the high interior. Five indoor and eight outdoor tennis courts, a spa, two swimming pools, and exercise equipment offer body reductions instead of price discounts.

⑦ Larkspur Isle

In 1972 Larkspur Isle Apartments was one of the first developments built over the former marsh on dredged fill. While the adjacent arks were designed for a water location, the first phase of the 26 one- and two-bedroom, two-story units taught a number of lessons about construction on filled marshlands the hard way. During the winter storms, the heavy rainfall runoff and high tides flooded the surface streets and some lower units. Settlement caused the ground to drop away from the units as much as 13 inches, disconnecting utilities and cracking paved patios. Tenants had to be moved out while the rigid utility connections were replaced with flexible ones to adjust to the land settlement. The foundations were raised three feet and new entrance stairs were designed to connect to the ground.

In 1977 after the repairs, the original 186 rental units were converted to condominiums and 20 were sold as affordable units to Ecumenical Association for Housing (EAH), which first rented them and then later sold some as condominiums with deed restrictions.

Flooding still occurs in the streets and paths adjacent to the creek when seasonal high tides and major winter rains coincide. In 2005 a number of the surface streets were re-graded to improve drainage, particularly at the corner of Larkspur Plaza Drive and Creekside Drive. Despite the natural problems, residents like the downtown location and its easy access to bike paths, creek and mountain views, and downtown restaurants, as well as the Canada geese and other wildlife ambling through the complex.

North of Larkspur Isle was another area with man-made changes. After the tree cover was cut from the hills in the 1850s and 1860s, the runoff from the bare slopes filled the creek with mud and silt so that old-timers remarked that by 1913 "even a rowboat must wait for the high tide."

LARKSPUR ISLE

"Larkspur Isle boasts 186 units and 186 cats in addition to a coyote who has been known to roam through the grounds at night and whose howls entertain residents with a taste of the wild."

— John Carr, longtime Larkspur Isle resident

▲ 8.40: To avoid appearing like a tract development, the roofs and front façades of Creekside homes were individualized, 2007.

⑧ Creekside

According to the 1871 map, two drainage channels crossed the marsh to the creek: one parallel to Larkspur Plaza Drive and one between Creekside and Edgewater. The site, created by the U.S. Army Corps of Engineers Flood Control Project in 1967 and 1968, had always been considered for development. The arks of Boardwalks #2 and #3 were removed and a dike was built 80 to 150 feet from the creek edge. Hydraulic fill approximately 5 to 6 feet deep was pumped behind the dike. According to the 1985 Escalle Environmental Impact Report, "unsupervised fill was added to the site from 1972 to 1976." Grading equipment was frequently parked at the north end of the site.

The last straw came in 1972 when developer Adolph Tiscornia proposed removing 40 feet from the top of Little King Mountain in back of the Escalle winery to raise the creek-side site. When the unauthorized clearing of the top of Little King was done, the city blew the whistle on the plans at a special emergency hearing *(see pages 258-260).*

Before Creekside was finally built, a succession of development proposals were submitted for the 25.8-acre site between 1975 and 1981. An early proposal in 1974 called for a maximum of 169 townhouses and flats plus 30,000 square feet of restaurants, offices, and a library site, with a net 10.5 units per acre, then later decreased to 104 units in total. Seventy units were finally approved in 1988 at less than 4 units per acre.

LIFE AT CREEKSIDE

"Neighbors got to know each other, held block parties, or shared a spur of the moment get-together in the street on sunny afternoons, and held annual Easter egg hunts and communal brunches in the park."

— Ventana Amico, artist

The 1988 proposal had to satisfy major concerns about drainage, settlement on the filled land, circulation, traffic, and limitations such as the line of flood control and the required setback from the creek. The Environmental Impact Report recommended "leveling jacks in conjunction with wood joist floors to allow for leveling of structures." A cluster design with zero lot lines and a series of cul-de-sacs achieved 44% open space, a greater amount than required and three times the required wetlands mitigations. Additional conditions of approval required the dedication of an affordable housing site to Ecumenical Association for Housing (EAH) and two vehicle access points.

To cope with the runoff from Little King, three major drainage flows were designed: one similar to the original one that tied into the marsh at the west end; one below ground under an open-space corridor through the middle of the project; and the historic one along the eastern end parallel to Larkspur Plaza Drive. A wide 100-foot bermed buffer along Magnolia

▲ 8.41: Creekside homes were designed in a cluster housing plan that allowed for over 44% open space, composed of marsh and parklands, including small neighborhood parks and an interior path system, 2010.

was created to buffer traffic noise and screen the Magnolia Avenue view. The conflicting philosophies of public access and wetlands preservation were reconciled by providing access to the creek with walkways and a new bike path, balanced by providing three times the required wetlands.

Since Creekside was built in two phases, many residents moved into the area at the same time, sharing stories and comparing notes about how their new homes were functioning and what questions needed to be addressed. Creekside resident and artist Ventana Amico believes the cul-de-sac layout of the neighborhood with the combination of walking paths, wetland views, and parks "facilitates a friendly neighborhood atmosphere." Creekside has escaped flooding, and the small trees and shrubs of the original landscape now reach two stories and provide welcome shade.

In 1989 Creekside homes from 1,879 to 2,651 square feet were selling in the low $500,000s. A second phase of homes was built on the remaining section in 1997. In 2010 resale prices averaged $1,300,000.

⑨ Marsh

Although the top of Little King Mountain was spared, the dredging spoils from the 1965 Flood Control Project and subsequent filling had obliterated the marsh. The restoration of the marsh was an important element of the Creekside development in 1991. Today the area once shared by arks and swimmers is home to ducks, native and domestic geese, and other seasonal visitors. According to Amico, the feathered fellows have provided background entertainment and spirited discussions, particularly about "Mother Goose" who for many years fed the geese she had rescued.

▲ *8.42: Marsh restoration with geese, 2007.*

▲ *8.43: EAH's Edgewater apartments, 1991.*

⑩ Edgewater

Award-winning apartments adjacent to a marsh preserve and Corte Madera Creek with a view of Mt. Tamalpais are not the usual perception of affordable housing. Edgewater scores on all those points. The 27-unit affordable housing complex developed by Ecumenical Association for Housing (EAH), the City of Larkspur and the Creekside developer in 1991, is located on two acres at the north end of Creekside. In 2007, according to Mary Murtagh, chief executive officer of EAH, 52% of the apartments were rented to people who work for Marin-based companies and includes teachers, accountants, medical assistants, and retail associates. Thirty-three percent were retired and 15% disabled. She counters critics and asserts that EAH annually verifies the incomes of all residents through employers and often reviews tax filings and bank statements.

· · · · ·

In 2010 Corte Madera Creek and the marsh are again an integral part of the daily enjoyment of homeowners, bicyclists, pedestrians, and wildlife. Trees have grown up to shade and soften apartments, condos, and single-family homes.

NORTH MAGNOLIA
Early homes and a pioneer winery overlooked extensive salt marshes.

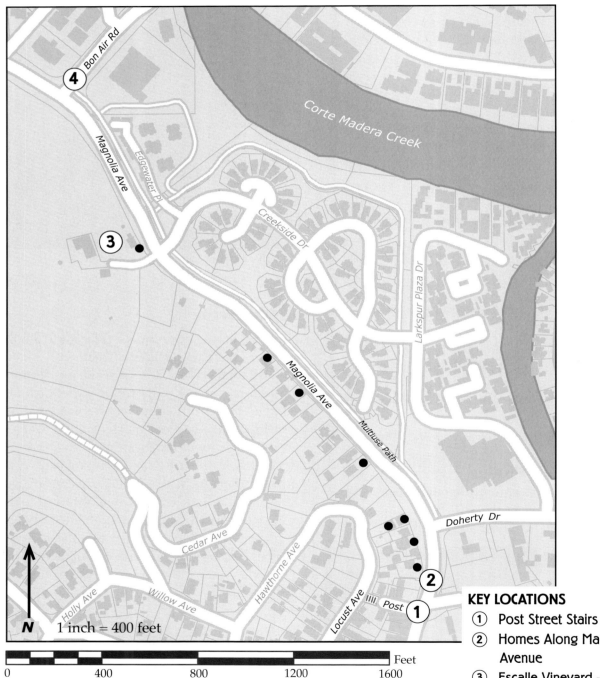

 A walk along the multi-use path between Doherty Drive and Bon Air Road on the east side of Magnolia Avenue provides views of some of Larkspur's early homes. Parking is available at Larkspur Plaza.

KEY LOCATIONS
1. Post Street Stairs
2. Homes Along Magnolia Avenue
3. Escalle Vineyard - Tiscornia Property
4. Bon Air Road at Magnolia Avenue
- Addresses of Note

NORTH MAGNOLIA

The majestic valley oak *(Quercus lobata)* next to 577 Magnolia Avenue marks the end of the downtown and the beginning of one of Larkspur's earliest neighborhoods. As Magnolia Avenue heads north, the road hugs the lower slope of Little King Mountain and the former edge of the marsh.

• • • • • • • • • • • •

Woodcutting and grazing from the 1850s to 1890s contributed to heavy erosion of the hillsides causing the creek channels to fill with silt. In the 1870s the marsh extended up to the edge of Magnolia Avenue. The first homes in the late 1800s were built on the southwest slope above the road. These homes were not crude cabins but substantial permanent homes for the elite. That stretch of the road was considered the nice part of town where people wanted to live, according to Mildred Young who grew up at 655 Magnolia Avenue.

Until 1913 Magnolia Avenue was a dirt road that "wandered up and down over the hill," reported Judge Samuel Gardiner. Vestiges of

▲ 9.2: *The large valley oak next to 577 Magnolia Avenue, 2008.*

▲ 9.1: *Magnolia Avenue with a boardwalk-type sidewalk, looking north towards Escalle winery building and vineyard. Beyond the vineyard the road climbed up the slope of Little King Mountain, about 1910.*

NORTH MAGNOLIA BEFORE 1913

"The railroad tracks were almost at marsh level, but the old road was on the hill above the railroad."

— Judge Samuel Gardiner

▲ 9.3: *Some of the earliest 1900s homes were built on the hillsides of Magnolia Avenue north of the center of town, 1979.*

the old road as it rose to higher ground above the current roadbed are visible at several points today, particularly opposite Bon Air Road.

① Post Street Stairs

With no cars and few streets above Magnolia Avenue, early twentieth-century homeowners and renters built stairs to get from downtown Larkspur and the train station to their front doors. The Post Street stairs just north of the Lark Theater connect Magnolia with Locust Avenue. Farther north, Alta and Opal Streets formerly connected Magnolia and Cedar Avenues. When these homes were constructed, automobile parking and storage was not a consideration but became challenging when cars arrived on the scene.

② Homes Along Magnolia Avenue

There is some confusion about the addresses of homes built on the slope between Magnolia, Locust, and Cedar Avenues since street numbers sometimes came into use after the homes were built. Over the years some of the original homes have been drastically changed, some raised to add garages, and some given incongruous additions. The McCormick house at **577 MAGNOLIA AVENUE** had retained its Greek Revival style until it was sold by descendants of its original owners in 1972. Dormer additions, out of character with its classic style, detract from the symmetry of the building so that it has lost much of its original integrity. The gable additions not only cause a visual pain they have chronic leaks.

The large valley oak next to the house was noted as a reference point for surveyors and was identified as a white oak on an 1871 map (*see page 219*). The Canary Island date palm flags the date of the house's construction since it was a popular specimen planted at the turn of the last century.

James and Mary Jane "Jennie" McCormick built the Greek Revival-style house between 1910 and 1912. Their youngest daughter, Gertrude McCormick Sheldon, said in a 1975 interview, that she thought it had been built by Larkspur architect and builder Gustave Nagel, or by a man who spoke German and referred to her mother's flower beds as "der rosengarten."

Nell Doherty, a friend of the McCormicks from the time of her arrival in Larkspur in 1906, recalled that she had sketched out the rough floor plan for the house. Two granddaughters of the McCormicks, Jane Sheldon Muzio and Patricia Sheldon Trembley, have a copy of a 1912–1913 tax bill signed by Frank Ambrose indicating $18 was paid in taxes on the property.

The McCormick family history was typical of newcomers to Larkspur in its early days. According to Pat Trembley, her great-grandfather Stephen James McCormick arrived in Oregon from New York in 1851 after an eight-month voyage around Cape Horn. He married her grandmother Anna en route. McCormick, a writer and newspaper editor, was not only the founder of the *Daily Advertiser*, publisher of the first Portland directory, and founder of McCormick's *Oregon Almanac*, he also served several terms as a member of the legislature. When

Oregon became a state in 1859 he was elected mayor of Portland.

The McCormicks' son James was born in Portland, Oregon in 1858. In 1882 the family moved to San Francisco where James became the editor of the Catholic publication *The Monitor*. While living there, he met Jennie Dolan, whose father had come to San Francisco in 1853 and was a member of the importing firm of Macondray & Co. James and Jennie were married in San Francisco in 1885.

After a severe bout of pneumonia, James moved to Larkspur about 1898 with Jennie and their four daughters Alice, Clare (Marian C.), Ella, and Gertrude. He hoped to find a more relaxed way of life than that allowed by his McCormick Bros. Printing and Publishing Company at Clay and Kearny Streets in San Francisco. In 1900 James and Jennie became the managers of the Hotel Larkspur (later the Blue Rock Hotel), known then as "a family resort" hotel owned by James Costello. They remained the managers until 1910.

Family members recalled that during the early morning of the 1906 earthquake, bricks from all the chimneys toppled onto the roof. Daughter Alice said that her bed rolled around her room. The family and guests left the building and sought the safety of open space in the street. Telephone service was interrupted. The trains made their scheduled runs south to Sausalito but did not return on their usual schedule. Since there had been only minor damage in Larkspur and central Marin, no one at the hotel realized how severe the quake had been until quite late in the day when word finally arrived that San

▲ 9.5: *The McCormick house at 577 Magnolia Avenue, with dormer additions, 2001.*

▲ 9.4: *The McCormick house at 577 Magnolia Avenue in 1913.*

▲ 9.6: Fragments of wallpaper found at 577 Magnolia Avenue, 2004.

LIFE AT 577 MAGNOLIA

"James, a tall, dark-eyed, dark-haired, fine-looking man was also loved for his wit and charming, personable manner but he was quite strict with his daughters. One story often repeated by his daughters was his habit of pacing back and forth on the veranda, his pocket watch open in his hand, making certain that his daughters and their companions arrived home at the appointed hour after an evening's social engagement."

— Pat Trembley, about her grandfather, James McCormick

Francisco was in ruins and ablaze. Three or four days later, when the fires were out and the train and ferry services were restored, James and his daughter Alice went to San Francisco and walked through the rubble to see if their relatives were all right.

"Everyone loved Jennie, the heart of the home," reported granddaughter Pat Trembley. Pat recalled, "All the housework was accomplished in the morning. The afternoons were devoted to visiting, entertaining, needlework, music, and drawing."

Neighbor and writer Stephanie von Buchau remembered that "Alice kept those floors polished so you could see your face in them."

Alice was interested in Larkspur residents and history, and enjoyed setting a pretty table with the lovely things her grandparents had brought with them around the Horn. A marble-top sideboard was in the dining room. The bedroom had an 1885 walnut bed set with a high headboard and footboard, a marble-top dresser, and a commode. "I remember quite a few oriental objects, particularly a pewter bowl that was very old and had either gone through the fire and quake or something because it had dents in it and looked burned," recalled Pat.

James McCormick died in 1913. His widow Mary Jane died in 1933. A family member occupied the house until 1971. The house was sold in 1972.

Living in an old house provides fun discoveries according to current owners Dena Van Derveer and John Gillespie, who have raised their son and daughter here since 1987 and have discovered both treasures and surprises. Fragments of Art Deco-era wallpaper were uncovered behind a stairway, and an obsidian arrowhead, champagne bottles, and china fragments were unearthed in the backyard. Like a page out of a Nancy Drew mystery, they found a secret passage to an attic room off a third-floor bathroom.

Since most of the homes along this section of Magnolia Avenue were built in the early 1900s they provide a sampler of the popular

▲ 9.7: James McCormick, manager of the Hotel Larkspur from 1900 to 1910.

▲ 9.8: The home at 599 Magnolia Avenue in the early 1900s.

▲ 9.9: Much of the original exterior character of 599 Magnolia Avenue has been retained, 2001.

design features of the day. The bell-cast curve of the roof design of both 599 and 603 Magnolia Avenue was a favorite of builders for some of the modest bungalows along the street. Architectural historian Dan Peterson suggests the flared, hipped roof may have stemmed from a South Seas influence.

Unlike many of the homes along the street, **599 MAGNOLIA AVENUE** has seen few changes over the years. The curved roof of this house is suggestive of the arks that populated the creek. The house has all of its original trim, doors, and fir floors. The crown moldings in the living room, dining room, and master bedroom and the fireplace are also original. Half of the gutters are still wood. The Esmoils lived here in the early 1900s, according to Glenn Courtright. In the 1920s the Goldsmiths lived here and later San Francisco assessor Russell Wolden Sr.

Alfred and Ingrid Drumright purchased the home as well as the two houses above it in 1964. The prior owner was Edmund Buck who had owned the house since 1949. The Drumrights, who spent time living and traveling in Japan, installed a Japanese garden with two koi ponds, Japanese maples, azaleas, rhododendrons, ferns, and camellias, as well as Japanese lanterns and gongs. A small garden behind the house was designed by Katsura Garden which, according to Mrs. Drumright, designed for the San Francisco Japanese Tea Garden. A shallow well on the site was used to water plants and still exists. An early Larkspur map shows a spring in the area where the garage is today. The Drumrights owned the home until Alfred passed away in 2004. The house stayed in the family when Mark and Elise Semonian bought it later that year (Elise's father was Ingrid Drumright's cousin). As of 2008 Ingrid was living in Baden Baden, Germany and turned 80 that year.

· · · · ·

The two early twentieth-century homes at **607 MAGNOLIA AVENUE** and **146 LOCUST AVENUE** stepped up the slope between Locust and Magnolia Avenues one behind the other and were only accessible by a private stairway from Magnolia Avenue. The first of the two to be built, 146 Locust was constructed with an interesting bell-cast gable roof with a mix of stucco, brick, beams, and shingles within the gable.

The original owners, Bertha and Vincenzo di Teresi, met in a pattern typical of the late nineteenth century – on a boat coming to America. Bertha was originally from Alsace-Lorraine, and Vincenzo was a diamond cutter from Sicily. They married, had two daughters Amanda and Carlotta, and built 146 Locust Avenue as a summer home. When their San Francisco home was destroyed in the 1906 earthquake, they removed to their house in Larkspur.

Amanda built the house at 607 Magnolia Avenue, just below her parents' home, now distinguished by a dramatic buckeye tree that marks the seasons with new leaves in spring, blasts of flower spikes by the Fourth of July, and loss of leaves in late summer.

Both Amanda and Carlotta became professional musicians. Amanda was a pianist who married Edwin Burns of Virginia. Charles Young remembers her as "quite an elegant lady" who taught piano and dressed very stylishly. In 1976 Mrs. Theodore Marilli recalled that "she went back to New York at some

▲ 9.10: 146 Locust Avenue above 607 Magnolia Avenue, 1990.

MEMORIES OF STEPHANIE VON BUCHAU

About home builders

"People had problems with construction rip-offs just like today. The builder cheated Amanda by installing (at great cost), blue rock fireplaces which didn't work because the flues were too small."

About her great-grandmother

"Bertha had a posh childhood with a live-in Chinese cook who used to threaten the kids if they bothered him while he was cooking. 'I jump down your throat and dance on your liver,' he would yell waving his cleaver."

— Stephanie von Buchau, 1991

point and all her nice things got ripped off. She was a talented musician and gave piano lessons."

Carlotta was a singer who headed east to New York City to sing professionally, according to her granddaughter Stephanie von Buchau. Stephanie's mother, Guinevere, was the daughter of Carlotta and her first husband, Ercole Sasso, who was from Naples. When they married in New York, Carlotta gave up her singing career, but returned to it when Ercole died in 1919. After a second marriage to Al Drago, a factory foreman, she toured on the East Coast vaudeville circuit where she hit the big time when Irving Berlin reportedly wrote a song for her.

When her husband's factory was lost during the Depression, they moved back to Marin. During the 1930s they ran the Redwood Lodge Restaurant where the Skylark Apartments are now located. Carlotta was a strong-minded woman who enjoyed singing at San Francisco's Black Cat bar during the 1960s Beatnik era and mingling with the liberal-minded patrons. She lived at 146 Locust Avenue until her death in 1981.

Stephanie von Buchau was a feisty writer and critic of classical music, dance, movies, and food from the 1970s until 2006, and was published in many bay area and national publications. She was noted for her blunt but witty insightful style of criticism and sometimes wrote under the byline of "Tiger Hashimoto." She often could be spotted wearing her baseball cap over her long, thick, blonde braid, crossing Magnolia Avenue at Doherty Drive to climb the steps to her home. After her death in 2006 the house was badly in need of repairs. In 2009 the two homes at 607 Magnolia and 146 Locust were purchased and a combination of restoration and additions are in progress by owner Gary Dowd and architect Jeff Kroot.

• • • • •

▲ 9.11: The homes at 146 Locust Avenue and 607 Magnolia Avenue are both undergoing renovations in 2010.

The Eastern shingle house with the "Raejoe" sign at **627 MAGNOLIA AVENUE** follows the pattern of early Larkspur homes that were given names instead of being referred to by an address. The name was in honor of early owner Joseph Harris and his wife, Rae Friedberg. Built in approximately 1895 by Ben Nelson, who was an importer of European glass, the house has retained its bell-cast gable roof, dormers, bay window, and a number of push-out casement windows. The Canary Island date palm in the front yard was a favorite tree of early 1900s landscaping plans.

Joseph Harris owned and ran a ship supply store in San Francisco, the "Joe Harris Company." He purchased the house in 1904 and moved his family to Larkspur in 1906. His children Perry, Wilfred "Biff," and Shirley were born here.

According to Biff Harris, his parents paid $5,000 in gold pieces for the house. "In those days you had to pay cash because no loans were available." One of Biff and wife Nadine's three children, Joan Hendrick, reported that the original house sign read "Carolben." She said her grandparents wanted to keep with the tradition of the house, so they carved their names on the back of the existing sign. She also pointed out that the house's original door faced Magnolia Avenue. When cars came along in about 1914, the house was raised to add a garage.

The house has not only an architectural history, it boasts a naughty reputation. A door at the back of the garage leads to a former bar and possible speakeasy. According to Joan Hendrick, there was a painting of a reclining nude, "Stella," that hung on the west wall of the room behind a curtain. When she was in fifth grade, Joan and her friends would sneak down and open the curtains to see the painting. Although she doesn't know the origin of the name, or what happened to the painting, she still has the wooden sign that hung on the "speakeasy" door: "May the hinges of friendship never grow rusty." Joan mentioned that her grandfather and his cronies used to hang out in that room, but that he died before she was born. "He was quite a figure on the waterfront." There was a liberty ship named after him – the SS *Joe Harris*.

Biff and Nadine Harris lived in the house until his death in 1981 and her death in 2001. At a real estate open house in April of 2001, all the equipment and furnishings were still in place down to the last dusty bottles of unopened spirits. Brad Beard, who had done gardening work for Nadine Harris, reported there were

▲ 9.12: 627 Magnolia Avenue with "Raejoe" sign, undated photo.

▲ 9.13: Many early Larkspur homes had names. "Raejoe" was named by early owner Joseph Harris and his wife, Rae Friedberg.

▲ 9.14: Raejoe at 627 Magnolia Avenue, in 2010.

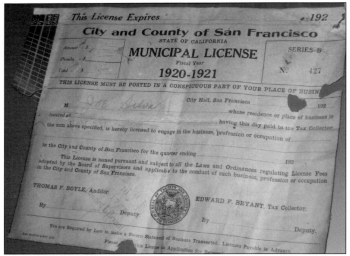

▲ 9.15: *Liquor license found in the bar behind the garage at 627 Magnolia Avenue, 2001.*

three slot machines in that back room. Two were draw poker machines – a Cowper and a Victor; the third was a dice machine. He said all three dated from the 1890s to the 1920s and were in bad shape.

Tom and Linda Chauncey purchased the house in May of 2001. They found dice, poker chips, shot glasses, a corn pipe, and a few 1920s-era documents in the back room when they moved in, as well as an old nylon stocking that dropped down from a ceiling beam in the garage more recently. The original "speakeasy" bar remains. Many nautical items were left behind, including two brass portholes, a ship's bell and light fixtures. According to Joan Hendrick, the upside-down champagne bottles that surround the holly tree on the south side of the house were remnants of her sister Gail's engagement party in 1958.

In 2009 the Chaunceys completed extensive restoration of the house's historic features while adapting it to twenty-first century living.

* * * * *

The bungalow-style homes with either shingles or shiplap siding at 631, 633, 639, 641, 645, 647, and 653 Magnolia Avenue are typical of the summer homes built in Larkspur in the early 1900s. Most have been modified. According to Biff Harris "all the places on Magnolia had apartments added to them during the 1940s" when the pressure for housing workers from Marinship was great. At that time the zoning was changed from single- to multiple-family residential. In the 1980s the zoning was returned to single-family residential, but many apartments remain.

Harris reported that the attorney who kept Cap Larsen out of jail after the water scandal *(see page 95)* lived at 631 Magnolia Avenue. One of the uphill houses north of number 627 was occupied by Mr. Hill who owned Hill's boathouse on Corte Madera Creek.

One of the few unchanged Victorians along this corridor is **655 MAGNOLIA AVENUE**. Its twin next door has been extensively remodeled although it retains a relationship to its neighbor. A covered veranda with square columns wraps around the front and south sides of each house. The house at 655 Magnolia has a high-gable roof with bell-cast dormers containing shingles in a wave pattern. The dormers have arched vents with a pair of windows below. At the north end of the house are Queen Anne bay windows with diamond-shaped panes in the upper sections.

▲ 9.16: *The Victorian house at 655 Magnolia Avenue has retained its original character, 2006.*

▲ 9.17: *The home next door at number 659 has been remodeled but echoes the look of its neighbor, 1990.*

Len Young, who ran the Larkspur Bar and then a café in the Brazil building on Magnolia Avenue, lived here with his family from 1920 to 1940. The house had a fireplace in the dining room and in the living room. There were four bedrooms, two screened-in porches, and two kitchens. The older kitchen had a coal stove. Len's son Charlie grew up in this house and, until his retirement in 1988, ran the butcher shop in Rainbow Market. Charlie remembered, "On cold days my mom would take the lid off the coal stove, wrap it in a towel, and bring it to us kids to put our feet on to keep warm." Mildred Young, Charlie's sister, remembered 20 sacks of coal being delivered to the house and carried up the stairs in the winter.

"The marsh was our playground. We never sank in the mud. When you walked on the grass, you didn't sink in so we stayed clear of the mud," recalled Charlie. When Charlie was growing up, a lot of sewage was dumped into the creek from a big drainage ditch outlet by Larkspur Lumber Co. but that didn't stop kids from jumping into the water.

> *"The creek was where we learned to swim. We'd walk down to Boardwalk #4 and jump off the wharf. We hunted rabbits in the marsh with a .22 rifle. We'd take a boat out and fish. We didn't catch much – only some perch."*
>
> — Charlie Young

Landscape features also contribute to the historic character of a neighborhood. The blue rock retaining walls and columns along Magnolia Avenue and in older Larkspur neighborhoods are composed of graywacke quarried in the canyon and on the hillsides. The grout between the stones is sculpted into raised, rounded lines that create a design itself.

The one-story 1909 bungalow at **671 MAGNOLIA AVENUE** has a totally different early 1900s design that contributes to the street's sampler of period architecture. The house has a stucco front with a pair of gables at either end, supported by bracket overhangs, and is flanked with a center-porch arbor. A large, fixed center window with two smaller casements on each side is centered in each gable. The lower portions of the windows have one pane, while the upper sections have two rows of ribbon windows – sixteen on the center window and six on the side windows.

The sides of the house have flush-board siding with a gable overhang. The railing across the porch has wooden uprights on the lower portion and diagonal inserts in the panel under the railing. The motif is repeated in the stair railing and the valances across the top of the ground floor windows.

Charlie Young remembered that Henry Meyers, who owned the Hotel Sausalito and other Marin County properties, lived in the house in the 1920s and went duck hunting with his father, Len.

Because of the city road easement, most of the front yards along this section of Magnolia Avenue belong to the city. Parking and backing up into oncoming traffic have always been irritating for residents. Garages had to be dug into the hillside or large retaining walls constructed. The 1919 city council minutes indicate that the city attorney was

▲ *9.18: The stucco-fronted house at 671 Magnolia Avenue was built in 1909 with two gables and a center porch arbor, 1990.*

▲ *9.19: The grout lines on the gray stone pillars and retaining walls at 671 Magnolia Avenue give them a unique appearance.*

MAGNOLIA AVENUE GARAGES

▲ 9.20: *A garage in the 600 block of Magnolia Avenue, since torn down, 1983.*

▲ 9.21: *Hillside garage and stairs near 679 Magnolia Avenue, built for a home once located on the slope between Magnolia and Cedar Avenues, 2010.*

"instructed to prepare a traffic ordinance and look into the matter of garages built on the street near Escalle's."

Ironically, the parking constraints helped to solve a fuss when the city's first bicycle and pedestrian path was proposed in 1970, according to council member and former mayor Joan Lundstrom. The bike path was approved and parking remains on the west side of Magnolia.

Just north of 679 Magnolia Avenue the false-front garage with the name "Hillside" in the rough stone stucco outlining the wood frame is typical of the detached garages built in the early days of automobiles. The garage and steps belonged to a house that was located on the slope between Cedar and Magnolia. After the house burned, the land-locked lot has provided a challenge to any construction on the site.

③ Escalle Vineyard – Tiscornia Property

When Baltimore and Frederick Mining and Trading Company member Daniel Taylor arrived at the shore opposite **771 MAGNOLIA AVENUE** in 1849, he wrote glowingly of the beauty of the hills. At the time of his arrival, Marin was considered the home of Indians and wild game. The hills were studded with oaks and madrones.

In 1874 Patrick King leased the land to Claude Callot, a French baker. Callot bought the property from King in 1879

▲ 9.22: *Escalle Winery in the early 1900s. Clockwise from center left: the barn, the water tank, the house, and the winery. In the foreground is the flared, gabled drinking and dining room. The brick Limerick Inn is located at the far right, but not in this photo. Two ark dwellers are carrying buckets of water from the water tank to Boardwalk #3. Gus Frizzi is making the weekly wine delivery with the horse and buggy.*

▲ 9.23: *Escalle Station on Magnolia Avenue, about 1930.*

ESCALLE STATION

"My brothers who came home on the train from San Francisco would go all the way down to Escalle instead of getting off at Baltimore Park … they'd go there and have a drink or two and walk home from there."

— Judge Samuel Gardiner

and began making bricks from the slope's clay. Transported by barges that pulled up to the dock opposite the kiln, the bricks were carried down Corte Madera Creek to San Francisco.

While brick making was initially Callot's primary business, changes came to the property in 1881 when twenty acres were set aside for vineyards, and another three acres for an apple orchard and a winery. The house, barn, winery, and water tank were built that year. Callot sent for his friend, 23-year-old Jean Escalle who lived in France. According to one story, Jean and his brother Pierre were hired to care for some valuable Clydesdales that Callot had purchased in France. The brothers soon became involved in the operation of Callot's various enterprises.

A *Marin Journal* article in 1887 stated, "C. Callot has added grape growing and winemaking to his former business of brick burning, and has succeeded in producing large quantities of excellent table claret which finds a ready market throughout the county."

After Callot's death in 1888, Jean Escalle married Callot's widow Ellen, 15 years his senior. When Ellen Escalle died in 1903, Jean married a German woman, Wilhelmina Vogel, who was called "Helma" by her friends.

The winery operated in the two-story false-front building that had a combination of a lower brick floor and an upper wooden floor. The grapes were brought into this upper floor and, according to Wilhelmina's foster daughter, Mrs. W. F. Wagner, were dumped onto the floor of the loft. As she explained, "Stems and all went onto the gleaning floor. The women then rolled them about with long-handled rakes, washing and separating them until they plopped into the vats in the darkness below." After being crushed, the grapes were put into the fermenting barrels. Wine was aged in casks one to eight years.

Although the winery's production of 12,000 gallons per year was modest, the quality was rated high. There were wine deliveries three times a week in a buggy drawn by a horse named Pedro – "just like a milk route," according to Randolph C. Doherty.

During Larkspur's resort era, the red brick Limerick Inn opened on April 20, 1894. It boasted bocce ball courts and gardens in the rear. In 1905 the Limerick Inn was rented to Nick Biegel, and later to Sam Orru. Outside the inn patrons enjoyed good food and wine at tables under a vine-covered trellis. A small bandstand provided entertainment. Customers arrived by train or buggy from miles around to sample and purchase wine, creating a relaxed, happy atmosphere that became the trademark of the inn. The train stop opposite the inn was called Escalle Station. Italian, French, and German societies from San Francisco thronged to the inn on weekends.

"Escalle's was a wonderful place," said longtime librarian Helen Wilson. "The French and Italians came here in droves on weekends to enjoy themselves. They brought their children and ate lunch. You could hear them singing all over town." A big celebration was held on Bastille Day and another in autumn called the "Vintage Festival" when winemaking was finished.

Winemaking wasn't Jean Escalle's only interest. He was prominent on the Larkspur political scene and was elected a city trustee in 1912, 1914, and 1918.

PROMINENT ESCALLE OWNERS

▲ 9.24: *Jean Escalle was not only involved in the brick-making operation but played an important role in the Larkspur political scene, 1881.*

▲ 9.25: *An undated photograph of attorney and land investor Adolph A. Tiscornia who at one point owned one third of the land in Larkspur as well as major holdings in San Francisco.*

He donated the bell for the first Catholic church on Cane Street.

Prohibition and *Phylloxera* spelled "fini" for grape production at the winery and ended wine selling in 1920, the same year Jean Escalle died. Wilhelmina continued to live in the big house until her death ten years later. She was buried at Mount Olivet Cemetery in San Rafael alongside Jean and Ellen.

Extensive litigation followed Escalle's death. Relatives in France kept the estate in limbo for almost twenty years. In 1940 when these matters were finally settled, the twenty-acre vineyard, winery, house, barn, and orchard property was purchased by Adolph Tiscornia. By the 1960s Tiscornia owned a third of the land in Larkspur, as well as land in Sausalito and properties in San Francisco and throughout the state.

Attorney and investor Adolph A. Tiscornia had become a legend by the time of his death in 1967 at age 82. A tough, canny entrepreneur, he gained a reputation for acquiring land cheaply and accumulating large blocks for back taxes during the Depression and then sitting on them until the price was right to sell.

"Other lawyers bought Cadillacs to make the public think they were rich. I say, if you make something, keep the seed so you have some money to put it in something else."

— Adolph A. Tiscornia

Herb Caen's June 2, 1957 comment about Tiscornia: "If I had a million, I'd... erect a 'spite wall' around A.A. Tiscornia's shameful row of eyesore buildings on Kearny at California, buy the Skid Road area and ship it to Nevada to be used as an H-bomb target."

Tiscornia held that same property for 30 years. When people complained of his run-down, unpainted buildings, he was quoted as saying, painting them "is like getting a shine on a pair of shoes that's full of holes." Prophetically he added, "There's no question but what something is going to happen around here sooner or later. We haven't any plans. We're waiting for other people's plans." And he was proven right. In 1963 he leased (not sold) the land for 99 years to the Bank of America who proceeded to tear down the crumbling structures and erect its fifty-two-story world headquarters.

Born in Calaveras County, Tiscornia graduated from the University of California and Hastings College of the Law in the Class of 1910. He cut his teeth as a lawyer by handling condemnation suits and legal matters involving land. As he began to make money in land he said, in a 1963 interview, that he held onto it to make more.

Over the years he made donations to many Marin County organizations and gave bonds worth $2,600 to the City of Sausalito with no strings attached. He was president of the Federal Ornamental Iron and Bronze Company in Sausalito and a director of the Orpheum Building Company in San Francisco.

Gossip and stories about Tiscornia abound. There were tales of him walking his Larkspur property with a shotgun to keep trespassers off, and roaring around the hills on heavy construction equipment.

One acre of his land was devoted to apple trees imported from France; a few of these trees remained in 2009. Some neighbors complained about the goats that grazed on the property and occasionally ended up in their yards.

Mary Tiscornia recalls that her grandfather, known for being a shrewd and successful businessman, was also a physical fitness buff who walked, boxed, and exercised at the Olympic Club. He spoke Latin and Italian and from time to time "did not hesitate to raise his voice."

He was a gutsy, active person even in his 80s. His wife had died previously. Newspaper reports told of him knocking down a 28-year-old assailant who tried to rob him. In a 1963 interview he reported that he kept fit by chopping trees on his Marin property, told of winning the Olympic Club Cup once for the Dipsea Race, and boasted of running up the flight of steps to his office. His only son, Marine Captain Edward Tiscornia, was killed in action in Okinawa in 1945. Tiscornia proposed the construction of a swimming pool in his son's honor at the corner of Magnolia Avenue and Doherty Drive, but the idea was rejected by the city, according to Charles Young.

After Tiscornia's death in 1967 his property was valued at $6.7 million and was held in trust until 1979 for his granddaughter Mary, by his longtime secretary and friend, Alice Copeland Vincilione, as trustee. Mary Tiscornia has handled the land with sensitivity and a careful stewardship. In 1990 an agreement with the City of Larkspur and Marin County was negotiated to sell 131 acres to be used for publicly-owned open space, another 129 acres of open-space easement, and a loop trail around King Mountain in exchange for a limited level of development on less than four acres of the property. In 2007 the Larkspur acreage had been reduced to approximately 23 acres owned by Mary Tiscornia.

▲ 9.26: *A 1979 sketch of the Escalle property shows the back of the Limerick Inn on the left, the barn in the center, and the winery on the right.*

The exterior of the house remained unchanged as of 2003. The horizontal wood siding, a brick foundation, a hipped roof, and a veranda on the front and side show the influence of French Colonial architecture. The main living area was restored by Mary Tiscornia's mother, Toni Heffelfinger, and stepfather. The blue rock fireplace in the sitting room and the antique furniture reflect the house's original, relaxed, turn-of-the-century character.

A spiral staircase connects the house and the two-story Italianate false-front building, which once contained a gravity-flow winery typical of the period. The exterior is a combination of brick on the first floor and flush wood board siding on the second floor with trim at the top. The brick 60- x 22- x 20-ft-high first floor cellar backs up into the hillside at the rear and originally had a large area for wine storage. Brick buttresses support the uphill foundation.

The winery's roof has a wide parapet on the front with brackets, which in turn is topped by a gable-shaped parapet inscribed with Jean Escalle's name and the date 1881. In early 1900s photos the words "Corte Madera Vineyard and Winery" appear on the false-front façade below the name and date (see figure 9.22). This was probably because Larkspur had not been incorporated at the time the building was constructed.

A gable roof is behind the false-front façade. The four-over-four double-hung tall, narrow second floor windows on the front originally had shutters. Four brick buttresses support the brick foundation at the front base with two small windows above (see figure 9.26). Vestiges of wine production can be glimpsed inside the winery with its large planked wooden floors and heavy beamed ceilings.

The only alterations to the exterior of the winery building are at the rear of the winery where they are not visible to the casual eye. An upslope, hipped-roof-shed addition now extends across the second floor from the house to the old grape transfer area where grapes were brought to the second floor crushing area. New windows have been added to this addition and a deck has been added as well.

Three other original structures are still on the historic site. A two-story wooden barn with a gable roof, trusses, and a teardrop finial is located south of the house. The building has stables on the first floor that are accessed through sliding doors on an outside track. The second floor loft is accessible by doors centered under the gable at both ends. A nearby water tank with a hexagonal roof that appeared in a 1909 ad dates back to the late 1800s brick-making operation. A two-car garage is built into the slope near the gully where a debris

▲ 9.27: *The Limerick Inn was reborn as a festive center for one night in 2008 when the Centennial Rose Bowl dance placed it in the limelight again.*

avalanche came down in 1982 and swept through the third original structure, the Limerick Inn.

After a period of disrepair, the brick shell of the Limerick Inn was stabilized and tie rods installed to support the walls and parapet in 2003. In that same year, nearby elms that were hazardous to the structure were removed, and new trees were planted. Although it is a structural ghost now, its arched doorways and windows, false front with corner pillars, and column-framed center parapet bearing the Escalle name provide a reminder of its historic past.

In 2008 the grounds and the Limerick Inn were spruced up both aesthetically and structurally for the Centennial Rose Bowl Dance when a thousand people danced and socialized under a full moon. For the evening, the grounds of the historic Escalle winery were transformed into a fairyland of twinkling lights and lanterns suspended over a vast dance floor. Dancers rested on hay bales, sipped and noshed at tables or upturned wine barrels, and enjoyed the music of the live bands. Up the hill, near the historic barn, Larkspur's volunteer fire fighters in traditional red shirts showed off the 1916 fire engine they had lovingly restored, and hosted another popular bar. Even the resident horses celebrated, taking off from the grounds to explore the neighborhood.

The Escalle Vineyard-Tiscornia property and buildings are considered significant because they have figured in every era of Larkspur's history: lumbering in the early 1800s, brick making in the 1880s, grape growing and winemaking from the 1870s to the 1920s, and resort partying from 1894 to 1920. Two prominent people – winemaker and early city trustee Jean Escalle and attorney and land investor Adolph A. Tiscornia – called the site home.

▲ 9.28: *Safeway at the southeast corner of Bon Air Road and Magnolia Avenue, 1975.*

▲ 9.29: *The plank walkway leads to Boardwalk #4 with construction of the new Bon Air Bridge at the center, 1959.*

The buildings on the site were given historic overlay H zoning in September of 2004. The overlay is restricted to a defined boundary area that ensures the protection and preservation of existing structures and the compatibility of new development with the historic elements.

④ Bon Air Road at Magnolia Avenue

For a long time the area around the north and south corners at Bon Air Road and Magnolia Avenue was vacant. When the Bon Air Bridge replaced the old wooden bridge across the creek in 1959, developers considered this area for a shopping center. Safeway built a store at the southeast corner. Assorted offices and a bank on the opposite side of the street provided the key elements for local shopping. In 1971 a commercial complex was envisioned that would have been an extension of the Safeway commercial area to the south. This plan was rejected, and the Creekside homes were built, leaving the existing commercial area in limbo. First Safeway relocated, then other businesses struggled for a number of years until medical-related facilities moved in – a logical fit given the proximity to Marin General Hospital. In 2010 despite Hillview-neighborhood protest, a commercial use moved into the northeast corner of the intersection when longtime family hardware store Corbet's Ace Hardware opened for business in the former bank building. ✣

HILLVIEW & KING MOUNTAIN
Larkspur's signature mountain gave birth to a subdivision and large apartment complex.

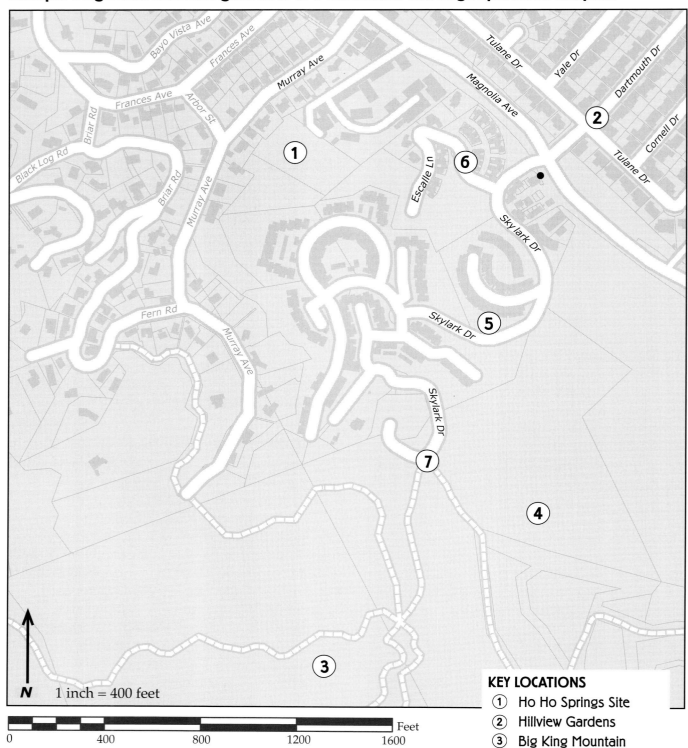

KEY LOCATIONS
1. Ho Ho Springs Site
2. Hillview Gardens
3. Big King Mountain
4. Little King Mountain
5. Skylark Apartments
6. Escalle Village
7. Open Space Access
• Address of Note

↪ *While this chapter is not designed as a walking tour, readers are encouraged to hike past Escalle Village and Skylark apartments up to the slopes of Big and Little King Mountains to enjoy fabulous views of Larkspur, Marin, and the Bay Area beyond.*

HILLVIEW & KING MOUNTAIN

Before the clear cutting of the trees on the slopes and the silting in of Corte Madera Creek, a wide creek channel had supported heavy boat traffic to Ross Landing. Magnolia Avenue cut across the base of Little King Mountain on the west and along the edge of the extensive marsh on the east by the creek, according to the 1871 map of the area *(see page 219)*. A portion of the old roadbed is visible on the slope opposite Bon Air Road.

▲ 10.2: King Mountain Trail, 1980.

• • • • • • • • • • • •

When William Murray and Patrick King bought the 1,233.75-acre lower Ross Valley property in 1869 from the Ross family for $4,500 (about $3.65 per acre), development of Larkspur advanced north of today's Bon Air Road. The two partners divided their land. Murray selected the northern portion, which later became Murray Park and part of Kent Woodlands. King took the southern half, which included eastern portions of Little and Big King Mountains and downtown Larkspur.

① Ho Ho Springs Site

An early 1890s destination was Ho Ho Springs, a recreational resort built by Joseph Has Brouck, a stockbroker and principal with Bancroft-Whitney Law Publishing Company. Located on the slopes above where the Woodlark apartments were built in 1963 at 965 Magnolia Avenue, the resort had an elaborate rustic layout consisting of five log cabins, tent sites, handcrafted twig benches and gates, horse stables, and a water supply from a hillside spring. Meals were served in an open-air pavilion. Guests gathered in a party room in front of a brick fireplace framed with timbers and decorated with oriental art pieces.

Little King Mountain is Larkspur's gateway to mountain trails and offers panoramic views of the Ross Valley.

▲ 10.1: A panoramic sketch from the Larkspur Open Space Bond flyer, 1975.

▲ 10.3: In 1890 Joseph Has Brouck built five log cabins and tent sites on the hill above where the Woodlark Apartments are today.

▲ 10.4: A spring on the site supplied water to the rustic cabins tucked into the hill. Note the tree growing through the porch roof.

▲ 10.5: Ho Ho Springs party room where visitors gathered for festivities.

Friends of Ho Ho's owners entered through ornamental gates and traveled on footpaths to the log cabins scattered around the area. All that remains on the site is the destroyed shaft for the spring. Development on the site has been in limbo since 1981 due to access problems.

Although some Murray Park homes were built up the canyon on Murray Avenue in the early 1900s, the steep terrain to the west and the marshes to the east of Magnolia Avenue between Bon Air Road and Murray Park were a challenge to development. The marshes were not just the habitat of feathered friends but also of vacationers escaping San Francisco's summer fog. Squatters floated in arks at high tide and anchored them on the upper mud flats creating Boardwalk #4, just north of the Bon Air footbridge. The arks were accessible by boardwalks laid across the marsh from Magnolia Avenue.

▲ 10.6: Dinah's Shack, a restaurant and bar at the corner of Magnolia Avenue and today's Skylark Drive, 1920s.

DINAH'S SHACK

In the early 1900s Larkspur was a recreation destination. Few permanent homes were built, and construction catered to summer visitors. During this time, Dinah's Shack, part of a chain with restaurants in Palo Alto and Santa Barbara, was located at the southwest corner of Magnolia and today's Skylark Drive. It was a favorite gathering spot, featuring "half a spring chicken on toast for 50 cents" that you "eat with your fingers," until it was razed by the fire department as a fire hazard.

▲ 10.7: Fill from Little King Mountain created the site for Hillview Gardens, 1955. Boardwalk #4 stretched along the edge of Corte Madera Creek. A wooden footbridge crossed the creek to Marin General Hospital.

▲ 10.8: Hillview Gardens, 1955. Dinah's Shack is on the right, in the foreground.

② Hillview Gardens

The post-war housing boom made developers take another look at the sites along Corte Madera Creek – sites they had sneered at earlier. With the steep lands of Little King Mountain just across the road, a source of fill was handy. In 1954 the lower slopes were gouged out and trucked to fill the marsh and create land for the 116 ranch-style homes of the Hillview Gardens subdivision.

Joe Monestier, Larkspur Public Works superintendent from 1952 until the 1980s commented, "They took out a whole hill, where Skylark is now, to build Hillview Gardens. They moved a lot of dirt. That was only the beginning."

Robert "Bob" Smith (who was on the City Council from 1962 to 1966) along with his family, was among the first residents of Hillview Gardens. The homes were built from 1954 to 1956 and cost in the low $20,000s. They attracted young families, many with several children. Smith commented, "In fact, it was because of the Hillview development that Henry C. Hall School was built in 1956. In 2007 there were only 10 of the original owners who still remained and under 60 kids in the neighborhood."

Bob Smith got involved in local politics when residents became concerned about the land around Hillview being zoned for commercial development. At this time, the same concern lured other Hillview residents to throw their caps into the political arena: longtime City Council member Al Malvino, who was mayor of Larkspur for six terms and served on the City Council for 25 years, Paul Cane, and Art Storhaug.

▲ 10.9: The original Hillview Gardens homes had a mix of horizontal siding and brick or stucco façades, 2007.

▲ 10.10: A Craftsman-style façade and second-story addition, 2007.

▲ 10.11: The most controversial and creative remodel was designed to protect neighbors' views of Mt. Tamalpais, 2007.

▲ 10.12: Big and Little King Mountains deserve their royal status and lord it over the Ross Valley with only Mt. Tamalpais overruling them, 2007.

Hillview residents were also concerned about floods when heavy rains and high tides caused Corte Madera Creek to overflow. Mud from the quarried slopes of Little King clogged the drains. To prevent flooding, King Mountain Creek drainage was improved, and additional catch basins were installed, as well as tide gates on the storm drains to prevent high tides from invading Hillview.

According to longtime resident Bill Webb, Hillview traditions included the Halloween parade, led by a Larkspur fire truck with red lights and sirens blazing, followed by adults and children in costume, and an annual barbecue block party.

Hillview Gardens has changed the most dramatically of all the Larkspur neighborhoods since its initial construction. The 1950s tract look has been replaced by two-story additions that have created a mixture of styles and drawn both praise and criticism. Some homes have a stucco, Mediterranean style, some have flat roofs, and some have column-supported, front-porch gables. One creative home was designed with a second-story tower to protect neighbors' views of Mt. Tamalpais.

③ Big King Mountain

Eight hundred foot Big King Mountain and four hundred foot Little King Mountain lord it over the lower Ross Valley, visually providing a valuable ecological and recreational resource on Larkspur's doorstep and a backdrop for the community. Over the years fires in 1880, 1909, and one in 1915 that lasted five days, have taken their toll on the mountains. Between 1952 and 1960 trees on the top of Little King were cut, and 200,000 cubic yards of soil were graded off without any plan or authorization. The reason cited was to create a site for a water tank on the saddle for future development.

The 1965 Larkspur General Plan designated every square inch of land within city boundaries for development: no new parks, no open space, and homes on steep hillsides every quarter-acre. Public access to open space was limited.

The history of the Kings involved three strong-willed land barons: Adolph A. Tiscornia, Paul Vincilione, and Joseph Pell. Tiscornia, who died in 1967, had a reputation for being feisty and shrewd. During his life he had amassed a personal goldmine in land and real estate, the most famous being his 99-year lease of the San Francisco Bank of America site in 1963. In 1940 he purchased the former Murray lands from the Escalle estate, and by 1960 he owned one third of Larkspur lands reaching from Big and Little King Mountains to upper Baltimore Canyon.

Paul Vincilione, a contractor who enjoyed playing with his collection of heavy grading equipment in his spare time, was involved in a number of Big and Little King projects and had quarried the fill for Hillview. He was married to Tiscornia's secretary, Alice Copeland, who became the executrix of the Tiscornia estate after Tiscornia's death.

④ Little King Mountain

Before zoning codes were established in Larkspur, commercial, high density, and single-family homes were often jumbled together along Magnolia Avenue. Originally the lower slope of Little King, north of Skylark Drive, had two single-family structures, one owned by former Larkspur police chief Howard Clark. Due to Larkspur's hilly terrain, each new development was isolated and

THE 1972 TISCORNIA PLAN

- 310 ACRES (100 in Larkspur, 210 in county)
- 360,000 CUBIC YARDS OF DIRT from Little King to fill low land at southeast corner of Magnolia Avenue and Bon Air Road
- A COMMERCIAL CENTER
- 190 TOWN HOUSES
- 110 HOMES
- 150 ACRES DEDICATED TO OPEN SPACE

became a new neighborhood with its own distinct architectural character.

In 1969 the Tiscornia estate built a chain-link fence around the perimeter of its lands, cutting off access to the mountains' open space. In 1971 mayor and council member Joan Lundstrom reported, "Larkspur citizens challenged and won the right to cross the historical path on the then-private Tiscornia lands in Madrone Canyon." Times had changed. A new generation of Larkspurians appreciated the Kings as a major open-space backdrop to the city and as one of Larkspur's major gateways to the North Ridge. A proposal for grading and development on Little King set off a movement to protect Big and Little Kings, and to put a building moratorium on ridge lands.

Things came to a head when Tiscornia presented his ambitious 1972 development plan, a serious threat to Little King's regal status. The proposal was to grade 360,000 cubic yards off the top of Little King Mountain to fill in the low land near the southeast corner of Magnolia Avenue and Bon Air Road.

Citizens exploded. Marathon sessions were held by the City Council when the Planning Commission's denial was appealed to them. The council votes seesawed back and forth until unapproved grading on Little King earned a unanimous denial vote.

Attorney Peter Brekhus, who worked on the case with city attorney Joseph Forest, recalled that the attempt to grade Little King and cut trees was reported to the city on a Friday afternoon. The city wanted to stop the work immediately through a temporary restraining order. To do so Brekhus had to have it signed that afternoon by the judge. Brekhus found him at a Little League game in Tiburon, where the judge issued a stop work order.

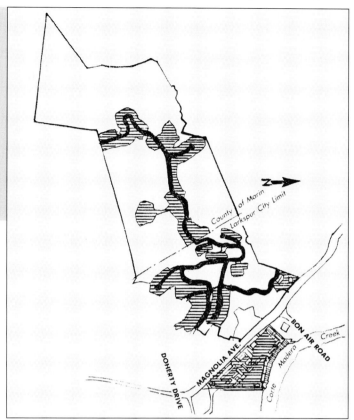

▲ 10.13: Tiscornia Plan, 1972 (see box).

A lawsuit followed with legal questions: Would the grading give the developer a vested interest in the land? Was a private venture in violation of public welfare? Could trees be cut when the city had no ordinance prohibiting their cutting?

The State Appellate Court ruled in favor of the city. The grading was illegal because the consequences of the massive grading were not taken into account. Attorney Peter Brekhus reported tires were slashed in parking lots outside the hearings because feelings ran so high.

▲ 10.14: The illegal grading on Little King Mountain triggered a lawsuit, 1972.

▲ 10.15: Skylark Apartments atop the old quarry that supplied fill for Hillview Gardens, 1971.

"The interesting thing about the grading of Little King and the suit that followed," commented former city manager Harlan Barry, "was that it was probably the first test that this community had of being in the forefront of an environmental suit, because the idea was to take down Little King and to fill the flatlands. From an engineering perspective that's a perfectly sound thing to do... but the city just said, 'No, it isn't going to happen. It's detrimental to the environment, and for a number of reasons we don't want this to happen.'"

⑤ Skylark Apartments

Polish-born Joseph Pell, a World War II Holocaust survivor who fled through Eastern Europe, reached the United States and then the Bay Area and ultimately became a billionaire real estate developer. One of his real estate investments was the purchase of the acreage that encompassed Ho Ho Springs and the future Woodlark, Skylark, and Escalle Village apartments and townhouses from the Tiscornia estate.

In 1969 Pell Development began construction of the lower 117 units of the 550-unit apartment complex of Skylark Apartments at 863 Magnolia Avenue. Designed by architect Richard Olmstead, the apartments climbed up the steep, quarried slopes that had been gouged out to fill the Hillview Gardens site.

⑥ Escalle Village

Between 1972 and 1979 several development projects adjacent to Little King sailed through approvals. The 28-unit Escalle Village was approved in 1975 and built in 1978. The earlier-built single-family homes were left stranded above the new development until they were joined by three new million dollar single-family homes.

The upper units of Skylark Apartments were built on Skylark Drive in 1979 and provided access to the future open space lands of Big and Little King Mountains. Because the hill above the apartments had many natural springs, slides and drainage problems have occurred over the years, sometimes man-made and sometimes natural.

⑦ Open Space Access

The City's philosophy about preservation of open space and ridgelines was mandated in the 1972 General Plan. The stage was set for a major public effort to purchase the lands. A $1,250,000 North Ridge Open Space bond issue was put on the ballot in 1975 to purchase 350.6 acres of Tiscornia land, but it fell short of the two-thirds vote needed to pass.

Two years later the name was changed to one word, "Northridge," when a 357-acre parcel was purchased for $850,000 with joint funding by Larkspur, Mill Valley, and Marin County thanks to individual citizen donations ranging from $2 to $2,000, and Clara-Belle Hamilton's $50,000 gift. Since the purchase did not include the Big and Little King lands, developments continued to be proposed.

Both Kings were threatened by development again in 1980 when 22 homes atop Big King Mountain and 125 units on Little King were proposed. The master plan called for 516 units, 25,000 square feet of office space, and a 36-room inn on the slopes and the flatlands across Magnolia Avenue.

In order to be pro-active, Larkspur set up a Citizens Advisory Committee (CAC) in June of 1980, headed by Maria O'Rourke. A hundred citizens got involved and closely analyzed, and then challenged, the Environmental Impact Report for the project. They called for scaling back the hillside development and transferring density to the flatlands. Issues cited included the cost of infrastructure services to hillside development, high visibility, loss of recreation potential, significant traffic impacts, potential for landslides and water run-off, and impacts on wildlife and vegetation.

"Enough people thought enough of this community to get involved," said former CAC leader Maria O'Rourke. "King Mountain today is proof that you

KING MOUNTAIN OPEN SPACE

"Preserving King Mountain as a woodland open space was a pivotal issue in maintaining the character and quality of life in Larkspur."

— David Moller, KMOSA chair

▲ 10.16: *A loop trail provides panoramic views, 1980.*

can make a difference … if you have the courage to get involved."

In 1981 the CAC's work paid off. Ridge development was postponed until the CAC completed a study of the cumulative effects of the entire development. Another option studied by the CAC was to buy King Mountain for open space. Discussions with the landowner were initiated, and on May 6, 1985, a purchase agreement was reached. The next task for citizens was to raise the money for the purchase and shift their focus to the filled land east of Magnolia Avenue where Creekside is today.

During the next two years, a one-hundred-strong citizens group formed the King Mountain Open Space Association (KMOSA) to put together a funding package for the $3.4 million open space purchase. After the Larkspur City Council formed the King Mountain Assessment District in 1987 to provide the city's portion of the cost, volunteers contacted 2,450 property owners within the district and worked tirelessly, canvassing neighborhoods to win support. KMOSA's slogan was: "For the price of two six-packs a month for 15 years, we can preserve King Mountain as open space." The campaign was successful, and with matching funds from the County Open Space District and the Marin Community Foundation, the land was purchased in 1990.

Commented David Moller, chairman of KMOSA, of the final purchase, "What we got out of this is 131 acres of publicly owned open space and 129 acres of an open space easement, a loop trail around the mountain, a limited development on less than four acres in the county, and strong controls to minimize visibility." Since 1990, the initially approved four homes atop Big King have been reduced to one mega-house on a 161-acre parcel. A 15,916-square-foot house with a 7,709-square-foot garage was proposed in 2007.

"Open space is most satisfying because it's there to see. You look up and all the hills around Larkspur are permanent open space that was bought through major citizen efforts," said longtime City Council member and six-time mayor, Joan Lundstrom.

Former Marin County supervisor Gary Giacomini reported of the purchase in 1990, "This has been done by the most massive involvement of the public I've ever seen."

Not only have the 481 acres of Big and Little King Mountains been saved but their natural environment is being preserved. The King Mountain Green Gorillas, started by Carl and Sylvia Thoelecke in 1991, logged more than 7,000 hours between 1994 and 1998, building trails and digging up non-native plants. Volunteers are still at work. As Carl Thoelecke joked, "We continue to be King Kongs."

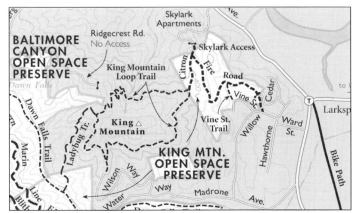
▲ 10.17: *Larkspur's prime access points to King Mountain trails are at the end of Wilson Way, at the top of Skylark Drive, and at the fire road off Willow Avenue, 2010.*

MURRAY PARK
Pioneer farmland gave way to homes and ever-evolving commercial uses.

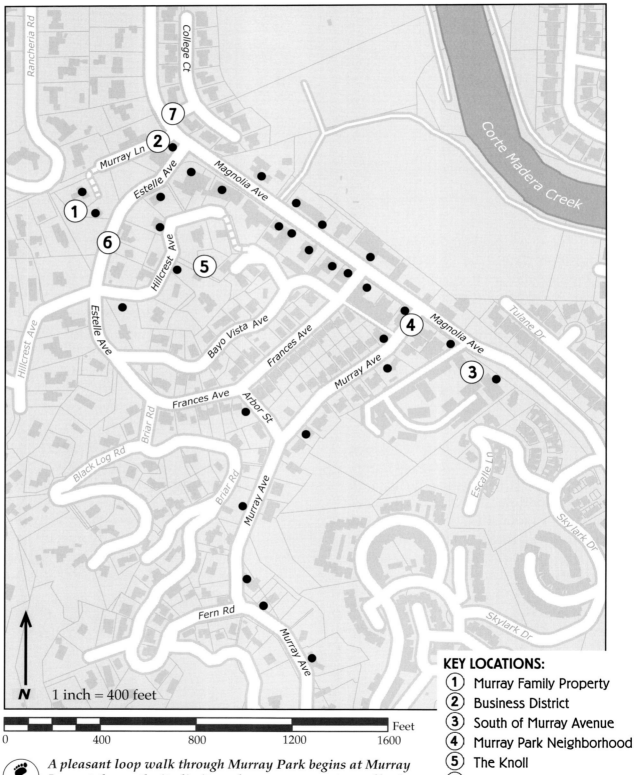

KEY LOCATIONS:
1. Murray Family Property
2. Business District
3. South of Murray Avenue
4. Murray Park Neighborhood
5. The Knoll
6. Estelle Avenue
7. College Park
• Addresses of Note

 A pleasant loop walk through Murray Park begins at Murray Lane at the north city limits and encompasses a tour of both the thriving businesses in north Larkspur and historic homes in the hills above. Limited parking is available along the side streets west of Magnolia Avenue, except Murray Lane.

MURRAY PARK

The Murray Park neighborhood of north Larkspur began in 1869 when William Murray and Patrick King bought the 1,233.75-acre lower Ross Valley property from the Ross family for $4,500, about $3.65 per acre.

• • • • • • • • • • • •

"Grandfather chose the northern half, and Paddy King chose the southern half which now comprises the town of Larkspur," explained granddaughter Estelle Murray Peterson in a 1985 interview. "The description of this land was strange," she continued. "It was always by stumps and trees and marshes and things like that." The northern portion became Murray Park and part of Kent Woodlands. The southern half included Little and Big King Mountains and downtown Larkspur.

① Murray Family Property

The Murray family played a vital role in the development of the lower Ross Valley. The Murray guest cottage and home at **5** and **9 MURRAY LANE** were built when the family moved to the area about 1869.

▲ 11.1: The Murray family home at 9 Murray Lane was surrounded by a cluster of guest cottages, about 1885.

▲ 11.2: The towering branches of old California black oaks near 9 Murray Lane, 2008.

CALIFORNIA BLACK OAKS

A series of dramatic California black oaks dotted the low lands of what is now called Murray Park in the 1800s. Their abundant crops of large and nutritious acorns were an important food source for the early Miwok residents.

The hundred-foot-high branches of the oaks retain their lofty presence above today's commercial buildings and residential homes along Magnolia, Frances, and Murray Avenues.

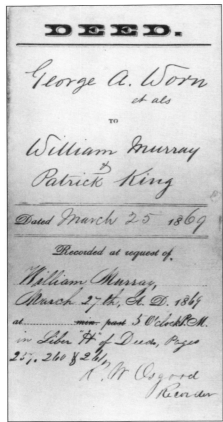

▲ 11.3: Early settler's property deed dated 1869.

William Murray was born in County Cork, Ireland, in 1826. He came to California in 1851 and mined in Sierra County. He went east in 1854 and returned that year with his bride, the former Maria Hogan. Their honeymoon included sailing to Panama, crossing the Isthmus on burros, and sailing on to San Francisco. Upon their arrival Murray put his wife and their personal effects in a white yawl and sailed across San Francisco Bay and up Corte Madera Creek to the site of the College of Marin that was called "Embarcadero" before John Reed changed it to Ross Landing in 1857.

The Murrays settled first in Fairfax where they owned a dairy ranch at the present site of the Fair-Anselm Shopping Center. Murray and a partner built a sawmill at San Quentin for Benjamin R. Buckelew whose land holdings included a section of Rancho Corte Madera extending from Ross to the bay along the north side of the creek.

While living in Fairfax, the Murrays were neighbors of Lord and Lady Fairfax, but Murray and Lord Fairfax didn't have a very congenial relationship. The story goes that during a flood, Lord Fairfax asked Murray for some potatoes. Murray threw the potatoes across the swollen creek, aiming at Lord Fairfax and finding his mark. Lady Fairfax and the Murrays had a friendlier relationship. In fact, she gave the Murray girls their first dolls.

William and Maria Murray had a large family of six sons: John, William, Vincent, Robert Thomas, James S., and Frank J., and three

▲ 11.4: Patriarch William Murray (center) with his family, 1900.

▲ 11.5: *This 1990 photograph shows the small cottage now at 5 Murray Lane. It was originally located at the corner of Magnolia Avenue and Murray Lane but was moved to its current site around 1971 when the bank was built.*

▲ 11.6: *The house at 9 Murray Lane, shown here in 1990, remains in its original location in 2010.*

daughters: Ellen and twins, Mary Frances and Margaret Rose, or "Rose."

When Murray and King divided the Ross Valley property in 1869, Murray moved his family from Fairfax to his newly purchased property. He built a home incorporating the small logger's cabin that stood on the property. The original timbers from that cabin are still in the roof of the Murray home. He also had a cattle ranch on the property where daughter Ellen liked to break in horses.

About 1873 Murray sold 400 acres to Albert Kent and retained 100 acres for his ranch. The Kent acreage became Kent Woodlands. From 1889 to 1901 Murray's house was a boarding house known as "Murray Farm" and was run by twins Rose and Mary. Behind the house there were several cottages that could accommodate about forty tenants who would normally arrive by train. Longtime resident Dorothy Boyd Sweet recalled buying eggs from the Murray girls, who also had a cow that Rose guarded. When Dorothy's father and his friends would come down to the cow pasture to play baseball, Rose would come out with her shotgun and chase them away because she said they bothered her cow.

"All the 'hoi polloi' went there," commented Lillian Murray Dodge, daughter of Robert Murray, in a 1975 interview. The sisters, she recalled, were excellent cooks who put on a "Christmas dinner with goose, ham, duck, turkey, loads of cakes, and a big pudding with flaming brandy." Added Estelle Murray Peterson, "The boarding house was very famous because they had great chicken dinners and their guests would go swimming in the creeks."

"A special treat at the Murray Farm boarding house was a cake baked with coins in it, and all the children wanted another piece."
— Lillian Murray Dodge

In 1912 the property was subdivided into building lots known as the "Murray Tract." Murray's sons and daughters formed a corporation that continued for 62 years until it was dissolved in 1974. The city limit dividing Larkspur and Kentfield now runs down the north side of Murray Lane.

Today the home at 9 Murray Lane has retained its tall, narrow, cross-gable form with a porch in front of the older section. The older section has six-over-six double-hung sash windows, while the addition has tall, narrow, four-pane windows. The addition has decorative bargeboard below the eaves of the gable.

The adjacent folk Victorian cottage at 5 Murray Lane was moved from its original site at the northeast corner of Magnolia Avenue and Murray Lane in the 1970s. It has a hipped roof with a ridge and a front porch with a separate hipped roof and arch frieze. The cottage had been originally used as a guesthouse and is the last of several accessory buildings that were part of the Murray compound.

Over the years the Murray property has faced a number of invasion threats to its idyllic setting because of its location adjacent to the commercial areas. In 1969 Charles McLeran asked to extend the commercial zoning into the rear portion of the 2.6-acre site that included the historic homes. He had purchased the land from John Murray, one of the

▲ 11.7: *Murray Park sign located at the north end of Magnolia Avenue at Estelle Avenue, 1945.*

⊃ *Continue south along the east side of Magnolia Avenue until opposite Murray Avenue.*

② Business District

The chaotic zoning history of Murray Park is reflected in the businesses along the three-block stretch from Murray Lane to the Woodlark Apartments. Murray Park was originally zoned residential by Marin County on February 4, 1947. Just five months later, the Vanzin Construction Company was the first to violate the residential zoning restrictions by installing a lumber and storage yard on the west side of Magnolia Avenue.

An influx of new residents created a demand for more commercial uses after World War II. Until the 1950s most of the commercial development in Murray Park had been low key – garages, markets, and two gas stations. When the railroad ceased operation and the tracks were torn up in 1942, the east side of Magnolia was ripe for development. Controversy swirled about the direction the development should take.

The 1948 Planning Commission minutes regarding zoning reported, "We have found that Larkspur is growing rapidly and in some instances there is a total lack of proper utilization of areas, which has resulted in a stagnant and unproductive condition of land potentially useful and valuable..."

Many people felt there should be fewer businesses. The intrusion of industrial-type uses raised some hackles. The west side was officially rezoned for commercial use in the early 1950s after Larkspur's annexation of Murray Park in 1950 and 1952. In 1956 the city drafted an ambitious plan that envisioned an 84-foot wide, 4-lane road with parking that would traverse north Larkspur. When commercial uses began rubbing elbows with residential uses, protests were ignited. Each era has left its mark on Murray Park's current commercial strip.

In the 1970s, **1177 MAGNOLIA AVENUE** was developed with a branch of the Bank of Marin on the site of the two Murray cottages. One cottage was relocated to 5 Murray Lane, the southwest corner of the property next to the old Murray ranch house, around 1971. The other Murray cottage was moved behind the Murray house onto Rancheria Road and was later replaced by a new house.

original descendants of the Murray family. McLeran's plan was to open an antique shop and an attorney's office in the 100-year-old Murray residence between Estelle Avenue and Murray Lane. He also wanted to build four shops on the three parcels of land to create a shopping complex that would "possess the charm of San Francisco's Jackson Square." The rezoning for the total parcel was denied, but commercial use was allowed on Magnolia.

In 2006 a request surfaced for a General Plan amendment to change 1.03 acres of the Murray property (between the Magnolia Avenue fronting parcel and the historic homes) from low density residential to medium density residential. After a strong neighborhood protest and the requirement for an environmental impact report, the project was withdrawn.

▲ 11.8: *The building at 1177 Magnolia Avenue replaced two Murray cottages around 1971 and was used as a bank branch for almost 40 years, 2008.*

▲ 11.9: *The Food Bank market at 1161 Magnolia Avenue, early 1950s.*

▲ 11.10: *Ambrosia Pizza and Village Peddler at 1161 Magnolia Avenue, 2008.*

Westamerica Bank replaced the Bank of Marin and is closing in 2010.

One of the early commercial buildings was the Food Bank at **1161 MAGNOLIA AVENUE**, a Quonset hut-style store built by Charles McLeran in 1946. After a fire in the early 1950s, the grocery store was rebuilt as "The Honeycomb Market." In 2008 Ambrosia Pizza and Village Peddler could be found at this location; later in the year the Village Peddler moved to 1111 Magnolia.

In 1946 McLeran also rebuilt the commercial area from Estelle Avenue to 1125 Magnolia into a series of shops with flat-topped Mansard roofs. In 2008 this block of shops changed hands.

FACELIFTS OF THE PAST

The wood mosaic façade of 1125-1127 Magnolia Avenue has been painted over to hide its hippie past, but a local history buff recalls when the X-rated movie "Behind the Green Door" was featured on its marquee for four months, when the theater was the Magnolia Cinema, a 144-seat venue. "The original concept approved by the city for the 50-seat theater was for an old-time movie theater featuring Laurel and Hardy and Shirley Temple films," he recalled. Promoters hoped that College of Marin students would attend during class breaks, according to another local. The alternate naughty use didn't last long.

▲ 11.12: *1127 Magnolia Avenue's wood mosaic façade, 1975.*

▲11.11: *Corbet's, shown here in 2008, was located at 1155 Magnolia Avenue from 1954 to 2010.*

A TRADITION OF GARDENS

In 1957 an early exception to the residential zoning was a nursery owned by Charles T. Kendall called "The Garden Spot" at 1144 Magnolia Avenue. It was granted commercial zoning on one acre that was College of Marin property. In 2008 the College of Marin reclaimed the site.

A combination of native plants, vegetables, and flowers has been planted at the Larkspur Center – Marin Brain Injury Network (MBIN) at **1132 MAGNOLIA AVENUE**, where garden projects are part of the horticultural therapy program, and continue the gardening tradition.

▲ 11.15: *Kentfield's post office, shown here in the early 1940s, was moved to 1129 Magnolia Avenue and is now a church.*

◄ 11.13: *This whimsical sculpture is in the garden at the Larkspur Center – MBIN at 1132 Magnolia Avenue, 2008.*

Jim Corbet's hardware store opened in 1954 at **1155 MAGNOLIA AVENUE** and soon expanded to encompass Myer's Plumbing next door. The popular store, whose helpful staff could replace any broken part, has maintained its small-town service tradition. In 2010 the Corbet family vacated the business from this building and moved to 800 Magnolia Avenue.

The building at **1129 MAGNOLIA AVENUE** was the final resting place for the Kentfield Post Office that was located, until the 1940s, where the parking lot of Kentfield's Woodlands Market is today. After passenger train service was discontinued in 1941, the Mediterranean-style building with a tile roof was moved to 1129 Magnolia and became the Paint Pot. Since then the building has had a variety

▲ 11.14: *A view of the Ross Valley Masonic Center at 1122 Magnolia Avenue, with the MBIN garden, College of Marin fields, Corte Madera Creek, and the Greenbrae hills in the background, 2010.*

▲ 11.16: Service station at 1118 Magnolia Avenue, 1970.

of uses. Currently St. Mark's Episcopal Church, 1928 BCP, holds services there.

Built in 1953, the Ross Valley Masonic Center at **1122 MAGNOLIA AVENUE** is one of the few buildings that has retained its original use and design over the years.

A gas station was built at **1118 MAGNOLIA AVENUE** in the 1970s and was later remodeled into the retail Folio shop that sells paper goods. The car ramps are still visible on the north side.

Before development, adults seldom ventured into the marsh, but children considered it a playground. A large pond, located east of the railroad tracks behind 1118 Magnolia, was a favorite destination due to its abundance of frogs.

· · · · ·

An address that could take first prize in a diverse history contest is **1115 MAGNOLIA AVENUE**. In 1914 James Murray built a home on this site designed by local architect-builder Gustave Nagel, who designed many Larkspur homes *(see Appendix D)*. Charles Young, who was raised at 655 Magnolia, remembers watching the Murray girls, all spiffed up in their Sunday clothes, driving to church each week in their family's Model T.

In the 1950s, 1115 Magnolia Avenue was purchased by Eugene S. Bissatini who originally had planned to fix it up but, according to his son Don, "It was in such bad shape that they tore it down and recycled the redwood." Instead he built a Texaco station where gas sold for 9¢ a gallon. Subsequently a fabric shop occupied the premises and, at one time, a produce-peddling truck called "Poor Richards" parked in the lot before moving to the corner of Murray and Magnolia Avenues.

▲ 11.17: *The Murray home at 1115 Magnolia Avenue, later owned by Estelle Murray Peterson, 1946.*

▲ 11.18: *Texaco gas station at 1115 Magnolia Avenue, 1950s.*

▲ 11.19: *The Magnolia Arbor at 1115 Magnolia Avenue, 2008.*

1111 MAGNOLIA AVENUE OVER THE YEARS

▲ 11.20: *Banfield's Rug Cleaners, 1970.*

▲ 11.21: *The Black Oak Saloon, 1975.*

▲ 11.22: *In 2008 the Village Peddler moved to Magnolia Place, 2010.*

▲ 11.23: *Airstrip seen in the marsh east of Magnolia Avenue with fire truck in foreground, 1920s.*

The next transformation was in 1976 when 1115 Magnolia Avenue was rebuilt by Don Bissatini into The Magnolia Arbor, a complex of small shops. In 1986 Gilardi & Co. purchased the building and converted it to an office building that they occupied until 2005.

• • • • •

1111 MAGNOLIA AVENUE was originally built as Murray's Garage in 1923 and was operated by Elmer Murray, grandson of William Murray. In the 1920s and 1930s, Murray, a pilot who did crop dusting, landed his plane at the airstrip in the marsh that stretched behind today's 1020 to 1110 Magnolia Avenue. The story goes that his wife hung a lantern in front of the family home to serve as a beacon to guide the plane into the landing strip at night. Dave Bettega, an over-90-year-old Kentfield resident, remembered seeing the Murray biplane land while looking through the window of his Kent School classroom. He said there was no defined landing strip. The plane landed in the large, salty mud flat where the current football field is located.

In the 1920s, when Larkspur hosted the State Fire Chief's Ball at the Rose Bowl, a major event was the demonstration of the Larkspur Fire Department's new Stutz fire engine. The Department tested the engine at the marsh, where the airfield can still be seen across the drainage creek.

Murray worked on his airplane in the service station shop. Speculation has swirled over the years about how he got his Jenny airplane from the airstrip, across the tracks with the hot third rail, and to the shop. One idea, that Cornelius "Conny" Oosterbaan of the Self Storage Emporium heard from an engineer, was that since the planes were made of wood and fabric, they were very light and could have been physically carried across the tracks. Conny was told that the trick was to lift the tail across the three tracks and then, with a crew of men, delicately lift up the wings in unison and gingerly walk it over the tracks. A safer bet was that, since the planes were simple crafts with few parts, they might have been disassembled and carried across piece-by-piece.

Ed Banfield's Banfield Rug Cleaners replaced the earlier Murray garage and endured a number of remodels and unsuccessful restaurant ventures after it was sold in the 1970s.

The most famous use at 1111 Magnolia Avenue was the Black Oak Saloon, named for the local trees. The vertical wood-paneled saloon blasted music during the 1980s and was a hot spot that riled neighbors over the noise and boisterous departing patrons. A

▲ 11.24: Dollars and Sense on Magnolia Avenue, 1970s.

▲ 11.25: Antone Motors at 1101 Magnolia Avenue, 1976.

testimony to the Black Oak Saloon's indecorous reputation was recalled by Piper Park tennis player Vikki Moreland who testified, "We even danced at lunchtime."

Gilardi & Co. purchased the building in 1988 and gave it a facelift that turned it into the more proper Magnolia Place. In 2008 the Village Peddler peddled down the street from 1161 Magnolia Avenue and parked its wheels there.

Until 1941 the railroad tracks, hot third rail, and the adjacent marsh discouraged development on the east side of Magnolia. After the railroad ceased its operation in 1941, controversy grew regarding the direction of development along this part of Magnolia Avenue. A yearlong battle ensued about changing the area from residential to commercial uses. Finally, at the end of 1958, the east side of Magnolia from 1108 to 1028 was zoned restricted commercial with a triangular buffer zoned office professional just to the south. The battle was led by Dr. and Mrs. Russell J. Merret whose Dollars and Sense, an updated version of the old 5 & 10 Cent stores, anchored the strip of new buildings. The store was a successful retail variety store and community favorite until its sale in the 1980s. Today a series of small shops occupies the strip along **1020-1110 MAGNOLIA AVENUE**.

▲ 11.26: Swiss Garage at 1101 Magnolia Avenue, 2008.

▲ 11.27: Self-Storage Emporium at 1023 Magnolia Avenue, 2008.

• • • • •

In the 1950s Corrigan's Corner was a grocery store at **1101 MAGNOLIA AVENUE** on the northwest corner of Magnolia and Frances Avenues with a cluster of buildings around it. Prefontain's service station, operated by Hugh McLeran, fronted Magnolia, and Antone's Auto Hospital was at the rear. When Corrigan's Corner was torn down in 1957, Antone built a more substantial brick garage. In 2010, 1101 Magnolia Avenue is occupied by the Swiss Garage.

Originally **1023 MAGNOLIA AVENUE** was built in 1949 for United Moving Company when commercial and semi-industrial uses began to infiltrate the area. Since 2001 it has been the home of the Self-Storage Emporium. Owner Conny Oosterbaan, a former

▲ 11.28: Conny Oosterbaan with model Jenny airplane, 2008.

▲ 11.29: *The judo school at the front of 1001 Magnolia Avenue and the original house in the rear, 1975.*

▲ 11.30: *Offices at 980 Magnolia Avenue, 2008.*

980 MAGNOLIA AVENUE: From Swim Club to Offices

A cluster of offices and professional buildings at **980 MAGNOLIA AVENUE** has replaced the Paul Daly Swim Club, originally built in 1957. At that time the Club was a compromise buffer between the northern commercial uses and southern residential uses. In 1977 it was zoned commercial except for a triangular parcel behind the Magnolia frontage area. Throughout the club's operation its marsh location created drainage problems for the swimming pool during winter storms because of the high marsh water table. The pool was filled in when the swim club moved to Bon Air Road in the 1970s.

▲ 11.33: *Woodlark sign at 965 Magnolia Avenue, 2008.*

member of the U.S. Marine Corps Air Wing, and an airplane buff, has mounted a tribute to historic World War II aircraft on his roof. He proudly flies a model replica of the Elmer Murray's Jenny airplane in his office.

The new commercial uses changed the look of the neighborhood. A judo school was built in front of the home at **1001 MAGNOLIA AVENUE** in the 1970s, retaining the original house at the rear. According to contractor Richard Torney, due to the basement's low ceiling, the taller students would hit their heads.

▲ 11.31: *Elite Rug Cleaners at 975 Magnolia Avenue, 1975.*

▲ 11.32: *Leif Petersen, Inc., an international furniture showroom, occupies the updated building at 975 Magnolia Avenue, 2008.*

③ South of Murray Avenue

In 1949 former city councilman Neil Brixon of Elite Rug Cleaners bought Vanzin lumberyard at **975 MAGNOLIA AVENUE**, continuing the invasion of the commercial uses into the residential area. It has since been transformed into a very contemporary modular building.

Real Estate developer Joseph Pell purchased acreage from the Tiscornia estate and built the 80 units of Woodlark Apartments at **965 MAGNOLIA AVENUE** in 1963 on the site of the former entrance to Ho Ho Springs *(see pages 255-256)*.

⊃ *Retrace your steps on Magnolia Avenue and turn west onto Murray Avenue.*

④ Murray Park Neighborhood

The Murray Park neighborhood is comprised of homes on Murray, Frances, Bayo Vista, Estelle, and Hillcrest Avenues and Briar Road. Some are in Larkspur and some are in the county. When the original Murray Tract was subdivided into building lots in 1912, all the homes west of Magnolia were in the county. The local guess is that the street names – Estelle, Frances, and Teresa (now called Hillcrest) honor various Murray women.

Larkspur annexed the neighborhood in 1950 and 1952. The new boundary lines that were drawn have led to much head-scratching since, in some places, the city/county line runs up the middle of streets and even slices through the living room of one home. One possible explanation, suggested in a letter from Robert Murray to the city, might be the city's high tax rate of 50¢-an-acre at that time.

"The boundary lines were weird," reported former businessman and Larkspur volunteer fireman Oakley Dexter. "The firefighters never knew if it was a Larkspur fire or a Kentfield fire."

Unlike other parts of the city only a few homes were built in the Murray Tract before the 1940s.

▲ 11.35: THE MURRAY PARK MYSTERY: *In the 1940s this Kentfield Victorian was loaded onto a trailer and moved to Murray Park, but nobody knows where it is today.*

"When I was kid in the '40s, Murray Avenue was just a gravel road," recalled Don Bissatini who grew up in a log house at 49 Murray Avenue. "There was nothing down to the corner except grass and trees." At that time his father, Eugene S. Bissatini, who was later involved in development in the area, bought five lots at $200-an-acre and five acres on the Ho Ho Springs property on the hill above.

The neighborhood provides an interesting mixture of architectural styles. Major changes have taken place in the last 15 years. Mid-century tract homes have been remodeled and expanded, cabins have

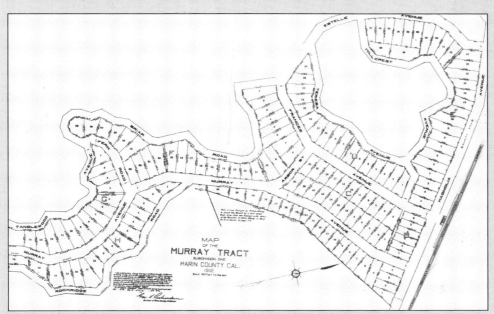

▲ 11.34: *On the 1912 Murray Tract Subdivision Map, the knoll was shown as one large parcel. The railroad is shown parallel to Magnolia Avenue.*

GROWING UP IN MURRAY PARK

"Growing up in the '40s, there were lots of places to explore. … We used to sneak into Escalle but we had to be careful not to get caught by Frizzi who patrolled with a shotgun."

— Don Bissatini

▲ 11.36: The house at 7 Murray Avenue was hand built by Raymond Thomas Olson and his oldest son, Merrel, who was paid a penny-a-piece for cleaning the salvaged bricks. Three-month-old son Ole supervised, 1946.

▲ 11.37: A four-sided gable cupola perched next to a chimney is designed with bricks circling its round form and a brick-supported arcade cap and finial at 7 Murray Avenue, 2008.

▲ 11.38: A hand-carved front door with the word "Liebesfreud," German for "love's joy," is framed by carved timbers at 7 Murray Avenue. Above the door there are leaded windows in a diamond pattern, 2008.

▲ 11.39: Raymond Thomas Olson's Timbrick house at 7 Murray Avenue when completed in 1946.

been replaced by the popular pseudo-Craftsman style of the 2000s. Only a few have retained their modest form.

The house at **7 MURRAY AVENUE** is an early survivor that everyone knows as the "Storybook" house. Built by designer-builder Raymond Thomas Olson in 1946, the combination brick, stone, and timber house with glass accents is Larkspur's prime example of what are often called "happy houses" or "fun houses" that interpret Old World vernacular designs with myriad variations. Officially the style, popular from the late 1920s until World War II, has many names: Storybook, Fairy Tale, Romance Revival, and "Timbrick" as Olson called number 7. According to his wife, Lucile, her husband bought ten lots at $1 each, then sold several for a profit and built the home at 7 Murray Avenue where they lived until 1951.

On a memory trip in 2006 to their former home, son Ole Olesen (note he changed the spelling of his name from Olson to the original Danish spelling) and his mother, Lucile, were pleased to see that no changes had been made to the house.

The hand-built house was constructed in nine months by Olson, who was a proponent of Timbrick houses. He used the style in homes in Kentfield, Ross, the East Bay, Washington, and Oregon. According to Lucile, her husband had never been to Europe but got his design ideas from reading and from his carpentry work.

A 1940s newspaper clipping reported that the house was the first Timbrick house in Marin and, "possibly the only one in Larkspur that employed the unusual construction method that had been used to build 500-year-old structures in Europe."

The two-story house has three heavy shake gable roofs joined on a diagonal. The house would have been considered a partially "green" building based on the recycled bricks, glass, and tiles that are incorporated into the design. Timbers, gable and eave trims, and door panels are hand carved. An apartment above the garage gable, accessed by the "Studio" door with Olson's initials "RTO," is connected to the main house bedroom by an interior bridge.

▲ 11.40: *Dormers that accommodate a new second story and a new porch design respect the Craftsman look of 51 Murray Avenue, 2008.*

▲ 11.41: *Luckily the family at 77 Murray Avenue was away from the house when a debris avalanche cascaded down the slope and through their home, 1982.*

At one time Bruce "Skipper" Sedley, the 1950s and 1960s local children's television host and puppeteer, lived in the house. Sedley invented what became the Magic Key for Children's Fairyland in Oakland and went on to become a successful businessman.

In the 1950s a series of tract-style homes, called "Greenberg" houses after the developer, were built along Murray and Frances Avenues. When commercial uses began to wall off the residential neighborhoods, an alley path was preserved east of **10 MURRAY AVENUE** to connect to the west of 5 Frances Avenue. Many of the homes along this stretch of Murray between Magnolia Avenue and Arbor Street have been remodeled or torn down and replaced by larger homes. Some have incorporated the flavor of the shingle-style architecture. The Craftsman-style bungalow with shiplap siding at **51 MURRAY AVENUE** has retained the original Craftsman character of the house while adding a second floor. Local architect Brock Wagstaff, who worked on updating the house with owners Sabrina and John Browne, said, "I wanted to retain the Craftsman look, but the house had a strange porch overhang that cut off the view and made the house dark inside. I designed a belly-band beam that wraps the supports and allows a view while retaining the Craftsman columns." When the Brownes bought the 1916-era house, it was the only one on the street with a front porch. They were told it previously had a pull chain toilet.

A number of homes on the south side of Murray Avenue connect to the street by bridges with arbors. However, the innocuous drainage channel that runs down the canyon turned into a monster in January of 1982. More than ten inches of rain fell in 24 hours causing a hundred-year flood as well as the loss of one home from a log jam and the destruction of 77 Murray Avenue when a debris avalanche roared through it.

High on the hillside above the creek, **80 MURRAY AVENUE** competes with 7 Murray in a contest for the most distinctive house. If a home is the essence of who lives there, then "Aubergine," the Gaudiesque home that marches up the hill at 80 Murray, reflects John Calella's multifaceted careers, which have ranged from hair dresser to radio show host to TV cook (where he earned the nickname "Organic John") and, in the 1970s, psychologist.

When Calella bought the small 800+ square foot 1910 cabin in 1968 at the top of a knoll above Murray Park, it was smothered in a heavy tree cover like a

▲ 11.42: *The house that steps up the hill at 80 Murray Avenue features a sampler of roof and house designs, 2007.*

▲ 11.43: *Exterior features and materials at 80 Murray Avenue are unified by the colors brown, yellow, and red, 2008.*

▲ 11.44: *Since the small 1960s homes along Frances Avenue do not fit the new century's lifestyle, some owners, like the one at 41 Frances Avenue, have considered adding a second floor, 2008.*

▲ 11.45: *This contemporary Craftsman-style house at 55 Frances Avenue was designed by architect Tom Hood and is part of the new generation of homes in the neighborhood, 2008.*

gangster's hideout. Recalled Calella, "It looked like something out of an old James Cagney movie."

The house was built creatively and imaginatively without any overall plans. The architectural sampler of modular structures that clamber up the slope is a fascinating, eclectic mixture and a far cry from Larkspur's usual California bungalows. Rectangular, square, and octagonal units with gable, shed, and ark-like roofs reflect Calella's appreciation of craftsmanship and design.

After redoing the old foundation, Calella fostered his love of cooking and did the first of four kitchen remodels in the old cabin. Working with skilled woodworkers, tile craftsmen, and designers, Calella winged the design as he went along. "I did the Neanderthal work of clearing the site," he remarked. The result is a delightful house with multiple individual nooks and crannies, niches for bird sculptures, oval swinging doors, and loft bedrooms for his teenagers. Guests can announce their arrival at his bright red front door by blowing a blast on a trumpet.

"I built around the original cabin and then worked my way down the hill," said Calella. "There's not a square room in the house.".

⮡ *Follow Murray Avenue to Estelle Avenue via Arbor Street and Frances Avenue.*

A large number of the modest homes along Frances Avenue have been remodeled and enlarged. At the corner of Arbor and Frances there are two homes designed by local architect Thomas Hood, who

UPPER MURRAY PARK

A number of older homes on the upper section of Murray and in the county's Briar and Fern Roads have not been researched. Several flagged for possible future research are:

❖ **101 MURRAY AVENUE**, a clapboard-sided cabin with an enclosed front porch.

❖ **103 MURRAY AVENUE**, a Prairie-style bungalow with extended brackets at the gable. The elaborate stone walls and terracing in this section were built by Italian stonemasons.

❖ **203 MURRAY AVENUE**, a 1920s cabin that has retained much of its original design on the interior but has a new roof and exterior shingles.

▲ 11.46: *View of The Knoll from Magnolia Avenue, 2008.*

served on the Larkspur Design Review Board in the late 1980s and early 1990s. He created a contemporary version of the Craftsman style with echoes of Frank Lloyd Wright at **55 FRANCES AVENUE**.

⑤ The Knoll

The small hill north of Frances Avenue, called "The Knoll" by locals, was shown as a single large lot on the Murray Tract map of 1912. Old-timers reported that in the early 1900s Richard Fontana Sr. owned the top and a large part of the western side of the knoll. The Puckett family owned acreage on the north side of the hill.

According to 85-year-old Dorothy Boyd Sweet who in 2008 lived in the house at **85 HILLCREST AVENUE**, the Boyd family purchased the front section of The Knoll in 1925 from Richard Fontana Sr. The Boyds built the two-story house with shiplap siding and a shallow gable roof that is visible above the tennis court that Dorothy, an avid tennis player, added at the corner of Hillcrest and Estelle Avenues. The house itself is only visible from across the tennis court on Estelle.

A sign of the times in the 1920s was a restriction on the house deed for 85 Hillcrest Avenue, which stated that no grapes were permitted to be grown on the property.

↪ *The following properties on The Knoll are only visible from private driveways.*

Around 1903 Richard Fontana Sr. bought the hilltop property and built a small summer cabin and barbecue pit at **49 HILLCREST AVENUE**. In 1926 Fontana and his wife, Anna, and their two children, Richard Jr. and "Pinky," moved into a permanent home designed by a student of Bernard Maybeck. Fontana surrounded the one-story, hipped-roof house with terraced stone walls and installed a pool with a fountain, a fish pond, and an elaborate garden. Between their house and 54 Hillcrest they planted a number of young giant sequoia trees that they brought back from a trip to the Sierra.

The Fontana family formed a compound on the hilltop with no fences separating the properties. When Pinky married, she was given the property across the back fence at 57 Hillcrest. Richard Jr., nicknamed "Noodles" because of his ownership of a spaghetti shop in San Francisco, married Arlene, and they lived in the house at 51 Hillcrest

▲ 11.47: *The Boyd family built this home at 85 Hillcrest Avenue in 1925. Tennis player Dorothy Boyd Sweet built the court at the corner of Hillcrest and Estelle Avenues, 2008.*

Avenue, built for him by his father in 1950. In 2008 the house was enlarged and remodeled.

The most spectacular addition was a railroad, similar to the Mt. Tamalpais & Muir Woods Railroad, that circled the hilltop. Arlene Fontana told railroad buff Richard Torney that the railroad was "built in the 1920s with design and construction supervision from their next door neighbor and Mt. Tamalpais & Muir Woods Railroad superintendent Bill Thomas. The train was powered by electricity, and the cars were modeled after the Crookedest Railroad's Gravity Cars."

▲ 11.48: *Richard Fontana Jr. operated the battery/electric engine and air brakes of the train car. His cousin Helen is seated next to him, 1935.*

▲ 11.49: *Although a deck circles 49 Hillcrest Avenue and the front porch has been enclosed, the house retains its Craftsman bungalow character, 2008.*

▲ 11.50: *The Puckett house at 56 Hillcrest Avenue, 2008.*

The train's open cars had electric controls powered by batteries and air brakes similar to gravity cars. After Richard Sr.'s death, Anna married Colonel Eastwald who maintained the railroad into the 1950s. When Eastwald died, Anna moved into the Tamalpais residential community. She lived into her 90s and died in the 1990s.

Richard Jr. died in the early 1990s. His widow, Arlene, lived at 54 Hillcrest until her death in 2006, when the house was sold. In 2008 the house underwent a remodel.

Anna Fontana sold 49 Hillcrest in 1969 to business litigation attorney Lynn McCarthy who gave the house a new life. She has not only preserved the Craftsman character but has revitalized the gardens and replaced the aged pool, fountain, and fishpond with new versions she designed.

Although the miniature railroad is now just the memory of old-timers, the terraced rock walls that encircle the hill are a reminder of its past.

The Puckett family home at **56 HILLCREST AVENUE** on the

north side of The Knoll was built in 1929 for $4,000 according to current owners Andrew and Caroline Silverman. The Pucketts owned the northeast side of the hill down to the current commercial area including a section of Estelle Avenue and the home at 15 Estelle Avenue. Since number 56 originally faced downhill, a recent remodeling moved the entrance to Hillcrest and added a new entry gable that retains its early twentieth-century charm.

6 Estelle Avenue

Early Larkspur's balmy fog-free climate tripled its population in the summertime when vacationers stayed at its local resorts or built homes on the hillsides. Number **15 ESTELLE AVENUE** is a typical 1920s summer home with board and batten siding instead of the usual shingle siding. Perched up on the wooded hillside, the house, part of the Puckett property on the northeast corner of The Knoll, features a continuous row of casement windows with wood mullions and transoms that line the north and east façades of the uppermost floor under the overhanging low-hipped roof.

⟲ *Return along Estelle Avenue then cross to the east side of Magnolia Avenue and head north. Take a right on College Court (at one time the continuation of Murray Lane) to explore the College Park neighborhood.*

7 College Park

College Park is east of Magnolia Avenue in a former marsh where cows got stuck in the mud and would have to be pulled out by horses. Soon after the end of electric interurban service in February of 1941, the railroad removed one of the double tracks and the third rail on both tracks. College Park was the first subdivision laid out east of Magnolia Avenue. Built in 1949 the houses, like others in Larkspur's 1940s and 1950s developments, have been brought into the twenty-first century in a variety of ways. Some College Court homes have added second stories and others have kept their basic bones but have had a facelift.

Although Murray Park is a hodgepodge of city and county boundary lines, the neighbors ignore city limits and gather together at sporadic block parties that have been held since 1988. Longtime resident and city council member Joan Lundstrom reported, "We've always had a great cross section of people at our block parties. Old timers, newcomers, out-of-town guests from as far away as Scotland, people in wheelchairs, children checking each other out, all mix under the redwood trees with a background music of smooth jazz to meet neighbors, share food and wine."

▲ *11.52: Some College Park homes have retained their original hipped-roof, single-story 1949 design like the one at 10 College Court, 2008.*

▲ *11.51: The wrap-around sleeping porch at 15 Estelle Avenue was a popular feature in early vacation homes to accommodate frequent guests, 2008.*

▲ *11.53: A number of College Park homes have added second stories but most have done simple facelifts that bring them into the twenty-first century, 2008.*

GREENBRAE & BON AIR
Homes and apartments wrap the hillsides of Larkspur's northern half.

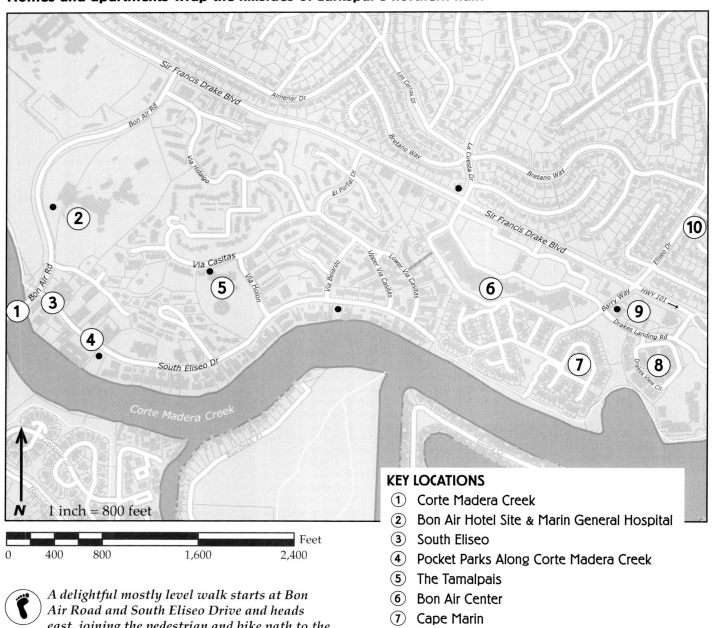

KEY LOCATIONS
1. Corte Madera Creek
2. Bon Air Hotel Site & Marin General Hospital
3. South Eliseo
4. Pocket Parks Along Corte Madera Creek
5. The Tamalpais
6. Bon Air Center
7. Cape Marin
8. Drake's Landing & Drake's View
9. Larkspur Fire Station No. 2
10. Green Brae Ranch Site & Development
• Addresses of Note

A delightful mostly level walk starts at Bon Air Road and South Eliseo Drive and heads east, joining the pedestrian and bike path to the Greenbrae interchange (Highway 101). A loop through the Bon Air Center and Cape Marin connects back to South Eliseo.

GREENBRAE & BON AIR

The Greenbrae and Bon Air areas of Larkspur are portions of a Mexican land grant named "Rancho Punta de Quentin," originally granted in 1840 to a New England sea captain named John Rogers Cooper. First arriving in California in the early 1820s, Cooper regularly traded across the Pacific Ocean between China, Hawaii, and California's leading port of Monterey. Finally settling in Monterey in 1827, he was baptized a Catholic as "Juan Bautista Rogers Cooper." The same year he married Encarnación Vallejo, a sister of a 19-year-old soldier named Mariano Vallejo, who later became the military governor of Alta California.

▲ 12.1: Aerial view of Corte Madera Creek and the Greenbrae area, looking west, 1947.

Cooper, a shrewd, politically-connected trader, began to amass land in the Monterey area and further north. His holdings eventually included the Rancho El Molino in central Sonoma county, Rancho Nicasio, and the Rancho Punta de Quentin, an 8,877-acre tract that stretched from Point Quentin to modern-day Fairfax, including Larkspur, Ross, and Kentfield. Cooper often visited the three ranchos, but continued to reside in Monterey.

Always short of cash, Cooper sold his Nicasio and Point Quentin ranches to Benjamin R. Buckelew in 1850. Buckelew engaged in a variety of ambitious undertakings, including the 1852 sale of a small portion of his land to the state to establish the San Quentin prison.

When his financial empire collapsed in 1857, Buckelew sold 8,840 acres to James Ross and his partner, John Cowell, for $30,000. The Ross family originated the name Green Brae, perhaps in memory of their Scottish origin. After Ross's death, his widow sold some of their land to Patrick King and William Murray in 1869, thus creating the source of land title for Larkspur on the south side of the creek.

The $50,000 sale of Ross's 680-acre "Green Brae Ranch" lands in 1890 to Patrick William Riordan, Archbishop of the Roman Catholic Archdiocese of San Francisco, allowed only limited development of the north side of the creek for the next fifty years, except for the ranch itself whose operators leased their land from the church.

① Corte Madera Creek

Up until 1906 clams were dug along the creek and according to Jim Nevil, whose parents summered at Boardwalk #2, "Martin The Clam Digger" dug clams daily to sell to San Francisco's Palace Hotel.

The diocese ownership of the land, the arrival of the railroad, and the geographic division by Corte Madera Creek determined the development and lack of development on its two sides. As the creek snaked down the Ross Valley in the late 1800s, it provided a waterway for barges hauling bricks, hay, and cordwood. Small brickyards occupied several spots along its banks, with a resort hotel on the north bank and a bathing house along the southern edge. Most of the northern edge was used for grazing.

In the early 1900s the creek was a playground for early settlers. At this time, the creek formed a large lake just below the Bon Air Bridge, and swimming and boating resorts were built at its edge. An 1897 *Sausalito News* article mentions a Mr. H. Varney who "owns and conducts the bathing and boating-house, a popular resort in summer time which is said to be the warmest saltwater bathing in central California. It is a great resort for cyclers and other summer excursionists. Moonlight boating parties have become quite the thing and their songs may frequently be heard until early morning floating up from the river."

CORTE MADERA CREEK

"We used to have a $5 bet on swimming from Hill's boathouse to the Greenbrae Bridge. We used to fish in the creek and take the carp out. Fisherman would pay us to get the carp out because they fed on the striped bass."

— Harold Kelly, who lived on Holly Avenue

▲ 12.2: *Hill's boathouse on Corte Madera Creek, about 1908.*

▲ 12.3: Bathing and boating on Corte Madera Creek opposite Escalle, early 1900s.

During the early 1900s Hill's boathouse, located just below the Bon Air Bridge, provided changing rooms for people who wanted to swim in the creek. Early developers boasted of "saltwater bathing" in their sales pitches.

According to Katherine Solomons Lilienthal, "Hill's Boathouse was located across from Escalle. A boardwalk was laid across the marsh to connect Magnolia Avenue with the boathouse. Boats were rented; changing rooms were there, although you had to bring your own towel. There was a diving float in the slough."

Recounting a typical summer day in Larkspur in the early 1900s, Lilienthal reminisced, "My friends and I would take the path down Hawthorne Avenue over to Hill's Boathouse. We would swim for the day and then return home for dinner. Then we would go to the Rose Bowl dance, which was great fun. If we were still feeling like it, we would go down to the Escalle Inn for a drink and sandwiches. Then return home and sleep in the tent. The nights were quite a bit warmer then."

Only crude connections linked the lands on the north and south sides of the creek. Early 1900s visitors to the Bon Air Hotel arrived by coach at Escalle Station and took a buggy across what was called a "corduroy road" to the hotel. A corduroy road consisted simply of logs laid side-by-side over the marsh.

The first Bon Air Bridge was a drawbridge operated by two men who lived on an ark anchored to the bridge. When Judge Samuel Gardiner was growing up, he recalled, "It was not much of a bridge. It was pretty dilapidated. I think it must have been built in the 1880s and was just planks. If you wanted, you could put your foot through it." Harry Richards, who was raised in Corte Madera, recalled fishing for perch from the bridge.

RECOLLECTIONS

"In the early 1900s, Marin was a place for summer visitors and bathing was a big deal. There was a wooden boardwalk from Magnolia for pedestrians over the creek at Bon Air. We'd cross that over to the Bon Air Hotel. The swimming pool was where the palm trees are now at Marin General Hospital."

— Estelle Murray Peterson

After a big 1922 flood damaged the bridge, it was condemned. A plank pedestrian bridge was the only crossing until a concrete bridge was built in 1959, repaired in 1969, and re-done in 1994. A new bridge designed by Bay Bridge architect Donald MacDonald is pending in 2010.

"The bathhouses were gone before I came along," commented Estelle Murray Peterson, "but we would swim in the creek, and it was very nice. The water was warm."

The character of the creek changed over the years. Run-off from the clear-cut hills filled the creek with so much mud and silt old-timers remarked that by 1913 "even a rowboat must wait for the high tide." About that time the ark communities of Boardwalks #2, #3, and #4 were developing along this stretch. *(See pages 224-232 for a history of the ark communities.)* Since the arks were not hooked up to a sewer system, the creek became progressively more polluted.

Commented Biff Harris, "One had to always swim the breaststroke in Corte Madera Creek to avoid all the sewage."

▲ *12.4: Bon Air Hotel, early 1900s.*

▲ *12.5: Swimming at the Bon Air Hotel, 1914.*

A final blow to creek swimming was the year the Ross Hospital sewer conduit ruptured and contaminated the area where people swam. Three of the Dell'Era children, whose family lived on the Bon Air Hotel grounds, contracted diphtheria, and one died from it.

② Bon Air Hotel Site & Marin General Hospital

Built in the late 1800s, the Bon Air Hotel was an elegant establishment capitalizing on the warm saltwater bathing available in Corte Madera Creek. Creek water was pumped into the hotel's cement swimming pool, the first pool in Marin County. Reno Dell'Era, a former Golden Gloves champion, recalled that his father planted the palm trees, but "the large eucalyptus tree was planted by me when I was about eight years old to provide shade for our chickens." He added, "If you yelled or called, you would get an echo from the pool's shallow end." Other hotel facilities included a bowling alley, a gambling room, and a dance pavilion, but there was no heating system. Reno's brother once found a $45 gold piece on the gambling room floor.

"The hotel was a mysterious place," recalled Judge Samuel Gardiner. "It was a good hotel but primarily a trysting place for San Francisco men who would take their girlfriends there." Mrs. Randolph Doherty recalled that many fancy dances were held at the hotel.

Like many of the other Larkspur resorts, fire was the Bon Air Hotel's downfall. Oakley Dexter's 78-year-old mother, Maggie, recalled in a 1975 interview that she watched the hotel fire and thought it was in 1923. The hotel at that time was deserted and people believed that some hobos who were living there started the fire. The hotel was subsequently demolished.

"The best blackberry patch in Marin was in the ruins of the old hotel where Marin General Hospital is now," recalled Susan Turner. "In one day we could pick enough berries to make two families jelly for a year."

Marin General Hospital, a major hospital in Marin County, was built on the hotel site in May of 1952, and enlarged in 1989 with a new façade at **250 BON AIR ROAD**. During the last decade the full-service hospital, which currently has 235 acute-care beds, faced several challenges, including the need for seismic retrofitting and technological upgrading as well as changes of ownership.

• • • • •

During the years of the Roman Catholic Diocese of San Francisco's ownership of the 680 acres of Bon Air and the Greenbrae hills, the areas were part of the county. Over the years various sections were sold to different owners who had annexed some to Larkspur. As a result, some lands remained in the county, some in the city. The houses along Bayview Road south of the hospital are in the county and have not been researched. Several of them date from the early 1900s.

The Schultz Building Company began in 1911 and developed 280 acres of Millbrae Highlands on the Peninsula in 1927, and other lands in Oakland, San Bruno, and Benicia before Marin caught Niels Schultz Sr.'s eye. In 1946, when he purchased more than 600 of the 680 total acres, the diocese retained the Marin Catholic parcel and the marsh. The Schultz Building Company at that time had become a family affair with Niels Schultz Sr. and his two sons, Alvin and Niels Jr., active in the company.

Until 1949 all of Greenbrae was within the county jurisdiction and construction of the first single-family homes was begun under county auspices. The county, however, had a restrictive policy about multiple-family housing. When the Schultz Building Company was ready to begin apartment construction on the hill adjacent to Bon Air Center, they petitioned and received approval after much controversy and a court hearing, for the annexation of the 75 acres of Bon Air Hill to Larkspur.

Judge Samuel Gardiner, who at that time was both Larkspur city attorney *and* the Schultz attorney explained, "The Schultzes did not like the county zoning and control … that would not permit apartments. When Schultz failed to get permits from the county for the apartments that he wanted to build on Bon Air Hill, I worked out an arrangement with the city to annex to Larkspur. The final annexation of the present apartment and condominium area was one on which I acted for both sides with full consent." A local agency formation commission did not exist at that time to regulate annexations.

"The Bon Air area was quite a controversial thing," recalled Miriam Austin in a 1985 interview. "The

▲ 12.6: *Marin General Hospital and Bon Air Hill with a single apartment building, 1975.*

▲ 12.7: *Marin General Hospital, 2007. The eucalyptus tree planted by Reno Dell'Era is at center, rear.*

old-time idea of Marin County was an absolute taboo on any dense development, which was why there was so much controversy about the proposal for a big subdivision." When Schultz proposed the development of the property that had been open fields and cattle-grazing lands, "the county flatly refused to permit it," explained Mrs. Austin. "They didn't feel that apartments belonged in Marin County so they (Schultz Investment Company) applied for annexation to Larkspur, and the City Council was quite willing to let them go ahead with apartments," concluded Mrs. Austin.

The Schultz Building Company had a long-range view. "Larkspur was beginning to look to its future and was ready to spread out," explained Niels Schultz Sr. in an April 5, 1972 interview in *The Ebb Tide*. "It should be pointed out that the Schultz family did not ask to be annexed to Larkspur. We were invited to do so by Mayor Joseph C. Thomas. We had a choice of accepting this invitation or annexing to Corte Madera or San Rafael. We chose Larkspur." Once annexed to Larkspur, the first apartments were built overlooking Sir Francis Drake

Boulevard on the north side of Bon Air Hill where they still retain their 1950s character and modest rents.

Prior to 1949, Corte Madera Creek curved north, close to Bon Air Hill, and along the back of the southeastern section of the shopping center. According to a March 17, 1949 *Associated Press* report, a bill introduced by Marin County representative Richard McCollister proposed to change the alignment of the creek. In the article Niels Schultz Jr. reported that his company "intends to develop a recreational area along the creek, including boating facilities." He felt that the realignment of the creek was the first step in what he hoped would be a coordinated program for the development of recreational facilities in the area. Newspaper reports at the time spoke of developing yacht facilities along Corte Madera Creek.

The old creek bed formed an arc that began near the drainage channel at the east end of the paved section of South Eliseo Drive, curved away from the creek, between Mollie Stone's Market and the apartment houses, and then headed back towards the creek, through what is now Niven Park. The realignment of the creek took place between 1950 and 1952 after the State Lands Commission worked out an agreement between the state and the Schultz Building Company. The actual deed transfer of the land was made sometime between 1954 and 1958.

The Schultz Building Company traded the waters of the creek for the land along South Eliseo Drive. After the old creek bed was moved southward and westward, the land area still required additional fill before building sites could be developed. In 1965 the U.S. Army Corps of Engineers' Flood Control Project supplied the dredging spoils that were dumped on this site, creating the land for the shopping center enlargement and the housing and office projects. Additional fill was supplied by lowering the hill behind The Tamalpais where the Spyglass Apartments are located. The channel was deepened and more fill was added to the land along South Eliseo Drive.

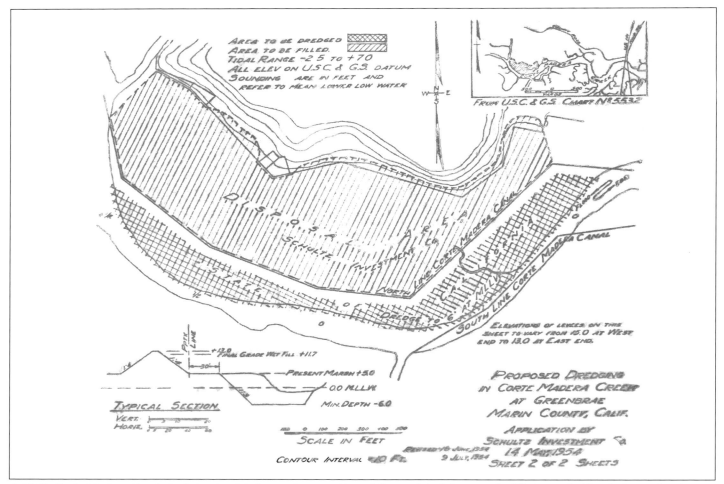

▲ 12.8: *Corte Madera Creek dredging traded the northern section of the creek bed for a newly filled parcel of land along what is now South Eliseo Drive, 1954.*

③ South Eliseo

Because of the proximity to Marin General Hospital, medical and dental offices were built close to Bon Air Road. The South Eliseo apartments were built individually between 1966 and 1970 without any master plan that would have laid them out in a controlled manner and integrated them with the environment. The Larkspur Town Meeting that was formed in 1970 attempted to put a cap on creek-side development but failed. In fact, one city councilman remarked in an *Independent Journal* article at the time, "Frankly, we don't need a citizen's committee to tell us how to run our affairs." However the town meeting group was instrumental in getting some new faces and a philosophy change on the city council, but too late to halt the creek development.

The intensive apartment construction stacked the units on Bon Air Hill and created what was called "a Chinese wall" of apartments along the creek. The construction came with a price. Slides have occurred on the upper slopes and when full moon high tides coincide with heavy rainstorms,

▲ 12.10: *A large billboard for the Bon Air Apartments on the Greenbrae hill facing the interchange raised the ire of aesthetic-minded drivers until the Larkspur city council ordered it removed in December of 1970.*

▲ 12.9: *Larkspur and Greenbrae viewed from Corte Madera Ridge, 1975. Corte Madera Creek, Larkspur Isle, and Boardwalk #1, foreground; the Tamalpais, South Eliseo, and Bon Air development, center; Greenbrae hills, background.*

creek waters lap at the pier foundations of some of the buildings.

The story goes that several teenage birdwatchers built a succession of crude duck blinds along the bank and had to knock them down and build new ones every time a new apartment house went up.

When the Larkspur housing study was done in the 1980s, the apartments and condos were predominantly occupied by seniors and retired people. According to Wanden Treanor, an attorney who specialized in condo law, the demographics of the area have changed because of the quality of the schools and high cost of freestanding homes. The population in 2010 is more evenly distributed between seniors and young families.

④ Pocket Parks Along Corte Madera Creek

Despite the early promises, not even a public path was laid out along the creek. The only recreational facilities constructed were a swimming pool and tennis courts exclusively for the apartment dwellers. The tennis courts were replaced by townhouses in 1992.

In 1972 the Schultz Building Company sold a one-third acre parcel at **594 SOUTH ELISEO DRIVE** to the city for $42,750 for park development. Sandwiched between apartments, Bon Air Landing Park was dedicated and opened in 1975 and features a fishing dock, sitting area, and picnic facilities.

Also in 1972 Clara-Belle Hamilton, a resident of The Tamalpais retirement community, looked down on the creek from her hillside residence and was concerned about the loss of public access to the shoreline. She purchased the last one-third acre lot remaining on the north side of the creek for $42,750 and dedicated it to the city for a park in 1975. The drought of 1977 slowed landscaping plans for the park, but in 1979, Hamilton Park at **1201 SOUTH ELISEO DRIVE** was finally completed, providing public access to the creek that is especially welcome to the numerous convalescent hospital patients in the area.

⑤ The Tamalpais

Although Larkspur citizens had been stewing about the creek side development in the late 1950s, their tempers boiled over when The Tamalpais high-rise senior residence was proposed for the top of Bon Air Hill at **501 VIA CASITAS**. Before Dr. John C. Siemens and Niels Schultz Sr. purchased Bon Air Hill, there were just cows grazing on the land, according to former councilman Robert Smith, who served on the Larkspur City Council from 1962 to 1966.

Today The Tamalpais looms large on the skyline of Larkspur, but its approval raised concerns in 1964. "The citizenship of Larkspur became enraged," recalled Smith. "Besides being an eyesore, it was simply too tall for the hill where it would be placed. However, the developers assured us that the structure would be no higher than the hill behind it." Ironically the hill behind the Tamalpais was bulldozed down for fill when the creek bed was moved and to create a level site on the top for the Spyglass condominiums.

In May of 1964 the Planning Commission turned the proposal down cold despite a newspaper ad that promised property tax revenues estimated at approximately $110,000. At the first public hearing before the council, few people were aware of the eleven-story building proposed on the hilltop. The vote was 3-2 to approve it on June 3, 1964.

▲ *12.11: Dedication of Bon Air Landing Park by city council members, Parks and Recreation commissioners, city staff and local residents, 1975.*

▲ 12.12: Construction of The Tamalpais, June 1968.

ON THE TAMALPAIS PROPOSAL

"One citizen paid for a helicopter to fly to the height called for in the proposal and rolled out a long length of material from the designated height to the ground. Then he hired a photographer to record it for publication."

— Bob Smith

When word of the approval got out, citizens began calling for a reconsideration of the vote. Over 1,200 signed petitions spurred the city council to agree to reconsider their approval. At the council meeting, a crowd of 340 protesters attended and it lasted seven-and-one-half hours but failed to change the original vote. The development of The Tamalpais high-rise "was a major fight," commented Judge Samuel Gardiner. "We had all kinds of hearings about that and tremendous opposition to it. Lots of people felt as I did that it was so much better to have 100 people in 100 rooms in a single high-rise than it was to have 100 single family dwellings scattered all over the county. I sat through these hearings as City Attorney, but the decisions were mostly policy matters." Judge Gardiner recalled in a 1985 interview, "the City Council at this time was a more friendly group and asked me about policy as well as the law."

Commented Councilman Vaughn Marker at the time, "I think a good part of this town is being bribed by money reputed to come in from taxes." Three years later, in 1967, the city received a rude awakening. The tax revenue had become a pipe dream. The ownership of The Tamalpais had changed from a for-profit organization to a non-profit. Between the time of the approval and final construction and occupancy in 1969, state legislation had been passed that exempted non-profit organizations from property taxes. Unfortunately a use permit condition did not protect the city from the loss of taxes, according to Gardiner.

According to *The Tamalpais, The Place and its People: A History*, by Loren L. Jay and Wanda Ramey Queirolo, 1989, The Tamalpais did agree to pay the City of Larkspur an amount 'in-lieu of taxes' equal to the amount that would have been assessed ... for services received, principally police, fire, sewage, and 911 emergency response services, and has been doing so since its inception.

Forty-one years later in 2010, 330 residents live in the high-rise that is a highly visible landmark. Despite the initial turmoil over its construction, over 20% of "Tam" residents hail from Larkspur and the Ross Valley – including some of its original detractors. Early residents included photographer Emma Gilman and philanthropist Clara-Belle Hamilton. More recently George Gmahling, who grew up on Hawthorne Avenue, and his wife, Georgene, moved in.

A waiting list of eight months to eight years for the 460 to 1,500-sq-ft apartments range from $75,000 to $500,000. Amenities include a dining room with Mt. Tamalpais and bay views, a swimming pool, fitness center, and library. On-site physician services, hospitalization, private assisted living apartments, and skilled nursing care is available at no additional cost. The Tamalpais is welcoming a second generation of Marin residents as the children of its original residents make it their home.

▲ *12.13: Development pioneers Niels Schultz Jr. and Niels Schultz Sr., 1983. In 1946 they bought 635 acres and developed more than 1,000 houses, 1,500 apartments, and scores of businesses between Highway 101 and Manor Road in Kentfield.*

▲ *12.14: Bon Air Logo designed by Michael Manwaring, and Dennis Patton's 1980 sculpture "Tamalpais, The Sleeping Maiden," a 17-foot COR-TEN™ steel tribute to Mt. Tamalpais, 2007.*

⑥ Bon Air Center

Before the realignment of Corte Madera Creek, it curved northward away from the current creek location, between the market and the apartment houses, and then curved back towards the current location, through what is now Niven Park west of Barry Way and Drake's Landing Road. The Coast Miwok once had a village at the west end of where Bon Air Center is today. Two of the original oaks are still there. A large buckeye tree may also hark back to the early days. According to a 1909 report by N. C. Nelson, a midden was located near today's office buildings. Rocks and trees are all that remain of a 25-foot-high mound that was graded down to provide fill for the surrounding marsh.

According to 1972 *Marin Independent Journal* interviews with Niels Schultz Sr. and Niels Schultz Jr., they envisioned a mixture of houses, apartments, offices, and businesses on the more than 600 acres they had purchased from the archdiocese. Single-family homes were planned on the north side of Sir Francis Drake Boulevard and multiple-family homes as well as commercial and professional offices on the south side.

"The center has evolved about the way we envisioned it because the original plan was broad," explained Niels Schultz Jr. in a 1983 interview. "The reason we have the depth behind Petrini's (in 2010, Mollie Stone's) is that in the original plan, the creek was right there and we had planned that the additions would be like an open 'V' with the apex at a junior department store, and then the center would swing back to Sir Francis Drake Blvd. When the creek bed was changed by the Flood Control Project, it allowed for a more flexible plan."

The first houses were constructed across Sir Francis Drake Boulevard near the La Cuesta intersection in 1948. The first structure in the shopping center was the Bon Air Super Market owned by James

▲ *12.15: A rock outcrop and heritage bay tree near an office building at Bon Air Center.*

▲ *12.16: Green Brae with Corte Madera Creek at top right and the future Sir Francis Drake Boulevard at left center, 1916. The line of oaks is where the west entrance of the shopping center is now.*

▲ 12.17: *Greenbrae, looking southwest, 1952: Bon Air Super Market (center); intersection of La Cuesta Drive and Sir Francis Drake Boulevard (right); Bon Air Hill apartments (upper right).*

Kilpatrick and built in 1952 at the west end of Bon Air Center. Petrini's market was added to the center in 1964 and was replaced by Mollie Stone's in 1996. In 1974 and 1977 major regional centers were proposed for the site and resoundingly turned down by the City of Larkspur because of the fear of traffic impacts.

In 1983 a more locally-oriented shopping center was designed with a commercial area of 166,000 square feet. All development on the site was limited to uses that would not generate more traffic than 4,500 additional cars per day. Face-lifts in 1985 and 1999, including new paint and awnings, created a more modern look. New landscaping continues to complement the remaining two large heritage oaks at the west entrance.

In 2010 Bon Air Center had over 50 stores, anchored by David M. Brian (a fine gift store), CVS Pharmacy, and Mollie Stone's, and everything from upscale women's clothing, shoe stores, and jewelry shops to a health food store, dry cleaners, an exercise studio, and four banks.

BEFORE BON AIR WAS DEVELOPED

"I remember hunting rabbits, squirrels, robins, quail, and raccoons. One day I found bones and brought them home. My mother was upset with me as I had disturbed the dead."

— Reno Dell'Era, who lived at the Bon Air Hotel

▲ 12.18: *Bon Air storefronts, 1960s.*

▲ 12.19: *Petrini's in the Bon Air Shopping Center, 1977.*

▲ 12.20: *Multiuse path along Corte Madera Creek and Cape Marin homes, 2007.*

▲ 12.21: *Eucalyptus picnic area and old arks location, 2007.*

▲ 12.22: *In 1983 a major drainage channel formed a lake at the end of what is now Barry Way. Local children called it the "Pollywog Pond."*

▲ 12.23: *The same view as above, with landscaped flood control pond by Cape Marin Community Center, 2007.*

⑦ Cape Marin

The new land created between the shopping center and the creek became the site of Cape Marin in the 1980s with a total of 129 single-family homes. Twenty affordable-housing units designed as duplexes were mixed in with the market rate homes and are difficult to distinguish or locate within the development. A pedestrian walkway located between Gregory Place and Mark Place connects the homes to the back of the shopping center and was remodeled in 1989. The old creek bed and drainage channel were incorporated into the landscape plan. The design of a water pond whose level can be controlled during heavy storms created a visual amenity as well as a drainage control area at the end of Barry Way, named in honor of Harlan Barry's services as Larkspur city manager in the 1980s.

To compensate for the lack of public bike and pedestrian paths along South Eliseo, parks and paths were required as part of the approval process for the addition of housing, offices, and commercial uses at the center. The path follows the creek edge and continues under the freeway to tie into the county trails system. A one-and-one-half acre grassy park was created between the knoll and the pond and was named "Niven Park" in honor of Jim Niven, the only Larkspur volunteer firefighter killed in the line of duty. In addition, two vista spots and a rest area were located at the creek-side edge of the park – one at the point, under a large eucalyptus tree, and another near the office buildings, in the flagpole seating area.

A clump of eucalyptus trees at the edge of the creek marks the approximate spot where a small number of arks were anchored until the Schultz Investment Company purchased the land. Some of the arks moved to Boardwalk #1 *(see page 232)* and some moved to the Greenbrae Boardwalk *(see page 305)*.

⑧ Drake's Landing & Drake's View

A popular bowling alley, Greenbrae Lanes, was located at the east end of the hill after the 1950-1952 realignment of the creek had filled that portion of the site. The Marin Airporter originally operated in the bowling alley area. According to Grace Hughes, her father William Melbern, who had a taxi service in Sausalito, realized the need for airport transportation and started a bus service with "Bouncing Betty," a yellow school bus, in 1975. As demand grew the bus service became the Marin Airporter, which moved to Larkspur Landing in 1985. The rest of the land stayed vacant until 1982 when the bowling alley building was torn down for the 122,000 square feet of Drake's Landing office buildings. The residential portion of this development began in 1988 with the 42 townhouses of Drake's View built atop the southern knoll above Niven Park.

▲ 12.24: Marin Rowing Association building, 2006.

▲ 12.25: Fire Station No. 2, 2007.

In 1959 a large 300-berth yacht harbor was proposed for the site just east of Highway 101 but was never constructed. Another boating facility was proposed for the state right-of-way on Corte Madera Creek, beneath the Greenbrae interchange, but it was never approved. Finally in 1991, the Marin Rowing Association (known as the "Marin Rowing Club" when it was located north of Wood Island) built a dock and boathouse, which combines boat storage and meeting space, adjacent to the southbound freeway on-ramp. Land for the facility was dedicated by the developers of Drake's Landing as part of the approvals for the office project. In June of 2004 a modern-style, 13,700-sq-ft building designed by the team of John Winder and Geoff Gibson of Winder Architects and Sandy Armstrong of Marin Rowing Association enlarged the crew's boat storage facility.

⑨ Larkspur Fire Station No. 2

The Larkspur Fire Station No. 2 was built at **15 BARRY WAY** to provide protection for the Greenbrae area. Completed in 1991, this station replaced the original 1960s station that did not meet seismic safety standards, was not accessible to the handicapped, and was flooded in the heavy rains of 1982. A plaque commemorates the dedication of the building to Alfred J. Malvino, a 25-year member of the Larkspur city council from 1966 to 1991. Malvino was a long-term resident of Hillview Gardens and a well-liked and widely respected man.

The two-story building meets all code requirements and houses three fire fighters daily around the clock. Sleeping quarters are upstairs with a traditional fire pole connecting the two stories. Because of heavy traffic on Barry Way, there is no room for fire engines to maneuver in the street and back into the station. Hence, this is a "drive through" station with engines entering from the rear of the building and exiting at the front.

The modest rise southeast of Fire Station No. 2 and above Niven Park is all that remains of what once was a small hill that created a dramatic curve in the creek. Known to picnickers and boaters as "Poison Oak Point," the hill appeared prominently in period photographs and was often the vantage point for early views westward across the salt marshes toward Mt. Tamalpais. By 1950 the hill was ringed by a dirt road that gave access to a few houseboats at the creek's edge.

⑩ Green Brae Ranch Site & Development

Before development of the lands south of Sir Francis Drake Blvd., the Green Brae Ranch had been the only development on the north hillside. Tasmanian-born James Ross managed his family's 900-acre Green Brae Ranch until his death in 1875. The land continued as a dairy farm in the swale marked by today's Eliseo Drive and Bretano Way until acquired by the Schultz Building Company in 1946.

The elder Schultz was questioned about using the name "Greenbrae" for the proposed development. Recalled Schultz, "Green Brae was the recognized train stop for San Quentin and everybody discouraged us from using 'Greenbrae' because of the link with the prison. I liked the name and I'm not sorry we kept it."

Niels Schultz Jr., who had been serving in the military in Italy at the time of the Green Brae land purchase, reported, "The project was pretty well initiated when I got back. The first thing when I got back was to take a look. Initially it had some trees on the hills but it was a beautiful piece of land along the road and the land got steeper as you went up."

Explained Schultz Jr., "Greenbrae was planned as a total community because the prospective streets had to be planned into different areas and had to go with the terrain.... The roads traverse the slopes on the grade. Only two major entrances were designed [in order] to restrict access to Sir Francis Drake Boulevard." According to a 1998 article in the *Twin Cities Times* by Ellen Murphy, Niels Schultz Sr. took great pains to engineer the roads and driveways around the majestic oak trees to disturb as little of the terrain as possible, to split roads that crossed slopes, and to include cul-de-sacs.

When ground was broken on the street work in May of 1946, all of Greenbrae was within the county jurisdiction. Construction of the early single-family homes was begun under county auspices. The first 197 homes were built in the lower area along Bretano Way and Corte Morada with the main entrance at La Cuesta Drive. The first house completed was at 21 Via Cheparro and was occupied by Niels Schultz Jr. from May of 1947 to September of 1955.

The Schultz sales office operated out of the old ranch house until 1949 when it moved to the turreted mini-castle sales office at **500 SIR FRANCIS DRAKE BOULEVARD** (the corner of Sir Francis Drake and La Cuesta). Designed by architect Albert Farr of Piedmont, it was built in the French Chateau style, a Farr specialty. According to Niels Schultz Jr., the intent of the building was to contribute to the landscaping and entrance character of the development behind it without being dated to the styles of that time.

The early homes sold for the high price of $10,500, a far cry from the often multimillion dollar price tag in 2010. An early sales brochure called it "a model community... with its own modern shopping district, schools, churches and a well-balanced residential district of beautiful homes."

When the later phases of the Greenbrae hill development were proposed in 1951, those sections were annexed to Larkspur, which had less stringent site requirements than the county. Commented former city councilman, Charles Curley, "It was a win-win situation for both because the City Council got the increased tax revenues and Schultz got much more lenient multiple dwelling and single-family ordinances. The minimum county lot size was a quarter-acre; Larkspur's was an eighth-acre. Schultz was able to double the land use in the remaining part of Greenbrae. If you were a bird looking down on a map of Greenbrae, you could clearly see the line where all the Larkspur houses are with little patches around them, versus where the Greenbrae county houses are surrounded by a lot of land."

"The Schultz property brought in a different type of resident to Larkspur," commented former police chief Howard Clark. "A higher class resident, really … and it changed from the shipyard-type employee to those who were business-type men, lawyers and doctors."

The annexation of the Greenbrae lands to Larkspur created a hodgepodge of city and county boundaries. Commented reporter and longtime resident Beth Ashley, "Some people are

▲ *12.26: Green Brae Ranch, viewed here from Sir Francis Drake Boulevard in 1920, was located where Parkside Way (off Eliseo Dr.) is today.*

▲ *12.27: New homes in Greenbrae with Greenbrae Company building (center) at the intersection of Sir Francis Drake Boulevard and La Cuesta Drive with empty hills beyond, 1949.*

in Larkspur and their next-door neighbor lives in the county. When we moved here, we had a San Rafael address, but my zip code is Kentfield. Part of Greenbrae is in San Rafael and part is still in the county. The only part of Larkspur I identify with is the Larkspur Library."

Many of the subsequent homes, whose style was often referred to as "Burgar homes" after their builder Edward W. Burgar, Inc., were built in groups of 30 to 50. Roads were engineered so building pads could step up the slopes. Divider strips to preserve the oaks and cul-de-sacs were part of the design.

A number of the landslides that have plagued the hillside areas of Greenbrae resulted from the early grading, according to a June 14, 1974 report by city engineer Roy H. Hoffman. The report stated that, "The slide experiences in the area [Greenbrae] point almost exclusively to the classic situation of uncontrolled surface and subsurface waters activating movement of fills which were made in gullies."

In 1949 part of the old ranch house site near Eliseo Drive was donated by the Schultz Building Company to the Kentfield School District for the Greenbrae Elementary School. The school was completed in 1951 and became a major community gathering place. Since neighbors' homes were on different levels, chitchat over the fence and casual meetings were difficult. "The school was the big glue that tied the parents and kids together," commented Beth Ashley. "Everyone met at the school. The kids came through my back fence gate to go to the school and to my cookie drawer, and I went through the fence to the PTA meetings. However, we didn't know where people lived."

The school buildings, although long a centerpiece of the community, were demolished in 1986 after declining enrollment forced consolidation with the Bacich School further west. "When the school closed, I was very sad," sighed Ashley. "Although a park was required, it is surrounded by large homes and not inviting to outsiders." The seven-acre school site was developed as a block of 19 homes along Parkside Way, surrounding the newly created Greenbrae School Park. Most of those homes were built in 1988 and 1989.

Although the trees have grown up and blocked Ashley's view of Mt. Tamalpais, the changes to the basic ranch-style homes have not been as dramatic as in other sections of the city. The neighborhood has been kept up and people have planted gardens in the dividers between the uphill and downhill sections of some streets.

"Today, there are virtually no empty lots in Greenbrae," reported Greenbrae resident and former Larkspur city councilman Donald Graff. "Expansion in the area is limited to increases in individual home size, with some of the original single-level Burgar homes now having a second level. The attraction of the area remains – its convenient location to shopping, to transportation facilities such as the freeway, bus and ferry, and its outstanding schools. In 2007 the population of the Greenbrae portion of Larkspur was approximately equal to the Larkspur population south of Corte Madera Creek."

▲ 12.28: *Reporter and longtime Greenbrae resident, Beth Ashley, 2007.*

NEIGHBORHOOD CHANGES

"Most women work and people don't meet in the street and talk casually. There are all different ages but mostly younger and fewer older people. I don't even know the names of my neighbors. The loss of the school changed it all."

— Beth Ashley, 2007

▲ 12.29: *Known as "The Castle," the original Schultz Development sales office has been replaced by a local real estate company, 2007.*

SAN QUENTIN PENINSULA
Quiet neighborhoods and transit facilities surround a famous prison.

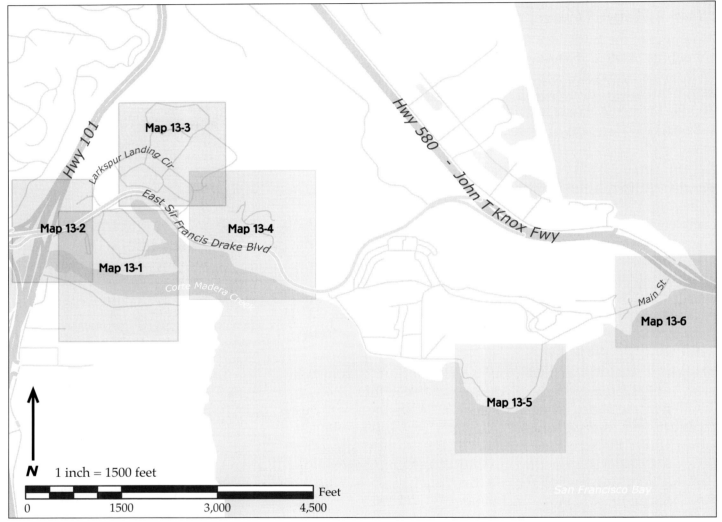

▲ 13.0: *Reference map of the San Quentin Peninsula. Each sub-chapter has a detailed companion map (see key) featuring general and specific points of interest highlighted in the text.*

MAP KEY
13-1 Ferry Terminal, Greenbrae Boardwalk & Environs *page 298*

13-2 Southwest San Quentin Peninsula *page 309*

13-3 Larkspur Landing *page 314*

13-4 South Central San Quentin Peninsula *page 319*

13-5 San Quentin State Prison* *page 328*

13-6 San Quentin Village & Point* *page 334*

*Although San Quentin State Prison and San Quentin Village lie outside of Larkspur's city limits, they are included in this book because their opportunities and challenges fall within Larkspur's sphere of influence and play an important role in the city's political, economic, and visual life.

SAN QUENTIN PENINSULA

San Quentin Peninsula, the smallest of Marin's peninsulas, has the longest recorded history. Although it is the site of a much disputed landing spot for Sir Francis Drake, no one challenges the fact that three Miwok Indian villages, one of which may have been the largest in Marin County, were situated there until the middle of the nineteenth century.

• • • • • • • • • • • • •

The Spanish first explored northern California in the early 1600s, but they did not discover San Francisco Bay until 1775. In 1804 Spain made California a province and began establishing ranchos. The peninsula was called "Punta de Quintin Corte Madera, la Laguna y Cañada de San Anselmo" by the Spanish land grant. The peninsula's history changed again when the lands became part of the Mexican Republic in 1824.

During the Mexican-Indian conflicts in California, a Miwok Chief named "Marin" was hotly pursued by Mexican troops and took refuge in the small islands lying near the entrance to a creek known as "Estero de San Rafael de Aquanni." Seeing the islands

▲ 13.2: Sculptor Dennis Patton installing the Sir Francis Drake statue at the eastern entrance to Larkspur in 1989.

◀ 13.1: Aerial view of San Quentin Peninsula; Highway 101 (foreground), Hutchinson Quarry, Sanitary District No. 1 treatment plant, and Remillard Brick Kiln (center), San Quentin State Prison and San Quentin Village (background), 1960.

surrounded by rafts, the Mexicans assumed they were outnumbered and retreated to a nearby neck of land, where they met strong resistance from a Miwok warrior named "Quintin." The battle was the Miwok's last stand. The Mexicans captured Quintin and detained him in San Francisco for two years. Because he was a good sailor, he was employed subsequently by the missionary fathers and put in charge of a trading vessel that made frequent runs between Sonoma and San Francisco.

In later years, after Quintin was captured, he was unofficially glorified as a "saint." The point where he had been captured came to be known as Punta de Quentin (Quentin's Point), later changed to Punta de San Quentin (Point San Quentin).

In the 1840s California was a political hotbed. Not only did Mexico relinquish its claim to California, enabling it to join the United States, but gold was discovered in 1848, resulting in a meteoric increase in the population. The politically and financially pressed Mexican governor, Juan B. Alvarado, deeded the land known as "Punta de Quentin" to Juan B. R. Cooper, a brother-in-law of General Mariano Vallejo, to repay a debt of $5,250. For that small sum, Cooper received the major part of Ross Valley, including what is now Kentfield, Ross, and part of San Anselmo, plus the San Quentin Peninsula.

Cooper, an absentee landowner, hired Timothy Murphy to look after the cattle he grazed on part of the property. Local Native Americans supplied the labor force and raised their own crops of beans, watermelons, and corn on the land.

In 1850 Cooper sold Punta de Quentin to Benjamin R. Buckelew. Two years later, Buckelew sold the State of California 20 acres of land along the southern shore of the point for San Quentin State Prison. In 1969 the City of Larkspur extended its city limits by annexing 200 acres of the peninsula east of Highway 101 up to the boundaries of San Quentin State Prison.

Today the San Quentin Peninsula presents an unusual mix of history and progress. Beginning with San Quentin Village and the prison at the eastern end, which date back to the mid-1800s, the history moves westward into the early 1890s, with the stack and kiln of the Remillard brickyard serving as a reminder of the bustling brick-making community. All that remains of the mid-1900s Hutchinson Quarry operation are the rugged 120-foot-high gray stone cliffs from which the gray rock was blasted.

A survivor from the 1920s and 1930s is the Greenbrae Boardwalk ark community that grew up along the creek across from the peninsula. In 1978 the Larkspur Landing offices, apartments, and shopping center were developed at the base of the cliffs. In 2009 the bulldozers went to work again re-contouring the land for the next phase of development.

LARKSPUR FERRY TERMINAL, GREENBRAE BOARDWALK & ENVIRONS

The San Quentin Peninsula tour begins at the south end of the ferry terminal parking lot.

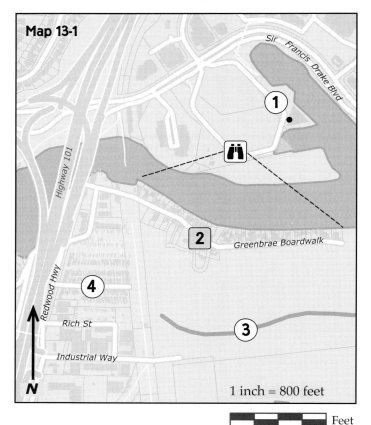

KEY LOCATIONS
1. Ferry Terminal
- Greenbrae Boardwalk Viewpoint
2. Greenbrae Boardwalk
3. Corte Madera Marsh Ecological Reserve
4. Industrial Area
• Address of Note

▲ 13.3: *View of the Larkspur Ferry Terminal site and Greenbrae Boardwalk; Wood Island is the dark hill on the right, 1945.*

① Larkspur Ferry Terminal

The patchwork of the old and the new on the peninsula is dramatically visible in the juxtaposition of the Larkspur Ferry Terminal and the Greenbrae Boardwalk, which is visible across the creek from the south end of the ferry parking lot. Between 1970 and 1973 a major controversy swirled around the location of the proposed ferry terminal. Conservationists pleaded unsuccessfully with the Golden Gate Bridge District to build it close to Point San Quentin, where historically a ferry terminal had operated.

Instead, the terminal was located at **101 EAST SIR FRANCIS DRAKE BOULEVARD** on a 25-acre site at the mouth of Corte Madera Creek. Designed by the architectural firm of Braccia, DeBrer, Heglund, and built by contractor Williams & Burrows, Inc., the intent was to "blend the architecture with the landscape." The mammoth, triangular steel-frame roof over the main terminal weighed 350 tons and cost about $1.5 million.

Dedicated on December 11, 1976, the Larkspur Ferry Terminal was described as a "16,000-square-foot triangular space frame." Critics called it a "Tinkertoy® building" that offered no protection from the foggy summer winds nor the winter rains. One satirical headline scoffed, "A Lavish Project – Three Years Late and $9 Million Over Budget."

Others disagreed. Ferry manager S.M. Kowleski countered, "When you build a ferry terminal like this, you want to do it right." Gene Rexrode, 1990 Bridge District secretary, commented, "Recognition of this effort has been made by the granting of three awards by the American Institute of Architecture and the American Institute of Steel Construction in 1977, 1980, and 1982."

Not only was the design of the structure dramatic, but construction was a challenge. Larkspur City Engineer

▲ 13.4: *Early construction of the Larkspur Ferry Terminal before dredging, 1975.*

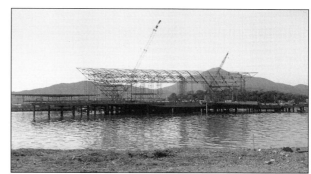

▲ 13.5: *Larkspur Ferry Terminal almost complete, 1975.*

▲ 13.6: *Larkspur Ferry Terminal, 2008.*

Phiroze Wadia, who worked for Kaiser Engineers at the time and was involved in the design of the ferry terminal, commented in 2009, "The foundations go down 150 feet, as the soil is very soft there. When the ferry boats hit the pillars coming into dock there are big lateral loads."

Ferry access required dredging a two-mile approach channel, a turning basin, and berthing areas. The original parking lot was designed to accommodate 888 vehicles; it was expanded in 1989 to hold 1,149. By 2009 the number had climbed to 1,800. In addition, racks have been provided for over 70 bicycles.

The GT *Marin*, powered by a gas turbine engine, was the first of the Golden Gate

Bridge, Highway, and Transportation District's three 750-passenger ferries that went into service for the Larkspur-San Francisco run in 1976. After the ferries had been in service for a short time, they were ordered to reduce speeds when approaching and departing the Larkspur terminal because of excessive water movement and erosion along the shore caused by the ferry-generated wave action.

The troublesome gas turbine engines were converted to diesel engines in 1985, and the commute service was expanded. The biggest boost in speed came in 1998 with the addition of the high-speed catamaran, MV *Del Norte*, which cut commute time to 30 minutes. A second high-speed catamaran that was added in 2001 increased the number of round-trips from 26 to 40. The spirits of commuters rose in 1986 when a new shelter was built with tables, chairs, and an energy-saving heating system.

The ferries came to the rescue and carried record numbers of commuters in January of 1982, when mud slides closed the Waldo Grade, and again after the Loma Prieta earthquake in October of 1989. By 2008 the ferries transported approximately 1.4 million people a year between Larkspur and the San Francisco ferry building.

Some 30 years after the advent of ferry service, the terminal faces the challenge of success. Since public transit connections are limited, the parking lot overflows onto landscaped areas and adjacent parking lots. Ferry ridership has increased 45% since 1997, and another increase is projected if a train connection is developed between Larkspur and Sonoma County. Plans to build a two-story parking structure to handle the heavy demand are still pending in 2010.

The design of the ferry terminal, which was originally controversial, has become an accepted part of the landscape. Phiroze Wadia is proud of how the building has matured, and commented, "It still looks like new. It is a landmark structure and the entrance to Larkspur from the bay. No other cities have this kind of entrance from the bay."

▲ 13.7: *The end of the original Greenbrae Boardwalk was approximately where the cruiser is docked at number 51, 2008.*

② Greenbrae Boardwalk

↪ *The Greenbrae Boardwalk points of interest can be seen by looking across the creek from the south end of the ferry terminal parking lot. Ark numbers are also address numbers on the boardwalk.*

Corte Madera Creek acts as a moat between the Greenbrae Boardwalk, the activity of suburbia, and the drone of Highway 101. "You can be in the bustle of San Francisco and drive 20 minutes, and your neighbors are clapper rails," said attorney Wanden Treanor, an 18-year boardwalk homeowner. A world unto itself, the 2,000-foot-long Greenbrae Boardwalk is bordered by Corte Madera Creek, San Francisco Bay, the Corte Madera Marsh Ecological Reserve, and busy Highway 101. Although it is partially surrounded by Larkspur (except for the marsh), the boardwalk is unincorporated and falls under county jurisdiction.

By viewing the boardwalk from the ferry terminal, the fronts of the homes are visible, and more of their character is revealed than from the boardwalk itself. As local historian and longtime resident Lee Miller commented, "Homeowners consider the creek to be their front and the boardwalk to be their back."

Ark communities are a unique development in the San Francisco Bay Area. The original houseboats of the Bay Area are built on the center of a barge that provides a surrounding deck area. The barge floats the house and allows it to be anchored on the water, on mud flats, or even on dry land. When living quarters were added to them, the houseboats were similar to a ship's cabin mounted on the hull. Although many of the structures have been altered or destroyed over the years, the arched roofs and shiplap siding of some arks are still visible.

Only a few arks are still mounted on the original barges upon which they floated, such as **49 GREENBRAE BOARDWALK**, three houses to the east of the hexagonal tower at 41 Greenbrae Boardwalk, and **111 GREENBRAE BOARDWALK**, six houses east of the canal. In 2009 it was the only one that still floated, according to Ed Epting.

The saga of the ark at 111 Greenbrae Boardwalk is typical of the unique development of the boardwalk. Built in Islais Creek in San Francisco by Ed Winters and Lou Kearny, the ark has a concrete hull divided into six compartments. Epting's father told him that the concrete of the hull was mixed with some "stuff" that came in bales from Austria and made the concrete waterproof. Whatever the "stuff" was, the ark has never leaked. The ark was towed over to 111 Greenbrae Boardwalk when it was completed in 1903 and has been there ever since.

Greenbrae Boardwalk residents live in 49 dwellings that are frequently clusters of structures with curved ark roofs, shed roofs, hipped roofs, and gables. Entrance decks and those that encircle the houses are common features. Many early arks came from Belvedere, the Oakland estuary, Santa Venetia, and other Bay Area locations, and were floated to the boardwalk when development encroached on them or ownership changed. According to Lee Miller, "In the 1920s they were used as weekend retreats. There were no house numbers, but the places had names such as *Anchorage, Snug Harbor, Tranquility*, and *Pirates Roost*. If someone asked where so-and-so lived, we would say, 'Go down to the *Mudhen*, and it is two more down.'" The favorite swimming hole at the time was on the west side of Wood Island.

Unlike other ark communities, the Greenbrae Boardwalk calls all the units "homes." The typical house foundation is a wooden stud construction sitting several inches below the mud level to prevent marine life from eating the sill. Stud replacement varies depending on the material used and tidal flows. The foundations of more recent homes at **61** and **125 GREENBRAE BOARDWALK** use galvanized steel pipe and I-beam studs, which rest on well-sunk wooden mud sills that allow for wider spans and a longer life. Two-story buildings are viewed with concern by the residents, who fear they are setting a precedent for future remodeling or construction on the one remaining vacant lot that lacks waterfront access.

Today Federal Emergency Management Agency (FEMA) and Greenbrae Boardwalk permits require the floor level of a new house or a remodeling project to meet a specified height above mean lower low tide. Access to the boardwalk had a history of flooding until the January of 2008 storm. Boardwalk resident engineer Peter Hogg and county public works engineer Jack Curley stemmed the high tide during a severe storm with a 40-foot-long polyurethane tube filled with 2,240 gallons of water, which blocked floodwaters at the entrance to the boardwalk.

▲ *13.8: Arks that retain their barge foundations, such as the one at 49 Greenbrae Boardwalk, were often refugees from other ark communities that were destroyed by flood control projects, 2008.*

▲ *13.9: The only original ark that still floats is at 111 Greenbrae Boardwalk. It is set lower to the marsh than newer ones, which have had to comply with FEMA requirements, 2008.*

▲ 13.10: *Greenbrae Boardwalk with just two arks anchored there. Note the barge hull of the ark in the foreground, early 1920s.*

Before 1930 there was no Highway 101. The way to reach Green Brae was by ferry from San Francisco to Sausalito, and then by train to either Baltimore Park or the Green Brae Station. An unimproved road went from Kentfield to San Quentin, and an unimproved county road that paralleled the present Highway 101 crossed Corte Madera Creek with a wooden approach and wooden hand-cranked lift bridge. The only portion of that county road remaining is the 400-foot section of frontage road now used for the Greenbrae Boardwalk parking.

The earliest dwellings evolved from duck-hunting shacks and arks that people just used on weekends. Recalled early fisherman Charlie Flynn Sr., in a 1978 newspaper article, "On the weekend, they'd all be fishin' and huntin', layin' around. … During the Depression, they stood here. It was a lot cheaper than San Francisco." In 1918 Lee Miller's father, who lived in Corte Madera, had a hunting shack on the boardwalk and a duck blind with portholes and seats covered with palm fronds, which was located on the eastern shore of the salt marsh.

Life on the boardwalk was not an idyllic vacation. When the original *Mudhen* (which is still at 121 Greenbrae Boardwalk but has since been remodeled) was floated over from Santa Venetia by Les Crump in 1924, he recalled that "there was no boardwalk at that time. Food was brought by boat, and water in large milk cans. There was no electricity, and a Coleman lantern was used for light. Wood and coal were used for heating. Ice for the cooler was delivered. They even came by boat to collect the rent."

Although the railroad trestle was built in 1884, the first bridge to connect the boardwalk to land was not built until 1917. Everyone had a rowboat, and local lore boasted that a precise timing of the oar strokes attracted the fish to the surface and the waiting hooks. Fishermen got their bait fish and pollywogs in the quarry ponds and smelt at the end of the peninsula. Lucky fishermen would have their pictures taken when they caught a bass. Local raconteur Ed Epting reported that the best spot for catching fish was by the point and that one time someone even hooked a ferryboat, but added, "You know what liars fishermen are."

Epting's uncle, who worked as a brick mason at the Remillard brick kiln across the creek, built one of the earliest homes at 33 Greenbrae Boardwalk in 1903 with his father. According to Ed, his uncle and grandfather first built a 40- x 30-ft house on stilts. Then they built a barge behind it, upside down, and then turned it upright. At a high tide, they floated the barge under the house. Because it floated, it suffered no damage in the 1906 earthquake. In 1922 they added a regular foundation.

In the 1930s, according to old-timer Dorothy Wilmes, land across the natural marsh inlet at

▲ 13.11: *In 2008 90-year-old Ed Epting's family still owned one of the early larks at 33 Greenbrae Boardwalk.*

▲ 13.12: *The original 50-50 Club, far left, was the social gathering place and arbiter of boardwalk life in the 1920s. The hexagonal tower at nearby 41 Greenbrae Boardwalk was built in 1990, and is shown here in 2008.*

BOARDWALK RECONSTRUCTION

The main boardwalk has been replaced three or four times over the years. In 1930 it was expanded to three boards wide for half its length and two boards wide the rest of the way. When the 1930 boardwalk was replaced in 1940, the boards ran horizontally. In 2009 composite boards of wood and plastic fibers were installed up to the bridge over the slough just past 69 Greenbrae Boardwalk. Some of the residents objected to the composite boards, so wooden boards were installed when the final section to 145 Greenbrae Boardwalk, naturally called "The Last House," was redone.

▲ 13.13: *Greenbrae Boardwalk undergoing renovation, 1940.*

the beginning of the present main boardwalk (where the concrete canal easement is located) was leased for approximately $2 a month. When the land was subdivided under the Marin County Subdivision Act of 1933, lots were put up for sale by Hugh Porter, who also sold the lots on Boardwalk #1 in Larkspur.

Access to Corte Madera Creek by boat was required by the rules of subdivision formation at that time. The lots sold for $15-per-front-foot facing the creek (which was considered the road), and $10-per-front-foot on the marsh side. "The reason the lots are weird-shaped is that they just drew the lot lines around the existing houses," explained Miller.

Former longtime resident Katherine Whidden, whose family began coming to the boardwalk in 1922, recalled walking over from Baltimore Park to the creek, where they would rent a boat from Bill Kissling to go fishing. In those days the only house that was not an ark was **43 GREENBRAE BOARDWALK**, the 50-50 Club, which is visible across the creek one house to the left of the hexagonal tower building. The shingled club is a cluster of small buildings with different roof forms – several shed roofs and a gable.

In the 1920s the all-male club, which contained a bunkhouse and club room, was the focal point of activity. According to early member Don Crews, the club was formed by a group of San Francisco tradesmen who came to the creek to hunt, fish, and drink but "never to play cards because that could lead too easily to fights." Crews continued, "The 50-50 meant share and share alike. The members shared equally in the work and the fun."

In the 1930s the portion of the boardwalk that extended from the unpaved county road to 69 Greenbrae Boardwalk consisted of three widths of 2- x 12-inch salvaged planks mounted lengthwise on the underframing of the boardwalk. A further extension was only two feet wide and used just two widths of boards. A thin galvanized wire rail running the length of the boardwalk provided some safety. The boardwalk felt like a springboard when walked on. The challenge was to try to run the length of the planks without falling off. "If you got drunk, you drowned," chuckled Charlie Flynn Sr., a former longtime resident.

Access to the boardwalk was not the only daunting problem faced by early residents. Obtaining clean drinking water was a major challenge that required rowing across the creek to a spring near the entrance to the Green Brae railroad tunnel, or to a beach called "The Springs" west of Paradise Cay in Corte Madera. Don Crews recalled an underground spring that could be accessed by a big rock on the Green Brae hillside. The Corte Madera spring was preferred because a "hobo camp" was located near the railroad tunnel.

Although there were only six ark dwellers in 1921, their request for water service from the Marin Municipal Water District was approved, and a two-inch line was connected to a twelve-inch pipe on Sir Francis Drake Boulevard. Four hundred feet of pipe were installed over the county road's wooden lift bridge and connected to the homes. Residents got their water, but the system suffered freezing and billing problems over the years until 1969, when the

▲ 13.14: *Home of early resident Lee Miller at 69 Greenbrae Boardwalk with boat lifts located at the slough inlet, 2008.*

present four-inch pipe system and individual water meters were installed.

Nevertheless, the severe temperature in December of 1990 still caused the above-ground water pipes of many boardwalk residents to freeze. Neighbors pitched in and worked continuously to preserve the water system. With typical resourcefulness, residents wrapped the above-ground pipes with everything from conventional insulation to shag rugs, chenille bedspreads, and fancy towels. The Boardwalk Water Association managed the system and billed the owners until 1993 when management of the water system was taken over by the Marin Municipal Water District.

Amenities were lacking in all of the early homes. Postal delivery did not begin until 1948, and sewage lines were only installed in 1961. Drinking water had to be carried over the pickleweed or by boat from the 50-50 Club to the outer homes before a bridge connection over the middle slough was constructed. In some homes a wood-burning stove was used for heat and cooking. In others, kerosene was used for portable stoves and, in some cases, lamps. Residents of homes beyond the early boardwalk had to wait for low tide to get across the marsh. The tides also influenced basic functions before there were sewer hook-ups. According to Ed Epting, "We had to do our serious business when there was an outgoing tide."

The Miller family has owned the property at **69 GREENBRAE BOARDWALK** since the 1920s. Purl Miller, who was an avid hunter, heard about Green Brae, as it was called at that time, around 1918. After camping on a launch near Wood Island, he built a hunting shack at what is now number 69.

When the Depression hit in 1930, the Miller family moved from 114 Willow Avenue in Corte Madera to the hunting shack. "Our family consisted of my father Purl, my mother Jessica, and my two sisters Shirley and Margaret, and myself, seven years old," recounted Lee Miller in 1991. "We took all our belongings down from the county road on a 6- x 14-ft barge … including a large, upright piano. The hunting shack consisted of one bedroom and a half. There was a separate 10- x 12-ft building, which was a combination kitchen and tool house. … We had to store all of our furniture in one bedroom, and we all slept out on an open porch. When it rained, my father threw a heavy canvas over our bed covers."

In those early days, the Millers were among the few people who had telephones. Purl and his wife Jessica groaned when popular Mildred Chamberlain, who lived at the far end of the boardwalk, got a call. "One of us had to run 1,100 feet down the boardwalk to get her because she didn't have a phone," recalled Miller.

Over the years, 69 Greenbrae Boardwalk has been jacked up to avoid flooding, remodeled, and enlarged. "Our present workshop was built from the materials of the original two-story Larkspur-Corte Madera School," remarked Lee Miller. "When the school was torn down, it was taken down piece-by-piece by the Cleveland Wrecking Company. The nails were removed and the pieces and doors sold."

REFUGEE ARKS

▲ 13.15: *In 1923, the ark at #29, at the left, was floated across the creek from Wood Island, 2008.*

▲ 13.16: *The Hodges' ark being towed from Rocky Point in Greenbrae to the boardwalk, 1947.*

▲ 13.17: *In the 1940s the ark at #107 was barged from Greenbrae in three sections, 1991.*

Miller has been a driving force on the boardwalk and was instrumental in marshalling support to raise the funds for the purchase of the Heerdt Marsh, now the Corte Madera Marsh Ecological Reserve. The bridge that crosses the slough just east of his house is dedicated to Lee Miller in appreciation of all his efforts to preserve the boardwalk.

Refugee arks that lost their anchorage at other Marin locations began to arrive in the late 1940s. When the Greenbrae Land Company purchased the land west of the freeway from the Roman Catholic Archdiocese of San Francisco in 1946, arks that had been located along the creek in Bon Air were given 30 days to move. Lillian Hodges, who was also known as "Ola," had photographs of the journey of her home from the Greenbrae site, through the open drawbridge of the roadway. It was located at 19 Greenbrae Boardwalk until it was replaced with a new home.

Four houses to the east of the canal is *Norah's Ark* at **107 GREENBRAE BOARDWALK**, another refugee that arrived at the boardwalk in the 1940s and has typical ark design. By 2009 its original shiplap siding, arched roof, and diamond-shaped windows on either side of the front doors were hidden behind a new gate and formal entrance.

The appearance of the boardwalk changed in the 1940s, not only with the influx of arks from other ark communities, but also with the construction of permanent buildings. In 1940 the boardwalk's biggest and most notable landmark, the Greenbrae Rod and Gun Club (also known as the "Rod and Gun Club"), was built by club members, several of whom had also belonged to the 50-50 Club. The clubhouse at **18 GREENBRAE BOARDWALK**, whose gable and hipped roof can be seen just above and beyond the railroad trestle, became the social community center for the area. When it was dedicated on July 20, 1940, H. C. McLaughlin was president, Dave Campbell served as secretary, and George Walcom was treasurer.

Former resident Ola Hodges, whose husband Walter was one of the founders and managed the Rod and Gun Club for 15 years, had photographs of the day-long fishing trips planned by the club for boys from Sunny Hills and St. Vincent's School for Boys and for disabled veterans from Hamilton Air Force Base. Potluck dinners, Christmas parties, and St. Patrick's Day corned beef-and-cabbage dinners were regular events at the club.

The Rod and Gun Club membership was comprised entirely of men. In 1949 the Greenbrae Improvement Club (GIC) was formed. Composed of tenants, residents, and owners, it quickly became the voice of the boardwalk. Commented Lee Miller, "The Rod and Gun Club and the

▲ *13.18: Newly constructed Greenbrae Rod and Gun Club at 18 Greenbrae Boardwalk, 1940.*

▲*13.19: The Greenbrae Rod and Gun Club hosted fishing parties and picnics for 125 children from Sunny Hills and St. Vincent's School for Boys, 1940s.*

▲ *13.20: In 1979 the old Rod and Gun Club became the Crossley Bridge Center, 1991.*

Greenbrae Improvement Club are separate entities, although the GIC held their monthly meetings and pot luck suppers there."

In 1979 the Rod and Gun Club was sold to Lura Crossley, who had leased it in 1971 for the Crossley Bridge Club. Despite much controversy over the use of the club for a bridge center because of the traffic and tight parking situation in the neighborhood, the use was approved. In 2009 Lura Crossley was involved with the club, but her son Bob was the manager.

▲ 13.21: Wood Island (at left) and Greenbrae Boardwalk before the Corte Madera Flood Control Project, 1948.

▲ 13.22: Wood Island after the flood control project during a 1974 flood.

Houses on the boardwalk stayed the same until about 1960, according to Lee Miller. Up until that time, many of them served as weekend homes. Not everyone was happy with the new homes being built on the boardwalk. Commented Ed Epting's mother at the time, "When people start living here (instead of just visiting on weekends) the Greenbrae Boardwalk will be ruined." Ed added, "She was right." In 1948 half the residents were permanent, and half were vacationers. By 2009 the number of full-time residents had grown to 85 percent.

Community spirit is vigorous when controversial issues affecting the boardwalk arise. Residents have banded together to fight development at the entrance to the boardwalk, to fight successfully for and obtain a parking lot, and to get riprap installed along the south shore of the creek to prevent further erosion of their boardwalk lands by the ferries. The residents not only protect their area from the ravages of the elements that sometimes cut them off by flooding but, through the Greenbrae Improvement Club, can marshal the troops to preserve their community and their unique lifestyle.

In 1965 and 1966 the community faced a threat when the Marin County Flood Control District proposed removing 19 houses in order to dredge a new creek channel. The residents' original protest was rejected, but they persevered, banded together, and wrote individually to President Lyndon Johnson, who passed their letters on to the chief of the U.S. Army Corps of Engineers. The result was the approval of an alternative plan. The deep water channel was moved to the north side of the creek, and required severing approximately 40 feet from Wood Island. Only two boardwalk homes were lost.

Although today's boardwalk residents do not live like pioneers in the sense of hauling their own water and roughing it, their lifestyle still requires plenty of grit. In the winter cold winds blow off the bay. Rainstorms make hauling groceries and garbage unpleasant, and often wet, chores. Bicycles, three wheelers, and even an occasional motorized wheelchair help. With their isolated location and limited government services, residents take responsibility for maintaining the infrastructure of their community.

Special skills are required. Residents have to practice how to hook a hose to the fire hydrant. All owners are responsible for broken boards in front of their homes. Construction materials have to be

WHIMSEY ALONG THE GREENBRAE BOARDWALK

Owners personalize the 23- x 20- x 13-in water meter boxes that are mounted along the boardwalk with bright paint, decorative objects, and plants.

◀ 13.23-25: Decorated water meter boxes along Greenbrae Boardwalk, 2008.

hauled in either by water or on lumber carts. To avoid wear and tear on the boardwalk, the owner of 58 Greenbrae Boardwalk arranged to have the building supplies brought in by helicopter. The house, which is not visible from the ferry terminal, was designed with a plywood skirt that was treated to look like concrete and a 36-foot-diameter main living section that is a circular form suggestive of a Mongolian yurt.

Another builder solved the challenge of constructing a house on the marsh in a unique way, although not without controversy. In order to receive approval to build, the buyer was required to purchase comparable mitigation land, which would be turned into replacement wetlands. The COR-TEN™ steel home at **125 GREENBRAE BOARDWALK**, designed by engineer Peter Hogg, adapted to the weather conditions, which have given the exterior a soft patina. The steel foundation allows wider spans and avoids periodic replacement. A steel skirt screens the house from plant growth under the foundation.

Nature still plays an important role in life on the "boards," as some people call it. Water and boating have always attracted people to the boardwalk. Docks on the creek side provide an anchorage for boats. Several residents have added boatways for lifting their boats out of the water and repairing them. One with high crossbeams is visible just to the right of the central slough.

The 1989 Loma Prieta earthquake did significant damage to what had been the only unchanged house (127 Greenbrae Boardwalk) on the boardwalk. A section containing a bathroom toppled over into the marsh. The entire dwelling now has been extensively remodeled. "The area got the worst shake since the community's inception," recalled Lee Miller.

The boardwalk has never been a "little Bohemia" but, rather, has been primarily a family neighborhood where children have grown up, and frequently several generations of families have lived. In 1991 there were ten children living on the boardwalk. At that time, activist Skip Henderson of 39 Greenbrae Boardwalk commented, "One of the things that is emerging is the increase of families. When I first came on the boardwalk, there was just one child. It has been interesting to watch the slow change. Now five mothers share in the school car pool." In 2009 there were a dozen residents under the age of 18.

▲ 13.26: *The COR-TEN™ steel house at 125 Greenbrae Boardwalk was designed for its marsh location and has an ark roof that echoes the historic look, 2008.*

The real estate market on the boardwalk is just as pricey as the rest of Marin. In 2008 one home was advertised for $700,000. Some residents move from one location on the boardwalk to another, rather than move away when they need more space. Boardwalk residents are just as varied as their homes. "We are a mixed group of people in every way," remarked resident Edith Witt, who was an avid letter writer and familiar face at public hearings in the 1980s. "We're mixed in age, in occupations, in economics and politics. What binds us together is our love of living here and that we depend on one another to maintain our community." In 2009 artists, engineers, lawyers, computer techies, sailors, nurses, teachers, and a judge all called the boardwalk home.

Residents may have free spirits, but they must obey strict rules. Because the boardwalk passes over wetlands, and the areas to the south and north are part of an ecological preserve and reserve, there are strict caveats about disposal of hazardous waste. Pet ownership is not exempt from regulation. Owners must take their animals out on a leash and clean up

▲ 13.27: *After a series of rip-offs, the tough decision was made to keep the mailboxes for messages but at a secure location, 2008.*

after them. Scoopers hang on the back side of the railing along the path.

The Greenbrae Improvement Club meetings are notorious for lively debates about issues but, according to Wanden Treanor, "I suspect we could agree that one of the biggest challenges is preserving the identity of this waterfront community in harmony with its history. We would hope to preserve the simple life, simple homes, and residents connected to the environment, knowing the birds, and the cycles of the moon and tides."

③ Corte Madera Marsh Ecological Reserve

The Greenbrae Boardwalk neighborhood is adjacent to the diverse plant and animal world of the marsh. Raccoons scoot through the pickleweed, saltgrass, cordgrass, marsh rosemary, *Jaumea*, and birds beak. Egrets, rails, gulls, pelicans, willets, butterflies, and blue herons do flyovers, and ducks vary by the season. One interesting form of wildlife on the boardwalk is spiders, which feast on the large number of insects that inhabit the marsh but who, unlike regular spiders, do not spin webs.

A 95-acre tidal marsh south and east of the boardwalk covered extensive ground in 1920. Over the years, several proposals were aired for development of the marsh area. The most surprising one that didn't fly was in 1945, when Corte Madera approved plans for an airport with three 3,000-foot runways, administrative offices, and a restaurant.

To forestall future development, Lee Miller spearheaded a drive in 1972 to "Save the Heerdt Marsh" by raising the $289,000 needed to buy the land. The purchase was successful in 1976, thanks to a combination of local and state funding. The salt marsh was renamed the Corte Madera Marsh Ecological Reserve, and came under the supervision of California's Department of Fish and Game. Commented Lee, "I'm pleased with the purchase. It was a little thing to do in life but a big reward, and it satisfies my heart."

In 1990 the reserve was enhanced when a new channel was dredged through the marsh, creating an island high-ground refuge for the clapper rails. The work allows the high tide to flood an additional three-quarters-of-an-acre of the marsh and gives a needed upland area for the birds to hide from hawks and other predators during high tide. The $48,000

▲ 13.28: *The industrial development east of Highway 101 has paid the price of a zero water table by suffering flooding when tides and severe storms coincide, 1978.*

project, mitigation for a 1988 sewage spill, was paid for by the City of Larkspur and the Central Marin Sanitation Agency.

④ Industrial Area

The industrial area east of Highway 101 includes two mobile home parks that provide affordable housing, parking lots for cement trucks, auto repair shops, and artists' studios, as well as services for pets and shoppers.

Cost Plus Plaza, sandwiched between Highway 101 and the Corte Madera Marsh Ecological Preserve, is a major retail area. In 2005 it was transformed by landscape designer Topher Delaney into a fanciful freeway oasis. Palm trees now grow in raised beds flanked with undulating aluminum supports. Concrete planters shaped like paper bags mark the store entrances. Large boulders were studded with glass geodes. When Trader Joe's joined the center in 2009, the streams of shoppers became almost constant.

▲ 13.29: *Cost Plus Plaza features "paper-bag" planters, metal sculptures, and boulders studded with glass crystals.*

▲ 13.30: *Ribbon cutting by vice-mayor Joan Lundstrom at the opening of Trader Joe's in 2009.*

▲ 13.31: *A view from the ridge across Hutchinson Quarry to Wood Island and the Greenbrae interchange, late 1960s.*

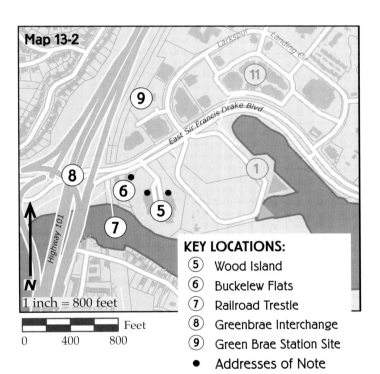

KEY LOCATIONS:
- ⑤ Wood Island
- ⑥ Buckelew Flats
- ⑦ Railroad Trestle
- ⑧ Greenbrae Interchange
- ⑨ Green Brae Station Site
- • Addresses of Note

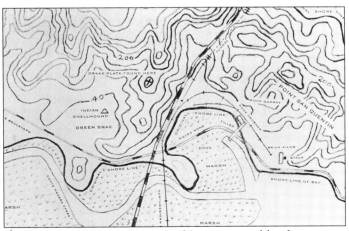

▲ 13.32: *In 1936, as shown in this map, marshlands extended north to the approximate location of today's Larkspur Landing Cinema.*

SOUTHWEST SAN QUENTIN PENINSULA

⤴ *Park at the Larkspur Ferry Terminal parking lot or, if continuing the peninsula walk, proceed to East Sir Francis Drake Boulevard and walk southwest.*

The lands east of the Greenbrae interchange and Highway 101 have been dramatically changed by development in the last 75 years. Hills have been topped, the marsh has been filled, and the former Hutchinson Quarry now houses apartments, offices, and a shopping center.

⑤ Wood Island

The 5.99-acre Wood Island stands as a sentinel at the entrance to the San Quentin Peninsula. At the end of the nineteenth century, the island was called Dean's Island after the two brothers who owned it. The Deans used the south end during the summer as an anchorage for their large ark and dock.

Over the years, the oak-covered knoll has suffered topographical indignities, such as having its peak cut off twice since 1912, and a 40-foot section taken off its southwestern side.

During the Depression, the next owner, Captain McCarthy, who was a coffee importer, built a lovely 3,200-square-foot home on the island. According to Greenbrae Boardwalk resident Lee Miller, Captain McCarthy lived in a house on the marsh in the area of the ferry terminal while he was building his 11-room house on the south slope of the island. Stories conflict as to why the house was torn down after it was sold in 1947 or 1948. One version is that

▲ 13.33: *View of Wood Island from Greenbrae Boardwalk, with Captain McCarthy's house on top, early 1940s.*

the house was vandalized by hippies. Another is that it was removed when the island was cut back 40 feet or more during the flood control project in 1965.

A succession of potential owners eyed the hill in the 1950s and 1960s. Some decided against the purchase because of Larkspur's 35-foot height limit. In the mid-1970s the J. Vanderjogt and Duzo Development Company constructed a 76,735-square-foot, four-story office complex at **60** and **80 EAST SIR FRANCIS DRAKE BOULEVARD**.

▲ 13.34: *Sculptor Dennis Patton at Buckelew Corners surveying the construction of his 30 foot-tall horse made of recycled lath, 1975.*

The architecture of the buildings visually re-contoured the hill and preserved its woodsy feeling. Originally the corporate headquarters of the Victoria Station restaurant chain was located there. Some relics of the past, such as a midden, remain on the southern slope. Blue herons and egrets still perch on nests in the trees.

⑥ Buckelew Flats

The low-lying area northwest of Wood Island, known as "Buckelew Flats," has been home to a potpourri of uses throughout the years from recreational, to hippie salvage, to a mixture of sports rental and retail.

Beginning in the early 1920s, Charlie Flynn Sr., who spent 55 of his 65 years in the area, summered with his family at Lucky Point, just west of Wood Island, abutting the county road leading to the wooden drawbridge. He occasionally trapped wild mink in the marsh and enjoyed watching the flight of the curlews and clapper rails. In 1923 the arks anchored on the west side of Wood Island were torn down.

At that time a boat rental business and store called "Duck Inn," run by Bill Peterson, was located in the general area of **14 EAST SIR FRANCIS DRAKE BOULEVARD**. Later, a store that sold gasoline and groceries to boat owners did business there. For a time the building was unoccupied until furniture manufacturer Sam Davis leased it in the 1960s. Davis first sold flea-market finds and later branched into designing and manufacturing oak reproduction furniture and antiques. He dubbed his shop "A Growing Concern." The name proved ironic when it was discovered that the expansion beyond the original gas station building was done without city permits.

To publicize the site, wood and metal sculptor Dennis Patton, who lived in one of the buildings, refaced and created an addition to the original shacks in a topsy-turvy manner and created a three-dimensional old west-style "town" dubbed

"Buckelew Corners." The faux old-west buildings gained national fame when VISA and Yamaha used them as locations for television commercials.

Patton's oversized sculptures were eye-catchers. He had built a 30-foot-tall recycled lath horse on this site in 1975. It was relocated to the Marin County Civic Center, where it remained until it was burned by vandals. In the 1960s he constructed a smaller 17-foot-tall Trojan horse made of driftwood that was located at the end of Lucky Drive near Highway 101, but it is no longer there.

A succession of dealers selling antique reproduction furniture occupied the buildings over the following years. In 2010 the "old west" look was painted out, and the buildings now house more traditional retail shops, while the grounds provide extra parking for the Wood Island office complex.

Until its new rowing clubhouse and dock were constructed west of the freeway interchange in 1991, the Marin Rowing Club, also known as the "Marin Rowing Association," used one of these buildings and its dock for rowing club activities. Kayak and canoe rental facilities still maintain the boating tradition.

⑦ Railroad Trestle

The railroad trestle that spans the mouth of the creek is the last vestige of the days of railroad travel across Corte Madera Creek. In the late 1800s scows and steamers, such as the *Ida* and the *Tamalpais*, plied the creek to Ross Landing (at today's intersection of Sir Francis Drake Boulevard and College Avenue in Kentfield), hauling cargoes of hides, tallow, cordwood, rough lumber, swine, and cattle.

When the San Francisco & North Pacific Railroad built its line between San Rafael and Tiburon in 1884, the Corte Madera Creek channel had to be kept open for freight boats to pass through, so the railroad constructed a single-track trestle and lift span over the creek. According to writer and railroad buff George H. Harlan, this original railroad was a separate entity for construction use only.

With increased traffic and the advent of heavier locomotives, the Northwestern Pacific Railroad replaced the existing bridge and trestle with a double-tracked 51-foot 6-inch bascule lift span and

▲ 13.35: *Corinthian yachts on Corte Madera Creek, southbound train on trestle (right), with Mt. Tamalpais and King Mountain in the background, early 1890s.*

▲ 13.36: *Northwestern Pacific Railroad trestle at Green Brae looking north, about 1914.*

▲ 13.37: *Northwestern Pacific Railroad trestle at Greenbrae, closed. In background, left to right, Wood Island, San Quentin State Prison, and Greenbrae Boardwalk, 1945.*

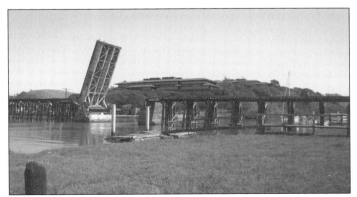

▲ 13.38: *The railroad bridge raised, with Wood Island in the background, 1991.*

a double-tracked 1,741-foot-long wooden trestle on the original alignment in 1924. The lift bridge and most of a single track portion of the trestle still exist.

In its early days, the trestle stilt-stepped across the marsh all the way to the Green Brae tunnel. Later a dike and raised railroad bed were built.

Former longtime boardwalk dweller Katherine Whidden recalled in 1978 that in the 1920s, when the barge came up the creek to bring hay to the Green Brae Dairy, it would wait for the bridge to open in the channel opposite the boardwalk. Four or five men were needed to operate the hand crank that raised and lowered the cumbersome bridge so a roving crew was dispatched from the Northwestern Pacific Railroad's headquarters in Petaluma. The bridge was usually closed during weekdays and raised on weekends to allow passage of masted pleasure boats.

Today the railroad drawbridge belongs to the Golden Gate Bridge District, which purchased the railroad right-of-way when freight traffic was stopped. Following an agreement developed in 1982 between the Golden Gate Transit District, the County of Marin, and the Marin Transit District, the 2½-mile stretch of roadbed between Paradise Drive in Corte Madera and Bellam Boulevard in San Rafael was purchased by the Golden Gate Bridge District in 1985.

Of the 200 movable bridges that have spanned waters of the bay and its tributaries since the 1880s, only 76 were still intact in 1976. The Greenbrae trestle is part of today's landscape and is not forgotten. Its raised roadbed signals to freeway traffic, and it features in every conversation about another creek crossing. In 2008 on East Sir Francis Drake Boulevard, a westbound big-rig, with a crane that exceeded the bridge height by a foot, plowed into the roadway section of the bridge, moving it 2½ feet. The major damage required the removal of one hundred feet of the trestle over East Sir Francis Drake Boulevard.

⑧ Greenbrae Interchange

Although San Quentin and the adjacent village was one of the early Marin settlements, access was circuitous. In order to cross the creek, travelers had to go to San Anselmo and then down the Ross Valley to get from one side to the other. An early stage-

▲ 13.39: *The old wooden drawbridge for cars and horses. The bare Green Brae hills are in the background, 1929.*

coach route called "Bret Harte "ran along the top of the ridge.

The introduction of the San Quentin prison population years earlier eventually triggered the construction of the Green Brae Station by the San Francisco & North Pacific Railroad in about 1884. At that time, Green Brae was spelled as two words. In 1917 a hand-operated wooden drawbridge that straddled the creek was reached by a rutted dirt road across the marsh just west of the railroad bridge. Kerosene lanterns on the county road provided light until 1926.

In 1928 the unpaved, two-lane Redwood Highway north of Larkspur was located approximately where the Redwood Highway frontage road now lies. A three-lane Highway 101 was built in 1930 and was replaced 15 years later by a four-lane bridge with multiple on- and off-ramps, the first phase of what today is called the "Greenbrae interchange."

By 1952, when longtime employee Joe Monestier joined the Larkspur Public Works Department, traffic had increased so much that a traffic light was

▲ 13.40: *The four-lane Highway 101 bridge and junction at Sir Francis Drake Boulevard, looking south, before a traffic light was installed, 1945.*

installed at the intersection of Highway 101 and Sir Francis Drake Boulevard. Monestier recalled that people would take picnic lunches and sit near the intersection to watch the traffic accidents that occurred with some frequency before installation of the traffic light. A second wooden highway bridge was removed in 1960, when the present structure was opened to traffic.

The marsh under the freeway interchange, which was targeted in 1969 for an elaborate boating facility that never got launched, became a sightseer's attraction in the 1970s. Larkspur sculptor Dennis Patton created a 27-foot-tall Don Quixote statue that was installed there. His tall sculptures were popular with motorists, and received international press coverage, including an article in an Egyptian newspaper, until the powers-that-be condemned them as a driving hazard. In the 1960s Patton's wood-mosaic truck was as familiar a sight on the peninsula as Merry Prankster Ken Kesey's bus was in the old-town area.

Today a steady stream of traffic occupies the eight traffic lanes of Highway 101 between Larkspur and Greenbrae, and the transportation authority of Marin is reviewing alternatives for the improvement of the interchange.

9 Green Brae Station Site

The Green Brae Station was originally built about 1884 for transporting prisoners to San Quentin. The long, narrow, hipped-roof station was located along the raised railroad bed behind the present Marin Airporter terminal site. When the Schultz family began building houses in the 1940s, their development was called "Greenbrae in the Oaks," which was later shortened to Greenbrae. At that time the Northwestern Pacific Railroad was extended south from San Rafael by owner Peter Donahue to provide a direct commute line to Point Tiburon.

The California Park railroad tunnel was dug through the hill between Greenbrae and San Rafael, and was used until rail freight traffic was discontinued in the 1980s. Over the years adventurous youths pedaled their bikes through the tunnel to get to San Rafael, dodging the occasional freight trains and sleeping transients. In 1982 the tunnel was part of a Golden Gate Bridge District

▲ 13.41: *The Green Brae Station, looking north, 1906.*

▲ 13.42: *A Eureka-bound passenger train heading toward Tunnel #3 and San Rafael, 1938.*

▲ 13.43: *As part of the new railroad connection between Cloverdale and Larkspur, the old NWP Tunnel #3 is being rehabilitated as the Cal Park Hill Tunnel, 2008.*

railroad purchase. As with other Marin railroad tunnels, fires have plagued it. The most recent fire in 1990 caused it to be closed.

In 2009 voters approved a quarter-cent raise in the local sales tax to implement the Sonoma-Marin Area Rail Transit (SMART) project. In 2010 the Cal Park Hill Tunnel is about to reopen for bikes and pedestrians.

▲ 13.44: *The San Quentin Peninsula from the Richmond-San Rafael Bridge to San Quentin State Prison and the Hutchinson Quarry, 1975.*

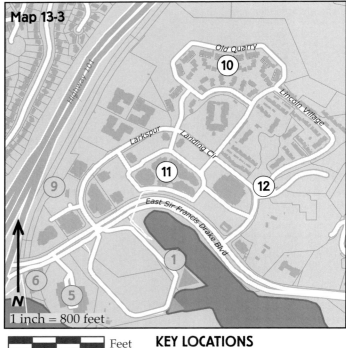

KEY LOCATIONS

⑩ Hutchinson Quarry Site
⑪ Marin Country Mart (Larkspur Landing Center)
⑫ Remillard Cottage

▲ 13.45: *Hutchinson Quarry, Remillard cottage and kiln, Sanitary District plant and San Quentin State Prison, 1975.*

LARKSPUR LANDING

⤴ *Walk the Larkspur Landing loop road beginning at the west end of Larkspur Landing Circle.*

⑩ Hutchinson Quarry Site

The Hutchinson Quarry, with a sagging rock grinder that was a prominent sight for travelers heading north on Highway 101 for years, has been transformed into a high-density center of activity. Before any development could occur at the quarry, 120-foot-high cliffs had to be stabilized, ponds and marshlands had to be filled, and the 48-foot-tall swayback grinder had to be demolished.

The Franciscan sandstone, commonly called "graywacke" or "blue rock," was first noted on the site in 1852, but was not recognized as a marketable product until 1891, when Pierre Remillard purchased 150 acres of the Green Brae Rancho, part of the Punta de Quentin property, from David Porter. In 1903 Dwight Hutchinson, who had quarries in El Cerrito, Richmond, and Palo Alto, was looking for a new quarry site for crushed rock and became interested in the San Quentin Peninsula site.

In a 1974 interview, Ike J. Ely, a Hutchinson relative, pointed out that gravel comes from river and creek bottoms, whereas crushed rock is quarried.

From 1891 to 1915 the quarry lands were part of the self-contained community that made up the Remillard brickyard. Beef and dairy cattle grazed on the lands at the west end of the property. Serious operations at Hutchinson Quarry didn't start until 1924, after a complicated purchase transaction by J. J. Moran combined the lands on the north side owned

▲ 13.46: *Hutchinson Quarry had two main sites separated by a knoll. The eastern site had a series of ponds for washing the rock, 1975.*

by George McNear with a portion of the Remillard lands owned by A. J. Paulsen. Marin's first asphalt plant was built at Hutchinson Quarry in 1927.

Before a Marin County market was developed, the quarry rock was barged by way of Corte Madera Creek for sale in other locations around the Bay Area. In 1930 the edges of Treasure Island were fortified with huge rocks shipped from the quarry to support the fill for the Golden Gate International Exposition. The quarry rocks were in demand when access roads were needed for the Golden Gate Bridge. Millions of yards of material were removed from the property and supplied aggregate for Marin highways and roads.

A boardinghouse, located at the quarry and run by Mr. and Mrs. John J. Kelly from 1927 to 1937, was famous for the dinners Elsie Kelly served to the 20 bachelors living in the bunkhouse. The Kellys' son Vince, the quarry's first truck driver, recalled hiking over the hill on the quiet dirt road (where Highway 101 is today) to a San Rafael school. A three-lane road was not built until 1930.

The quarry consisted of two main excavation sites from which the rock was hauled to the large lopsided quarry bunker for processing. The rock was conveyed from the bunker by an overpass to the barges that pulled into a dock in the area where the East Sir Francis Drake pedestrian overpass is now located. Rock was barged out from the quarry until the late 1950s. Clint Eastwood fans remember the quarry site and trestle from the movie *Dirty Harry*, when the area was used for a spectacular chase scene.

The quarry bunker, according to Ike Ely, was built on landfill and started to sag shortly after it was built because the bottom boards had been laid on the ground. When the boards rotted, the weight of the heavy rock passing through the screens caused the boards to slip, carrying the superstructure with them on a crippling slant.

In 1929 a five-foot-thick cement-and-steel floor was installed but failed to stabilize the structure; a 1939 addition of concrete fared no better. In 1941 Forrest Brown, an office boy and longtime associate of the Hutchinsons who had purchased the site, had the entire building covered with Gunite to prevent its collapse. While the unstable-appearing building looked like a pushover, it took eight hours and many loads of dynamite to demolish it in 1977.

Early in 1969 the winds of change were blowing through the site. The City of Larkspur annexed the 75-acre Hutchinson Quarry site, and six months later annexed the 85 acres between the quarry and

▲ 13.47: *The graywacke quarried at Hutchinson Quarry was carried across an overpass to a loading dock at the creek inlet, 1970.*

▲ 13.48: *The knoll between the two quarry sites was dynamited and lowered to create the Marriott hotel site, 1980.*

▲ 13.49: *Larkspur Landing shopping center office (far left) and shopping center construction (center), 1979.*

the San Quentin State Prison property. At that time the area had fewer than 12 registered voters, so the annexation did not require an election. In 1972, after Brown's death, the property was sold to Title Insurance of Los Angeles and attorney John Ford, and subsequently to Lincoln Property Company of Texas, also known as "Lincoln Properties." An early plan that envisioned a multiple-unit housing project, a 300-room lodge, 14 sunken tennis courts, and an exhibition amphitheater impelled the City to take an innovative approach; the City wanted a say in how the site should be developed.

Rather than allowing a developer to dictate how the site should be converted from hard rock to a money-making enterprise, a citizens' committee was formed, and an environmental impact report (EIR) was mandated. Despite widespread community involvement in the approval process, one error slipped through unnoticed: the cliffs were counted as buildable land in computing the density. The result was an allowable density of 25 to 27 units-per-acre, rather than the 12 to 14 the City had visualized.

The development plans for the first phase of 478 apartments sailed through the approval process, as the only residents that showed any interest in the site were the thousands of swallows that returned every spring.

⑪ Marin Country Mart (Larkspur Landing Center)

To prepare the site for construction of the apartments, offices, and shopping center, the cliffs had to be stabilized, and other site preparation had to be accomplished. In the course of grading the site, a geological cross section created by the College of Marin geology program shows evidence of volcanism by exposing rhyolites and pyrite between the predominant graywacke and shale, particularly on the hill site of today's Courtyard by Marriott.

When construction at Larkspur Landing Center was begun in 1978, the San Quentin Peninsula was like an orphan that had been little noticed and was off the beaten path. Lincoln Properties initiated and planned the project and developed

LARKSPUR LANDING CENTER IN THE 1970S

▲ 13.50: *Victoria Station, which built its headquarters at the top of Wood Island, had a restaurant nearby at Larkspur Landing Center, 1975.*

▲ 13.51: *Sculptor Dennis Patton designed Larkspur Landing's iconic fountain, 1979.*

▲ 13.52: *A facelift of the Larkspur Landing Center eliminated the "New England"-style look, 2008.*

▲ 13.53: *The 1891 Remillard Cottage, now a nursery school, is located next to the Larkspur Shores Apartments, 2008.*

the residential portion of the site. W. R. Grace created the commercial center and christened it Larkspur Landing Center, a name contributed by Greenbrae writer Beth Ashley, who did public relations work for the center at that time. The original center was designed to resemble a seaport town in New England. When it was being planned, people scoffed at the idea of a shopping center in an abandoned rock quarry, next to a sewage treatment plant, and a half mile from San Quentin State Prison.

When the project opened in December of 1978, there were 13 businesses; by 1983 there were 55. Initially the businesses were geared to a tourist market, but later shifted to a more local orientation. With the opening of the Courtyard by Marriott hotel in 1987, followed by the construction of 250 condominiums in 1991, the neighborhood became the self-contained community that was originally envisioned.

Many of the early tenants, such as the Victoria Station restaurant that served up food in a collection of box cars and a go-cart track, as well as old-timers like A Clean Well-Lighted Place for Books, Scoma's, Yet Wah, and Fry's Grocery, have disappeared. In the early 2000s the shopping center changed hands again and, despite a facelift, struggled. Management blamed the poor economy; tenants blamed the high rents. Only three original businesses remain from 1978: The Ragged Sailor Framery and Gallery, Lark Shoe Repair, and Norman Mahan Jewelers. Other "longtimers" are Marin Brewing Company and the Asher Clinic. A farmer's market is held on Saturdays from May to September.

More recently, Larkspur Landing housed 38 businesses, with Bed Bath & Beyond as the big draw. After years of pressure by residents and the City of Larkspur, a small grocery store was opened but it has since closed.

Hope appeared on the horizon in 2009 when J.S. Rosenfield & Co. purchased the 16-acre, 173,000-square-foot shopping center, and hired BALDAUF CATTON VON ECKARTSBERG Architects, who were responsible for the magic retail make-over of San Francisco's Ferry Building Marketplace. New owner Jim Rosenfield, who paid $65 million for the center, reported that he'd had his eye on the center for about two years. "I'm going to focus on local services, exceptional food purveyors, and charming boutiques," he said. The firm envisions everything from book and toy stores to restaurant and food vendors selling produce, cheese, and charcuterie. Gardens and playgrounds are also on the improvement application, as is a name change to "Marin Country Mart."

The new look should be welcomed by residents and office workers. Major changes in the demographics of the housing have resulted in a different market than was originally anticipated. Most 2009 renters agree with former Larkspur Parks and Recreation director, Nancy Spivey, who loves the location. "It's centrally located in Marin with easy access to the ferry terminal and the freeway," said Spivey, a resident of Larkspur Courts, which is oriented to families and seniors. According to Lindsay Sullivan, a resident of Larkspur Shores, which was scheduled for a facelift in 2009, it is a pet-friendly, middle-income apartment complex with few children and elderly. Gossips say "it's where dads go when families split up." At least a quarter of the residents commute to San Francisco, most of them by ferry. Few work locally but would welcome food services and conveniences within walking distance of their homes.

(12) Remillard Cottage

At the eastern end of the shopping center, the new meets the old. A nineteenth-century remnant of the peninsula's history is Remillard Cottage at **2900 LARKSPUR LANDING CIRCLE**. The modest hipped-roof Victorian cottage constructed about 1891 for the superintendent at the Remillard brickyard is a visual reminder of the bustling community that existed on the peninsula in the early 1900s.

According to John Tacchi, who was raised in the area, Frank dePue, a fingerprinting expert who worked at San Quentin, lived in the gray Victorian cottage in about 1906. The cottage, which is visible on John Tacchi's map *(see page 322)* and in old photos in the Heritage Preservation Board files, had a peripatetic history. Originally it was located at the quarry bunker site. When the bunker was built, the cottage was moved farther east, near the location of the pedestrian overpass that now spans East Sir Francis Drake Boulevard.

When Larkspur Landing construction began in 1977, the cottage was under a death sentence and was scheduled to be burned in a Larkspur Fire Department exercise. Former Larkspur city councilman Robert Lee, who owned the adjacent Remillard brick kiln and stack, persuaded the Larkspur City Council to rescue the historic cottage and cover the $3,800 cost of moving it.

In 1978 the cottage, which was purchased by the City of Larkspur for $1, was first moved adjacent to the brick kiln, but its troubles were far from over. By 1985 the council was anxious to unload the structure, for which it had been unable to find a buyer. The creek and the lack of clearance under the bridges prevented its being moved to another section of the city.

Rather than sacrifice the building, the city donated the cottage to the Remillard Cottage Board of the San Rafael Cooperative Nursery School, which was looking for a new location for its school. After a fund-raising effort, the cottage was again hoisted on moving blocks by Wacker and Sons and hauled to its present location on the community center site of Larkspur Landing in 1984. Since then it has echoed with children's voices in its new life as a nursery school, and it is listed in the National Register of Historic Places.

REMILLARD COTTAGE MOVES AROUND

▲ *13.54: In 1977 the superintendent's Victorian cottage was located approximately where the pedestrian overpass is today.*

▲ *13.55: The superintendent's Victorian cottage being moved by Wacker and Sons, 1979.*

▲ *13.56: Anne Jeschke of the San Rafael Cooperative Nursery School accepts the donation of the Victorian cottage from city councilman Robert Lee at its current and final location next to Neighborhood Park, 1984.*

SOUTH CENTRAL SAN QUENTIN PENINSULA

⤴ *A walk can begin at the Victorian cottage on Larkspur Landing Circle, or all the locations can be viewed from Remillard Park and the Sir Francis Drake statue. Tubb Lake and Miwok Park can be reached by a public access easement at the end of Drake's Cove Road. A future public access point will connect to Larkspur Landing Circle.*

▲ 13.57: *Tubb Lake (foreground), Sanitary District (middle left), and Quarry (far right middle), 1972.*

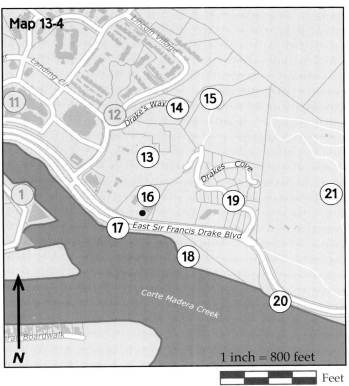

KEY LOCATIONS
- ⑬ Ross Valley Sanitary District Site
- ⑭ Drake's Way
- ⑮ Tubb Lake & Miwok Park
- ⑯ Green Brae Brick Yard
- ⑰ Sir Francis Drake Statue
- ⑱ Remillard Park
- ⑲ Drake's Cove
- ⑳ Windsurfing Beach
- ㉑ San Quentin Graveyard
- • Addresses of Note

⑬ Ross Valley Sanitary District Site

Across from the Victorian cottage on the eastern end of Larkspur Landing Circle, another major topographical and land-use change has occurred. The former Ross Valley Sanitary District site has been demolished and the land filled. The hill behind it has been lowered and graded, and 24 affordable homes have been constructed.

A large prehistoric village was situated on the San Quentin Peninsula, according to an investigation report prepared by archaeologist William Roop in 1979. A smaller midden of more recent origin extended from the sanitary district site south to the Remillard brickyard stack and possibly beyond to Sir Francis Drake Boulevard and the adjoining strip park.

Another report in 1997 referred to both a Chinese village and a prehistoric archaeological site. Archaeological consultants Holman & Associates found evidence of circular beehive kilns predating the Hoffman-type kiln.

During early development on the peninsula, archaeological sites were not on the public radar. Major destruction of part of the Native American midden within the sanitary district site occurred in 1948, when the plant was built, and in 1975 when it was expanded. Destruction of other parts had occurred when East Sir Francis Drake Boulevard was built. The 1979 report stated that undisturbed remains still existed in the area and that "Human burials are more likely to be within the grounds

▲ 13.58: Major grading was required to prepare the former sanitary district and EAH sites before construction could begin, 2008.

DRAKE'S WAY CONSTRUCTION

"We like to joke that we got the land for $1 and overpaid ... The engineering challenges of the site – the jagged spine of hard rock – have been every bit as difficult [to grade down] as we had feared."

— Andy Blauvelt, EAH Project Manager

of the Marin Sanitary District or under Sir Francis Drake Boulevard." In 1999 and 2000 additional remains and artifacts were unearthed during removal of the district's old tanks to make way for new development. Two reburial ceremonies were conducted by the Federated Indians of Graton Rancheria, according to Nick Tipon of the Sacred Sites Protection Committee.

The sanitary district moved its treatment operations to a new location on Andersen Drive in San Rafael in 1984-1985, but retained an office at 2000 Larkspur Landing Circle. In 2003 the Campus Property Group's co-partners, Robert Upton and Michael Hooper, proposed the 2000 Larkspur Landing Circle development for the nine-acre site. A mixed-use project was approved in 2006 for a 100-room extended-stay hotel and 126 townhouses and condominiums. In 2009 residential and hotel construction was halted until toxic soil problems could be resolved.

14 Drake's Way

As part of the approval of 23 market-rate units at Drake's Cove *(see page 326)*, developer Monahan Pacific donated an eight-acre site to the Ecumenical Association for Housing (EAH) for affordable housing and deeded 2.5 acres for open space in 2002. EAH provided an additional three acres of private open space. In 2008, after the former quarry spine was leveled to create a building site, construction began on EAH's Drake's Way, a project consisting of 24 townhouses above the 2000 Larkspur Landing Circle site.

Funded by federal affordable-housing tax credits, the project had a groundbreaking ceremony in May of 2008, and EAH opened the $14 million development in late 2010. Funding and leveling the ridge were just two of the problems EAH faced. Controversy also swirled over where to haul the dirt. "Despite it all, after 10 years of work, the families moved in for the holidays in 2010," said EAH president and CEO, Mary Murtagh. "Drake's Way not only meets the needs of low-income households, but has been given LEED certification," she added.

15 Tubb Lake & Miwok Park

Eight acres of open space lie to the east and south of Drake's Way at Tubb Lake and Miwok Park. The surrounding slopes once provided the clay for brick production. Although created by a man-made dam, Tubb Lake not only supplied water for the brick-making process, it was also a source of water for a wider area, and served as a favorite recreation spot.

▲ 13.59: The Ross Valley Sanitary District sewer plant, shown here in 2008, was demolished in 1999.

▲ 13.60: *Artist David Morris's house and studio were at the upper end of Tubb Lake, 1975.*

Greenbrae Boardwalkers Charles Flynn and Don Crews reported that they got drinking water in a spring near there in the 1920s and that Tubb Lake was their favorite swimming hole. Helen Wilson recalled that in the 1930s people who swam and picnicked there had to pay someone who lived in a nearby cottage to use the lake.

Catherine P. Robson, a descendent of Frank Pixley, wrote in a 1986 letter that "Lucky kids around here stole surreptitious swims, and fishermen baited traps to catch the crawdads in the lake."

Don Zubler of San Quentin Village recalled, "On the other side of the hill from Tubb Lake was the Cardoza Ranch, where the sewer treatment plant is today. The railroad tracks ran through the ranch, and boxcars were stacked up along the tracks. We kids used to play in the boxcars and run along the top of them."

Decades ago willows took root around the dam holding back the lake waters. Over the years cattails have choked the banks, and parrot-feather plants have spread into the lake, so that it has become more like a pond, providing nesting spots for American coots.

Master potter David Morris and his son Nico built a studio and home on the edge of Tubb Lake in the 1960s when his Sausalito studio burned down. They fired their work in a kiln named "El Corajudo" (the old grouch) because of its unpredictability. Morris's high-fired stoneware earned him national recognition. He had exhibitions at the Smithsonian Institution in Washington, D.C., the San Francisco Museum of Modern Art, and the Oakland Museum.

When the lands were to be sold, Morris worked out an agreement with the city that allowed him to continue at Tubb Lake for a number of years. When

TUBB LAKE REFLECTIONS

"My mother, Grace Jenny Duffy Zubler, told me that there was an old watering trough in the middle of the lake, and so the original name was Tub-A-Lake, which got condensed over the years to Tubb Lake.

… One time someone threw some goldfish into the lake, and they grew and grew. We would take a bent pin and a worm and catch dozens of goldfish."

— Don Zubler, San Quentin Village resident

▲ 13.61: *The idyllic setting of Tubb Lake sits below the EAH site on the skyline, 2009.*

▲ 13.62: Pierre-Nicolas Remillard, founder of the Remillard Brick Company, undated photo.

REMILLARD BRICK COMPANY

"Up near the highway and where the bunker was located, we have the dairy cows and beef cows. Coming down the road a ways, we have the barn, stable for horses employed in the kiln operations, cook house, where three Chinese cooks were hired during the season to prepare meals for 30 to 55 brickmakers. ... Drinking water came from what is now known as Tubb Lake."

— John Tacchi

development plans were later approved, the house and kiln were torn down. The north end of the lake has now reverted to its natural, idyllic state.

As part of the approval of the preliminary plan for the development proposed by Lincoln Properties, eight acres, which included Tubb Lake and the adjacent hillside environs of Miwok Park, were dedicated to the city. The Environmental Impact Report on the San Quentin Peninsula in 1975 stated, "The visual quality of Tubb Lake and its environs is unparalleled in the area.... Tubb Lake, though small in scale, [is] the center of interest, with the vegetation at the edge of the lake forming a natural transition to the surrounding hillsides."

A 1983 habitat report by the Marin Audubon Society noted that Tubb Lake is a beautiful little freshwater lake that provides good wildlife habitat for such rare species as common gallinule, pied-billed grebe, and Virginia and sora rails, which have been known to nest there.

16 Green Brae Brick Yard

A major concern when reviewing development on the sanitary district property was that the new construction not block the view of the National Register of Historic Places landmark Green Brae Brick Yard, also known as the Green Brae or Remillard Brick Kiln at **125 EAST SIR FRANCIS DRAKE BOULEVARD**.

During the heyday of frantic building in San Francisco in the late nineteenth century, bricks were a hot commodity. Canadian-born Pierre-Nicolas Remillard, also known as "Peter," worked at a brickyard in Oakland and eventually became owner of the

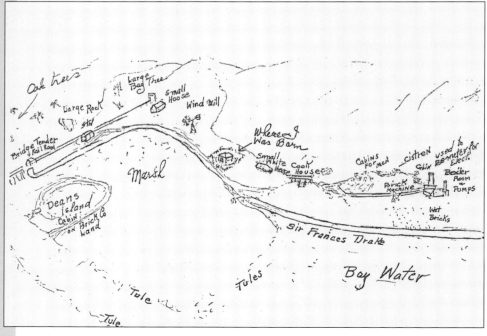

▲ 13.63: John Tacchi, born in the hipped-roof Victorian Remillard Cottage...

business. His two brothers joined him and formed the newly named Remillard Brick Company, which later incorporated in 1879.

Their first Marin County venture was located on 75 acres along the Gallinas Creek near the Civic Center and Santa Venetia in 1870. Reportedly, bricks from this yard were used for the original Palace Hotel in San Francisco. Seeking to extend the operation, Pierre purchased 150 acres of the Green Brae Rancho from Mary Tunstead, widow of John Ross, and part of the Punta de Quentin property from David Porter in 1890. The following year, the Remillard brothers established a brick-making plant on the San Quentin Peninsula, and Pierre sold the land to the new company.

Early resident John Tacchi's father helped construct and manage the Remillard brick kiln and the 130-foot-tall stack, which replaced an old beehive kiln that had been built on the site of an ancient Coast Miwok midden. In 1974 he drew a picture for the Larkspur Heritage Committee of the self-contained community centered around the brickyard that existed there when he was growing up.

He recounted, "…on the property was a blacksmith's forge that was not only used for shoeing the horses but for making tools. The workers were given cabins to live in, and, at 'happy hour,' it was steam beer brewed below their cabins. There were pig sties, gardens of vegetables and fruit, and fishin'-a-plenty across the road."

Bricks were shipped to San Francisco on four company schooners – *Virginia, Olga, Frances,* and *Lillian.* The *Lillian* was named for Pierre Remillard's daughter, Lillian, better known as 'Countess Dandini.'

In a 1973 newspaper interview, Countess Dandini chuckled about her boat namesake, "It was always on the rocks and in the newspapers, and the family had the greatest time with me."

▲ 13.64: Countess Lillian Dandini, Pierre's daughter, solely owned the Remillard Brick Company from 1934 until her death in 1973.

REMILLARD BRICKS

From 1891 to 1915, the Remillard Brick Company, the largest brickmaking firm on the Pacific Coast in 1900, produced some ten million bricks – 500,000 a year in the Green Brae kiln alone. At its peak production, the brick company served as the chief supplier of bricks for the entire Pacific Coast. Remillard bricks helped rebuild San Francisco after the 1906 earthquake and fire.

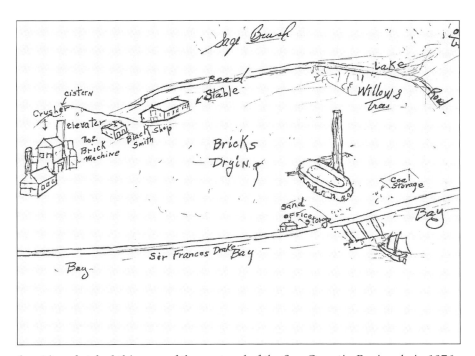

(cont.) …sketched this map of the west end of the San Quentin Peninsula in 1976.

▲ 13.65: When future owner Bob Lee first visited the Remillard brickyard in the early 1970s, only the stack was visible.

▲ 13.66: *When the brush was cleared away, the kiln entrances were exposed, 1976.*

OTHER USES OF THE KILN

John Kelly, whose family lived at Hutchinson Quarry in the 1930s, recalled a "grappa" still in the kiln run by local Italian-Americans, who "added the cheap brandy to their wine to give it more kick."

In a 1976 interview Virginia O'Conner of Greenbrae reported that an industrious innovator had used the kiln in the 1940s to grow mushrooms.

▲ 13.67: *Seismic retrofitting was done on the 130-foot-tall stack by bonding a concrete slab and steel bars to the interior walls. Restoration of the kiln included replacing missing bricks, 1989.*

The dock for loading the finished bricks onto the schooners was directly across the road from the kiln. The bricks were piled three feet high and covered the decks from bow to stern. Large clay deposits situated on the flatlands lying between San Quentin State Prison and Highway 101, and on the hills, were excavated and formed into bricks at the kiln that was built on the site.

One of the few remaining examples of the Hoffman-type kiln in the United States, the Green Brae kiln, with its circular firing chamber and offset stack, is an engineering landmark of statewide significance. Unlike the usual batch kilns, a Hoffman kiln could be fired continuously, and new green bricks could be added as the already fired bricks were being removed.

The continuous-firing kiln was fed coal through openings in the ceiling. The stack, connected underground to the kiln, was a source of ventilation. After the bricks were formed six at a time in wooden molds and air dried, they were stacked in the kiln and removed through the 14 arched openings on the sides. The kiln operated 24 hours a day from April or May to November, but not during the rainy season, although a metal shed-roof building covered the kiln.

When Pierre died in 1904, ownership of the Remillard Brick Company passed to his wife, Cordule Laurin Remillard, and one of their daughters, Lillian. Two of their four children, Walter and Philip, had died in 1879 and 1901 respectively. The Green Brae brick kiln closed in 1915 after operating for 24 years. Local gossip suggested that the McNears, who owned a competing brickyard in San Rafael, pressured the Remillards to cease operations in Marin. After Cordule's death in 1934, Lillian solely owned the company.

Lillian, who at age 52 married Count Alessandro Olioli Dandini, twenty years her junior, was a spirited woman who said she had helped Jack London through a French course when they were both at Oakland High School. She had wanted to follow a music and voice career, but the idea was squelched by her family. She was a patron of the arts for many years.

When the elaborate Chateau Carolands estate in Hillsborough was threatened with destruction in 1950, she traded rock from her San Jose brickyard for ownership of the four-story Beaux Arts-style Pullman mansion. Interestingly, the mansion had been built with Remillard brick. Countess Dandini ran the business until the last brick plant closed in 1968. She died in 1973 at the age of 93.

- - - - -

In 1971 only the stack of the kiln was visible, but it piqued the interest of history buff and former Larkspur city councilman Robert Lee. He traipsed over to the site with heavy-duty pruners and hacked his way through the brambles until he discovered the kiln openings. He connected with owner Countess Dandini through Andre Bose, a cousin of the Remillard family. Commented Lee in a 1977 interview, "I think she became convinced of our sincerity in preserving the kiln. She was quite a woman. She cherished her father, and she saw what we were talking about doing as a memorial to him." Lee and Bose purchased the property in 1973.

Next came a ten-year "sleeping beauty" stage, when blackberries again covered the kiln, and small eucalyptus trees sprouted from its five-foot-thick walls. Frosts loosened the bricks on the north side of the stack. During the ten-year hiatus, various projects for the site were proposed, but none came to fruition.

Efforts to preserve the historic resource continued. In 1978 the Remillard brick kiln and stack were included in the National Register of Historic Places and the kiln declared a State Historical Landmark. Finally, in 1989 a building designed by James Maxwell was proposed by Intermark Interests, Inc. The industrial character of the building preserved the integrity of the stack and the kiln and echoed the historic use. To justify the $7.5 million cost of the restoration project that preserved the kiln and stack, a 29,500-square-foot office building was allowed. In 1991 the Remillard brick kiln received the Pacific Coast Builders Gold Nugget Merit Award for "the best rehabilitated commercial or industrial project."

The office building was set back from the kiln and stack to preserve their presence on the street. The barrel-vaulted kiln was transformed into a 5,000-square-foot upscale restaurant called "Remillards." Since then several other restaurants have served a variety of foods under the brick arches of the kiln. In 2009 the Melting Pot was offering a unique fondue menu.

⤴ *Cross East Sir Francis Drake Boulevard to the Sir Francis Drake statue.*

⒄ Sir Francis Drake Statue

For generations the area called Drake's Bay at Pt. Reyes has been unofficially recognized as the site where Sir Francis Drake landed in 1579 for his 36-day stay. The road from San Francisco Bay to Point Reyes Lighthouse also bears Drake's name and winds through other potential landing sites.

Like any good mystery, there is little solid evidence but many clues, all of which have triggered vigorous arguments and sometimes heated debates. The facts are that the English sea captain set out in 1577 to sail around the world and returned to England in 1580. Drake and his five rickety ships sailed down the east coast of South America and around the Straits of Magellan, and then headed north, hugging the coast, periodically taking the time for a little recreational plundering of Spanish vessels and settlements.

By the time he reached the Oregon coast, he was down to one ship, the *Golden Hinde*. Bad weather forced him to abandon his search for a route home via the Orient, and he set sail to the south. On June 17, 1579 he anchored off the northern coast of California and named the area Nova Albion. Unfortunately, Drake never published any account of the trip, and later accounts varied in specifics, including what was called the "conuenient and fit harborough" where he summered. One set the location at 48 degrees latitude; another at 38; and yet another at 30 degrees, 30 minutes. A map published in 1589 and written reports that talked about white cliffs, summer fogs, and a "faire and good Baye" only widened the areas of speculation.

▲ *13.68: The Remillard Brick Kiln and the Sir Francis Drake statue welcome people to Larkspur, 2009.*

As if there weren't enough confusion, a brass plaque surfaced on a Green Brae hillside in 1936. Purported to have been placed there by Drake to claim the land of Nova Albion for Queen Elizabeth I, the plaque started a controversy of its own. Was it a prank by students or the real thing? Even carbon dating failed to silence the debate. The best conclusion is that in 1579 Sir Francis Drake landed somewhere between the beginning of Sir Francis Drake Boulevard on the San Quentin Peninsula, and the Point Reyes lighthouse.

In 1988 big-thinking sculptor Dennis Patton offered to donate a piece of public art to the City of Larkspur. The 30-foot-tall stainless and COR-TEN™ steel statue of Sir Francis Drake was installed at this location with a backdrop of the creek, Northridge, and Mt. Tamalpais.

When asked about his large-scale sculptures, Dennis Patton explained, "I want to give a story to people. My job is to make public art that touches minds."

"It's like Marin's Statue of Liberty," commented a bystander at the dedication ceremony in 1989. The statue takes some artistic liberties. The squat, chunky English explorer has been transformed into a tall, slim gentleman in his metal version. The pilings in the bay adjacent to the statue are remnants of the wharf where bricks were loaded on barges to be hauled around the bay. Although the sculpture was presented to the City of Larkspur, its construction and site preparation were funded by private contributions.

Patton, who was raised in Larkspur and whose parents owned Casa de Art in the downtown area of Larkspur, produced a number of other public art pieces in Larkspur, most notably the large reclining woman, "Tamalpais," who greets shoppers using the center entrance to the Bon Air Center. Others include "Two Boys Fishing," which formerly was at Larkspur Landing; and a driftwood sculpture that once graced the façade of Hall Middle School.

⑱ Remillard Park

Just beyond the statue of Sir Francis Drake, what used to be an unofficial playground for children became Remillard Park when it was added to the Larkspur park system in 1986. The seven-acre freshwater marsh is one of the few remaining freshwater environments around the bay. The pond is a valuable natural resource, providing a habitat for the western pond turtle, migrating birds, American wigeons, soras, and ring-neck ducks, among other species.

Funding for enhancement and improvements was gradual in coming. Before its purchase, the pond had deteriorated from siltation and the invasion of cattails. The first order of business when it joined the park system was to restore it to a healthy condition through the cooperative efforts of the City of Larkspur, Marin Audubon Society and the California Coastal Conservancy. The areas around the pond and the walkways were designed to preserve the delicate environment. Native plants were installed for both erosion control and ambience.

⑲ Drake's Cove

Although controversy swirls about where Drake landed in Marin, developers have adopted him and

▲ 13.69: *View across Remillard Park's freshwater pond to the former rifle range, 1985.*

▲ 13.70: *Major grading was required to create the building pads for Drake's Cove homes, 2008.*

▲ 13.71: *Windsurfers gather at the small beach just before the prison gate, 1991.*

20 Windsurfing Beach

In the 1980s when windsurfing became a popular sport, surfers headed to the beach, located between Remillard Park and the west gate of the prison, to catch the strong prevailing westerly winds that swept through the area in the summertime. When the wind is up, wet-suited sailors still can be seen careening across the creek and dodging ferryboats. On calmer days kayakers and canoeists take advantage of the creek-side location to paddle to the bay.

love to use his name for their projects. As of 2009 the most current was Drake's Cove on the hillside above Remillard Park. In return for the city's approval of a multi-unit development of 24 luxury homes, with selling prices of around $2 million each, land for affordable housing and open space was deeded to Larkspur by developer Monahan Pacific. Providing pads for the homes required major grading of the slopes and 20-foot-high retaining walls. A connecting road provides access to Tubb Lake, Miwok Park, and 2000 Larkspur Landing Circle.

21 San Quentin Graveyard

On the north ridge above East Sir Francis Drake Boulevard just beyond the city limits is San Quentin Graveyard, an old prison burial ground. Simple wooden markers bear the numbers of the 694 nameless inmates who were either executed or died while in prison and are buried there. Men whose bodies were not claimed were interred on this hillside between 1857 and 1947. An ancient Miwok burial mound is located nearby.

⮑ *Return to the ferry terminal parking lot, and drive to the visitor parking lot just to the left of the east prison gate for the San Quentin Village and Prison walks.*

▲ 13.72: *A prison cemetery was located on the hillside above East Sir Francis Drake Boulevard, date unknown.*

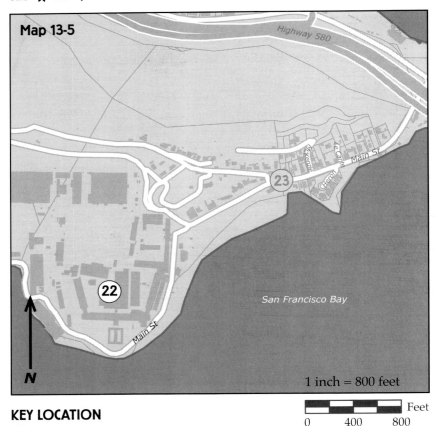

KEY LOCATION

㉒ San Quentin State Prison

↪ *Limited parking is available on Main Street or the prison's East Gate lower visitor's parking lot.*

▲ 13.73: *In 1913 new buildings, housing, and a school designed by state architect George Clinton Sellon had been added to the original 20 acres of San Quentin State Prison.*

▲ 13.74: *The prison dominated the San Quentin Peninsula landscape in the early 1900s.*

SAN QUENTIN STATE PRISON

In 1824 the San Quentin Peninsula was the end of the road for Miwok warrior Quintin. Now the peninsula has the last Marin turn-off before the Richmond-San Rafael bridge on I-580, and is the "end of the road" for 5,300 San Quentin State Prison inmates.

At the height of the Gold Rush in the 1850s, ships were being deserted at the foot of Jackson Street in San Francisco when their crews took off for the gold fields. San Francisco quickly grew from a village into a brawling city of 57,000 with more than its share of thieves and murderers. Since California at that time had no prisons, criminals either got off scot-free or were tossed into the abandoned ships, which were equipped with makeshift cellblocks and were nicknamed "hell ships."

Until 1852, 150 male and female prisoners lived on a 268-ton bark, the *Waban*, in squalid conditions, anchored off Point San Quentin. At that time Benjamin R. Buckelew sold the State of California 20 acres of land along the southern shore of the point for San Quentin State Prison. Although the state paid $10,000 for the land, the original prison was a private facility.

The boat prisoners helped build the first catacomb-like basement cellblock with rock quarried on the site. In *Chronicles of San Quentin* Kenneth Lamott reported that the first cellblock, called "The Stones," was completed in 1854. Overcrowding was a problem from the early days, when 150 prisoners were crowded into the dungeon's cells that were built to accommodate 45. By the end of the first year, the number had doubled to 300. Flogging and an early version of "water-boarding" were standard punishments. Escapes were common in the early days of the prison. In fact, one story has it that the incorporation of San Rafael was initiated in order to create a police force that could guard the citizenry from escaped San Quentin convicts.

Early traveler Daniel Taylor of the Baltimore and Frederick Mining and Trading Company (see pages 99-100) reported in his journal, "In those days the convicts were hired out in work gangs. The state prison at that time had no walls, a circumstance that gave rise to one of the most sensational prison breaks ever recorded. In the 1860s, 400 [other reports say 150] convicts broke prison, taking with them as a hostage the lieutenant governor [John F. Chellis], who, by law, was then the resident warden of the prison. They marched him along the rear of this lawless army to prevent the guards from firing on them, and only liberated him after hurrying him for three miles, on one of the hottest days of the season, to what was then Ross Landing, now Kentfield. Then the outlaw band scattered, making for the hills of Ross and Larkspur."

Dick Nelson, prison historian and associate warden from 1958 to 1998, reported in 1991 that many escapees voluntarily returned to prison after a short taste of freedom. They found life on the outside rough and wanted to be guaranteed a roof over their heads and a daily meal.

One of the most comic and, for a short time, successful prison escapes was the voyage of "Rub-A-Dub-Dub." Three felons hid the makings of a sailboat and, upon escaping, assembled it at the water's edge. As they paddled up Corte Madera Creek, the guard in the tower, mistaking them for boaters on an outing and seeing their rickety boat, called out to see if they needed any help. The trio waved back and paddled the leaky vessel up the creek to temporary freedom.

In another failed attempt in 1976, three inmates burrowed a 10-foot-deep tunnel under a utility alley behind a locked door. The tunnel, which stretched 67 feet and came within 50 feet of the San Francisco Bay, was supplied with an electronic warning system that allowed the inmates in the tunnel to talk to other prisoners.

* * * * *

Convict labor was widely used in the early days. Prisoners in chains and leg irons were frequently hired out for such diverse work as harvesting potatoes, cutting timber, building roads, and erecting cottages and commercial buildings. (Many brick commercial buildings in San Rafael were constructed with the help of convict labor.) During those early days, the prison was a self-contained community growing its own vegetables, raising hogs, and baking bread for prisoners and residents alike.

Over the years the work ethic flourished at the prison. Skilled inmates tanned hides and made shoes and harnesses, while unskilled convicts were put to work at the rock pile and brickyard. In 1880 the prison opened a jute mill that for years supplied farmers across the state with grain sacks until it burned down in 1951. Crafting fine furniture for public buildings has continued until the present time, with the most notable examples being the furnishings in the warden's office and the handsome Frank Lloyd Wright-type furnishings at the Marin Civic Center. However, until 1937 prisoners were never allowed to forget their status. An early gallows, where hangings took place on Fridays at 3 o'clock sharp, remained in the entrance yard of

▲ 13.75: *In 2005 controversial plans for a death-row center on the western section of the prison were on the drawing boards.*

the prison long after that form of execution had been discontinued.

If a prison could have a golden era, it would have been in the period between 1912 and the late 1920s. According to Don Zubler, nephew of Clinton T. Duffy who was warden from 1940 to 1952, there were Sunday marching band concerts, with the inmates decked out in John Philip Souza-style uniforms. Sarah Bernhardt and her company of actors presented *Une Nuit de Noel* on an outdoor stage. The Olympic Club sponsored annual track and field days. Comic costume parades were held, all belying the harsh realities of prison life.

Other times the convict ensemble played in the large gazebo by the warden's office that overlooked the manicured knot garden, called "Garden Beautiful," with its flowers, shrubs, and a birdbath. Festive events were held at the warden's impressive Victorian home located on a knoll above the prison grounds. The house overlooked the formal garden containing monolithic concrete sculptures and embossed arches, balls, and towers.

Over the years since its entertainment heydays, the prison has welcomed modern-day performers as well. In 1969 country music artist Johnny Cash recorded a live album there and performed for the prisoners on three separate occasions. More recently in 2003, the local rock band Metallica shot a video at the prison, with the prisoners as their audience. In 2009 prisoners themselves took the stage and entertained their fellow inmates with a performance of a play by William Shakespeare.

▲ 13.77: *Prisoners crowd the yard to watch entertainment on the stage at the left, 1913.*

Many of the early amenities and landscape features have disappeared. The warden's house was torn down in 1955. Commented former associate warden Dick Nelson, "The termites took it down." The Stonehenge-like monolithic sculptures of the formal gardens are now overgrown. Only a Norfolk star pine that towers over the older prison buildings has survived. The pine is one of two that were brought around Cape Horn and are believed to have been planted by Dr. Alfred Taliaferro, the visiting prison doctor from 1869 until the early 1870s.

The hospital building was originally constructed in 1885 as a women's center. Later the first floor was taken over as a hospital. After scandalous stories circulated and a number of pregnancies were reported, women were moved to a separate

▲ 13.76: *Prisoners made the desk and other furnishings in the office of Robert L. Ayers Jr., who was warden from 2006-2008.*

▲ 13.78: *Sunday afternoon band concert at San Quentin Prison, 1920s.*

▲ 13.79: *The façade of the 1885 hospital building and the lower dungeon were preserved when the building was razed. A new hospital facility was under construction in 2009.*

▲ 13.81: *The twenty 18-inch beams of the former hospital truss ceiling were recycled and re-used, 2007.*

prison in 1933. A library replaced the hospital. As a result of a 2006 lawsuit, the hospital building has been razed and replaced by a new, improved healthcare facility. The Italianate façade and the dank, crypt-like basement dungeon under the original hospital have been preserved under the new building. The dungeon is believed to be the oldest surviving facility constructed by the state, according to historians.

"In the '30s and up until the '60s," commented Don Zubler in 1983, "there was a different class of prisoner – mainly men in on burglary charges." Zubler's family hired convicts for household chores, selecting those who had been sentenced for "crimes of passion." Explained Zubler, "My father figured that that sort of crime only happened once in a man's life, so he was a good risk. Through the '30s, San Quentin was populated by men who had been caught stealing to keep their families going. Now the men inside are hardened criminals."

Major changes in the approach to prisoners took place when Clinton T. Duffy became warden in 1940. The son of a San Quentin guard, Duffy had been born and raised on the prison grounds. He began progressive rehabilitation programs for the "men," as he called the inmates. The airless cells of the dungeon were closed. Torture and physical punishment by whipping were abolished. A night school, cafeteria, and prison newspaper were introduced. His pioneering agenda changed the whole atmosphere of the prison.

The rehabilitation approach was continued from 1983 to 2006, when the Reverend Earl Smith was the Protestant chaplain at the prison. He helped

▲ 13.80: *This late 1920s photograph shows the knot garden in front of the building housing the "Captain's Porch" on the first floor and the women's prison on the second floor. The formal semicircular garden is in the center, with the warden's house above on the hilltop.*

▲ 13.82: *Impressive formal gardens, shown here in 2007, were located on a knoll above the prison in the 1920s.*

EMPLOYEE HOUSING

One of the sections of the prison that is most familiar to the general public is the housing for prison employees visible from East Sir Francis Drake Boulevard just past the west gate. Some of the 85 rental homes, with their hipped roofs, date from the 1880s. Others were built before World War II. The homes are now inhabited by key prison personnel who would be needed in an emergency.

▲ 13.85: Homes on the prison grounds, originally called "The Gulch," were more recently called "The Reservation," 1991.

PRISONER HOUSING

▲ 13.83: An arched-roof cell in the original dungeon, which was sealed off by an iron door with a small slit, was called a "Judas hole," about 1940s.

▲ 13.84: The West Cell Block houses prisoners in five stories of 6- x 8-ft cells, 2007.

form a mass choir, played chess with inmates, organized prison football and basketball teams, and launched a college education program. "I wanted to show that even in a place like this, people could find … something of value," he told a reporter when he retired. In the early 2000s writer and San Quentin recreation supervisor Don DeNevi served up a schedule of tennis activities that mixed local players with inmates.

The policy of providing rehabilitation activities that can teach useful skills to future parolees was enhanced with the renewed publication of the award-winning *San Quentin News* in 2008, after a 16-year hiatus. The *News*, which has a circulation of 7,500, is one of only two prison papers in the country. Inmates can also participate in the gardening program, which is designed to teach them marketable skills they can use when they are paroled. Inmates fear the loss of these programs if a prison sale should result in their being sent to another facility.

The San Quentin Museum's collection of photographs and memorabilia, assembled by former associate warden Nelson and historian Jeff Craemer in 1991, is open on an appointment-only basis. Housed in a single-story hipped-roof cottage just inside the east gate, the museum contains historic treasures, such as the unpublished manuscripts of Prison Doctor Leo Stanley.

Over the years the prison has had its share of famous prisoners who peered out from behind its bars, such as "Black Bart," Charles Manson, Sirhan Sirhan, Eldridge Cleaver, Richard Ramirez, and Merle Haggard to name a few.

Controversy has always surrounded the medieval, castle-like structure, with its turrets and arched cathedral windows. Talks of closing the prison have been frequent over the years. In 1934 a move to Angel Island was suggested and, even as late as 1971 and 1976, talk of closing the prison made developers sit up and take notice. However, with the new construction that was authorized in 1991 and the addition of 2,650 more prisoners since then, the idea of closure seemed far from any official minds.

▲ 13.86: *The stucco schoolhouse, with its interesting concrete "eyebrows" over the arched windows and doorways, was built in 1924. Between the schoolhouse, shown here in 2007, and the bay is the section targeted for the new prison development.*

The area of the prison lands has been increased to 432 acres, but overcrowding continues to be a problem. Some of the buildings are in a decrepit state, with rebar exposed, stucco missing, mosaics damaged, and murals faded. Repair of the 100-year-old buildings is not an easy task. Although some buildings have been retrofitted with buttresses and painted, others do not yet meet seismic standards.

The most controversial item to heat up state, county, and local meeting rooms in the early 2000s was the proposed $360 million, 750-bed complex for condemned inmates on 40 acres on the west side of the prison. Opponents of the prison expansion argued that the project would cost far more than predicted and that the bay front land would be better used for a mixed-use transit center. Controversy and funding questions continue in 2010.

Running San Quentin in 2010 is no small task, as the recently named Warden Vincent Cullen knows. The prison has an annual budget of $184 million and employs 2,000 workers in the care and feeding of the 5,200 inmates. More than 650 men are on death row alone.

Besides being visually prominent, the prison is a major player in Marin's economy and is the biggest water consumer in the county. It even has its own zip code. Its scale dwarfs that of the 50 homes in the nearby village, and the two jurisdictions maintain a touch-and-go relationship. As former associate warden Nelson summed up, "We coexist with the community and make a dedicated effort to be good neighbors."

▲ 13.87: *Four epic 12- x 100-ft long murals depicting California history were painted in sepia tones by artist-prisoner Alfredo Santos between 1953 and 1955 while he was incarcerated. The murals decorate the walls in two of the three separate dining rooms, 2007.*

▲ 13.88: *The fortress-like prison was called the "Bastille by the Bay" by San Francisco Chronicle columnist Herb Caen, 2007.*

▲ *13.89: Ferry passengers get the best view of San Quentin Village, 2008.*

SAN QUENTIN VILLAGE & POINT

⤴ *Park at the visitor's parking lot below the east gate of the prison and walk up the hill to the post office.*

Not only is San Quentin Village the last exit from Marin County off Interstate 580, it also perches at the edge of an almost forgotten time. According to the State Historic Commission, San Quentin Village is one of the last remaining working villages in Marin County. Its main street is more reminiscent of rural West Marin than the dense urban corridor of Highway 101.

One small signpost lures sightseers to its single main street and 50 homes. The last grocery store went out of business in the early 1960s. Except for San Francisco Bay, the village is completely surrounded by state-owned land: the freeway, the prison, and open space. It boasts no school, no church, no community center, no police station or fire department, and no mail delivery.

San Quentin Point is now a dead-end road for villagers and for prisoners, just as it was in the early 1800s for one of its original settlers, Miwok Quintin, who made a last stand there. Although he lost the battle, he subsequently won the honor of having Marin's smallest peninsula named after him. Spain made California a province in 1804, and the lands became part of the new Mexican republic in 1821. Local legend has it that John Frémont first glimpsed San Francisco Bay from Cypress Point.

However, the point became the beginning of the road for settlers in the 1850s. Daniel Taylor, an early

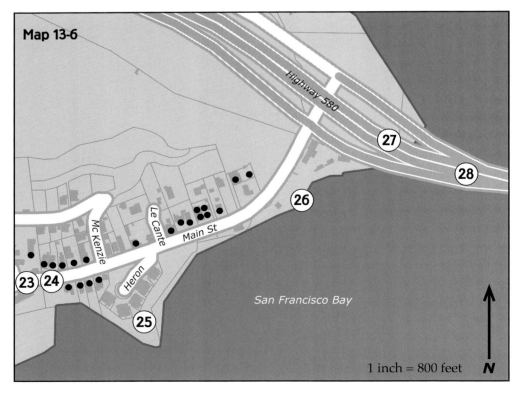

KEY LOCATIONS
- ㉓ San Quentin Prison – East Gate
- ㉔ Main Street Houses
- ㉕ Cypress Point
- ㉖ Old Salt Water Pump House
- ㉗ San Quentin Point & Agnes Island
- ㉘ Richmond-San Rafael Bridge
- • Addresses of Note

member of the Baltimore and Frederick Mining and Trading Company, journeyed from San Francisco to what is now Larkspur in 1849 to set up a lumber mill in "Baltimore Gulch." Recounted Taylor in a 1914 interview, "As we neared San Quentin, a few Indian wigwams were noticeable on a rancheria where the prison hog yard is now located."

In 1850 Juan B. R. Cooper sold Rancho Punta de Quentin to Benjamin R. Buckelew, a New York jeweler and entrepreneur who had journeyed west in 1846. Buckelew dreamed of creating a new metropolis, but decided that San Francisco was nothing but a sandy, thistle-covered land, so he sailed across the bay, first to Tiburon and then to Point San Quentin. He called it his "empire on the bay" and named it "Marin City." However, before he could start, he had to go to court to settle his claim for the land under its original Mexican land grant. Title was confirmed to him in 1854.

William Murray, who purchased property and settled in the northern part of what is now Larkspur, built a sawmill at San Quentin for Buckelew. The mill, which later burned down, was located near the first cluster of eucalyptus trees on the bay side of Main Street just south of the causeway, by the pump house.

Captain Charles Mastron, whose steamers plied the waters of Corte Madera Creek and the bay to San Francisco, had the lease for the San Quentin terminus and erected the first wharf at Point San Quentin. At that time, three years before the prison was built, there were four buildings on the street's north side. Two houses (8 and 6 Main Street) were on the hill across the street from the beach and today's modern-day condominiums. A duplex (24 and 22 Main Street) and the Bay-View Hotel (26 Main Street) were farther up the street.

The town grew after the opening of the penitentiary in 1854. In the early days, when the prison was managed privately instead of by the state, the superintendents built homes and lived in the village. A surveyed map of the Point San Quentin tract was first recorded in 1897 and showed homesites of varying sizes that already existed. Today lots vary in size from 1,500 to 18,800 square feet.

By 1900 the village was sparsely settled. According to a 1950 *Independent Journal* article, on the south side of the street were the Sheppard Hotel, a lumber mill, and the stage-line terminal; on the north side were 63 Main Street and the office at number 64, which had a barn in back for horses and buggies. The article also stated that one of the prison superintendents (who owned a sash-and-window factory) lived at the Sheppard Hotel, which was on Cypress Point. (A condominium development now stands on the site of the former hotel.) The superintendent's lighting was supplied by candles or lanterns, and his water came from artesian wells in the hills. The village had no gas or electricity until 1908.

(23) San Quentin State Prison – East Gate

San Quentin State Prison has always loomed over the village and dominated the lives of families who live there. Clinton Duffy, the warden from 1940 to 1952 who was raised at 100 Main Street when his father was a prison guard, said kids didn't play cops and robbers, but rather prisoners and guards.

As the town grew, the majority of the houses were built facing south, which afforded them a spectacular view of the bay, but for a price: they

▲ 13.90: The towers of the prison loom at the end of Main Street in the village, 2009.

▲ 13.91: *The original San Quentin Village school house remains behind the San Quentin post office, 2010.*

▲ 13.92: *66 Main Street in 1991.*

▲ 13.93: *62 Main Street in 1991.*

got the first blast from the winter storms as they roared in, unimpeded, across the bay. In addition to the weather, residents faced a number of other challenges. Until a sewage system was installed in 1969, the prison and village dumped sewage into the bay and earned the dubious distinction of being the thirteenth-worst polluter, as determined by the San Francisco Bay Regional Water Quality Control Board.

Although official fire protection is provided by San Rafael, the prison fire department will answer calls unofficially until fire fighters from San Rafael can get there. With the re-institution of the death penalty, traffic and protesters jam Main Street when an execution is planned. If the proposed prison expansion is approved, the resultant increase in the convict population will mean more visitor traffic and noise along the tree-lined street. Installation of a speed bump is currently under consideration.

The proximity of the village to the prison does not raise any goose flesh on the residents. Villagers still chuckle over the excitement one balmy summer's evening, when, as former resident Pat Orr recounted, "Every cop car in San Rafael and southern Marin descended on the area. Helicopters, Coast Guard boats, and floodlights illuminated the night, searching for two fellows who 'invaded' into the prison grounds. The two teenagers had begun their ill-starred caper by stealing a car in Larkspur, ditching it near the West Gate, and then [jumping] the prison fence into the housing area, where they were spotted, and the alarm sounded."

The transition between the prison and the village is the San Quentin Prison East Gate, where the prison gift store offers warmth, hospitality, and help for prison visitors. Volunteers occasionally are called upon to help female visitors choose "appropriate attire" from a stack of used clothing before entering prison grounds. The dress code for visitors prohibits blue and denim clothing, yellow rain gear, orange pants, skirts, and jumpsuits, and revealing clothing.

Property owners in the village realize they live on a prime piece of land that is extremely attractive to developers. They frequently hear from realtors inquiring if they are in the market to sell, despite the fact that many of the homes do not have central heating. In 2009, for instance, some properties went on the market for over a million dollars.

Residents have respected and preserved the historic character of the area. Many of the homes along Main Street look the same today as they did in historic

ARE RESIDENTS CONCERNED?

"Having a prison as a neighbor is probably better than a K-Mart, a pickle factory, or 1,000 condos."

— Patt Orr, former San Quentin Village Association president

▲ 13.94: *Villagers are more concerned about the wild turkeys ambling down the street than with the possibility of escaped prisoners, 2008.*

▲ 13.95: 58 Main Street in 1991.

▲ 13.96: 54 Main Street in 1991.

photos. Horses still graze on the state-owned hills north of the homes, nibbling at the poppies and wildflowers that are prevalent in the spring. Some of the Norfolk star pines, fig trees, and exotic trees planted by an avid gardener between 1860 and 1870 remain. The black-crowned night herons still nest in the eucalyptus trees and nightly wing their way out to forage for food.

㉔ Main Street Houses

A walk along Main Street from the prison's east gate is a trip into the past, when the two-lane road was called San Quentin Street. Because there has never been mail delivery to the village, residents have always picked up their mail at the post office and were free to choose whatever numbers they liked for their homes. The result is a non-sequential mixture of odd and even address numbers that is completely perplexing to first-time visitors.

⟳ *Walk on the southwest side of the street.*

Until 1924 the first San Quentin schoolhouse with a tall bell tower in front was located behind the lot where the 1930s-era blockhouse-type post office at **162 MAIN STREET** is today. When a new school was built on the prison grounds in 1924, the original school building was remodeled into a home. Not only does the home remain intact today, but the hardy Mexican fan palms and the Norfolk star pine, which have survived since the 1870s, still grace the property.

The simple, steep-gable-roof houses at **66** and **62 MAIN STREET,** with off-center front doors, have retained their basic lines and are typical of modest nineteenth-century homes, particularly those in company towns. These may have been built in the late 1800s for prison superintendents.

The two-story Victorian house at **58 MAIN STREET** originally had porches with turned-rail posts on both levels and an off-center entrance on the left. Interestingly, the front had a combination of wide-board shiplap siding under the porch and narrow-board shiplap on the rest of the house. Over the years locals referred to the house as the "Chinese house," possibly because of the frequent use of Chinese labor in the prison in the early days. In 2009 the owner had a surprise visit one day before a scheduled prison execution: a surveillance crew commandeered the house as a lookout spot from which to monitor the invasion of protestors into the village.

The one-story hipped-roof cottage at **54 MAIN STREET** was once inhabited by Helen Wills, a pro tennis star in the 1920s and 1930s. Despite some changes, it has retained the flavor of its 1900 folk style, with its mansard roof and front porch. A terraced landscape steps up from the street, and the tall, narrow windows, which originally may have had transoms above, have been replaced. A new front door with a window was added, although the old transom above it has been preserved.

Continuing a tradition of successive generations remaining in the village, the granddaughter of long-time resident Minnie Zappetini Detmayer is the current owner. In 2009 Mrs. Detmayer's daughter was living at number 23.

The homes at **44, 42, 23,** and **38 MAIN STREET,** along the south side, are some of the earliest houses built after the prison opened. Judy Alstrom, former Point San Quentin Village Association president, who lives at 44 Main Street, is the second-generation

▲ 13.97: Homes at 38, 23, 42, and 44 Main Street in 1991.

THE DUFFY HOUSE

"They called it 'Duffy's corner.' They used to say the Duffys ran the town. They did, sort of."

— Don Zubler,
Clinton Duffy's nephew

▲ 13.98: The Duffy house at 100 Main Street in 1991.

owner of the house that her father, Wyman McClure, bought in the 1970s. The Alstroms are unperturbed about having a front-row view of the prison from their back deck, preferring to watch the black-crowned night heron that sleeps in their eucalyptus tree during the day.

An old building at number 44, which originally housed the Snack Shop, was partially removed when the parking ramp was constructed in the early 1990s. In 2009 it was being used as a studio/storage building.

The addresses of these homes exemplify the mixture of non-sequential, odd-and-even numbers on the same side of the street.

The modest home at 42 Main Street, with an unusual side entrance, was on the market in 2009 for over a million dollars.

The gingerbread trim is a more recent addition to 23 Main Street, but the gable-roofed house still retains its tall, narrow, original windows and the basic lines of its late 1800s vintage. Minnie Zappetini Detmayer lived there with her husband for over 31 years. They had picked the spot because of its water location. "Things really grow here," commented Minnie in 1991.

Although the two-story house at **100 MAIN STREET** has been remodeled, it retains vestiges of its original character, such as the arched and trimmed windows on the side bays with brackets. The hipped-roof house, which now has an enclosed front porch, was the second home of former San Quentin prison warden Clinton T. Duffy. The Duffy family first lived on McKenzie Street. Clinton was born in 1898 and lived there until he was ten years old.

Duffy's father, William Joseph Duffy, had come to San Quentin in 1894 from San Pablo. Commented Clinton Duffy in 1950, "Dad didn't like farming, and when he was offered a $60-a-month job as a San Quentin guard, he jumped at the chance. He was later a prison steward." Clinton, who spent his teens in this house, was unique in that he was born in the village, went to school there, married a local girl, and later became the prison warden.

In a 1950 newspaper excerpt from *San Quentin is My Home*, by Clinton T.

Duffy, as told to Dean Jennings, Duffy recalled that he first realized his life was different from that of other families after the 1906 earthquake. The night after the quake, he saw his father standing in front of the house with a rifle. "The San Francisco police had evacuated the jails, loaded the prisoners into a ship that had anchored offshore opposite our house. There was a rumor that the prisoners were plotting to seize the ship as part of a mass prison break, and worried San Quentin guards patrolled the waterfront."

At that time, William Duffy may have set the tone for his son's future sensitivity to prisoners and his desire for rehabilitation programs at that time. Duffy remembered that his father had said, "Now look, kids, go on and play, and forget those poor fellows on the ship. They're probably wet and hungry and scared, and they're not going to bother anybody."

Clinton's childhood was influenced subtly by the prison. The kids fished, climbed fruit trees to claim succulent prizes – "usually the pomegranates around the warden's house" – and had paper routes. "On Sundays we would hike up the north hill and look down into the yard and would occasionally see the men in stripes and the few who were forced to wear red shirts, so as to be better targets for the riflemen patrolling the walks."

Duffy, who married Gladys Carpenter, the daughter of a prison guard, served in the U.S. Marine Corps during World War I. From 1940 to 1952 he was the warden of the prison.

In keeping with his sensitivity to prisoners, one of Duffy's first acts as warden was to eliminate the whipping post and close the dungeon. Although an outspoken opponent of capital punishment, in his role as warden he had to officiate at 90 executions. His comment about the executions, "In the 60 years that I have been around prisons, I have never known of one man who had wealth or position who was ever executed."

When Duffy retired, he was appointed to the adult authority board and served on the parole board for five years. His interest in penology continued to be strong, and he spoke frequently against capital punishment. Clinton Duffy died in 1982 at age 84.

Don Zubler, a historian whose memories spanned the golden era of the prison and the Warden Duffy reign, lived in the former Duffy house at 100 Main Street in 2000. His father Ernest, who was married to Grace Jenny Duffy, was superintendent of the prison jute mill, a major manufacturing part of the prison that turned out five to six million grain sacks a year. The mill burned down in 1951. Don has fond memories of growing up in the village. He

▲ 13.99: During his term as warden at San Quentin State Prison, Clinton Duffy introduced shows in the entrance stage courtyard and brought in entertainers, such as comedian Joe E. Brown, pictured here, 1940s.

WARDEN DUFFY

"I've thought of men behind bars as my father saw them – human beings in trouble and needing a helping hand."

— Clinton Duffy

attended the new school when it was built on the prison grounds in 1924. The two-room building housed grades 1-4 and 5-8. The 50 children who attended were taught by Gladys Duffy, Don's aunt and Duffy's wife.

A favorite sport of village kids was to make sleds out of the pickets in front of the houses.

"We'd take two pickets, a square from an orange crate, and another smaller piece and mount the pickets on them. We'd grease the backs of the pickets with bacon rinds and then go up on the hill behind the village and slide down the grasses."

— Don Zubler

---

(25) Cypress Point

While the storm winds that blow off the bay are a natural risk for the village, those that bring change and "progress" are an even bigger concern for the residents.

Cypress Point, which pokes up from the edge of the bay and bears the brunt of winter winds and summer fogs, bore the first threat of development. When early settlers landed on the peninsula, they replaced the Coast Miwoks. They planted the cypress trees and built a lumber mill and the Sheppard Hotel, where the Heron Court condominiums now stand.

The large two-story hotel was an early example of recycling. Lumber that had been shipped around Cape Horn was originally used to build a structure at *El Campo*, later called "California City" near today's Paradise Cove on the Tiburon peninsula.

▲ 13.100: *The Sheppard Hotel, circa 1900s.*

▲ 13.101: *Cypress Point and condominiums, 2008.*

When a number of structures in that area were dismantled in the 1870s, the lumber was barged over to San Quentin to construct the hotel. The gabled structure was the scene of many social functions and had quarters for transients, workers, and sightseers. Many of the rooms were rented by people who were welcoming released prisoners. The hotel saloon was the most popular of the five in the village in the early days. The hotel was torn down in 1962.

Another threat to the point came in 1976, when high-rise condominiums were proposed for the 2.24-acre Cypress Point site, where the old Sheppard Hotel had once stood. The village community banded together and fought a six-year battle that resulted in a drastic reduction of the density from forty units in ten two-story buildings, to ten units in five two-story buildings. The 1981 approval included a permanent open-space easement for the cypress-studded bluff and the beach area on the east side. A trail leads down from the point to large flat rocks that project out into the bay.

During the fight over the condominiums, villagers had feared that construction of such a large project would irrevocably alter the historic character of their environment. Ironically, the new condo owners are some of the strongest supporters of the community and of retaining the village's historic qualities.

↪ *Continue walking east on Main Street.*

A painting by former warden Duffy captures the look of 97, 95, and 26 Main Street. The gable roof of number 97 is all that remains of its former appearance. Number **95 MAIN STREET**, built about 1860, was originally the post office. It later became a grocery store, first operated by Bill Kinney and later by the McCarthy family, who still owned the building in 2009, although it has been converted from a store into a residence. At one time it was nicknamed the "cowboy house" because of its western façade, but when the building was converted to a duplex, its original architectural character was changed.

Both **63** and **64 MAIN STREET** have also been converted to homes, but in their early days they had other personalities. The gabled-roof building at 63 Main Street was the stagecoach terminal, and 64 was the office. When the trestle to the ferry terminal was condemned, a new railroad terminal was located at 63 Main Street.

The significant-looking, two-story brick building at **26 MAIN STREET** was the Bay-View Hotel in the early 1900s. Over the years it housed a bordello and later a grocery store called the "Hitching Post." At one point in its history, Henry Le Cante operated a hotel there.

In 1991 when the building had fallen into disrepair, former New Orleans resident Walter Villere remodeled it into a single-family dwelling with an attached in-law apartment. According to Villere, the two-story brick building was retrofitted with "a steel cage on the inside that holds the floors and roof up if the walls collapse." Two inches of the old sand concrete on the exterior walls had to be dug out and replaced. Villere replaced the old fenestration with mahogany-framed windows, which he installed himself. The project maintained the historic character of the building and gave it a French-Quarter look with its wrought-iron railings.

The single-story duplex building at 24 and 22 Main Street, and the adjacent two-story fourplex at 20A, 20, 18A, and 18 Main Street are in early photos.

The home at **16 MAIN STREET** is a good example of how an 1870 home can be updated into the twenty-first century, while retaining its historic character. In 1991 the cross-gabled, two-story house was badly in need of both cosmetic and structural help. It has now been restored and remodeled into a three-bedroom, two-bath home with an income unit. Michele Barni, who is acting president of the Point San Quentin Village Association in 2010, and her husband, David, are the owners. Fishscale shingles, a stained glass window, and new gable trim have spruced up the gable area above the two-story bay. Porch railings

▲ 13.103: Bay-View Hotel at 26 Main Street in 1909.

▲ 13.102: Clinton Duffy's painting of 97 (second house from left), 95, and 26 Main Street.

▲ 13.104: 26 Main Street in disrepair, 1991.

▲ *13.105: 16 Main Street in 1991.*

▲ *13.106: 16 Main Street in 2009.*

have been replaced. The shiplap siding and brackets under the eaves have been painted.

As with other residents, the proximity of the prison doesn't light up the worry meter for the family. Commented Michele in a *Marin Magazine* interview: "The village is a low-crime neighborhood. If someone escapes, they're not going to hang around here, where the law enforcement is nearby."

The hipped-roof Victorian houses at **6 and 8 MAIN STREET,** visible on the hill above the north side of Main Street, date from the late 1800s. Number 8 has had a front addition, which obliterated its original porch. Number 6 has retained its wrap-around porch, front dormer, and its Victorian-cottage appearance.

㉖ Old Salt Water Pump House

Periwinkle Beach, the quiet cove southwest of the Richmond-San Rafael Bridge, not only mixes the old and the new, but provides an interesting juxtaposition of the bustle and noise of traffic with the quiet feeding of sandpipers. The old Salt Water Pump House harks back to the early 1900s, when the salty bay water was pumped to a hilltop reservoir for the prisoners to bathe in.

㉗ San Quentin Point & Agnes Island

San Quentin Point and Agnes Island were hubs of transportation in the late 1800s. Point San Quentin ferry service was started in 1855 by Charles Minturn, called "The Ferryboat King" because of his monopoly on trans-bay traffic in that period. A deep-water wharf built on Agnes Island by Martha Buckelew, Benjamin's wife, was connected to the mainland by a causeway, where the bridge approach is today. A 25-cent toll road connected the wharf with San Rafael. Ferries and barges put in at the

▲ *13.107: 6 Main Street, 2009.*

▲ *13.108: The Old Salt Water Pump House, 1991.*

wharf, as did prison supply boats. Boats brought loads of fruit from the Sacramento Valley for transport to Ross Valley.

In a 1900 photograph, two buildings were situated on the wharf: a hipped-roof station and a saloon. The first post office was at the ferry terminal, which had a large deck to connect it with the ferry for easy passenger transfer. The ferry ran between the point and Richmond until 1955.

Marin's first railroad, the San Rafael & San Quentin (SR&SQ), built in 1870, ran the 3½ miles between the ferry landing and San Rafael. In the early days a train trestle extended on piles from near the Greenbrae Rod and Gun Club (see page 305) to the Agnes Island wharf. To make other connections, a stage-line terminal was near the causeway by the pump house.

In the 1920s a bay shrimp processing factory was located next to the train station at the point. In later years, when the trestle was declared unsafe, the station terminal was moved to 63 Main Street.

Old-timers still smile about the day a lot of chickens learned to swim. The story goes that after the station had been moved to the Main Street terminal, the train would halt before the trestle and switch to the spur track into the village. However, on this one day, the train sped out to the end of the line on the trestle and dumped the conductor, his engine, his fireman, and engineer, along with a trainload of chickens, into the bay. No one was hurt, but many a squawking fowl learned to swim. Don Zubler recalls swimming in the waters of the bay near the old pier and finding large train wheels imbedded in the mud, perhaps corroborating the story.

The Bay Conservation and Development Commission (BCDC) controls construction within

▲ 13.110: The "Klamath" auto ferry arriving at Point San Quentin from Richmond, 1945.

100 feet of the shoreline and will review any development proposals for the point.

㉘ Richmond-San Rafael Bridge

The actual Point San Quentin and Agnes Island disappeared under the approach lanes when construction of the Richmond-San Rafael Bridge was completed in 1956, and the approach leapfrogged from the point to Agnes Island and across the bay. After the rejection of a Frank Lloyd Wright design, the state designed the 5½ mile-long, two-deck bridge that became known as the "roller-coaster span" and "the swayback bridge." The engineers explained that the unusual shape of the bridge was dictated by the angles required to connect the highways at either end. The undulating form was to accommodate the navigational channels that pass under the bridge.

During the 1977 drought, a pipeline across the span carried precious water to Marin. After the mud slides on the Waldo Grade in 1982 (when the Golden Gate Bridge was closed) and, again, after the 1989 Loma Prieta earthquake (when a section of the Bay Bridge collapsed), bridge traffic boomed. In 1969 an average of 15,489 vehicles crossed the bridge each day; by 1982 the count was 32,500 vehicles a day; and in 2009 the count was 70,000.

Like many aging citizens, the bridge is currently suffering from joint problems, which lead to the creation of potholes on its surface. However, an even more ominous black cloud on the horizon, for the village and the wider area, is the pending enlargement of the prison and the uncertainty over its impact on traffic, noise, and the historic character of the San Quentin Peninsula. ✦

▲ 13.109: Early 1900s view of San Quentin Village, the railroad connection to the mainland, and Agnes Island (at right), as seen from Cypress Point.

EPILOGUE

Only one day a year is the moon centered over Mt. Tamalpais… but you can celebrate living in Larkspur every day of the year.

14.1: Moon over Mt. Tamalpais, timeless.

Over the years man has been lured to Larkspur because of the creek, the tall redwoods, and hillside views. Homes were built creating distinctive neighborhoods in its canyons, along its creek banks and on its slopes with views of Mt. Tamalpais.

The downtown began as a cluster of Native American villages that were replaced by lumber mills, livery stables, and shipping docks and evolved over the years first to ranch lands and hillside vineyards then to local hardware and grocery stores. In 2008, the city's Centennial Year, the butchers, bakers, and bars have been replaced by bistros, boutiques, and baby shops.

Yet Larkspur has preserved its historic essence. The basic elements of the town are positioned at the junction of Magnolia Avenue and King Street – a residential home, a commercial building, a church and a city hall and library. The false front store facades, the Mission Revival style church and city hall, the early Queen Anne Victorians and the Blue Rock Inn all evoke the essence of the city's past and present a capsule history of the town in its two block downtown. On its 100th birthday Larkspur's downtown still retained the flavor its bawdy past. Old buildings have been gussied up and even the Silver Peso has been painted.

Although development has filled most of the vacant land, far-sighted citizens purchased open space, required marsh dedication and took strong stands on heritage tree preservation.

What hasn't changed is Larkspurians' love for their community. The active involvement of concerned residents in proposed changes to the areas they care about so deeply still provides protection that ensures Larkspur's special qualities will be looked on with pride for years to come.

Although descendants of the reported 375-pound bear hunted by early loggers no longer roam the canyon slopes, deer, raccoons, squirrels, and laurels, madrones, oaks, and wild flowers abound.

14.2: Baby strollers, bikers, and diners have replaced grocery and hardware store shoppers, 2008.

The city still lures people to its creeks, its heritage oaks, and its majestic redwoods that inspire a special, quiet aura, dwarfing human intrusions. Views of Corte Madera Creek, Mt. Tamalpais, Big and Little King Mountains, and Northridge are coveted.

As it enters its second century Larkspur remembers its colorful past while making room for present-day challenges and opportunities. In the words engraved on the Centennial plaque before City Hall, Larkspur is a city that preserves and honors its history and small-town character. This book is a tribute to that spirit.

Appendix A: PRESERVING LARKSPUR'S PAST
How Citizen Volunteers Helped Save a City's Heritage

"Much of Larkspur's charm and character come from its rich architectural heritage. Its historic resources are irreplaceable assets that contribute to the special and unique character of the city and are a source of identity and pride for its residents." — Larkspur General Plan, 1990-2010

Larkspur's rich historic character exists today because for 40 years citizen volunteers have played a key role in recording, honoring, and preserving the city's colorful past.

It all began at the end of 1970, when 250 citizens attended the first Larkspur Town Meeting and made several recommendations, including the creation of an "aesthetic" volunteer committee to deal with the renovation and beautification of what was called "the shabby downtown with empty storefronts." Larkspur residents Nancy Curley and Helen Heitkamp volunteered.

"All we were going to do was take the poorly framed old photos in City Hall down from the walls, write captions, reframe them, and find more photos in the library," said Curley. "But we couldn't find more photos." Fireman Doug Archer came to the rescue with negatives from the Larkspur Fire Department's collection and the city's photo archives began.

When Heitkamp tried to write the captions, she could find little documentation of Larkspur's history. So she went to the person in town who knew more about Larkspur than anyone – Helen C. Wilson, longtime librarian and city clerk – and began recording the city's history.

Curley and Heitkamp were joined by a group of volunteers, and the Larkspur Heritage Committee was formed. The committee set about interviewing longtime residents, collecting and copying historic photos, and publishing walking tour brochures of historic locations, culminating in 1979 with publication of the first edition of this book. A second edition followed in 1991.

But the committee members wanted to do more than research Larkspur's history. They moved to provide official protection for the city's historic resources by drafting a historic preservation ordinance for consideration (and ultimate adoption) by the city council and creating an inventory of historic buildings, homes and sites that would become Larkspur's official historic resources inventory.

The committee succeeded in 1982 in having "Old Downtown" Larkspur recognized as a Historic District in the National Register of Historic Places. Placement in the register provides incentives and benefits to property owners of historic buildings and enhances a community's ability to preserve them. Historic plaques can be seen on buildings in the district, listing characteristics that give them special status. Other historic Larkspur structures in the National Register of Historic Places include the 1888 Dolliver House on Madrone Avenue, the 1927 Alexander Avenue Bridge, and the 1891 Remillard Brick Kiln on East Sir Francis Drake Boulevard, which was also declared a State Historical Landmark.

In 1978 the City Council adopted the Heritage Preservation Ordinance and at the same time created the Larkspur Heritage Preservation Board, an official arm of the city, to oversee the elements of the new ordinance. Members of the old heritage committee continued to work on, and with, the new board.

In recognition of the downtown's historic importance, its zoning emphasizes historic preservation, providing planning tools needed to ensure that new and remodeled buildings reflect the area's historic character. "We treasure our downtown," said Larkspur city councilmember Joan Lundstrom, who initiated and chaired the Larkspur Town Meetings in the 1970s and helped spark Larkspur's interest in its history.

Over 77 homes with special qualities that have contributed to Larkspur's essential character are recognized on the city's *Historic Resources Inventory*, initially approved by the Larkspur City Council in 1979 and updated in early 2009 following a series of public hearings held by the board. Such recognition provides benefits to homeowners and preserves the exterior of homes that the public views.

The work of the board is reflected in the city's official mission statement: "The City of Larkspur is committed to providing the best possible service to the community, preserving the City's unique historic character, and maintaining its total environmental balance."

Larkspur Heritage Preservation Board

The Larkspur Heritage Preservation Board was established by ordinance in 1987. It currently consists of volunteer members of the community, a member of the Planning Commission, and a member of the Planning Department. Members are appointed by the City Council and serve a term of four years. It is an advisory committee to the Planning Commission and its powers include review of building applications for homes and structures on the Larkspur *Historic Resources Inventory*, recognition of outstanding preservation work on historic structures, and periodic compilation of resources to be added to or deleted from the inventory.

The following standards must be met for the Board to recommend approval of applications:
- The proposed work will be compatible with the exterior architectural character of the historic resource and neighboring historic resources.
- The proposed work will maintain the integrity of the historic resource.
- The proposed work will not significantly diminish public view of the historic resource.
- The proposed work will not adversely affect the historic, architectural, or aesthetic character of the neighborhood.

Historic Preservation: Benefits and Incentives

In addition to the emotional link to the past and the prestige that historic resources provide, there are practical benefits to an historic designation as well as incentives offered by the City of Larkspur:
- 2009 *Historic Resources Inventory* identifies buildings with historic significance. Early awareness of the historic significance of a property will assist property owners in preparing appropriate remodeling plans.
- Awards Program for Historic Restoration/Renovation honors notable historic renovation of both residential and commercial properties.
- Greater flexibility for variances and exceptions to zoning regulations helps preserve existing historic residences and allows for appropriate additions.
- Application of the Historic Building Code* allows more flexibility in meeting building standards, provided there is no conflict with health and safety. Consult with the city's building inspector before designing additions and alterations.
- Mills Act Contract Program* provides a limited number of qualifying historic single-family residences with property tax reductions in return for active restoration and maintenance of the resource.
- Varying tax credits* have been available over time for the rehabilitation of historic structures that are income generating properties (apartments and commercial). Credits apply only to the original structure itself, not to any additions.

The State Office of Historic Preservation website http://ohp.parks.ca.gov has information on the Historic Building Code, Mills Act Contracts and tax credits. The office can also provide a list of grants and funds that may be available for designated historic structures.

A HISTORIC TOWN MEETING

In 1970, Larkspur citizens looked around at some disturbing trends:

❖ Apartments were walling off Corte Madera Creek and a high-rise rose atop a hill;

❖ All hillsides were proposed for development, with the population expected to almost double in 15 years;

❖ Historic downtown buildings were falling into disrepair, with competition from shopping centers looming.

Newcomers Joan Lundstrom and Helen Heitkamp decided to take a page from New England history and organize a Town Meeting to make the public aware of all the proposed changes and their implications for Larkspur's small-town character. The two women recruited a committee of 50 citizens to plan a public meeting where such issues as coping with population increases, saving open space, and improving the appearance of downtown could be explored.

Public support seemed evident when 250 citizens showed up on Nov. 21, 1970 and adopted a set of 15 resolutions profiling concerns on residential and commercial development, preservation of open space, and creation of hiking and biking pathways. When the resolutions were rebuffed by the City Council, that sparked a genuine political revolt. Three more Town Meetings were held in 1971, 1972, and 1974, demonstrating broad support for new approaches. Lundstrom was elected to the Council, and Heitkamp was appointed to the Planning Commission. The 1973 General Plan reflected the Town Meeting resolutions. And work began to chronicle and preserve Larkspur's history.

Seeking National Recognition For Larkspur's Downtown

In 1982 Larkspur's downtown was listed in the National Register of Historic Places and designated a Historic District -- providing formal recognition of our city's historical significance based on national standards used by every state. Citizens researched the area's history and worked with city officials to prepare the application for placement in the register. Excerpts follow:

(Excerpts from National Trust Application)

★ **THE DISTRICT IS SIGNIFICANT because of the high percentage (72%) of buildings, particularly commercial ones built between 1880 and 1930, that remain.**

Progress has been gentle to Larkspur. Growth and development have not eliminated its historic essence. Brad Paul, regional information Officer of the National Trust, commented that Larkspur is fortunate to have so many of its early buildings still intact.

It is significant that so many of the original buildings representing the commercial, civic, religious and residential life of the community retain their human scale, intent and design. The changes that have been made are reversible so that many remodeled buildings could be taken back to their historic form.

★ **THE DISTRICT IS SIGNIFICANT because it has the ambience of a typical California small town between 1900 and 1930.**

The downtown district is a three dimensional portrait of how people lived in small towns at the turn of the century. Its commercial store fronts with residential units above, its eclectic look resulting from the mix of styles that infilled during different architectural periods and its blend of residential styles from modest Queen Anne to California bungalow-all convey the feeling of the past.

The Blue Rock Hotel, the bank, the theatre, the Silver Peso (Bob's Tavern), the barber shop and City Hall – all still house uses similar to those for which they were used in the 1900s.

Although the railroad tracks have been removed, the station, the cluster of railroad buildings, the concrete platform and the arched trees still evoke the feeling of the days when trains instead of bikes roared down the tracks.

Magnolia Avenue has been paved and the bare electric light wire strung across the street has been replaced by underground wiring, but the streetscape still has the echoes of the look and human scale of a small bedroom community of the 1900s.

The palm tree, typical of the favorite trees of the 1900s, is a reminder of the civic activities of the Larkspur Woman's Improvement Club that developed the park in front of the railroad station in 1913.

The Mission revival-style civic buildings – the library, city hall and firehouse – within the District are typical of small town public buildings in the 1900s.

Unlike other towns that have evolved into suburban bedroom communities, Larkspur has retained its small town commercial character. The purchase by the city of the Northridge open space lands has preserved the natural backdrop of the city so that the view looking south along Magnolia Avenue through the District is visually the same as it was in the 1900s.

★ **THE DISTRICT IS SIGNIFICANT because of the part it has played in the history of the Bay Area.**

In the hectic 1840s when gold rush fever created a run on building materials in San Francisco, Larkspur had a deep water port that was officially designated by Capt. J.B. Montgomery, USN, located at Sawmill Landing a block and a half from the northern end of the District boundaries. The oxen that hauled logs down Magnolia Avenue from the city's two sawmills loaded them on barges at Sawmill Landing for transport to San Francisco.

When the passenger railroad station was built in 1891, summer vacationers discovered Larkspur's congenial climate. They rented rooms at the Blue Rock Hotel or one of the cluster of bungalows on Magnolia Avenue that leased for $12 a month.

Refugees from the San Francisco earthquake raised their tents across the street from Crazy Murphy's house, and many San Franciscans who had summer homes in Larkspur, such as the Costellos who had purchased the King house, moved into them permanently.

In the 1900s the Rose Bowl dances first held in the park in front of the railroad station drew 3,000 to 4,000 people weekly. Dancers took the ferry to Sausalito or San Quentin and the train to Larkspur to attend the dances.

★ **THE DISTRICT IS SIGNIFICANT because of its reflection of Marin County's unique history.**

While modest examples of the architectural styles of the 1800s and 1900s, the commercial, residential and civic buildings in the District are a capsule history of the early lumbering, ranching and dairying, marketing, vacationing and living patterns that were prevalent in small Marin County towns. The wealthy summer visitors headed for Ross or San Rafael, but Larkspur summer residents built more modest homes such as the Frizzi home and the Costello home or rented bungalows on Magnolia Avenue or campsites under the redwoods across from Crazy Murphy's house.

Located on a major county road connecting Sausalito and Tomales and the prime route to the Russian River, Larkspur's Blue Rock Hotel was the stopping off spot in the early days.

County-wide crowds were drawn to the back of Frizzi's saloon and the old Lynch building to cheer on the name prizefighters who sparred there.

The Fourth of July Booster Day Parades held from 1909 to 1913 quick-stepped down the length of Magnolia Avenue within the District drawing crowds from all over – a tradition that still exists today at the annual Fourth of July Parade.

★ **THE DISTRICT IS SIGNIFICANT because of the typical small town architectural styles represented.**

Although the residential and commercial buildings within the District were built over a period of years between the 1870s and the 1930s, the scale of the streetscape has been maintained so that the Historic District is a cohesive unit of commercial and residential buildings documenting by their architecture the various periods of growth and history in Larkspur.

CITY OF LARKSPUR DOWNTOWN HISTORIC DISTRICT

BOUNDARY ▰▰▰▰▰▰

SCALE: 1 inch = 100 feet

STRUCTURES AND SITES

 Contributing

 Non-contributing

CONTRIBUTING BUILDINGS
for Larkspur Downtown Historic District, 1982

234 Magnolia Avenue
236, 238, 240 Magnolia Avenue
242, 246, 250C, 260, and 270 Magnolia Ave.
274 and 274A Magnolia Avenue
276 Magnolia Avenue
278 and 280 Magnolia Avenue
282, 284, and 286 Magnolia Avenue
105 King Street, Costello House
400 Magnolia Avenue, Larkspur City Hall
401 Magnolia Avenue, St. Patrick's Church
420 Magnolia Avenue, Larkspur Fire Station
15 Rice Lane
435 Magnolia Avenue
444 Magnolia Avenue
450 Magnolia Avenue
455 Magnolia Avenue
457 Magnolia Avenue
460 Magnolia Avenue
464 Magnolia Avenue
467 and 471 Magnolia Avenue
468 Magnolia Avenue
469 Magnolia Avenue
472 Magnolia Avenue
474 Magnolia Avenue
475, 479, and 481 Magnolia Avenue
480 and 482 Magnolia Avenue
483 Magnolia Avenue
488 and 490 Magnolia Avenue
489 Magnolia Avenue
494 Magnolia Avenue
499 Magnolia Avenue
503 Magnolia Avenue
107 Ward Street, *now 115 Ward Street*
507 Magnolia Avenue
2 Ward Street
4 Ward Street, *now 504 Magnolia Avenue*
531, 533, 535, and 537 Magnolia Avenue
541 and 545 Magnolia Avenue
549 and 551 Magnolia Avenue
552 Magnolia Avenue
552 ½ Magnolia Avenue
Railroad platform and right-of-way

Appendix B: TYPICAL HOMES OF LARKSPUR

B.1: Victorian farm house, Murray Park, 2001.

B.2: Craftsman style, Baltimore Park, 2009.

B.3: Canyon summer shack, Baltimore Canyon, 1990.

B.4: Prairie style, Baltimore Park, 1990.

B.5: California Bungalow, South Magnolia, 2010.

One of the charms of Larkspur is that its neighborhoods present a capsule history of the town that is subtly reflected in its architecture. Architectural periods ranging from Victorian, California Craftsman, Mission Revival, and California Bungalow to the tract and ranch homes of the 1940s to 1960s are represented.

Because of the city's proximity to San Francisco, Larkspur home builders were aware of a wide range of architectural details that they combined with local natural elements such as redwood, brick and blue rock. The local lumber yard could mill all sorts of details and combine design features from all styles often making the pinpointing of a period of construction difficult. Early builder Gustave Nagel produced and remodeled homes from 1888 to the 1930s representing a wide range of styles and details.

"What makes Larkspur's homes unique," explained architectural historian Dan Peterson, " is that instead of being generated by professional designers, they have been done locally. The homes are very personal and individualistic."

Although most of city's built environment is composed of modest structures, it reveals a way of life as clearly as do more sophisticated structures. They show how average people lived in the late nineteenth and early twentieth centuries. While individually the homes may not be significant, collectively they contribute to the total character of the area. In many neighborhoods, homes of vastly different sizes and prices are often side-by-side.

The earliest neighborhoods developed along Magnolia Avenue and the hills immediately west of it. Baltimore Canyon homes began as summer cabins for summer vacationers and for permanent residents after the 1906 earthquake.

Some neighborhoods such as Baltimore Park, Heather Gardens, Meadowood, Hillview, and Greenbrae were developed as total units at one period of time, creating a large concentration of homes, in the same style and scale. By 2010, many of the original homes had been modified, remodeled, or replaced and mingle with lovingly maintained homes from the early 1900s and 1920s and 1930s.

Larkspur has many homes 50 years or older that have not been detailed in this book but contribute to its general ambience. Before remodeling them, owners are urged to check with the city for guidance. The homes highlighted in the book not only meet the age requirement of 50 years or more but many are also related to a person or event of historic importance within the city.

B.6: Mediterranean bungalow, Baltimore Park, 2009.

B.7: World War II tract home, Heather Gardens, 1990.

B.8: 1960s house, Meadowood, 2009.

C.1: Beta Street at 110 Madrone Avenue originally connected up to Hazel Avenue, but only the lower steps are still available to the public and the local deer, 2008.

C.2: Path and stairs between 2 and 4 Shady Lane to Piedmont Road, 2008.

Appendix C: PAPER STREETS, STAIRS & PATHWAYS

In the car-less days of the late 1800s, early hillside residents ran errands and visited friends using neighborhood pathways, steps, and lanes that often appeared on maps as streets but were little more than mostly unimproved public rights-of-way.

The original Larkspur survey map, drafted in 1887 by H. C. Ward for the American Land and Trust Company *(see page vi)*, the city's first developer, included named streets in the hills that were designed to provide connections to the few existing streets on the flats. But the streets on paper didn't match Larkspur's topography of steep slopes and gullies, which made these "paper streets" – streets that appear on maps but don't exist in reality – difficult if not impossible to improve as streets for public use. Subsequent subdivision maps designated walking routes for Larkspur pedestrians.

Paper streets have had disputed, confused and changing legal status over time. It's been reported that when Charles Wright was subdividing Larkspur, his wife Georgiana wanted 64 "rights-of-way" preserved as open space until they "reverted" to the Wrights' ownership "in the future." The underlying fee-title ownership of what turned out to be inaccessible rights-of-way ultimately reverted to the Wrights and their heirs.

Some of the stairs and pathways have become overgrown; some right-of-way easements have been abandoned by the city; and some have been paved. Although they may only be occupied by a pedestrian stairway or drainage and utility easements, some of the paper streets are retained as public property, and continue to be recognized as public streets maintained by the City of Larkspur.

In the twenty-first century residents are rediscovering Larkspur's informal networks of paper streets, pathways, and stairs that offer faster ways to get around town without using cars. They're seen as important escape routes in case of fire, as shortcuts for children to get to school, and as venues for healthful exercise.

Some of the original paper streets, such as the Arch Street stairs, Post Street, Eden Street, and the path between lower Elm Avenue and Bayview Avenue path/stairs, continue to be used by pedestrians and athletes in training. In 2008 Post Street and the lower Elm to Bayview path received federal grants totaling $307,875 for repairs that would help people get around on foot and reduce time needed for pedestrian travel.

WHERE ARE THEY?

These paper streets, stairs, and pathways are maintained by the City of Larkspur. Addresses are given for the downhill side.

DOWNTOWN:
- **Arch Street** – stairs between 255 & 285 Magnolia Avenue to Walnut Avenue.
- **Post Street** – pathway and stairs just north of the Lark Theater (549 Magnolia Avenue) to Locust Avenue.

OLD HOMES
- **Eden Street** – stairs between 2-4 & 11 Eden Lane to Laurel Avenue.

CANYON
- **Beta Street** – stairs from street to sidewalk at 110 Madrone Avenue.

BALTIMORE PARK
- **Stradway Lane** – stairs between 233 & 247 West Baltimore to Coleman Avenue.
- **West Baltimore Avenue** – stairs between 265 & 273 West Baltimore Avenue to Coleman Avenue.
- **Shady Lane** – stairs between 2 & 4 Shady Lane to Piedmont Road.
- **Shady Lane** – stairs between 3 & 11 Shady Lane to Piedmont Road.

PALM HILL
- **Lower Elm Avenue** – stairs and pathway between 80 & 88 Elm Avenue to Upper Elm Avenue.
- **Bayview Avenue** – pathway between 44 & 56 Bayview Avenue to Lower Elm Avenue.

HEATHER GARDENS
- Stairs from Heatherwood Park to Meadowood.
- Pathway from Heatherwood Park to Midway Road.

GREENBRAE & BON AIR
- **Lower Via Casitas** – pathway, stairs, and bridge from the north end of Bon Air Center to between 160 & 210 Via Casitas.

D.1: Portrait of Gustave Nagel, late 1880s.

Appendix D: GUSTAVE NAGEL - LARKSPUR'S ARCHITECT

The structures that versatile local architect-builder Gustave Nagel built in Larkspur ranged from modest homes to pretentious mini-castles and public buildings.

A facile designer, Gustave Nagel changed his architectural style to match the fashion of the day. In the 1890s and early 1900s he designed Victorian homes with dropped siding, brackets and turrets. Nagel also did remodeling and repair work, including the completion of Judge Mahoney's home at 74 Hazel Avenue in the 1890s after a lawsuit was brought against the original contractor. In the 1920s and 1930s he switched to the bungalow style with shiplap siding, covered verandas with pillars and low pitched hip roofs or a gable roof with a front dormer. During Prohibition, he went with the times and added secret 6- x -8-ft rooms that could be used for stashing contraband.

Born in 1860 on a farm outside of Chicago, he learned the carpentry trade there before moving to San Francisco where he operated the Oyster Depot. After he married Emilie Lanouette in 1884 and had two daughters Eda and Delma, the family moved to a house on Walnut Avenue in Larkspur, and he began his building career. When the home burned, the family returned to San Francisco but fled back to Larkspur after the 1906 earthquake when their city house burned. They stayed initially with Emilie's sister Carolyn, and her husband Charles Rice. While the new house at 126 Magnolia Avenue was under construction, Nagel lived in a small rear cabin in the backyard until it was completed in 1907 *(see page 182)*.

Between 1925 and 1927 Nagel created a family compound with shared backyards for his daughter and in-laws while he designed an adjacent home at 116 Magnolia and two at 8 and 10 Alexander. After his death in 1943, his daughter Eda lived in 126 Magnolia and kept it in vintage condition, maintaining the original furnishings until her death in 1984 at 96.

Because Larkspur had its own lumber and mill yard, Nagel often drew up his own architectural plans and incorporated design elements for all periods gleamed from Maybeck, Coxhead and Polk homes around the Bay Area. Inside, Nagel like to include a stone or brick fireplace, wood paneling, a built-in bookcase and a buffet with leaded or stained glass.

Time and wage books, written in penciled longhand by Nagel, show that his highest paid carpenter in 1920 earned $44 a week for 5½ days at $8 per day. For a job on Ward Street that same year, Nagel recorded the following: 5 sacks cement for $16.50, lumber nails and carpenter for $12.50, ¼ load of sand for $1.25.

An impressive number of Nagel homes are still part of many Larkspur neighborhoods.

The Nagel Larkspur structures identified on the opposite page were verified by his daughter Eda Nagel, his great-granddaughter Joan Dougherty, and by county records. Homes that have been extensively remodeled or have lost distinguishing features are not included on this list.

"If at first you don't succeed, the hell with it."

— Gustave Nagel

GUSTAVE NAGEL HOMES and OTHER PROJECTS

Address	Original Owner	Structure	Date
58 Madrone Ave. *(p 106)*	Ann Dolliver	House	1888
95 Laurel Ave. *(p 90)*	C. E. Basebe	House	1888-90*
771 Magnolia Ave. *(p 248)*	Jean Escalle	Limerick Inn	1890*
74 Hazel Ave. *(p 88)*	Judge Mahoney	House remodel	1890*
15 Sycamore Ave. *(p 72)*	Henry Thornton	House	1893
531-533-537 Magnolia Ave. *(p 47)*	Fritz Goerl	Commercial building	1891
105 King St. *(p 6)*	Burtchaell (King)	House remodel	1892
126 Magnolia Ave. *(p 182)*	Gustave Nagel	House	1907
507 Magnolia Ave. *(p 41)*	William Stringa & Serafino Marilli (owners of the Blue Rock Hotel)	Hotel remodel	1910
27 Bridge Rd. *(p 167)*	Ignacio Escobosa	House	1911
10 Rice Lane *(p 18)*	Father Conlan	Rectory	1915
12, 16 & 22 Onyx St. *(p 108)*	Ellen Dolliver Jewell	Houses	1920s*
33 Bridge Rd.	Unknown	House	1922
8 & 10 Alexander Ave. *(p 180)*	Helen Bain	Houses	1927
116 Magnolia Ave. *(p 182)*	Mert Bain	House	1926
134 Magnolia Ave. *(p 184)*	Rudolph Rummel	House	1925

The following buildings were constructed by Nagel but are no longer standing:

Address	Original Owner	Structure	Date
20 Magnolia Ave. *(p 176)*	School Trustees	Two-story school	1895
557 Magnolia Ave. *(p 54)*	Anton Brazil	Saloon remodel	1895
5 Ward St.	Mr. Harris	House remodel	1929
1115 Magnolia Ave. *(p 269)*	James Murray	House	1914

House rumored to have been built by Nagel:

Address	Original Owner	Structure	Date
577 Magnolia Avenue *(p 240)*	James McCormick	House	1910-12*

*Estimated date

D.2: The Gustave Nagel family camped out behind 126 Magnolia while it was being built, about 1907. Gustave is second from left.

D.3: The Nagel family in front of 126 Magnolia Avenue, 1929. Left to right: Daughter Eda, Gustave Nagel, grandchildren (daughter Delma's children) Dorothy and Lois Bain, and wife Emilie Nagel.

Appendix E: LARKSPUR WOMAN'S IMPROVEMENT CLUB

Larkspur feminists were activists before the Nineteenth Amendment was passed in 1919.

The Larkspur Woman's Improvement Club was founded on April 12, 1912 when 29 women met at the Baltimore Canyon home of Belle and Mary Brown. Belle preferred to be known as the cofounder with Mrs. James A. Gardiner, who became the first president. Their goal was "to promote Civil, Educational and Social Measures and Community Affairs."

Their first project started at ground level. The club cleaned up accumulated rubbish around town, loaded it into 24 large trash cans at selected locations, and paid $30 annually to have the cans emptied from 1912 to 1917.

E.1: In this undated photo, members of the Larkspur Woman's Improvement Club ride in a Booster parade. Their automobile was not driven by a man.

Encouraged by its success, the club looked to fulfill the "improvement" part of its name. It promoted a $45,000 bond issue for Larkspur to pave Magnolia Avenue and lateral streets and build a town hall. Members mounted a vigorous campaign, and, despite strong opposition, the measure passed the following August, thanks to the club's intense political efforts. The streets were paved, and City Hall was constructed and dedicated in 1913.

Next on the club's agenda was the establishment of the Larkspur Library, one of its finest achievements *(see page 11)*. In December of 1914 a club committee opened a library with 265 books and a few magazines in a small City Hall room. For the next nine years, the committee raised funds to finance and run the library by sponsoring thrift shop sales, fashion shows, afternoon teas, and other social affairs. Members bought and maintained the books and staffed the facility at no cost to the city. By 1923, when patronage had grown too big for the club to handle, it presented the 2,100-book library to the City of Larkspur as a gift valued at about $4,000.

Other credits on the club's resume include the improvement of the downtown park at the northeast corner of Magnolia Avenue and Ward Street. The club provided for a fence, a lawn, and plants, and paid the park's water bill until 1923. During the same period it provided improvements to the auditorium on the second floor of City Hall and equipped a kitchen there. In return, the group was allowed to use the room for its meetings.

Eventually the city assumed responsibility for large-scale improvements, but the women continued to sponsor a variety of social and service activities under an amended name, the Larkspur Women's Club. During World War I, the women prepared bandages for the Red Cross and sponsored several French orphans. In the 1950s they purchased picnic tables, benches, and a drinking fountain for Dolliver Park, and paid for a part-time director to supervise children.

The evergreens planted along Magnolia Avenue between Doherty Drive and Bon Air Road and those around the old Greenbrae Fire Station are also on the club's credit sheet. Over the years the club treasury provided scholarships to Redwood High School students, helped deserving Girl Scouts go to camp, and supported a myriad of charities.

The Larkspur Women's Club disbanded in 1976. Its final act was to support Larkspur's parks and history by donating its remaining funds for the Northridge open space purchase and to the Larkspur Heritage Committee, a predecessor of the city's current Heritage Preservation Board.

Appendix F: TIMELINE - SUMMARY OF LARKSPUR'S HISTORY

Period of Transition - The Native Inhabitants' Last Days (1500-1840s)

Pre-History
: Coast Miwok rancherias existed near today's Heather Gardens and on the San Quentin Peninsula.

1750 Landmark valley oak, *Quercus lobata*, begins growing at 205 Baltimore Ave.

c1805 Sea otters and seals were hunted on the shores of San Quentin Peninsula and their skins shipped to the Orient.

1816 Mexican soldiers developed a landing somewhere on the shore of Corte Madera Creek.

1817 Mission San Rafael Archangel established.

c1824 Miwok warrior Quintin captured on Point San Quentin by Mexican forces.

1834 Rancho Corte Madera del Presidio, including today's Larkspur south of Arroyo Holon, granted to John Reed.

1840 Rancho Punta de Quentin, including today's central Larkspur and Greenbrae, granted to New England sea captain Juan B.R. Cooper.

The Days of Lumbering, Sawmills & Creek Barges (1840s-1890s)

1846-47 Folsom or "Government" Sawmill established near today's Hall Middle School, and nearby Sawmill Landing designated as an official port by Captain J.B. Montgomery, USN.

1848 Captain John Van Reynegom arrives by schooner, settles in the area now called Chevy Chase.

1849 Baltimore and Frederick Mining and Trading Co. begins sawmill operations at the Canyon's mouth.

Early 1850s
: Bowling alley, one of California's first, constructed in Canyon near sawmill.
: Bickerstaff and Brown families begin farming near today's downtown.
: Today's Magnolia Avenue is the major land route between Sausalito and Mission San Rafael.

1850 Rancho Punta de Quentin sold to Benjamin J. Buckelew.

1852 Buckelew sells part of his land to the state for the establishment of San Quentin Prison, then acquires Baltimore Co. sawmill; later moves it to Pt. San Quentin.

1854 San Quentin Prison opens and village settlement begins.

1855 Ross Landing grows into busy shipping point.
Point San Quentin Ferry Service begins.

1857 Buckelew sells Punta de Quentin to John Cowell and James Ross; Ross family names it Green Brae.

c1860 John Van Reynegom files claim to 160 acres in Chevy Chase area.

1880 Prison's jute mill opens, producing grain sacks.

1880s Construction begins on housing for prison employees.

Ranching, Dairying & Resort Days (1869-1900)

1869 For $4,500, Patrick King and William Murray purchase 1,233 acres covering most of what is known today as Old Larkspur and Kent Woodlands.

1870 San Rafael-San Quentin railroad links ferry landing with San Rafael.

1871-72 Alexander Forbes and William Coleman purchase Brown and Bickerstaff lands that encompass much of Larkspur and Corte Madera.

1874 Claude Callot begins brick making on property later converted to vineyard and winery by Jean Escalle.
North Pacific Coast Railroad begins freight service from Sausalito to Tomales Bay through area that later becomes Larkspur..

1877 Coleman and Brown lease out Quarry Ravine for production of graywacke or "blue rock."

1880 Patrick and Bridget King sell their King Ranch to William F. Mau; as Secretary of American Land & Trust Co., Mau later transfers that land to the corporation for about $21,000.

1881 Pixley fire sweeps over much of south Marin and up Mt. Tamalpais.
House, barn, winery and water tank built on Callot/Escalle property.

1884 First railroad trestle across Corte Madera Creek.
Green Brae Station built.

1885 Frank Pixley, Van Reynegom's son-in-law, receives quitclaim to Van Reynegom lands, buys more acreage, and establishes Owl's Wood.

1887 American Land & Trust Co. begins development of subdivision called "Town of Larkspur." C.W. Wright has land surveyed and begins selling lots.

1890 Green Brae lands sold to Roman Catholic Archdiocese of San Francisco for $50,000.

1890s Giant sequoia planted at Olive Avenue-Madrone intersection.

1890s	Baltimore Canyon used for summer camping ground and vacation cottages.
	Ho Ho Springs rustic resort built on slopes above 965 Magnolia.
	The Larkspur Inn, an 80-room resort hotel, built at the end of Sycamore Avenue.
	Hill's boathouse offers boats and changing rooms for swimmers at Corte Madera Creek.
1891	Remillard Brick Company adds the kiln on the San Quentin Peninsula to its vast Bay Area operations. Remillard Cottage built, later moved to its present location.
	North Pacific Coast Railroad opens Larkspur Station for passenger service.
	Hotel Larkspur (today's "Blue Rock Inn") opens to the public.
	Bon Air Hotel built on present site of Marin General Hospital.
1892	Rice Stable opens on Ward Street.
1894	Wood-framed Larkspur-Corte Madera School built with two stories, four classrooms.
	Limerick Inn opens in brick building on Escalle property.
	Frizzi's Bakery opens at what later became 499 Magnolia Avenue.
1896	Redwoods Presbyterian Church established.
	Glen Addition subdivides upper Canyon land parcels.
1899	First St. Patrick's Church opens.

Early Growth & Booster Days (1900–1919)

Early 1900s
    Earle Doherty opens Doherty Lumber Yard, later renamed Larkspur Lumber Co.
    Home construction begins in Murray Park.

1902	North Pacific Coast Railroad reorganized as North Shore Railroad.
1903	North Shore Railroad adds electric passenger trains.
1905	Limerick Inn adds gardens and bocce ball, attracting international visitors.
1906	Bricks topple from Larkspur chimneys during the 1906 earthquake; population of year-round residents increases.
	Volunteer Fire Department organized.
	Historic catalpa trees planted along Olive Ave.
1907	First Baltimore Park subdivision created.
	Demand for lots stimulates Laurel Dell subdivision on Madrone Avenue.
	North Shore Railroad becomes Northwestern Pacific Railroad.
1908	Larkspur incorporates; first town trustees elected.
1908	First "Booster Day" celebration and dance to raise money for the Volunteer Fire Department.
	City Park developed on NE corner of Ward and Magnolia.
	"Three Sisters," Costello rental homes, constructed.
1908	Tracks of Northwestern Pacific Railroad altered at Baltimore Park to branch off toward San Rafael.
1910	Model Bakery opens at 475-479 Magnolia Avenue.
	Hotel Larkspur sold, remodeled and renamed the Blue Rock Hotel. It remains under the same ownership until 1938.
1912	Murray Park development begins.
1913	Snow falls in Larkspur on January 9.
	City Hall built for $15,110.50.
	Rose Bowl outdoor dance floor constructed; dances continue until 1963.
	Palm Hill and second Baltimore Park subdivisions begin.
	Madrone Avenue paved around the existing redwoods and Magnolia Avenue macadamized, a first in Marin County.
	Railroad builds passenger shelters, promoting easy San Francisco commute.
	Mexican fan palms planted down Baltimore Avenue.
c1913	Corte Madera Creek silted in; Boardwalk communities begin.
1914	Railroad trestle over Corte Madera Creek rebuilt with double track.
1915	Remillard brick kiln ceases operation.
1916	Two-story addition built onto Larkspur-Corte Madera School.

War & Post-War Years (1940–1959)

c1940	City purchases 43-acres for use as dump; eventually it becomes Piper Park.
1940	Lark Theater opens. Closed in 1999, it is restored and reopens in 2004.
1941	New St. Patrick's Church opens.
	Rod and Gun Club built on Greenbrae Boardwalk.
	Adolph Tiscornia buys Escalle property.
	Northwestern Pacific Railroad stations closed.
1941-45	Marin population increases for World War II Marinship yards in Sausalito.
1941	Historic *Magnolia soulangeana* planted at 125 Magnolia.
1942	Heather Gardens developed.
1945	Northwestern Pacific Railroad trestle closed.
	Fourth lane added to Hwy. 101.

1946 Schultz Building Co. buys 600 acre Green Brae Ranch; "Greenbrae" development begins.
Film *Impact* shot at Probert's service station and home on Magnolia Avenue.

1947 American Legion acquires former railroad section foreman's home at 500 Magnolia.

1948 Postal delivery to Boardwalk begins.

1949 Subdivision map filed for College Park development.
75 acres between Sir Francis Drake Boulevard, Bon Air and Corte Madera Creek annexed to City of Larkspur.

1950-52 Corte Madera Creek channel moved westward.

1951 Redwoods Presbyterian Church built on Magnolia Avenue.

1952 Marin General Hospital built on site of old Bon Air Hotel.
Greenbrae hill and Murray Park lands annexed.
Bon Air Super Market opens as first structure in Bon Air shopping center.
Traffic light installed at Hwy. 101 and Sir Francis Drake Blvd.

1953 Richmond-San Rafael Bridge built on Point San Quentin over Agnes Island.
Ross Valley Masonic Center built at 1122 Magnolia Avenue.

1954 Lower slopes of King Mountain removed to fill marsh for Hillview construction.

1955 Hillview Gardens developed.

1957 Proposal for Mt. Tamalpais aerial tramway defeated.
City assumes control of the Fire Dept.

1958 Redwood High School opens.

1959 Henry C. Hall School opens.
Joe Wagner baseball field and concession stand open.
First concrete bridge built over Corte Madera Creek.
Rice Livery Stable demolished.

Flight to the Suburbs (1960s-1970)

c1960s Fire Station #2 built to protect Greenbrae; rebuilt 1991.

1961 Madrone Woodlands opened for development.

1962 Silver Peso supercedes earlier taverns.

1963 Greenbrae Marina opens for development.
Volunteer Fire Department closes Rose Bowl dances.
St. Patrick's School opens.
Woodlark Apartments opens.

1964 Construction of The Tamalpais is approved.

1964-66 Army Corps of Engineers' Flood Control Project eliminates Boardwalks #2, #3 and #4, removes 40 feet of Wood Island, and deepens creek channel while adding fill to South Eliseo Drive.

1966-70 South Eliseo apartments constructed.

1967 Meadowood opened for development.

1968 Greenbrae Marina (later Larkspur Marina) built on soil dredged from creek.

1969 The Tamalpais retirement community opens.
Skylark Apartments constructed.
Approximately 200 acres of San Quentin Peninsula annexed by City of Larkspur.

Build Out (1970-2010)

1970 First Larkspur Town Meeting organized.
City's first bike-pedestrian path approved along Magnolia Ave.

1971 Larkspur Plaza developed.
Second Town Meeting held.
Lark Creek Inn restaurant and shops developed.
Piper Park opens.
Larkspur citizens win right to use historic paths on Tiscornia property in Baltimore Canyon.
Rail service between San Rafael and Sausalito via Baltimore Park discontinued.

1972 Doherty Park opens on Magnolia Avenue near Doherty Drive.
Third Town Meeting held.
Bon Air Park sold to city.
Temporary police station opens at Piper Park Corporation Yard.
Larkspur Isle Apartments built on filled land over former marsh; later rebuilt, sold as condominiums.

1973 Bon Air Landing Park and dock developed.

1974 Fourth Town Meeting held.

1975 Hamilton Park dedicated.

1976 Larkspur Ferry Terminal dedicated, with three passenger ferries.
Marin County Open Space District acquires 357 acres of recreational land above Canyon.
Recontoured Wood Island adds four-story office building.
Corte Madera Marsh Ecological Reserve named.
Marin Plaza developed.

1977 Heatherwood Park opens to serve Meadowood and Heather Gardens.
Northwestern Pacific Railroad ceases Larkspur operation and removes tracks.
During drought, emergency pipeline carries water to Marin over Richmond-San Rafael Bridge.

1978	Larkspur Landing development opens with shops, offices and apartments.
	Tubb Lake and Miwok Park dedicated to the City.
	Dolliver house listed in National Register of Historic Places.
	Remillard Brick Kiln listed in National Register of Historic Places and declared a State Historical Landmark.
	Escalle Village built.
1979	Skylark Apartments, upper units built.
	Former Larkspur-Corte Madera School closes, becomes Marin Primary.
	Rod and Gun Club becomes Crossley Bridge Club.
1981	Neighborhood Park completed.
1982	"Old Downtown" Larkspur declared an Historic District and included in the National Register of Historic Places.
	"Hundred Year Flood" damages many homes in canyon with mud and debris flows.
	Community Garden opens.
	Henry C. Hall School becomes Hall Middle School, serving grades 6-8; grade 5 added in 2006.
1983	Alexander Avenue Bridge listed in the National Register of Historic Places.
	Library facilities updated and expanded.
	Bon Air Center enlarged.
1984	Remillard cottage restoration completed.
1985	Drake's Landing Office Park and housing development constructed.
1986	Remillard Park added to Larkspur park system.
1987	Greenbrae Gardens developed.
	Community Fields installed adjacent to Redwood High School.
	Pasticceria Rulli opens downtown.
1988	Greenbrae School Park developed.
	Jim Niven Park opens.
	Cape Marin developed.
	72 Creekside homes approved with 42,800-square-foot marsh restoration project.
	Railroad Open Space Association (ROSA) formed to purchase railroad land for multi-use path near Baltimore Park.
1989	Marin General Hospital enlarged.
	Remillard offices and restaurant construction allows preservation of the historic kiln and stack.
c1990	Statue of Sir Francis Drake installed on East Sir Francis Drake Boulevard.
	Agreement with Tiscornia Estate allows development of approximately four acres in exchange for purchase of 131 acres as publicly-owned open space and another 129 acres as open space easement and loop trail around King Mountain.
	Canine Commons opens near Boardwalk #1.
1991	Edgewater Place developed northwest of Creekside.
	New Larkspur Fire Station #2 opened in Greenbrae.
	Downtown railroad station buildings restored, leased to small businesses.
	Marin Rowing Association dock and boathouse built near Drake's Landing.
1995	Twin Cities Little League creates Susan Johann Gilardi Field.
1999	Eight homes approved in Elm Crest neighborhood.
1999-2000	Indian remains, artifacts uncovered during removal of Sanitary District Tanks at Larkspur Landing; reburial ceremonies conducted.
2002	Blue Rock Hotel, badly damaged by fire, undergoes reconstruction.
2004	New multi-use field opens at Piper Park.
2008	City celebrates its Centennial with year-round festivities.
	24 townhouses, 23 market-rate homes begin construction at Drake's Cove.
2009	Magnolia Ave. Park improved, renamed Centennial Park.

• • • • • • • • • • • • •

Population Statistics from U.S. Census Bureau

CITY OF LARKSPUR

Year	Population
1910	594
1920	612
1930	1,241
1940	1,558
1950	2,905
1960	5,710
1970	10,487
1980	11,604
1990	11,070
2000	12,014
2010	12,200 (estimated)

City of Larkspur - Contact Information

Address: City Hall – 400 Magnolia Avenue, Larkspur, CA 94939
Phone: (415) 927-5110
Website: www.larkspurcityhall.org

Appendix G: CREDITS

This book is a project of the Larkspur Heritage Preservation Board, which maintains the Larkspur Heritage Archives from which many of the images used in the book are drawn. Further information about the archives and about the board and its activities can be obtained by contacting the City of Larkspur (415) 927-5110 or viewing its website at http://www.ci.larkspur.ca.us/.

Forwards
1 Heitkamp Archives
2-5 Rita Nattestad
6 John Gillespie
7 Heitkamp Archives
8 Jack Wilson
9 Jude Mooney
10 Jack Wilson
11-12 Heritage Archives

Chapter 1 - DOWNTOWN
1.1 Larkspur Centennial Committee
1.2-3 Snyder Collection
1.4 Heitkamp Archives
1.5 Penna Collection
1.6 Bancroft Library
1.7 Penna Collection
1.8-9 Heritage Archives
1.10 Heitkamp Archives
1.11-12 Heritage Archives
1.13 Richard Cunningham
1.14 Heitkamp Archives
1.15-16 Richard Cunningham
1.17 Heritage Archives
1.18 California Room
1.19 Larkspur Fire Dept.
1.20-21 John Gillespie
1.22-23 Heritage Archives
1.24 Heritage Archives, Ken Anderson photograph
1.25 Heritage Archives
1.26 Heitkamp Archives
1.27 Snyder Collection
1.28 Heritage Archives
1.29 Bancroft Library
1.30 Snyder Collection
1.31 Richard Cunningham
1.32 Larkspur Fire Dept.
1.33 Bancroft Library
1.34-36 Heritage Archives
1.37 Bancroft Library
1.38 Larkspur Fire Dept.
1.39 Heritage Archives
1.40 Jack Wilson
1.41 Richard Cunningham
1.42 Heritage Archives
1.43-44 Heritage Archives, Ken Anderson photograph
1.45 Heritage Archives
1.46 Snyder Collection
1.47-48 Larkspur Fire Dept., courtesy Mrs. Doherty
1.49 Heritage Archives, courtesy Marty Weissensee

> **ABBREVIATIONS FOR CREDITS:**
> **Sources of photos, maps, and other images**
> - Bancroft Library – Courtesy of the Bancroft Library, University of California
> - Heitkamp Archives – Archives of Helen A. Heitkamp
> - Heritage Archives – Larkspur Heritage Archives
> - California Room – Courtesy of the Anne T. Kent California Room, Marin County Free Library
> - NWPRRHS Archives – Collection of Fred Codoni, Northwestern Pacific Railroad Historical Society Archives
> - Snyder Collection – Newall Snyder Collection
> - Penna Collection – Courtesy of Paul Penna, Will Penna, and Rosemary Penna U'Ren
> - SQMA – San Quentin Museum Association

1.50 Penna Collection
1.51 Bancroft Library
1.52 Heritage Archives
1.53 Penna Collection
1.54 Heritage Archives, Ken Anderson photograph
1.55 Bancroft Library
1.56 Heritage Archives
1.57 Bancroft Library
1.58-59 Snyder Collection
1.60 Heitkamp Archives
1.61 Heritage Archives
1.62 Helen Frizzi Enyeart
1.63 Frizzi Collection
1.64-65 Heritage Archives
1.66 Heitkamp Archives
1.67 Bancroft Library
1.68 Richard Cunningham
1.69-70 California Room
1.71 Heritage Archives
1.72 Larkspur Fire Dept.
1.73 Nagel Archives, courtesy Joan Dougherty
1.74 Snyder Collection
1.75 Heritage Archives
1.76 Snyder Collection
1.77 Bancroft Library
1.78 Frizzi Collection
1.79-80 Archer Family Collection
1.81 Heritage Archives
1.82 Snyder Collection
1.83 Heritage Archives
1.84 Snyder Collection
1.85-86 Heritage Archives
1.87 John Gillespie
1.88 Snyder Collection
1.89 Richard Cunningham
1.90 Heritage Archives
1.91 Bancroft Library
1.92 Snyder Collection
1.93 Heritage Archives
1.94 Snyder Collection
1.95 Heritage Archives, *Marin Independent Journal* photograph
1.96 Snyder Collection
1.97 Frizzi Collection
1.98 Larkspur Fire Dept., courtesy Mrs. Doherty
1.99 Heritage Archives

Chapter 2 - OLD HOMES
2.1-4 Snyder Collection
2.5 Heitkamp Archives
2.6 Frizzi Collection
2.7 Snyder Collection
2.8 Larkspur City Survey 2003
2.9-10 Snyder Collection
2.11 Heitkamp Archives
2.12 Heritage Archives
2.13 Penna Collection
2.14-15 Heitkamp Archives
2.16 Heritage Archives
2.17-19 Heitkamp Archives
2.20 Marilyn River
2.21 Snyder Collection
2.22-27 Heitkamp Archives
2.28 Snyder Collection
2.29 Larkspur Fire Dept.
2.30-31 Snyder Collection
2.32 Larkspur Fire Dept.
2.33 Heritage Archives, William Stringa photograph
2.34-35 Heitkamp Archives
2.36 Redwoods Presbyterian Church
2.37 Penna Collection, courtesy June C. MacCourt
2.38 Penna Collection
2.39 Penna Collection, courtesy June C. MacCourt

2.40 Heitkamp Archives
2.41 Heritage Archives
2.42 Heitkamp Archives
2.43 Maria O'Rourke, Eric Voorsanger photograph
2.44-47 Heitkamp Archives
2.48-51 Heritage Archives
2.52 Penna Collection
2.53-59 Heitkamp Archives

Chapter 3 - Baltimore Canyon
3.1 Larkspur Fire Dept.
3.2 Humboldt State University Library, A. W. Ericson photograph
3.3-4 Heritage Archives
3.5 Penna Collection
3.6-7 Heritage Archives, courtesy Joy Jaegeling Best
3.8 John Gillespie
3.9 Heritage Archives
3.10 Charles Ford Collection
3.11 Heritage Archives
3.12 John Gillespie
3.13 Heritage Archives
3.14 Richard Cunningham
3.15-16 John Gillespie
3.17 Heritage Archives
3.18-19 Richard Cunningham
3.20 Heritage Archives
3.21-26 John Gillespie
3.27 Heritage Archives
3.28 Heitkamp Archives
3.29 Richard Cunningham
3.30 John Gillespie
3.31 Heritage Archives
3.32 Richard Cunningham
3.33 Marin County Assessor/Recorder's Office
3.34-35 John Gillespie
3.36-37 Richard Cunningham
3.38 California Room
3.39-41 John Gillespie
3.42 Heritage Archives
3.43-44 Heitkamp Archives
3.45 Richard Cunningham
3.46 Heitkamp Archives
3.47 Snyder Collection
3.48 Heritage Archives
3.49-50 Heitkamp Archives
3.51 Heritage Archives
3.52-53 Heitkamp Archives
3.54 Heritage Archives
3.55-57 Richard Cunningham
3.58 Heritage Archives
3.59 Richard Cunningham
3.60 Marin County Open Space District

Chapter 4 - BALTIMORE PARK
4.1 Bancroft Library
4.2 Marin County Assessor/Recorder's Office
4.3-4 Heritage Archives
4.5 Heitkamp Archives
4.6 Richard Cunningham
4.7 Heitkamp Archives
4.8-9 Richard Cunningham
4.10-12 Heitkamp Archives
4.13 Richard Cunningham
4.14 Heitkamp Archives
4.15 California Room
4.16 Heitkamp Archives
4.17-18 Richard Cunningham
4.19 NWPRRHS Archives
4.20 Richard Cunningham
4.21-22 Heitkamp Archives
4.23 Richard Cunningham
4.24 Heritage Archives
4.25 Heitkamp Archives
4.26-27 Richard Cunningham
4.28 Heritage Archives, *Marin Independent Journal* photograph
4.29-30 Richard Cunningham
4.31 Heitkamp Archives
4.32 Richard Cunningham
4.33 Heritage Archives
4.34-35 Heitkamp Archives
4.36 Richard Cunningham
4.37 Heritage Archives
4.38 Richard Cunningham
4.39 Snyder Collection
4.40-41 Richard Cunningham
4.42-43 Heritage Archives
4.44 Bancroft Library
4.45-46 Heitkamp Archives
4.47 Heritage Archives
4.48 Richard Cunningham
4.49 Heritage Archives
4.50-51 Richard Cunningham
4.52 Heritage Archives
4.53 Richard Cunningham
4.54 Marin County Assessor/Recorder's Office
4.55 Heritage Archives
4.56-58 Snyder Collection
4.59-64 Richard Cunningham
4.65 Heritage Archives
4.66 Heitkamp Archives
4.67-69 Richard Cunningham
4.70 Heitkamp Archives
4.71 Snyder Collection
4.72 Richard Cunningham

Chapter 5 - SOUTH MAGNOLIA
5.1-3 Snyder Collection
5.4 Charles Young
5.5 Heritage Archives
5.6 Schultz Building Company
5.7-8 Heitkamp Archives
5.9 Bob Collin
5.10-11 Heitkamp Archives
5.12 Thomas McCarthy
5.13 Heritage Archives, Carlton Cherry photograph
5.14-16 Heitkamp Archives
5.17 Snyder Collection
5.18-22 Heitkamp Archives
5.23 Snyder Collection
5.24-29 Heitkamp Archives
5.30-32 Heritage Archives
5.33-32 Heitkamp Archives
5.35 Heritage Archives

Chapter 6 - PALM HILL
6.1 Heritage Archives
6.2 NWPRRHS Archives
6.3 Heitkamp Archives
6.4 Emagene Boero
6.5-11 Heitkamp Archives
6.12 Irene Clark
6.13 Heitkamp Archives
6.14 Dena Van Derveer
6.15 Heritage Archives
6.16-17 Laverne Ball
6.18-20 Heitkamp Archives
6.21 Crowell-Collier Publishing Co.
6.22-23 Laverne Ball

Chapter 7 - HEATHER GARDENS & MEADOWOOD
7.1 Heritage Archives
7.2 NWPRRHS Archives
7.3 Nancy Curley
7.4-6 NWPRRHS Archives
7.7 Nancy Curley
7.8-9 Heritage Archives
7.10 Nancy Curley
7.11 Laverne Ball
7.12 Nancy Curley
7.13 Heitkamp Archives
7.14-15 Penna Collection
7.16 Heitkamp Archives
7.17 Larkspur Fire Dept.
7.18 Nancy Curley
7.19 Heitkamp Archives
7.20 Jay Graham Photography
7.21-23 Heitkamp Archives
7.24 Anthony Epidendio
7.25 Heritage Archives, *Marin Independent Journal* photograph

Chapter 8 - PIPER PARK, BOARDWALK #1 & CREEKSIDE
8.1 California Room
8.2 Heitkamp Archives
8.3-4 Penna Collection
8.5-6 John Gillespie
8.7-8 Heitkamp Archives
8.9 Nancy Curley
8.10 John Gillespie
8.11 Dena Van Derveer
8.12-14 Heritage Archives
8.15 John Gillespie
8.16 Snyder Collection
8.17 Bancroft Library
8.18 Phil Frank

8.19 John Gillespie
8.20-21 Heritage Archives, Ken Anderson photograph
8.22 John Gillespie
8.23 Heritage Archives, Ken Anderson photograph
8.24-32 Heitkamp Archives
8.33 Twin Cities Police Department
8.34-35 Heitkamp Archives
8.36 Larkspur School District
8.37-42 Heitkamp Archives
8.43 Jay Graham Photography

Chapter 9 - NORTH MAGNOLIA
9.1 Heritage Archives
9.2 Heitkamp Archives
9.3 Snyder Collection
9.4 Larkspur Fire Dept.
9.5 Heitkamp Archives
9.6 Dena Van Derveer
9.7 Heritage Archives
9.8 Mildred Young
9.9-10 Heitkamp Archives
9.11 John Gillespie
9.12 Joan Hendrick
9.13 Linda Chauncey
9.14-17 Heitkamp Archives
9.18 Schultz Building Company
9.19-20 Heitkamp Archives
9.21 John Gillespie
9.22-24 Heritage Archives
9.25 Heitkamp Archives
9.26 West Marin Senior Services
9.27 Heritage Archives, Jude Mooney photograph
9.28 Heitkamp Archives
9.29 Heritage Archives, *Marin Independent Journal* photograph

Chapter 10 - HILLVIEW & KING MOUNTAIN
10.1 Heritage Archives
10.2 Heitkamp Archives
10.3-5 California Room
10.6 Snyder Collection
10.7 Penna Collection
10.8 Heritage Archives
10.09-12 Heitkamp Archives
10.13 Heritage Archives, *Marin Independent Journal* photograph
10.14-16 Heitkamp Archives
10.17 Marin County Open Space District

Chapter 11 - MURRAY PARK
11.1 Heritage Archives
11.2 Heitkamp Archives
11.3-4 Heritage Archives
11.5-6 Heitkamp Archives
11.7 Heritage Archives, Carlton Cherry photograph
11.8 Heitkamp Archives
11.9 Larkspur Fire Dept.
11.10-13 Heitkamp Archives
11.14 John Gillespie
11.15 Richard G. Torney Collection
11.16 Heitkamp Archives
11.17 Larkspur Fire Dept., courtesy W. C. Cornwell
11.18-21 Heitkamp Archives
11.22 John Gillespie
11.23 Larkspur Fire Dept.
11.24-33 Heitkamp Archives
11.34 Heritage Archives
11.35 Richard G. Torney Collection
11.36 Olesen Family
11.37-38 Heitkamp Archives
11.39 Olesen Family
11.40-47 Heitkamp Archives
11.48 Richard G. Torney Collection
11.49-53 Heitkamp Archives

Chapter 12 - GREENBRAE & BON AIR
12.1-3 Heritage Archives
12.4 Larkspur Fire Dept.
12.5-6 Heritage Archives
12.7-8 Heitkamp Archives
12.9 Heritage Archives
12.10 Heitkamp Archives
12.11 Heritage Archives
12.12 Bancroft Library
12.13 Schultz Building Company
12.14-15 Heitkamp Archives
12.16 Heritage Archives
12.17 California Historical Society Library
12.18 Twin Cities Police Department
12.19-25 Heitkamp Archives
12.26 California Historical Society Library
12.27 Niels Schultz, Jr.
12.28-29 Heitkamp Archives

Chapter 13 - SAN QUENTIN PENINSULA
13.1 Heritage Archives
13.2-3 Heritage Archives, Carlton Cherry photograph
13.4 Heitkamp Archives
13.5 Heritage Archives, Carlton Cherry photograph
13.6-9 Heitkamp Archives
13.10 Lee Miller
13.11 Wanden Treanor
13.12 Heitkamp Archives
13.13 Heritage Archives
13.14-15 Heitkamp Archives
13.16 Heritage Archives
13.17 Heitkamp Archives
13.18-19 Heritage Archives
13.20 Heitkamp Archives
13.21 Lee Miller
13.22-27 Heitkamp Archives
13.28 Snyder Collection
13.29-32 Heitkamp Archives
13.33 Lee Miller
13.34 Dennis Patton
13.35 Bancroft Library
13.36 Heritage Archives
13.37 Heritage Archives, Carlton Cherry photograph
13.38 Heitkamp Archives
13.39 George Walcom Collection, donated by Lee Miller
13.40 Heritage Archives, Carlton Cherry photograph
13.41-42 Bancroft Library
13.43-60 Heitkamp Archives
13.61 John Gillespie
13.62 Ronald Eustice
13.63 John Tacchi
13.64-65 Heritage Archives
13.66-71 Heitkamp Archives
13.72-73 SQMA
13.74 USGenWeb Archives
13.75 MediaNews
13.76 Heitkamp Archives
13.77-78 SQMA
13.79 Heitkamp Archives
13.80 SQMA
13.81-82 Heitkamp Archives
13.83 SQMA
13.84-90 Heitkamp Archives
13.91 Linda Chauncey
13.92-98 Heitkamp Archives
13.99 SQMA
13.100 SQMA
13.101 Heitkamp Archives
13-102 SQMA
13-103 Walter Villere
13.104-108 Heitkamp Archives
13.109 Bancroft Library
13.110 Heritage Archives

EPILOGUE
Ep1-2 Heritage Archives

APPENDICES
A.1 Heritage Archives
B.1 Heitkamp Archives
B.2 Richard Cunningham
B.3-4 Heitkamp Archives
B.5 John Gillespie
B.6-8 Heitkamp Archives
C.1-2 Heitkamp Archives
D.1-2 Nagel Archives, courtesy Joan Dougherty
D.3 Heitkamp Archives
E.1 Heitkamp Archives

Appendix H: CONTRIBUTORS

The following people and organizations helped make this book possible by contributing their time, memories, photos, and documents.

Bruce Abbot
Wendy Abrams
Doug Allen
Judy & Dale Alstrom
Ventana Amico
Doug Archer
Ron Arlas
Cathy Bain
Laverne & Greg Ball
Barbara & Norman Beal
Joy Best
Sandy Blauvelt
Emagene & Roger Boero
Ron Bradley
Anne T. Kent California Room,
    Marin County Free Library
Donna Cameron
John Carr
Dr. Robert & Nancy Ceniceros
Fred Codoni
Bob Collin
Patti Cooke
Jim Costello
Jeff Craemer
Kathi & Pete deFremery
Monte Deignan
Karen Deist
Reno Dell'Era
Amelia De Mello
Joan Dougherty
Barbara Dubuc
Paul & Christine Elmquist
Bill Epidendio
Rich & Debbie Epidendio
Ed Epting
Lois & Don Errante
Dale & Ann Eubanks
Dee Fratus
Dennis & Susan Gilardi
John Gillespie
George & Georgene Gmahling
Jim & Polly Gorder
Frances Gordon
Don & Theo Graff
Jay Graham
Jana Haehl
Lilli Hart
Kathy Hartzell
George & Mildred Heierle
Joan Hendrick
Katharine Hermann
James Holmes
Bill Howard

Audrey Hulburd
Dottie Ioakimedes
Katherine Jones
Pat Kaiser
Kathleen Kearley-Green
Kendall & Mary King
Michael & Eliza Koeppel
Cathy Lane
Bob & Leena Lee
Sue Lessin
Jill Lerner
Joanie Levinsohn
Joan Lubamersky
Christine Main
Glen March
Marin History Museum
Joanie Maroni
Nancy Martin
Tina McArthur
Chris McCluney
Jim & Eileen McGowan
Bill & Brenda McKowen
Brian & Laura McLeran
Scott Metcho
Laura Moe
David & Robin Moller
Jocelyn Moss
Thorley & Bob Murray
Mike Myers
Ruth Nash
Rita Nattestad
Steve Nicol
Cyndi Niven
Ole Olesen
Lucile Olson
Merrel Olson
Maria O'Rourke
Dennis Patton
Paul Penna
Bette Peters
Dan Peterson
Valerie Pitts
Marianne Rafter & Peter Martin
Phil & Kathy Reilly
Barbara Reinert
Lt. Samuel Robinson
Teresa Rose
Gary Rulli
Daniel Sadowski
Barbara Salzman
Craig Scherfenberg
Gary Scott
Mark & Elise Semonian

Tom & Stevie Serleth
Miriam Silver
Robert Smith
Newall Snyder
Nancy Spivey
Steve Stein
Carol Svetcov
Phil Terry
Carl & Sylvia Thoelecke
Laurie Thompson
Eleanor Tierney
Richard Torney
Wanden Treanor
Ellen Turner
Rosemary U'ren
Carol Uhrmacher
Walter Villere
Eric Voorsanger
Phiroze Wadia
Shay Walling
Kay Washburn
Catherine Way
Bill Webb
Marty Weissensee
Molly Wuthrich
Charles Young

Appendix I: ADDRESSES & PLACES OF NOTE

The following are addresses, structures, or other places of note that are discussed in the text and found on the maps in this book.

ACACIA AVENUE
18 Acacia Ave
200 Acacia Ave

ALEXANDER AVENUE
Charles Holcomb Bridge
  (Alexander Avenue Bridge)
8 Alexander Ave
10 Alexander Ave
12 Alexander Ave

ARCH STREET
Arch Street Stairs
9 Arch St

ARDMORE ROAD
9 Ardmore Road

BALTIMORE AVENUE
Palm trees along Baltimore Ave
1 Baltimore Ave
2 Baltimore Ave
  (Calvary Baptist Church)
5 Baltimore Ave
101 Baltimore Ave
107 Baltimore Ave
118 Baltimore Ave

BARRY WAY
15 Barry Way
  (Larkspur Fire Station No. 2)

BON AIR ROAD
250 Bon Air Rd
  (Marin General Hospital)

BRIDGE ROAD
Rustic Bridge
1 Bridge Rd
15 Bridge Rd
16 Bridge Rd
19 Bridge Rd
25 Bridge Rd
27 Bridge Rd

CANE STREET
476 Cane St
502 Cane St
505 Cane St
508 Cane St

CHANTICLEER AVENUE
5 Chanticleer Ave
9 Chanticleer Ave

EAST SIR FRANCIS DRAKE BOULEVARD
14 E Sir Francis Drake Blvd
  60 E Sir Francis Drake Blvd
  80 E Sir Francis Drake Blvd
  101 E Sir Francis Drake Blvd
  125 E Sir Francis Drake Blvd
    (Remillard Brick Kiln)

ECHO PLACE
1 Echo Place ("The Maples")
3 Echo Place ("Echo")
4 Echo Place ("Vernon Dale")

ELM AVENUE
3 Elm Ave
70 Elm Ave
106 Elm Ave
109 Elm Ave
130 Elm Ave
375 Elm Ave
385 Elm Ave
395 Elm Ave
410 Elm Ave
455 Elm Ave

ESTELLE AVENUE
15 Estelle Ave

FRANCES AVENUE
55 Frances Ave

HAWKINS WAY
11 Hawkins Way

HAWTHORNE AVENUE
21 Hawthorne Ave
121 Hawthorne Ave
201 Hawthorne Ave
219 Hawthorne Ave
234 Hawthorne Ave

HAZEL AVENUE
10 Hazel Ave
74 Hazel Ave

HILLCREST AVENUE
49 Hillcrest Ave
51 Hillcrest Ave
56 Hillcrest Ave
85 Hillcrest Ave

HOLCOMB AVENUE
409 Holcomb Ave
431 Holcomb Ave
437 Holcomb Ave
441 Holcomb Ave

KING STREET
105 King St (King-Costello house)
114 King St
115 King St
117 King St
120 King St
115 King St
125 King St
131 King St
133 King St
135A King St
135B King St
143 King St

LARKSPUR LANDING CIRCLE
2900 Larkspur Landing Cir
  (Remillard cottage)

LA ROSA WAY
8 La Rosa Way

LAUREL AVENUE
95 Laurel Ave

LOCUST AVENUE
11 Locust Ave
37 Locust Ave
51 Locust Ave
108 Locust Ave
113 Locust Ave
125 Locust Ave
127 Locust Ave
146 Locust Ave
148 Locust Ave

LOMA VISTA AVENUE
8 Loma Vista Ave
12 Loma Vista Ave
20 Loma Vista Ave

MADRONE AVENUE
41 Madrone Ave
47 Madrone Ave ("The Redwoods")
53 Madrone Ave
55 Madrone Ave
58 Madrone Ave
63 Madrone Ave
68 Madrone Ave
69 Madrone Ave
82 Madrone Ave
83 Madrone Ave
87 Madrone Ave
88 Madrone Ave
94 Madrone Ave
96A Madrone Ave
96B Madrone Ave
96C Madrone Ave
105 Madrone Ave
109 Madrone Ave
110 Madrone Ave
118 Madrone Ave
123 Madrone Ave
124 Madrone stone wall
124 MadroneAve ("Holmestead")
130 Madrone Ave
136 Madrone Ave
  ("Sunshine Villa")
143 Madrone Ave
  ("Honeymoon Cottage")
146 Madrone Ave
147 Madrone Ave
148 Madrone Ave
150 Madrone Ave
151 Madrone Ave

157 Madrone Ave
160 Madrone Ave ("The Catalpas")
163 Madrone Ave
167 Madrone Ave
171 Madrone Ave
205 Madrone Ave
207 Madrone Ave
217 Madrone Ave
221 Madrone Ave ("The Shambles")
222 Madrone Ave ("Elfdale")
228 Madrone Ave
234 Madrone Ave
250 Madrone Ave ("Ridgewood")
259 Madrone Ave
260 Madrone Ave
263 Madrone Ave
264 Madrone Ave
265 Madrone Ave
268 Madrone Ave
271 Madrone Ave
272 Madrone Ave ("El Cabana")
300 Madrone Ave
337 Madrone Ave
   ("Forget-Me-Not")
339 Madrone Ave
370 Madrone Ave
377 Madrone Ave

MAGNOLIA AVENUE
20 Magnolia Ave
93 Magnolia Ave
110 Magnolia Ave
116 Magnolia Ave
125 Magnolia Ave
126 Magnolia Ave
130 Magnolia Ave
134 Magnolia Ave
141 Magnolia Ave
143 Magnolia Ave
144 Magnolia Ave
145 Magnolia Ave
150 Magnolia Ave
214 Magnolia Ave
215 Magnolia Ave
223 Magnolia Ave
234 Magnolia Ave
245 Magnolia Ave
265 Magnolia Ave
274 Magnolia Ave
275 Magnolia Ave
282-286 Magnolia Ave
320 Magnolia Ave
400 Magnolia Ave
401 Magnolia Ave
409 Magnolia Ave
420 Magnolia Ave
426 Magnolia Ave
428 Magnolia Ave
435 Magnolia Ave
444 Magnolia Ave
450 Magnolia Ave
452 Magnolia Ave
455 Magnolia Ave

457 Magnolia Ave
460 Magnolia Ave
464 Magnolia Ave
465 Magnolia Ave
468 Magnolia Ave
471 Magnolia Ave
472 Magnolia Ave
473 Magnolia Ave
474 Magnolia Ave
475 Magnolia Ave
476 Magnolia Ave
477 Magnolia Ave
478 Magnolia Ave
479 Magnolia Ave
480 Magnolia Ave
482 Magnolia Ave
483 Magnolia Ave
484 Magnolia Ave
485 Magnolia Ave
488 Magnolia Ave
489 Magnolia Ave
490 Magnolia Ave
494 Magnolia Ave
499 Magnolia Ave
501 Magnolia Ave
503 Magnolia Ave
505 Magnolia Ave
507 Magnolia Ave
515 Magnolia Ave
529 Magnolia Ave
531 Magnolia Ave
532 Magnolia Ave
533 Magnolia Ave
537 Magnolia Ave
539 Magnolia Ave
545 Magnolia Ave
549 Magnolia Ave
552 Magnolia Ave
557 Magnolia Ave
570 Magnolia Ave
577 Magnolia Ave
599 Magnolia Ave
600 Magnolia Ave
607 Magnolia Ave
627 Magnolia Ave
   ("Raejoe")
655 Magnolia Ave
671 Magnolia Ave
771 Magnolia Ave
863 Magnolia Ave
965 Magnolia Ave
975 Magnolia Ave
980 Magnolia Ave
1001 Magnolia Ave
1020-1110 Magnolia Ave
1023 Magnolia Ave
1101 Magnolia Ave
1111 Magnolia Ave
1115 Magnolia Ave
1118 Magnolia Ave
1122 Magnolia Ave
1125-1127 Magnolia Ave

1129 Magnolia Ave
1132 Magnolia Ave
1155 Magnolia Ave
1161 Magnolia Ave
1177 Magnolia Ave

MAIN STREET
6 Main St
8 Main St
16 Main St
23 Main St
26 Main St
38 Main St
42 Main St
44 Main St
54 Main St
58 Main St
62 Main St
63 Main St
64 Main St
66 Main St
95 Main St
100 Main St
162 Main St

MEADOWOOD DRIVE
10 Meadowood Dr
15 Meadowood Dr

MILLARD ROAD
20 Millard Rd
24 Millard Rd
45 Millard Rd
56 Millard Rd

MONTE VISTA AVENUE
2 Monte Vista Ave
5 Monte Vista Ave
8 Monte Vista Ave
9 Monte Vista Ave
   ("Whiteacres Cottage")
14 Monte Vista Ave
19 Monte Vista Ave
20 Monte Vista Ave
23 Monte Vista Ave
28 Monte Vista Ave
31 Monte Vista Ave
32 Monte Vista Ave
40 Monte Vista Ave
112 Monte Vista Ave
116 Monte Vista Ave
118 Monte Vista Ave
122 Monte Vista Ave
202 Monte Vista Ave
203 Monte Vista Ave
208 Monte Vista Ave
210 Monte Vista Ave
211 Monte Vista Ave
215 Monte Vista Ave
219 Monte Vista Ave
226 Monte Vista Ave
230 Monte Vista Ave
232 Monte Vista Ave
234 Monte Vista Ave
237 Monte Vista Ave
250 Monte Vista Ave

MURRAY AVENUE
- 7 Murray Ave ("Storybook House")
- 10 Murray Ave
- 51 Murray Ave
- 80 Murray Ave
- 101 Murray Ave
- 103 Murray Ave
- 203 Murray Ave

MURRAY LANE
- 5 Murray Lane
- 9 Murray Lane

MYRTLE AVENUE
- 29 Myrtle Ave
- 33 Myrtle Ave

NIVEN WAY
- 3 Niven Way
- 24 Niven Way

OAK ROAD
- 20 Oak Rd
- 45 Oak Rd

OLIVE AVENUE
- 1 Olive Ave
- 16 Olive Ave
- 18 Olive Ave
- 20 Olive Ave
- 25 Olive Ave
- 53 Olive Ave ("Brantwood")
- 55 Olive Ave
- 57 Olive Ave

ONYX STREET
- 1 Onyx St
- 11 Onyx St
- 12 Onyx St
- 14 Onyx St
- 15 Onyx St
- 16 Onyx St
- 17 Onyx St (Schula's Grove)
- 22 Onyx St

ORANGE AVENUE
- 9 Orange Ave
- 11 Orange Ave

PALM AVENUE
- 30 Palm Ave

PIEDMONT ROAD
- 10 Piedmont Rd
- 18 Piedmont Rd
- 24 Piedmont Rd
- 25 Piedmont Rd
- 27 Piedmont Rd
- 30 Piedmont Rd
- 52 Piedmont Rd
- 57 Piedmont Rd
- 62 Piedmont Rd
- 65 Piedmont Rd
- 66 Piedmont Rd ("Old Glory")
- 81 Piedmont Rd

POST STREET
- Post Street Stairs

REDWOOD AVENUE
- 1 Redwood Ave
- 11 Redwood Ave
- 33 Redwood Ave

SHADY LANE
- 3 Shady Lane
- 4 Shady Lane
- 11 Shady Lane

SIR FRANCIS DRAKE BOULEVARD
- 500 Sir Francis Drake Blvd ("The Castle")
- Bon Air Center

SOUTH ELISEO DRIVE
- 594 South Eliseo Dr (Bon Air Landing Park)
- 1125 South Eliseo Dr (Hamilton Park)

SYCAMORE AVENUE
- 12 Sycamore Ave
- 15 Sycamore Ave
- 16 Sycamore Ave
- 22 Sycamore Ave
- 40 Sycamore Ave
- 117 Sycamore Ave

VIA CASITAS
- 501 Via Casitas (The Tamalpais)

WALNUT AVE
- 3 Walnut Ave
- 7 Walnut Ave
- 19 Walnut Ave
- 33 Walnut Ave
- 55 Walnut Ave
- 60 Walnut Ave

WARD STREET
- 2 Ward St
- 5 Ward St
- 7 Ward St
- 11 Ward St
- 12 Ward St
- 25 Ward St
- 115 Ward St
- 122 Ward St
- 133 Ward St
- 134 Ward St
- 136 Ward St
- 143 Ward St

WEST BALTIMORE AVENUE
- 203 W Baltimore Ave
- 204 W Baltimore Ave
- 205 W Baltimore Ave
- 215 W Baltimore Ave
- 222 W Baltimore Ave
- 223 W Baltimore Ave ("Baltimore Lodge")
- 229 W Baltimore Ave
- 232 W Baltimore Ave
- 233 W Baltimore Ave ("Sequoia Lodge")
- 249 W Baltimore Ave
- 250 W Baltimore Ave ("Twelve Trees")
- 263 W Baltimore Ave
- 264 W Baltimore Ave
- 273 W Baltimore Ave
- 320 W Baltimore Ave
- 330 W Baltimore Ave
- 339 W Baltimore Ave
- 346 W Baltimore Ave
- 374 W Baltimore Ave
- 380 W Baltimore Ave

WILLIAM AVENUE
- Electric Booster Station
- 7 William Ave
- 12 William Ave
- 15 William Ave
- 106 William Ave
- 110 William Ave
- 116 William Ave
- 121 William Ave
- 123 William Ave

GREENBRAE BOARDWALK
- 18 Greenbrae Boardwalk (*Rod and Gun Club*)
- 43 Greenbrae Boardwalk (*50-50 Club*)
- 49 Greenbrae Boardwalk
- 61 Greenbrae Boardwalk
- 69 Greenbrae Boardwalk
- 107 Greenbrae Boardwalk (*Norah's Ark*)
- 111 Greenbrae Boardwalk
- 125 Greenbrae Boardwalk

BOARDWALK #1 ARKS
- Ark #8 (*Star*)
- Ark #9 (*Pacific Striped Bass Club*)
- Ark #15 (*Redwing*)
- Ark #22 (*Standard*)
- Ark #26 (*Sea Gull*)
- Ark #28 (*The Mooring*)
- Ark #32 (*Sea Lark*)

INDEX

50-50 Club *302*, 303
1871 map *219*, 240
1906 earthquake 70, 76, 83, 98, 118, 139, 153, 241, 243
Agner Variety Store 31, 32
Agnes Island 342–343, *343*
airstrip *270*, 270
Alexander Avenue Bridge *179*, 194
Allen, Harris S. "Harry" 123–125
Allen's Press Clipping Bureau 124
Alpine Garage 15
Ambrose, Frank *13, 24*, 69
Ambrosy, Joseph A. *22, 24*
American Land and Trust Co. ix, 1, 5, 7, 41, 44, 48, 50, 59, 90, 106, 110, 117, 126, 132, 140
American Legion 40
American Trust Co. 34
Ammann, Frederick 172
Ammann's corner 172
Anderson, Kenneth "Ken" 27–28
Anglo-American Land Co. 75
Archer, Clifford "Cliff" *45*, 45
Archer, Douglas "Doug" *45*, 346
architects
    BALDAUF CATTON VON ECKARTSBERG
        Architects 317
    Braccia, DeBrer, Heglund 299
    Brown, B. Allen 66, 74, 85
    Buckley, Vincent 9
    Clausen, Charles O. 10, 176
    Clinch, Bryan 18
    Constable, Arnold 8
    Grommè, Mulvin & Priestley 210
    Heiman, Samuel 12
    Hood, Thomas B. 44, 276
    Horstmeyer, Arend L. "Buzz" 208
    Kroot, Jeff 244
    Littlefield, J. H. 41
    MacDonald, Donald 284
    Maxwell, James 325
    Minton, Henry A. 11
    Morgan, Julia 85
    Nagel, Gustave 7, 18, 39, 42, *43*, 47, 54, 72, 88, 90, 106, 108, 133, 167, 168, 176, 180, 182–183, 184–185, 240, 269, 350, *352*, 352–353
    O'Brien, John 232
    Olson, Raymond T. *274*, 274
    Peterson, Dan 72
    Polk, Willis 85
    Sally Swanson & Associates 11
    Sellon, George C. 328

Wagstaff, Brock 39, 121, 147, 153, 162, 275
Welsh, Thomas J. 8
Arch Street stairs 79–81, *80*, 351
Arkites Association 227, 231
Arroyo Holon 101, *140*, *166*, 186, 216
    See also Larkspur Creek
Asher Clinic 317
Ashley, Beth 294, *295*, 317
Ayers Jr., Robert L. *330*
Azevedo-Foster Dairy 56, 214, 216
Azevedo, Ignacio F. 42, 48, 53, 214
Baeza, Bernice 49
Bain Family 180
Bain, Henry 13
Bain, Jim *24*
Bain, Merton *63*, 180
BALDAUF CATTON VON ECKARTSBERG
    Architects *See* architects
Ball, Laverne "Suzy" 201–202, *203*
Ball, Neil 201
Baltimore and Frederick Mining and Trading Co. 99–101, 144
Baltimore Canyon 97–141
Baltimore Gulch 97
Baltimore Park 143–173
Baltimore Park Associates 208
Baltimore Park signal tower
    See railroads
Baltimore Park Station *See* railroad stations
Banfield Rug Cleaners 270
Barni, Michele 341
Barry, Harlan 149, 260
Basebe, Col. Charles E. 90–91
Basebe house *79*, 90
Basebe, Rosa 90
Bay Conservation and Development Commission 343
Bay-View Hotel *See* hotels
Beleney, George 66
Beleney house *41, 79*
Bergeron, Victor 86
Bernhardt, Sarah 330
Beta Street 87, 112, *351*
Bickerstaff adobe *52*, 52–53
Bickerstaff, Ann Teresa 52–53
Bickerstaff, Jonathan 52–53, 143
Big King Mountain *258*, 258, 260, 261
Bissatini, Eugene 269, 273
Blauvelt, Sandy 134, *222*
blue rock 43, 141, 247, 251, 314 *See also* gray stone, graywacke
Blue Rock Hotel *See* hotels

boardwalks
    Boardwalk #1 *221, 224*, 224–232, *287*, 303
    Boardwalk #2 *224*, 224–226, *225*, 236, 284
    Boardwalk #3 224–226, *225*, 236, 248, 284
    Boardwalk #4 224–227, *225*, 253, 256, *257*, 284
    Greenbrae Boardwalk 292, 298, *300*, 300–308
Boardwalk Water Association 304
Bob's Tavern 23
Bon Air Apartments *287*, 291
Bon Air Bridge *225*, 283
Bon Air Center *290*, 290–291, *291*
Bon Air Hill *285*, 285–289, *287*, 291
Bon Air Hotel *See* hotels
Bon Air Landing Park *See* parks
Booster Day 1, 19, *21*, 47
Booth & Little 14
Booth, Harry 156
"Bouncing Betty" 292
bowling alley *109*, 109–110
Braccia, DeBrer, Heglund
    See architects
Brantwood 123–126, *124, 125*
Bray, Elizabeth 117
Brazil, Antonio "Antone" 48, 54
Brazil-Azevedo building *47, 48*
Brazil building *35, 46, 49*, 54, 247
Bridge Road 112
Brixon, Neil R. 216, 272
Brown, B. Allen *See* architects
Brown, Belle 11, 18, 103–104, *104*, 117, 354
Brown, Helen 52, 144
Brown, Joe E. *339*
Brown, Mary 18, 103, 117, 354
Brown, Richard S. 52, 103, 144
Buckelew, Benjamin R. 100, 264, 282, 298, 328, 335
Buckelew Corners 311
Buckelew Flats 310–311
Buckelew, Martha 342
Buckley & Company 33
Buckley, Vincent *See* architects
Burgar, Edward W. 295
Burgar homes 295
Burtchaell, James T. 7
Cal Park Hill railroad tunnel
    See railroads
Callot, Claude 248
Calvary Baptist Church
    See churches

Canine Commons *See* parks
Canyon Express Co. 22, 23
Cape Marin 292, *292*
Carillo, Leo 85
Cash, Johnny 330
Centennial Park *See* parks
Chapman Tunnel *See* railroads
Charles Holcomb Bridge *See* Alexander Avenue Bridge
Chevron station 45
Chief Marin 297
Chronicles of San Quentin 328
churches
 Calvary Baptist Church *161*, 161
 Presbyterian Church 79, *81*
 Redwoods Presbyterian Church 157, 175, *180*, 180–181
 St. Mark's Episcopal Church *268*, 269
 St. Patrick's Church 7, *11*, 11, *17*, 17–18, *18*, 22
 Rectory *8*
Citizens Advisory Committee *See* Larkspur, City of
City Council *See* Larkspur, City of
City Hall *See* Larkspur, City of
Clark, Chief Howard 64, 233, 258
CLASP *See* Larkspur, City of
Clausen, Charles O. *See* architects
Clinch, Bryan *See* architects
Cloney, Michael 40
Coleman and Forbes 194, 199, 208, 214 *See also* Forbes-Coleman Tract
Coleman, William T. 53, 144–145
College Park 279
Collier's magazine 13, 202
Collman, Arthur D. 149, 162
Community Fields 210
Community Garden *See* parks
Conlan, Fr. John G. 18
Constable, Arnold *See* architects
Cooper, Juan B. R. (John R.) 281, 298, 335
Coquelicot 37
Coral Beauty Salon *35*, 35
Corbet's Hardware Store 268
Corrigan's Corner 271
Corte Madera Creek 282–284
Corte Madera Grammar School *See* schools
Corte Madera Marsh Ecological Reserve 308
Corte Madera School *See* schools
Costa, Giacomo 15-16, 32, 33
Costa, Henry 16, 21
Costello, Ellen 7–8
Costello, James M. 7- 9, 17, 18, 42

Cost Plus Plaza 308
Country Gardens 31
county road 2, *143*, 175
Courtright, Glenn 195
Courtright, Gordon 184, 195
Courtright house 195–196, *196*
Courtright, Mary L. 195
Courtright, William L. 145, *150*, 167, 176, 194, 195–196
Courtyard by Marriott *See* hotels
Cowell, John 282
Craemer, Jeff 332
Craig, Frank 10, 118–120
Crandall, Llewellyn D. 94
Creekside 221, *236*, 236–237
Crossley Bridge Center 305
Cummins, Neil 179
Cunningham, Richard 170
Cunningham, Susan 170
Curley, Charles 199
Curley, Nancy 178, 199, 346
Cusimano, Chief Todd 233
Cypress Point *340*, 340
Dandini, Countess Lillian 323
Danenberg, Zvi 80
Daveler, Lesly 66
David M. Brian 291
Day, Joan 164
Dean's Island 309
Deignan, Monte 201, 203
Delaney, Topher 308
DeLegons, Jack 23, 28
Denton, Mary 201, 203
DePue, Frank 181
de Veuve, Henry 101, 187
de Veuve house *187*
Dinah's Shack *256*, 256, *257*
Dineen, Chief John M. 34
Dirty Harry 315
DJ Chinese Cuisine 15
Dodge, Charles C. 110
Dodge, George M. 146, *165*
Dodge, Lillian M. 110
Doherty, Earle 29
Doherty house *57*
Doherty Lumber Co. 29
Doherty, Nell 24, 29, 57, 240
Doherty, Randolph "Dolph" 12, 13, 16, *20*, 21, 24, 25, 27, 29, 55, *55*, 55–57
Dolliver, Ann 106
Dolliver house *106*, 346
Dolliver Park *See* parks
Dolliver, Sewall 108–109
Dolliver, Thomas 106
Donut Alley 25
Drake's Cove *326*, 326–327
Drake's Landing 292–293
Drake's View 292–293

Drake's Way 320
Duck Inn 310
Duffy, Clinton T. 330, 331, 338–339, *339*
Durston, George 6
Duzo Development Co. 309
Eastwood, Clint 315
Ecumenical Association for Housing 235, 236, 237, 320
Eden Street 91–92, 351
Edgewater 237
Electric Booster Station *See* railroads
"Elfwood" 74–75, *77*, 79 *See also* Charles W. Wright
Elm Crest development 202, *209*
Emporio Rulli 25, 26, 27, 28
Epidendio, Bill 216
Epidendio, Ernie 32, 150, *217*
Epidendio Gardens 215–217
Epidendio, Mary 216–217
Epidendio, Pietro "Peter" 32, 53, 208, 216–217
Epting, Ed 301, *302*
Escalle, Ellen C. 18, 249
Escalle, Jean 18, 249, *250*
Escalle Station *See* railroad stations
Escalle Village Apartments 260
Escalle Vineyard & Winery 224, *239*, 248, 248–249, *251*
Eubanks, Katherine 28
Ezekiel, Leslie 68, 177
Fabrizio Ristorante 16
Fairfax, Lord & Lady 264
Federated Indians of Graton Rancheria 320
fires 55, 128, *129*
Fire Station No. 1 *See* Larkspur, City of
Fire Station No. 2 *See* Larkspur, City of
floods 101, 118, 131, 139, 220-221, *308*
Foley, Eleanor 135–136
Foley Jr., John T. 10, 68, *135*, 136
Foley Lane 111
Fontana, Richard 277
Forbes, Alexander 53, 144–145
Forbes-Coleman Tract 144 *See also* Coleman and Forbes
Ford, William "Bill" 226
Foster, Enos 214
Frank, Phillip "Phil" 224, 225
Fremont, John C. 52
Friedberg, Rae 245
Frizzi, Adelina 19
Frizzi, August "Gus" 34–37, 61
Frizzi Electrical Works 35
Frizzi, John 13, *13*, 19

Frizzi, Julia   34–37
Frizzi's saloon   *36*, 36–37
Frizzi's Sweet Shop   37
Frizzi, Walter   *31*, *45*, 63
Frizzi, William "Willie"   *21*, 35, 62–63, 215
Gallery Bergelli   32
Garcia, Jerry   95, 134
Gardiner, Adda H.   187
Gardiner house   *104*, *175*, *188*, 187–189, *189*
Gardiner, Judge Samuel   188–189
Gardiner, M. T.   9
Gardiner, Rev. James A.   9, 101, *185*, 187–189
Gardiner, Robert S.   194, 195
Gilardi, Andrew   25, 158
Gilardi & Co.   270
Gilardi, Dennis   32
Gilardi's Delicatessen and Catering   25, 158
Gilardi, Susan   32
Glen Addition   121, 130–134, 136–138, 139, 140
Goerl building   *47*
Goerl, Fritz   47
Golden Gate Cleaners   *6*, 28
Grace, W. R.   317
Granger, William F.   *6*, 23, 26, 27, 30, 34, 148, 152, 166
gray stone   *247*, 251   *See also* blue rock
graywacke   43, 169, 247, 314, *315*   *See also* blue rock
"Greenberg" houses   275
Greenbrae   281–295, *287*, *291*
Green Brae   *290*
Greenbrae Boardwalk   *See* boardwalks
Green Brae Brick Kiln   *See* Remillard Brick Kiln
Green Brae Brick Yard   322–325
Greenbrae Improvement Club   305
Greenbrae interchange   *309*, 312–313
Greenbrae Land Co.   305   *See also* Schultz Building Co.
Greenbrae Lanes   292
Larkspur (Greenbrae) Marina   223
Green Brae Ranch   282, 293–294, *294*
Greenbrae Rod and Gun Club   *305*, 305
Green Brae Station   *See* railroad stations
Green Brae Tract   293–295
Green, Chief Phillip "Phil"   233, *234*
Grommè, Mulvin & Priestley   *See* architects
Hall, Henry C.   23, 177–178, *178*

Hall Middle School   *See* schools
Hamilton, Clara-Belle   141, 260, 288, 289
Hamilton Park   *See* parks
Hargens, Charles   27, 28
Harris, Biff   69, 245
Harris, Joseph   245
Harry Allen Trail   124
Heather Gardens   *204*, *210*, 212–214, *213*, *214*, 221, *223*
Heatherwood Park   *See* parks
Heerdt Marsh   305, 308
Heierle, George   147
Heierle, Otto   147, 201
Heiman, Samuel   *See* architects
Heitkamp, Helen   198, 346
Heritage Preservation Board   *See* Larkspur, City of
Hillenbrand, Heidi   49
Hillmer, Dan   213
Hill's Boathouse   *225*, *282*, 282–283
Hillview Gardens   221, *257*, 257–258
Historic Resources Inventory   *See* Larkspur, City of
Ho Ho Springs   255–256, *256*, 260
Holcomb, Charles   154–155, *156*
Holme, Garnet   122–123
Holmes, Jack   115
Holmes, James   127
Honeymoon Cottage   *115*, 115
Hood, Thomas B.   *See* architects
Horstmeyer, Arend L. "Buzz"   *See* architects
Hotel Larkspur   *See* hotels
hotels
   Bay-View Hotel   *341*, 341
   Blue Rock Hotel   1, 8, 37, 41–44, *43*, *46*, *63*
   Bon Air Hotel   283, *284*, 284
   Courtyard by Marriott   316, 317
   Hotel Larkspur   8, 19, 35, 37, 41, *42*, *45*, 53, 241
   Larkspur Inn   73–74, *74*, 77, 180
   Larkspur Villa Hotel   65, *65*, *66*
   Sheppard Hotel   335, 340
Howard, H. William "Bill"   25, 26, 65
Hughes, Grace   292
Hurst, Frederick   153
Hurst, Mary   153
Hutchinson, Dwight   314
Hutchinson Quarry   *297*, 298, *309*, *314*, 314–316, *315*
Impact   4, 13, 159
Intermark Interests, Inc.   325
Jaegeling, Dr. Julius P.   102
Jaegeling, Dr. Thurlow C.   14, 25, 184, 195
Jag Town   61

Java   6
Jeschke, Anne   *318*
Jim's Tavern   23
Jones Way   136
Joplin, Janis   134, 170
Jossa, Joseph   65–67
J. S. Rosenfield & Co.   317
Kaiser-Frazer showroom   4
Karl's Grocery   *16*, 33
Katherine Eubanks' Florist   *6*, 28
Kearley-Green, Kathleen   67, 95
Kennedy, William J.   10, 119
Kent, Albert   265
Kent Woodlands   263, 265
Kesey, Ken   64, 313
King Mountain Assessment District   261
King Mountain Green Gorillas   261
King Mountain Open Space Association   261
King, Patrick   ix, 3, 5, 6–7, 17, 18, 248, 255, 263, 282
Kirby & Yates Liquors   *16*, 17
Kokjer, Ralph L.   23, 28
Kott, Gerald C.   172
Kott house   *171*
Kroot, Jeff   *See* architects
Lagan, Rev. Hugh   17–18
L'Ambiente   30
Lamott, Kenneth   328
Landmark Oak Tree   *See* trees
landslides   *See* mudslides
Lark Creek Inn   3
Lark Shoe Repair   317
Larkspur Association of Volunteer Firemen   *13*, 13, 19, 20, 55, 62, 70, 95, 130
Larkspur Bakery   *28*
Larkspur Cash Grocery   *16*, 23
Larkspur, City of
   1965 Larkspur General Plan   258
   1990 Larkspur General Plan   207, 346
   2008 Centennial   ix, 1, 2, 22, 252
   Citizens Advisory Committee   260
   City Council   9, 11, 12, 38, 53, 55, 102, 318
   City Hall   ix, *5*, *9*, 9–16, *11*, 22, 25, 354
   city limits (extension of)   298, 315
   CLASP   53, 229
   Fire Station No. 1   *12*, 12-14,
   Fire Station No. 2   *293*, 293
   Heritage Preservation Board   346, 347, 354
   Heritage Preservation Ordinance   346
   Historic Building Code   347

Index, continued

Historic Overlay H Zoning 253
Historic Resources Inventory ix, 232, 346, 347
    Larkspur Board of Trustees 9, 10–11, 83, 93, 101, 118, 119, 136
    Larkspur Heritage Committee 346, 354
    Larkspur Library 11, 139, 354
    Mills Act Contract 67, 347
    Tidelands Ordinance 232
    Twin Cities Theatre 10
Larkspur-Corte Madera School *See* schools
Larkspur Creek 101, 112, 216 *See also* Arroyo Holon
Larkspur Dairy *See* Azevedo-Foster Dairy
Larkspur Dry Goods 26
Larkspur Ferry Terminal 298–300, *299*
Larkspur Food Center 33, 48
Larkspur Food Store *33*, 33
Larkspur Garage 23
Larkspur (Greenbrae) Marina 221, 223
Larkspur Hardware 23, *23*, 25, *28*
Larkspur Inn *See* hotels
Larkspur Isle 221, 235, *287*
Larkspur Landing Center ix, *316*, 316–317, *317*
Larkspur Library *See* Larkspur, City of
Larkspur Lumber Co. 21, *24*, 25, 29, 46, 53, 55, 229
Larkspur Meat Market 25
Larkspur Pharmacy *27*, 48
Larkspur Plaza 55, 229
Larkspur School *See* schools
Larkspur Shores Apartments *317*
Larkspur Station *See* railroad stations
Larkspur Villa Hotel *See* hotels
Larkspur Walkers 221, *222*
Larkspur Water Co. 77, 95, 140
Larkspur Water Co. dam 140
Larkspur Women's Improvement Club 10, 103, 354
Lark Theater *49*, 49–50
Larsen, Arthur W. "Cap" 13, 21, 95, 246
Laurel Dell Tract *117*, 117–118, 126, 129, 131
Lauterwasser parcel 173
Lauterwasser, Russel W. 173, 186
Lee, Bette 102–103
Lee, Robert 102–103, 318, 325
Left Bank Brasserie 44
Leo's Restaurant and Cocktail Lounge 55

Lewis, Huey 134
Limerick Inn 248, 249, *251*, *252*, 252–253
Lincoln Property Co. of Texas 316
Little, David C. "Doc" 14, 234
Littlefield, J. H. *See* architects
Little, Frank 14
Little King Mountain 236, 237, *258*, 258–260, *259*
London, Jack 121, 324
Lundberg, Debbie 86
Lundstrom, Joan 11, *308*
Lynch house *41*
Lynch, Richard 42, 45, 47
Lynch's Hall 10, *35*, 42, *45*, 45–47, *46*, *47*
MacDonald, Donald *See* architects
MacKillop, Angus 133-134
Madrone Canyon *See* Baltimore Canyon
Madrone Woodlands 138, 139
Mahoney house *79*, *88*, 88–89, *89*
Mahoney, Judge William 88–89
Malvino, Alfred J. 257, 293
Marie's Tavern 55
Marilli and Stringa Saloon's 36–37, *37*
Marilli, Elizabeth 36, 43, 62, 68
Marilli, Serafino 34, 36, 42–43, 62, *63*, 68
Marilli, Theodore 62, 68
Marin Airporter 292
Marin Audubon Society 211, 322
Marin Brain Injury Network 268
Marin Brewing Company 317
Marin Country Mart 317
Marin County Flood Control District 306
Marin County Open Space District *141*, 173
Marin County Subdivision Act of 1933 303
Marin General Hospital 284, *285*, 287
Marin Municipal Water District 303, 304
Marin Primary & Middle School *See* schools
Marin Rowing Association 293, *293*, 311
Markham, Edwin 121
Martin, Peter 135
Mastron, Capt. Charles 219, 335
Mau, William F. 7, 42
Maxwell, James *See* architects
maypole *178*, 179
McCluney, Christopher 231
McCormick house 240–241, *241*

McCormick, James *42*, 42, 240–242, *242*
McCormick, Stephen J. 240
McLeran, Brian 200
McLeran, Charles "Charlie" 70, 199, 265, 267
McLeran property *202*, 203
Meadowood *215*, 215–216
Mercantile Trust Co. *34*, 34
Merwin, Edmund L. 46
Merwin's General Merchandise *41*, 46
Metallica 330
middens 52, 151, 319, 323
Millard, Frank B. 120–122, *121*
Miller, Lee 304-305
Mills Act Contract *See* Larkspur, City of
Minton, Henry A. *See* architects
Minturn, Charles 342
Miwok ix, 52, 101, 215, 219, 290, 297
Miwok Park *See* parks
Miwok Warrior Quintin 298, 328
Model Bakery *24*, 27
Morgan, Julia *See* architects
Morris, David 321
Mt. Tamalpais Railroad *See* railroads
Mt. Tam Racquet Club 235
mudslides 118, 131, 136, 139
Muender, Christian 24
Muir, John 121
Muir Woods Railroad *See* railroads
Murphy, Catherine 23
Murphy, J. Frank *13*, 13, 23, 39
Murray house *263*, *265*, 269
Murray Park Neighborhood 273–279
Murray, Robert 24, 38, 86
Murray Tract 265, 273, 277
Murray, William 6, 255, 263–266, *264*, 335
Nagel, Gustave *See* architects
Nardene Beauty Shop *28*
National Register of Historic Places 2, 106, 194, 318, 322, 325, 348–349
Neighborhood Park *See* parks
Neil Cummins School *See* schools
Newsom, Gavin 171
Niven, Cyndi 40
Niven, George 160–161
Niven, James 40
Niven, Jim 292
Niven Park *See* parks
Niz Brown Realtors 47
Norman Mahan Jewelers 317
North Pacific Coast Railroad *See* railroads

Northridge open space   141, 260, 354
North Shore Railroad   *See* railroads
Northwestern Pacific Railroad
    See railroads
O'Brien, John   *See* architects
Ogden, Bradley   5
Oglesby, John C.   194
Old Salt Water Pump House   *342*, 342
Old Sawmill Landing   225
Olson, Raymond T.   *See* architects
Oosterbaan, Conny   270, *271*
O'Rourke, Maria   85, 260
O'Rourke, Michael   72
O'Shaughnessy, Michael M.   60
Owl's Wood   *190*, 190–191
Palm Hill   *192*, *193*, 193–203
paper streets   67, 72, 84, 92, 199, 351
parks
    Bon Air Landing Park   *288*, 288
    Canine Commons   222
    Centennial Park   *178*, 178
    Community Garden   222
    Dolliver Park   102, 130
    Hamilton Park   288
    Heatherwood Park   211–212, *212*
    Miwok Park   320–322, 327
    Neighborhood Park   *318*
    Niven Park   292
    Piper Park   ix, *219*, 221, 221–222, *222*, *223*
    Remillard Park   *326*, 326
Pasticceria Rulli   *See* Emporio Rulli
Patton, Dennis   297, *310*, 310–311, 313, 326
Paul Daly Swim Club   272
Pell, Joseph   258, 260, 272
Penna, Guy   *32*
Peterson, Dan   *See* architects
Peters, Richard   19, 39
Picco Restaurant   6
Piper Park   *See* parks
Piper, Ron   221
Pixley, Emma   127
Pixley Tract   121, 127, 132
Pixley, William C.   126–127, 128
Pizzeria Picco   6
Point San Quentin Village
    Association   341
Polk, Willis   *See* architects
Porter, Hugh B.   227, 303
Post Street stairs   *68*, 240, 351
Presbyterian Church   *See* churches
Probert, Hildred "Hil"   3–4
Probert, Mildred   3–4
Punta de Quentin   227, 298
Punta de Quintin   297

quarries   141, 169   *See also* Hutchinson Quarry
Raejoe   *245*, 245–246
Rafter, Marianne   135
Ragged Sailor Framery and Gallery   317
Railroad Open Space Association (ROSA)   159, 207
railroads
    Baltimore Park signal tower   151
    California Park railroad tunnel   313
    Chapman Tunnel   206
    electric booster station   207–208, *208*
    North Pacific Coast Railroad   ix, 7, 50, 60, 205
    North Shore Railroad   50, 151, 205
    Northwestern Pacific Railroad   51, 159, 193, 205, 311–312
    trestles   *211*, 302, 311–312, *311*
    San Francisco & North Pacific Railroad   *311*, 312
    San Rafael & San Quentin Railroad   343
    "The Cutoff"   205
railroad stations
    Baltimore Park Station   145, 151, 159–160, *160*, 206, *207*
    Escalle Station   *249*, 249
    Green Brae Station   206, 302, 312, *313*
    Larkspur Station   50, 51, *60*
Rainbow Market   31, *32*, 217, 247
Rancho Corte de Madera del Presidio   143
Rancho Punta de Quentin   110, 117, 281–282, 335
Red Robin Catering Co.   33
Redwood High School   *See* schools
Redwood-San Andreas Marsh   209–211, *211*
Reed, John   143, 190
refugee arks   *304*, 305
Remillard Brick Co.   322–325
Remillard Brick Kiln   297, *322*, *323*, *324*, 324–325, *325*
Remillard Cottage   314, *317*, *318*, 318, 322
Remillard Park   *See* parks
Remillard, Pierre-Nicolas   314, *322*, 322–324
Rice, Carolyn   24, 38–39
Rice, Charles "Charlie"   38–39, 193, 199, 352
Rice house   *39*, 44
Rice, Joseph B.   38, 199
Rice Livery & Express Co.   38–39,

39, 44
Rice Stable Court   39
Richardson Island   209, *210*
Richmond-San Rafael Bridge   343
Ridgeway Lane   130–131
Roman Catholic Archdiocese of San Francisco   282, 305
Rose Bowl Chateau   14, 15–16, *16*
Rose Bowl dance   19, 19–22, 21, 61, 62, 130, 154, 157, *252*
Ross, James   282, 293
Ross Landing   2, 219, 255, 264
Ross Valley Masonic Center   *268*, 269
Ross Valley Sanitary District   297, 319, 319–320
Rulli, Gary   26
Rulli, Jeannie   26
Sally Swanson & Associates
    See architects
Sandra Marker Path   208, *217*
San Francisco & North Pacific Railroad   *See* railroads
Sanitary Barber Shop   28
San Quentin is My Home   338
San Quentin Point   342–343
San Quentin State Prison   297, *328*, 328–333, *329*, *330*
    dungeon   332
    East Gate   336
    employee housing
        "The Reservation" ("The Gulch")   332
    graveyard   327, *327*
    hospital   331
    jute mill   329
    knot garden, "Garden Beautiful"   331
    prisoner housing   332
    prison labor   329
    San Quentin Museum   332
    San Quentin News   332
    schoolhouse   333
    The Waban   328
    West Cell Block   332
San Quentin Village   297, *334*, 334–342, *343*
    Main Street Houses   337–342
    school house   336
San Rafael Cooperative Nursery School   *See* schools
San Rafael & San Quentin Railroad   *See* railroads
sawmill site   99–100
Schmalfeld, Karl   16, 23, 33
Schmitt, Caroline   208, 209
Schmitt, Frank   208, 209
Schmitt Chicken Ranch   *208*, 209

Index, continued

schools
   Corte Madera Grammar School   177
   Corte Madera School   177
   Hall Middle School   221, 234, 257
   Larkspur-Corte Madera School   *143, 160, 176,* 176–180, *177, 179*
   Larkspur School   177
   Marin Primary & Middle School   179
   Neil Cummins Elementary School   234
   Redwood High School   209–210, *219, 220,* 221
   San Rafael Cooperative Nursery School   318
   St. Patrick's School   9, 12, 18
Schultz Building Co.   285, 286, 288, 293–295
Schultz Investment Co.   292
Schultz Jr., Niels   286, *290,* 290, 293, 294
Schultz Sr., Niels   285, 288, *290,* 290, 294
Scott Lane   123
Sedley, Bruce   274
Sellon, George C.   *See* architects
Shady Lane stairs   168, 351
Sheppard Hotel   *See* hotels
Shropshire, Dr. Elmo   73
Shula, Anton "Tony"   108–110
Siemens, John C.   288
Silver Peso   23
Sir Francis Drake statue   *297, 325,* 325–326
Skylark Apartments   *260,* 260
Solomons, Lucius   82–83
Sonoma-Marin Area Rail Transit   313
Soroptimist's Grove   *See* trees
speakeasy   245
Spivey, Nancy   *222,* 222
Spyglass Apartments   286
Steffe, Joseph P.   30
Stephens, Mabel G.   27, 45
St. Mark's Episcopal Church   *See* churches
Stoll, Christian   27, 28
Stolzenberg, Hugo   9, 25
Stolzenberg's Meats   *16, 22, 24,* 25
Stolzenberg, Sophia   9, 25
"Storybook" house   274
St. Patrick's Center   12
St. Patrick's Church   *See* churches
St. Patrick's Rectory   *See* churches
St. Patrick's School   *See* schools
St. Patrick's Thrift Shop   16, 17
Stringa, William   36, 42–43, *43, 63,* 68

Swiss Garage   271
Tacchi, John   322–323
Tamalpais Grocery Co.   7, 26, *33*
Tamalpais, The   286, *287,* 288–289, *289*
"Tamalpais, The Sleeping Maiden"   290
Taylor, Daniel   329, 334
"The Castle"   295
"The Knoll"   *277,* 277–279
"The Redwoods"   103
The Woggle Bug   226
Thoelecke, Carl   73, 261
Thoelecke, Sylvia   73, 261
Tidelands Ordinance   *See* Larkspur, City of
Tiscornia, Adolph A.   76, 88, 236, *250,* 250–251, 258
Tiscornia Estate   141, 258
Tiscornia, Mary   22, 251
Tiscornia Plan, 1972   259
Todsen, Theodore   162
Torney, Richard   278
tramway   130-131
trees
   California black oaks   263
   Douglas fir   119, 135
   giant sequoia tree   120
   heritage Eucalyptus trees   *179,* 179, 284, *285*
   landmark magnolia tree   *184,* 184
   landmark oak tree   *100,* 101, 163
   Mexican fan palms   160
   redwood trees   102, 130, 169
   Soroptimist's Grove   150
   tall trees in the Canyon   119
   valley oak   101, *239,* 240
Tubb Lake   *319,* 320–322, *321,* 327
Twin Cities Police Authority   *233,* 233–234
Twin Cities Theatre   *See* Larkspur, City of
Uris, Leon   172
Vallejo, General Mariano   101
Van Derveer, Dena   242
Van Reynegom, Capt. John   190
Vanzin Construction Co.   266
Varsi family   208, 212
Varsi Hill   *56, 204,* 209, 211, *212, 214,* 215, 217, 220
Vegetable Man "Gow"   187
Victoria Station   *310, 316,* 317
Vincilione, Alice C.   251, 260
Vincilione, Paul   258, 260
Vogt-Schmalfeld building   32, *33*
von Buchau, Stephanie   67, 242, 244
Von Meyerinck, Anna   92–94
Von Meyerinck, Wilhelm   11, 92–94

Waban, The   328   *See also* San Quentin State Prison
Wagstaff, Brock   *See* architects
Walcott, Joe "The Barbados Demon"   *36,* 62
Ward, H. C.   61, 67, 79, 351
Ward Street Café   38
water scandal   95, 246
Way, Catherine   203
Wegner, William F.   110, 152, 154, 155, 158, 171
Weissensee, Marty   31
Welsh, Thomas J.   *See* architects
Wheeler, Almon C.   3, 161, 196
Wheeler, Burt C.   57, 161, 196
Whiteacres Cottage   *146*
White, Charles   146
Wilfert house   169
Wills, Helen   337
Wilson, Helen C.   11, 76, *138,* 138–140, 346
Wilson, Jack   84
Wilson, Sallyanne   84
windsurfing beach   *327,* 327
Wood Island   299, 301, 304, *306, 309,* 309–310, *310, 311,* 316
Woodlark Apartments   260, 266, 272
Woods, Alfred E.   11, 83
Wright, Charles W.   ix, 59–60, 70, 73–76, *75,* 351
Wright, Georgiana A.   60, 75-76
Wright houses   *69,* 70
Wright, Thorpe   72–74
Young, Charles "Charlie"   32, 55, 247
Young, Leonard   *13,* 13, 55, 247
Zampetti, Giuseppe "Joseph"   23
Zaro, Prosper   *13,* 13, 19, *31,* 32, 129–130
Zubler, Don   339